The Miser's Son: A Tale

Richard Bedingfield

Printing Statement:

Due to the very old age and scarcity of this book,
many of the pages may be hard to read due to the
blurring of the original text, possible missing pages,
missing text, dark backgrounds and other issues
beyond our control.

Because this is such an important and rare work, we
believe it is best to reproduce this book regardless of
its original condition.

Thank you for your understanding.

THE

MISER'S SON:

A TALE.

BY

R. BEDINGFIELD, ESQ.

AUTHOR OF 'CRIME,' 'THE PEER AND THE BLACKSMITH,'
&c. &c.

WITH ILLUSTRATIONS.

———————

LONDON:

R. THOMPSON, JAMES STREET, GRAY'S INN LANE;

STRANGE, PATERNOSTER-ROW; BERGER, HOLYWELL-STREET

AND ALL BOOKSELLERS.

ENGRAVINGS.

The Skeleton of the Lane

DEDICATION.

TO Mrs. THAYER.

My dear Aunt,

That I cannot inscribe to you a book which might go down to posterity with a brightness commensurate with your merits, is a mortification, in one sense, to me ; but I know that the tribute of esteem and admiration I offer to you, will not be less kindly received because of that unworthiness : for nothing prompted by sentiments of affection is insignificant to those who accept the poor offering they dictate ; since those sentiments are of the heart more than the intellect.

Whatever the faults of " The Miser's Son," I hope and think that the most fastidious will not conceive they are imbued with anything in any degree hostile to the cause of truth, or inimical to that of virtue. And the true and the good, I know, are loved and sought by yoo, who are so quick to perceive a merit ; because it is with intuitions of moral beauiy, as with perceptions of external form, and those so ready to notice the one, possess a clear sense from within of the other.

Even were I capable of writing such a work as I desire, I

could add nothing to your excellence, I could not increase by a single iota the estimation you are held in by the world. I acknowledge, therefore, a selfish motive in dedicating "The Miser's Son" to one so far removed from my ability to elevate in the eyes of men, and whose fine and cultivated taste can so readily detect errors, even while the kind and liberal heart is so free to encourage the dawn of Thought and Imagination.

That you may long continue to delight with the charms of conversation, and the exercise of those rare acquirements you possess, is the fond desire of your affectionate Nephew,

RICHARD BEDINGFIELD.

Upper Montagu Street,
   September 1844.

INTRODUCTION.

T H E Fiction now ranks but little below the Epic, the Drama, or the Essay; and combines the essence of them all. The names of Cervantes, Fielding, and Scott, if they do not occupy so high a place as those of Homer, Virgil, and Milton, are bright and glorious exemplars of the majesty of Romance. They stand round about the Sun of the eternal poetry of Nature, searching into the dark nooks and quiet spots of the human heart: and if they do not rise, like the great Dramatists of Greece and England, to the vast and the sublime; though they excel rather in the natural and the beautiful, the humorous and the satirical, than the awful, the stupendous, and the terrible—all honour be unto them.

Cervantes was the first Novelist who thought below the surface; he had, most undoubtedly, fine intuitions into the truthful and the fine, but he did not attempt to unravel the intricacies of the passions in their grander aspects: his imagination was subtile, rather than intense. Fielding was a philosopher: but he was a one-sided thinker. He delighted to view humanity physically, to search deep into the material and sensual portion of our being, but not to soar to abstract feeling and sentiment. He had no idea of the spiritual, but he embraced all that is real, actual, and common-place. And did Scott take a higher flight? Was *Truth* the element in which he lived? Yes; he was *true*. There never was a more perfect master of what lies on the surface of humanity than the great Magician of the North:—the august of passion, the terrible of nature he was not able to embody: yet all that he has done, who *but* he could have effected? I shall go into this subject more fully presently, in order to give a cursory view of the history of Fiction—a most important portion of letters in modern civilization.

A higher order of writing than was sought for a century ago, is now required to meet the intelligence of the age. De Balzac and George Sand in France have attempted the philosophical and metaphysical in Romance, while in our own country we are frequently surprised in perusing a Novel, to find it embody principles of abstract reasoning, and to advance into theology for the development of a peculiar character. Comic literature is now the most successful in France and England— witness the writings of Dickens, Lever, and Paul de Kock: but we know not, if out of what is meant solely for amusement, a great moral power may not come forth. There is no reason, it is indisputable, why the moral should be conveyed through the medium of Heraclitean philosophy, and if it be possible to amend the heart and to amuse the fancy at the same time, so much the better. Sir Walter Scott has accomplished an infinity of good by his bright, cheerful humour, as well as his exquisite pathos: there is a human kindness in him truly delightful; but Scott, in some respects, was rather the Novelist of the Past than the Future. His pleasant, mirth-moving fancy, his quaint originality, his fine insight into the ridiculous, remind us more of a century or more age—indeed, they carry us back even as far as Chaucer—than our own age. Chivalry he admired more than our modern Humanity, and his heroes are almost all physical warriors, like those of Homer and the ancients. There is no reason why we should not have pictures of the chivalrous ages: but why have almost all our Novelists neglected to give us the philosophy of epochs; why have we not the characters of *moral* heroes? When we admire the courage and gallantry of the soldier, cannot we adore the constancy and faith of that man who fights against evil passions and subdues them? A dog may be as courageous as William Wallace; but he cannot love his country, he cannot reason against desire. Surely, such divine examples of patience and heroism of mind as sages and philosophers have set, might be productive of more than Spartan virtues.

Few of our Novelists have either attempted to anatomize the secret mind of man, or penetrate into motives. In *Hamlet* we have the metaphysics, the morals, the poetry of the Prince of Denmark. All Shakspeare's characters develop the *whole* individual; but Scott's, for the *most* part, are but flesh and blood, bones and muscles, without the vital principle which sets them in action. Yet, I repeat, Scott was great on his own ground. He is the undoubted King of modern Romance:—but there is no reason, I think, why there should not be an Emperor. Marlowe preceded the dramatists of the age of Elizabeth; and may not Scott be the precursor of a greater than himself? We want some pioneers to clear the way, to prepare the public mind, which will not receive *Genius* at once; among these pioneers I would, with humility, advance. Talent is the pioneer of Genius, and *that* exists. Great is the demand for fiction, and vast the supply: but it were absurd to look for more than one master-spirit in a century. But he will come in the course of years. The majority of our Novelists seldom rise far above the prettiness or imitation that we skip over, and think no more of, though there may be half-a-dozen endowed with subtle and poetical insight into the human heart,—who can delineate the progress of a mind, and write dramatic and spirit-stirring scenes, and lofty sentiments, such as would not have disgraced the great ones of the Past.

The object of Romance, however, is scarcely ascertained, and so vast are the varieties of opinions upon it, that it would be difficult to fix its legitimate boundaries. Poetry and Philosophy are indissolubly connected, for Plato, Kant, and Berkeley are all sublime poets, and Shakspeare, Milton, and Wordsworth profound philosophers ;—while Romance is so comprehensive, and its space so large, that it is not obliged to cast away the materials which the Poet must reject, and connects Thought and Action, combines description and sentiment, allows the Author to illustrate his own creations, and obviates the difficulties a Dramatist must necessarily experience ; so that we may say Fiction is subject to no fixed rules, but is free as the air, except it impose laws on itself. For Poetry must sacrifice Philosophy ; and Philosophy, Poetry ; while Romance can do as it will.

We are surprised that antiquity should not have used this vehicle for the expression of ideas; but in a state of simple semi-civilization, the complex machinery which the Novelist now commands was not set in motion. The world was then divided into two great classes—tyrants and slaves :—though some of those tyrants were more slavish than their bondmen,—and superstition and ignorance prevailed everywhere, to the prevention of science being diffused; so that readers were but few, and writers of rare occurrence. But Printing spread abroad the means of knowledge, and in proportion as education was universalized, men of narrower acquirements than great Thinkers and Scholars were desirous of being entertained as well as enlightened ; the bondage of credulity was modified, but the love of the marvellous increased,—from that inherent love of contemplating the distant which is natural to all who have souls,—and tales of wild knight-errantry were eagerly devoured by all classes, until the genius of the middle ages was superseded by a totally dissimilar spirit—in creating which, might not Cervantes have exercised an influence ?—The cycle of Chivalry having run its course, there was a violent re-action, and instead of the improbable and the impossible, the real and actual existence of man was worshipped. Instead of shadows —the array of spectres and demons, and giants—all was earthly, and the philosophy of cold Materialism created the literature of heartlessness and sensuality, which lasted, with little intermission in England, from the reign of Charles the Second down to that of George the Third.— And now shall we not arrive at the golden mean between the dreamy and the sensual—both equally false—shall we not have the ideal, the poetical, the *true?* I contend we are yet in the infancy of Fiction, and it is not ascertainable how great an influence it may exercise over posterity. It is likely to be more general than any poetry, than science, than ethics, in its application.

The few read works of abstruse reflection, the many devour those of imagination, and if, through the instrumentality of Romance, kindly, generous, and charitable feelings may be generated, who will be hardy enough to contend that it is not an engine in the hands of Providence for the exaltation of man?

But are we to amuse, as well as to instruct? Why not? We cannot

be always thinking, and it is better we should find some innocent pleasure, than be sad, idle, or excited by dissipation. It is probable that
Romance must ever in some degree avail itself of those melo-dramatic
materials which are neither calculated to awake the reasoning faculties
(in those that are not reflective), nor to evolve the moral nature; but in
the scheme of Creation we perceive how minute circumstances act upon
the mighty system, and become the agents of Good; and it may be that
while we play with the fancy, we excite a desire of something higher
than the fanciful, we rouse the soul to pant after what is beautiful and
great. How insensibly the child sickens of his fairy-tales, and gets to
like Scott, gets to like Shakspeare, and enjoys as a youth, in the end,
Locke and Bacon! Where there is a mind at all, the love of reading
engenders the love of study, and the love of study, that of Truth. When
this is accomplished, we have a man to deal with—and oh, a sincere
man, a thinking, rational, intellectual being, is a noble piece of work!
Almost every novel, from ' Tom Jones' down to ' Oliver Twist,' is in some
way melo-dramatic; but the Illegitimate enhances the enjoyment of the
Legitimate; and after some scene of wild excitement and suspense, how
lovely and holy appears a touch of Nature, such as may be found in the
last work referred to,—simple, pathetic, purifying, and tender! Light
and Darkness, Darkness and Light,—such is the law of the Universe.

But it is singular that those men of antiquity, with their " great, deep
hearts," when Nature was naked before them, and their fierce passions
were unrestrained by Christianity and knowledge, should have thronged
to the Theatre—with them a national want, *not* a recreation—to hear
cold, abstract poetry which few even now can enjoy! *We* want the
contest of fierce passions, while *they* appeared content with calm, uniform action:—for the shadow of the coming Fate was ever before their
eyes. The inexorable Destiny allowed no scope for melo-dramatic interest; and description was substituted for the vitality of dramatic situation, to the destruction of all that is stirring, animating, and graphic.
But their poetry was their religion: it was invested with a solemn interest, and there was an awe upon their hearts when they listened to the
stately and majestic verses of their Æschylus, such as we feel when
gazing into the awful mystery of the heart of Things. They knew that
nothing could avert the course of Fate, and their Gods and their Demi-
gods, their Heroes and their Prophets, were but as the exponents of the
grand and terrible doctrine of Predestination. We, on the contrary,
believe in no such stern Necessity: we know not even if the Will of the
Eternal with regard to us is fixed and unalterable; the Heaven and the
Hell are above, around,—the Everlasting Fiat has not gone forth, and
every petty and trivial accident evolves the inexpressibly important
Drama in which we are all the Actors. The philosophy of Necessity
was the Genius of Ancient Literature, and that of Free-will the permeating principle, the gigantic interest, the integral action of our own.

The Miser's Son.

BOOK I.

We know not where we go, or what sweet dream
  May pilot us through caverns strange and fair
Of far and pathless passion, while the stream
  Of life our bark doth on its whirlpools bear,
Spreading swift wings as sails to the dim air.
                        The Revolt of Islam.

Winds behind, and rocks before.—WORDSWORTH.

THE

MISER'S SON.

CHAPTER I.

A tall and proper man, well skilled in war,
The other, deeper, subtler.—*Old Play.*

THE SOLDIER — THE STRANGER — AN ADVENTURE — REFLEC-
TIONS.

 HEN the last faint rays of a glorious summer sun
were sinking beneath the horizon, and the fair
pale crescent of the silver moon was just apparent
in the soft azure of the cloudless sky, a solitary
horseman pursued his way over one of those fertile
and cultivated tracts of land, peculiarly characteristic of our England's inland counties, having deserted the high road previously, in
order to save a circuit which it made.

His was one of those powerful and majestic forms which the writer
of romance is wont to ascribe to some of the mail-clad heroes of distant and chivalrous ages : a form combining strength with elasticity,
height with the most symmetrical proportions, vigour, agility, and
length of limb, with ease, grace, and firmness hardly to be excelled.

The age, too, of the young man had arrived at that culminating
point of perfection when the high and buoyant spirits of the youth are
beginning gradually and imperceptibly to blend with the dignified
composure, the thought, and reflection of the energetic, ardent, and
impassioned man ; and though perhaps the lofty and ingenuous, but
yet somewhat narrow forehead of our traveller did not exactly indicate
the wild enthusiasm, the unconquerable daring, the ambition and rest-

less enterprise of a singularly powerful or peculiar mental composition, the cool courage which was imprinted on each line of his remarkably handsome and intelligent countenance---the fire of his large and splendid eye---the kindliness, mingled with firmness and sagacity, that played around his mouth, and, indeed, infused expression and character to each feature of his face---denoted a being decidedly superior to the ordinary run of common-place and worldly mortals; a being probably devoid of profound and philosophic qualities of mind, but quick, stedfast, ardent, and impenetrable to selfishness, invulnerable to little pride, or feelings of petty enmity, envy, or anger.

Such was Captain Charles Walsingham, as brave a soldier as ever supported the honour of England and the Hanoverian line of monarchs, and whose erect bearing, soldier-like apparel, and general deportment, added to the fine and fiery steed (whose lion-like eye and haughty neck seemed eloquent of battle) which he rode, and a scar upon the brow, denoted to every eye his military profession.

While we are accompanying the gallant warrior on his lonely road, it may be as well briefly to state that he had been ten years in the service of his country, and had passed the greater part of that period in an eastern clime with his regiment, with which he had recently returned, and was now hastening to visit some relations who had not seen him since he was a stripling of sixteen, when he had just mounted his epaulettes, and attained the tall stature of a man—a stature which he had now overgrown two inches.

Those who had not beheld Charles Walsingham since his colours were first presented to him, would scarcely have recognised the graceful, slight, and beardless boy, in the athletic, powerful, and almost colossal man, while the bronzed cheek, the bearded mouth, the originally fair hair turned to a dark brown, altered, though it did not entirely metamorphose the expression of lineaments such as Titian or Michael Angelo would have been delighted to have been able to impart to a picture or statue of some old Roman hero. But the bright, sanguine, noble, and generous nature remained the same, while the tincture of chivalry and romance, which he had imbibed in his boyhood, had deepened into a quiet enthusiasm, which his military habits of self-control taught him to disguise on ordinary occasions; and it was only when the latent poetry of his character was elicited by some strong appeal to his warm and overflowing heart, that any, save the close observer of mankind, could have distinguished in him the fire and the glow which in fact constituted his very inmost idiosyncracy itself.

But the reader will judge of the gallant captain by the events to be detailed hereafter, and so it will be better to eschew unnecessary illustration, and hasten to narrate the adventure (for which, doubtlessly, the greater portion of those who peruse these pages, and works of fiction in general, are ever most anxious) which has been promised in the heading of this chapter.

Well, then, the young soldier, as his horse turned a right angle of the road into which he had again struck, encountered a mounted traveller, who was emerging from a clump of tall chesnut trees, from a cross path, and whose father progress appeared to tend in the same direction as that of Walsingham.

There was something so remarkable in the appearance of this stranger, that the captain, taught by custom to examine the outward man of those he met, and to bestow a more than passing attention on forms of uncommon strength and vigour, could not help taking a rather protracted survey of the person of the horseman, who for his part was equally rude in the surprised regard with which he surveyed the soldier from head to foot.

The stranger's age exceeded that of the soldier by about a dozen years; his height was less by nearly a whole head, and his body considerably longer in proportion. His cheek, too, originally fair, had become brown from long and continual exposure to the inclemency of the weather and the heat of the sun, and, singular enough, there was a large scar on his brow, in a position very nearly similar to that on Walsingham's. There was thought, there was intellect, sagacity, and daring, mingled perhaps with a dash of savage hauteur, in a far greater degree than in the face of the other, while the irregular features derived a grace and radiance from the working of his quick, active mind, such as it is almost impossible to convey, either by the pen or pencil.

The figure was built rather for strength than elegance; but, nevertheless, was not by any means inclining towards the unwieldy. The chest was broad and deep, the head finely placed on the magnificent shoulders, and the arms (perhaps a trifle too long for a stature of five feet seven or eight) of prodigious bone and muscle. He was mounted on a small but apparently most powerful horse, of the pony formation, and which bore the same physical analogy to him as did Walsingham's charger to his master, and his dress was plain and gentlemanly, consisting of a sad-coloured coat, made so as to button completely over the chest, black inexpressibles, riding boot, and hat of the Spanish fashion, slouching over his face.

The two horsemen, then, involuntarily drew up their reins, rapidly reading what has occupied us so long in description, probably comparing their respective strength and capabilities, and the high and fearless daring which so singularly animated their countenances. The stranger had first completed his scrutiny, and with a smile, courteously addressing Walsingham, in a deep and distinct voice said—

"Good evening, sir. Are you proceeding towards Uskedale?"

The soldier returned this salutation with frank affability, and answered the query thus conveyed in the affirmative.

"I think, then, that a portion of my journey may be in your company, if you have no objection," said the stranger.

"I shall be delighted with your society."

So on the two travellers journeyed.

"I believe," said the unknown, "we were mutually engaged in determining the relative powers of our bodies, just now. You can endure enormous fatigue, I should imagine?"

"My horse and I have already made a march of six-and-forty miles to-day, and the roads over which we have travelled are hilly."

"Well, you will hardly believe, perhaps, seeing the freshness of my little steed, that we have exceeded the distance which you named considerably since morning; but he is a paragon of a beast," and the stranger patted his horse's neck affectionately, while the animal tossed up his pretty head, and snorted proudly at the notice taken of him.

"He is a compact little fellow," observed the soldier, carelessly surveying the beast which his companion appeared to hold in such high estimation, and then bestowing a stroke on the glossy skin of his own charger.

"Ay, and the finest trotter that the world ever witnessed," was the rejoinder. "He makes no difficulty of carrying me sixteen miles an hour, and can maintain that pace through half the day. Poor Dickon! Good horse! For leaping, bearing fatigue, for sense, and for strength, I will back him against the world. See, there is a broad ditch before us, and the opposite bank is high and steep. Do you think that your steed would take such a jump?"

The soldier paused, as he surveyed the awful chasm denominated "a ditch."

"You do not surely mean to say that that little——"

" You shall see," interrupted the stranger. " Ho, Dickon!" and in another instant he had cleared the space, which was, in fact, an excavation in the earth of such depth that at the bottom there was a large quantity of water.

Now it so chanced that by leaping this chasm, a feat rarely indeed attempted by the boldest huntsman in the county, a circuit of nearly a mile was obviated ; and the young soldier, deeming it impossible but that his noble animal could achieve what had been performed with such apparent ease by the comparatively diminutive horse of the stranger, put spurs to his steed, who willingly took the leap, but stumbled, when he had gained the opposite side, on the rocky and precipitous bank, and the head of Walsingham coming in contact with a gnarled trunk, he was stunned, and lost his seat.

Beloved Reader—How often do we behold some fine, high-spirited fellow, carried away from reason's high road by the force of emulation, galloping furiously onward in the great steeple chace of ambition, now stumbling, now fainting, now renovating—still dashing madly over hill and dale, and hurdles—and the deuce knows what all—straining every nerve, and sustaining his soul with the hope of winning that breath, that bubble Honour—at length, in some insanest insanity, attempt a thing, the nature of which he is ignorant of, and break his neck down a precipice at last !

CHAPTER II.

Rons. The service of a gentlewoman consists most in chamberwork, and sick men are fittest for the chamber. I prythee, give me a favour.

Casta. Methinks you have a very sweet favour of your own.

Rons. I lack but your black eye. *Cyril Tourneur.*

THE LEGITIMATE SCOPE OF FICTION DISCUSSED—THE AUTHOR'S AIM IN WRITING THIS WORK—WALSINGHAM IN SICKNESS.

" It may possibly be all very sound philosophy, Mr. Author, that you were talking at the tail of your last chapter, but what the d—l (saving your presence) do we who read novels care how a parcel of fools knock out their brains in the manner you described ? I tell you, Sir,

that the way for a Novelist to succeed eminently in these days is to
rush through thick and thin, haling along no-matter-what improba-
bilities, or impossibilities, hair-breadth escapes, fearful murders,
daring burglaries, tremendous passion, awful catastrophe, &c. &c.
forming, with a few spectres, the entire elements of that universe—
that little, pleasing, moving, bustling, fictitious, real, foolish, sensible,
and confoundedly amusing rubbish, which may by possibility excite
the tears of bread-and-butter young ladies, and raise the hairs on
the heads of susceptible young gentlemen who breakfast on bread
and milk, through the space of ten or a dozen months, and then is
consigned to the tomb of all the Capulets (namely, the cheesemonger's
shop), to make room for more nonsense, and more outrageous anomalies !"

"But, my dear sir, recollect that an author, being as it were a god
in his own peculiar creation, should construct those spiritual and immaterial beings of the mind————"

"Pshaw, now you are going to metaphysicize, and we all know
what metaphysics mean. Metaphysics! otherwise a parcel of d---d
incomprehensible words, tickling the ears of those who fancy they are
philosophers, but who no more deserve the name than any of the
gentlemen who experience the knowledge of evil in the realms of Tar-
tarean night! I tell you what it is, Mr. Author---philosophy consists in the science of being pleased, and I will write a treatise
some day (only I fear no one would comprehend it) on the method
of employing our time to the best advantage, making money, health,
and spirits all at the same time. I will bet you £100 (when I get
them), I will write much better sense, and *ergo*, infinitely better philosophy than ————, or ————, or ————, should I ever be induced
to become a scribbler."

"But you will allow me to say a few words?"

"Oh, talk---do! I know all that you will utter."

"An author, then, most lively and loquacious sir, when he sits
down to compose a work, should imagine he is going to create an
intellectual world, and people it with thoughts and reflections, as well
as beings and incidents————"

"Stuff and nonsense---there is no creation in creation. Therefore a book being, according to you, a creation, if it be a novel, the
just and legitimate scope of fiction is interest. Now, there is no interest in morality, considered in the abstract; for what are all morals
but sober facts, and not ideal images?"

"Talking metaphysically against metaphysics, for *they* integrate the whole system of ethics! But there shall be no speculations in this tale of mine, but such as necessarily and unavoidably arise from character and from circumstance, without whom, Fiction were not."

"Let character and circumstance speak for themselves, and you will please your readers better than if you introduce your own sentimentalities, theories, and platitudes. In one word, dismiss all your imaginary philosophy, and stick to imaginary *facts*, for you perceive that on facts all reasoning must be built, despite the ravings of your *à priori* gentlemen, who contend that solid matter is mind, and gull the foolish with their laughable mysticism. Depend upon it, Sir, that action, action, and nothing else, is all that the writer of romance should aim at."

"And how shall he ' point the moral' of his tale?"

"Who cares about the moral of a novel? If there be one, all well and good. Those who are eternally prating concerning the expediency of integrating every work with the spirit of ethics in their practical utility, should take into consideration, that when a person flies to romance for amusement he does not go to school for instruction. Take my advice. Look at Scott, Ainsworth, Dickens, Paul de Kock, and all the great novelists of the nineteenth century, who have pocketed from £1500 to £15,000 per annum. Have they been any of your Kantesians, or your Cousinites? Deuce a bit of it! Be amusing, and that's enough. You will make your fortune if you can cram this tale with exciting incident, never permitting the interest of it to flag for a single instant, even for the finest moral precept that ever fell from the lips of a Seneca. Never philosophize—always talk good common sense—people fancy it a tacit compliment to themselves now-a-days, and strive not to amend the morals you never made."

Such is your clever man of the world. With an immensity of that faculty of observation on the surface which he deifies under the denomination of common sense, with an inexhaustibility of animal spirits, with a little wit, a great deal of good humour, and some sarcastic shrewdness. Perhaps a few of my readers may resemble him, many imitate, and one or two despise. I speak plainly out. Utter worldliness in every modification is altogether despicable—though a spice of it may be necessary to enable a man to bustle through the business of life—and can never lead to true wisdom, or real and substantial

c

happiness. The enduring beauty of Love and Faith constitutes the bright poetry which lends existence heaven.

The tale before you is neither a psychological system, a wild and thrilling romance, a heartless sneer at mankind, such as might emanate from a disciple of Voltaire, or of that crazy but extraordinary man, Byron; but if there be adventures to entrance the spirits of the ardent and the dreaming; if there be sentiments to move the enthusiasm of the pure and tender; if the cheek of beauty, like the rose, should be moistened and beautified with the pearly dew from the unpolluted springs of an innocent and sympathizing heart—more will have been achieved than the aspirations of the solitary individual who in silence and meditation has composed a work which he earnestly hopes "the world will not willingly let die," have ever dared to picture to his soul : while if the sorrowful should receive some drops of consolation, if the sad should derive entertainment, and the wretched should be led for a season to forget their troubles, the El Dorado of the author's visions, the Ultima Thule of his desires, will be in every respect fully accomplished.

When Walsingham recovered from the stunning effects of the blow which he had received, be found himself in a small, darkened apartment, and stretched on a bed, while the figures of two females were dimly visible as they sat behind the curtains, engaged in conversation carried on in whispers so low that the mere murmur of it was the uttermost that his ear could catch.

Does it not seem a strange thing that the iron muscles, and the proud strength, and the buoyant spirits, which a few brief moments previously appeared fresh from the joyous springs of immortal life and vigour, should by one little accident—one trivial circumstance, which the mind had not regarded for an instant—be reduced to less than baby helplessness ? The man of gigantic energy enfeebled to so great an extent as to be incapable of giving utterance to his wants and wishes—in fact reduced to a condition, no atom more powerful than when he first issued from the womb into consciousness ?

The soldier in vain attempted to rise from his recumbent position, or to articulate inquiries concerning his whereabouts, but a faint groan escaping from his lips, as the motion he made in his fruitless exertion caused the blood to flow upwards to his head—the only part that had been severely injured—one of his nurses, a woman whose age appeared to be verging towards senectude, by the streaks of grey and white which mingled with her dark hair and the many wrinkles that were implanted in her forehead and face, advanced to the assistance of the patient.

Descriptions are almost invariably tedious, or it would be worth while to dilate upon the countenance and figure of that woman, as it arose in a sort of weird-like grandeur to the faint eyes of the suffering soldier.

She was tall, thin, pale, and sallow; her eyes of the deepest grey, her nose somewhat beyond the aquiline, her lips promising firmness and resolution of character, and her brow, high and commanding, with something of that wild and enthusiastic energy which occasionally may be remarked in that feature.

She must once have been strikingly beautiful, but time and sorrow had left their dark and indelible lines of ravage upon her haughty and majestic form, and dimmed the fire of her eyes, so piercing and so splendid still, but not with the radiance of hope and life; yet, perhaps, like the ruin which the tempest and the lightning have scathed and desolated, decay, in destroying the grace of beauty, had added to the picturesqueness of its effect. She was dressed plainly, not to add coarsely; but as has been said, there was a grandeur and rugged dignity in her deportment which evinced, at all events, her mind was of no vulgar cast.

"You must be quiet, or the pain you endure will be greatly aggravated," she said to Walsingham, in a voice wherein pity appeared to struggle with habitual command. "You are in the hands of those who will take the greatest care of you, and your friends shall be made acquainted with the accident which prevents your joining them at present. Now try and take this draught."

Feebly and with difficulty the poor soldier, who perceived the necessity of rendering implicit obedience to the injunctions of his imperious nurse, swallowed the nauseous contents of the phial she held to his mouth, and sinking again on his pillow, was speedily buried in profound sleep. How long he thus remained happily insensible to pain, he knew not, of course, but on awakening found the mellow and the softened light of the noon-day sun streaming through the partially-closed shutters of the apartment.

But what was his astonishment, as he opened his eyes, to perceive one of the loveliest visions of female beauty that had ever presented itself to his ardent imagination, tenderly bending over him, and appearing to have watched with the greatest solicitude his tran-

quil and unbroken rest, one of her sunny ringlets which had escaped
from her head gear, almost touching his cheek. He could half have
fancied that he was still locked in the embrace of Morpheus, but when,
on perceiving that Walsingham was awake, a carnation blush overspread the modest cheek of the young girl, and she retired a pace
from the bed, he could not mistake the evidence of his senses.

She could scarcely have numbered more than sixteen summers,
though her form was rounding into the mature grace of consummate
womanhood, and there was a refinement and a delicacy in the expression of her sweet face which clearly demonstrated that the cultivation of her mind had not been neglected.

" I hope that you feel better now," were the first accents which the
lovely stranger addressed to Walsingham, as he contemplated with
bewildered amazement the charms presented so unexpectedly to his
notice.

" Thank you, I believe I have not a great deal the matter with me,"
replied the soldier, gradually recovering a perfect recollection of all
that had occurred ; " but where am I now, and to whom am I in—"

" You had better not speak any more at present," interrupted the
young girl ; " at all events, until you have taken this broth, for you
must be exhausted with all you have lately undergone."

" My sleep has greatly invigorated me, yet I do, certainly, still
feel rather weak," returned Walsingham. " I have been bled profusely, have I not ?"

" Yes, yes ; but pray take this broth, and then I will go and
fetch your real nurse and physician, who has been sitting up with
you all night, and as soon as it was morning went to bed, and I
took her place. Oh, here she is ! Elizabeth, your patient feels
greatly better now !" and with these words, much to the chagrin of
the soldier, the lovely girl glided out of the chamber.

" Pray, who is that young lady ?" inquired Walsingham, of the
same stern and stately woman who had administered to him the
draught, the results of which appeared to have been so happy.

" I cannot allow you to speak, or to be disturbed," was the rejoinder. " Your recovery entirely depends on perfect quiet."

Walsingham could almost have laughed, notwithstanding his pain
and vexation, that he, who from his boyhood had been accustomed
to exert undisputed authority over veteran warriors, should thus be
schooled and commanded by a woman, but deemed it best to submit without expostulation.

CHAPTER III.

We rest—a dream has power to poison sleep ;
We rise—one wandering thought pollutes the day ;
We feel, conceive, or reason, laugh, or weep,
Embrace fond woe, or cast our cares away.—SHELLEY.

———— A shape like to the angel's,
Yet of a sterner and a sadder aspect.—BYRON's *Cain.*

DANVERS—ELIZABETH—AND A NEW CHARACTER.

IT is now indispensable to the current of our narrative (the Hibernicism about to follow must be forgiven) that we retrograde a few hours, in order to follow the movements of the individual, to whose boasting admiration of the qualities of his horse, the accident of Walsingham might be *prima facie* attributable.

What a blessed thing it would be, if the wretched mortal who has involved himself in a labyrinth of inextricable difficulties, who has plunged in a moment of ebriety and folly into irremediable guilt and misery, could, like the Novelist, hold the tangled skein of destiny in his hands, and, when he has made a *faux pas*, by a little care and attention apply an efficient remedy to the mischief he has entailed on himself and others. But the annihilation of one single little act by an insignificant worm, the merest atom in the infinite universe—whose vast and incomprehensible involutions of cause and effect should demonstrate to the philosophic inquirer into nature and mind that there must be some pivot upon which the great whole revolves and moves, inscrutable to the keenest and most penetrating intellectual eye, whose range is limited by time and space—the blotting out and erasing of a single manifestation of being, is beyond the power of the Arch-Cause of All, without the destruction of its work. A thought becomes an act—an act, an eternity!

The stranger, then, whose jumping Bucephalus had just performed so prodigious a feat, beheld the impetuous leap to which the soldier urged his splendid charger, and on perceiving the manner in which it was manifest he intended to clear the wide space intervening between them, called out to warn him of his danger, but his shout was too late: for the head of Walsingham came in contact with the trunk of the stunted tree, almost simultaneously with the echo of the unknown's voice, as its deep intonation rang in his ear; and immediately hastening to the assistance of one in whom he had taken a singular degree of interest, even on first beholding him, discovered that he had sustained a severe injury, though happily on that part of the head where the structure is most condensed.

"Fool that I was, to tempt the rash boy to this venture," muttered the stranger, as his hawk-eye seemed to gather at a glance the amount of damage which the cranium of the luckless Walsingham had received, "but he should not have expressed such a supercilious contempt for Dickon."

Raising the soldier in his athletic arms, as if a weight of at least thirteen stone was that of the merest stripling, Danvers (as we shall, for the sake of perspicuity, henceforth term him) cast his eye around in the hope of finding assistance.

"He ought to be bled immediately," he said; "but hang me if I like to turn apothecary on him. That lip, that face—so like—"

It was at this juncture that a well-known voice, from behind an enormous oak that grew in the centre of a narrow cross-road, accosted him with,

"What have you here, Walter? Surely, you have not wounded this young man?"

"God forbid, my dear mother," exclaimed Danvers, with emotion, as the erect and haughty form of the woman whom the reader knows by the name of Elizabeth stood before him, "it is fortunate that you are on the spot; for I am grown a child while looking on him."

"Ha," ejaculated Elizabeth, as she stooped to examine the injuries of Walsingham, while Danvers still sustained him in his arms, "you are right, it can be no other than the young Charles. But how did this unlucky accident occur?"

Danvers briefly narrated the incidents of the adventurous leap, as the female produced a lancet, and at once proceeded to perform the act of phlebotomy on the muscular but motionless arm of the soldier.

"Do you not think he is like her, mother?" inquired Danvers, as

soon as the incision which Elizabeth had made was bandaged up;
"and yet," he added, "the relationship between them is not very
intimate,"

"Ay, ay, he has proud blood in his veins," returned the woman,
seeming little to heed the question put to her, "pity that it should
have been shed in the cause of the tyrant and the usurper."

"What shall we do with him now?" inquired Danvers, doubtfully,
"he is severely hurt, and it is more than two miles to the village."

"Poor boy, poor boy," said the woman tenderly, her stern and
masculine nature apparently mollified by the helpless condition of the
soldier; "it would be dangerous to take him so far, and he need
never know—"

"Say no more," interrupted Danvers, eagerly, "lead the horses
and I will carry him, and as the motion will be easier up this irregular ascent than if he were carried by Dickon or his own beast, I
can easily manage to bear him so short a way."

With these words the powerful fellow bore the insensible Walsingham with much gentleness along, and having reached the top of a
steep acclivity, proceeded down a somewhat precipitous path, which
terminated in a pleasant valley, where, embosomed among tall and
ancient sycamores, stood a pretty little cottage, and into which he
conveyed his burden, and deposited it on the identical bed where
Walsingham found himself on recovering from his stupor.

Having performed this prodigious feat of strength with much
ostensible ease, though it might well have tried the thews and sinews
of the most redoubtable hero that ever figured in history or romance,
Danvers addressed Elizabeth, who had closely followed him, and said,

"I cannot stay, but I know that he will do well in your hands.
Dispatch some person you can trust to Walsingham Hall, to prevent
uneasiness on his account, of course disguising the place of his present abode, and so good bye, dear mother, till to-morrow."

Thus having spoken, Danvers kissed the forehead of Elizabeth
affectionately, quitted the cottage, and mounting his good horse
Dickon quitted the valley at a canter.

The country through which he now proceeded was of a hilly and
not very cultivated character, but the picturesque and frequently
majestic beauty of the bold and variable scenery amply compensated
the want of those verdant thick-set hedges, green pasture lands, and
golden corn-fields, which so peculiarly distinguish the prominent
features of truly English landscape. Here a broad and impetuous

river, with noise and foam poured along its clear and sparkling tide,
and when it was obstructed by the vast fragments of rock which
arose from the water, and frequently assumed fantastic, grotesque,
or beautiful shapes, a column of the glittering lymph shot upwards
to the sky, and was painted by the declining sun with all the colours
of the rainbow. Sometimes thickets of grand and towering trees,
the growth of centuries, impeded the view of the cheerful river ; and
glimpses of the blue hills, forming an amphitheatre in that direction,
were dimly visible in the quiet distance, like those fairy castles which
the eager fancy of visionary youth builds for itself to luxuriate upon,
seen through the vista of happy years, which, alas, the silence of the
tomb may alone fill up ! Bright and delusive phantoms of the buoyant imagination ! Though, as we advance in knowledge, we perceive
and smile at the dreamy enthusiasm of the boy, yet the cheat has
been productive of many pleasant hours which might otherwise have
been spent in dejection and despondency, or worse, in those vicious
pastimes which heedless youth seeks, to beguile time of its wearisomeness, and too frequently, we find, instead of the roses of pleasure,
discovers the briars and thorns where pain and perdition lurk.

Blessed be the imagination ! without which, indeed, our common
life were a burthen almost intolerable : and evil be to those—and
they create their own misery—who would exclude that best and
brightest gift of heaven from the sad philosophy of life.

"Happy is he who imagines himself so," thought Danvers, a train
of reflections not very dissimilar from those into which we have inadvertently been betrayed, having passed through his mind ; for
though by no means of a moralizing or meditative temperament, still
the most thoughtless have their periods of grave and melancholy
retrospection, and our traveller was of by no means contemptible
understanding, with respect to that comprehension which our German
neighbours have categorized under the head of subjective, although
his element was action—wild, adventurous, and romantic action,
such as distinguished the career of a Montrose and a Claverhouse,
in common with whom he shared many remarkable qualities of mind
and nature.

"Yes, I was once happy," he continued, slackening his pace, and
resigning himself to the thickly-thronged visions of the gone, " at
least I appeared to live in a sweet and dreamy Paradise, and thought
not of the future or the past, but as things peopled with beings and
things of brightness and of joy. Surely all pleasure consists in the

pursuit and anticipation of it; for when we clutch the shadow that
appeared so divinely radiant in our eyes, like the golden fruit which
appears so lovely and delicious before we touch it, the dream, the
passion, and the glory crumble to dust, the odour and the sweetness
disappear, and what—oh, what remains to us? Corruption, corruption, corruption! Behold the history of man !"

The moralist paused. In the intensity of his abstraction he had
given vent to his surcharged feelings in words, and suffering his horse
to crop the short grass which grew beneath his feet, he appeared
lost in bitter regret.

" What might I have not been," he continued, as he wandered in
fancy over the actions of his past life, " but for the influence of those
dark omnipotencies which men call chance and circumstances? With
a mind whose inexhaustible energies have never failed me, with a
body whose iron vigour defies fatigue and hunger, and loss of sleep,
might I not, under a happier fate, have been the leader of victorious
armies, and spread the glory of my achievements over the whole
earth."

He was startled and interrupted here in his soliloquy by a taunting
and scornful laugh, which, on lifting up his eyes from the ground,
on which he had unconsciously fixed them, as he remained in motionless inactivity, he found must have proceeded from a youth of
apparently about eighteen years of age, though the depth of his voice,
as it rang in the ears of Danvers like one from the tomb, with its
mocking and ironical tones, and the thoughtful pallor of his sallow
cheek and ample forehead, appeared appertaining to a person more
advanced in life. But such a singular personage should not be introduced at the end of a chapter.

CHAPTER IV.

We wither from our youth, we gasp away,
  Sick, sick,—unfound the boon, unslaked the thirst,
Though to the last, in verge of our decay,
  Some phantom lures, such as we sought at first,
But all too late—so we are doubly cursed,—
  Love, Fame, Ambition, Avarice : —'tis the same,
Each idle, and all ill, and none the worst ;
  For all are meteors with a different name,
And Death the sable smoke where vanisheth the flame.
                          Childe Harold.

THE EPICUREAN.

IT was a form which, once having been beheld, no length of time could possibly obliterate from the recollection. There was nothing very remarkable perhaps in the features or the figure themselves, except that they were handsome and well proportioned ; but the power, the passion, and the splendour of that dark and piercing eye, the mind which was stamped upon that haughty and scornful brow, the strength and sensuality which a physiognomist would have instantly detected in the powerful jaw, and the large though well formed mouth, and the deep lines of reflection already discernible in the colourless cheek, plainly and unmistakably marked a character for the study of the philosopher, as also physically and metaphysically for the sculptor, the painter, the poet, and the man of genius in general, irrespectively of those adventitious circumstances from whence the peculiar rauge of his observation arises.

And there they stood—the being of stern, of fierce, and bloody action—the being of enterprise, of daring, and indomitable resolution, and the boy of premature and lofty manhood, of aspiring intellect, and of dreamy, meditative, slothful, and uncertain habits, with powers of body, though undeveloped, little inferior to those of Danvers, and with abilities of a rarer and a far profounder quality.

"I think you spoke to me," observed Danvers, after a pause of some duration, and still continuing his survey of the singular indi-

vidual before him—a survey borne with unquailing disdain, such as
few indeed ever long maintained beneath the scrutiny of his penetrating glance—but the master-spirit of the eagle, even when youngest
and weakest, will not cower beneath the soaring ambition of the
falcon.

Danvers had broken the deep silence of the sequestered nook
where this strange encounter of two such singular and opposite natures was held beneath the canopy of the unclouded heaven.

It was an epoch in the sublime history of that psychology which
the bright spirits of the beatified may love to contemplate—a psychology teeming with high and mighty interest—the active influences
of mind in its wonderful development, when Hell looks on with
anxiety, and all but *One* are uncertain of the result ; when the spirit
of the individual, aroused from its passive condition, exerted itself to
the uttermost in the trial of strength—when the resources of learning,
of intellect, of memory and experience were all vivified and awakened
—the trembling scale, perhaps, about to be decided—the Angel or
the Demon Fate becoming the eternal ascendancy, and inexorable
misery or happiness, undeterminable by all the philosophy, the
genius, and the patient investigation of science, to be fixed, unalterably fixed, perhaps, in the annals of the Book.

Such are the inevitable results of contact with high and original
Mind, when the wavering opinion becomes formed and rooted ; but
who ever gives a single thought to the great Epic of the Soul, that
is everlastingly in the vast interest of action ?

" You were saying," replied the youth, a slight and almost imperceptible sneer communicating itself to his voice and face as he
answered Danvers, " that you *might* have been the leader of victorious armies, and ' spread the glory of your achievements over the
earth.' I had been reading, under this tree ; reading Plato, and
was musing on the mysteries of life, when I heard the words,
' *Corruption, corruption, corruption ! Behold the history of man !*'
I lifted up my eyes and perceived you. I saw the workings of your
mind as plainly as if they had been spread out in a book before me
—the progress from the deadened worm of the heart, which we call
Retrospection, to the ardent hope, the advance of the torpid blood,
as the enthusiastic aspiration entered your heart—I saw it all ; and
as I traced ' *corruption, corruption,*' I could not choose but
laugh."

The lad (if so he could be called who was evidently no despicable philosopher) finished, and Danvers, after a brief silence, replied,

"The glory which the great spirit of man may accomplish, is worthy of the toil and labour which are necessary for its achievement; and though I acknowledge that fame is not *alone* enough for happiness or even *content*—since the more we possess the more we desire—yet I am unacquainted with any worldly good which the greatest and wisest of mankind have more earnestly wished for. In fact, it is the object of each person in the aggregate of active existence, and without its stimulus to exertion the mind would sink into lethargy, and our entire moral world become a chaos, a void, a dream!"

"And what other is it than nothingness? Whence did it arise? You cannot answer me. So," continued the boy sarcastically, " having determined the value of the world within, may I ask you how much has ever been gained by this idol—this god—this master passion, consuming and overpowering every other. Is the dead man happier for its miserable and uncertain tenure? Is its possession a means of adding to the pleasures, real and substantial, of the living? Its POSSESSION! Pshaw! you cannot, nor I cannot, nor the wisest sage of sages (letting the old Greek metaphysician drop to the earth) could not command it for a single instant beyond the decree of fate. I had almost fancied you a philosopher, when I heard you speak of the omnipotencies of chance and circumstance. I find you but a very sorry——never mind what! Good morning to you!"

"Stay," said Danvers, surprised and fascinated by the extraordinary discourse of the boy moralist, "I should like to hear the object in *your* belief most proper and desirable to attain. Pleasure of body cannot long endure; indeed, if we seek it, we lose the power of its attainment in the search. Pleasure of mind, or *happiness*, is a thing descanted on very gravely by our great ethical writers, as an absolute entity attainable by every individual; but can this be the case?"

"Certainly not," replied the youth " for the mind being constituted in a determinate manner, and acting, and being reacted on by external objects, according to the laws of that organization, we must still depend on external circumstances for *that* happiness."

"But is any kind of happiness attainable?"

"You are anxious for it, 'twould seem," returned the lad, with his strange smile, in which there was a mixture of profound sarcasm, sadness, scorn, and desolation. "You, who are double my age, ask my advice? What thing in existence is most pleasant to you?"

"I can hardly answer that question; and, if I am not mistaken, although I am no logician, it is an incongruous sort of proposition, if you intend to apply it as a rule of action. What, to-day, I wish to possess, I would not give the value of a farthing for, to-morrow, and *vice versa*; so that when you ask me what I consider most pleasant, you merely inquire a state of mind."

"Even so, my friend; the weed grows beside the flower, and the flower withers; the flower blooms, and the weed is scattered to the winds! Behold an emblem of the mind and its pursuits. In the freshness of infancy it is a thing wherein a canker lurks; weeds grow up around it, and it fain would lift itself from out the rank atmosphere they generate. In maturity it aspires to gain the possession of its childhood's dreams; but then those very objects it disdained are those which it would acquire, from the innate tendency of our incomprehensible nature to acquire what it is unable to reach. All things pass away into the nothing from whence they *are*. The bright, the beautiful, the loathsome, the sweet, the disgusting, become commingled, and finally reproduce new forms of being. Eternal change marks the current of our feelings, and we know not how chance or necessity may modify the emotions which constitute the existence of our sensations. How, then, should we act, in order to obtain happiness? Catch the present moment of enjoyment—eat, drink, sleep, love, hate (they are all means of pleasure in their turn), and finally descend into the charnel! So, farewell," and the boy of deep, dark, morbid reflection, disappeared.

There is a melancholy of the gloomiest hue inseparably attendant on every profound poetic or philosophic discourse, except where a glimpse of some more bright and enduring state of existence is pointed out as the goal where the immortal spirit within us may rest and weep no more. For the inevitable result of all experience in the pleasures and gratifications of earthly being—pleasures and gratifications unavoidably counteracted and destroyed by the repletion and the satiety superinduced by frequent practice, or leading to schemes of unwise ambition, vice, and selfishness—is the conviction of the utter hollowness of all human power, pride, wealth, honour, and glory. We imagine, perhaps, that we have discovered some divine El Dorado for ourselves; we picture scenes of smiling love,

of peace, fame, applause ; we fancy ourselves beloved and respected,
our wishes strenuously supported by hosts of friends, of faithful adherents, and enthusiastic admirers, and *perhaps*, after having exhausted a youth of intellect, power and vigour, and a glorious manhood of strength, health and consummate knowledge, we gain that
point to which all our fondest anticipations once tended ; and,
behold, the bubble bursts ! Envy, hatred, artifice, machinations,
disappointment, environ the *fortunate* fool, who has wasted
thought, who has squandered the heart's best wealth—affection,
love, peace, hope—and for what ? A GRAVE.

CHAPTER V.

O happiness ! our being's end and aim !
Good, pleasure, ease, content ! whate'er thy name ;
That something which still prompts th' eternal sigh,
For which we bear to live, or dare to die,
Which, still so near us, yet beyond us lies,
O'erlooked, seen double by the fool and wise.—POPE.

THE MISER.

"AND is it even so ?" muttered Danvers, as he pursued his
lonely way ; "and is it even so ?" His ambition had been awakened a few moments before his rencontre with the boy philosopher,
and the latent springs of action, which can never remain long dormant in such a nature, aroused by the conviction that he possessed
within himself powers capable of carrying him on in the race of life
to the station that appears so enviable to those who have not experienced its cares, its anxieties, and defeated projects, had communicated an elasticity to his frame such as is not ordinarily felt, except
in sanguine youth ; but the evident belief of the singular being from
whom he had just separated, of the folly and the vanity of all ambitious struggles, had imparted a portion of sadness to his own more
buoyant spirits, and recalled the painful associations which he had
been on the point of banishing from his recollection.

So the traveller increased his speed, and was borne rapidly along

through a less sterile part of the country than that he had left behind him, abounding in rich pastures, in orchards, woods, and corn-
fields, while farm-houses and cottages, all neat and clean and comfortable, plainly evinced the flourishing condition of the inhabitants
of the neighbourhood.

It has often been observed that there exists a nameless something,
endeared and rendered delightful to the feelings of an English heart,
in the cheerful aspect of the scenery in which our noble little island
so extensively abounds, that may in vain be sought throughout the
sunnier and more splendid climates scattered through the European
division of the globe; and probably that charm, though not merely
one arising from pride of country (since it is noticed by our conti-
nental and other visitors), derives its principal and most enduring
interest from the evidences which it affords of our agricultural pre-
eminence, and the advantages arising from the natural productiveness
of the soil, superadded to the idea of comfort and happiness conveyed by the order, neatness, and regularity of the humble homes of
our peasantry. Here there are no prodigious mountains which
impress the intellect with the sentiment of the insignificance of the
individual in the mighty infinity of creation, no stupendous chasms
or caverns, for the possession of which a landscape almost invariably
sacrifices whatever of quiet, gentleness and smiling beauty it might
otherwise present to the senses and subdue the heart with—by that
inconceivable influence the external exercises over the mind within—
but a succession of objects, well calculated to please, if not to
astonish, to awe or to appal.

Danvers, though he could not be said to be an enthusiast in his
admiration of the works of nature, which he surveyed not with the
eye of the painter or the poet, was never callous or insensible to anything that was able to amuse the fancy, to awake the imagination,
or to satisfy the judgment; and the soothing and balmy tenderness
of the lovely evening, with its twilight and its silence, the distant
and scarcely audible song of the husbandman borne on the soft and
languid gale of summer, as after the toils of the day he returned with
a jocund heart to his peaceful happy home—the solemn grandeur of
the heavens above, the low rustling of the boughs as the birds, before
closing their eyes in sleep, hopped from branch to branch—and the
sweet breeze made music among the luxuriant foliage—all tended to
sadden and subdue, yet not to excite a dark degree of melancholy

in his bosom, for as fine old Wordsworth observes in his beautiful
" Excursion"—

> " We live by admiration, hope, and love,
> And even as these are well and wisely fixed
> In dignity of being we ascend.

If the heart refuse to cherish each impulse which directs its dormant
energies to something good, and pure, and noble, then indeed nothing
in the fabric of this goodly world can excite more than a transient,
fleeting, pleasurable sensation; but images of beauty carefully gar-
nered up and stored within the soul, mingle with our aspirations,
blend with our associations, and spiritualise and exalt our being by
their everlasting holiness.

The evening was now fast declining into night, and the pale and
radiant Hesper which, from the beginning of time, (since with time
poetry began and has been idealised) came trembling, like the tear
on the cheek of beauty, into life, and love, and radiance.

Sweet star! the emblem of a divine spirit, watching over and
brooding on some glorious world of fancy—then retiring into the
depths of its own being, and feeding on the light of its own substance!
But the lofty soul which creates and verifies an universe of ideal
splendour, unlike that mild, bright orb, fades—fades away from the
earth which it illuminated, for ever, and perhaps ascends into some
distant world to subsist upon truth, knowledge, and virtue, those
heavenly visitants of mortality, " few and far between" indeed, but
yet of occurrence sufficiently frequent to convince the sceptical of the
existence of a principle that could not have sprung from dust.

Descending into an abrupt semicircle, the declivity by which Danvers was now wending his way became extremely rough and precipitous; but before he had gained the bottom of the hill, an opening in it
discovered a gothic cottage in somewhat ruinous condition, and immediately dismounting he knocked at the door, which was opened
presently to him; and unceremoniously entering, he found himself
in a square apartment—the flooring of which was in a dilapidated
condition, and the walls and ceiling in by no means perfect repair—
in company with a tall, emaciated man, whose dress was threadbare,
but in whose countenance there were decided indications of a noble
and ancient lineage. But, nevertheless, there was in the restless
grey eye, in the contracted, though lofty forehead, in the thin lip,
and the hollow cheek, so strong and indelible an impression of mean-

ness, of avarice, and of narrow, selfish, grasping littleness of mind, that the eye turned away displeased from a countenance which must once have been moulded in the greatest regularity of outline, and still retained some portion of former beauty, though the glorious spirit, the aspiring intellect, the feeling, the passion, and the becoming pride, were not to be discerned, for the component parts of his nature were all absorbed in the ruling vice of his soul.

It was a Miser who confronted the liberal, free-hearted, but sanguinary Danvers.

Of all the dark, the grovelling passions which transform the sublime image of the Divine Sculptor's hand into clay and rottenness, and pestilence—of all the wretched frenzies that ever possessed the brain of fallen, poor, and pitiable mortality, that of avarice is probably the most despicable, the most to be commiserated and wondered at in the category of inexplicable paradoxes which baffle the acuteness of the philosopher, as he endeavours to assign adequate and probable causes for the effects he witnesses in the world of morals. In itself an anomaly—its essential elements it is, of course, in vain to attempt any analysation of; but in following out the strange and intricate paths, in which the human heart appears to take a wayward delight to wander, we are frequently surprised at witnessing things, the sources and the springs of which are perfectly inscrutable, if they exist at all; and as we speculate upon the gigantic mysteries of being in the abstract, we are lost in astonishment at the frequent manifestations of recondite philosophy implicated in the very simplest effects it is possible to imagine. Whence is all this complicated machinery? Whence is all this wonderful organization, this universal involution of the materials of intellect and circumstance, yet so evidently the result of design, of thought and preconception? How can man have become what he is, when he might be (if we are to draw any inference from that standard of illimitable perfection which certainly subsists in *idea*) almost a god in his strength, his majesty, his capabilities? The metaphysician will go to the origin of evil; but with all his vast ingenuity, his sagacious research, his infinite patience, labor, and investigation ten-fold investigated, the more he thinks, the more he is convinced that his soul is the repository of that cryptic secret which is beyond the capacities of sense, though present to that principle which acts upon it, and clearly and most unequivocally attesting and developing to the inferior understanding that it is merely a small segment of that colossal universe with which

E

it is indivisibly connected here. We breathe, as it were, our own divine eternity in time. But digressions, although sometimes nearly unavoidable, are never wise or pleasant in any species of composition ; and it may often, perhaps, excite a smile on the lip of the philosopher, when he finds the individual who has been endeavouring to elucidate a dark enigma, himself involved in difficulty—a mystagogue, incapable, like Protagoras, of teaching to *his own mind* the subtle, baffling, and eluding ideas which he fancied, because he experienced, might therefore be explained.

To return, then, from the discussion of motives to the illustration and unravelling of character and events, let us proceed to recount the interview between Danvers and the Miser ; two men, who in former years had been of congenial habits, at all events, but were now——oh, how changed ! The mind moves, the nature departs. " Strange !"

CHAPTER VI.

You cast the event of war, my noble lord,
And sum the account of chance.—SHAKSPEARE.

Fortune may smile upon a future line,
And Heaven restore an ever-cloudless day.—BYRON.

DANVERS AND THE MISER—WALSINGHAM'S LIBERALITY—A
LITTLE MYSTERY AND SOME REFLECTIONS, &c.

"WELL, Walter Danvers," said the Miser, after a silence of some
minutes, "what brings you here?" and his voice trembled perceptibly as, with even more than customary suspicion in his glance, he
perused with furtive quickness the striking face turned towards him.
"If you want money," he continued, writhing under the terror of
parting with his beloved gold, "you know that I am poor, that I
ruined myself by the excess of my youth, when you——"

"Pshaw, man!" interrupted Danvers, contemptuously, "if I
wanted your gold, it were easy enough for me to force it from you.
No doubt you have plenty in that iron box you watch with such
nervous anxiety! But you need not turn so pale, for I require not
money now. I am come, according to the intimation conveyed by
the letter which you of course received from me, to communicate
with you on a subject of importance; and should you accede to the
propositions I am about to make, your wealth and influence will be
extensively magnified."

It was curious to watch the operation of the Miser's mind, as
they imprinted themselves on his wasted and prematurely wrinkled
countenance, while the bold and mysterious being before him, with
a clear and rapid utterance, spoke; but curiosity appeared the paramount feeling within him, as Danvers concluded.

" I do not understand you," replied the Miser, as he still fruit-lessly endeavoured to glean the purport of Danvers' visit by stealthily observing his gestures and general bearing. " But I cannot trust you, Walter ; for I know that you have become . . . Well, well, *that* does not matter to me. What brings you here now ?"

" Well, then, listen ; and remember, that if you should dare to breathe a syllable of what I am about to communicate, to any person hostile to the cause I am attached to, I can blast your name for ever ; and by heaven !——"

" Nay, nay, good Danvers ! kind, generous Walter !" exclaimed the Miser, shaking in every limb, as if afflicted with a fit of the ague. " You know that I—I—you will not betray me—you cannot—and of what advantage would it be to you, who are implicated——"

The utterance of the Miser here became so thick, that it was im-possible to distinguish what he attempted to articulate ; but it was evident that he suffered acutely from some unknown cause, perfectly understood by Danvers, as, quivering from head to foot, he cower-ed in a supplicating attitude before him, casting terrified glances from his person to the iron box, the utility of which he seemed so well acquainted with ; as if revolving how much it would be neces-sary to part with of that glittering dust, which is as the heart's blood to the avaricious man, to preserve the secret—the disclosure of which, even though merely hinted at as a possibility, almost petrified him with horror, and fear, and agony.

Danvers appeared to enjoy the dismay evinced by the Miser, as he sat in imperturbable composure, striking his boot with the butt-end of a heavy riding-whip which he carried.

" Be easy, Everard Walsingham," at length returned Danvers, " I am not the man to discover what indeed would not benefit me, though it would destroy you, without a very sufficient motive ; nay, if you comply with the terms I am about to make you, I will take any oath you like to impose, never to reveal your secret to man."

" Oh, Walter ! I am poor, I tell you," replied the other. " You cannot expect that I should give you a great deal out of my little ; but if a thousand guineas—ugh ! did I say a thousand ?—would—purchase the oath you talk of, you should have them forthwith."

Danvers opened his eyes. Great, indeed, must have been the desperation of the Miser, which could have induced him to offer such a sum for anything on earth, save what was certain to increase his store : and after he had ejaculated the astounding sentence, he clenched his bony hands, and remained the very image of hopeless misery, doubting not that his munificent offer would be accepted, and the gold depart from him for ever. But he was mistaken in his man.

"Zounds, Walsingham! I never thought to hear you tender a thousand guineas for any one's acceptance," exclaimed Danvers, "even to save you from perdition; but, I repeat, I want not your money, and your secret at present is safe with me."

The Miser breathed freely again. His face became radiant with satisfaction; and taking Danvers cordially by the hand, he said :— "Well, then, my good, liberal, and disinterested friend, what is it that you would have? I suppose that you are planning some scheme to enrich yourself at the public expense; but take care. Oh! take care, Walter—ugh! You might, when in prison, be induced to betray—ugh!" and again his cheek became blanched with apprehension. "Indeed, you had better accept my offer." His trepidation now became still greater. "If one thousand pounds be not sufficient, I will make it—yes, I will make them two thousand!—Oh! two thousand pounds!—to be wasted in riot and extravagance;— horrible! I cannot contemplate the picture."

Danvers, still more astonished at the liberality of Everard Walsingham, replied :—" I *have* a scheme; but it is not my own, but one concocted for the restoration of the rightful monarch of the British crown to his throne; and although our plans are as yet immature, our resources will be great, our friends multitudinous, and you are invited by the king himself—the *true* king, who is resolved to die, or regain the legitimate sceptre of his ancestors—to unite in the confederacy now organising for the purpose of expelling the Elector of Hanover from these dominions. In which case, he promises to grant you the forfeited estates of your family, seized upon by the rapacious hand of William of Orange; and, in addition, to elevate you to the dignities of a duke, with all the privileges and immunities held—Ah! what was that?" suddenly ejaculated Danvers, hastily interrupting himself, and rising from his seat.

" Did you hear a noise?" inquired the Miser.

" Yes. Have you any domestic?"

" No, no; I can't afford to keep a servant. You must certainly be mistaken."

" And yet I could have sworn it was a stifled cough."

So saying, Danvers opened the door of the cottage, and looked around; but though the moon was shining brightly, no living object, save his own horse, quietly nibbling the short herbage, was discernible.

"Perhaps it was the horse that coughed?" suggested the Miser.

"Well, it might have been; but the sound did not seem to proceed from that direction. However, as you say there is nobody in the house except yourself, I suppose I was deceived."

The conference was resumed; but Everard Walsingham, notwithstanding the glittering bait which Danvers held out to him, did not appear to relish the proposals made.

"If the plot were discovered," he said, "I should lose all! All the savings of nine long years; for which I have pinched myself, and denied my miserable body almost the necessaries of life. Nor should I, perhaps, obtain the estates you referred to, after all; for we all know that princes in power are not what they are out of it. I would rather not engage in the plot personally."

"What!" returned Danvers, impetuously; "do you think that the Stuart would forfeit his kingly word, for which he has here transmitted a document, signed and sealed by himself, and which I am commissioned to deliver to you? Shame on such a vile and unworthy suspicion! Wherefore should you doubt a pledge so sacred?"

"It would not be the first pledge which a Stuart has broken," replied Walsingham; "for when my brave ancestor, John, demanded from Charles the Second the restoration of those estates, which had been confiscated by Oliver Cromwell, during the Protectorate, for his adhesion to the royal cause, he was answered with insult; and, old, feeble, and impoverished, was obliged to quit the Court."

"But James the Third is not Charles the Second," responded Danvers, biting his lip; for the well-known ingratitude and selfishness of the Stuarts had already often baffled this warm adherent of their cause, in many exertions he had made in it.

It is a remarkable feature in the peculiar physiology of the Miser's ruling passion, that, although earnestly set on acquiring wealth, he is cautiously alive to the slightest risk in doing so: and probably this characteristic in their commerce with mankind, has materially aided the Jews—those most avaricious of the human race—in frequently amassing such prodigious riches, and also in keeping them. But Danvers had fancied that the covetousness of Walsingham would immediately induce him to join the league, of which he was an agent. It was not a little, however, that could overcome the perse-

verance, or baffle the ingenuity of the shrewd, powerful-minded man,
than whom, the cause he upheld could scarcely have chosen a more
sagacious, cool, active, and bold instrument for the furtherance of
those schemes which were, in the course of a few years, to plunge
England into civil war, and create a clashing of those elements, held
together by union, without which it is a moral impossibility for any
system of polity for any length of time to subsist. The consequence,
in the abstract, of a disunion in, and disorganization of, the established opinion which rules the majority of the mass, although it may
only be apparent for a brief period, is productive of effects seldom
calculated by the ordinary politician, who habituates himself to consider that the expediency of the hour is *all* that should be consulted
in legislating for an empire. The philosophic mind, however, perceives results more remote, and is accustomed to contemplate the
action of causes apparently the most nugatory in the succeeding
effects.

The infamous abuse of the Stuarts of the powers entrusted to
them by the nation, induced that dormant spirit of liberty to germi-
nate, the vast effects of which are now visible in " the wreck of old
opinions," in the abhorrence of oppression, and contempt of systems
and dogmas, based solely on the authority of the past. In vain
does tyranny endeavour to shackle the gigantic energies of the human mind when once aroused ; in vain attempt to stem the tide of
popular sentiment, as it rushes ocean-like through the whole body of
laws and institutions, carrying away with it bloody enactments and
iniquitous statutes, but perhaps annihilating much that might, with
gentle modifications, have been productive of beneficial results, in its
eager desire to witness the purification of the universe from the taint
of the cruelty and the ignorance of our predecessors ; while the individual mind, unchanged, mocks at the futility of intellectual enlighten-
ment for the entire regeneration of the faculties which constitute
our moral being. The optimist imagines, as he perceives that
progression in science appears to be a law of development, that the
mental organization of the rational and intelligent creature must inevitably act upon the *heart*, and consequently that virtue must ultimately reign throughout the world ; but, alas! nature is too strong
for all the wisdom, the knowledge, the power, and the experience of
man ! Change pervades all things in time ; and, indeed, without it,
time would not subsist ; so that even, if we attained to perfection itself, a change would necessarily cause imperfection. With the Great

Disposer of events alone exists the means of turning the hearts of the
disobedient to the wisdom of the just. How impotent, in his *power*,
is man!

CHAPTER VII.

What have we here?—a man, or a fish?
Legged like a man, and his fins like arms.
    What's the matter? Have we devils here?
Do you put tricks upon us with savages, and men of Inde?
SHAKSPEARE'S Tempest.

THE CHILD AND THE MONSTER.

AGAIN, gentle Reader, the Author has to solicit your indulgence
for his offence in launching forth into an argument on the possibility
of perfection being rendered permanent in anything in time, though
in a preceding chapter he expressed his opinion of the inexpediency
of introducing digressions, when not necessitated to do so; but remember, in mitigation of the offence, that we are, all of us, for ever
promising amendment, and for ever renewing our transgressions.
But how many kindly and generous feelings of the soul are elicited
by the reciprocal forgiveness of trifling injuries, the recurrence of
which (if they do not swell into great outrages) are productive of such
ameliorating influences with those, imperfect indeed, but yet possessing the right stuff of humanity within their secret bosoms, that it
might well reconcile us to being created less than the angels, when
the sweet smile, and the tearful eye, and the trembling lip, all fondly
assure us of the entire forgiveness of a hasty word or omission, and
render all the privileges of dear, social intercourse and mutual love
and aspiration endeared to us, beyond expression of such a pen as
inscribes these humble pages.

Considered rightly, then, there is no evil which has not its due
counterpoise of good, whatever Byron, Shelley, and other mistaken
sceptics have asserted to the contrary.

But lest, in entreating pardon for the offence which has been
deprecated, a second and more mortal reiteration of the crime be
unintentionally committed, let us, without attending to the turn of

a fluent sentence, recommence the narrative from which we have diverged.

Notwithstanding the reluctance of the Miser to involve himself in any scheme which might endanger his safety, Danvers possessed a power over him—a power which he had been accustomed to exercise, and the weak Walsingham acknowledge and obey in years past,— against which he vainly attempted to struggle; so that after a pro- tracted visit, the political agent quitted his ancient friend fully assured that he had gained over a valuable adherent to the cause he served. Taking leave of Walsingham, he mounted Dickon, and proceeded to retrace a portion of the way he had previously traversed; but did not observe, as he quitted the place, that a female form emerged from behind a projection in the wall of the cottage, and gazed after him with a malicious grin, in which there was much mischief lurk- ing; for, engrossed in his own reflections, plans, and intricate plot- tings, he suffered his horse to walk leisurely along in the direction of a village, at the distance of about a mile.

"What a strange being is that Walsingham!" thought he; "but I have him fast; although I would not trust him otherwise; for he would sell his soul for gold: and at present the Elector of Hanover can bribe more highly than James the Third. But the time is coming quickly when England will be aroused to a sense of the injustice she has committed in suffering these foreign rascals to occupy the an- cient throne of her legitimate monarchs; and then—and then I shall not be what I am now! an outlaw, a robber—aye, so should I be called by those conventional people who judge of men entirely by externals. But I shall have high military rank; I am promised a Colonel's commission for these services, and then surely I shall be able to wipe away the stain that clings to my name. From a Colonel to a General there is but one step, and why should not I be a second Marlborough, in the service of my true sovereign? Yes, yes, I feel that I shall rise; that I was never destined to play a subordinate part in the great game of life; ultimately, I may be ennobled, and my children, my dear children——"

As the ambitious man recurred to the images of those beings who in infancy had fondled and clung to him, and had entwined them- selves around the branches and fibres of his heart, an unwonted tenderness entered his soul, and his eyes moistened.

"My Ellen, my own Ellen! and my dear boy—bright children of a most unworthy mother! how proudly they will adorn the station

F

at which I now aim!   It is for them I plot, and scheme, and waste
the night in thought; without them, I were but a blighted tree, and
existence would be objectless!"

Intent on these desultory dreams and musings, Danvers had come
suddenly upon a scene so singular that our history must make a
backward movement, in order that it may be distinctly pourtrayed
to those who peruse it.

A young boy, of about nine years old, was occupied in eating a
large slice of plum cake, as he walked across a broad green park,
and had just struck into the midst of an avenue of magnificent trees,
when a strange object, which might well have startled into horror
any ordinary child of his age, so grotesque and hideous was its
almost indescribable appearance—on a sudden came upon him.
This was a creature with long and matty locks of a rusty hue, with
a dull, stony eye, a forehead apishly low, a vast mouth, stretching
from ear to ear, a flat nose, a gigantic head, arms of most dispropor-
tionate magnitude to the body, which was hardly that of a lad of
thirteen in stature, but nevertheless was marvellously muscular and
sinewy, and a strange mixture of the man, the boy, and the brute in
his whole appearance.

No sooner did this frightful being behold the tempting cake that
the young boy was munching, than he rushed forwards and attempted
to snatch it from his hand.   But the brave little fellow, nothing
daunted, withheld the object which had excited the desires of the
unnameable creature, and doubling his fist, with flashing eyes and
dilated figure, dared him to despoil his grasp of the plum cake. The
nondescript, upon this, uttered a most hideous cry, resembling, in
some degree, that of a monkey when infuriated, and darting on the
little boy would speedily have inflicted a severe punishment on him,
had he not eluded the long horny nails, resembling the talons of a
wild beast, which were aimed at his face, and dealt his enemy a
hard blow on his bare and hairy chest.

Howling horribly, the creature again attacked the child, who
took to his heels, closely pursued by his foe, and they were now
within a few paces of the spot where Danvers had arrived.

"Oh, help, help!" cried the poor little fellow, as the detestable
creature at length overtook him, and threw him violently to the
earth, "he is choking me!"

"The devil!" exclaimed Danvers, leaping from his horse's back,
and hastening to the child's assistance.

The Boy, Brute, the Ape, and Little George.

Page 35.

Had he been a few seconds later, the fiendish being, whom we know not how to designate, save as the boy-brute, would absolutely have strangled the child; but bestowing a buffet on his huge ears, which for an instant stunned the nondescript, he released the struggling and panting object of pursuit, who clung to him now fairly terrified and trembling.

But it appeared that the contest might not be so easily terminated; for as the boy-brute, his ears gushing with blood, recovered himself and uttered a mighty yell, an ape suddenly rushed forwards, and clasping him in its embrace surveyed Danvers and his *protegee* with vindictive hate.

"Never fear, my pretty boy, they shall not hurt you," he said, encouragingly, and had hardly spoken, when the boy-brute hastily broke a branch from off a tree beneath which he stood, and dividing it between himself and the ape, assumed an offensive attitude, whirling his weapon rapidly round, and making gesticulations of menace, which excited nothing but a smile from Danvers, who, notwithstanding, could almost have fancied himself in one of his childhood's dreams of fairy land, so incomprehensible and wild was the whole affair.

The boy-brute again advanced to battle, and had even the audacity to direct his attack on the formidable protector of his former adversary; but he, stepping briskly forwards, seized him by the throat. Demoniacal was the rage of the boy-brute, as he writhed in the vice-like grasp of his powerful antagonist; and, gigantic as was the strength of Danvers, it required no common exertion of it to restrain his furious endeavours to inflict some injury upon him. The ape now came to the assistance of its bestial friend, and though its teeth chattered with fear, having gathered up some large stones from the road, might have seriously hurt Danvers, when the young boy, similarly armed with flints, discharged a volley of those missiles at the animal, which caused it to retire. Still the engagement was not over. The ape having climbed the tree from which the boy-brute had broken the bough, commenced hurling the stones with unerring aim at Danvers, whose only resource was to cover himself behind the body of his foe, whom the ape at length wounded in the head with a stone intended for the other.

Perceiving this mis-adventure, which was succeeded by a sharp cry of pain from him who had suffered by it, the ape descended, and, emboldened by its strange affection, actually struck at Danvers with the stick previously given to it. Angered and provoked, Danvers on a sudden drew his sword and aimed a blow at the ape, which, had it fallen on the skull, must inevitably have severed it, but, instead of doing so, cut off the nose, as it fell in a slanting direction, and together with it a portion of the face. With agonized screams, the miserable beast fled, and Danvers permitting the nondescript to escape from him, they were soon both out of sight.

Now, my sweet, pretty little maiden, whom I value beyond all my readers for the tenderness and romance in that little heart of thine, and for whom I intend something better than has hitherto appeared in this true chronicle, don't shake your glossy ringlets with that incredulous look of dissatisfaction at what may appear to your sagacious judgment a recurrence to the style of the old impossible stories which you have discarded with your dolls and the nursery with very proper disdain, for the character of the boy-savage will not probably fill a very prominent part in the tale before you ; and, moreover, though he is a kind of Casper Hawser, or Caliban, or one of those monsters which fact and which fiction have occasionally presented to man, you may, after all, find him a remarkably amusing kind of brute, and as original as a fancy portraiture of the ideal in the author's mind can make him.

But it is time to hasten onwards before the curiosity and sympathy of my lovely friend have subsided in the affairs of Captain Charles Walsingham.

CHAPTER VIII.

I do believe as whirlpools to the sea
Love is to life.—*The Sea-Captain.*

Dost thou not breathe a spirit like the morn,
That warms like blood, and bids thee on to something?
      *   *   *   *   *
I know no more of this than that 'tis evil.—G. STEPHENS.

ELLEN DANVERS AND WALSINGHAM—THE SECRET CONFERENCE.

WHO would not be an invalid, if, on condition of a little corporeal suffering, he might have so sweet a nurse as that unlucky,
lucky dog, the Captain—watching his slumbers, smoothing his
pillow, administering his medicines, speaking the kindest, softest
words, in accents of such honied music! O Jove! and O Cytherea! I must not permit my imagination to conjure up the delights of
such a sick room, or in a fit of temporary madness I may go and
throw myself out of window, on the speculation that some fair
daughter of Eve, witnessing the catastrophe, may take compassion
on *me*, also, and then, and then—Tush, whither am I rambling?

Charles Walsingham was a romantic young man, as has been
already observed, and a fellow of all others calculated to excite
a tender emotion in the heart of a not less sensitive young maiden of
sixteen. Handsome in person, chivalrous by nature, gentlemanly,
ardent, and now suffering from a broken head, he was altogether
irresistible; and destiny ordained that Ellen Danvers—gentle, compassionate, warm-hearted girl---should witness how nobly he could
endure great suffering, restrain the natural irritability and impatience of illness, and most unmistakeably admire her budding
charms.

There is something in the atmosphere of a sick room (could I not find some oriental metaphor now, such as so abundantly adorns the glittering sentiment of Lalla Rookh?) which apparently predisposes to the melting sensations of Love; not that pity alone is entirely sufficient for kindling such a passion, which indeed would soon expire amidst such roses as Mr. Moore was in the habit of continually pelting us withal; for it requires a sustenance more solid than the perfumed breath of flowers, and gums, and spices; there must be something ever to counteract the effects of excessive sweetness---innumerable collaterals must combine to excite those impassioned feelings, which thrilling each fibre of the sentient being, pervade also the spiritual framework of intellect, and evoke from its " vasty deep" the undeveloped sympathies and dormant sentiments, the associations and the poetry which constitute the great elements of the existence of that divinity,

> " ———Without whom
> The earth would seem—like what it is—a tomb."

How rich, how exquisite, would be that page which could accurately pourtray the progress of a pure and innocent love, carrying away by its aerial impetuosity all the ideas which had preceded the epoch of its first nascent fascinations, creating a new universe, full of hope, and aspirations, and joyous dreams, and while elevating and etherealising our belief of its holiness and immortality, most irresistibly convincing us, despite the sneers of the sensualist, and the invectives of the ascetic, that its origin---if in its object and as an effect it is human---in its cause cannot be otherwise than divine!

Yes, there she sate, her large, azure eyes at one time tracing the bold and noble outline of the soldier's features, and at another fixed thoughtfully on the ground, and then raised to the heaven that appeared through the little casement in all the cloudless beauty of serenest summer, while her heart was palpitating with the gushing sentiments which were slowly beginning to centre themselves in the not unworthy object who lay asleep before her. Elizabeth had again quitted her patient, and Ellen was filling her spirit with those bright and ecstatic, but delusive dreams, which are for ever melting in air, and again returning upon the imagination with a redoubled splendour.

A few brief months, and where shall the radiant vision have departed? The remembrance may exist; but the principle which nourished and mingled with it—the hope, the passion, and the fancy, shall *they* return again?

> " A shadow shall come, and the light of that sky,
> Like the song of the swan, in its own glory die."

Ellen sunk into a deep reverie. Her transparent temples pressed by her lily hand, and her arm resting on the table placed by the bedside of Walsingham, her regular and soft breathing, and the faint respiration of the sleeper, were the only sounds of life distinguishable there. Suddenly the eyes of the soldier unclosed, for he had been merely dozing, and the mellow radiance of the harvest moon poured down on the fair young face that was presented to his view.

" How like an angel she does look!" thought he, endeavouring to discover what might be passing within her bosom by earnestly studying the expression of her ingenuous face; and, fearful lest he should disturb her from a position which afforded him a perfect prospect of all her virgin and delicate loveliness, he remained hushed and mute; "I wonder if there *can* be anything more beautiful in heaven?"

Take care, take care, Charles Walsingham! When young fellows of your age launch forth into rhapsodies about angels, and compare their *possible* graces with those of an earthly creature, there is danger, *very* great danger, indeed, to their quiet and peace.

At length, Ellen looked up, and encountered the tender and rather passionate gaze of Charles.

" Oh, how kind you are," he exclaimed, " to take all this trouble about me. I know not whom I am addressing; but permit me to assure you that the gratitude I feel for your goodness towards one so totally unworthy of it——"

" Hush, hush, I beseech you," interrupted the maiden, the warm blood mantling to her temples, " any over-exertion on your part might be fatal. Are you well enough to take anything to eat?" And Ellen timidly tendered some delicious fruit.

" Thank you, thank you, I feel almost *quite* well now, I assure you;" but, as Walsingham spoke, he experienced a throb of pain, the most acute he had yet suffered, which caused him to turn to an ashy paleness; but, with a great effort, he mastered the anguish he endured, and smiled upon his beautiful attendant.

The maiden after a silence of several minutes spoke, and said,

"Your nurse has been called away unexpectedly, and, as you are not fit to be left alone, I—I—"

Why was it that Miss Danvers could not conclude that sentence? There was nothing in it; but there arose such a fluttering at her breast that, for the life of her, she could not articulate one single syllable further.

Walsingham was rejoiced somehow that she was confused. He would not have had her calmly kind, on any account, and so he did not attempt to assist her out of her dilemma. But why attempt to describe all the sweet falterings, and the broken accents, and unfinished sentences, and the nameless nothings, which invariably characterise the growth of a First Love (for, though the soldier had accomplished six-and-twenty mortal years, he had never once experienced a throb of passion, save in his wild enthusiasm of fancy, and Ellen had not even dared to *dream* hitherto)—a love which was ordained to undergo many vicissitudes, but one which was as warm and disinterested, and free from "baser stuff," as our great poets have ever succeeded in delineating it. Suffice it, then, that about one hour of uninterrupted intercourse, in which hardly ten ideas were interchanged, determined Ellen and Walsingham that they were respectively the most charming young lady and gallant cavalier in the whole world; and, if ever they *did* marry, each was the model of the other's *beau ideal* of a wife and husband.

What a pleasant thing it must be to credit that there is one being in this wide universe of wickedness, folly, and moral deformity in every various phase, free from a single taint of its corruption!

When Miss Danvers quitted the brave, the enthusiastic Walsingham, no wonder if the excitement produced by her presence on his nerves were productive of some slight augmentation of fever; nevertheless, his strength appeared to recruit itself, and though occasionally visited by sharp twinges, he forgot almost entirely the object of his interrupted journey into that part of the country, and indeed every thing under the sun, except the adorable, the angelic Ellen. Again the soldier dozed, and presently his chamber-door was softly opened by the stately Elizabeth, who, conceiving him to be in a sound sleep, cautiously retreated.

Soon afterwards there issued from the adjoining chamber a sound of voices in earnest conversation, and Walsingham awoke, with the sense of hearing rendered painfully acute by the irritable state of his nervous system.

Through a small chink in the wall, which was of no great thickness, he perceived a light, and could catch a glimpse of the figure of a man, although he was not able to discern his features.

" The cause advances bravely," said the voice of Elizabeth, in answer to something that had been previously uttered by the individual Walsingham had perceived, " but nevertheless, more, much more, remains to be accomplished. We want money beyond every thing ; yet we must not by any means neglect to secure as many adherents as possible."

The soldier, if his curiosity were somewhat aroused by the mystery which lurked in this conversation, aware that it was not intended for his ear, was about to endeavour to turn his attention to some mental exercise (no very hard one probably, but redolent of love and his inamorata's loveliness), when he heard his own name spoken.

" Touching this same Captain Walsingham," exclaimed the voice of the man, " I should fear it is almost an Utopian scheme to attempt to divert him from his loyalty ; nevertheless, I know that Danvers has an oily tongue, and a subtle wit ; and, if we *could* gain him over to our cause, he would be a most————"

" Hush, do not speak in so loud a tone," interrupted Elizabeth. " I left him buried in sleep ; but a slight noise frequently disturbs an invalid."

An answer was returned, but in so low an accent, that even the soldier, all attention, and with a preternaturally excited sensibility of hearing, could only catch a few detached sentences.

" When will Captain Danvers return ?" inquired the strange man, after a debate of some duration, apparently upon the expediency of a measure, the nature of which Walsingham could not clearly comprehend—although he could not divest himself of the notion that, throughout, himself formed a topic of discourse.

" A few hours hence, at all events, but he is extremely uncertain in all his movements," responded Elizabeth.

" I must see him to-morrow, before I leave England ; but must now be in motion again without delay, as the friends of the good cause expect me at the distance of nearly ten miles, in the course of an hour and a half ; and I would impress upon you the necessity of exerting whatever influence you may possess to make this young man our own. Be not sparing in your offers, and be assured that *he* will ratify them ; but be cautious lest you unwarily betray—"

" *I* betray, Sir Agent ! *I*, who hand and heart am bound up

G

in—" (here a few words remained, not overheard). " I, who every hour that—" (again some sentences were lost on the listener), " fear not *my* discretion."

" And if, and if—the young maiden could do anything to serve———"

" Speak no more of that !" exclaimed Elizabeth, hastily, " *her* safety must not in any case be imperilled ; and were we to lay a snare in which she might hold the net, she might suffer—" another *hiatus* here ensued in the conversation, and immediately afterwards the man took his departure, Walsingham remaining a prey to doubt and conjecture.

Under ordinary circumstances, he would have been the last in all the world to play the eaves-dropper ; but uniformly in sickness the mind is agitated by an under-current of fancies and feelings, which in health would never for an instant cross it.

Our soldier, too, was beginning to experience very serious sensations about the regions of the heart, of which the idea of Miss Danvers formed the nucleus ; and probably he thought he might by possibility discover something relative to her also. However the case may be, he remained restless and uneasy during that whole night ; and, when he again sank into a state of unconsciousness, he dreamed confusedly of treasons, plots, and love-makings ; sometimes fancying that he had become a statesman, and was involved in a thousand intrigues, which, when awake, would never have entered into his honest soul to conceive ; sometimes imagining that the syrens were tempting him into interminable dangers and difficulties, out of which the hand of the faithful lady of his heart could alone extricate him.

END OF BOOK I.

BOOK II.

The past is Death's—the future is thine own.

The Revolt of Islam.

Our ancient crown 's fa'n in the dust,
  Deil blind them wi' the stour o't;
And write their names in his black beuk,
  Wha ga'e the Whigs the power o't.
Grim vengeance lang has ta'en a nap,
  But we may see him wauken;
Gude help the day when royal heads
  Are hunted like a mauken!—BURNS.

BOOK II.

CHAPTER I.

Yes, be the glorious revel mine,
Where humour sparkles from the wine.
MOORE'S *Anacreon.*

Away, away, for only flight can save you.
Richard III.

THE TAP-ROOM—CORPORAL FIGGINS—THE BEARDED WOMAN—
A PLOT, AND MYSTERY—DANVERS—THE CHILD.

EATED in the tap-room of a small hostelry, whose outward sign was a flaming picture of a very red-nosed lady, somewhat damaged by storm and wind, and which, as the large letters beneath informed the wayfarer, was intended to represent Britannia, were several jolly topers, many of whom were already in that blissful state of semi-intoxication and unconsciousness, which is the Drunkard's Paradise; and the greater number essentially elevated beyond the ordinary pitch of their spirits; while a few—a couple, or perhaps three, old steady, regular, not-to-be-made-drunk-with-drinking tipplers, retained their wonted equibility,—only their eyes were a thought more sparkling, and their noses a degree more crimson than when for a brief interval they refrained from paying their devotions to the god of wine.

Among those of the latter denomination, whose proboscis was redder, and whose whole appearance was more indicative of long-continued habits of adoration to Bacchus, than that of any other person present, was a huge brawny man, with a face of extraordinary breadth, bearing some slight resemblance to that of a certain celebrated Irish barrister and political luminary of the present day, and who was evidently "the star of that good company," occupying the seat of honour, and appearing the cynosure of attraction to every gaze present.

There was so much shrewdness, good humour, cunning, wit, and joviality in this worthy's face, that he would have been invaluable to a painter of the Dutch school, whose peculiar merit lies in delineating features illustrated by breadth and originality of character, while his tall stature, his vast shoulders, and a certain soldierly erectness of carriage that he maintained even in his easy posture, although they might not exactly add dignity to his form, imparted a sort of antique, burly, and stalwart formidability, which carried the imagination back to the days when hard blows and deep drinking constituted the chief delights of such a sturdy, terrible, merry and boon a fellow, as was that whom our artist has pourtrayed in the engraving, with a tankard of humming ale in his great coarse hand.

"Come, Corporal Figgins, jolly Corporal Tom, tip us a stave of the right sort!" exclaimed an individual, who with some difficulty maintained his equilibrium, as he sat opposite to the person he addressed.

"Ay, a song, a song!" shouted the whole party, unanimously; "a good song, and a merry tune to it."

"With all my heart, good gentlemen," quoth Figgins, tossing off the remainder of the contents of his tankard, and immediately calling for more. Clearing his throat, and elevating his head, while his small twinkling grey eyes glittered like those of a snake, the Corporal immediately trolled, in a voice of gigantic power, and with great animation and effect, the following words to a favourite air of the time.

"Hurrah for the ale! for the jolly jolly ale,
    That fills the heart of man with gladness;
If the soul should be sick, and the spirit fail,
Quaff the ale, quaff the ale, the jolly, jolly ale,
    And, d——e, 'twill away with all sadness!

"Look around—as the ale, as the jolly, jolly ale
    Fills the breasts of good fellows with mirth,
While it circles and warms, it tells a tale,
That there's strength and bright life in all jolly ale,
    'Tis man's constant good friend upon earth.

> " Drink away, drink away! and if drinking we die,
> Why the Devil will say as he takes us,
> (What the parson may preach is all my eye,
> For he drinks himself, though he well can lie,)
> ' What splendid fine devils ale makes us.'

" There, my lads, I made all that as I sang," said Corporal Fig-gins, as he finished his Bacchanalian ditty amid thunders of ap-plause. " It is my opinion, gentlemen," continued he, with a look of genius, as he again moistened his throat with the beverage he loved, " that there's something more than the mere spirit itself in choice liquor—'tis the essence of wit, the nourisher of good fellow-ship, the promoter of mirth and love; it darts through all the veins and arteries, and calls to the brain, I know not how, at once, every pleasant sensation the body can experience. Gad's my life! they say that it's a friend of old Satan, and sends many to the bottomless pit; but let me ask all here present—and I could not find a more unprejudiced jury---if it be reasonable to believe that what makes us all so happy, can come from the realms of woe?"

" Bravo, Corporal, you are right, old boy."

" Gentlemen," rejoined Figgins, " I used to hear some of my officers, when I served in the Royal Horse Guards, affirm that wine is the nectar of the Gods. I don't know precisely what nectar means myself, being no scholar; but, blood and 'ounds, I know that a couple of pots of this ale elevates my spirits to the moon; a third, to the stars; a fourth, to the sun; and a fifth, up to heaven itself! So, here goes now for another song of my own.

> " When I was a boy, and my chin was yet smooth,
> I fell into love, and I snivell'd away,
> I prayed and besought her, but never I caught her,
> For then I knew not Love's only right way.
> But soon I grew wiser, I flew to the glass,
> I kissed her, I fondled, as much as I chose,
> For the juice of the grape, and drink in each shape,
> Makes a man, makes a man—in her favor I rose."

The Corporal was proceeding to improvise some more verses for the delectation of the company, when he was suddenly pulled by the sleeve; and, on turning round, beheld a very ugly old woman, of forbidding aspect, who whispered a few words in his ear.

" Well, mother Stokes," he exclaimed, " what the deuce brings you?"

The presence of the new comer instantaneously damped the joviality of the assembled topers; and, indeed, her presence was not calculated to inspire pleasurable emotions of any sort. She was low of stature, of swarthy complexion, with a dark beard on her chin, now mingled with grey, and her eyes were sinister, and her wrinkled brow scowling; while there was a fierceness and a maliciousness in the entire expression of her countenance, such as we usually associate in idea with the witches of Macbeth.

"Wherefore delay?" returned the woman, in answer to Figgins, and in a low voice, at the same time unceremoniously helping herself to drink, at the expense of a more than two-thirds fuddled individual who sat on the right of the Corporal, "you will lose a prize, such as may never fall to your lot again, if you don't quickly bestir yourself."

"Well," replied Figgins, unwillingly quitting his seat, and following the hag out of the room.

They proceeded into a small apartment, which, it being nearly midnight, was dark as pitch, and the female then eagerly exclaimed,

"Walter Danvers is here!"

"Ha!" ejaculated the Corporal, evidently not a little startled.

"You know the reward offered for his apprehension formerly, and we have him now beyond the possibility of escape. Let us at once bar all egress from the room he occupies."

"But," said Figgins, irresolutely.

"Do you hesitate?" was the rejoinder; "nay, then, I myself will secure him, and obtain the reward of one hundred pounds."

"Stay, mother Stokes," said the Corporal, detaining her as she was on the point of leaving him, "I do not hesitate; but we must be cautious how we proceed. You know, Danvers———"

"Fear not," interrupted mother Stokes, "I have a hold on him you know not of. Come this way; I have the key of the padlock that secures the outer door leading to his chamber. Vengeance, vengeance! Curse him! I shall soon see the villain suspended on a gallows. Oh, that I might tear the heart out of him!" And with these words, the amiable female and Figgins proceeded to consummate the scheme that the former had projected.

Leaving these worthy coadjutors to their business, let us run up a flight of stairs, advance through a long, gloomy passage at whose extremity there is an oaken door of great thickness, and again up two or three steps, at the end of which there is another and common door; and taking the liberty of peeping through it, by an exercise of the faculty that is spiritual within us, behold an old acquaintance, in the person of the identical Danvers, whose adventures have occupied perhaps the greater portion of our first book.

Yes, there he is, leaning on one hand, and apparently buried in thought. He seems melancholy, and often lifting up his eyes to the glorious heavens, spangled with " stars innumerable," is engaged in a train of fancies, indefinable even by poetry or philosophy, but yet sometimes experienced by every created being with soul and feeling—fancies steeped in the relics of passion, and hope, and rapture, occasionally presenting some fixed image indeed ; but yet, notwithstanding the predominance of a particular phase of reflection, still made up of a hundred associations, connecting themselves with the visions of the past, the present (if there *be* a present) and the future; like those beings created by the vivid imagination of some lofty dreamer, as they flit before him in dim reality, in all their pensive, their radiant, and solemn show.

" Poor, poor Harriet," he exclaimed, in a tone of remorse and sorrow, " how I loved her ! Oh, God ! oh, God ! And I know— I am *sure* that I was dear to her also ; but destiny battled against us. She was too pure and perfect for such a world as this. Peace be with her !"

He relapsed into silence, and completely concealing his face with his hands, appeared to sleep, though he was only in a kind of torpor, totally oblivious of the actual world around, and from which he did not arouse himself for a considerable period.

During this interval, had he not been so deeply abstracted, he might have heard a grating sound, as of the drawing of a bolt outside his door; but the report of a park of artillery would hardly at that particular time have caused him to start ; so that although he was conscious of perceiving a slight noise with his outward senses, the mind within took no cognizance of it, and consequently his reflections were in no degree disturbed.

Presently, however, there was a tapping at the window of the room from the outside, the continued recurrence of which for several minutes at length broke the spell that bound his soul. He arose from his seat, and gazing out of the window beheld the figure of the very same child whom he had rescued from the clutches of the savage a few hours before, standing on the topmost branch of a tree that

H

grew at the distance of two or three yards from the wall of the house, and making gesticulations of alarm to him.

"What is amiss?" he inquired, immediately throwing up the casement.

"Hush!" returned the boy, who had been throwing pebbles at the window, "I fear you are in danger; but know nothing about it yet."

"In danger!" echoed Danvers, mechanically catching up his pistols, and examining the priming, "from whom?"

"They have been fastening you in," was the whispered response.

Danvers rushed to the door, and found it was bolted. With an oath, he applied his shoulder to it, and broke it down in an instant; but having done so, soon discovered a farther obstacle to his departure.

CHAPTER II.

For life and death he flies; indeed,
Like Death's upon the wind his speed.—MS.

MOTHER STOKES AND HER FAMILY—THE LADY IN THE STRAW —DANVERS AGAIN—THE PURSUIT.

UNWILLING as the Author may be to tantalize the patience of his Readers, he is unavoidably constrained to take up the narrative where it broke off in the seventh chapter of the first book; but religiously promises not to presume hereafter upon a quality excessively rare with us poor imperfect mortals, and should not that promise satisfy any fair lady or noble gentleman who is desirous of instantly following up the adventure that has befallen Danvers, it is only necessary to pretermit the intervening matter, which will not occupy a very considerable space.

"By Jove!" said Danvers, when the savage and the ape had both vanished, "this has been a most extraordinary scene!" Then turning to his *protegé* he asked, "Have you ever seen that strange being before?"

" Yes, sir, I've seen him once," answered the child.

" And what is your name, my little fellow ?"

" My name is George."

" And where are you going?"

" Oh, not a very long way from here! I am so grateful to you, sir, for your kindness to me, and, though I am a poor boy, God will hear me when I pray for you !"

Danvers was touched at the earnest gratitude of the child's manner. " I will see you home, if you do not live far hence, then," said he, and mounting Dickon offered to take him up before him. The child was delighted, and Danvers found on inquiry that he was returning to the identical Inn where he had resolved to sojourn the night. " And have you a father and mother?" he inquired of little George, as he put his horse into a trot.

" No father," answered the boy sadly, "and my mother is ill now, and away from me."

" And what is your mother ?"

" Oh, she is an actress, and I act with her very often, and dance on a rope, and sing."

" Indeed ! And how long have you lived thus ?"

" Ever since I can remember—about five years."

" Have you been to school?"

" Never, sir; but I have learned to read, and oh, I am so fond of books, they are friends to me."

" Fond of books are you ? What books do you read ?"

" Any that I can get, but I like plays best."

" Whose plays do you prefer ?"

" Shakspeare's !" replied the child, with sparkling eyes, and subdued enthusiasm in his sweet voice, which, strange to say, though Danvers was quite certain he had never before beheld him, seemed familiar as a remembered music to his ear. " Yes, Shakspeare is so grand," continued George, and, when his characters speak, I can see them before me, as if they were really so !"

More and more interested in this singular boy, Danvers proceeded to put several questions to him, which he answered with intelligence beyond his years; and when he arrived at the Britannia Inn, he told him to be sure and come to him the following morning—a request with which George gladly complied.

Meanwhile, the savage had run after the ape, whose howlings and groans were still continued, and had hardly overtaken it, when a female arrived on the spot.

"Who has done this?" she screamed, on perceiving the piteous condition of the animal.

The boy-savage made no reply, but pointed in the direction Danvers had taken, and the woman, ascending an eminence, immediately saw him as he rode along with the child. Dire were the threats of vengeance that she uttered as she descended to the aid of the luckless ape, and applied such bandages as were within reach to the injuries. She then, followed by the savage and the brute, directed her steps to a hovel, at a few furlongs distance, and entering it, vented her indignation and wrath in audible curses.

"What is the matter?" asked a faint voice from the farther end of the room, which (with the exception of a kind of loft) was all the hut could boast.

"Matter, wench!" replied the woman, striking a light, and seating herself beside the bed of a female, who held a sleeping infant in her arms, of which she had been apparently delivered but a few hours; "but I'll be revenged; yes, Master Walter Danvers, I have you!" and the hag chuckled fiercely.

"Walter Danvers!" repeated the lady in the straw, who, though passed the perfection of her beauty, still retained many traces of it, "what of him?"

"Look at that poor ape; niece Sophy, _he_ has done it—curse him, curse him!"

"I do not understand you; do you mean my——"

"Husband! Yes. Ha, ha, you love him, and he loves you, as one devil loves another. Haw, haw!"

"But, mother Stokes, if you _have_ seen Walter—"

"I saw him about three hours ago, as I was watching the Miser's house, and I listened, long, and heard them hatching treason. I shall wring money from the avaricious dog's fears _now_; and for your husband, he shall swing, —— me! Figgins is at the Britannia, and I will go to him directly. Poor ape, poor ape; and my grandchild, too—the only things I do not hate in all this cursed earth. Oh, he shall suffer!"

Mistress Stokes, thus having spoken, fortified herself with a deep draught from a bottle of spirits, inquired whether the newly-delivered lady needed anything, and being answered in the negative (for it was evident nothing could be elicited from the hag to satisfy curiosity), soon afterwards quitted the hovel, and wended her way in the same direction Danvers had taken. And now the adventures of that personage, against whom so much mischief is brooding, may be resumed at once.

Having by main force broken down the door of his apartment, Danvers rushed forwards, but found that the outer door, which was of immense strength, was fastened on the outer side. In vain he strained his prodigious muscles to burst it off the hinges (for none but a Sampson could have achieved such a feat); and now voices and footsteps approached up the stairs. His only resource was to draw a bolt on the inner side, and return to his apartment.

"Hasten,' cried the voice of George, who remained on the tree, " here is a rope, and I will fasten it to this branch. There are soldiers below." So saying, the little fellow threw Danvers a rope, which he caught, and at the same time heard a great noise at the outer door, and immediately afterwards it fell with a crash.

Delaying no longer, Danvers sprang out of window, and was soon standing foot to foot with his young ally.

"I have taken out your horse for you," said the little fellow quickly, " there he is—good bye."

Hastily descending the tree, Danvers was soon on *terra firma*, and he had no sooner reached the ground, than several persons appeared at the window, which was twenty feet from it, and a pistol-ball whizzed past him, grazing his cheek. He uttered a shout of defiance, and vaulted on the back of Dickon; but, before he could quit the place, a gigantic hand arrested him.

With the swiftness of thought, the pursued dealt his opponent an awful blow on the face, which for a moment stunned him, and in that moment Danvers was off like the wind.

"Pursue!" cried Corporal Figgins, who had just received the stroke of that iron fist, and suiting the deed to the word, he mounted a large, powerful animal, belonging to a dragoon, and urged it on to its greatest speed. Half a dozen soldiers instantly dashed forwards, and seizing their horses, leaped into the saddles, and joined in the chase.

O'er hill and dale, on, on they went, leaping ditches, gates, and precipices, Corporal Figgins shouting, at the top of his stentorian voice, " Fifty pounds for the man that takes him! Spur onwards, my lads!"

But Danvers was at least three hundred yards in advance of his pursuers, and Dickon, having rested nearly two hours, was almost as fresh as ever.

The country that they traversed became gradually more level, and less intersected by streams and morasses, and Danvers, after the lapse of half an hour, during which he had left nine good miles behind him, was well nigh out of the range of the soldiers' sight. Striking into a cross road, he was congratulating himself on his escape, when on a sudden he beheld the glittering of steel, as the moon burst forth with dazzling brightness, at no very great distance in advance.

The path was narrow, so that more than two horsemen could not conveniently ride abreast, and his eagle eye at once discovered that a considerable body of cavalry was approaching him. On one side there was a river, broad and deep, on another there was a ploughed field, and in the van and rear the troops and his pursuers.

Without a moment's hesitation he plunged into the water, and swam Dickon across. But the stream was remarkably rapid, and unfortunately the beautiful planet which had directed his observation to the cavalry shone with undiminished and sun-like splendour on him. Corporal Figgins, rising in his saddle, discerned the troop, of whom the handful that had joined in the pursuit of Danvers formed the advanced guard, and bawled out, as the best means of directing their attention to the fugitive—" A Deserter !" In an instant the whole troop was led on to secure the runaway, and dispersed in various directions ; some swimming their horses after him, some taking a short cut by a bridge thrown across the river, and others flying to prevent him from gaining a valley on the other side, which he had now nearly reached ; and, thus hemmed in on every side, escape seemed next to impossible. But Walter Danvers was a lion, though in the toils, and his hunters were not to make him their prey without a violent and bloody struggle.

CHAPTER III.

Sae rantingly, sae wantonly,
Sae dauntingly, gaed he.—BURNS.

And therefore, when he ran away, he did so
Upon reflection.—*Don Juan.*

THE CHASE CONTINUED—DANVERS DISPLAYS HIS POWERS.

BULLETS whizzing past his head, and encompassed by foes on every side, the desperate courage and cool self-possession of Walter Danvers did not for an instant desert him. His resources, his powers, like those of all persons pre-eminently gifted with a quality on a sudden called into operation, rose with the occasion ; and every expedient of his fertile ingenuity passed through his brain with the swiftness of lightning, while he crossed the rapid stream, holding his pistols with one hand, so as they might not be injured by the water, and with the other grasping the bridle,—his docile horse apparently understanding the whole affair as well as his master, and obeying the slightest impulse of his arm.

There was a peculiarly precipitous bank on the other side, which the enemy, conceiving it impossible for Danvers to ascend, neglected to guard ; and he thought, by making a feint, as if he would dash among the thickest of them, and then mounting the steep abruptly, he might gain a considerable start, and then, still trusting to the prowess of the paragon he bestrode, he conceived that in the open country he might easily elude them all.

Acting upon this resolution he caused Dickon to strike out towards the land where it was level with the stream, and then suddenly turning, before his opponents could catch the drift of his manœuvre, he had actually gained the bank, and without stumbling or accident ascended it.

One alone had the quickness to conceive the whole stratagem
before it was completed, and that one was the redoubtable Figgins,
who had reached the opposite side, and instantly dashed forwards
to prevent Danvers from making good his landing, while he was
yet contending with the tide. He was just in time to meet the fugitive hand to hand ; and, burning with rage at the memory of the
tremendous blow he had previously sustained at his hands, he
struck at his head with a huge broadsword.

Danvers arrested the heavy blade as it was descending on him
impelled by tremendous force, and turning it aside with his weapon,
aimed at the Corporal with one of his pistols ; but a small portion
of water, notwithstanding the care he had taken, had entered the
barrel, or Figgins would never have wielded sword again. They were
equally matched ; but Danvers had no time to lose in " exchanging
hardiment," if he desired to make his escape ; and therefore wheeling round, and dealing blows like hail upon his burly antagonist,
dashed past him, and was borne along a nearly open country, still
followed closely. The Corporal was well-mounted, and bent on
capturing the runaway ; but his bulk was very great (not less than
eighteen stone of mortality encompassed his heroic soul), and caused
a considerable deterioration in the speed that he might otherwise
have used.

Dickon, however, although unequalled in his way, was still a mere
earthly horse, and Danvers was most reluctantly compelled to relax
his celerity at this juncture, notwithstanding that he perceived
several of the soldiers were rather gaining on him than otherwise.
Nevertheless he had left the great body of his pursuers far in the
rear, and he hoped he should be able to cope singly with the very
stoutest that might choose to try his mettle. Accordingly he examined his remaining pistol, and found it was fit for immediate use,
calculating that at all events he might despatch one of his opponents
with that. Bracing up his sinews for the encounter, he now fronted
the advancing foe, and with deadly determination on his brow,
though without the quiver of a muscle, levelled the pistol.

There is something peculiarly calculated to daunt the boldest
heart in that calm passionless aspect and immoveable rigidity of
position, especially when they sit on the face and form of so fierce
and bold a man as Walter Danvers. A tall dragoon, a young officer, and Corporal Figgins were the first to come within range of fire ;

yet, though heated and inflamed by the wild ferment superinduced by a hard chase, when they observed the cold, keen eye fixed sternly upon them, and felt the fearful accuracy with which the steel-strung hand would direct that little weapon it grasped, they prudently retired behind a vast tree, and one of them discharged his carabine at him. The shot would have taken effect, had not the pursued (to use a familiar phrase) ducked, and conceiving that it might be better policy to meet one at a time if possible, he adopted the stratagem of the old Roman hero, pretending again to fly, and the officer imprudently quitted the shelter of the tree, heedless of the warning voice of Figgins, who was not deceived by the feint. Danvers turning in his saddle perceived how matters stood ; but the beardless face and stripling form of the rash boy who dared to put his puny power in competition with one of the most redoubtable warriors of his day, then saved him from a death which would certainly have met a sturdier soldier.

" Poor fellow, he is like Harry !" muttered Danvers, as he dropped the arm that he had raised with the intention of firing. Figgins and the dragoon now emerged from behind the tree, and resumed the chase. " They shall have it, d—n them !" exclaimed the pursued from between his clenched teeth, as their shouts became more loud and exulting ; for they saw that the strength of Dickon was beginning to diminish, and had been fearful lest the wind of their own beasts should soon fail. Again wheeling round and facing the enemy, he awaited their coming with the same stern and statue-like calmness which has something in it so far more appalling than the wildest desperation.

The young officer, anxious to display his courage, with reckless impetuosity spurred on his charger, and called on Danvers to yield, threatening to blow out his brains, if he refused. The only reply was a slight laugh, which so irritated the lad, from the contempt it appeared to throw upon his prowess, that drawing a pistol from one of his holsters he aimed at the " tiger at bay," and grazed his forehead with the ball. Nought, perhaps, stirs up the blood of a nature like that of Danvers, as the ignominy of being hunted like a wild beast, and when excited he was indeed like the fiercest animal in his ferocity.

" Fool!" he exclaimed, as the officer now engaged with him, hand to hand, " I spared you once." Then, with one stroke of his weapon disarming him, he rushed upon the ill-fated boy, and with the butt-end of his pistol struck him on the temples. Danvers had not intended to deal a death-blow on his insignificant antagonist; but the weight of his unarmed hand alone was such that it might well have annihilated the stripling, particularly when nerved as it was by resentment; and, uttering a sharp cry of agony, he fell lifeless from his horse, as the hard iron of the pistol-barrel entered nto his brain.

"Come on !" cried Danvers, as the Corporal and the dragoon deliberately advanced like veterans, as they were, to the attack, and his voice was hoarse as he spoke, for somehow, despite himself, he felt pity for the unfortunate youth he had destroyed in the fair promise of his spring, and sought to turn aside the feeling of remorse which he experienced by venting his anger on a foe equal to combat with him. Nor did he long wait the expected assault. Figgins, sword in hand, spurred on his horse, and the dragoon followed his example. Danvers, had he chosen, might have killed one with his pistol; but he thought it might yet stand him in good stead, a more urgent occasion requiring, and therefore refrained, relying on his admirable and almost unequalled swordmanship.

It was a tremendous struggle, and one which tried the strength, and skill and quickness of the fugitive to the uttermost. Parrying, striking, wheeling, feinting, never exposing himself for a single instant but of necessity, he realized all the achievements of ancient chivalry; for taller, more powerful, and more consummate soldiers than the dragoon and the corporal seldom, if ever, swelled the ranks of the British troops. And now the shouts of the advancing cavalry were distinctly heard by Danvers, who felt that to be taken was to be executed, and that the contest he now maintained could not he greatly prolonged. Flinging the pistol that had previously proved useless with wonderful precision at the Corporal, it struck him full in the face; and, before he could recover the shock of the concussion, closed with his other opponent, seized him by the neck, and whirling him from his horse with the strength of a giant, threw him to the earth, so as he might fall on the head, and stun himself in doing so.

Again he was compelled to trust all to the wind and limb of Dickon, who exerted himself with almost incredible spirit, as if aware of the urgency of the occasion, and carried his rider in a few minutes beyond the sound of the lusty vociferations of the pursuers. Still Danvers did not flatter himself that he was by any means secure—

the more so that he knew he was now in a tract affording but few facilities of escape, and he was certain that some portion of the enemy had taken a course so as to encounter him in the van, and cut off the possibility of his retreat.

Under these circumstances, it was necessary again to have recourse to stratagem. One road would only have led him back to the river; and he was shut out from taking the opposite direction by the knowledge that a chain of hills extended in that line, the ascent to which, on that side, was impracticable. Revolving swiftly in his mind these difficulties, he directed his glance along the champaign which extended far as the eye could reach, and discerned a pretty and romantic little cottage embowered among trees of luxuriant growth, and appearing the only place of refuge, far or near.

Dickon was almost exhausted, and even Danvers himself experienced some sensations of fatigue; for he had taken no rest at all, and all the previous day had been in the saddle. Irresolute how exactly to proceed, the first faint streaks of morning tinted the horizon, and again the voices of his pursuers were borne upon the wind. As he expected he also thought he could hear indistinctly the cries of those sent round to take him in the van, and hesitating no longer, quitted the back of Dickon. "Be careful of yourself, my horse," he said, as soon as he had dismounted; and pointing out to him the direction he wished he should take, the sagacious animal trotted off towards the river. Danvers then strode hastily forward, leapt the low wall that encircled the isolated cottage, and was speedily lost to view.

CHAPTER IV.

Pale as the marble covering thrown aside,
    And scared as he were peering in some tomb
    To confront horrible death—So looks Castaldo.
                                    G. STEPHENS.

THE SILENT CHAMBER—A RHAPSODY OF BEAUTY—THE UN-
    EXPECTED MEETING—SHADOWS OF THE PAST—DANGER.

IN a small but elegantly-furnished apartment, adorned with pictures executed with the most masterly and exquisite taste, and furnished with unpretending yet admirable simplicity of effect, there
lay a woman of strange beauty, the faint moon-beams throwing a
weird light on features as perfect as ever Phidias moulded, and a
mind, a spirit more divine in the expression than any save God
himself could impart to clay.

She was extended on a couch, having apparently fallen asleep
over a book that was spread before her—an Italian copy of the
great Dante's Divina Comedia, of which there were some fine trans-
lations and criticisms—evidently in a lady's hand-writing on the
blank leaves of the volume.

Some eight-and-twenty summers had laid their hands upon that
woman's form; but her unequalled loveliness had apparently increased rather than diminished with time. Her brow and cheek
were both like Parian marble; not a ray of colour could be discerned
in her chiselled face; yet the absence of what may lend a lustre to
the charms of others, imparted a more seraphic glory to her splendid and unearthly beauty.

The characters of profound thought, of deep sensibility, of imagination, purity, and the lofty aspiration that becomes a part of being,
were imprinted on her snowy forehead, and appeared to quiver on

her arched and open lip, which exposed to view a row of pearly teeth (but pearls were never so dazzling and unspotted), and around a mouth where poetry and passion breathed a spiritual radiance such as never vivifies even the eyes of common souls. Her hair was of dark brown, silken, glossy, and luxuriant; her skin fair and delicate, and her voluptuous figure combining dignity, modesty, and softness, appeared instinct with a life of pervading grace. But never, had I the pen of a Shakspeare or a Milton, and the pencil of a Raffaelle and Titian, could I convey any correct idea of the loveliness I have feebly sketched, hopeless of conveying *more* than the outline to the reader's fancy.

Such forms have flashed on the dreaming spirit of the rapt poet, as his winged imagination has wandered among the stars, and in moments of wild inspiration he has been able to " turn them to shape," yet never to convey the divinity he has witnessed to any other intellect, though it may catch some faint glimpses of the meaning that struggles through shadowy metaphors, and of which the following description of a divine enthusiast in ardent youth may give an illustration.

" Seraph of Heaven! too gentle to be human!
Veiling beneath that radiant form of woman
All that were insupportable in thee
Of light and life and immortality!
Sweet benediction in the eternal curse,
Veiled glory of this lampless universe!
Thou moon beyond the clouds! thou living form
Among the dead! thou star above the storm!
Thou wonder, and thou beauty, and thou terror!
Thou harmony of nature's art! thou mirror
Wherein, as in the splendour of the sun,
All shapes seem glorious which thou lookest on."

How wonderful is the human face! Now sad, now joyous, now tranquil, now impassioned, now darting fire, now smiling fondest love, and, while overshadowed or unclouded, never, never the same, but borrowing the Spirit's genius, and glassing the emotions of the heart. In sleep, too, there is something inexpressibly touching, and calculated to excite the deepest sensibility in every brain and bosom where there exist feeling and fancy—when the hushed breath, and the closed eyes, and the motionless form, present a lovely likeness of the image we must all assume at last, before our dust mingles with the dust whence it arose—when the mighty spirit of life is stirring indeed, but so still, so calm, and, in natures like that of the beautiful woman, so innocent in its visions, thoughts, and ideas.

And it is a strange mystery, with its pomp, its darkness, its fierce, but melancholy and brief delight, that seems an antepast of eternity, to wean us from the world (if we could but see Heaven, who could endure existence here?) leaving darkness and desolation behind—hopes, cares, sorrows and despair alternating! Then we again live over our childhood's days—our sins, our griefs and joys—now passing from life to death, now beyond time and space, now in some little spot of earth, with some dear human tie to bind us closely to it; then in the heaven of heavens, with the Great Omnipotence beaming upon our immortalized being :---at one moment in the empyrean of God, with the blue and glorious floods of ether around, around, around, and instantaneously precipitated into the lowest abyss of hell, all agony, and gloom and horror! Is it possible, is it conceivable, that aught but an immaterial principle could perform these most antithetical of operations so immediately that they hardly appear an act of the will? Truly may it be said the Creator has made us in his own image. As in the beginning God said, " Let there be light, and there was light," the human mind compels eternity to be present to it, evoking the darkness to its conceptions, or soaring above it with eagle wings---creating an universe in the illimitable resources of ideas---rushing beyond the bounds of its own great thoughts (for it is not itself subject to limits) making chaos into beauty, vivifying, destroying, annihilating---it sinks, it rises, for ever baffling conception, for ever active in sleep or wakefulness—so grand, so august, so awful, and incomprehensible!

There was a settled expression of pensiveness which even in slumber did not depart from the countenance of the lovely being who might well have been mistaken for an angel by those who believe in pure intelligences having shape (but I myself am Kantian enough to believe that there is no such thing as form in the abstract, and that what is purely spiritual can have no location but in the mind---though I do not contend for the nonentity of matter), as she slept so peacefully.

On a sudden the door of the apartment was slowly and cautiously opened, and the figure of a man darkened the space it occupied previously. The moon had withdrawn her light, so that he did not instantly perceive the contents of the room, and having closed the

door, had advanced some paces; so that he was within a foot of
the sleeper (though, so soft and regular was her breathing, he could
not hear a sound), when again the radiant planet burst forth, and
revealed her to his gaze. As if by the effect of electricity his whole
strong frame shook, convulsed, contracted—then became still as
death—his lips quivered, but uttered not a syllable; his eyes became
fixed and ghastly—the very life seemed issuing from his heart. He
fell upon his knees, he clasped his hands in supplication; and never
did pious Papist address his patron saint with more devout worship
than did that man adore the sleeper.

"Great God!" he at length articulated, "can it be? The dead
returned to life! I dream, or is it her spirit? Dear ghost, wherefore art thou here? Alive or dead I'll touch her!" He bent down,
and kissed that pure, bright brow. The breath of the lady fluttered
on his cheek. "She lives, she lives!" he exclaimed wildly. "It is
herself! My Harriet, my first—last beloved!"

The sound of that deep and thrilling voice, as it burst forth in
accents of passionate joy, of wonder, and of tenderness, awoke the
sleeper. She gazed around with bewildered looks.

"Ah, I am ever dreaming of him," she said. "Great Heaven,"
(perceiving a man on his knees before her,) "help, help!"

"Harriet, it is I—who have thought you dead," replied the
intruder, in a tone that could never be forgotten, suffocated though
it were from the effects of excessive emotion.

"Walter Danvers!" exclaimed the lady, almost sinking to the
earth, and her knees trembling under her.

"Yes, Harriet Walsingham. After long, long years of agony and
desolation, we meet again," responded Danvers. "Oh, Harriet, to
find you thus, when I thought that those matchless features were
mouldering in the silence of the charnel; and that glorious form——
my God, my God!"

And the being of haughty, of fierce, and desperate daring, who,
a few minutes before, had been engaged in bloody and mortal strife,
was humbled in the dust before a helpless woman, trembling and
quailing before her gaze, and unable to give voice to his feelings.

The lady regained her composure with a mighty effort, and
steadily regarding the face of Danvers, an expression of mingled
pride and detestation infused itself to her own. Her stately and
perfect form erect, her pale cheek, if possible, a shade paler than
usual, she appeared like a being of another world, addressing a

mortal abased by the deep consciousness of crime and inferiority, as after a long silence she calmly and firmly spoke.

"Man of blood!" were her first words, "what do you here?" Then apparently relenting from the sternness of her purpose, before an answer could be given to her question, added, "I thought you would never dare to present yourself before me again. I never thought to see you more!"

"Oh, Harriet, Harriet," cried Danvers, despairingly, "you know not what I have suffered. I know that I acted like a villain towards you, but indeed I am not so guilty as you imagine. Your image has pursued and haunted me day and night. Life, love, hope—all that we poor things of dust prize in the sanctuary of the heart of hearts, you have been—you yet remain to me. Pardon me, pardon a guilty wretch, whose greatest crime was a wild adoration of your divine perfections, and who never---never can forgive himself the misery he has caused you."

"Alas," returned the lady, evidently touched by the profound humility and agonized remorse depicted on the face of Danvers, "I have little to forgive, and never harboured for an instant a vindictive feeling towards you. Oh, Walter, Walter——" sobs choaking her utterance (for her previous tranquillity had been indeed only on the surface), "how could you---how——"

"Angel of light!" exclaimed Danvers, "you have never experienced the wild throbs of burning passion; the frenzy and hopelessness and anguish unutterable of an eternal but desperate love! Yet I call God to witness that despite the deadly sin, which nothing can efface, that love I bore for you was pure, was sacred; say that you but pardon me, sweet saint, that I may go forth——oh, heaven, and having found you thus—alive, compassionate, I must quit you for ever! Death, oh Death, would that I were thine!" And as he spoke he struck his forehead with his clenched hand, and writhed in fearful agony.

"Nay, Walter, this must not be!" ejaculated the beautiful woman, "whatever your crimes, God is merciful, and if you sincerely repent—Ha! what is that noise?"

A sound of many feet was heard approaching the cottage.

"They come to take me," answered Danvers, without stirring an inch, or moving a muscle of his face, though the inward conflict of many passions was vast and tumultuous. "It is well; I shall make no more resistance."

" To take you!" echoed the lady with dismay and horror in
every line of her speaking countenance, and her frame shaking
with the wild excess of sudden emotion, " no, no, no—they shall
kill me first! Come this way, I do entreat you! Make haste—oh,
make haste, for the love of heaven! Ah, I hear them below at the
window. For mercy's sake, Walter, come!"

" No," he replied, abstractedly, " wherefore should I ? My hour
is come—let fate do its worst."

" Hark, Walter, they are on the stairs—for *my* sake, Walter—by
the memory of that fatal passion, I implore you, come, come!"

He shook his head. " It were vain," he answered.

" Not so, not so—they are here at the door," (her voice sinking
to a thrilling whisper) " but I will lock it; there, now I know that
I can conceal you in the adjoining room."

Still Danvers remained rooted where he was. Steps and voices
were now indeed to be distinguished, though the fears of the lady
had made her imagine them before they were actually heard. She
threw herself on her knees before him, and raised her beautiful and
glorious orbs to his moveless face.

" You *must*, Walter," she exclaimed, in low and startling tones,
that searched his very soul. " Shall *I* thus prostrate myself before
you? *I!* Now they are here; they will burst open the door; if
you ever loved me---*me*, who idolized you, and, oh God, even now,
in spite of all that has passed, cherish a guilty and eternal love—"

" Enough," interrupted Danvers, a violent and electric shock
convulsing him, " dispose of me as you will," and they entered the
inner chamber without further delay.

CHAPTER V.

Passion! I see: Passion! 't has many senses;
And plays in each the abortive casuist.
A startling paradox is passion, sir;
Wormwood and honey! brief as mortal thought!
Eternal as the everlasting word.—*Martinuzzi.*

Sævit amor, magnoque irarum fluctuat æstu.
                                    VIRGIL.

CORPORAL FIGGINS' DISCERNMENT—THE SEARCH—DEVOTION.

CORPORAL FIGGINS, foremost in the chase of Danvers, when he
found that the fugitive had again obtained a start, and that the
horse he himself rode was not able to sustain his great bulk much
longer in such a pursuit, lost no time in ascending a tall elm, though
it was with difficulty he managed to do so---the boughs being
hardly able to bear him—regardless of the insensible state of the
dragoon, who had been so signally worsted. He was thus enabled to
reconnoitre his movements for a considerable distance, but at length
an angle in the road concealed him from sight. Descending with
all expedition, and finding that the dragoon was gradually recovering, he left him to the care of his comrades, who were now within
musket-shot, and re-mounting, again spurred forwards until he
reached the spot where Danvers had disappeared. Just at this
juncture he saw Dickon at a great distance in full career, and without a rider. The Corporal put his finger to his nose, and thought.
" That fellow would never be thrown," he exclaimed aloud, after
a minute's pause; " no, no, it's a stratagem of war. Monstrous
clever dog !"
Again he continued his course, carefully marking the prints of the
horse's hoofs; but there had been a recent, mounted traveller on
the same road, so that he was somewhat puzzled exactly to trace

the fugitive as, farther on, it was evident that Danvers had not taken the same path as his precursor. Accordingly, once more he had recourse to his peculiar ratiocinative process, which, although not conducted by any rules of the dialecticians, was simple, shrewd, and astute.

"Let me see," quoth the Corporal, "one of these two roads here he *must* have taken, and this one he surely would not have thought of, as it is so exposed. But then, I should think he must be aware that the other would only lead him into fresh peril. Ah, I have it! He is hiding in the shrubbery yonder, and wishes us to imagine his horse threw him into the river—that must be it, for I see the cavalry sent round to take him in the van—the cunning rascal!"

And with these expressions Figgins immediately proceeded to the garden wall that Danvers had leaped. His quick eye detected a foot-mark in the sod, and finding that the soldiers were close at hand he shouted to them to follow, and with elephantine agility threw himself over, and cocking a pistol began to look about for more unmistakable traces of the fugitive.

He was not long in discovering the fresh marks of his feet, and followed them up to the house in which he had taken refuge. "How could he have got in, for he must be in the house!" meditated Figgins. He tried a door, which was locked; but, on turning his eyes upwards, descried a window that was not quite closed, about seven feet from the earth. "So, so, he must have had a hard scramble up there," thought the Corporal, "I shan't attempt to follow." He returned to the garden wall.

"Surround the house!" he cried to the dragoons who now, to the amount of a dozen, had arrived, "and one or two of you come with me, for he is a desperate dog."

The Corporal now returned, burst open the door, and entered the house, a couple of troopers having dismounted and followed him. By this time nearly half the detachment had reached the scene of action, and several of them made for the dwelling, and having gained it, every practicable, and indeed impracticable mode of egress was speedily guarded. Meanwhile the Corporal cautiously made his way along a dark passage, and entered a room, where he found a female domestic buried in deep repose, and having struck a light and found that Danvers was not there, he proceeded up a flight of stairs, and discovered an open door.

" Where the deuce can he be ?" muttered Figgins to the soldiers,
" he is not in this room."

" No, there is the mark of a dirty shoe," was the rejoinder of
one of the dragoons, " this way."

They were now at the door of an apartment, which it was evident
Danvers had entered, and perceiving it was locked they hesitated for
an instant how to proceed. " Down with it !" at length exclaimed
Figgins peremptorily, and throwing himself against it, his own weight
alone sufficed to demolish the panels. He had scarcely effected an
entrance, when a form of grace and majesty advanced from an inner
chamber, a lamp in her hand, and confronted the intruders.

There was something so august in the beauty presented to their
view, that the rude troopers instantly doffed their helmets, and
Figgins, viewing the lady with astonishment, ejaculated,

" What! do I see Miss Walsingham ?"

" How is it," said the lady with stern and haughty accents, " that
you thus violently invade the privacy of my house at such an
hour ?"

" I beg your pardon, Miss Walsingham, but we are in search of
a culprit who is hiding here," returned Figgins, reverentially, " and
indeed, madam, I didn't know you were the mistress of the house,
or I should have used more ceremony ; but we must not delay.
Will you allow us to continue our search ?"

" Certainly," answered Miss Walsingham calmly ; " but I cannot but think that your conduct has been most unwarrantable, in
breaking open this door, before applying for admittance ; and as I
have been sitting up hitherto, and no person has passed through
this apartment, I must request you to retire forthwith."

Corporal Figgins hesitated to comply with this demand. " Forgive me, madam," he said, " but we saw the print of a dirty foot at
the door, and I perceive it in this chamber, and therefore duty—"

" Impossible !" interrupted Miss Walsingham, " unless it be my
own footstep. I was in the garden late this evening."

The Corporal fixed his keen, penetrating eye on the beautiful
face before him, and he thought he could detect a slight—a very
slight blush on it.

"That footmark cannot be yours, madam," returned Figgins ;
" your shoe is very small ; pray, permit me to pass you ;" and so
saying, he was about to enter the inner apartment, when the lady
prevented him.

" Not one step farther," she said, in a voice that awed the firm heart of the Corporal, so steady, so proud and commanding was its clear, bell-like sound and articulation. " I have told you already—"

" Pardon me, madam, but I think I heard a sound issue from your chamber, just then."

" That is my sleeping apartment," rejoined Miss Walsingham, with an increase of dignity, " and none *can* be there. I command you to retire."

" Indeed, madam, I should be sorry to offend you, but I believe I have no alternative as to my conduct. I do not, of course, doubt your word, but the man may have stepped by, unobserved by you ;" and hearing the voices of several soldiers, as they ascended the stairs, Figgins again attempted to proceed in his investigation.

With flashing eyes, with frowning brow, with erect stature, and lips that seemed, as it were, instinct with passion, yet in a voice subdued almost to a whisper, Miss Walsingham caught the arm of the Corporal, and exclaimed,

" Beware ! I will not endure insult. I have told you it is impossible that any person can have entered this chamber ;" and, perceiving that an officer was now present, she added, " I believe, sir, your name is Captain Norton. Will you have the goodness to order your men to withdraw ?"

" I should be loth, dear madam," returned the officer, in that Grandisonian style of gallantry that characterised the politeness of the middle of the eighteenth century, " I should be loth to invade the sanctity of a lady's chamber, more especially that of Miss Harriet Walsingham, whom I heartily rejoice to see after an interval of so many years; but, really, I—I cannot exactly perceive how it is possible to comply with your wishes under the circumstances of the case, and as it cannot pain you———— "

" Your ear, one moment," interrupted Miss Walsingham, trembling violently, and agitated beyond expression by some inexplicable feelings, on perceiving that she had nothing to hope from the civility of Captain Norton, who was a rigid disciplinarian, and would not have sacrificed a single *iota* of duty for all the ladies in the world, despite the veneration in which he held them ; (" yes, it is the only way to save him," she thought to herself with agony), and whispered, " Oh, sir, you are an old acquaintance of my family, save—save my honour !"

" Good God !" ejaculated the officer, with undisguised horror, but before he could recover his utter astonishment at receiving such an intimation, Figgins, taking advantage of Miss Walsingham's forgetfulness of having left sufficient room for a person to pass by her, darted into the inner room. Uttering a scream of agony and dismay, Miss Walsingham rushed after him.

"Back, my men!" ejaculated Captain Norton, finding that the dragoons were pressing forwards, and hastily endeavouring to avert an exposure, the idea of which filled him with repugnance. But, before he could himself enter after the Corporal and the lady, and close the door, there was the sound of a blow loud as the report of a pistol.

The scream of Miss Walsingham reached the ear of Danvers, who had been concealed by her in a closet, and bursting forth with rage and indignation, imagining that she had received some outrage, and perceiving that she clung struggling to the arm of Figgins, who, in his efforts to disengage himself, threw her down, he struck him so desperately as to dash his huge form motionless to the ground. Raising the scarcely less inanimate body of Miss Walsingham in his arms, he chafed her hands, and tenderly besought her to be comforted. Then perceiving the presence of Captain Norton he drew his sword ; but instantly changing his determination, said,

"I am the man you seek. I yield my weapon to you."

"Mr. Danvers!" cried Captain Norton, "I am all wonder! Ah, I have discovered the mystery now. Oh, Miss Walsingham, you should not have thus imposed upon me—though, indeed, I could not for an instant believe that as pure a saint as ever graced the courts of heaven, could be guilty———"

"What," exclaimed Danvers, impetuously, gathering in an instant the whole enigma, "did she indeed say *that* ? Oh Harriet, Harriet—and for me—such a worm—for me, too! God—God bless you !"

And heedless of the presence of the officer, he knelt down and pressed the hand of that lovely and devoted woman to his lips, while tears rolled rapidly upon it, and sobs heaved his broad Herculean chest. The Captain was deeply affected, notwithstanding his decorum and dignity.

"What devotion !" he inwardly exclaimed. "Such a love as this woman must entertain for this man is beyond conception priceless."

Woman's love is indeed a treasure, which transcends the power of thought to conceive. I speak not of the ordinary love of ordinary woman; but of a devotedness like that just displayed, which *their* good sort of inoffensive commonplace natures cannot comprehend. True love almost appears to reverse the general laws of our being, and to make us infinitely more anxious for the welfare of the one object than our own. Well might the poet exclaim that it is not of earth, but it is *in* the earth as a solitary Angel, cheering, supporting, strengthening; and affording no dim, nor faint, nor shadowy and uncertain image of the ETERNITY IT BRINGS DOWN TO TIME.

CHAPTER VI.

Nay now bestir thyself; there is no time
For long delays and council. Let the wind
Bear on its wings thy heart and thy resolve.
Old Play.

Sleep stays not, though a monarch bid;
So I love to wake ere break of day.—COLERIDGE.

LITTLE GEORGE AND HIS ADVENTURES—SHOWING THAT THE INFLUENCE OF A PRETTY MAIDEN IS UNIVERSALLY POTENT.

WHILE Danvers was engaged in the terrible struggles detailed in the foregone chapters, the noble little fellow, whose gratitude for the service he had rendered him had prompted to such great exertions in his behalf, did not remain inactive; for overlooked in the precipitation of pursuit, he was able to enter the apartment of his new friend and ally unobserved, and to discover an open letter which he had dropped accidentally, bearing his name and address. George ruminated an instant.

"I wonder whether he will escape," he murmured; "if not, what is best to be done?" This was a puzzling question to the boy, whose only object was to be of service to his benefactor, towards whom he felt a sentiment of kindness and affection, which he had never before experienced for so recent acquaintance. "Let me see,"

continued the thoughtful child, "if he is taken they will put him
into prison, and his friends will be anxious about him at any rate.
Either way, I of myself can do nothing to serve him, and so I think
I will try and find out this place." Thus resolved, George descended
cautiously, and looked around him. All had vanished from the
place, eager to behold as much as possible of the pursuit.

"I will saddle the landlord's pony, and so save time," said the
boy. And proceeding to the stables he there found, as he expected,
a diminutive steed quietly reposing on his straw, and speedily completed arrangements for the journey on which he had determined.
Mounting the pony, he was about to quit the stable when a sturdy
lad, who was help to the hostler, upon a sudden made his appearance.

"I say, young gemman!" exclaimed this functionary, on perceiving George all equipped for a ride, "what be you a-going for
to do with that 'ere powney?"

The child made no reply; but knowing the great necessity for
dispatch, if he wished to get clear away, he bestowed a hearty
smack on the pony, and immediately galloped from the spot.

Indignant at this supercilious disregard of his authority, the
stable-boy quickly pursued, and another hard chase was the result.
George was a good rider, considering his years, a circumstance in a
great measure owing to his once having been engaged in some
equestrian performances something similar to those now exhibited
at Astley's, and although the ground was extremely rugged, bravely
kept his seat, and urged on the pony both with voice and hand.
The stable-boy was nimble of foot and sound of wind, so that the
little steed was not much more than a match for him in swiftness;
but his present rider was of very little weight, and he was fresh
after a long repose.

But an unexpected difficulty here assailed poor George; for
several persons were approaching towards him down a narrow lane,
which he had chosen to thread, and he knew that he must be inevitably captured by them, if they heard the lusty voice of his pursuer
vociferating "Stop him!" Indeed he discerned that they belonged
to the Inn, so that he was certain to be recognised. At once taking
his resolution, he abruptly turned, and dashing back, made a desperate charge on the stable-boy, who was so unprepared for such a
fierce attack that he was knocked down, and George obtained a
start of nearly a hundred yards. With loud shouts of triumph he

continued his flight, cleared a low hedge, bounded over a clover field, and ultimately, after a chase of half an hour, succeeded in baffling all pursuit. Victorious thus far, his next consideration was how to find the locality to which he was directed by the letter he had picked up; and the moon shining forth with splendour, he took the epistle out of his pocket, and, after a moment's hesitation, perused it.

The hand-writing was fortunately clear and large, or George could not have deciphered it; but as it was, he had no difficulty in reading the bold characters, and was rewarded by a clue to his object of search. The following was the purport of the letter:—

"MY DEAR DANVERS,

"I have just seen Harry, and we are now proceeding to the village of A * * * *, in order to communicate with several persons favourable to the good cause. Your exertions, I know, are unceasing, and, I cannot but think, will ultimately be attended with success. Walsingham will be a great acquisition, as he can lend money, for which, I have no doubt, we shall be able to offer him excellent security. I shall be with you in two or three days at farthest, and meanwhile, if you want to know anything of my movements, if you call at a little cottage, just out of the London road, and about half a mile from Y * * *, the owner of which is an old friend of yours, as I shall call there to-morrow (probably, your son with me), you will be able to obtain accurate information of yours, very truly, "A. NORTON."

"Norton—I have heard that name," thought George, "oh, I remember a Mr. Norton has the fine house about five miles away. It is possible it may be him. But my best plan will be to make at once for A * * * *, and try to find the cottage mentioned here. I wonder who he is—my kind friend? His name is Danvers; *that* I overheard when I found that old witch and Figgins were plotting mischief against him. But A * * * * is a very long way off, and I have no time to waste." So putting the pony into a fast trot, George resumed his journey.

The bell of a church-clock tolled the hour of one as he passed the village of A * * * *, and descending a short hill looked around him for the cottage indicated in the letter. In vain, however, he directed his gaze now here, and now there, for the moon had chosen

L

to withdraw, and the trees grew to so great a height, and in such
thickness in every direction, that it was probable a small cottage
might be entirely concealed by them.   It was not likely that he
should obtain any directions at such an hour, and perplexed and
fatigued he knew not how to act, when he heard the clattering of
horses' hoofs advancing, and two men emerged from an opening
among the trees, apparently engaged in interesting conversation.
Again the moon shone forth, illuminating every object, and disclosing
the persons of the horsemen to George.   One was a middle-aged
man, of gentlemanly exterior, and mounted on a fine grey mare; the
other, a slight and graceful youth, of some seventeen years of age,
whose horse was of admirable proportions, and whose dress was
studiously neat and plain.

   " Ha !" exclaimed the adventurous child, as he gazed on the
latter of these individuals, " how like—how *very* like to Mr. Danvers he is !   There can be no harm, at all events, in asking him his
name--perhaps he may be the son spoken of in this letter." Accosting the travellers, who now had reached the ground where his pony
stood, George inquired " Pray, gentlemen, are you acquainted with
—with Mr. Danvers ?"

   The persons thus interrogated were startled at the abruptness of
this address, and surveyed George with curious and rather mis-
trustful looks.

   " I think, sir," continued the young boy, appealing to the youth,
" I think you must be Mr. Harry Danvers ?" and he waited
anxiously the rejoinder.

   " And if I am, what do you want with me, my lad ?"

   " But *are* you the son of Mr. Danvers ?" asked George.

   " What is your motive for inquiring ? I am the person you seek."

   " Then, sir, I think that your father is in great danger, for he is
pursued by soldiers."

   " What—pursued ! where ?" exclaimed the youth and his companion in one breath.

   " Ah, I don't know where he is *now*—but I will tell you all I
can about him."   And with these words George proceeded to recount with brief simplicity the escape of Danvers, and his own
instrumentality in facilitating it; and finally produced the letter he
had picked up in the Inn.

   " This is most unfortunate, Harry," said the gentleman who
accompanied young Danvers.   " I wrote that letter to your father

yesterday, and sent it by my own groom. I know that my brother, the captain, is out also with a troop of dragoons, and, from what I can gather from this lad, in the direction he has taken in flight; so that Danvers will surely be intercepted."

"Prompt measures must be pursued to save him," rejoined Harry Danvers, with the decisiveness of his father. "Suppose you ride to ——— (which is not above half an hour's gallop hence), and consult with the meeting now held there. I will proceed to the Inn which this little fellow mentions—gain farther intelligence, and rejoin you with all despatch. I wish I could communicate with our good Elizabeth, too—she might devise something in case of his being already captured."

"Can I be of use to you?" inquired George.

"You are a brave boy—yes." Tearing out a leaf from his pocket-book, Harry Danvers wrote a few words with a pencil, and gave it into George's hand. "Make what speed you can," he said, "to ———, which is about eight miles from this spot, if you are not too fatigued, and you will easily find the house mentioned in the direction of this letter. If possible, get into the cottage without any noise, and ask for Mrs. Elizabeth Haines. Take these ten guineas, and God speed you—many thanks for your assistance."

Before George could make a reply of any sort, Harry Danvers had thrust some money into his hand, and, striking spurs into his horse, was, together with his friend speedily out of sight.

Wearied as he was, the child did not loiter on his journey, but manfully bearing up, before the first peep of dawn was in front of the cottage of Danvers. Dismounting, he reconnoitred the house, and finding that all was buried in profound repose, hesitated, in compliance with the instructions which he had received, whether to disturb the inmates. Conceiving, however, that anything was preferable to delay in so urgent an affair, he was about to knock for admittance, when he heard a window thrown up above him, and perceived a fair face looking out of it.

"Can I speak with Mrs. Elizabeth Haines?" inquired George, of the person thus presented to his notice.

"At this time? What do you want, child?"

"I must deliver my message to her myself, pretty one."

"Saucy boy," was the reply, accompanied with a musical laugh, "Mrs. Haines cannot be disturbed at present, without sufficient cause."

" But indeed, indeed," returned the child earnestly, " I *must* see her, if she is within."

" From whom do you come ?"

" I don't mind telling you, because you have such a sweet face," said George, " and I think you must be related to him, from your likeness—from Mr. Harry Danvers."

" Indeed, little flatterer—and what does my brother want ?"

At this juncture another window was thrown up, and a more majestic, but less lovely face, became apparent.

" What is the matter ?" asked the stern voice of Elizabeth.

" I have a note for Mrs. Haines, from Mr. Harry Danvers," was the answer.

" Then give it to me—here, tie it on to this string."

" Are you sure you are Mistress Elizabeth Haines ?"

" Yes, yes ;" and, drawing up the missive, Elizabeth read.

" Is anything amiss ?" inquired Ellen Danvers, (whom the reader may have recognized in the lady George first accosted.

" Why, no—I think we need not alarm ourselves," returned Elizabeth. Then, addressing the little messenger, she observed, " You look tired, child, and must need rest. I will come down, and let you in directly."

" But is Harry ill ?" said Ellen, anxiously.

" No, he is quite well," answered George, readily, while Mrs. Haines threw on her habiliments and descended to admit him.

" But what is the matter? pray tell me, pretty boy, if you know," said Ellen, imploringly.

The appeal was irresistible, and George replied, " Mr. Danvers, who, I suppose, is your father, has been pursued by some soldiers."

Before he could conclude the sentence, Mrs. Haines had opened the door to him, and frowning at his indiscretion told him to enter.

CHAPTER VII.

Oli. What's a drunken man like, fool?

Clo. Like a drowned man, a fool, and a madman; one draught above heat makes him a fool; the second, mads him; and a third, drowns him.—SHAKSPEARE.

Peopled with unimaginable shapes.---SHELLEY.

HARRY DANVERS AND THE LITTLE FUDDLED PHILOSOFHER—THE OLD WOMAN—ASSOCIATION OF IDEAS.

MEANTIME Harry Danvers, not a little anxious on account of his father, with all speed made towards the village where the Britannia Inn was situated, and reached it without any adventure. Aware of the necessity for caution in his proceedings, he looked about him, for the purpose of examining the premises, that he might discover whether any one were in motion to whom he might direct his inquiries; but for a considerable time his search was crowned with no success. The denizens of the Inn had at length retired to rest, and were buried in sleep.

Debating with himself whether he should arouse the somnolent inmates, or endeavour to procure his information by other means, he observed not a rotund figure progressing towards him with uneven steps, now and then breaking forth into snatches of song, the burthen of which it was not a very easy matter to catch (so thick was the minstrel's utterance), but which contained allusions to wine, to women, to love and the devil, in conjunction with sundry other ladies and gentlemen, and *et cæteras,* " altogether too numerous to mention."

Harry turned in his saddle, as his ear caught a fragment of the melody which the fat individual was delighting himself withal; and saw the diminutive figure of a man, with a tolerable protuberance of

stomach, who had evidently been indulging in copious libations, and
who was directing his steps to the door of the Inn where the youth
had halted.

Hesitating whether he should address the pinguid little stranger,
Harry remained stationary, while the other reeled onwards, inter-
larding his musical performance with a variety of ejaculations, some
of which were so strange and incoherent, that they gave the hearer an
idea that he was labouring under some extraordinary hallucination,
independent of that produced by the fumes of alcohol on the brain.

"Bright are the heavens!" exclaimed the stranger, as he neared
the youth, "bright with stars—but thy dear eyes are more divinely
bright! Wine, wine, drink the wine—the ruby, ruby wine!" and here
he broke forth into incomprehensible song; but, suddenly staggering against the horse of Harry, he tottered, reeled, and fell to the
earth, where he lay, looking upwards with a most ludicrous expression of countenance, that at any other time would have excited a
hearty burst of merriment from the youth; but now he was aware
that he might not delay an instant longer than was absolutely requisite, wishing to succour his father. Accordingly, he addressed the
fallen gentleman, who was making vain, though violent efforts to
recover his centre of gravity, his corpulent person wagging up and
down in the exertions he made to rise, and said,

"Can I assist you to stand?" holding his hand to the unknown.

"I thank you, gracious stranger!" responded the fat little personage, with theatrical pomposity, and availing himself of the proffered help. "I come from far this light—this night, and long to
reach—ah, what was I saying? I beg your pardon, sir—but I'm a
man so crossed by fortune, and by fate so stung—the black and fell
ingratitude of man hath overshadowed so my mind of life—(that's
fine—*mind of life*—damme, eh?")

"My good sir," interposed Harry, impatiently.

"My mind of life! it is metaphysical, psychological, ontological;
you perceive it is an imitation of the Elizabethan dramatists, whose
peculiar forte lay in happy allusion, analogy, and correct expression
of ideas."

"I want to ask you——" commenced the youth, but he was not
permitted to conclude his sentence.

"The lucid and divine perspicuity, perspicacity and comprehensiveness of the most abstract ideas in poetry—the bringing down of
lofty and immortal truths to the intelligence of the ignorant vulgar,

is a privilege appertaining to Genius only. There's a fluent period for you, full of strength and harmony! Come, I'll give you a song now, if you like."

" Friend, I am in great haste, and desirous of know——"

" There's a great mystery in poetry—a very—very great one!" continued the poet stranger, without noticing the impatience of his auditor; " and I can demonstrate to you that the heart of this mystery may be found in the combination of abstract ideas——"

" D—n abstract ideas!" exclaimed Harry, angrily.

" No, no, don't damn abstract ideas!" said the little man, with drunken gravity, " for you perceive that the imagination is evidently affected by——"

" I cannot stay to dispute the point with you, my friend. Have you seen——"

" Seen, seen! what have not poets seen?—and I have once a poet been! As the wild music of the spheres revolves—Ha, I wonder what makes the earth totter so under one's feet? It's a philosophical problem, that has never yet been solved by the ingenuity of man.—My worthy sir, I pray you, leave me not, but check impatience even in the bud. I say, it's a problem ——"

" Confound the fellow," muttered the young man, as the tipsy individual caught him by the arm, and prevented him from quitting so unprofitable a companion.

" It's a philosophical problem whether what we call motion be not the tendency of the mind to activity—whether motion be not in the mind—no, that's not it—how shall I state the proposition?"

" I can stay no longer," exclaimed Harry, roughly, " for I see you are drunk, and can give no information."

" Drunk, sir! What do you call drunk? An affection of the external senses is not drunkenness, or you would be drunk—as you imagine I am so. No, I define the idea of drunkenness to be motion in——"

Here Harry, finding that the fat individual was resolved on detaining him in order to deliver his (i. e. the fat man's) overflowing soul of its superabundant riches, with a sudden jerk pitched him again to the earth, where he measured five feet one on some mud and dirt that lay conveniently for his reception: thus affording a complete and practical illustration of the philosopher's idea, by making him exhibit motion in filth.

While the genius lay kicking and bawling lustily, Harry again revolved the difficulties of his position.

"What the deuce shall I do?" he muttered to himself. "I fear from my likeness to my father I should be suspected; but better incur the risk than remain inactive. I suppose I must knock up the landlord—that drunken little brute can't give a rational reply?"

He was relieved from his embarrassing dilemma by the appearance of a female, who, on perceiving him, gave a start of surprise, and appeared undecided how to act. Harry accosted her, without allowing her time for thought however, (as she seemed wavering whether to retire or advance,) saying,

"I find that there has been a remarkable event here—the capture of a prisoner, was it not."

"O, yes!" replied the woman, mysteriously surveying the youth with an air of confidential significance, and approaching nearer to him, she whispered, "He is not taken, Master Danvers, he is safe."

Harry was put off his guard by the woman's manner, and though surprised at the familiarity of her address, inquired with breathless interest, "Where is he?"

"He is hiding; but this is not the place for such a confidence as ours. We might be watched, and you arrested on suspicion, for the authorities are all alive, since the discovery of your plot. Follow me, and you shall learn further."

Harry paused irresolute; but conceiving, even if treachery were meditated, that the strange female could not have any motive for leading him away from a place where he might easily have been captured—fatigued as was his horse with a long journey—moreover forgetting, in the excitement of the moment, the singular resemblance he bore to his father, and thinking that she could not have recognised him so immediately, unless entrusted by the object of his inquiries with a special communication, he yielded to the impulse of his feelings, in the hope of being able to extricate Danvers from difficulty.

The woman hobbled briskly onwards, maintaining an unbroken silence, and apparently engaged in her own cogitations. Occasionally, she would mutter to herself indeed, indistinctly, almost inaudibly, and direct furtive glances at Harry, displaying a sort of unsteady vigour and agility, which her apparent decrepitude hardly intimated she could possess.

At length, as they reached a green knoll, surmounted by a growth of underwood, the female abruptly stopped and said, "Your father commissioned me to seek you, and to say——" The sentence was interrupted by the apparition of a strange creature whom Harry at first imagined to be a large ape, but which, on nearer inspection, he perceived to bear some resemblance to a human being, and whose speed was astonishingly great, as it bounded toward the spot where he stood with his guide.

A wild confusion of ideas and associations rushed on his mind. He seemed familiar with something about the woman, and was convinced that he had before seen a shape similar to the nondescript's; but all was like a dream of the past—more vivid than a mere vision indeed, but connected indissolubly with the fantasies and recollections of his childhood.

That wonderful association of ideas---so complex, yet so clear--- so undefinable, yet so self-evident, so wild, and strange, and unaccountable. The relations of things intermingling with the shadows and chimeras of the brain! the infinite and indefinite contrasting the definite and finite! Oh, the vast mysteries of mind---the interminable diversities of sensation! What power is it that binds all these together---that abstracts and generalizes, that forms, combines, and modifies?

What wonder, if individuals of lofty intellect, plunged into the glorious and stupendous ocean of mental philosophy, are apt to contemn the tangible and the real, the palpable and material, for the beautiful ideal of the spiritual and metaphysical! The speculations of abstract philosophy must ever teem with lofty and divine interest; and the bias of fine souls and original idiosyncrasies for ontological studies, clearly demonstrates the magnetic influence which the unseen and the invisible exercises over the immaterial principle within; and which is developed in proportion as the understanding is directed from the common concerns of this common, vulgar life, to that which exists within the radiant and beautiful heaven of pure intelligence. *Here* is nothing to clip the wings of the spirit! Little though the one being may appear in his own estimation, when overwhelmed with the majesty of the Eternal Universe, the ability to comprehend a portion of that infinity, elevates while it depresses. Thank God for that innate conviction of the bright Immortal which he has stamped upon the spirit of the brain in His own divine and indestructible characters, which, the more that reason is brought into action, expands and quickens. That conviction vivifies many

M

a lofty aspiration—profoundest breathings of the heart and the
imagination—desires after the existence beyond the grave—a poetry
wherein passion becomes celestial, and love is extended to all, with
hope, and faith, and joy. The poet and philosopher, who has a
high and holy mission to fulfil, realizes frequently, in his sublime
reveries, pictures far too ethereal and exquisite for the pencil or the
pen to embody, to be felt rather than analyzed, and yet in some
degree to be imparted by the eloquence of his glowing genius,
simply through that same marvellous faculty of association in others
that perceives occult meanings, and dim revealings of loveliness that
never cast its spell upon earth,—reason approximating to imagination (is not the highest philosophy poetry), and imagination streng-
thened by the very power it antagonizes. Yet we cannot fathom the
depths of our own hearts, nor understand the connexion and analogy between external objects and mental phenomena. Still, the
very mystery is awfully delightful, and in tracing the delicate filia-
tions of mind, although much is incomprehensible, dark, and dream-
like, the soul is filled with moral beauty, and drinks of the undefiled
waters whence angels quench their thirst. Knowledge is happiness,
for it is *within*; but to fancy, in grasping a segment of it, we have
reached *all*, produces scepticism and foolishness—pride—vanity—
TO KNOW OUR IGNORANCE IS TO BE WISE.

BOOK III.

Man's yesterday may ne'er be like his morrow;
Nought may endure but mutability.—SHELLEY.

No doubt our souls can conjure with strong thoughts,
Which are but dreams till their effects be tried,
Nor yet ensnared in the web of destiny,
Whose objects, who can reach?—G. STEPHENS.

BOOK III.

CHAPTER I.

A noble spirit in that lady dwells,
Gentle as morn, and radiant as is Day,
Her heart ne'er cherishes one mean desire,
Her soul is truth, her mind is virtue's angel.
Old Play.

Deep thoughts are ever dangerous.—R. H. HORNE.

NIL ADMIRARI—HARRIET WALSINGHAM'S CHARACTERISTICS—
THE EPICUREAN AND HIS SOLILOQUY.

IT is a wonder (though nothing is to be wondered at, considering the endless series of miracles, which attract no attention whatever) that the constitution of the human mind should admit of the susceptibility to excessive joy and anguish, which so frequently succeed each other; and it only evinces that all things—moving in an eternal cycle—that the transition of sensations is an effect of an exhaustion of the segments that compose it, and in order that a new succession of feelings may be evolved, a process in some degree similar to that material substances undergo, before they can be restored to their primitive elements from the corruption of decomposition, must take place. And thus it is. We cannot remain stationary in Time; and consequently, when we attain the pinnacle of bliss, a fall is certain, is inevitable; and the contrast is so vivid, that what under ordinary circumstances might seem a common misfortune is an irremediable woe—a spectral memory, a haunting dream of darkness—a ruin, and a desolation. Beautiful is the harmony preserved even in the

economy of what men term evil. If we do not experience a very
great amount of happiness, we are better prepared for a reverse of
fortune; and the true philosopher will regard absolute wretchedness
as but the prelude to a comparative heaven, and therefore to be endured with fortitude and resignation. But there are some characters
whose organization is so peculiarly sensitive and delicate, that it is
morally impossible for them to govern their passions and feelings by
a rule which even the sternest of Stoics have not always been able
to carry out in practice; and their acute sufferings are not to be
assuaged by all that old moralists have written, and deep sages enunciated. There are some whose hearts are so fine and fragile, that a
rude touch will break the exquisite existence which they breathe, for
ever; and nothing save the bright vision of immortality—God's
last, best gift to man—can compensate the dreary loss.

Happily, there is a limit to all mortal misery, and in proportion as
grief is violent, is the period of its duration brief or long. The mind
of Harriet Walsingham, it is vain to attempt a full development of.
The depth of her spirit was commensurate with the ardour of her
passion, and in the violent contest to which they were continually
exposed, there was an intensity of high dramatic poetry, never to be
all embodied. Profound feelings are seldom demonstrative. The
breaking heart is silent as the charnel. A smile has frequently more
agony in it, though quiet and transient, and conveys more eloquence
of deep and voiceless woe to the soul capable of appreciating high
and rare natures, than even the groan wrung from the tortured bosom; and so a common observer would not have dreamed that she
was a woman with the most fiery emotions, nor imagined there was
' a very life in her despair,' which was only to be exterminated with
the source whence it sprang. Highly imaginative persons, it has
been asserted by a great poet of this century, impair the power of
passion in their own breasts, by the tension of their souls in the
lofty ideal they cherish; but, although there may be some instances
of the truth of this aphorism, it is not either rational theoretically,
nor visible practically, since it appears indisputable that the quality
of a fine imagination necessarily depends on the force of feeling and
sensation, and how can they be vivified and engendered, except by
the impression made upon the heart itself? And this refined sensibility existing, it is impossible that it should all be dissipated in
idealism.

Certain it is, that Harriet Walsingham, eminently gifted with the highest attributes of fancy—in fact, a poetess from childhood,—was a woman in tenderness, a man in mind and energetic impulse and resolution, yet, despite her gushing feelings, and overflowing soul, calm in the command which she usually exercised over her inclinations, and almost unalterably determined in the course which she considered that of rectitude and virtue.

She was seated in an arbour, the fragrance of the wild honeysuckle and the music of the thrush and lark exciting no observation nor delight in the spirit ordinarily so sensitive to them. It was a lovely spot, realizing the beautiful description in the strange, wild, and spiritual imagination, which imparts so all-pervading a charm to the verses of my favourite dreamer, in one of his latest poems.

> Broad water lilies lay tremulously,
> And starry river buds glimmered by,
> And around them the soft stream did glide and dance
> With a motion of sweet sound and radiance.
> And the sinuous paths of lawn and of moss
> Which led through the garden along and across—
> Some open at once to the Sun and the breeze,
> Some lost among bowers and blossoming trees,
> Were all paved with daisies and delicate bells,
> As fair as the fabulous asphodels.
> And flowerets, which drooping as day drooped too,
> Fell into pavilions white, purple, and blue
> To roof the glow-worm from the evening dew.

How that pure, bright creature, who there sat engaged in painful meditation, would have adored the divine idealism of the ill-fated Shelley, had he lived in her day; for, although her own fancy was not of that vivid description, which seems to intensify every object into a species of self-life, and although sufficiently material to love the real for its own sake, she often craved for a food capable of filling the mysterious void which all fine minds experience, in the imagination as well as the heart, at frequent epochs of mental progress.

The real of itself is not sufficient for the aspirations excited by it, and hence the fascination of poetry is enhanced by the state of the mind searching for the spiritual and divine; and the ideal becomes, in some instances, a haunting passion, from the magic associations evoked by those feelings which but the few strongly experience, and can never analyze. As the tone of the universal mind is elevated by the external influences of science and philosophy, an inner growth of

sentiment requires sustenance, and thus the wildly fanciful acquires
a factitious popularity unheard of in the first stages of civilization.
It is a gross error to suppose that nations immersed in ignorance and
superstition are capable of liking, far less of appreciating, the higher
order of poetry; for though such an order may *exist*, how can it be
felt and understood by those who have not rendered up their secret
souls to the enchantment of elevated and sublime trains of ideas?
We may depend upon it, that the grand and shadowy intimations of
a mysterious beauty, irradiated by a passionate adoration of the spirit
of their material forms, must possess within them a charm for future
generations, independently of the intrinsic value of their sentiments;
for the farther we advance in science, the more we pant for the unattainable and the unseen.   But, not to digress any farther, and to
return to the immediate interests of the poetess.

The traces of tears and emotion were yet visible in her sculptured
lineaments, yet an air of tranquillity was diffused through the veil of
her sorrow and sadness, like the pensive radiance of a star, shining
through clouds and gloom.   Her white hands clasped on her knees,
her proud head meekly bent, and her beaming eyes suffused with a
gentle moisture, no better image of patience could have been desired
as a model by the sculptor. Yet she had but just attained the victory
in a terrible struggle with herself, and although the tempest was
hushed, it had left its scathing marks upon the very centre of her
being.

"He is changed," she murmured, her low but clear voice
sounding sweetly and plaintively in the stillness, "but still he is the
same. Nothing can ever destroy the character of his noble form.
Time may plant wrinkles in the open brow, and dim the fire of the
eagle eye; but in the decay of youth, and the utter blight of the
heart, and the storm of raging passions, the traces of the irrevocable
past will burn forth and be discernible as the sky, over which vast
and innumerable shadows have passed. Poor, poor Walter! Guilty
though he be—steeped in crime though he be—I am certain he is not
lost to good. God will forgive him! And shall we poor things of
dust and corruption judge one like ourselves? Who can answer
what would have been his own actions, if exposed to sore temptation?
The best of men may become the worst, and the worst the best. If
we have not strong passions we are but negatively virtuous in acting
rightly, and if we *do* possess them, it is hardly possible for us to
conquer our nature. We can only triumph over ourselves by the

help of Heaven. I—I myself have only been rescued from deadly sin by the mercy of that Great Being who saves us from our own defeat by decreeing pain and anguish for our lot ; for what a mighty spirit of evil is inherent in my nature! Had I been a man, I shudder to think of the deeds I might have committed."

While Miss Walsingham was yet soliloquising (a habit of the existence of which those who indulge in it are hardly aware,) a form darkened the pleached entrance to the arbour, and lifting up her eyes, she saluted her visitor with—

" Well, William, have you learned anything ?"

" Danvers will be examined before the magistrate to-morrow," answered he to whom the question was addressed, a young man of appearance as remarkable as that of the lady. And he seated himself beside her.

Harriet Walsingham was silent for some seconds. Thought was evidently busy in her brain, and her companion contemplated her curiously, as if he would have read all that was passing in it. But even he, close observer as he was, could not fathom the soul of such a woman. Indeed, it appears problematical, whether we of the ruder, can ever accurately interpret the softer sex. It is evident we must not judge them by an arbitrary standard, deduced from our own experience, for their feelings are frequently in total opposition not only in degree, but in kind, from ours. Their passions are not only more rigidly subdued, and their feelings more exquisitely sensitive, but they appear in the most antithetical phases, and flow in the most dissimilar channels. The very simplicity of her pure and lovely nature makes woman incomprehensible to any save the inspired poet, who possesses, as it were, the elements of two distinct beings, in his intense appreciation of beauty in the abstract, which becomes a part of his own nature, and the less subtile and delicate operations of his own weak human heart ; and notwithstanding both these advantages in conjunction, it is by no means indisputable, that he can depict with perfect nature, the sensations he imagines, rather than feels. The imagination of feeling is distinct from the feeling of imagination, and, consequently, the two distinct natures which a highly ideal being may possess *in* himself and *out* of himself, are absorbed and blended in the interest of the one, or centred and combined in the passion of the other. Miss Walsingham at length divulged the result of her self-communings ;—

" William, I rely upon your aid. You will, I know, render me

N

what help you can, and I have great reliance on you when you *will*
exert yourself."

"My hand, and heart, and life shall be devoted to your service.
What would you have me do?"

"The service that I shall ask will be of no personal peril to yourself; but I, as a woman, could not so well execute it. Leave me for
a few minutes, that I may consider the feasibility of the scheme I
contemplate."

In silence the young man acquiesced in the last request of Harriet Walsingham, and, quitting the arbour, directed his steps along
a gravelled walk, terminating in a labyrinth of various trees, imper-
vious to the light of the sun, so closely were they interwoven. There
is something very pleasant in a labyrinth, as there always is in
everything imbued with a slight degree of mystery; for, our curiosity
excited in however small a ratio, the mind is necessarily amused,
and imagination plays her aëry gambols, much to the delectation of
vivid associations, and in contempt of the very troublesome and impertinent monarch, Reason. So throwing himself on a rustic bench,
and lazily reclining on his arm, the youth resigned himself to reverie. "This is what I like," he thought to himself, "almost for-
getful of existing, and yet enjoying the full force of animal life.
Let those who style themselves philosophers talk what they will of
the gratification resulting from the exercise of our moral and intellectual powers; or silly sentimental poets rhapsodize about the unintelligible ecstacies they assert they experience in evoking bright
forms of grace and splendour—give *me* a soft breeze just fanning
the cheek through the interstices of green boughs, and perfumed
with the rain-sweetened breath of flowers and new-mown grass.
Oh, the senses are the sole source of pleasure."

Thus cogitating, the Epicurean lapsed into a sort of doze, such
as excessive indolence alone knows the delights of, resolutely shutting out every thought, in the absorption of sensuous being. Thus
he remained for at least half an hour, when rousing himself he took
a pocket volume in his hand, and began to peruse it.

"Admirable Wycherly," he exclaimed, after reading a few sentences, "what fine nonsense in your wit. The world—the old,
canting, hypocritical, lying, and face-making world—thinks you excessively immodest now, and *modest* maidens colour at the mere
mention of your name; but I will maintain that there is excellent
morality in what you have written. Your plots are all licentious—

What of that—is not the life we all lead so? Your characters are almost all vicious—the parallel will hold again. Your humour is ribald—granted; so is that of all men. Your wit is indelicate— acknowledged; I never knew any otherwise.* Your scenes are the *ne plus ultra* of shameless indecency; but had they been less so, they would not have represented man as he is—man as he must always be—a low, sensual brute in nature, despite his endowments of mind, and knowledge, and fancy. True, true to the very life you are, oh witty, wicked Wycherley! Though you do not search each corner of the heart, and anatomize the grander passions of man, like Æschylus and Shakspeare, you paint with a master's hand the filth that comes forth from what some dunces call an immaterial soul, and expose the profligacy and natural——pshaw, what folly I am talking! *All* is irresistible necessity! There is no such thing as vice, properly speaking; but it is as well, perhaps, if we wish to let man take his station above the other animals, we should let him *think* there is."

Here raising his eyes, the Necessitarian encountered the calm, tranquil, and pitying gaze of Miss Walsingham, who had followed him to the labyrinth, aware of his propensity to idle away hours, in total oblivion of having promised to execute any commission. He arose, his sallow cheek slightly tinged with crimson, which instantly vanished, and stood listlessly regarding the weeds that grew in rank luxuriance beneath his feet.

"William—William Walsingham, why have you adopted these vile and miserable sophistries," said the lady, with suppressed indignation, " when you must feel, in your heart, that they are irrational and mischievous? I beseech you to weigh the matter dispassionately, and believe not that we, with such glorious intellectual and moral powers, are the vile slaves of organization and external circumstances, which may modify, but cannot mould the actions."

The Epicurean smiled, and there was a bitter sneer lurking beneath, "You women," was his answer, "argue from the heart, and not the head. I have no eloquence, and therefore have no chance with you. How can we possibly act, except from the original bias given us in our formation, and the effects produced on us by the circumstances of time, and place, and society, acting upon the organization?"

* The reader will be pleased to recollect that the Epicurean was speaking "Tom Jones" was a picture of manners.

"But the human mind, being an essentially active principle, is capable of building up its component parts from volition. Circumstance must and will have an effect; but when you talk of original formation, in conjunction with it, being all-powerful, you are in fact what logicians, I think, call merely begging the question."

"I really cannot see the necessity for such an inference. Who ever exercised that which you call volition in coming into existence, more than a plant or blade of grass? and who ever ordered the train of events that formed his character?"

"Certainly, we have not exercised volition in coming into existence. But, my dear nephew, the mind creates circumstances. All action proceeds from mind."

"Ay, but the cause for the effect! Motives, feelings, convictions, call them what you will, all spring from external circumstances, over which it is impossible we can exercise control. The mind is but a machine set in motion, say what you will."

"Nay, mind must will either to act or be inert, and while motives sway, and feelings and convictions urge to deeds, they in themselves are merely passive in their influence. They cannot organise action. Where do they operate in any way *without* the mind? Therefore it is reasonable to conclude that the will is sovereign and supreme over motives."

"Answer me, do we not desire to will, not will to desire?"

"Surely not. The desire and the will may possibly be simultaneous; but it is impossible desire can precede volition, and for this reason. There must be an effect for a cause, as you have already asserted. There cannot possibly be an infinite succession of effects, but a starting point there must exist. Then the first cause of desire must originate somewhere, and a cause must be active. Circumstances act upon the mind; but that mind, being a superior principle to the external agency, they cannot necessitate its operation."

"Ah, you have had a lesson from Spenser, I perceive. I will answer your objections in a few words. The mind *must* either act or be inert, you say. Truly so. *Must!* you used the word. Then, if you tell me it is free to do either, you are involved in an anomaly of terms. Motives, feelings and convictions, according to you, are passive, and have no existence without the mind. Then how can passive causes (a ridiculous solecism in speech, as well as sense) produce active effects? The desire and the will again you assert are at all events simultaneous. There must be a motive for all volition. Then, whence that motive, but for the external influences around? As to the impossibility of an infinite series of effects, something must be infinite, and the original cause must be produced."

"I see you fancy you have obtained a victory, but I will not allow it; neither do I admit that my arguments were furnished by Henry Spenser. I speak according to my best judgment, and, though I pretend not to philosophy, I *do* to reason. I will reply to what you have said, and then we will quit the subject until we have more leisure. The mind *must* either act or be inert. (I believe that argument of yours is a plagiarism from Hobbes.) Then what is it that constrains action or inaction? Does the mind, or does it not? If not the mind, then it can have no agency at all, and of course cannot be concerned in the matter. In fact it could not be said to exist, and no materialist denies that it does. I *will* act, I say, or the reverse. Then, if I say I *will*, at any rate there is a counterbalancing anomaly in terms for your *must*, if I cannot, The motives and feelings are all vivified by mind, and made active agencies by it; so that the will is established, whether we act or otherwise. For the production of an original cause—everything has a beginning in Time, though connected with Eternity, and consequently volition is a cause for action, and so the first."

CHAPTER VII.

Man is of dust ;—ethereal hopes are his,
Which when they should sustain themselves aloft
Want due consistence.—*The Excursion.*

Respecting man, whatever wrong we call,
May, must be right as relative to all.
What makes all physical or moral ill ?
There deviates Nature, and here wanders will.—Pope.

THE EPICUREAN AND HIS ATHEISM—THE ANGLER AND ANGLING —THE OLD MAN'S PHILOSOPHY.

" She is a splendid woman that Harriet Walsingham," thought the Epicurean, as he quitted his aunt (for, though she was so young, such was her relationship to him), after having held a conference with her at the termination of the dispute in the last chapter; " but her reasoning is inconclusive. I hate arguing with females—particularly when they possess beauty. What man with any soul can resist the bright eloquence of pleading eyes? Pshaw ! and then they never allow us to meet their reasonings, but appeal to our passions, not our judgment, and we all know very well that in such a contest the feelings predominate over the convictions, and solid sense goes to the devil, for the sake of a radiant glance, or musical tone. But she *has* a mind as well as a heart, by Jove ! None of us understand Harriet."

Thus ruminating, the young man striking into a path divaricating from the high road, and pursuing multifarious sinuous fancies, ascended a green hill upon which several sheep were grazing, and from whose pine-crowned summit a landscape of considerable beauty stretched away far as the eye could reach ; hamlets, villages, and towns picturesquely insulated in the general area they occcupied.

The scenery of England is characterised by little bold variety, or striking grandeur, so that, in all descriptions of it, frequent repetition becomes nearly unavoidable---a fact which some of our novelists who sometimes usurp their privilege of prescriptive infliction in prosing on the beautiful, would do well to consider. Yet who is there with any feeling for country or Nature, who will not linger over the graphic pictures which some of our rural poets have been so happy in the execution of, and among which the following, from the " Excursion," is not the least delightful nor applicable to that on which the Epicurean gazed from the hill.

> " In rugged arms how soft it seems to lie,
> How tenderly protected! Far and near
> We have an image of the pristine earth,
> The planet in its nakedness ; were this
> Man's only dwelling, sole appointed seat,
> First, last, and single in the breathing world,
> It could not be more quiet."

" How wonderful is Nature," said the youth, musingly. " How marvellously sustained the vast whole by the unerring laws which Necessity organizes. Thou vital and permeating principle of the universe! Beautiful and incomprehensible Necessity! Thou art no solitary sovereign, exhausting the powers, and destroying the harmonies created by himself, but in the immensity of what we call space, diffusing life, and light, and motion ; and maintaining through countless mazes the eternal series of causes and effects of which thou art the first and the last! Necessity! Where does it not exist? What is not in fact Necessity? It is the nucleus of all things, and the heart and centre of the interminable systems which baffle the conception of the finite mind. And yet---and yet---millions live, and suffer, and die; and convulsions of Nature scatter anguish, and woe, and desolation, demonstrating thou art imperfect and deficient in the power which we call intellect. If there were one to controul and regulate thine operations, we should not behold the elements of evi nor the discordancies of moral and physical agencies. What ha: man in truth to hope? Nothing can ever satisfy the inordinate desires of his aspiring mind, nor fill the scope of his wants and his ambition. It is singular, but incontrovertible, that all other animal: are satisfied with their condition, and he, though nothing more tha . an intellectual animal, is always sighing after the unattainably pe .

fect. I know not how to account for this, because we do not find that the amount of pleasurable sensations among other living creatures is in anywise proportioned by the amount of understanding that they possess. The stupid insect is as happy as the sagacious dog— it lives, it flutters, and becomes extinct. Difficulties surround the mind on every side, and I have almost come to the conclusion that one creed is as reasonable as another; though I did not think so four years ago, when I first embraced materialism with such ardour. Strange—most strange! that our sentiments and feelings should undergo such an entire revolution in so brief a space of time; but every thing is mutable in matter: and so we cannot expect mind, which is only the highest attribute of it, to be stationary."

Descending the hill, our philosopher found himself in a pleasant and fertile valley, through which a river of some length extended, and on the banks of which were seated, at far distant intervals, two or three anglers, earnestly and silently engaged in their piscatory occupations. The youth smiled, and he never did so without a mixture of scorn and sarcasm.

"It amuses me to remark on what trifles the mind, whose cravings after perfection I was just admiring, will frequently fritter away its noble and lofty energies. But, so it is. One man is endeavouring to make the conquest of the world with all its multitudes of rational beings; another is wasting his time in absurd pastimes and frivolous pursuits. Here is an old, grey-headed man, now, who, in other circumstances might have been a Newton, entirely absorbed in watching that childish toy that flaunts so gaily with its gaudy paint on the stream. He considers not the tortures of his unhappy victims, not he; but he is acting from impulse—from an inherent instinct,— even as the great Necessity, itself necessitated to perform its intricate evolutions, unmindful and ignorant of the effects which its multiform operations must cause. As the human being unconsciously inflicts torture and misery on myriads of living things, so the first cause of his existence is eternally occupied in a blind arrangement of Nature, and hence the earthquakes, tempests, and innumerable plagues of earth; which all, however, alternately increase the aggregate amount of enjoyment and collective happiness. I'll speak to this fellow." And as he repeated the words of Shakspeare's divine conception, the Materialist addressed the personage, whose keen and anxious glances at his float had so much excited his contempt and wonder-

The Young Philosopher and the Old Moralist.

P. 97.

ment—for he had some greatness in him, though he had adopted false and distorted principles.

The old man was as unique a specimen of the disciples of Walton and Cotton as can be imagined. He was decidedly diminutive in stature, and his hair was perfectly white with the snows of nearly seventy winters; but his well-natured face was rosy, and his eyes were still eager, and bright, and animated. The Epicurean accosted him, saying,

" You have a fine day for your sport, old man."

The angler appeared surprised at the freedom of this address, and answered in a manner far above the station of life he seemed to fill would have intimated a probability of——

" Ay, I have travelled almost twenty miles this morning, in order to arrive at this spot, where I am told there are some particularly fine fish. Have you ever caught anything rare about here, young sir ?"

" Very silly fish," returned the youth with his cold sneer.

" You think that they seldom venture into such shallow water," said the old man, hardly noticing the contemptuous tone in which he had been answered, " but you may find—ah, ha! a nibble! Now, my fine fellow—my delicate trout! you *are* a beauty! Look at him, friend! Remark his colour and size! What do you think he weighs?"

" He ought to weigh a good deal heavier than some brains, in order to recompense your trouble."

" Trouble—trouble, quotha? Fishing is never a trouble, young gentleman. I have pursued it, solely for the pleasure I find in the pursuit, for fifty years. In all weathers you might have seen Roger Sidney (ay, and though he is in his 70th year you may see him now) with his rod in hand, and basket on arm, early and late, winter and summer—whenever anything was to be caught. By Bacchus! Another bite! I have him safe enough! A fish for a king! Beautiful! Magnificent !"

And the old man rubbed his hands, which, from long exposure to the inclemency of the weather, were hard and horny, in the rapture of his soul, as he safely brought to land a second trout of magnitude.

" Wonderful !" muttered the young philosopher. " A man on the verge of threescore years and ten, with one foot in the grave, delighting, mind, and heart, and body, with all the exuberant gaiety of youth, in a cruel pastime, unworthy the intellect of a child. A wretched fool!—But he imagines himself well-pleased, and so I

o

know not why I should spurn him. Man! oh, man! Slave of mean vices! Abject worm! unworthy of the prerogative which chance affords—the lordship of the universe! only maintained by a superior organisation, for other animals have far nobler instincts. I wonder if this man have the least atom of a heart, or an understanding?"

As the Epicurean was thus engaged in his own bitter and peculiar strain of moralizing, the angler had been busy in making preparations for departure, and having completed them, looked into his face with a gaze of inquiring shrewdness and penetration, such as a spectator would have deemed it impossible for him to wear, who had just displayed such childish eagerness, in his somewhat inhuman sport. He appeared to gather the import of his companion's cogitations, for observing the deep abstraction into which he had fallen, he fidgetted for some moments, and finally addressed him thus—

"You are amazed that a person of my age should fritter away the valuable and irrevocable time apportioned for preparation for a higher state of existence in the pursuit of an idle pastime, which can neither intellectualize his mind, nor elevate his moral being. I have not done so without consideration, I assure you. But life is so overshadowed with the clouds of fate, that to divert the soul from booding upon it is something; and I am content in my old age, having scarcely a connexion in the world, to wander about at will, to observe the loveliness of Nature in her varied aspects, and to render up my spirit to quiet meditation. For you will observe, that while the uncertainty of success in angling amuses the mind, it does not prevent it from pursuing trains of thought, while the quiet necessary to be observed, is calculated to arouse reflection; and undisturbed by the sound of human voices, as the stream ripples past in the light of heaven, and the birds sing blithely, and the very air is instinct with pleasant sounds, the soul abstracts itself from the present, while the senses are gratified also, and engages in devout meditation."

"Amazing!" ejaculated the Epicurean, raising his eyes to the firmament. "What! You engage in ' devout meditation,' and raise your mind to the infinite and eternal, while you are occupied in watching a little float upon the water, and eagerly anticipating the moment which shall deliver your innocent and unsuspecting prey into your hands? You can delight in such a sport, when you know the agonies you inflict upon your wretched victims, and can etherealize your being as you describe, while playing the butcher's part?"

The old angler appeared momentarily offended at the bluntness and severity of the censure passed upon himself and his favourite recreation ; but after reflecting for a little, he replied, mildly—

" It has pleased God that countless myriads of harmless creatures should suffer a brief—a very brief physical struggle, and a termination is put to their life. It is evident that all things that live, must cease to do so, and does it matter in what way an end is put to existence, so that needless torture is not inflicted ? Indeed, young sir, you attack the pursuit I love with too much harshness. It has none of the wild frenzy which appears to animate the hunter, but allows ample scope for contemplation, and is calculated to engender thought even in the thoughtless."

" But do you consider the agonies of the poor fish as it writhes beneath your skill and cunning ? Do you reflect that its little life is all it possesses, while you are endued with lofty mental energies, and capacities for pleasure, in which it is impossible that beings of a less elevated order can participate ? Nothing can restore the life that we destroy, and to what we usually call the purely animal, the *sense* of it alone is unending satisfaction, if enjoyed under no bodily affliction. Do you not think, if we regard not the sufferings of the lower order of animals, we may be apt to forget the claims of the highest on our humanity ? If your pastime have not the wild frenzy of the chase, it seems to me of a much meaner madness. I saw that your eyes glittered, even now, with as much glee as if you had made a nation happy, instead of putting a period to the existence of a poor trout."

" But you are aware that we are necessitated to give pain and inflict death upon multitudes of living creatures totally independent of volition. Every inspiration that we draw probably destroys more than one animalcule ; but the capacity of that animate atom for enjoyment is proportioned to the brevity of its existence. I allow that for a few moments the sufferings of a fish caught by the rod are excessive ; but I am careful to terminate them as speedily and mercifully as is practicable. And does not the Creator himself thus act towards me ?"

The aspect of the Materialist's face darkened.

" Is it not infatuation, ignorance, and superstition, to imagine that a Being infinite in power, illimitable in wisdom and knowledge, eternal, holy, pure and beneficent, would permit a state where such wretchedness is paramount, and such crimes and cruelties are almost universally perpetrated? The amount of actual acute and unmitigated suffering in this world is altogether incalculable, it defies conception, it baffles mathematical powers. Wherever we go we see it. Not a sweet breath of air but arises from the pain of some portion of animated Nature. Even allowing that man is given volition, and therefore is accountable for his actions, surely these poor brutes and insects, which have nothing save instinct to direct them, should not undergo the penalties of sin and transgression. They have never sinned, nor are they capacitated to disobey the moral law."

"I am speaking to an atheist," said the old man, sadly, when Walsingham had finished. "Well, I once had my doubts, and God forbid that I should judge harshly of any frail, erring human being whose opinions differ from mine. The arguments you have used may have some force, but are not by any means unanswerable. Many a time, while following my silent and lonely occupation, I have deeply reflected, as far as my poor intellect would allow, on the vast mysteries by which we are surrounded; and the existence of evil, moral and physical, has been a subject of engrossing interest. That there *is* evil, both in the moral and material universe, none will controvert. Neither will you deny that there is good also. If there be more good than evil in the world, then we are justified in concluding that, supposing an Intellectual First Cause, His attributes are benevolent. I assert, after long and patient investigation, that the amount of good is greatly more than that of evil, morally and physically. If evil predominated, we should then be authorized by reason in calling into question the beneficence and intelligence of the First Cause; since *those* qualities would, of course, organize happiness. But, surely, sir, you will allow that more experience an amount of pleasurable than painful sensations in some way? We are discontented from the very amount of good that we are susceptible of, and proportionally with the blessings we have received is the reluctance to endure that evil that generally succeeds. You must here acknowledge the preservation of a beautiful harmony which reason, pure reason, and nothing else, enables all men who will think to descry. If we suffer intensely *now*, by so much the more is our capacity for future fruition enlarged; according to the contrast of pain is the intensity of pleasure enhanced. Indeed we must suffer the one, in order fully to appreciate the other. Are we to charge omnipotence with partiality in the distribution of its good? I answer, that we make or destroy our own happiness, and that the Creator is just in the apportioning of His benefits. There is always some counter-balancing advantage or disadvantage in every situation. The beggar has health and rags, the king sickness and purple. The one has a cheerful mind and poverty, the other riches and discontent. Circumstances may create character in some measure, and modify our feelings in various methods; but, you perceive, that if they antagonize with what is usually termed good, they produce a power of contrast, which enables what is evil to one man to afford pleasure to another. So that in the moral government, search where you will, examine how you may, there is evidence of a good, merciful Providence, even though evil is so widely diffused over its works."

" I hardly expected to encounter so formidable an opponent in an angler," said the materialist, as the old man paused to breathe and allow an answer, before resuming his forcible and logical argument. " But I will disprove that evil under any circumstances is good, or that there is an equipoise of happiness in the distribution of it. We cannot conceive that one man enjoys this existence as much as another, when millions drag on a weary burthen of poverty and destitution, constrained to actions by stern necessity at which they shudder and recoil to think of. Have not Circumstances---the gods of Time!--- created all this misery? And if a Supreme Being exist, has He not ordained those circumstances? If not, He could have had no purpose in creating. But——"

" Wait! I did not say there is equality of *happiness*. Happiness is essentially a state of mind. We make our own happiness or moral misery; but we do not order the series of causes and effects around us. Pleasure is external, and happiness internal. As to the millions who endure a wretched physical life, of course we do not pretend that they are privileged in the same measure as ourselves. Still, according to the amount of physical evil they endure, is the exquisite sense of pleasure if it arrive. Give a man the whole world and he will be heartily sick of it in a short time. We always wish for something that we cannot attain, and so are dissatisfied with all that we possess. Surely this fact, instead of being an argument against, is a strong reason for the existence of a future state? Then, as to God having ordered all things, we must be careful to draw a line of demarcation betwixt creating and permitting. We ourselves suffer what is evil to remain (though it would be a crime to cause it), in order that more might not arise by the extinction of it. Look through all Nature! Is anything done ill or amiss? All things indeed contain the elements of decomposition, but are made fresh from the hands of the immortal, and are excellent in kind, whatever they may be in degree. All things certainly become corrupt, but we see they are not created so."

" A distinction without a difference, to my mind."

" Pardon me---God creates the elements of evil, because what He *creates* must be less perfect than himself. Everything out of God is liable to change. He can sustain a being beyond the possibility of falling; but sustentation would prevent free-will; but if that being is not God, the inference is obvious. So that, in causing the elements of material decomposition, He adapts the material to our necessities, and affords a clear analogy of our own state, with this difference, that if we depend upon the changeable we must, like other substances, become corrupt; but if on the unchangeable, we cannot fade away. Thus in the moral universe (the analogical deductions from which and the material demonstrate that they are from the same hand, for they are truly wonderful) man may do well or ill, but he rises or sinks by his own exertions. All living things are subject to death, but here secondary causes are the agencies which the Eternal employs for the operation of what we ignorantly term evil— since death is none in the abstract. The animal world having no sad experience nor dark anticipation enjoy more good than evil, even in the extremest limitation of existence, so that they are not entitled to another life. Man alone aspires after the everlasting. And to him alone, as he possesses that aspiration, is the everlasting due."

Frequently as the young Materialist had heard arguments similar to these urged with yet greater eloquence and power, there was a simple energy and an earnest faith in every tone and look of the old man that made a greater impression on him than he cared to avow; and it may be remarked, in passing, that these are the keys of persuasion and conviction. The discussion between the old and young man was here interrupted, but in what manner a succeeding chapter must solve. It is now requisite that we quit the personages who have occupied the more prominent stations in our tale, to detail events remotely to be connected with them.

CHAPTER III.

My name d'ye see's Tom Tough,
I've seen a little sarvice.—C. DIBDIN.

THE MAIMED SAILOR—THE SCHOLAR, AND A VISITOR.

A SMALL but neat habitation, containing two or three rooms, and thatched with admirable ingenuity, comprised the small portion of mortality which belonged to the excellent Mr. Samuel Stokes. Nature had once bestowed on Mr. Stokes the ordinary stature of a man, but the " unspiritual God" had deprived him of a quantity of those useful and ornamental appendages, called legs.

Beneath an ancient oak slowly falling into decay, the sun streaming down upon his sun-burnt and weather-beaten features, reclined the aforesaid Samuel, upon a crazy bench, a pipe in his mouth, and a mug of beer in his hand. His face, though not exactly handsome, according to the models of Grecian antiquity and the analysis of Hogarth, was certainly very far removed from what we include in the category of ugliness. Though his nose inclined to the snub formation, it was a good nose—full of good nature and simplicity, not of impudence and conceit, like many such noses; and though his eyes were of a greenish grey, a colour not generally preferred to black, or brown, or blue—though the cheeks were too fat, and the chin enlarging into the Siamese-twins contour, there was an indescribable something in it---a real, honest English courage and kindness that absolutely irradiated it into pleasingness, such as Phidias could not have permanently imparted to stone. His hair was grey, his frame strong and firmly set, and his years amounting to about six-and-forty. Thus, apparelled in a sailor's jacket and straw hat, with a long staff supporting him crutch-like beneath his arm, and his unfortunate legs defended at the extremities with manifold pieces of hard leather, in order that when he walked---which he did without artificial support—he might not wear out his bones and flesh more than was inevitable, we have a picture of a maimed British tar of the last century, and as good a specimen of honesty, valour, good nature, and cordial feeling as ever existed.

Mr. Stokes was engaged in, apparently, no very pleasant reverie, for occasionally he would heave a sigh and exclaim, "Oh, Sally, Sally, cruel Sally!" Then he would drink about half a pint from his mug, and resume his occupation of puffing clouds and turning up his eyes to heaven, as if to request a special interposition in his favour. "I don't know," sighed Stokes, having at length finished his beer, and nearly exhausted his tobacco, and reasoning the matter over with rueful earnestness, "why I should take on so, seeing as how I'm getting into middle age, and in the course of natur' must soon slip the cable; but flesh is flesh, and blood is blood, and cousin Sal—is cousin Sal anyhow." He paused, as soon as he had enunciated these incontrovertible propositions, and seemed to ruminate whether there existed any new aspect in which he might regard his peculiar position. "Sartinly," continued Sam, after an interval of some minutes, "I oughtn't to have expected Sally, after my misfortin', to take me for better for worse; but considering what *did* pass—well, I suppose it's a punishment I desarve for having taken advantage of her youth and innercence—though I'd ha' married her over and over again, for that 'ere matter, d—n——I wish as I could conker that evil habit o' swearin', as I've caught—but habit is natur, or maybe natur's habit. Ah, Mr. Smith, how goes the world with 'ee?"

"Thank you, Samuel, pretty well," answered a little man with a protruding stomach, who had come upon Stokes as he was moralizing on the force of habit. "What was it that I heard you say just now?"

"I was a-thinkin' how unpossible it is to get over bad habits. Sit down, sir, and I'll go and make some grog ready in a jiffy"

"No, Sam, no, I'm much obliged to you, but I exceeded the bounds of moderation last night—in point of fact, I got drunk."

"I hopes that aint your common custom, sir?"

"Why, Sam, the truth of the matter is, that my ardent temperament aroused, it outstrips my judgment, and enthrals my reason too frequently. Stokes, I am now engaged in multifarious occupations, and when any one of them is crowned with success, I indulge too much in the bottle—I make too great sacrifices to Bacchus, from the exuberance of joy I then experience."

"Ah, Mr. Smith, I'm glad I'm no scholar. I always see as you learned, clever gentry never does well in the world. It seems as if stupidity was the best quality for use."

"You may be in some measure right, my worthy friend. Dull rascals stick to business, and diligence is one chief element of success. *They* never make excursions into the regions of divine philosophy, nor indulge in the poetic raptures which persons of cultivated minds derive so unappreciable a gratification from. But I do not doubt but that I shall ultimately succeed in my present pursuits. The manager of a theatre has half promised to accept a tragedy of peculiar construction, combining the classical elegance and majestic grandeur of the Grecian drama, with the glorious nature and passionate power of the tragic writers of the Elizabethan era. O! I must succeed! A radiant future lies in the perspective of my aspirations, and instead of drudging on as an obscure village schoolmaster, I shall attain to the pinnacle of fame, and be crowned with the laurels of eternal ages. Stokes! I could not be content with competence and obscurity. I must have the acclamations of multitudes. I must hear the shouts of admiring thousands. I must possess the renown of genius and of scholarship. For these I have toiled by day and night. For these I have abandoned the 'ignorant present,' and I live and breathe in the far future, encircled by a living halo of light and glory."

During this eloquent oration, which Mr. Smith delivered with due energy and emphasis, marking the periods of his fluent sentences with a flourish of his short arms, Samuel Stokes remained gazing on him in silent admiration, as if an eighth wonder of the world had visited his lowly dwelling. When the speech was finished (Mr. S. was practising prior to the time when he hoped to make his public *debut* as a second Cicero), Sam slowly recovered from the effects of the bewilderment he felt at hearing such a vast explosion of intellect and fine words, and though much had been incomprehensible in the declamation, to his unsophisticated mind, yet catching the substance of the rhapsody, he replied—

"You are a wonderful man, Mr. Smith, that's sartain; but I can't myself understand no how, why anybody should bother hisself arter fame, and honner, and all that sort o'thing; when it aint possible for him to enjoy it. What I means is this. Our great folks as wins battles, and our wise men as governs the affairs of state, and our clever men as writes books, what none but clever folks like themselves can comprehend, don't they take all their trouble for no reward

P

at all ? No one talks well of 'em when they're alive. It's only arter they die they becomes famous."

"Nay, Samuel, there are many illustrious persons who reach the goal of their ambition, even in life. There are many whose glory is now shining above the horizon with intense lustre, and which will increase in radiance to the end of time."

"The gole of their ambition, d'ye say, sir ? I don't know ixactly what gole is ; but this I knows, those folks never seem satisfied, when they've got all they wanted. And I've had sad exper'ence of that 'ere myself—not as I would compare myself with them. I did think when I got lots of rhino, and a nice bit of a cabin like this, I should be as happy as the day is long. But disappointment follows us all through life. I hopes when we goes aloft as we shall leave it behind for ever."

"True, Sam, very true," responded Smith, "and I have frequently thoughts of abandoning the dear and bright schemes I have laid for immortality, when I consider the instability of all things here. I certainly should be inclined to do so, if I might enjoy the blessings of domestic felicity, far from the folly and contention of cities. But circumstances have urged me on. You know that I placed my early affections upon an eminently worthy object—O, she was so good, so pure, that—upon my soul, Sam, I can't speak of her *now* without playing the woman! She was taken from me—and I feel very, *very* desolate sometimes still. I would give all I may ever possess to hold poor Rose to my heart again."

The worthy Mr. Smith here turned away, and honest Sam appeared to sympathize deeply with him ; 'one touch of nature' making 'the whole world kin.' A few minutes previously the scholar was unintelligible to the sailor ; but now he was reduced to the standard of his own humble affections, and he felt for him like a brother. "Poor fellow," he exclaimed, brushing away a tear.

"God has bereaved me, and so I must submit," resumed Smith ; "but I see a visitor approaching, and so I will leave you at once." Thus saying, he shook the sailor by the hand, and hastened away.

"A visitor! who can it be?" ejaculated Stokes, "shiver my timbers, I should know him ; but I can't, for the life of me—ah, surely I do, though, and yet it can't be, its quite unpossible. But he is so like his father, there can't be no mistake. Master Francis ! is it you, sir ? Lord bless us, what a man you *are* grown, to be sure."

Uttering this exclamation, Stokes grasped the extended hand of a fine gentlemanly-looking young man of perhaps nineteen, attired in a naval uniform, and whose warm and hearty return of the rough tar's violent shaking of the limb evinced that their acquaintanceship was one of long duration.

CHAPTER IV.

O cauld—cauld now those ruby lips
I aft hae kissed sae fondly;
And closed for aye the sparkling glance,
That dwelt on me sae kindly.—Burns.

THE SCHOLAR AT THE GRAVE OF HIS BELOVED—THE STRANGE UNKNOWN—THE PACKET.

Mr. Smith, after quitting the abode of his humble friend, struck into a path, which communicated at its opposite extremity with an old church-yard, where yews and willows sighed mournfully in the faint, sweet breeze; and where numerous wild-flowers contrasted with the more pretending cultured ones, which the hand of affection had planted over the graves of the lost and loved; as if to show that Nature can mourn her children with as much fragrant sorrow in her tranquil, sweet, sad face, as any emblems that man in his vanity may rear.

Here a monument of marble erected its stately head, to commemorate the virtues, the rank, or the celebrity of the senseless dust beneath; and here a rude stone was carved with some pious and affectionate sentiment, indicative of the simplicity of the living grief, and the reality of the departed worth; while the greater number of green mounds, over which the pretty daisies and the golden buttercups grew in great luxuriance, possessed no other external mementoes, nor afforded the slightest clue to what the beings, once so full of life and elastic vigour, and who now slept so movelessly a few feet below, had appeared to those, so soon to share a similar fate— oblivion, ashes, nothingness!

And must we all come to this? Must the smiles we treasure, must the looks we cherish, and the hearts that make us rich, though poorest, with their sacred wealth of tenderness, fade, fade away,

and be no more beheld? The delicate loveliness, the haughty
beauty, the lofty and divine intelligence which breathes in human
lineaments are scattered in abhorred dust—first worshipped in the
zenith of their glory—the theme of poets, the admiration and model
of painters—giving light to passion, and inspiration to song—next,
a banquet to the hated worms of the earth, and finally portions of
that earth we so carelessly tread upon.

The scholar—for despite his pedantry and extravagance Smith
was really such—pursued his way over the burying-ground, until he
reached a grave, over which there was a low stone, whereon was
engraved in rough and inartificial characters—indeed so clumsily
executed that it was not easy to spell them; but in its sentiment
full of pathos and affectionate sorrow.

" ROSE STOKES, DIED MAY 17, 1720, AGED NINETEEN YEARS.

> " No marble consecrates the dust that lies
>   In mouldering silence 'neath this lowly stone—
> That dust once bright as are the summer skies,
>   The soul that lit it—like itself ALONE.
> Lo! yon blue cope is beautiful and fit
>   To cover even my pure angel's head,
> But the great God so loves and prizes it,
>   His bosom keeps it safe and blest instead."

" Ah, how I am altered since that time," murmured the little
man to himself, " strangely altered altogether! Ten years—is it
possible? Ten years since my dearest left me, and I wrote that inscription there! How often we used to wander together in this—
then to us—pleasant, though melancholy place, and talk about
future happiness—never, never to be attained! Little did I think,
ten years ago, I should be gazing on this stone, and be standing
above the corruption that was once more dear—"

He left the sentence unfinished, and seating himself upon the
grass was lost in the abstraction of memory. Poor fellow, with all
his absurdity and vanity, he had as warm and kind a heart as ever
beat within human bosom; and isolated as he now was, he clung to
the past with a tenacity such as those only in similar circumstances
of bereavement can comprehend. Though he frequently looked forward to a golden future of splendour and renown, his first warm
affections were buried in that lowly resting-place, and all appeared
as nihility to him, in comparison with his irreparable loss. What

was fortune, what power, what popularity, when he had no one to share them with him, when no fair face would smile upon his own, no gentle voice partake in joy the elation of his prosperity.

Mr. Smith was the son of a poor farmer, and by his own almost unaided industry had acquired sufficient learning, by the time he had grown to man's estate, to capacitate him for a private tutor, which situation he was fortunate enough to obtain. He afterwards accepted an engagement as master to the foundation school of his native village, and in which village we find him at present; an office which he filled with diligence and respectability for a period of some years.

He had fixed the affections of his heart on a pretty, ignorant girl, who was related to Samuel Stokes, and had all his good qualities, and applied himself assiduously to effect the removal of her mental darkness; but having succeeded in intellectualising her, even beyond his most sanguine expectations, " fell death's untimely frost" suddenly deprived him of his darling, and instead of receiving a loving wife to his bosom, as he had hoped, in the course of a single week she occupied the narrow mansion where no sounds are heard. So great was the agony of his loss, that he found himself unequal to the office he had hitherto filled, and having nobody dependent on him, retired from it, much to the regret of his scholars, by whom he was almost universally beloved. In order to divert his grief and melancholy, which preyed on his mind to so great an excess that at one time there were serious fears of his becoming a lunatic, he subsequently engaged in a multiplicity of the most heterogeneous pursuits—now joining a party of strolling players, now undertaking to instruct some aspirant to dramatic honours (to which indeed he was fully competent,) now composing verses, some good, some indifferent, and many nonsensical, now conceiving various works of science, imagination, criticism, or erudition, and not unfrequently betrayed into excess in his libations, hoping to dissipate the weight that oppressed his spirits, in everything he did. In some measure he was successful in this object, but the respectability of his character had suffered materially from the extravagances in which he indulged, and he was often hard-pressed to procure even the necessaries of life, though too proud to acknowledge the fact; but occasionally he obtained a windfall, for he really possessed abilities, which when directed into proper channels, were by no means contemptible. Not possessing a single relation of any kind, he was accustomed to take up his quar-

ters in all parts of the country which he traversed, never remaining
stationary for three weeks together. Such was the eccentric character
introduced to the reader's notice in the last chapter, and in whom
may possibly be recognised the fuddled gentleman from whom Harry
Danvers had found it impossible to extract any available or useful
information. It was astonishing, however, when his feelings were
thrown into their old phases, how they resumed the truth and purity
of nature, and how his pedantry and hyperbolical expressions dissipated with the delusive mists which he was in the habit of conjuring,
to beguile himself from himself.

He was startled from his contemplation by hearing a sob or groan
at a little distance from him. The church-yard was so remote from
any habitation, and was so rarely visited except on the Sunday (for
there was a shorter cut to the cottage occupied by Stokes, than that
which terminated in the burying-ground), that Smith was surprised
at discovering that he was in the vicinity of a human being. A high
grave-stone was placed at about a dozen paces from that on which
he leant, and directing his eyes to it, he saw a head bent toward the
earth and over the stone, the lower part of his face resting on two
emaciated hands.

Rising from his stooping position, then, he surveyed the tall, thin
figure which had been previously concealed from his view, and fancied that he was familiar with it, but could not make up his mind
whether imagination cheated him or not. The stranger, unconscious
of the proximity of another person, indulged his emotions, and from
the agitation of his bony and angular frame, it was quite evident he
endured no ordinary degree of suffering. Again he groaned, and this
time spoke aloud, not hearing the cough, by which the scholar
deemed it right to intimate his presence.

"Crime, oh deadly crime! What can erase from my soul the red
spots upon it? Blood—ay, blood!" and he shuddered visibly.
"Where is the water that shall wash it out? Oh, God, there is no
mercy for me! No hope, no pity, no forgiveness! No comfort for
me on earth, and horror and despair petrifying me when I dare to
look into futurity!"

It would be difficult to describe the appearance of fear and wretchedness which imparted a ghastly and livid hue to the naturally
almost death-like pallor of the stranger's sunken cheek; his chest
wrung with the anguish of his repeated groans, and his hands
clasped together, and now pressed upon his high, narrow forehead,

on which large drops of agony were standing. He was not old, and yet he appeared, in some respects, to have passed middle age, though in fact his years were short of forty; his grey hair, which had nearly deserted the temples, his wrinkled brow, and the deep lines in his cheeks, appearing the effect of excessive misery, and of passions in contention, rather than the ordinary result of the certain and gradual operations of the destroyer Time. He fell down upon a sudden, in a species of stupor, and his face became as vacant as that of the dead.

The scholar approached him, and, as no notice was taken of his presence, he became apprehensive that the unknown had been seized with a fit. Acting upon this supposition he was on the point of attempting to raise him in his arms, when he abruptly started to his feet and exclaimed with wild and intense energy,

"My gold! my gold! thou shalt not have my gold—Hell shall not wrest it from me. I tell you that I have sacrificed Heaven for it—I have committed mur—ha, ha! I will take it down with me to the grave, and it shall be placed here, here!" putting his hand to his heart, "so that in the great day of account, when I shall be asked wherefore I did the deed—I may point to the glittering dust and say, 'Avarice was made my master passion, and I was not given help to struggle against the temptation.' Avarice and Jealousy are the fiends of fate, and bear down the unwilling soul to the depths of perdition!"

With such rapidity were these incoherent words ejaculated, that it was impossible for Smith to get in a sentence. He now was inclined to think the unhappy man a maniac broken loose from prison, and, desirous of soothing his excitement, said,

"My good friend, your gold shall not be taken from you," (a likely thing he should have any, was Smith's inward thought, with such a coat as he wears,) "and I shall be happy to render you service?"

"What do you say? who are you?" returned the stranger with quickness, and not waiting for an answer continued, "I am not in need of your assistance;" saying which, he strode rapidly away, and was lost to sight in the winding of a road which extended almost in a circle to the churchyard. Smith, crossing his arms, lapsed into a musing attitude.

"I do not think he is insane," he thought, "but how awfully he looked and spoke. I am certain I have seen that man before—but where, I cannot conjecture."

Thus engaged in cogitation, his eyes happened to fall upon the spot where the mysterious being had stood, and were arrested by a small packet which, it seemed, he had dropped. He picked it up, and hastily followed in the direction which its owner had taken, with the purpose of restoring it to him; but, far or near, he had not left a vestige behind.

"There's a terrible mystery about this fellow, which it is impossible to fathom," again meditated the scholar. "He talked of blood and murder; and his face—upon my soul I shall never forget the aspect it wore."

Returning to the churchyard, he lingered at the grave where the stranger had remained so long, and read, though not for the first time,—for he was familiar with every tombstone there,—the inscription on its marble tablet. It was simply this——

"F. W. DIED 1721, AGED 28.

"SHE SHALL WAKE, TO WEEP NO MORE."

There was nothing farther of any kind to distinguish what the occupant of that dreary abode had been; and Smith recollected a funeral which he had accidentally witnessed, at which there was no mourner present, terminating there. The church clock reminding him that it was time for him to fulfil his engagement, he quitted the burying-ground and walked briskly on his way.

"I can't make out the business in any way, so it is useless to waste farther time in thinking of it," said the worthy ex-pedagogue to himself. "I will keep this parcel safe, and leave it with Stokes, that it may be returned to its legal possessor, if he inquire for it." And so, he endeavoured forthwith to dismiss the inexplicable matter from his mind.

It is a very singular fact, and one which future metaphysicians may discuss until discussion be exhausted, (a period which, our American friends would say, extends "from July to Eternity") that in proportion as the human mind endeavours to dismiss a theme from the sphere of its apprehension, so it is magnified into consideration and importance; and hence we may conclude that the very best method of getting speedily rid of an insuperable difficulty within the regions of intellect, is to permit it to have its run—to let it get out of breath, in whirling round the cycle of the brain, till dizzy and tired,---for here the sad fruits of Mother Eve's fatal

indiscretion are distinctly apparent, in the perversity with which the
soul ever turns to a prohibited subject; for no other reason in the
world than because it is so. But there are exceptions to this general
rule, for the lucid exposition of the first principles of which, you may
consult the "Metaphysic of Ethics," or the heavenly mysteries of
Emanuel Swedenborg, or, if you prefer it, the "Transcendentalism" of
Mr. Thomas Carlyle, or any other book dealing in subtile casuistry
and ontological illumination, and which some of our ignorant English
critics, not yet inoculated with German mysticism, have the strange
audacity to denominate incomprehensible. Not that old Kant, and
Swedenborg, and Mr. Carlyle are not all excellent in their way
" as their sceptical adversaries allow" even to the understandings of
beer-bemuddled English brains; but the deuce of the matter is, that
when you have arrived at some sort of definite conclusion as to their
doctrines, you discover that they only tell you what might have been
explained in a dozen common-sensical sentences—but then we
should lose all their acute reasoning, analysis, synthesis, and obscurity.

So our scholar bothered his sensory with the operations of conjecture, just like many wiser—or, as others may conceive—more foolish
fellows, from the Stagyrite down to the Mathematicians who occupy
themselves in the attempt to effect the quadrature of the circle. It
was ordered, however, by the stern sisters that an end should be put
to his surmises, before imagination run riot could be guilty of any
very grave extravagancies, as, fortunately for themselves, the force
of utilitarianism brings down psychology to the earth and constrains
its votaries to follow the business of life. But hang the doctrines of
Bentham, as well as the antitheses of the others. Benthamism is
good, and so is idealism; but what is there beneficial in extremes,
whether in science, politics, or philosophy? Mischievous materialism
and absurd abstraction from the world for which we are created, are
equally at variance with sound wisdom, happiness, utility, and
truth.

CHAPTER V.

" Here" he was interrupted by a knife,
    With " Damn your ayes! your money or your life!"
                                    Don Juan.

Ha, ha! what a fool honesty is! and trust, his twin brother, a very foolish gentleman. I see this is the time that the unjust man doth thrive.—SHAKSPEARE.

THE OLD STRANGER—A POETICAL DISCOURSE UNPLEASANTLY BROKEN IN UPON—OLD ACQUAINTANCES.

As Smith was preparing to pursue the vagaries of fancy, instead of
the logical inductions of the higher faculty of reason, a remarkable
figure arose from beneath a hedge, and gave him a good-morrow.

The individual in question was an old man, of rather venerable
appearance, with long white hair and bushy eyebrows of the same
colour, a large mouth, furnished with white and even teeth, in a
high state of preservation for his years, a nose of the aquiline order,
and forehead puckered up into wrinkles, though the remainder of
his face was smooth, and even youthful in its freshness. There was
a lurking expression of cunning about the corners of the mouth, and
a dash of ferocious daring in the keen grey eye, scarcely in accordance with the other characteristics of his general appearance.

His stature must once have been very great, for, although he
stooped a great deal, it was above six feet, and his dress was composed of an old, shabby hat, a long, faded, threadbare coat, and
unutterables so ancient that it appeared a question whether they
could ever have been made for him, old as he was.

It is delightful weather," observed the old man, slowly dragging
on his gigantic legs, and keeping pace with Smith, who was trotting
along as fast as his little members would permit.

" Very pleasant, indeed, answered the scholar; " but you seem
fatigued, my good man, will you lean on me?"

" No, I thank'ee, sir ; I'm not quite sure that I could manage to do so, however well inclined," he replied, with a smile, looking down upon the short man.

Smith was the essence of good-nature, and could take a joke with perfect equanimity, so that he merely returned the smile of his new acquaintance, nor heeded the implied insignificance of his personal appearance, and rejoined—" We appear to be journeying in the same direction, and as I have heard of frequent robberies in this part of the country, we shall be a mutual protection to each other ; for although neither of us be very formidable—you, from your age, being feeble, and I, from my original organization, not being gifted with great strength—robbers seldom attack more than one person at a time ;—not that either you or I probably possess much to tempt rapacity."

" Why, as for that matter, sir," returned the old man, " I shouldn't like to lose what little I have; for though my dress is beggarly, my purse is not empty—but I am imprudent in talking thus, in spite of the respectability of your appearance," he added, with a peculiar expression of countenance. " I have just been to market, and my horse having met with an accident, I thought I would walk home; for I didn't like the useless expense of hiring another. But what of these robbers you mention ?"

" I have heard there are two men, of absolutely gigantic stature, who usually infest this road, and have been known to stop a dozen farmers and others returning from market, one after another, when no one is near. But, little as I am, I would show fight, and you, I am sure, with that long staff of oak, would second me. You must have been a terrible fellow when young, judging from what you now are. It is not often a person at your time of life can show such a muscular hand."

" I'm a peaceable man, now ; but I believe I could wrestle and use a cudgel with most fellows, certainly ; but I don't think I should be able to do much now. Still I would stand by you—Ah ! that looks a suspicious character approaching on horseback now— that tall man in a long cloak !"

" Fortunately, however," remarked Smith, " I can perceive two labouring men advancing down the lane."

As he was yet speaking the object of the old man's trepidation, a rather handsome, dashing fellow, with a black patch on his cheek, put the large well-made horse he rode into a canter, and met them.

A look of significance passed between Smith's companion and the mounted traveller (unobserved by the little scholar), and the latter, with a polite bow to them, continued his journey.

"Well, I'm glad we've escaped from the scoundrel, if he be the highwayman," said Smith, whose heart had been beating a trifle faster than was its wonted impetus, though he was no coward, "for he certainly is a terrible fellow to look at, and I am, unfortunately, quite unarmed."

The pedestrians now descended a winding path, intersected by a stream that, with gentle plash and sparkling foam, coursed along and divided the lofty trees, which grew even into the water, and from whence no trace of man or man's abode could be descried. It was poetically lonely, and the birds and the gay insects that fluttered and flew through the clear air, were the only things of life perceptible by any of the senses, far or near; save when at intervals some finny tenant of the river rose above the surface, or some reptile ran into its hiding-place, at the unusual sound of footsteps in that sequestered valley.

Smith's romance was excited by the subdued and picturesque beauty of the spot, and falling into an attitude half natural, half theatrical, he exclaimed,

"Divine loveliness of Earth! How tranquil is the charm you wind around the heart, and how soft and delicious the calm that dwells in all your secret nooks! As we wander among your varied landscapes, and read the excellent lessons you afford to the meditative mind, the soul expands to moral beauty, and we feel more of the dignity of our nature, than when encircled by the noise and turmoil of crowded cities; for there issues from the mysterious recesses of life that aspiration after the true which manifests itself in the love of the ideal, and the ideal becomes, as it were, an abstraction of the ethereal and the everlasting. In the lines of the admirable Pope, the first of our living geniuses---

> ' Happy the man who to the shades retires,
> Whom Nature charms, and whom the Muse inspires,
> Whom humble joys of home-felt quiet please,
> Successive study, exercise, and ease.' "

During this long effusion, the old stranger had manifested very evident symptoms of *ennui*, and not appreciating the excellence of

Mr. Smith's ideas, nor the appositeness of his quotation, he broke in upon the harangue, and said,

" I think we had better make the best of our way onwards, for this is an unfrequented place, and the labourers you saw just now will soon be out of the reach of your voice, though you seem to have good lungs," (Smith had the voice of a Stentor) " so that should the robbers you are apprehensive of——"

" True, true, you wisely act the Mentor to my forgetfulness. As we proceed, I can as well discourse," returned the scholar, " after the manner of the Peripatetics. I have a notion of establishing some sort of institution, for the purpose of instructing adults in classics and philosophy, and I think I shall resume the ancient practice of Aristotle, and in fine weather deliver——"

In the middle of his sentence Mr. Smith was suddenly and most disagreeably interrupted ; for the huge hand of his companion was placed on his throat, so as to prevent the possibility of his crying out, and in an altered voice the old man said,

" I didn't come here to be humbugged with your nonsense, my rum chap! Come, fork out what you've got. I am one of the gentlemen you bestowed the very complimentary epithet of scoundrel on, just now."

" Oh, the devil!" ejaculated Smith, speaking with difficulty, from the compression of his new friend's fingers on his throat, which was so intense as to threaten his windpipe with adhesion, " indeed, indeed, Sir, if you recollect, I didn't call you a scoundrel. Pray, relax your grasp, or you will throttle me. I have got nothing to give to you, upon my word and honour as a gentleman."

" Pshaw, don't think to gammon me, old cock! As for your not calling me a scoundrel, you applied the term to my partner and relation, as well as insulting my professional dignity, and those in the same house of business, you know, are one and the same. Otherwise, for your civility in offering your support, believing me to be infirm, I *might* have let you off. I'm hard up for cash, and so I must search your pockets, not doubting your word of honour as a gentleman, but conceiving it is possible your memory may not be so good for the common concerns of life as it is for Pope's poetry."

With these words, delivered with much urbanity and humour, the robber proceeded to take cognizance of the contents of Smith's pockets, and rifled them of a pen-knife, a pocket-book containing only some memoranda, a Greek Homer, and a very few half-pence, all of which the highwayman politely restored to their owner, adding,

"I believe you have told me truth, Mr. What's-your-name, and, somehow or another, folks so often forget their morality in that respect, when speaking to me, that I suppose I must let you off, though I can tell you that I didn't endure the bother of your company so long for nothing. I promise you that you shall not be troubled with me again, till you carry something more substantial with you than the stuff you've got in your brains. But wait a moment—I see something in your breast—allow me to inspect it. You shall have it again, if it is as worthless as all the rest about you."

"No, Mr. Robber, you shall not have that; it isn't mine!" exclaimed the scholar, vehemently struggling in the nervous grasp of the gentleman footpad, "and I must and will retain it, in order to return it to its lawful owner."

But the robber threw Smith on his back, and easily deprived him of the object of contention, while the victimised party vociferated with lungs which had been exercised in several barns in such characters as *Richard* and the fiery spirits of the drama. Nor were his cries long unavailing; for while the footpad was leisurely examining the contents of the parcel which the scholar had accidentally picked up, two persons appeared from behind a broad tree which had concealed them, and Smith recognizing one shouted,

"Oh, Master Walsingham, help, help me!"

The robber, thrusting his spoil into his dress, drew a long rapier from under his coat, and assumed a defensive attitude, at the same time hurling away the unfortunate scholar with such terrific violence as to throw him stunned and senseless, at the distance of some yards, upon the earth.

William Walsingham (for it was no other than the Epicurean and his acquaintance of the rod, who had heard the cries of Smith, and hastened to the scene of action to render their assistance) lost no time in unsheathing his weapon, which he, like almost all gentlemen of the age in which he lived, habitually wore, and, gathering at a glance the state of affairs, attacked the robber who instantly drew up his tall form to its real altitude of six feet four, and with menacing brow appeared to think it probable that his gigantic appearance would intimidate so young a foe into retreat. But Walsingham was a lion in daring, nor was he unskilled in the use of the weapon which he wielded, so that he was by no means an insignificant antagonist, even when opposed to such an one as the tall footpad.

Every vestige of age and infirmity had vanished from the robber, as if by magic, and his slender but sinewy and towering figure, and the way in which he flourished his rapier, showing great scientific accomplishment in the swiftness of his cuts, demonstrated that the disparity in numbers (for the old angler with the butt-end of his rod was preparing to aim a blow at him) would be counterbalanced by his superior agility, strength, stature, and skill. Walsingham now parrying a thrust from the footpad, commenced a vigorous assault, but his weapon was made rather for ornament than use, and the length of his opponent's blade, as well as his extraordinary extension of limb, were fearful odds against him.

Seconded by the angler, however, who, if he could not seriously injure, could annoy and harass the robber, he maintained the combat with the highest credit to his coolness and self-possession, until his ill-tempered blade was shivered beneath a well-directed stroke of his antagonist's sword, and he was left defenceless. In an instant the footpad's steel was at his chest; but here the angler rendered good service, by striking it away with his fishing-rod, and Walsingham suddenly closing with his enemy, endeavoured to pinion his arms. But he was struggling with one of the most vigorous and gigantic men in England, and though his own muscular powers were great for his age, he had not exercised them so that they could avail much against the practised skill, and steel-strung sinews of the robber. Nor could the disciple of Walton and Cotton be of efficient assistance; for, though hale and strong, he was more than commonly diminutive in person, and wholly unaccustomed to the violent and terrific struggles, which can alone develop the energies and capacities of the body, so as to make them serviceable in contests of such a description.

The scholar still remained insensible, and before he recovered, the contest had terminated; for the footpad, with a mighty effort, aided by the vast advantage which he derived from his extraordinary height, succeeded in raising his opponent from the ground, and in hurling him nearly to the spot where the other lay, when, knocking down the angler with his fist, he took to his heels, and was speedily lost to view among the surrounding trees.

The cause of his precipitate flight, after so signal a victory, was soon apparent; for the brawny figure of a man might have been discerned, hastening down a sloping path, and in a very few moments the discomfited combatants were joined by one, who had he been previously present might have turned the event of the day. He was indeed equal in point of strength and swordmanship to the gigantic robber.

"If you had been here a minute sooner, Figgins," said William Walsingham, who regained his faculties almost before the footpad had fled, "you might have secured the rascal; but he has such confoundedly long legs that he would outstrip anything but a racer, much more such a huge unwieldy fellow as you are. Let us see how Smith is faring! O, he has recovered!"

The scholar was gazing around with bewildered eyes, and slowly shaking off the effects of his stupefaction, and woefully rubbing his head--which did not feel any the better for having come in hasty contact with the hard ground--he strove to collect his scattered thoughts and address his allies.

"The villain! Is he gone?" asked the poor scholar; "well, he completely bamboozled me, hang him! Master Walsingham, I hope you are not hurt? I see the scoundrel has served you as he served me!"

"I shall have some sore bones to-morrow, nothing more," replied the Epicurean. "I will wish you good bye."

"But you are not going the road the robber has taken," exclaimed all in one breath, as the young man shook the angler by the hand, and nodded familiarly to Smith.

"*That* is my direction," he answered, haughtily. "Figgins, perhaps you can lend me a pistol?"

"Certainly," was the reply, "but if I might advise———"

"You know I never take advice," interrupted the Epicurean. "I will wish you all a good day. Lend me the pistol at once. I hope, Sir, (turning to the old man of the rod), that we shall meet again, and have our argument out;" and so saying he took his departure, having received the pistol.

"An audacious boy," muttered Figgins, "yet I like him for his pluck. "Mr. Smith, are you better now?"

"Thank you, Corporal, I shall do very well; but I am sorry the rascal has robbed me of that packet."

"We must try and catch him," observed Figgins, "but he has got such precious legs that he would lead the devil himself a chase from here to Africa!" With a bow to the old man, Figgins then resumed his way.

With the reader's permission (perhaps, it is to be feared, without it) the course of the narrative shall follow Figgins's thoughts, and tread on his heels, and we shall thus obtain some further insight into the peculiar character of the Corporal, who, no doubt it is perceived, is a bit of an original, in his way; and originality is always amusing, whether it be that of eccentricity, roguery, or intellect—a fact which Will Shakspeare's genius took cognizance of, when it created that marvellous monstrosity, which is so life-like that we all know him as well as if we had been intimately acquainted with his fun, his joviality, and his cunning, our whole existence—no need to add that the fat knight is alluded to.

Taking a cross-road which terminated in a common of considerable extent, Corporal Figgins resumed the train of thought which had been broken in upon by the recent adventure. " So, we have got Danvers safe, but I think it would have been better policy to have left him alone. Yet the reward is worth having, and I owe the fellow a grudge, so I shall not be sorry to see him swing. I am getting on in the world; but I must be careful of my character, and Danvers *could* reveal what I don't wish known. But I shouldn't think he would consider it worth his trouble to blab; and, should he even do so, my credit is better than his. And I remark that in this life the man whose character for honesty stands highest is almost certain to maintain it, unless there be damning evidence against it. Who will believe a murderer like that fellow? Oh, I'm safe! Then, this business with Sophy is a cursed nuisance. Who would have imagined that the woman at her age would have taken to child-bearing? I might as well have taken a younger one. I must exert my wits, and keep a sharp look-out, or I shall get into a mess with the perils and difficulties which are gathering round me. That boy, William Walsingham, suspects me, and he is confoundedly clever; but then, I know his intrigue with Sophy's cousin—so that there I have him in my power, for he would not like that the matter should be made public, if I know anything of him. I don't care much for any one else. I am universally thought as honest as I am shrewd—ha, ha! But what man ever rose to consideration by probity? Humbug! No, no—the knaves of this world talk a deal about virtue and truth, and all *that* cant and stuff, and the fools believe them, and so they are properly and egregiously gulled. Why not? They were made, like silly brutes, without strength, to be preyed upon by the cunning and powerful; and so the world goes

R

on, and the devil is amused. The devil! I wonder if there *is* a
devil? He must be a queer chap, at any rate. That young William
doesn't believe even in a God, I fancy—but *that*—hum! I don't
think I could bring myself to think so—though I might be more
comfortable, if I could."

Such was the substance, though not the exact phraseology of the
mental operations of the selfish and hypocritical man of the world ;
and we shall soon see that his theory and practice harmonized. He
had by this time arrived at his destination.

CHAPTER VI.

Foul murder has been here, and treachery
Still meditates some dark and horrid deed.
Within this place how easy 'twere to strike
At unprotected life.—*Old Play.*

HARRY DANVERS FINDS MORE NOVELTY THAN PLEASURE—
THE SKELETON.

It will be remembered—by those who take the trouble to remember anything in a work of this description—that Harry Danvers, at
the end of the last chapter of the last book of this veracious chronicle, having accompanied a woman as far as a hill crowned with
trees, as he was, he hoped, about to hear a communication from his
father, was surprised by the apparition of a strange creature ; and
that the scene in which he found himself conjured up one of early
life.

That scene was fraught with horror, and had never been effaced
from his memory ; so that when he found himself in the very spot
where it had taken place, all the circumstances connected with it
returned with vivid force upon his mind, and he was convinced that
he had been betrayed, and that he might be murdered by some lurk-

ing assassin, if he did not instantly make his escape. Before he could act upon the resolution which he had taken, the witch-like female he had followed seized the bridle of his horse, and the undefinable being whose hardly human appearance had made so great and indelible an impression on his boyish imagination that, though he was greatly altered, it at once recalled the whole terrible drama he had seen enacted, so long antecedently, to his brain, appeared to be prepared to prevent his flight, if it were meditated.

" You must dismount," said the woman to Harry, " your father is concealed within a few yards——"

" Devil hag !" interrupted the young man, with fierce indignation, " you would have imposed on my credulity ;" and for the first time in his life raising his hand against a woman, Harry struck her with his riding whip, and wheeled round.

Unfortunately, the ground was slippery, and his horse stumbling, the youth lost his balance and his seat, and, before he could recover himself, a bear-like paw was laid upon his throat, and he was struggling for life and death. Though his form was slight, Harry was vigorous, and accustomed to act in emergencies, so that disengaging one arm from the claw of his enemy, he drew a dagger which he wore, and endeavoured to plunge it in the body of the savage.

But, before this could be accomplished, the female had darted upon him, and, uniting her strength with that of the nondescript, strove to prostrate the youth, who had succeeded in regaining his feet, and who, rendered desperate by the conviction that his life would be taken, if he were vanquished, made agonized exertions, and ultimately was enabled to strike his female adversary with the handle of his dagger, and by so doing felled her to the earth.

Still his remaining adversary held on to him with ferocious tenacity, and he could not release himself with all his efforts, nor stab him effectually with his weapon. In the contest he also struck his head against a tree so violently as in a great measure to confuse his faculties, and prevent him from acting with the promptitude and decision which he would otherwise assuredly have displayed. At length, however, by a sudden jerk, he was able to spring from the clutches of his wild enemy, and to dart into his saddle, for his horse had been accustomed to stand still in action, and was ready to receive him.

Drawing a 'pistol from the holster, Harry discharged it at the savage—but the ball merely grazed his ear—and then stuck spurs

into the noble beast that bore him. Fate, however, was unpropitious
to the youth, and in his haste he took a path which led into a hollow
overgrown with underwood, and from which there was no outlet on
the other side, except for an active pedestrian.

Turning with all speed, and with a second loaded pistol in his
hand, Harry galloped back, and found the hag and the savage
ready to receive him, one armed with a long pole, and the other
with stones and similar missiles, which were hurled against him with
rapidity and effect.

Again Harry fired, and this time wounded the savage severely in
the left shoulder, and making a charge, soon cleared a passage, and
was congratulating himself on his fortunate escape, when a heavy,
slanting blow, directed from behind a tree, alighted on his head, and
he fell without sense or motion from his horse.

When he recovered from the stupor thus produced, he found
himself in almost total darkness, and felt also stiff and sore from the
effects of the bruises which he had received in falling. Arising, he
gazed around, as far as the dense obscurity of the place permitted,
and discovered that he was in a cave of some extent, but was unable
to find any indication of an outlet, though there was a very small
aperture at the top, through which a few broken rays of light were
streaming. He had been deprived of his weapons, but otherwise no
farther outrage than the spoliation of liberty had been inflicted on
him.

"Cursed fortune!" he cried, "what will become of my father?
Oh, if I could but escape!"

In vain the prisoner endeavoured to penetrate into the secret of a
mode of egress, though he struck against the clay walls of the cave
with his fist, and made an attempt to clamber up to the aperture in
the roof—which was only of half a foot in circumference, and was
at the height of several yards from the earth.

For his own fate—as far as danger was concerned—he entertained
no care. He had so often looked on death face to face, that he had
acquired an absolute indifference to personal peril, natural as it was
for one so young to cling to a life which was opening with such a
spring of bright promise to his eyes. Yet, when he recollected the
awful catastrophe which he had witnessed in his childhood, and felt
that he was in the power of the very miscreants who had committed
a deed which he shuddered to contemplate, he could not entirely
divest himself of a fear lest he should fall ingloriously by an assas-

sin's knife; and he had fixed his heart upon the attainment of military glory, and, if destiny so willed it, an honourable death, and a fame which should long outlive his perishable dust. But it was for his father that he was most anxious, for Danvers had been an exceedingly affectionate parent, and Harry was a youth of warm feelings, and loved and admired him with heart and soul. Still so confident was he in the inexhaustible resources of that father's ingenuity, which he had seen successful in circumstances of difficulty so fearful, that other men would have been hopeless to extricate themselves from them, that he entertained no apprehension but that he would ultimately baffle the toils of his hunters, and elude the vigilance, activity, and indefatigable exertions which were at work for his destruction.

Animated by this hope, he roused himself from the lethargy into which he had fallen, and determined on setting to work, in order to effect his own restoration to freedom. He had a pocket-knife of more than usual size, which he had used when a young boy for cutting sticks, and which had not been taken from him, with his other more formidable weapons; and again sounding the walls, that he might discover where the thickness of them was most inconsiderable, he commenced operations, and in the course of a few minutes he had made a hole of some size in the clay.

Hours passed on, and still Harry Danvers was busy at his employment; and at length his exertions were in some degree successful—though not so much so as he had anticipated—for he had effected an aperture, large enough to admit of his body passing through it: and he then found that there was a second and smaller cave, entering which he perceived that there were numerous articles scattered about, which he should not have dreamed of finding in such a place. Doubting not that these were stolen goods, so deposited in order to be safe from discovery, he walked onwards as far as the limits of the second cave would allow, but it was so dark that he could with difficulty distinguish anything in it. Setting his brains to work, that he might procure a light, he picked up a flint, and a piece of dry wood, and striking the former with the blade of his knife, was thus furnished with the requisite means for exploring the cave.

It descended into the earth to a greater depth than the other, and had evidently been in frequent use; but the prisoner could detect no door, or any other mode of escape. Nevertheless, he continued to prosecute his search with diligence, for he argued that he could not have got where he was, unless some such door or aperture existed, and he industriously hammered all around, to learn the hollowness and thickness of the walls.   But still his long-continued investigation was frustrated, and at last, thoroughly fatigued with the unusual labour he had undergone, he sat down to rest himself, and at the same time take a minute survey of the place.

The wood to which he had set fire threw a dim and flickering light over the desolate cave, and revealed, though indistinctly, an object at the distance of a few paces from the spot he occupied. At first, Harry could not distinguish its shape or outline; but becoming more and more accustomed to the darkness, he was startled to find that it bore the semblance of a human figure, and rising from the ground, he approached it, when, to his horror and dismay, on touching the rotten clothes with which it was covered, they fell off, and a fleshless skeleton was grinning ghastly before him.

Strong as were the nerves of Harry Danvers, they were not proof against the surprise and terror of this loathsome sight, and in spite of himself he uttered a cry which echoed drearily through the dismal place; but with an effort mastering his feelings, he resumed his examination, and lifting up the tatters that still adhered to and concealed some of the bones, a pocket-book in a state of decay fell into his hand.

There were some papers in it; but the light was so insufficient, and the characters so defaced by damp, that he could not, with every wish to do so, decipher them; so, putting the whole into his pocket, he again turned his attention to the skeleton. He possessed sufficient knowledge of anatomy to know that it was that of a man, and probably in the prime of life when he died, and on looking steadily at the skull, that it had been fractured by a blow, but otherwise he could not obtain any trace whereby to ascertain aught relative to the deceased.   But he had a clue to the dark affair, in the reminiscences of his childhood, and he could not doubt but that these were the mortal remains of him whom he had seen savagely murdered so many years before.

"And is such the accursed fate reserved for me?" exclaimed Harry, with natural repugnance.   "O God, have mercy on me!" He relapsed into a state of deep despondency; but, after a few minutes, summoning all his energies to his aid, and obtaining an accession of light by means of some more wood which lay near him, he looked around for some better instrument to carry on his work than the blade of a pocket-knife afforded. A rusty pick-axe, that had previously escaped his notice, was at the feet of the skeleton, and, furnished with this, hope resumed its empire in the youth's heart, and he recommenced his labours with renewed vigour.

All-sustaining Hope! without thee, how should we poor, wretched mortals journey on through the vast wilderness of the world! Without thee, this earth so beautiful, as Shelley sadly but perhaps truly predicates, would indeed seem " like what it is—a tomb!"

It was a singular scene, and one well worthy the attention of a painter—particularly one excelling in those strong lights and shades that so marvellously distinguish the pictures of Rembrandt. There was the human being, so young, so comely, so active, and so energetic. The efforts of mind were visible through the traces of extreme fatigue upon his fair smooth face; while the symmetrical limbs were in motion with the life of his hope, and appeared to adapt themselves naturally to a labour that fatigues even the brawny arms of the sturdy operative.

And there was the silent skeleton, with the eyeless sockets and the ghastly nose, and the hair still clinging to the ugly skull—so unsightly, so grim, and useless. But for the hand of death those motionless bones might have stirred as bravely as the ardent youth's, and the brain have acted in obedience to the mind of which it is the organ, with as resolute a firmness, instead of lying there, of no more value than the vile and inanimate matter to which it was mouldering fast. What is this death? this omnipotent of earth? The nothing, the shadow which is the crowned King of Time ? The stern severer of affections, the destroyer of beauty, the conqueror of conquerors, the victor of heroes, the exterminating angel against which all genius and love and passion are unavailing.

But the strength of Harry could not endure much longer, and finding that the progress he had made was not sufficient to justify him in hoping that he should speedily consummate his work, he threw himself on the earth, and gradually sleep stole over his senses.

How calm and happy the poor boy looked, as he reposed in that dark abode! The dying embers of the fire he had kindled sufficed to throw a faint and sickly light on his pale tranquil face, while his now nerveless hand grasped the pickaxe by which he had hoped to free himself, and with which he would have defended himself if any attempt were to be made on his life.

He had quite forgotten all his troubles and anxieties in the dreamless slumber resulting from extreme fatigue, and if he had slept on down, surrounded with adherents, and certain of peace and prosperity, as far as any can be certain of them in this life, on the morrow, could he have enjoyed as undisturbed and delicious a repose?

We have now arrived at a point in our tale, when the events crowded together in a few hours are to be developed in the course of months and years. There may be bitter regrets and wasting memories, tears and lamentation—thoughts like spectres—haunting ghosts —and burning passions urging along and destroying the very vitality they arouse: but still the current will bear the actors on, and the child will become the youth, and the youth the man, in ignorance of the elements that form his destiny. Mind may expand, and wisdom unfold, but the bias who shall predict? Can any one foretel whether the fate of an individual will be dark or bright, whether he will be good or depraved, seek the praise of man or God, drag on obscure life, or dazzle a nation with his glory—whether in the shadow of the tomb his memory will live, and his good deeds smell sweet ; or whether he will be execrated, pitied, forgotten ?

BOOK IV.

Whence are we, and why are we ?   Of what scene
The actors or spectators ?   Great and mean
Meet mass'd in death, who lends what life must borrow :
As long as skies are blue, and fields are green,
Evening must usher night, night urge the morrow,
Month follow month with woe, and year wake year to sorrow.

SHELLEY.

Some joys, some woes, some hopes dispersed in air,
Some vain contentions, and some black despair,
Some dark delusions, and some gleams of truth,
Old Age's shadows, and the dreams of youth ;
Passion and weakness, vanity and pride,
And the broad stream down which we ever glide
And vainly strive, is past—Sage ! what is there beside ?—MS.

BOOK IV.

CHAPTER I.

Cold—dead!—what is this thing? It is not mine!
The empty casket is not what I want;
Give me my treasure—rob me not of that!
My all—my priceless, and my beautiful!—*Old Play.*

CAPTAIN NORTON — CORPORAL FIGGINS — THE DEAD BOY —
AGONY.

OME few hours before the time when the preceding Book closes its brief but eventful act, a person was seated in a neat and well furnished apartment, dedicated to the purposes of study, in a musing attitude. It was no other than the officer in command of the troop, by whose indefatigable exertions the redoubtable Walter Danvers had been captured. He was of elderly appearance, and of somewhat low stature, with gray hair, a long, but tolerably well-shaped nose, eyes without much lustre or expression, and severe determination of character on his wrinkled forehead; yet a disciple of Lavater would have conceived from these general features, taken in combination, that he was strictly conscientious, and that he possessed qualities of head and heart, which, if not very remarkable, were of much respectability,—and he would not, certainly, have greatly erred in his estimate of Captain Norton.

The officer was of an ancient family, which had of late years fallen into decay, and no longer enjoyed the celebrity of being the wealthiest commoners and most extensive landowners in the county; but still he was not absolutely a poor man, and his aristocratic connexions were ready to further his interests at court, in which hope of aggrandisement, the Captain, after a long interval of idleness, had resumed the profession of arms, and was now in expectation of the promotion to a Majority, which he had been promised. But it is desirable, before the narrative recounts any further particulars of this worthy, that the reader should be put in possession of a few facts relative to him, which had occurred antecedently.

It will be remembered that Walter Danvers, in the desperate struggle he had been engaged in, had unintentionally destroyed a youth, whose daring had vastly overstepped his discretion. The Dragoon whom he had unhorsed, a man of Brobdignagian proportions, in the very perfection of his active as well as his muscular powers, on recovering from his stunning and unexpected fall, descried the body of the poor boy lying at the distance of a few yards, just as the main body of the military was in sight; and although he had previously given not a thought to the fate of the hapless stripling, in his eagerness to obtain the reward offered for the taking of Danvers, he now hastened to the spot where the motionless clay reposed, and raised it in his arms.

"Why, Jennings!" exclaimed a Serjeant of the horse, who was the first to arrive, "is Cornet Norton there killed?"

"Quite dead," answered the Dragoon, "nothing's to be done for him."

"We must not let the Captain see the body of the poor boy," said an elderly man, who was now present, and was also the second in command of the troop; "Jennings, take the corpse on your horse, and convey it to the nearest cottage. I must think of some means of breaking the piteous matter to my friend—his bereaved relation. What a dreadful stroke it will be to him, for he doted on the ill-starred youth—and he was a fine, high-spirited fellow!"

It was extraordinary to mark with what entire calmness the veteran who had just spoken seemed to contemplate the dire calamity of one he had known from boyhood, and the untimely death of a most promising lad he had nursed in his infancy; but he had fought in a hundred fields, and had seen his dearest friends fall around him like daisies beneath the scythe of the mower; so that a solitary misfortune made small impression on him, though he was by no means an unfeeling person. It is astonishing how gigantic an influence the circumstances in which they are placed will exercise on similar dispositions; if he had not been the warrior of so many hard-fought battles, he would probably have been affected even to tears, by such a catastrophe occurring to an intimate acquaintance. Jennings surlily obeyed the mandate of his officer, for he had made up his mind to come in for something handsome by personally capturing the fugitive, and raising the dead body on his large steed, he departed with it.

Scarcely had he disappeared, when Captain Norton was seen galloping to the spot where this halt had occurred, and the chase was renewed with vigour. After Danvers had been taken, and placed in close imprisonment, Norton proceeded to his own house, which was at no great distance, and left the command of the troop to the officer who had ordered Jennings to remove the corpse of the young Cornet. Unwilling to agonize the feelings of his friend by detailing the circumstances of the young man's death, ere it was absolutely imperative so to do—for singular to state, he would much rather have witnessed a thousand deaths of torture on the "tented field" than have lacerated the heart of one individual by his own words—the second officer assumed the head of the cavalry, and Norton cantered off to his mansion, at which he arrived in less than half an hour.

And the tale may now return to him in his solitary study, where he spent the greater portion of his time in general, reading works on military science, or in perusing the elegant literature afforded by the works of Addison, Steele, "*et id genus omne.*"

"I wonder what makes Percy so long coming!" muttered the Captain to himself, "I left directions for him to ride home without delay. How I love that lad! And he is a noble boy! His mind is so elegant, his habits and feelings so refined, he must do honor to his name, and the profession he has adopted. I wish that he had not been so anxious to enter the army—he will be exposed to so many perils, and he is so ardent and daring! But Heaven will protect him—the gallant youth! He will be a hero, I am certain.

Oh, that he should be the offspring of illicit passion! I can never
—*never* forgive myself—at an age when the fever of youth had
subsided—but then how could I marry his mother,—the mistress
of another previously? Well, she is gone, and my darling boy is
almost the only tie that endears existence to me."

He lapsed into silence, but after an interval of some minutes
added, " I expect my Majority in a few days, and then I will go
to London, and see what I can do by pushing my interest with
the King. It was most unfortunate that my deceased father
should have been so warm an adherent of the Stuarts. I fear, I
am looked upon with distrust—the more so, that my brother is
well known lately to have had an interview with the exiled James
abroad. I am glad, yet sorry, that this man Danvers is taken,
and through my instrumentality. My loyalty will receive some
proof of its stability by his capture—but poor Miss Walsingham
will be dreadfully pained and shocked. He will be hanged—the
evidence against him on that trial was conclusive, and he was
condemned—how he contrived to escape, is a mystery to this
day. And, upon my word, I am even sorry for him. I have
known him from his early manhood."

As Norton ended these disjointed sentences, there was a very
heavy footstep outside the door, a hesitating tap, and, on the
" come in" of the Captain, a burly form became visible.

" Well, Figgins," exclaimed the officer, " and so you were the
first mover in this business of Danvers, I hear."

" Y-e-s, your honour," replied Figgins, uneasily.

" He is a terrible fellow, Corporal, and must be strictly guarded.
You know he killed a sentinel when he effected his escape so
long ago, although *he* was unarmed! But have you seen aught
of my—nephew? He ought to be home by now."

The Corporal cleared his throat, and seemed about to speak,
but whatever he was going to say stuck in the passage out of
which so much mischief and evil continually issue. There was a
brief silence.

" He is a fine boy—my dear nephew Percy," said the officer.
" How admirably he rides that fiery horse he would make me
give him yesterday," and added anxiously, " I hope he will not
be thrown. He is very late."

"Hem! yes, your honour—a splendid young gentleman he is every way."

"He has been taking lessons of you, Corporal, in the use of the broadsword? He could not have a better master, I am convinced, in all England."

"You make me proud, Captain—I see the sun has risen."

"Ah! I hear the clattering of the hoofs of Percy's horse," ejaculated Captain Norton, suddenly leaving his seat, and going to the window. "What can this mean?" he exclaimed, in an accent of alarm, "I trust that vicious animal has not kicked him off!"

The officer was about to quit the apartment, but was prevented by Figgins—"If it please your honour, Master Percy will not be home just yet—he—has—"

"What! he is ill—he is hurt? for the love of mercy, tell me," cried, or rather screamed the agonized father (for such, indeed, was the relationship he stood in to the ill-fated youth.)

But Figgins held his peace.

"God of heaven! I see it all! That devil there has thrown my poor boy—and he is dead. Oh, misery, oh, wretchedness! My son, my son!"

"Bear up, your honour," returned the Corporal, with as much feeling as he could muster for the occasion, and, though a heartless man of the world, he was not altogether indifferent in reality, "he is indeed dead, but he died like a hero—he died nobly, as a soldier ought to die, and by the hand of one of the most able and valiant warriors in Christendom——"

"Ha! Walter Danvers—Danvers killed—ha, ha, ha!" interrupted the officer, with a sort of hysteric energy. "Yes, that was it—I see it all. Lend me your arm, Corporal, and lead me to the corpse. You see I am perfectly calm and unmoved. I must behold him, or I shall die!"

It was a strange sight to see that stiff, stately man, the creature of conventional proprieties, and ordinarily so cold and unimpassioned, tossed about on the raging sea of his convulsed feelings; trembling one moment—then rigid as a statue—reeling, shouting, whispering, laughing like a drunken man. It was horribly absurd; his eyes rolled wildly, his lips moved, but did not articulate when he attempted to speak, and cold drops of awful agony trickled down his face. Even Corporal Figgins felt compassion for his frenzy. He endeavoured to lead him to his chamber, and induce him to lie down, but could not prevail.

"No, Corporal, I must see him, and then I shall be quite content. Otherwise, there is something here," (pressing his forehead tightly with his hand,) "which will drive me mad. My horse is ready saddled—my Percy's horse—that he flattered himself would carry him so bravely to battle! My hero! he had too much of the Hotspur in him; but he was born to be a soldier. Yes, he might have been—but now, he is lifeless clay! You tell me that!"

The old man passed his quivering fingers across his burning brow. "I suppose it is the punishment of heaven for my great crime! Just—just are all its ways; but *he* was innocent. Oh, God! My pride! my hope! my passion! The only idol I have had for long, long years! Great Punisher, thou has left me *quite* desolate! I did not think to die childless!"

The wretched being ceased to speak, and smiled——*such* a smile! Years of anguish were concentrated in it. Figgins did not see his face, his back being turned to him, and deceived by his apparent fortitude, said,

"That's right, bear it patiently, your honour!"

"Oh, yes, I will see him now," exclaimed the old man, (he seemed to have grown old in the last few minutes), not noticing the words of the Corporal, "I must see him."

"I think you had better not, Sir. He is terribly disfigured."

"Oh, devil, to do that," cried Norton wildly, for singular as it appears, we find invariably that defacement on the senseless dust aggravates the grief of the survivors, and he was so proud of the personal beauty of his young son. "Tell me, where, where is the wound?"

"At the temple, Sir; but do not talk about it."

"Disfigured, is he! His only weakness was vanity in that respect, and he was wonderfully handsome. Come now, Figgins, I think I shall be better after I have seen the body; at all events, I cannot be satisfied until I have done so!" And with these words the Captain opened the door, and as he, on all occasions, military and domestic, exercised unquestioned authority, the Corporal obeyed, and they were speedily mounted.

At first, they proceeded at a slow pace; but in the course of a few minutes Captain Norton was dashing onwards at a gallop, and presently a cottage was seen, surrounded by several peasants engaged in earnest conversation. "That is the place?" asked the officer; and receiving an affirmatory bow he increased his speed, arrived before the humble abode, sprang with the agility of youth from his seat, and was immediately within the threshold and before the inanimate remains of him he had so much loved.

"Leave us alone!" exclaimed the Captain authoritatively to several persons collected around the corpse, and gazing with strange looks of horror, curiosity, or apathy upon it. And the room was quickly emptied of life, with the exception of that in Norton's desolated heart. The broad sun streamed brightly and cheerfully through the lattice of the cottage, and irradiated the pale face of the corpse.

The unfortunate boy was remarkably handsome, with long, soft, auburn hair, like that of a girl, and much intelligence of expression in his face, while despite the characters of intense pain stamped upon his smooth forehead, it retained a gentleness and a radiance which intimated that he united fire and kindness of disposition. But where the weapon of Danvers had entered the brain, there was a ghastly wound, and the passions in the fearful conflict had distorted the serene beauty of his perfect and Grecian lineaments. He was of tall stature for his years—which could hardly be said to have reached manhood—and his chin was as guiltless of beard as an infant's. The Captain bent down and kissed the white brow, which was stained with the life-blood of his only son. He removed the fair hair, clotted with gore, tenderly from the temples, and pressed it fondly to his lips.

It was an affecting spectacle, and one which might have brought tears into the eyes of the most heartless. The grey hairs of the bereaved father, as he stooped to kiss the yet warm remains, mingling with those silken ringlets of such womanly length and luxuriance; the contrast of the withered figure, and the graceful, but motionless form—the associations of glorious youth and the mangled features—oh, it was very dreadful! One moment and life, and grace, and power, in all their splendour and strength and beauty; another—and corruption, the worm, silence—nothingness. Who is there in the world unacquainted with death? Who

T

has not beheld the last moments of suffering humanity, who has
not seen the eye grow dim---the strength pass away, and heard the
voice fail---depart---and the tremendous stillness that succeeds---
save where the choking sob, and the stifled cry and the suppressed
groan attest the bereaved one's agony!

What more terrible than a father's grief over the remains of
his only child? The child he had clasped for so many years to
his bosom---the only thing that rendered the cup of existence
sweet---the being for whom he would have toiled and labored,
and been content and happy so to do for his excessive love---now
unable to respond to his endearments---to speak one word of
kindness or affection to sooth him in his affliction. The stern,
grave, haughty man, was there hopeless and humbled to the dust.
His pride, his pomp, his vanity---where were they? The tendrils
which had twined around his heart were broken---the music that
dwelt within his breast was crushed for ever, and life with all its
turmoil of ambition, its wild passions, its enjoyment and brightness, was without a joy for him. Inscrutable and mysterious
Providence! the pangs which thou inflictest on thy weak creatures
are beyond expression fearful.

"My blessed boy!" at length murmured the officer, whose
whole spirit had till then been absorbed in his eyes, "thou art
happy now! Thy life was virtuous—thou wert beloved on earth,
and thou shalt be blessed with Angels' love in Heaven! Still thy
face retains the majesty of its former radiance, but thine eye lacks
all its fire—stony, stony, lifeless! My brave, my beautiful! Pride
of my heart, and solace of my advancing age! To thee, my Percy,
I was not as I was to others! and even from thy childhood, thou
didst not fear me, but wouldst climb upon my knee, and kiss my
cheek, and clasp thy little arms around my neck—so fondly!
And while others dreaded to hear my voice—for I have been a
severe man too frequently—thou wouldst run unto me, and look
into my face, and smile on me—so that I could not be angry!
And thou wert ever ready to plead in behalf of others!—O me!
my soul is heavy!"

The desolate old man ceased speaking, but from the working of
his features it was plain that painful and agonizing thought was
busy within. "Now, then, I have nothing left to do in this life,"
resumed Norton, "I have only to pray for pardon and death.

Hadst thou lived, my darling! I would have strained every energy, I would have exerted every power of my brain, to place thee among the loftiest of the children of men! I *had* hoped to have held thy children to my bosom, and to have seen thee the admired and the honored among the great! But it is otherwise. A little while, and that most graceful form will lie within the tomb—a little while and the red worm will feast upon that warm and noble heart that used to beat with impetuous zeal,—and thou wilt be forgotten by all---except thy father. And *he!* Eternity could not efface thy recollection from his spirit. Thy memory will haunt him in sleep---thy presence---No more---no more! I shall go mad, if I do not tear myself away. That ghastly wound! My beautiful!—Cursed, thrice cursed be the bloody hand that struck it! I pray thee, Heaven! if that man have a child, to let him be childless also. If he have doted to idolatry upon him, if he have fixed every hope and aspiration of his mind and being upon him, centred each desire and thought in him---worshipped the very ground he trod upon---weighed rank, and friends and fortune as things of air in the balance with him——Vengeance, oh, vengeance! Let me be thine instrument!"

As the officer in his inexpressible grief and passion spoke these broken sentences, Corporal Figgins, who had hitherto remained outside, respecting the sacredness of a father's sorrow, ventured to enter, and suggest that Captain Norton had been long enough with the body.

"Oh, that I might die, and be buried with him," was all the reply of the heart-broken parent.

In vain did Figgins urge every argument his ingenuity could devise to draw the Captain away from his son. He would quit the corpse for an instant and advance to the door, but invariably returned and devoured the lifeless looks.

"Is he not handsome, Corporal!" said the fond father, with calm despair, "Oh, he is like some far-famed Grecian statue, and should remain a monument of beauty free, from corruption. He is far more gloriously lovely, even now, than ever breathing stone shaped by genius. Phidias and Praxiteles never formed an Apollo so perfect!"

Figgins feared that Captain Norton would go distracted, for he was habitually so cold and austere, that he never exhibited the slightest emotion of joy or sadness. "For God's sake, Sir, cease looking at the corpse in that way. Your eyes start from your head!" cried the Corporal. But no heed was given to what he said. As a last expedient to divert his attention by appealing to some other passion of his heart, he cried,

"And the culprit---the murderer---he must be punished. We must not allow him to escape."

"True, true," exclaimed Norton, as if awaking from a trance, and speaking with intense energy, "Hell itself shall not rescue him!" and imprinting one long, lingering, passionate kiss on the cold lips of the corpse, he departed.

Figgins remained gazing calmly on the rigid features of the dead, for the space of two or three minutes. "He was a fine lad, a very fine lad, indeed," he muttered, "and I'm extremely sorry for him. But we must all come to this, at last; so there's no use to make a fuss about it. What has become now of the soul of the unlucky boy? Humph, that's a troublesome thought, which connects itself with a hereafter---a d---d thought."

And, covering the body of the slaughtered youth with a cloak, the Corporal quitted the room and the cottage. It was some time after this that Figgins came upon the scene in which the tall robber was the principal actor; but as events of more importance than those in which he took a part are about to be evolved, we must take leave of the worthy Corporal for two or three chapters.

CHAPTER II.

Few of Earth's highest, happiest, do not deem
That youth's *least* joyous, tamest, dullest dream
Was brighter far than any actual bliss
Which gives its light to such a world as this.
                    Mrs G. Lenox Conyngham.

CHARLES WALSINGHAM—ELLEN—GEORGE—CYTHEREA'S WICKED SON.

Too long have we been altogether absent from the gallant gentleman who was the first to make his *debut* on the boards—or, should it be written, the sheets?—of " The Miser's Son," who was left in a terrible predicament in the last chapter of the first book, with Cupid's artillery playing on his ill-fortified heart.

I wonder what love *is* ? No one can analyze it—no one can even perfectly define it. Dr. Johnson's Dictionary only leaves one still more obfuscated than with ignorance. " Passion between the sexes," " kindness," " courtship," " liking," " fondness," " concord," &c. Really, the Doctor, though a very clever, intellectual man, must have been stuffed with turtle-soup when he gave such a definition. It is all moonshine. But who can give a better ? Who can tell how love grows ? Whether it is a plant of celestial sowing or growth ? What is its first cause ? And whether it is necessary, in order that it should be perfect, for the passion to be simultaneously reciprocal ? There was a singular old fellow by the name of Plato known among us, who had some figments in his head upon the subject—though he was, it is said, a terrible sensualist himself—which have been conventionalized among poets until they have become prescriptive in their authority; but then, prescription of any sort is now laughed at by our thinking men amazingly, and even the votaries of the Muses, compelled to exercise their powers of ratiocination to keep pace with the age, are beginning " to apprehend" that the ancient psychologist has enunciated an abstraction, and that the extreme idealism of the hypothesis is as opposite to truth as the converse of it. We shall get something better, it is to be hoped, one day, by way of *theory*; and as for practice, who ever lived to years of discretion without experiencing a stinging sensation, from the arrow glancing by and grazing the epidermis, or more frequently penetrating the outer covering of the organ through which all the blood and tender emotions must pass?

Captain Charles Walsingham was no ontologist, and so he did not attempt to trace to the source of pure being, feelings which were becoming so perilous to him; but in conformity with the indolent inclinations superinduced by languor and illness, occupied all his thoughts and fancies with the fair ministering spirit who hovered about his couch.

She was a charming creature—that Ellen Danvers---the child of nature, simple, pure, modest and tender-hearted. Her sensibility was not that of high imagination and romance, but emanated from the genuine warmth of her unsophisticated nature; and living entirely in seclusion, sentiment and feeling were nourished by the external calm and loneliness which she loved. It is impossible to prescribe any fixed period for the germination of the master-passion of our being. In crowded cities, the mind being distracted by a great variety of objects, the force of one feeling is in some measure counteracted, by the necessity for exercising the intellectual powers and using the physical organs. By all means, if you do not wish a young man and maiden, the vacuum in whose breasts is not pre-occupied, to yield themselves to each other, heart and soul, suffer them not to be together *alone* in the country.

Charles Walsingham was enjoying the delights of very excellent company---he was by himself. The morning star, " day's harbinger," was just apparent in the grey and silvery sky, over which a few soft purple clouds were sailing with silent grace, and the hush of the outward world was unbroken even by the sound of the matutinal lark's inspiriting song. He was gazing through

the half-closed shutters with languid eyes, and longing to behold
the sylph-like form of Ellen once more.

By referring to the place where we last shook hands with our
Captain, it will be found that he had passed the whole night in
dreaming confusedly of plots and treasons, of ambuscadoes and
love-makings, heaped together in heterogeneous masses, and that
the idea of Miss Danvers had been the nucleus of all. He awoke
unrefreshed and feverish, yet with a delicious tumult in his veins,
expecting soon to behold the lovely unknown, which he never remembered to have experienced. It was not of the same species
with that fiery ardour which used to rush through all his blood,
when he was in momentary expectation of encountering a foe;
but it was not less violent, nor less soul-absorbing. He had
almost entirely forgotten the mysterious conversation he had overheard the preceding night, and was just yielding up his spirit to
waking dreams, when the sound of a window being thrown up
attracted his attention, and his own not having been entirely
closed, as the weather was oppressively warm, his acute ear distinguished the bell-like tones of Ellen's voice, as she addressed
some person below.

What can all this mean? thought Charles. What can she want
to talk with any one at a time like this for? Well, it is nothing
to me, and it would be despicable in me to listen! Nevertheless,
Captain Walsingham *did* again play the eaves-dropper (how mean
in some respects the exalting sentiment of love will make the most
generous!) and became acquainted with the business which brought
little George to the cottage at so unseasonable an hour.

In the course of a few minutes afterwards Walsingham heard a
step approaching his door—was it light, fairy-like? No, it was
grave and majestic. Still he hoped on, till there was a knock,
and immediately a tall woman—how unlike the little sylph he
admired so much—entered and stood before him. Despite himself, the soldier felt peevish and angry. Yet he was one of the
best-tempered fellows in existence, and it was not a little, even
when he was suffering quite as acutely in the flesh as at present,
that could destroy his equanimity of mind.

Why was that old woman there, with her haughty gestures and
her commanding voice? He hated old women in a sick chamber,
and never liked them at any time too well: (of course he did not

say what he thought.) Elizabeth—for it was no less a personage, addressed him—

"I hope you have passed a quiet night, Captain Walsingham! Allow me to feel your pulse!"

"How did you know my name?" he asked quickly.

Elizabeth deigned to make no reply to this direct interrogation, but taking his wrist commenced counting the beatings of his pulse.

"I know not whether you should not be bled again—you have too much fever," she said. "I will give you some medicine to allay the heat of your blood," and so speaking, the imperious woman quitted the chamber.

"How in the name of wonder could she know my name?" exclaimed the invalid. "I might perhaps have talked about myself in some delirium of which I was unconscious. My name was not on the knapsack I carried with me, and which, I perceive, is by my side."

Presently Elizabeth returned with a draught, which she delivered to the Captain, and wishing him a good morning, again, without further parley, took her departure.

"What a stately old dame it is!" thought our soldier to himself. "I wonder if she is related to that sweet girl!"

Elizabeth meanwhile descended to the sitting-room, where she found George, to whom she had previously given some breakfast, which he was eating with a good appetite, and Ellen Danvers at the same time glided into the room.

Poor George, overcome with his extraordinary exertions and loss of sleep, could with difficulty keep his eyes open, and Elizabeth having extracted from him previously all the information she could concerning Danvers, desired him, in compassion to his drowsiness, to lie down and take some sleep; and the words had hardly quitted her mouth before the boy, suffering his weary eyes to close, and falling back in his seat, was buried in still repose.

"My child!" said Mrs. Haines, addressing Ellen; "I am compelled to leave you for some hours; but I will not be absent longer than is necessary. You will attend to Captain Walsingham, who is rather feverish this morning, and, if requisite, give him another composing draught."

"O, my kind nurse! I know that there is something amiss!"

exclaimed Ellen; "indeed that child told me my father is in danger, and if so, it is my duty to go to him."

"You could be of no service, and I think nothing is really to be apprehended," returned Elizabeth, peremptorily. "You will be cautious how you speak to this young man, who is a zealous adherent of the Elector of Hanover, while you are with him, and do not remain in his room longer than is essential. It is most unfortunate our servant should have been taken ill; but perhaps I can send you a woman from the village. God bless you, my daughter!" and kissing the fair brow of the maiden, Mistress Haines forthwith vanished.

Ellen gave herself up to thought. "I know my father is engaged in some hazardous scheme," she inwardly exclaimed, "thinking to serve *our* king, and I fear much it has been discovered, and therefore he is pursued. If so, and he is taken, no mercy is to be expected from the government, and they might even execute him. Oh, how dreadful---Almighty Father, protect and save my parent!"

Sinking on her knees, the pious and affectionate being offered up her prayers and supplications to the throne of mercy, and if ever the petitions of the purest and most innocent of His weak creatures are heard by the Omnipresent, surely the earnest and meek address of Ellen was not neglected then. Rising from her posture of humility, she surveyed the noble and tranquil form of the sleeping boy, over whose fair young face not a shadow nor cloud was passing. There certainly was something in the expression and contour of the two faces of the girl and the child, by no means dissimilar; but the latter's, notwithstanding his extreme youth, was decidedly most marked and bold. The countenance of Ellen was all love and gentleness---like that of a pellucid river gliding softly beneath the peaceful moonlight. No passion, nor haughty energy of disposition was impressed upon it, and yet, despite this lack of individuality of character, there was sense and sensibility, there was candour, intelligence, and sweetness; but though she bore a striking similitude to her father, the fire, the splendour, and the mighty thought of his striking face were totally absent from hers. The features of the young boy, on the contrary, promised boldness, decision, and originality of mind. Though they were not exactly regular, they were pleasing and

U

handsome, and his form was graceful, strong and active in a remarkable degree.

"I like the appearance of this child," said Ellen, "I think I know some one to whom he bears a striking resemblance---nay, I know not whether he be not something like myself."

There was a mirror at hand, and gazing into it, the maiden compared her own, with the countenance of the boy. "There is something more than fancy in this," she thought; "but still he is very different to me. If he do not rise to be a great, I am persuaded he will be a good man, and perhaps there is more real greatness in virtue, than in any powers of wisdom, or stores of learning and knowledge. He is more like Harry than myself, perhaps; but I have seen some one he yet more strikingly resembles. Who is it? Can it be Captain Walsingham?" Ellen blushed as she thought of the invalid. "Let me see;" she raised the fair hair from the white smooth forehead of the little sleeper, and looked at him narrowly. "The brow will be broader, but it is not unlike," she remarked to herself, "and the nose will perhaps grow like his, and the mouth---oh, there certainly *is* a likeness. And if he resemble *me* also, I must--what stuff I am talking---I am not in the slightest measure like him."

Nevertheless, Ellen Danvers was unaccountably pleased with the notion of her similitude to the sick officer, and after an interval spent in deliberating in what way they resembled each other, she thought she would go and see whether he wanted anything.

"And if he is asleep," she said to herself, "I will compare—pshaw, I will do no such thing!"

Having thus cogitated, as soon as the heightened colour brought to her transparent skin by the thought of Captain Walsingham in relation to herself, had subsided, she softly quitted the sitting-room, and ascended to the officer's apartment. Hesitating a moment at the threshold, she then tapped, and on being asked to enter, she did so, and inquired, in a voice in some degree tremulous, whether he would take any breakfast?

"You are very, *very* kind, to trouble yourself so much about me," answered Walsingham, "but I will wait an hour before I try to eat. *Might* I presume to request you, if not otherwise engaged, to sit a few minutes with a poor invalid?" (observing that the maiden was about to retire) " for I feel somewhat solitary, and my spirits are not so good as usual."

Ellen paused irresolute a few seconds, but in the guilelessness of her untainted heart imagining it impossible that there could be any impropriety in complying with the petition of the poor soldier, she took a seat by his bedside, as she had done several times before, in order to relieve Elizabeth.

" What a heavenly morning!" exclaimed Walsingham, as the sun burst forth with magnificence and power in the sky, and poured its effulgent beams upon the sleeping earth.

" It is, indeed, most beautiful," was the rejoinder of Miss Danvers.

" It is a glorious time—the early morning!" pursued the soldier, desirous of eliciting something more than a passing reply from his lovely companion, " and I envy not those who sleep it away in idleness and sloth."

Ellen bent her head, but made no response to this last observation. Walsingham looked rather disappointed, but continued,

" I think that the gentleman who, I conclude, so kindly assisted me after my unlucky accident, is your father, is he not?" This was hazarding a guess; but he thought it probable, from Ellen's resemblance to Danvers, and her attendance on him, that such was the case.

" Ye-es," replied Ellen, confusedly, recollecting the warning of Elizabeth, and determined to be discreet.

" I cannot express the feeling of obligation in my heart for his kindness," said the soldier, " I hope he will pay me a visit ere long; when I may personally thank him for the unmerited goodness he has extended to me. And the elderly lady who so kindly officiated as my physician, and to whose skill I am indebted for much, is——"

" She was my nurse," responded Miss Danvers, vainly struggling with her embarrassment, and meditating a retreat, in order to obviate the necessity for returning an answer to the questions of Walsingham.

" Pardon me, if my curiosity is impertinent," said the Captain, observing the hesitation of his fair companion, and with the delicacy of a refined mind, turning the conversation immediately. " I was a foolish fellow," he added, " to underrate the powers of that little horse which your father rode. I thought I was a better judge of horses."

"Dickon is truly a wonderful creature," returned Ellen, "and my father values him exceedingly." She moved to the window.

"May I trouble you to throw it up?" asked Walsingham, "the fresh air will revive me. I feel a little faint!"

Another paroxysm of pain paled to a deadlier hue than it had hitherto worn in illness, the cheek of the invalid, and alarmed Ellen not a little, as he could not help writhing under his agony. Oh, that sympathy for sick men in the female bosom! Sir Edward Bulwer asserts that a woman thinks it incumbent on her to give her heart to the man she has seen in his night-cap. Charles Walsingham did not wear that ornament, but he was suffering acutely, and as pity is near akin to love, it may safely be predicated that little Cupid was essentially assisted in his attacks on Ellen's sensibility by the force of that feeling toward the invalid. The pain subsided, and the sufferer smiled—and smiled brightly, for the maiden's eyes were fixed on him, suffused with a moisture evincing the reality of her sympathy for him.

"I am giving you a great deal of trouble," he said, "and I fear that I do not endure pain well; but, if you look so pityingly on me, I may feign it for the sake of having your compassion, which I prize so highly."

Ellen turned away her head, and tried to force a laugh.

"This is an exquisite spot, as far as I can judge," observed the invalid, "I could be content ever to dwell here."

"Indeed! you have not lived much in the country, perhaps."

"My early life was spent in it; but for ten years I have had little solitude. Yet I think we value all things by negatives, and I should enjoy a secluded life the more, as I have hitherto mixed much with men. Oh, the joys of the free air and the mountain breeze, the thunders of the cataract, and the low music of the stream, are no poor delights, when shared with one whose feelings are congenial with our own. What thrilling happiness to be able to impart every secret thought, and to share the unfettered confidence of a dear and affectionate being, whose every wish and thought is pure as the breath of heaven!"

Walsingham paused, partly from exhaustion, and partly because he hated to *display* himself. Ellen drank in his clear tones with "a greedy ear," and thought that he was passing eloquent.

" I wish," said the Captain, recurring to a theme which was uppermost in his mind, namely, the desire of knowing more about Ellen Danvers, " that I could be of assistance to your father. I—accidentally overheard—but I could not distinctly understand the matter—something concerning him, a short time ago, which led me to conclude he was exposed to peril."

No reply was given to this sentence. Ellen had almost forgotten the danger to which her father was exposed, in her admiration of the fine feeling displayed by Walsingham. " Who knows," she thought to herself, " whether this gentleman might not be of important service to him ? I know he is in the service of the government, and should suppose he is highly thought of. But I dare not—no, I dare not disclose—"

The officer appeared to read what was passing in the brain of Miss Danvers, for contemplating the shadows on her ingenuous face, he said, " I am not a person of great importance, being but a senior captain in the army ; but I have friends and connexions who have influence, and it would give me the sincerest pleasure if I could in any mode repay the obligations———"

" Talk not of obligations," cried Ellen, " we have only shown you the common duties of humanity ; but, if you would interest yourself in my dear father's behalf, I should be eternally indebted to you."

The maiden, in the fervour of her desire to procure efficient aid for her father, forgot herself entirely ; but when she saw the ardent eyes of Walsingham fixed almost passionately on her glowing face, she felt abashed, and could not proceed any farther in her appeal. Observing her confusion, he refrained from replying as he had meditated, and said,

" Most cordially I thank you for the confidence, however small, you have reposed in me ; and you may be assured, amiable girl ! that soul, and heart, and hand, Charles Walsingham is at your disposal. May I ask by what name I may think of you ? I only ask your Christian name."

Ellen had been warned not to disclose the appellation of Danvers, as they went by a fictitious name, but her own baptismal designation, she thought there could be no harm in telling ; so rising from her seat she answered " I am called Ellen ;" and disappeared from the enamoured eyes of the soldier.

CHAPTER III.

Man, one harmonious soul of many a soul,
    Whose nature is its own divine controul,
Where all things flow to all, as rivers to the sea :
    Familiar acts are beautiful through love ;
    Labour, and pain, and grief, in life's green grove
Sport, like tame beasts, none know how gentle they could be.

In the immense sum of human existence, what is a single unit. Every sod on
which we tread is the grave of some former being ; yet is there something that
softens without enervating the heart, in tracing in the life of another those emotions that all of us have known ourselves. For who is there that has not, in his
progress through life, felt all its ordinary business arrested, and the varieties of
fate commuted into one chronicle of the affections ?—E. L. BULWER.

THOUGHTS ON LOVE AND OTHER MATTERS—ELLEN AND GEORGE.

THERE are lots of people in the world, some good, many bad,
and the greater number very indifferent. Yet it is evident that
there must be no inconsiderable amount of virtue, or we should
not so often be condemning vice. There are people wrapt up in
self, whose every thought and desire is centered in that dear and
estimable being whom they value infinitely beyond all the residue
of humanity collectively (and they have a right to do so,---they
have a right to their own opinion on the estimate they form of the
universe in relation to the individual, if they like it; but they
may chance to find they make a bit of a mistake), and there *are*
persons continually mortifying the natural man, eschewing all
gaiety, sociability, and so on. These latter are excellent, but
perhaps deluded individuals, who are in the minority on all divi-

sions of the Great House of the entire Earth ; and then there are
those who live but in the reflected happiness of others, as the
globe derives all light from the sun---Oh, if the aggregate of
humanity could be composed of these ! But they are meteors far
too intensely bright to burn for long in such a sphere ! And lastly
there are " *the good sort of people*," among whom we all flatter
ourselves we may be classified, who possess sufficient good nature
to lend a hand to a friend, when doing so is not attended with
any very serious inconvenience to themselves, who scrub on from
day to day, eating, drinking, laughing, swearing, scolding,
bustling, smiling, crying, now elated with prosperity, now dejected
beneath adversity, one moment praising the wisdom and harmony
that subsists in Time, and another thinking in their hearts it is a
very scurvy and disagreeable order of things ; doing like others
for the sake of others' good opinion---or contempt ; neither religious nor profane, moral nor licentious, beloved nor hated, and
so the dream clouds, and brightens, lowers and clears---

> 'Till tir'd they sleep, and Life's poor play is o'er.

You will find their philosophy to consist in some such apop-
thegm as the following---"This is but a poor sort of existence ;
but we must make the best of it ; since theologians tell us we cannot help our calamities !" How the angels must laugh now and
then, if the celestials do not consider risibility incompatible with
the dignity of their immortality, over our common, humdrum,
sensible, absurd, preposterous ways, all tending to one common
centre in theory and supposition ; but as far from it as the stars
which Dr. Dionysius Lardner, and some greater astronomer before him, inform us are so distant from the earth, that there has
not been time yet for a ray of light from them to visit it, however
ancient may be the date of creation.

Ay, happiness ! We all want happiness ; but some fancy it
consists in anticipating eternity, and others in eating turtle, plum-
pudding or beef.

Is there no one in these days of Steam and Machinery to invent
an agent for Universal Felicity ? Something that may be so agreeable, and pleasant, and irresistible, that by the simple use of it,
we may forge fetters of brass for that old hag Care, and leap
about hither and thither, breathless with fruition, until we are

swallowed up in the great gulph of Death, and our materiality mingles with the huge, horrible, and monstrous thing, which we Philosophers---save the mark! are for ever bothering our subtile and queer brains about.

I dare say Captain Walsingham thought he was going to be very happy---no doubt he did---for we all commit that wise piece of folly, even when things appear least inclining to prosperity--- and probably pictured to his mind the delights of a quiet and undisturbed abode, with a sweet fair wife, and pretty playful children, all as amiable and loving as seraphim and cherubim; and cheated his imagination with dreams and phantasies, which hop about, Will-o'-the-wisp-like, over the universe, and plague, and tease and delight us alternately, as we fancy we catch them and they dissolve "in thin air," even as those dear creatures we love and worship so devoutly. The Captain was an excellent fellow, and though not utterly unselfish perhaps, had more in him of the qualities panegyrized above in the category of humanities beyond all the rest, than one in five hundred on the average of mankind. But he was not a philosopher. Who is? Those that style themselves such? Was Plato wise in *action*? Was Solomon? They were tremendous sensualists; and although William Walsingham might have admired their wisdom in that respect, while he ridiculed the spirituality of the one, and sneered at the lofty ethics of the other, depend upon it, Sir, epicureanism—which inevitably defeats its own object—is as great a piece of nonsense as the system of——but hang particulars and personals. We are all of us imperfect, and as philosophy is the love of perfection we shall adore its ethics; but give the lie to our delight in Wisdom by our practice. Oh, no! we are ever seeking amaranths among the flowers of earth, and find but roses, and few of *them*, poor frail, dying things, flowers that bloom for a day with an odour and a beauty of the eternal, and then are scattered by the winds of desolation. We may love, we may aspire, and adoration of and aspiration to some bright and divine ideal will afford us felicity awhile—a poetry of feeling that clothes the common and the real with splendor; but the loveliness is a shadow, and the passion is a phantasmal ecstasy; Sorrow lurks within the buds of Joy, and Despair in the germs of Hope—

" Ah, sister, Desolation is a delicate thing :
   It walks not on the earth, it floats not on the air,
But treads with silent footstep, and fans with silent wing
    The tender hopes which in their hearts the best and gentlest bear ;
Who soothed to false repose by the fanning plumes above,
   And the music-stirring motion of its soft and busy feet,
Dream visions of aërial Joy, and call the monster Love,
   And wake and find the shadow Pain, as he whom now we greet."

And Ellen—the good, gentle, innocent Ellen Danvers—who though *not* the heroine of this chronicle of the past, which it has been the author's aim to make a picture of life and man as they are, dark, radiant and variable—is not an unimportant nor, it is hoped, an uninteresting character in it—what did she think ? What thoughts occupied her heart ? I wish I were able to analyze them (you will find something like a description of their confusion in Shakspeare I dare say, for he understood what love is), but they were in such a chaos, I should have to write an Essay as long as Locke's on the Understanding, in order clearly to elucidate them. I should have to abstract and generalize on sensation and modes of sensation before I could make clear what she experienced ;—to classify and re-classify, and say the same things over and over again, like all other psychologists from Pythagoras to Schilling, and it may be after all to no purpose ; and so the well-natured reader's vivid imagination must help me out of the dilemma.

The more simple and true a mind, the more powerfully do new and strange sensations affect it. Hence it is that first love is the most pure, absorbing and intense ; but the component parts of it, I do most sincerely believe and avow, we are, and shall ever remain, in almost total ignorance of. I do not wish to recur to first principles, and abhor the useless repetition of such things as we see in the systems of ontology to no purpose (entity—non-entity and so on—an infinite deal of nothing unless employed to some real principle of being) from my soul ; and therefore I predicate that Love, in all its phases and modifications, is a great mystery, an arch enigma, and that every primordial substance of our complicated nature is far more susceptible of demonstration relative to its rise and progress than this. Therefore no more concerning the origin of love, which like that of evil, will remain

X

inscrutable, and yet continue to perplex the noddles of our profundities till we live in the empyrean, in an atmosphere unclouded and serene as virtue.

Every thing was propitious to the growth of the passion betwixt Ellen and Walsingham. It has been positively asserted that obstacles to love promote and cherish it into strength and vitality; but this appears to me the most problematical of postulates. Difficulties in the path of ambition may fire and energize the mind of genius; but the two passions are essentially dissimilar. We want soft odours and fragrant breezes, genial sighs and tender breathings, at the commencement of such a sentiment as the first, not gigantic aspirations, vast strugglings, august visions and proud dependence on self, such as must characterize the progress of an Alexander or a Napoleon. It seems to me as if, when the active powers of intellect are expanded, as they are in ambition, the passive feelings which have to be operated on by various latent principles, must be swallowed up in the fierce Maelstrom of the haughtier nature; that they cannot equally subsist together, and consequently the dreaming, the musing, on those imaginary perfections which are the lover's nympholepsy (for no earthly creature has more than a portion of them) would necessarily be obstructed. Thus, at all events in the first instance, the soul should not be diverted from brooding on its ideal by the compulsion of exercising its other faculties; the stream should glide deliciously and calmly on, that the light barque may speed swiftly under the impetus of favoring breezes—for too violent a sea would hurl it into destruction in a brief period.

I have never been in love myself since I was ten years old, when incontinently I adored every pretty little creature of every rank and style of beauty I encountered, but "I have had some dreams;" and whether silly or otherwise, dreams constitute the greater part of being. This was the case with Charles Walsingham, as far as the visionary business was concerned, and having arrived at an age when with such hearts as his there is an absolute necessity for loving, he was the more prepared to conceive a deep and lasting affection for so amiable a girl as Ellen. So, when she had left him, he thought he would have a resolute reverie on her charms of mind and person, real and imaginary, and rendering himself up to this delightful recreation and occupation, heeded not the flight of time.

One of the most singular features of "the divine passion" is its total forgetfulness of the measure of duration. To the Idealist the incontestable fact may afford a proof in favor of his system of non-entities, and to the Lover and the Poet it may demonstrate that it lives in eternity and has nothing to do with the hour; and certain it is that days may seem as minutes when the mind and heart are pre-occupied and take no cognizance of external objects, in some measure showing that our internal sensations act upon the outward world rather than the converse, and so mark the flight of the destroyer. But Time again is another great mystery.

It was noonday, and the sun was shining gorgeously, and creation smiled in the pure light of heaven as brightly as when the first man opened his eyes in Eden, and all but the lord of all and those subjugated to his tyranny and caprice were blithe and gay. The painted butterflies were thick in the radiance which displayed their splendid colours, and rejoiced in the ignorance— the happy ignorance!—of the brevity of their existence; the scarcely less glittering insects on the greensward and the flowers were eating their favorite food and basking in the heat, and the joyous birds were singing "and soaring as they sang." None would have imagined, if they could have been transported from some distant world among the stars, where sin and sorrow have never fixed their cruel fangs, that anything but virtue and happiness could exist in so bright an earth.

Walsingham was admiring the scene, which he could easily distinguish through his open window, and his heart was merry, for he felt better in himself than he had for many hours, and who is unacquainted with the delightful sensations of returning health? and anticipation was busy in his brain. "To share this cottage with *her!* To pour into her faithful bosom the transport, the romance, the feeling, excited by the beauty of God's sublime creation—it would be an antepast of heaven!"

So thought the soldier. "How gladly shall I resign the hope of renown, the ambition which so often proves a curse—the entire passions of my being to be the beloved of such a creature!"

As he was thus rhapsodizing he heard a voice which was hardly that of a child, but yet not that of a youth, carolling the words of a song which he remembered to have heard when he was a boy himself, and a flood of recollections burst upon him, as his ear distinguished the following words:—

" O, remember this life is but dark and brief,
  There are sorrows, and tears, and despair for all,
  And that hope and joy are as leaves that fall!——
  Then pluck the beauteous and fragrant leaf,
  Before the Autumn of Pain and Grief!

There are hopes and smiles with their starry rays,
  O, press them tenderly to thy heart!
  They will not return when they once depart!
  Rejoice in the radiant and joyous days,
  Though the light, tho' the glee but a moment stays!

As the dew-drops fall with their diamond sheen,
  They sparkle beneath the ethereal beam,
  And die in their light—like some Angel dream!
  Which is loved and is blessed, but no sooner seen
  Than it flies—O 'twere better it ne'er had been!"

The mournful pathos and artless melody of the young minstrel's song went directly home to the feelings of Walsingham, and raising himself in his bed he tried to look out of window; and succeeded in catching a glimpse of a childish figure walking across the plot of grass beneath.

He had not been the only listener to the ballad, for Ellen Danvers, who had been engaged in thoughts not very dissimilar to those that were passing through his mind when he first heard the song, recognized from her window the young boy she had left asleep below a few hours before, and immediately descended, and quitting the house joined him.

"I hope you have recovered from your fatigue, my little friend," said Ellen, offering her pretty hand to him.

"Thank you, sweet lady, yes!" returned the child, gallantly pressing the taper fingers of the maiden to his lips.

"What a pretty song that was you were singing just now," observed Ellen, smiling at the gallantry of the little fellow, "I should like to hear you repeat it."

"I think I must be going" answered the boy, sadly, "Oh, how I wish that I might live with you who look so kind and beautiful, and your noble father and brother. I should love you so very very much!"

"Have you no parents—no relations then?"

"Ah yes! I have a mother, but she does not love me," returned the child, "nobody ever loved me, as I could love. And yet many have been kind to me."

"Nay, that is impossible if you have a mother," rejoined Ellen, beginning to feel much affection for this singularly interesting and engaging boy. "I am certain you are good, and do not give her trouble."

"I try to be good," answered George, "but it is often very difficult to be so, when you are treated with harshness and unkindness; and if there did not exist a great God (as I have been told, and as I feel in my soul there must be) who protects all his creatures, and chiefly those who need his aid, I think I should almost be driven to despair and wickedness.

There were tears in the boy's eyes which demonstrated the earnestness and sincerity of his feelings, and his clear and musical voice, more than commonly manly for his age, was unsteady with emotion. Ellen took his hand in hers and pressed it warmly.

"You are a good child," she said, "but how is it that your mother does not love you?"

"I know not," responded George, "she has never done so, though I have often felt more love for her than I can tell you. She has met my fond kisses with coldness, and never returned my caresses. I have sometimes wept in secret, because I have seen other children pressed to their parent's breasts, and received with such looks of fondness. Oh, how happy are you, dear lady! to have such a father as I am sure you must have. He must love you as his own life! and I think I should love you too, almost as much, if I lived with you. Your looks have so much pity in them! I could almost fancy, as I look in your kind and gentle face, some good angel from heaven is gazing with compassion on me, who am doubly an orphan in having a mother but not sharing her love. Farewell! I will remember you in my prayers!"

"Stay, my young friend, you must not leave me yet. I have a great deal to ask you, and if you will kindly take upon you the office of my messenger, I shall thank you from my heart."

"That I will," answered George with alacrity.

"But I should wish you to wait a few hours, until we see whether my nurse will return. Meanwhile, let me hear the story of your life."

As Ellen Danvers finished speaking, the child and herself had entered a sort of summer house, rudely and recently constructed, and odorous with the pure breath of roses and violets and wall-flowers which grew around it in luxuriance. It was the place where Ellen was accustomed to read or amuse herself with draw-ing or embroidery while she listened to the jocund notes of the thrush, the black-bird, and others of the feathered tribe, who congregated in a clump of trees at the distance of a few yards, and appeared to emulate each other's strains through the day.

" I have not much to tell you," said the young boy, " though I have passed through more adventures than most children of my age; but they would not for the most part interest you. But my life has been one of thronging feelings, which I cannot well describe to you—and *would* not to all others. As you wish, you shall hear as much about me as I know myself; but I am afraid I shall often want words to paint what I desire. I will stay with you as long as you like, if I can be of use to you, for no one cares about me, and I am suffered now to do just as I like with my time."

The child passed his hands through his fair hair, and gather-ing his thoughts together, prepared to relate his tale. It was a pretty sight to behold those two young and bright-natured beings as they sat together, Ellen's dove-like eyes fixed with attentive interest on the boy's remarkably intelligent and sensible counte-nance, and he, though clothed in coarse apparel, which he had outgrown considerably, with his noble form and princely features, looking like one of Nature's own nobility, as he thus, with but little hesitation in his choice of phraseology, commenced the nar-ration of the incidents of his brief existence.

CHAPTER IV.

—— Have I not striven in vain
To bind one true heart unto me ?
                              Mrs. Hemans.

THE CHILD'S STORY.

" I know not where I was born, nor did I ever, as far as I know, see my father.   From my earliest recollection I have led the life of a vagrant, going here and there, and never remaining in one place for any length of time.   My mother followed the calling of a strolling actress, and was admired both for her beauty and abilities on the stage.   It is a beautiful art—that of acting, and I have loved it for its own sake, though I was compelled to study much for children's parts, in which it was said that I excelled.

" I was taught to read by a kind good man, who often acted in the plays I used to perform in, and gave me instructions in acting.   My mother hardly ever took any notice of me at all, except to scold or to beat me, yet for all that, if she would have let me, I could have been so fond of her.   From the time that I could make out the meaning of books by myself I have given up nearly every other pleasure for the sake of them.   It gave me much more delight to sit beneath a tree with a book in my hand, and passing hours fancying that the wonderful scenes in it were actually occurring before me, than to mingle with boys of my own age, and play with them.   The old man who was so kind in teaching me to read and act, was the only real friend I ever had, and he told me things I should never have heard of, but for him.

" When I was wretched, and I sometimes was most miserable, when I was very, very young, because my mother was unkind, I used to think it would have been better that I had never been born; but that good old man taught me what I had never heard of from my mother, and said there was a Good Spirit in all the world, watching over its creatures. And then I would ask him why, if that Spirit is so good, there should be such dreadful misery and wretchedness in the world, and he would answer me,

" ' My child, God creates us that we may be good, and raise ourselves above the poor nature he has given us; if he did not suffer evil to exist, how could this be accomplished? If it were not possible for man to do wrong, what merit would there be in his doing well?' And so, after thinking on the subject, I was satisfied, for when my dear friend first told me what God was— I never having heard his name unless when used in curses—I thought to myself, ' Why does not this Great Being interfere for our good? If I were God, I should wish all the universe to be as happy as myself.' But I could not doubt, when I came to reflect more deeply, that, according to the amount of temptation, is the virtue of resisting it. And so I used to pray to this eternal and mysterious power to make me a better child, and to give me purer desires, and to enlarge my mind, that I might understand what is wise to do; and to be present to my heart, and succour me; and after I did so, I was at peace in myself, and rejoiced that I lived, though unfortunate."

The boy paused, and appeared to be meditating. " I think," he continued, " that the most wretched have cause to be quite thankful that they have been called into life, since, if there *is* a God (and I cannot believe that any one who has heard what I have, can doubt that there *is*), He must have created them that they might all be blest. I have not had much to make me happy, as other children have—no dear eyes turned fondly upon me, no tender lips to press my cheek, no words of affection to soothe my sorrows—and more than anything have felt the want of such sweet things; yet I should not complain, for every thing in nature delights my senses, and my own thoughts are often most pleasant to me. For when I look above and see the blue sky, and hear mysterious sounds and melancholy music in the distance— sounds that I know not how they spring into existence—when I behold the bright stars and the holy moon, and the great earth seeming to sleep quietly and deliciously beneath them, I have almost imagined that pure and lovely creatures, with eyes more lustrous and ethereal than even the countless lights in heaven, whispered in my ear, ' O child, not only shall you have those things when you die and live with us, to gratify you, but our songs of joy and our looks of love, and, more than all, the melody and the radiance, the unbounded affection of your great Father will be yours.' And, lady, I have heard strange things—so wild and beautiful—seen such visions of glory and of bliss, that my soul has been transported, and with tears, instead of words, I have thanked the good Being, who permits me to enjoy such fair life. I love very often to sit upon some quiet grave, when the first stars come trembling sadly yet calmly, like glistening tears, into their brief but glorious splendour, and to think, when the undying soul goes forth, to what sweet world among them it may depart. I have supposed myself permitted to enter one of those bright places, and see vast hills and rivers, seas and forests. I have often fancied that in a tiny boat I have entered huge caves, and followed their windings among rivers of all strange hues, and as I lay plucked flowers that do not grow on earth, while my ear was ravished with songs more delicious and sounds more exquisite than those of the lonely nightingale. Oh, I love solitude, almost as much as faces which are as gentle and kind and fair to look on as yours, dear lady; for when I lie beneath the dark vault of Night, and try to count the diamonds (more bright than any that adorn a queenly brow) on her face, I feel sensations and thoughts which I shall never be able to describe—solemn, infinite, and shadowy as spectres, but arrayed in loveliness and light. And being able to read my favourite authors, some of which my kind old friend helped me to understand, I have traced in their beautiful imaginations and ideas the same feelings which have burned so deeply within my own breast, and *that* was most pleasant. But this is not the only delight I have in reading. When a noble action is supposed to be performed, how my blood dances and thrills, and how my frame becomes animated as if by magic! I think I stand in the same place myself—I think by my own exertions I may make numbers blest—relieving the wants of my fellow creatures, and restoring the poor and starving to plenty

Y

and peace. Oh, to pour comfort into the hearts of the afflicted, and to supply the necessities of all, should be happiness to angels, and to do these things, it seems to me, God created us.

"A year has now elapsed since I met with a terrible misfortune. My kind and good old friend was taken from me, and since then I have had no one to care for my affection, or to say one word of love and tenderness, and this is a dreary world without them. Strangers, indeed, have looked on me kindly; but otherwise I have been alone in the wide universe, and the sense of my solitary condition has only been relieved by indulging in those dreams I have described.

"I remember it was just such a mild and glorious day as this, when my benefactor, to whom I owe all the good in myself that I possess, ceased to breathe. I was sitting by his bedside, and praying that so good a friend might not be taken from me, when in a feeble voice he called me yet closer to him, and taking my hand, he pressed it in his own, and after a pause he said,

"'George, I am going from you, and you will have no protector but Him which is in heaven. You will be exposed to temptations you will find it hard to resist, but if you will only ask God fervently to help you, if you will only turn your thoughts to heaven when you are sorely tried, you will triumph over yourself and be happy.' How I have treasured up those last words in my secret soul! Day and night I have thought over them, and tried to put them in practice, and I have often had cause to thank God that I was induced to do so. Do you not think it is a glorious thing to be good. Nature gives mind, and strength, and beauty; but we ourselves raise ourselves above the low thoughts and base wishes which, if indulged in, make us no better than the brutes. So my old friend taught me, and all that he ever said I have considered over and over again; for almost all other persons I met with, wherever I went with my mother, indulged in riot and swearing, and vice of all kinds. My benefactor, after he had said those words that I repeated to you, drew a long breath, and then added,

"'My dear child, I have a conviction that you will one day become a great man, and there is a degree of mystery concerning your birth, which I cannot fathom. Time will perhaps reveal what is now hid in darkness, and I hope, meanwhile, you will try and fit yourself for a higher station in life than that you now fill. You have abilities, which from your peculiar situation have been early brought forth, and you have only to study and think to do great things. Nevertheless, be humble-minded, and recollect that I only conjecture what I have said about your birth. Continue to read those books I have put in your hands, strive to be good, and to serve all ; so you will employ your time to advantage, and be fit to mingle with virtuous and educated men, without having cause to blush for your own inferiority. I have begun the work, and you must complete it yourself. I leave my little library to you.' After he had said thus much, my poor friend sunk back on his pillow exhausted ; but after a time he revived and spoke again.

" ' Mine has been a strange life, George,' he said, ' and I never thought to end it as a strolling player. I was the son of a gentleman, and being left an orphan when a very young man, I plunged into dissipation, and soon squandered my small patrimony. I then tried to write for the stage, but I was not successful, for great wits were then dramatic authors, and I never possessed very rare abilities ; so finding that I could not succeed as an author, I turned actor, but was not much more fortunate in that capacity. And now for nearly thirty years I have wandered about like a vagabond, but I have thought much, and, I hope, improved my heart. Yet I have seen so much wickedness and depravity among the low fellows with whom you and I have been associated, that I earnestly hope you will escape all danger of the contagion, by abandoning the calling of a strolling player as soon as you can.'

" My dear friend was again obliged to be silent, from fatigue, and was never able to speak much more, What is heard from one we respect on the bed of death cannot be forgotten. I watched him as the dark shadows came across his face, and I knew that he was struggling with death. Then his hand which grasped mine became icy cold, and he gasped for breath, and presently there was a shudder and a sigh, and a noise in the throat, and after that rattling noise, which was so dreadful that it seemed to thrill through every part of me, he was as still as if he slept sweetly. And so he did! I saw him buried, lady, and often walk many miles to sit on his grave, and take fresh flowers to strew it with, and if I am mournful his spirit seems to comfort me. When I am dead, there will be none to mourn for me, perhaps."

" Dear child," said Ellen, her eyes suffused with tears, as the boy contemplated the earth, as if to measure out a quiet resting-place, " many will love you before you die."

" No," answered George, " I do not think I am to possess much good on earth, but I am content."

He then proceeded to detail the events connected with the capture of Danvers, with which the reader is already acquainted, bringing them down to the period when he arrived at the cottage, and adding,

" Mrs. Haines told me, when she let me in, not to say anything about the affair to you, till she came back herself; but as you heard that your father is in peril, I thought there could be no harm in saying what I knew. And if I can be of any use to you, dear Miss Danvers, I would risk my life for your sake. Though I have not known you many hours, it seems as if a brother's love were springing up in my heart for you. I could not have told any one else on earth what I have told you, for I do not like to display my feelings to those who are indifferent."

The boy ended and Ellen lapsed into reverie.

" I can do nothing before Elizabeth returns, or I know some further particulars," she murmured ; " my little friend, do you think you could ascertain the fate of my father, and let me know all that you can gather by nightfall?"

" That I will," said George, with alacrity. " The pony is refreshed, and so am I, and we will set off without delay."

The matter being thus settled, and Ellen having forced some provisions on her young messenger, he mounted his steed, and having received a kiss on his fair forehead from the velvet lips of Miss Danvers, immediately departed. Ellen watched him until he was lost in the distance, and then returned to the house in order to minister to the wants of Walsingham, who was still too weak by far to help himself, though he was rapidly regaining strength.

CHAPTER V.

What, Love and Danger ! By'r bright lady, they
Are themes of highest interest, without
Whose wild enchantment what would be romance ?
Old Play.

YOUNG LOVE—ELLEN—AN ADVENTURE OF A RATHER STARTLING DESCRIPTION.

I AM very fond of day, and still more so of night, and if ever there *is* anything approaching to poetry in my soul—if ever I rise above my materiality and rejoice in the glory of the nature which it has pleased Heaven to bestow on its terrestial creatures, it is when my fancy conjures aërial beings full of light and life and joy, disporting in the dewy air, and weaves wild thoughts together, while the bright islands in the sky perform their mystic evolutions, and I am sad and happy both at once,—sad because I know that all this solemn and majestic pageantry, this grand and beautiful vision we call the Universe, shall be as nothing to me ; and happy, since I am assured there are worlds more pure and capacities more vast, and feelings more exquisite and sublime than man has ever experienced. I marvel what we shall think of this life and this earth, when we have shaken hands with them, and commence our real rational and immortal being ? How we shall smile at the sordid passions and the abject desires, the mean pursuits, follies and ignorances, some of which men deify and deem most dazzling and august, which constitute the objects of great (?) men's aspirations, energies, ambition ! What will it matter whether we have been kings or cobblers, beggars or statesmen, famous or obscure, yielding, haughty, dunces, geniuses, Hottentots, or London exclusives?—Well, it was night, and there were two individuals, engaged in the contemplation of its glories. Their hearts were filled with pure and pleasant thoughts, and if they were pensive, they were not depressed. Those two persons, among earth's myriads, were Ellen and Walsingham. They were not together, but they had only just separated, the maiden having given the invalid his evening draught and having retired to rest. Let us look into their breasts, and see what is passing there. It may be observed, *en passant*, that the privilege of being able to read the most secret thoughts and feelings of those in whom we take an interest is one of the principal pleasures of Novel-reading. There is that dear, honest heart of the single-minded, valiant Charles, beating rather faster than usual, just because it has got a figment that Ellen is clasped to it. There she is, in the young soldier's imagination, so beautiful that she eclipses light, blushing and smiling and whispering his name, and he " my own dear wife!" he exclaims, "my gentle, my true, my lovely one! For thee, my Ellen, how joyfully could I resign the beloved radiance of Heaven, and the fragrant air, and the music of great Nature's lips to press thine thus, and to feel thy chaste kiss trembling and thrilling, and making thought and being cognizant of that alone--bliss so intense, transport so excessive —Elysium *here!*"

We weep, we love, we laugh, and mourn, joy and grief, hope and tears, and the little vision is dispersed, and there is silence —nothing more that we can know of! Poor enthusiastic Walsingham! He recked not of the "to come"—the departure of the golden splendors of youth and passion, dispersed like vapours as they are, and the chilling breath and the smileless void—but some of my readers would rail at me were I to anticipate all. Without uncertain specks and shapes in the dim horizon, where were the interest—the melodramatic and vulgar interest—of romance,—ay, and of life also?"

" I know not how it is!" thought the soldier, some few minutes after the delightful scene his vivid fancy had been performing in with his chosen. "I know not how it is, that I cannot for an instant dismiss the thought of this young girl from my brain. I have seen others more brilliant, polished and intellectual; she is the child of nature without guile or art—a wild rose, and owing all her charms to native freshness; but I love her;—the more I see of her the more my spirit clings to the genuine sweetness, tenderness and simplicity of her beautiful disposition. I have not been in her society, altogether, above half a dozen hours—I must not be too precipitate—another week, or another day before I determine, before I ought to determine—but love annihilates time---Pish! I have not the stability of a child. I must have her, existence would be an utter blank if not passed with her. Dear, dear Ellen!"

It has been observed that imagination is a most powerful auxiliary of the urchin archer we make so much of, in fact a duplicate of himself, and while the chief is employed in gratefully returning the kindness of those who kiss and hug him by sending an arrow to their hearts, the other is performing his operations by penetrating with a subtile fluid to the very centre of being. It may safely be asserted that there never was love without fancy. We must in solitude strain the ideal image to our bosoms, intensify the charms we admire, celestialize the virtues we know but little of, and do a thousand other wise or foolish things, quite impossible to be named, before we have imagined ourselves into being unalterably "fixed."

Charles Walsingham had a good deal of the faculty which Schelling and Coleridge tried to write a theory about, and could not, although he did not possess a highly imaginative mind. Fancy and feeling, closely allied and coalesced, were his paramount characteristics, but in that alliance and coalition his sound judgment had to contend with powerful enemies, on the principle that union is strength; for if he had had to fight with one only he would perhaps have conquered. Feeling, he was accustomed to habitually subdue in the presence of others, but it consequently exercised a redoubled force when he was alone. Then came the auxiliary with irresistible hues of loveliness, and in such a struggle his clear-headedness had a most tremendous hard tussle with his predominating nature. That he did make a faint attempt to give free play to reason has been seen; but he may be thought, by the calculating and prudent, a very silly fellow, to plunge head and ears into the ocean of passion, without knowing or stopping to examine any of the rocks and quicksands which environ that changing sea.

Now Ellen Danvers, being but sixteen, did not think at all. She let her feeling and her fancy perform whatsoever gyrations they pleased, and not knowing anything about the philosophy of the case, she blindly permitted herself to be guided by the hour and the circumstance. A woman is privileged to act unadvisedly; and a young girl may do almost as she likes. A young girl, Sir, makes even thought itself a phase of feeling; her head and heart, if not quite identical, do not admit of a line of demarcation betwixt them. Let us see now what the innocent creature is dreaming about.

"I feel things that never entered into my breast before. How very handsome, and kind and candid Captain Walsingham is! I wish that I might be equally ingenuous with him, and tell him as much of my history as he has told me of his! Ah, me! His is a proud destiny. Famous in arms, of a noble family, with all his mental and personal advantages! I think my father would like him!"

Now can any one, casuist, or poet, learned, or simple, tell me why Ellen Danvers enunciated the sentence above recorded? There she stood in her neat, pretty apartment, slowly and abstractedly proceeding to divest herself of her simple apparel, and revealing beauties to the enamoured gaze of the stars, and the beams of

> "The yellow-orbed maiden,
>   With white fire laden,
>   Whom mortals call the Moon;"

which might well have excited the jealousy of Mrs. Diana. There was indeed a chastity, a purity, and an innocence about the young girl, which encompassed her as with a supernal halo. There might exist shapes of far more ethereal symmetry—fairy-like though she was—there might exist shapes of far more grandeur and command—bosoms more admirably developed, and even complexions of more snowy whiteness (for in the last two particulars women improve after the age of Ellen); but anything more suggestive of the lovely Eve whom Milton describes, on the point of waking to consciousness, with all his intense beauty of conception, it is impossible to imagine. There could hardly have existed a sensualist so depraved as to harbour a base thought against that gentle, child-like being, womanly as was her appearance. The maturity of female loveliness is more voluptuous, if not less pure than that of a young maiden. We feel more towards the one as we do towards an infant, because we suppose her as ignorant. It is very ridiculous that we should associate aught impure with the works of that Great Being, whose architecture sculpture and painting, as developed in the heavens and the earth and the sea, are all surpassed by the glory of the human form. But our own grovelling passions deform the works of the Creator, and we dare to think that gross and sensual which proceeds directly from His divine hand, and could never have been imagined so, but for that vile stuff, which a most false and vain absurdity of feeling has generated, and a pseudo morality maintained. Ignorance! It is argued that God formed man ignorant. He did and he still does so; but where is the superiority of man over the brutes without knowledge, which is the only true morality? There can be no virtue in ignorance: wisdom and morality are the images of the divine. Nevertheless I am not going, as Lord Byron and Thomas Moore would perhaps have done, to paint the modest charms concealed from the view of any save the holy planets and the pure Spirits that hover in the air, as they were covered with the snowy night-gown which scarcely rivalled the whiteness of the smooth skin. That wild and exquisite minstrel who sang St. Agnes' Eve, from the delicacy of his intense fancy could alone adequately portray the grace and holiness of such beauty under such circumstances. If you have not read that delicious vision of one of the brightest spirits that ever adored the true, the unsullied, and ideal, you have a rich treat to come. I must indulge in a little quotation from it, because it will help out myself, and assist the unimaginative among my readers—those who can *feel* better than they can fancy——

> " She seemed a splendid angel newly drest,
> Save wings for heaven,"

as, before she entered her bed she addressed with clasped hands and uplifted eyes the Almighty—

> " She knelt, so pure a thing, so free from taint;"

z

when a noise at her window broke the spell of vision, and as she was in expectation of the return of George and of Elizabeth, who much to her disappointment and anxiety had sent no intelligence to her, although it was midnight, when overcome with fatigue she lay down to sleep, she immediately arose.

When we have made up our minds not to slumber very soundly a slight noise will often disturb us, and although the noise which had aroused Ellen was by no means loud it was sufficient to put her on the alert. Pity that she thus lost as pleasant a dream of the sick soldier as Morpheus ever vouchsafed to maiden or to lover, and especially as the interruption, she speedily discovered, did not make amends for the loss of sleep, or indemnify her for the imaginary delights of being with Charles.

Hastening to her casement she was about to throw it up, when a gruff voice, totally unknown to her, speaking in an undertone, excited no small alarm in her breast. A projection in the wall of the house prevented Ellen from descrying who it was that stood below, but her quick ear sharpened by apprehension instantly detected the sounds which were uttered by the unseasonable visitor. Nor were the accents uttered calculated to allay her terrors, for she rapidly gathered the intention of the nocturnal intruder as he spoke thus—

"I shall not need the crow-bar, Bess; the door is only locked I think; keep a sharp look-out, girl, lest—Ah, hist! No, I mistook. I thought I heard something then. It was only the whistling of the wind among the trees—I am not used to this sort of work, and so I'm rather sneaky. Curse these skeleton keys! I must either use the crow or try a window." And having said thus much the man was silent.

What was poor Ellen to do? She could not doubt but that burglary was meditated, and she had no means of raising an alarm, nor, if she had, was there any one near to aid her. No person was in the house save Walsingham, sick and ill, and unable to leave his bed; but she thought at all events it was better to seek him and ask his advice. But then, with the rapid apprehensiveness of growing love, she reflected that by exciting the invalid, he might be seriously deteriorated, and she would rather have sacrificed her life than that the poor fellow who had been a good deal better for the last few hours, should be thrown back.

Deliberating thus with herself, the minutes flew by, and she now imagined that an entrance had been effected by the robbers, and that she heard a footstep on the stairs. Actuated by terror, and losing all self-command, she uttered a faint scream and attempted to fly ; but she was as if in a dream, and she could not move a step. Still she retained sufficient possession of mind to run over the accumulating difficulties of her position, and she finally came to the conclusion that as Walsingham in all probability must be disturbed during the operations of the housebreakers, her wisest mode of action was to give the alarm herself with caution. Poor girl! she measured the strength of the soldier's nerves by her own, and did not calculate that, though weakened by loss of blood, the lion heart of him she loved could not quail beneath the presence of an earthly foe. At length, by a kind of frantic effort, Ellen recovered her capacity of motion, and opening her chamber door, with flying and noiseless feet hurried towards the room occupied by the invalid. She was necessitated to traverse a considerable space before she could reach Walsingham, as their chambers were the most distant in the house. She did not choose to occupy a room nearer to him, from motives she did not stop to analyse, but she now regretted that she had not, for she heard a stealthy step approaching, and knew, from the direction of the sound, that a robber interposed between her and Walsingham.

CHAPTER VI.

"———— This whole
Of suns, and worlds, and men, and beasts and flowers,
With all the silent or tempestuous workings
By which they have been, are, or cease to be,
Is but a vision ; all that it inherits
Are motes of a sick eye; bubbles and dreams ;
Thought is its cradle and its grave, nor less
The future and the past are idle shadows
Of thought's eternal flight."

THE EPICUREAN AND OTHERS.

WE left Walsingham the Epicurean pursuing the way he had
determined on taking, despite the perils which beset it, and as
he was a Necessitarian, and had made up his mind as to what he
should do, his fatalism led him on regardless of consequences.
The distinction betwixt the doctrines of necessity, and the less
intellectual one of destiny, is so subtle, that it requires a far abler
philosopher than I can pretend to be, I confess, to draw a line
of demarcation between them. The one indeed arrogates to itself
the freedom of choice—abstractedly considered, and pretends to
forethought, though it most positively contravenes the first, and
nullifies the last, when reduced to first principles ; while the other,
carried out to the extreme of Hindooism, blindly follows the demon
God ; but as a celebrated writer, who adopted the Necessitarian
doctrines, observes, " the farther we see, the more acutely we feel,
and the more deeply we understand, the less reason have we to
be attached to life—the more patient are we of hard necessity
and inevitable fate, because we have the less variety to gild our

chain." And the noble author subsequently adds, " Well then, caution avaunt! Let me plunge headlong into the stream of life, reckless of the consequences ; since they must follow, follow what will." Now these were the principles of William Walsingham ; they actuated the whole current of thoughts and actions with him, and will serve to illustrate the peculiarity of his character.

The Epicurean was now travelling along a wide undulating high-road, for the most part covered with clumps of birch, larch and smaller trees. He then struck into a more secluded path, the underwood of which occasionally obstructed his progress, winding along in the shape of a serpent. Here a gorgeous pheasant sprang timidly away, and here he disturbed a hare, or a rabbit, of which there were great numbers in that part of the country ; and now and then a lordly deer, bending his splendid antlers, darted away among the luxuriant foliage at the imminent risk of striking his ornamental head-gear against the dense branches of the low trees. The ilex and the chesnut at distant intervals spread their broad shade over the velvet turf, and tempted the indolent youth to repose under them ; but for once he restrained his inclinations (*the stronger motive predominating*), and continued to step forwards with tolerable briskness.

"I like this walk," thought the Epicurean to himself, "and to-day it is more pleasant and beautiful than usual. How delicious that stream looks through the opening there among the thickly thronging clusters of the young plantations, the air so serene, and the sky so gloriously blue and overhanging yonder little island, with its wild-flowers and verdure, make it appear a fairy place, suspended in an Elysian atmosphere. The mossy slope there above the quiet dell, and embosomed among the green banks which are so picturesquely situated, invites the weary traveller to repose. But no ; I will not yield to the temptation ; I am on Harriet's business. How exquisite would be the enjoyment could I share this lovely solitude with one possessed of a heart and mind—some fair and tender being whose whole existence were wrapt up in mine, lying together, "*sub tegmine patulæ fagi,*" and descanting on the scene around. I feel that I am under a necessity of loving ; nothing but passion can fill the void here ;— the vulgar and sensual intercourse in which I have hitherto indulged is insufficient and unworthy ; for I have, I think, capacities of enjoyment more refined and intense than brute pleasure can supply."

The youth was now involved in a dense labyrinth of brushwood, through the centre of which a glassy rivulet slowly trickled, and among the plentiful bushes it contained, blackberries and other wild fruits grew luxuriantly. He paused to gather some berries. A magnificent pine, whose head appeared to pierce into the blue heaven, grew in the midst of the thicket, which was strewn with its fallen leaves and branches. "That tree is still the king of this domain," thought the Epicurean. "I remember, when I was a young child, I used to love to come hither, and speculate, after my own fashion, on the mystery of things. How happy I was then; they called me a melancholy child; and I *was* devoted to solitary thoughts; but they were delightful from their vague pensiveness. I was ignorant then of those dark enigmas, good and evil." The Atheist smiled. Did you ever see a wild, fantastic light in the sky, when all was gloom and darkness? such was his smile then—most transient, undefinable, and adding dreariness to the night which was settled upon his brow.

"Ay, then," he added, "I saw the green leaves fall, I watched the brown foliage of rich autumn decline into the nothingness of winter. I saw all was rottenness and corruption, yet I believed that I myself was an exception to the general order of nature. I imagined that I was destined for some incorruptible inheritance among the everlasting stars, and fancied that I should traverse the ethereal space, hearing soft sounds and making melody. By Heaven! I think that ignorance, after all, is the very best privilege that man may enjoy. But the mischief is, it is impossible to restrain the inborn impulses of mind, and so, with infinitely loftier susceptibility to happiness than the brutes, we are immeasurably less content than they are, because we are more liable and sensitive to pain from forecast and reflection."

Thus musing, the philosopher cast his eyes in the direction of the pine tree, and they were instantly arrested by what they saw. A wild, unshapely creature, whom it would have puzzled a Naturalist whether to classify as belonging to the genus homo or not, was kneeling beside an ape which was bleeding profusely, and endeavouring to bind up some wounds, the bandages of which had been torn away by accident, having brought some water in his huge hands, which were so monstrous as more to resemble paws, and having previously vainly tried to tempt it with fruit. With all his errors, sins, and vile philosophy, the Materialist was humane to and universally beloved by the brute creation. He was also a little bit of a doctor, and not unskilled in the use of herbs. Advancing therefore to the ape, while he surveyed the other nameless thing with much curiosity, he discovered that the animal was almost exhausted from the loss of blood, and that its face was terribly mutilated. The nondescript gazed with mistrust and scowling suspicion on him, but when he proceeded to tear his handkerchief in half, and gathering some herbs, to apply a remedy, which proved efficient to the hœmorrhage from which the ape was suffering, his gratitude knew no bounds. He would have actually licked the hand of William Walsingham, if he had been permitted to do so; but raising him from the ground on which he was kneeling to him, the Epicurean put some questions to the " very strange beast," for the purpose of discovering whether he were understood.

The nondescript looked up to him with eyes half bestial, half human, and though he could not, it was manifest, exactly comprehend the meaning of what Walsingham said, it was also evident that he had some glimmering of reason, for he made various gestures not devoid of intelligence, which informed him that he was unable to speak. As the Materialist was at last about to quit this singular scene, finding that noon was fast declining, a female of forbidding aspect, whom he remembered to have seen before on several occasions, and whose name he knew was Stokes, appeared. The nondescript on beholding the woman instantly bounded up to her and performed violent gesticulations apparently quite intelligible to her, and which were in fact demonstrative of the gratitude he felt toward the youth for his timely aid to the ape.

" Well, Mistress Stokes," said the philosopher, " can you tell me what this wild being here is? I think I have heard of his existence, but was not prepared to behold so strange a thing."

" I am much obliged to you for attending to my ape," returned Mother Stokes, with infinitely more graciousness in her manner than was usual with her, though it approached to familiarity;

" for this boy, he is my grandson, and he has lived with me ever since he was born in my cottage."

" Can he speak in any manner, then ?"

" No," was the answer, " but I can understand what he means, and that is quite enough. I don't want to be annoyed with the gibbering of human fools, who are no better than brutes —if as good."

" Ha, ha, ha," laughed the young man, " so you are a misanthrope, Mistress! I should like to hear some particulars about that boy, or whatever he is, if you can spare time to walk this way with me."

Mrs. Stokes seemed irresolute. " Not now, not now," she replied. " Sally will tell you how to find my dwelling, and I shall be glad to see you—at least my daughter will bring you whenever you wish."

" Ah, Sally is your daughter, though she does not like to own the fact," observed the Epicurean.

" There are many things Sally wouldn't like to own," returned Mother Stokes, with a meaning leer at the young man.

The blood coloured Walsingham's sallow cheek for a moment, but returning no answer to the hag he passed on, while she muttered, as his proud and noble form vanished,

" He has a handsome face, and I don't wonder at the girl's taste. I can't be surprised that she will have nothing to say now to her crippled cousin. I must know more of that boy—he's a deep one."

And what thought William Walsingham?

" How the devil," he soliloquized, " did that old hag of hell discover my secret? Sally must have told—and if so, I will break off all connection with her. The wench is pretty enough, but I will not degrade myself to be laughed at and pointed out as the admirer of a servant. Yet what an ass am I! Sally Stokes with her ruddy cheeks, and coarse, though not deficient understanding, may be—*is* just as good as the painted harlot who moves in high and brilliant circles, and sells herself to the best bidder, or yields to the most adroit seducer. I do abhor seduction. I should never be expert indeed in the arts which win a woman's favor. I could never flatter, and cringe and bow to a meaningless, sordid creature, without heart or imagination, for the sake of

what compensation she could make me. I am sorry, very sorry
that I have been thus implicated with this low woman. I was
extremely young, when the affair first commenced—that is my
only excuse; for, without love, such intercourse is utterly brutal.
Pshaw! I am always yielding my mind to this old world nonsense.
I must rise superior to prejudice. Love! why have I been
thinking so much about it latterly? The cause for the effect.
The exigencies of my nature require a reciprocation of feeling and
passion; but there must be some more potent reason than this,
for the consuming principle growing up in my mind; because my
passions for a long time past have been as strong as they are now.
Do I—no, I cannot be what is called in the cant of dissemblers,
and the jargon of idiots, " in love." I have ever considered that
the confinement of feeling and sentiment to one object is absurd,
yet now—Down, demon, down! It shall never be said that
William Walsingham, the philosopher of eighteen—who, for four
years, has been firm and consistent in his principles and opinions,
despite the controversy, the bigotry, prejudice, and reprehen-
sion with which he has been assailed, is enslaved by that which
he knows is opposed to the good he worships. Harriet Walsingham—my father's sister! Yet the law will not recognise our
relationship. A bastard! How that word sticks in my throat!
I verily believe I should not be an atheist, if I were not what I
am otherwise. Weak fool! *thou* boast thyself a philosopher!
The minion not only of thyself, but the insane opinions of this
idle, crack-brained world's idolatry. Tossed upon the billows of
passion, wrecked on the quicksands of doubt and darkness—the
worm trodden under foot by those not worthy to stand beside
thee—ha, ha!" and he laughed bitterly.

The Epicurean, quitting the wooded country through which he
had been previously walking, struck into a part of the same road
where Mr. Smith had first encountered the seeming old man,
who had proved so disagreeable a personage. Leaving this also,
after traversing a few furlongs, he took a cross-path extending
for about a mile, and at the end of which might be seen an extensive park, in which herds of deer were grazing. He had hardly
quitted the high road ere he was joined by a handsome young
man of gentlemanly exterior, though with something bold and
saucy in his well-looking face, and mounted on a horse of high

2 A

blood. He was of tall stature, and if not robust, was by no means a stripling in figure. Accosting Walsingham politely, and as he took off his hat, displaying a profusion of dark brown ringlets, perfectly feminine in their length and fineness, the stranger said, "I think, sir, I shall be able to cross by yonder park, shall I not? By so doing I may save myself a considerable circuit?"

The young Materialist was struck with the face, the manner, and the voice of the unknown, though he did not at once recal where he had seen and heard those similar to them; for, engrossed in his own absorbing thoughts, he had totally forgotten his recent adventure with the footpad; but afterwards, in spite of the disguise which the robber had worn, he recognised a striking resemblance between them, and except that his new acquaintance was about two inches shorter, could have almost fancied that the form was the very same. Before however these thoughts presented themselves to his mind, he replied, "That park belongs to my friend Captain Norton, and it is not open to the public; but I shall be happy to use whatever influence I have to procure a passage for you."

"I am infinitely indebted to you," replied the agreeable stranger, with a fascinating smile of thankfulness, in the performance of which, he displayed a row of white teeth, and a mouth of such dimpled sweetness as would have been irresistible in a female. Indeed, but for his great height and martial figure, there was something which might have been deemed effeminate in the horseman, notwithstanding the boldness and freedom of his address.

The Materialist was one ever ready to penetrate into character, and remarking a brightness about the eyes of the unknown, which promised intelligence, he said, for the sake of drawing him out—

"How we subjugate the brutes to our imperious will! Is it not marvellous that so strong an animal as the horse, should be so entirely the servant of weak, impotent man?"

"Upon my soul, Sir," returned the other, "it is fortunate that the beasts have no more sense than they have, or man would be in but a poor condition. If the ox took it into his head to turn restive, how should we get on with the plough? and as for the horse, we never could do anything with him, if he had any more brains than he has. In what physical particular do you think we surpass brutes?"

The youth held up his hands.

"Without these," he answered, "where were the supremacy of man? Could we build houses, or fashion implements, or till the earth, or commit thoughts to writing, or perform any one of the operations by which alone we are distinguished from the beasts, but through *their* instrumentality? It is only a superior physical adaptation, it is only a more fortunate combination of the materials of the animal structure that enables man to consummate the glorious schemes of his ambition. Therefore it is rational to conclude that the intellectual organization is only the ultimatum of physical perfection, and not distinct from it."

"I don't pretend to be a philosopher," returned the stranger, "and therefore shall not attempt to argue with you upon the difficult point you were giving your opinions on. It seems to me, however, that mind and matter differ in essentials, and so they cannot be identical. But I really care not two pins whether my intellectual principle be like the earth on which we now tread, or of a totally dissimilar nature. What is it to me? Even could I obtain the knowledge of the components of my mind, should I be at all the happier? Deuce a bit on't. So I make up my mind to be satisfied with my condition and the extent of my capabilities, moral and physical. I sleep and try to have pleasant dreams, of love, wealth, and all that constitutes the substantial enjoyment of existence;—I drink and strive to get good society, and merry wits, humorists and boon fellows, and excellent wine to promote the flow of mirth;—I make love to all the pretty girls, and deceive as many as are silly enough to let me deceive them. And so I let life slip away, and like it as much as I can, convinced that that is the only wisdom."

"A pleasant, amusing fellow this!" thought the Materialist, an ill-suppressed sneer curling his lip, "he carries out my sentiments *ad extremum.*"

"You are quite right," he observed; "but do you find that you are ever ready for pleasure and never weary of it?"

"Oh, I feel satiety and disgust now and then, like others, I suppose; but as we take a dose of medicine and are then all right again, I swallow the blue devils as best I may, and then, hey for a lass and a glass! The capacity for enjoyment is not impaired by repetition; only we suffer a little bit now and then, that we may go to it afresh with keener relish."

" You are fortunate in being endowed with a nature so light and buoyant; and I congratulate you on the true philosophy which you exhibit. I am unhappily of a more sombre disposition, and so I cannot cope with the corroding thoughts which will oppress my brain."

" If you but try to drown thought with lots of good wine and jokes, you'll do it easy enough."

" I have tried, I assure you," answered the youth. " I am perfectly of your opinion that reflection is a very useless and excessively troublesome companion : but you know some things will ever adhere to others, from their properties having a power of attraction to each other. If thought fix on my mind, and mind— essentially inactive—cannot free itself from the force of circumstance under which it labours, why it must yield to the pressure, and be obedient to the laws by which it is organized, like any other principle in nature."

" Oh, you are going to reason! What the deuce should we reason for? No occasion in the world for that. I'll give you advice, far better than all the—the—what-d'ye call 'em?—the metaphysicians have left in their musty, unreadable nonsense. You say you must yield to circumstances. Very well. Plunge headlong into pleasure, and occupy yourself with that—*think* of nothing else as much as possible, and very soon you'll *care* for nothing else. I will introduce you to London life. I shall soon be returning to town, and know some capital fellows—actors, authors, wits, gamblers, gentlemen of the road—the most diverting of them all, when you are intimate with them—and all kinds of people, in fact, from the peer to the prig. I'll put you up to the rigs of London—get you a pretty mistress—procure you the best wine, and drink it with you ; I will, upon my——reputation ; and as you appear a fine sort of lad in your way, I'm convinced you'll be a first-rate luminary among us—for you know a clever man may excel in whatever he chooses. I am myself a smart sort of good-natured man. The ladies think me handsome—and the men agreeable. I play—the devil with the one, and cards with the other, as also on several instruments, and having a tolerable voice, sing songs amatory, bacchanalian, anacreontic, sentimental, &c. &c. I keep the best company—entertain myself with the most beautiful women, am universally popular, have the finest horses and table of any man I know, and though I've no real fortune to lose or to trouble me, thus live like an emperor—on reputation. My dear sir! throw away your books and thoughts. Let care fly about, and seize on those foolish enough to humour the grim fiend. You have as good a face as I have—probably more brains; the ladies like young men, and you will have—oh, here we are at the park. There's my address in London—' Sir Hippolitus Smithson, at the Jolly Fiddlers.'—I may always be heard of there, and am otherwise always changing my quarters, as also my brother, Captain Valentine, and we shall be delighted if you'll spend an evening with us."

The Epicurean bowed his acknowledgements, quite overpowered by the volubility of his gay companion, and having procured for him the privilege of crossing the park, inquired for Captain Norton.

Thus parted the man of pleasure and of the world, and the boy of the peopled universe of thought—soon to meet again.

In answer to Walsingham's interrogatories, he was informed that Captain Norton had not been home for many hours; but the servant who gave this information, added—

"I suppose, Sir, that you have heard of the late melancholy occurrence? I dare say that my master's at the cottage where poor Master Percy lies."

"What! I hope he has not met with an accident?"

"Accident! O, you don't know then that the poor dear boy is killed."

"Gracious Heavens! My old playmate—the constant companion of my childhood! Percy Norton killed! Poor Percy! Young, brave, generous, light-hearted and enthusiastic! Dead, dead! It is indeed very sad, very awful"—and William could not speak for unwonted emotion.

Turning away at once from the old and respectable domestic who had communicated this melancholy intelligence, in order to give vent to the sincere grief he felt at losing one of his dearest friends, the Epicurean hastily retraced his steps.

"An early plant, indeed, destroyed," half sobbed the Materialist, tears forcing themselves from his eyes and coursing down his cheeks in copious streams. "What power is it that blasts each promising flower, and leaves us but the thorns and weeds of desolation. Alas! nothing but necessity exists to carry on the system of the universe. O, that my power were proportioned to my will! how unboundedly happy all should be! Poor, weak, unintelligent nature! Thou didst not, couldst not know the agony thou didst inflict upon the poor, bereaved parent's heart, when thou didst strike this deadly and irrevocable blow! Accursed— thrice accursed passions of the human heart, derived from this gross nature of things. Wherever ye are there is ruin, and tempest and destruction. Why do we exist? Of what use is this goodly structure of the world, these pure and eternal heavens, these green hills and purling streams, the melody of happy birds, the rejoicing of the bright host of stars, and the resplendent sun, and the smiles of yon Queen of Night whom I now see trembling into her first soft evening life—when the intelligent and rational Lord of Earth—who measures the firmament, and describes the evolutions of those celestial bodies, notwithstanding his fine capacities of sense, and his exquisite organization for enjoyment, is less happy than the veriest reptile that crawls,—in the words of the old Jewish writer 'cut down like a flower, he fleeth as it were a shadow, and never continueth in one way.' Alas, alas, poor, poor Percy!"

Indulging in these lamentations and regrets over the untimely fate of his young friend, and hastening his pace, as if to smother his own feelings in the rapidity of motion, he speedily arrived at the cottage where the body of the hapless boy remained, and instantly supposing, from the numbers collected about the place, that it was there that the corpse lay, he merely stopped to make a brief inquiry, and passed into the cottage, where he was left alone with the remains of the young, the graceful, and admired of all; and gazing fixedly on the cold, white face, formerly so animated and rosy, he placed his hand on the icy brow, sorrowfully and affectionately.

It was the first dead person he had ever seen. A shudder passed over the strong frame of the Atheist as the chill of death shot to his heart; but speedily recovering himself, he continued his earnest scrutiny. Thus he remained for a considerable time, wrapt in feelings and thoughts too deep for utterance. Eternity, the charnel, the silent, slow, but sure corruption, and finally the reproduction of new existence from the calm and shapely form lying there, pressed on his brain. The tender moonbeams threw a silver radiance over the serene and faultless features of the dead, lighting them up with a splendor not of earth.

"And this is death?" soliloquized the Materialist. "It is a fearful thing. And yet how still, how beautiful! A little while, and a fleshless skeleton will stare with ghastly horror from the skin! And that will fall away, and loathsome insects sleep in the brain where subtile thoughts and fine fancies were. Earth's millions all come to this!—Poor Percy!—It was but the other day he was so proud, because he found he was taller than I am. Now that five feet ten of clay but encumbers the ground. I wish I might have perished for him!—I should not have been missed. He was better than myself—more pure, and gentle and beloved ;— with a mind which might have surpassed mine, and a heart which makes mine seem vile. He was a bastard, too,—and felt the degradation keenly ;—one reason why I pitied and liked him so! Farewell, Percy, I shall never look on your face again! Our dust may mingle in the vastness of matter; but we cannot interchange bright thoughts again; we—O, dreadful Death—robber and murderer of joy!—Curse thee, curse thee!"

Uttering this malediction, the Atheist left the place. Bitterness and desolation were in his heart, and from that hour his gloomy tenets became more rooted in him than ever.

CHAPTER VII.

O Liberty, so dear!   For thee
The meanest slave will venture life, the brute
Itself will peril life and limb.   Had God
So framed us that the most celestial good
Were not our choice, but forced upon our souls,
The spirit would rebel and evil seek,
That it might be its own Omnipotence.
Ethereal Being!—beautiful! sublime!
Lamp of the world! Stars, Sun, and Heaven combined!
                                        Original MS.

WALTER DANVERS—LITTLE GEORGE—THE SENTINEL.

Too long have we been necessitated to be absent from Walter
Danvers, whose fortunes may be considered as the nucleus and
active principle of the stirring events which have been narrated
in our Chronicle.   It is wonderful to contemplate the manner in
which the fate of individuals and of communities is evolved.
How events the most remote and seemingly the most nugatory
may effect the most extraordinary changes in the aspect of the
affairs of families, of localities and of nations.   It may well
humiliate the proud heart of the statesman involved in the intricate ramifications of policy, and of the subtle schemer who is
working his way, as he supposes, to place and power, that the
most trivial and inconsiderable of obstacles may overthrow the
long and deeply considered organization of his systematic operations, and with one fell swoop at last annihilate influence, party,
honor; and it may level the pride of our philosophy and intellect,

to behold the impossibility of calculating the action of causes and effects, beyond the passing moment which is our own.

It seems as if our knowledge directed into the future is but as a point, the height and breadth of which it were vain to predicate, because no one single link in the mighty chain in which we are all of us connected, but is inscrutable until it is absolutely riveted for all eternity.

Walter Danvers was alone and in prison. The long, soft twilight of early August was just commencing, and the breeze, though faint and indistinct, sighed mournfully through the trees, and blended with the thrilling strains of a solitary nightingale which seemed borne on the wings of a spirit, as it fell on the captive's ear. He was heavily manacled, and the bars of his prison window were thick and close; yet it had been considered expedient to place a sentinel outside his door; and the dull, monotonous, and measured tread of the ponderous soldier who had been selected for the duty, was the only other sound distinguishable far or near.

There was no change in the marked and striking lineaments of the prisoner. He had just awoken from an uneasy slumber into which he had fallen from pure exhaustion, in spite of the excitement under which he laboured; and was seated on a stool buried in meditation. It was not in the power of fate to bind that stern and unyielding spirit for any length of time, and surrounded as he was by apparently inextricable dangers, his own peculiar peril occupied but a very secondary place in his mind, which was "all armed in proof" against personal apprehension.

Natures like those of Walter Danvers which, if not very rare, are sufficiently original and powerful to be worth some study and illustration, possess a quality of endurance proportionate to the more active and energetic principle of character by which great deeds and glorious achievements are evolved. Though not a Napoleon in the comprehensiveness and brilliancy of his intellect, Danvers was eminently endowed with a gift of more sterling value and utility in action than velocity of thought and largeness of conception, though certainly possessing *them*. He had much of the disposition, as has been already said, of the Scottish Claverhouse, and his resources, his strength, and determination increased rather than diminished when terrible reverses depressed

2 B

the courage and destroyed the confidence of others. If not so buoyant and sanguine as many, with his colossal strength of frame and uninterrupted health he was not so subject to fits of despondency and of gloom ; but firmly and consistently pursuing the course of action he marked out for himself, he forecast events in his mind with caution, and modified his plans when necessary by circumstances.

He was now occupied with considerations which required all his sagacity and prudence; for he had strong grounds for fearing that his detention might overthrow all the plans which he thought were maturing so favourably hitherto for the restoration of the exiled royal family to their legitimate rights; and he was vainly attempting to conceive some practicable method by which to communicate with those engaged in the cause in which his whole heart and prospects were implicated.

At the period in question there were many contending factions and interests in the State, and it was hoped that, by availing themselves of the discontent and disunion which subsisted between parties and denominations, the adherents of the Pretender might be more successful in their exertions than in the ill-starred insurrection of 1715. To overturn any long-established system of polity it is of course necessary that the wealth and influence of a kingdom should in some measure be enlisted on the side of rebellion ; for, although there have been instances of an outraged people rising against their oppressors, and succeeding in liberating themselves without money or resources, unless there be some power at work which causes the indignation and universal hatred of a nation, it is vain to imagine that the great mass will plunge into disturbance and revolution without they can obtain some definite advantage by doing so. It is a mistake to suppose that the general mind is eternally operated upon by the love of change ; on the contrary there appears to be a common dread of violent dissolution of the entire elements by which we are surrounded, lest, in the convulsion of the moral body, personal interests should suffer, however fair the prospect of the change, and connexions and ties should be severed which custom has made dear and valuable.

Danvers was in what the Americans term " a fix." He had papers about him, which, although they had hitherto escaped observation, could hardly fail of being detected; and if he destroyed them, which was no easy matter, as his hands were in bondage, he must give up the hope of proceeding with his projected schemes when they were ripe for execution; yet if he chose to run the risk, and to preserve them, in the event of their discovery many of his own personal friends would be ruined, and the enemy be in possession of all the secrets of the conspiracy. If he could but have conveyed the important documents to one in whom he could trust, his mind would have been at ease; but unless his predicament were known, and some ally sent to him, the case was almost hopeless. All this he had been revolving previous to dropping asleep, and he had been unable to come to any satisfactory mode of action, in spite of the promptness of his judgment.

It was probable that his person would be more strictly searched than heretofore, prior to his examination on the morrow, and the only means he possessed of making away with the papers, was to bite away a portion of his dress in which they were concealed, and then to swallow them. He had no appetite for such a quantity of paper as he must thus demolish, though he doubted not but that his ostrich-like powers of digestion would enable him to do so without much inconvenience, and he did not think it safe even if he could tear the documents into the smallest possible pieces, to suffer them to lie on the ground. He had made up his mind, however, to the measure against which his stomach was insurrectionary, and had even bitten through his coat, and was on the point of masticating the most important of the papers about him, when he fancied something struck the pane of glass through which the light was admitted into the prison, and remembering the way in which little George had warned him of his danger at the Britannia Inn, and also hoping that a friend had learned the exigency of his position, he arose and walked as far as his chains would allow, but found that he could not reach the window.

Desirous of attracting the attention of the individual without, in the hope that he might be a confederate, he commenced humming an air which was a favourite with the adherents of the Stuarts, which he thought might at the same time divert the attention of his guard from the noise he now again distinguished, and which he could not doubt but was premeditated. He dared

not give intimation of his presence by calling out, lest his sentinel's vigilance should be aroused ; and his sole resource was to
whistle a tune popular only among the Jacobites, in order to
attract the notice of the person outside. This measure was apparently successful for the desired object, for immediately a piece of
paper was thrown in at the grated window, which alighted within
a yard of him. Picking this up with his teeth, Danvers managed
to read a few words scrawled in a childish hand-writing, the purport of which was simply—

"If your name is W. D., find some means to let me know it
is so. I am come from your daughter.

                                                  "GEORGE."

"If I could but get this boy—evidently the same who gave me
notice of the machinations of my foes a few hours ago—to take
these papers for me home, all would be well," thought Danvers,
with his usual rapidity of judgment ; "but these accursed bonds—
stop, let me see ! The sentinel paces from the cell, and cannot
distinguish words to a song through that thick door when he is
not close to it. This child is quick of apprehension and will understand my dilemma. I am certain he is to be trusted—but
how he has found me out here I cannot conjecture. There, now
the guard is at the door :—he pauses ; now he turns ! I will hum
an air—confusion ! he is coming in."

And as he spoke, the sentinel—the same tall, burly soldier he
had so signally defeated in the late pursuit—opened the door,
and in a surly and indeed savage tone, said—

"You'll be good enough, if you must sing and whistle, not to
make such a —— noise."

And closing the door, he continued his walk, while Danvers,
heedless of the interruption and the insolence of the man, sang
thus—

          "In prison and handcuffed, poor Walter in vain
              Strives a moment of freedom, my brave boy, to gain—
              The sentinel's coming,—without loss of time
              Try up to the high, grated window to climb."

"Curse your singing !" vociferated the guard, but without

entering this time. "If you ever pray, you'd better do it now than bawl those d—d Tory songs of yours,—you'll hang soon, my buck!"

Regarding not this brutal impudence, Danvers eagerly waited for some signal from his little friend outside, but for some minutes he waited in vain. At length he heard a noise above him, and on looking up, to his astonishment he saw a trap-door open at the top of the room, which was of considerable height, and perceived the figure of George standing in the aperture.

"Thank Heaven!" exclaimed Danvers, mentally, "now, if the discretion of this child be equal to his zeal in my service—all my present anxieties will be relieved. But I cannot write with my manacled hands, and I must tell my little ally what to do. I dare not raise my voice again, for the guard is near the door, and indeed, as it is, if he should come in a second time?—I'll stand with my back against the door—and giant as he is in stature and bulk, he shall not open it singly. Then the child may come to me."

This last thought had hardly suggested itself however to the mind of the prisoner, before it was dismissed, for he perceived that it was impracticable for George to descend from an altitude of above a dozen feet, and even if he could have done so, he saw no method by which he could raise himself again. But he had not calculated on the prudence and foresight of his little friend, who having soon completed a survey of the cell, produced a coil of rope from his dress and noiselessly effected a descent. Danvers motioned to him with his head to be cautious, and advancing to him the child whispered—

"I have brought you a file, and will soon release you from this chain, and then you can get up to the trap-door, and there is nothing to prevent your escape."

"But if the guard should enter, my boy, and you are discovered," answered Danvers, in a low voice, "you might suffer for your generosity. Here, take this packet, and conceal it carefully from all, till you can place it in the hands of my daughter, son, or Mrs. Haines, who I suppose you have seen, though I know not how you found them. Leave me to do what I can for my release. I think with this file I can free my hands."

"No, no," returned the boy, "don't fear for me. I will file through your handcuffs," and he commenced his operations.

Danvers, who felt that he could not have done this but in a great length of time, as he must have held the file in his mouth, unwillingly permitted George to proceed; nor did he prove an unskilful workman; but with little noise, in a few minutes enabled Danvers to use his hands. Seizing the file then, the captive proceeded to cut through the chain which withheld him; but in his eagerness forgot the requisite caution, and the sentinel instantly turned the key of the door; but the Herculean shoulders of Walter Danvers sustained the powerful impetus of the soldier's hand.

"Fly!" he whispered to George—"you have your directions—God speed you!"

George hesitated—but seeing he could be of no farther use to the prisoner, was about to comply with his injunctions; and was swinging his light weight to the ceiling, when the rope unluckily broke, near to the beam on which he had fastened it, and he fell violently to the earth; but alighting on some straw, which was placed there for Danvers to lie on, sustained no injury.

Meanwhile, the guard, exasperated at the resistance he encountered, and then hearing the noise of George's fall, shouted to the prisoner, and swore he would kill him if he did not admit him; and throwing his huge body against the door nearly broke it in, but did not displace Danvers.

CHAPTER VIII.

It was a piteous spectacle to see
His grey hairs in the dust, and in his eyes
Sorrow, and agony, and madness—Then
The vengeance fit swept o'er him like a blast
That spends its violence upon itself,
Howling and desolating; but the ruin there
Will not sweep o'er and die.

Old Play.

THE BEREAVED FATHER AND THE DESTROYER—THE INTERRUPTED ESCAPE.

NOTHING less than the vast strength of a Walter Danvers could have sustained the awful shock of the soldier's gigantic form, thrown violently against the panels; but, although he had undergone excessive fatigue both of mind and body so recently, the emergency of the occasion seemed almost to endow him with supernatural power, and he did not move an inch, though the stout hinges and thick oak of the door appeared on the point of being demolished.

" Hide!" whispered Danvers to George, who in an instant caught the direction of his eye, and recovering from the effects of the concussion he had undergone, crept beneath the straw which had previously rendered him such good service; and, covering himself with it, lay completely concealed from observation. The captive hastily cast in his mind whether it were better to admit the rude sentinel without farther obstruction, or to endeavour to exclude him from the cell. If he did the latter, others might come to the guard's help, and resistance on his part must inevitably be overpowered; but then George at all events might be saved, if he could manage to gain the trap-door, which standing open would discover all, if observed.

" Blood and thunder," vociferated the soldier, " I will shoot you like a dog, if you don't let me come in," and again dashing against the door with his shoulders, the panels gave way, and Danvers had given himself up as lost, when a footstep was heard approaching, and immediately the sentinel, recognising an officer, ceased his efforts to effect an entrance, which Danvers felt he could not long have withstood, the fellow being in mere animal strength equal to himself.

But then the trap-door! It was growing rapidly darker and darker, and he hoped, in the dusky twilight, that it might not be discovered. In any case he could do nothing more, and standing away from the door, it was almost instantaneously thrown wide open, and an elderly man, with wild, haggard, and distorted lineaments became visible.

" Shut the door," said the officer, whom Danvers did not directly recognise, so strangely was he altered in the course of a few hours, and his orders having been obeyed with military promptitude, yet with surly obedience, he confronted the captive, who had placed himself in such a manner as to render a view of the open trap-door as difficult as possible, and at the same time to prevent the officer from approaching the straw under which George was lying.

The unwelcome visitor gazed with a wild glare on the haughty and commanding countenance of the prisoner, as it stood out in bold relief in the midst of the apartment, the stature appearing taller, and the whole form more grand and majestic than usual in the uncertain light. I wish I were a painter, that I might convey to the eye as well as the understanding an idea of the singular scene—The dusky and swarthy line of the captive's cheek and brow assumed a still deeper colour in the light in which he stood, and his broad chest and brawny shoulders contrasted strongly with the thin, shrivelled figure of the officer, whose pale, sunken face, whose white lips and starting eye-balls were terribly distinct in the gloom, appearing like those of a spectre rather than of a living man, while, though within an inch of the other's height, he seemed shrunken into a pigmy, as he bent and shook and twisted with the excess of terrible and convulsing passions. But there is no Rembrandt now to represent the strong and weird lights and shades, no inspired hand to trace the awful agonies and emotions on the spectral lineaments of the officer.

Long, long was the fierce, the terrible, the indescribable gaze, in which the hate and misery of ages seemed concentrated, of that desolate being on the man who had deprived him of his cherished-all-on-earth. He gnashed his teeth, though not loudly, but otherwise was almost breathlessly still and silent, while Danvers, amazed at his strange and ghastly looks, did not utter a word, but waited for some explanation—and it came at last, like the thunder broken loose after "a portentous pause," deep, intense, and tremendous.

"Murderer of my son!" said the officer, in a voice at first preternaturally low but distinct, and gradually rising into passion and violence the most frantic as he proceeded—" Cold-blooded murderer! To butcher one who had but just passed childhood! How could you look upon his young, fair face, and find the heart to strike him with your powerful hand? O devil! Walter Danvers! I knew your father and your mother, and have held you in these arms when you were as helpless as the poor dust of my only child—ay, you may start, he was——"

"Good Heaven! Captain Norton, was that rash boy——"

" Yes, he was my son! I do not disguise it *now!* I care not for the world—I care not for earth—for life—for rank and riches! That boy you have so cruelly destroyed was all these, and more—much more to me. O man, man! Have you known what it is to have one to whom you gave life cling to you fondly—clasp you in his little arms—call you endearing names, weep when you suffered, smile when you were glad—have you known this—I have heard you are a father—and yet—my God! What demons do thy creatures become?—Yes, let my reputation, and all I have held most dear depart from me,—let the fools, and knaves, and slaves around me sneer and taunt, and laugh—let them all point at the cold, proud, austere man whose character for morality was so unblemished! I have nothing left me to render what mankind can say of consequence! O misery!"

2 c

The broken-hearted old man ceased his broken sentences, and covering his grey hairs with his hands, remained fixed like a statue—the very image of despair; while Danvers, not a little affected, was respectfully, if not reverentially silent, and struggled not with the remorse that clung gnawing to his heart.

The mood of Captain Norton now changed. The darker and fiercer passions of his stern nature painted themselves on his wasted cheek in fell gloom and shadow, and, his parched lips at first moving inarticulately, while his eyes rolled with frenzy, he exclaimed—

"Monster of guilt! I did not come here to expose my wretchedness, but to bid you prepare for the fate awaiting you. A jury of your country has long since condemned you to a well-merited death, and though you escaped from punishment by your cunning, the execution of the law shall be no longer delayed. You will be taken before a magistrate to-morrow, and being identified as the murderer of Mr. Walsingham, it will be unnecessary to try you again as the destroyer of my son. You will be conducted immediately to the gallows, and there expiate your dreadful crimes; and if you can murmur a prayer, pray,—pray, that you may not be sentenced to the lowest abyss of Hell for ever and for ever!"

"I expected to hear what you have told me, Captain Norton," answered Danvers, with astonishing calmness and composure; "and though I most indignantly deny the justice of that sentence which pronounced me a malefactor of the deepest dye, I *will* endeavour to make my peace with Heaven, for I, like many others, am a great sinner. Believe me, I sympathize most sincerely with you under your great affliction, and deplore beyond all expression the unhappy accident which occasioned it—blaming myself for want of temper, but asserting, emphatically and solemnly, that my intention was not to have destroyed the poor fellow——"

"Talk not of pity, ruthless ruffian!" interrupted Norton in a voice hoarse with rage and hate. "If you find not more, when you appear before the tribunal of the Eternal Judge, than you have shown—tremble, tremble! You will not live to be what I am, alone and desperate! You will not live to miss the smiles, the kindness and affection which are dear as the drops of heaven to the consuming plant—life, love, hope—all; but your punish-

ment, if God is just, will be, as you wander in the world of dreary
shadows, to behold a spectre haunting you with looks of mourning and desolation,—ever, ever, ever present, and groaning for
his murdered child. Through ages and ages will that image follow you, and never more shall you know one moment's peace.
In the grave it shall sit upon your heart like an incubus, in time
it shall make your last moments a horrid antepast of eternal damnation, and in eternity it shall overshadow all things for you—shut
out the blue air—the bright angels—the songs—the melody—
the splendour, joy and effulgence of the lost heaven! It shall
darken all light, cloud with blackness the sun, glare into your
soul, obscure the hope of pardon, and obstruct the mercy of the
Omnipotent!"

Uttering these words of imprecation with maniac vehemence,
the unhappy man rushed away, like some whirlwind which had
previously been scattering death and destruction around. Such
a curse pronounced with such fearful energy, might well have
struck some terror into the boldest breast, and it was not without
its effect on Danvers, though he pitied the bereaved father more
than he quailed beneath the vindictive foe. It had been fortunate
that Captain Norton in his frenzy thought of nothing but his own
woes, and vengeance against the destroyer of his son, so that he
had not removed his eyes for an instant from the face of the captive, or he must have detected the trap-door which opened to
the top of the house.

It was now perfectly dark, and even the moon had withdrawn,
so that when the surly guard opened the door again, he did not
discover either that Danvers had his hands free, or that there
was anything remarkable in the appearance of the place.

" You won't have any light, my man," said the amiable sentinel, " and so you had better go to sleep, or say your prayers;
and I'll tell you what, if you dare to prevent my coming in again,
I'll knock your brains out, and save the hangman a job!" And
having uttered this polite intimation the soldier vanished.

Danvers now recurred to his own predicament, the difficulty
of which was increased from the circumstance of the panels of
the door being broken in, so that the slightest noise might arouse
the suspicion of his guard, and frustrate the possibility of escape.
If he could but reach the trap-door, all impediment to his depar-

ture, would, he doubted not, be removed; but the rope having broken, and the loftiness of the room being more than usually great, he did not see how he could effect this desirable object. He was again assisted by the ingenuity of little George, who rising from beneath the straw which had concealed him as soon as the sentinel had retired, whispered—

"I can climb up to the ceiling with your help and fix the rope again; but I am afraid it will not bear such a weight as yours. Isn't there a blanket or something of the kind about the room?"

"No;" answered Danvers, "but by tying some of my clothes together, and by the help of this short chain, the difficulty may be got over if you can reach the trap-door. But how can you climb such a height?"

"You shall see," cried the child, "and hark! the guard ceases walking—he is going to sleep, perhaps. Now, then, raise me on your shoulders—oh! that is not high enough! You are sufficiently strong to lift me by the feet. Now I can very nearly reach the ceiling. You can see a beam which runs across the room with large nails in it; they will bear me, and so I can get across to the other side, and reach the trap-door."

"But you may fall again, my little fellow, and hurt yourself."

"Don't fear for me—a mountebank taught me these things." So saying, George grasped a huge nail which projected from the beam he had mentioned, and a row of which, of singular size and strength, as we said, extended across the apartment, about a foot apart. With astonishing agility the boy grasped nail after nail, swinging lightly in the air, and arrived in safety at the trap-door. Meanwhile Danvers with his liberated hands immediately commenced filing the remaining chain; and soon after George had reached his destination, was entirely free from it. By means of the two yards of rusty iron which this chain afforded, Danvers principally relied on being able to reach the ceiling, and George letting down the rope which had proved so rotten, cautiously drew up the chain, which Danvers tied to it, and fixed it to a staple in the beam. Removing the stool, which was the sole article of furniture the cell afforded, to beneath the trap-door, the prisoner stood upon it and found that by so doing he could grasp the chain. But not having been accustomed to the gymnastics in which the boy was so adroit, he experienced considerable difficulty in raising himself, having nothing to keep his feet; and it was only the extreme exigency of the case which enabled him to accomplish the ascent.

" Now," said George, "I think we shall soon be safe; but first I will remove the chain and close the trap-door."

Having performed this business, the clever little fellow motioned to Danvers to follow him, and walked across the roof until he came opposite to a tree.

" You can leap, I suppose;" said George, "if not, that thin bough will bear me, and I will go and fix the chain for you to that thick branch yonder."

" I think the last plan will be the best," returned Danvers, "for I am unaccustomed to jump, and should I fall and disable myself, all is lost."

The child accordingly clutched a bough which was within a yard of the roof, and speedily reached the thicker branch which was not by any means too strong to bear Danvers.

Fortune had hitherto favoured them; but the fickle dame now veered round, for as the child sheltered himself in the tree a sound of voices approached.

" Lie down," said George to Danvers, the quick ear of the former having detected the unwelcome person's approach before the duller sense of his companion.

Perceiving that something was amiss, and having good cause for confidence in the sagacity of the boy, Walter Danvers obeyed the directions given him without question; and it was well that he did so; for the bright moon now burst forth in all her summer radiance, and revealed every object with the distinctness of noon-day. He now distinguished voices and footsteps, and presently could discern a party of soldiers, some of whom he remembered to have seen among those by whose exertions he had been taken. George was perfectly concealed from view by the thickness of the foliage of the tree, but the roof of the house on which Danvers lay being nearly flat, he was unavoidably exposed in some degree to observation, nor did he choose to risk discovery by creeping back to the trap-door. His only hope was that the soldiers would not be star-gazing, and by lying perfectly still he trusted he should escape notice. They were now within a few yards of the tree where George was lurking, and Danvers perceived that several, if not all of the party were the worse for liquor. The soldiers on a sudden came to a halt, and one of them proposed "for a lark" to climb the tree, and look for birds-nests.

It was an awful moment to Danvers and George, especially when a two-thirds intoxicated man began to ascend. The boy, active as a squirrel, finding that he must inevitably be detected if he remained where he was, at once with the utmost caution crept along the bough; but not so noiselessly as quite to escape notice.

"Is that an owl?" exclaimed one of the soldiers below. "Catch him, Tom, and we will have some fun with him."

Tom, however, could not preserve his equilibrium so perfectly as to be sufficiently expeditious to catch the supposed bird; for when he reached the top of the tree he had disappeared.

"I think the creetur's gone down the hollow trunk somehow," remarked the climber, "and it's too small for me to follow—I'm fat!"

"Throw some stones at him then, lad," returned another fuddled fellow, "I warrant you'll soon bring him out, if he's there!"

"Good God! they will kill the child!" thought Danvers, "what shall I do? Better sacrifice my own life than let his be destroyed!"

He was not allowed much time for deliberation, for the soldier who had ascended the tree, having been furnished with some large pebbles again climbed upwards; and Danvers was just about to discover himself in order to save the noble little boy, when his generous intention was unexpectedly diverted.

CHAPTER IX.

To have an open ear, a quick eye, and a nimble hand is necessary for a cut-
purse. A good nose is requisite also to smell out work for the other senses. What
an exchange had this been without boot? What a boot is here with this exchange?
SHAKSPEARE's *Winter's Tale.*

> Why what a world of pain and care do we incur
> Who thus in plots and in conspiracies
> Do peril all that wisdom holds most dear?
> Indeed, my lord, you act but Folly's part
> In risking life and fortune on this chance.
>
> *Old Play.*

THE MISER—THE ROBBERS—THE HIGHWAYMAN'S ADVEN-
TURE—THE ALARM AND THE PURSUIT.

THOUGH unwilling to tantalize the reader by leaving Walter
Danvers and George in their critical position, it is of imperative
necessity, as will hereafter be discovered, that this true narrative
do proceed to recount particulars which are of vital importance
to it, inasmuch as they develope adventures which, if less exciting
than those recorded in the last chapter, may not be pretermitted
without sacrificing the perspicuity of the whole. And here it is
proper to observe, that, if the Author's integrity be but implicitly
credited, and his kind and indulgent friends will but yield themselves up to his humour, he will be careful to refrain from tres-
passing too largely on their goodness, and while he may apparently shake off the crises of his principal characters' fortunes un-

necessarily, he is only preparing materials which shall evolve
events of loftier interest, and further the progression of the story
—rather than obstruct it.   Only don't abuse the "trickery" of
melodramatic uncertainty.

It may be remembered that there was a certain mysterious man
who dropped a packet in a churchyard where the excellent Mr.
Smith had repaired, and which he also picked up.   That person
is now the one who must occupy some portion of our attention.
After his abrupt disappearance from the ex-schoolmaster, he lost
no time in striking into the most sequestered and unfrequented
path, the multitudinous windings of which, almost all forming
acute angles, ultimately conducted him to a fair and pleasant spot
where the waters of the chief river of the county, fed by many
tributary streams, had collected themselves into a basin, in the
centre of which grew a lovely island, where stood a pretty little
half-ruined building, in which a hermit, it was the tradition, had
passed his life in days of yore.   The hermitage was sometimes
visited by small parties who loved to explore its mysteries, but
ordinarily was as still and undisturbed, save by a few swallows
and other birds who luxuriated in the shady retreats of the picturesque spot, as the mountains inaccessible to human feet.   The
stranger, apparently insensible to the beauty of the place, and
utterly indifferent to everything but its extreme loneliness, sank
down beneath a venerable oak and groaned.   That stifled sound
was the only one distinguishable in the seclusion ; for the very
air and stream had ceased to whisper and to ripple—

> " It was a beauteous evening, calm and free,
>   And quiet as the bosom of a nun
>   Breathless with adoration, the broad sun
>   Was sinking down in its tranquillity——"

But look through earth, and where is there not some blighting
touch of human woe, of misery and guilt ?

The solitary abandoned himself to dark and painful thoughts,
the nature of which it was only possible to gather from the con-
traction of his brow and the quivering of his lips ; for he had shut
his restless grey eyes and subdued every other external emotion,
but the entire expression of his still fine and handsome though
distorted face, was remorse in the utmost intensity of its charac-

teristics.   How strangely passion does modify the materiality of
man? How suddenly will it metamorphose the appearance of the
face? It is hardly possible to recognise the same individual sometimes when under the influence of highly-excited feelings and in
the more common routine of existence.   The miserable man at
length sunk into a doze.   The slanting beams of the declining
orb of day gradually quitted his pale, thin countenance, and he
dreamed.   Still he thought the green banks and the silvery river,
the verdant trees, the grass and the wild-flowers, with the quiet
and peace of the solitude and gentle evening, were present; but
there gathered portentous and tremendous appearances in the sky,
some of which assumed the shape of men and seemed to look angrily on him.   The blue heaven became of a leaden hue, and the
entire arch was spangled with stars, all red-and fierce and unnatural; and then a vast gulf yawned beneath him, and sights
and sounds of horror and dismay proceeded from the bowels of
the earth. Having been tormented for some time by this hideous
phantasm, which all the vivid power of reality could scarcely have
surpassed, a scene even more fraught with fear and agony to him
flashed upon his brain—a scene which had recurred too often to
his visions to startle him from them, but yet terribly distinct, real
and sensible.

He imagined he was walking with an old associate among poplars and other large trees, which entirely concealed all other objects from view.   They sat down together and conversed familiarly ; when a wild frenzy seized upon him, and he thought he
was possessed by a demon which urged him to commit murder
on his companion.   And with a knife in his hand, which was
furnished by the fiend, he stabbed his unarmed friend, from
whose breast the blood began to flow.   Then came the desperate
struggle—the cries, the groans, the prayers and the curses horribly intermixed.   The hand of the dying man clutched his throat
with a convulsive energy, and he gasped, and panted, and thought
he should be choked himself.   Then came the death-groan—the
groan of despair and pain and misery—and the gurgling noise in
the throat, and the reproaching eyes turned upon him with a gaze
which petrified his soul—O, the agony, the wretchedness, the
hell of that imaginary scene. Surely even here the bad man pays
a deadly penalty for crime.   It is not only in reviewing the past

2 D

he is accursed; it is not only that the present has no substantial joy, that the future has no hope, no brightness; but all singly and collectively in sleep arise to torture and drag him down to perdition; while on the contrary the virtuous and innocent enjoy feelings of rapture and delight, while locked in the embraces of that angel of mortality, which mercy has given, as one of its best boons to its suffering creatures, when sin has not stamped its leprosy on the heart.

Awaking with an oppression on every sense, as if death were struggling with him, the stranger---in whom some sagacious reader may, or may not have detected Walsingham, the Miser—endeavoured to start to his feet; but the effort he made to do so proved ineffectual, for all his members seemed growing into stone, and his muscles would not obey his will. While he was thus contending with the effects of the nightmare, which had paralysed all his body in the space of little more than an hour, he beheld at the distance of half a dozen yards two figures, and near them as many horses which they had quitted, in order to regale themselves with some provisions which they were demolishing. They were both of great stature, and of not ungentlemanly exterior; but yet there was something about them which excited the darkest suspicions in the Miser's breast.

He was in such a position as to be able to descry all their motions, and to have a perfect view of their faces, which were rather handsome than otherwise, while he remained unseen behind the trunk of the oak. They spoke in a low tone; but the hearing of the Miser was sharpened by a sort of anxiety, which he could not define, and by listening attentively he was able to distinguish all that they said, with the exception of a few monosyllables.

"Well, Bess, I suppose you haven't been doing anything to-day?" observed the taller of the strangers to his companion, whose elegant figure was dressed in a suit of new and fashionable clothes, which could not have been worn half a dozen times.

"O yes, but I have! How d'ye think I came by these togs, my good Peter?"

"I thought you were given them by the young Lancashire squire who had a fancy for you, and from whom you, by way of joke, begged his best finery. Ha, ha! Bess! sister Bess! you are a rum one, upon my soul—a regular devil!"

"No such thing! the squire's clothes were not large enough for me, and so I swapped them for a bag and sword. I will tell you how I got the togs. You must know that as I was riding along, just after I left you alone with the little fat man, I came up with a lanky coxcomb, mounted on a vile horse which I would not give three shillings for in any case, and perceiving he was a spoony sort of a fellow, I accosted him, determined that I would profit by his softness in some way, fair or foul. Putting on my very best manners I addressed him thus—

"Good day, sir! I think that I have seen you in London at a friend's of mine—the Duchess of Mountcastlebury's? Your name, if I am not mistaken is——"

"'O sir, I believe you are in error,' responded my gentleman with a simper. 'Gad's my life!' he added, 'the Duchess of a—a—the Duchess is a charming woman. I *do* know her intimately.'

"'Yes, she has a great admiration for tall and strapping fellows like you and I,' was my answer. 'Sir Hippolitus,' (that's the name I generally give myself, you know, Peter, when I want to come it flash,) 'My dear Sir Hip,' said the lovely Duchess to me one night at a grand masquerade given by the king in our honour, 'do you know that elegant young spark there, almost as tall as yourself, whom the Marquis of Rattleton brought to my rout?' So recognising you, sir, by your distinguished air and stature, I replied that I did not, but must try to make your acquaintance. I could not get an introduction to you then, and was detained by some of the royal family in conversation, and you know the bore of court etiquette does not permit us to quit the blood royal at pleasure. But I hope that now we are so happily met you will waive ceremony, and admit me to your friendship. My name is Sir Hippolitus Smithson; I was at one time a Colonel in the army, and the Duke of Cumberland having taken a fancy to me I was knighted, and now hold a place at Court.' My spark brushed up at this address, and cried—

"'Gad's my life! some mistake; but shall be most happy, Sir Hippolitus, of your acquaintance.' And producing a kerchief, highly scented, he wiped his nose with an air. 'I am just going to—ahem!—to propose for a lady—an heiress from London; and so you see—Gad's my life! damme—I should be most happy to

stay with you, and treat you to a bottle of wine at the next house
of entertainment; but the urgency of the case, you know—
damme!—'

"'Oh, my dear sir! don't use any ceremony with me,' I replied. 'But where, may I ask, did you get these clothes?—
Your tailor has made a damnable bungle. Did you have them
from London or not?'

"'Why, 'pon my life!—hem!—Sir Hippolitus, I thought they
were pretty tolerable. I went to town—ahem!—for them; and—
and—the tailor assured me I should have them first-rate. I paid
him twenty guineas for the suit. I did, damme! I'm sorry you
don't like them;—a—a—for the lady I'm going to—a—propose
to give up my liberty to—ahem!—being an heiress from town—
a——You see, she's particular about the mode; and you—a—
Gad's my life!—eh?'

"'I would advise you strongly to change your clothes ere you
enter into the lady's presence,' I answered, gravely; though I
had no little difficulty in restraining my mirth at the ass's folly;
'for though your appearance is naturally elegant, dress, you
know—damme!—' And I imitated his own manner.

"'I'm glad to find, by your air, that I have *modelled* mine
aright, Sir Hippolitus,' returned the fop. 'Of course I know—
hem!—what's right—a—but you, just being Come from court,
you know—a—hem!—damme! But, Gad's my life! I'm sorry
to find I'm wrong about the clothes. I am, stap my vitals, cursed
sorry! There's no remedy for it, either; for it will take a week
to have them from London, and by that time my heiress may be
flown. This is a cursed bore, isn't it—eh?—Oh, damme!'

"'I can suggest but one alternative,' I cried. 'I will lend you
the clothes I wear, which were made by the Court tailor two or
three days ago, (they were as old as the hills, Peter, you know,)
and will wear yours for an hour or two, as no one will see me.
You can then return them to me, having gained your suit; and
I shall be happy to have you, if you will do me the honour of
remaining with me, to dinner at my hunting-lodge, which is about
a league hence.'

"'My dear sir,' answered the would-be coxcomb, eagerly, 'I'm
infinitely obliged to you, Gad's my life, stap my vitals, damme!'
and almost immediately proceeded to undress. But you know,

Peter, I'm particular; and so I would not divest myself of my apparel before him, though I don't know that such a donkey would have made discoveries. So I said:—

"' When you've taken off your clothes, I would advise you to have a bathe in the river, there; it will wonderfully improve your looks, for you are pale, and it is the fashion at this time to have a colour. Some men paint, indeed. I always remain half an hour in a bath myself, before I dress. I do, damme! I would advise you to keep in the water for the same length of time; and as I take very long to undress, my clothes will not till then be ready for you.' So the addle-pated fellow obeyed my directions, and plunged into the water. I had a good mind to have taken his togs, and run, but I had compassion on him; and as my old things were of no use to me, I took them off, retiring behind a hedge to do so; and having re-dressed, mounted my horse, and called out to the fop, who was still in the water, I would return to that place in an hour, and wait for him; and then we would repair to my lodge, and drink his mistress's health. I took with me a purse, a watch, a gold chain, and diamond buckles—the first of those articles containing ten guineas, and the three last being worth twenty more—and cantered coolly away, regardless of my spark, who called out to me that he had left his purse in his breeches."

This adventure was narrated with so much humour, spirit, and vivacity, that the other tall individual indulged in many hearty bursts of merriment, in which the Miser, however, did not feel at all inclined to participate. He recollected that he had money about him, to a large amount, and if he should be discovered by the robbers,—for he could not doubt that such they were,—he had nothing but a slight rapier to defend himself with; and he remarked, that the objects of his well-grounded suspicions were armed with pistols and broadswords, besides being two of the most formidable-looking fellows he had ever beheld. In his own house, the Miser kept weapons of all descriptions; but not being personally timid, he was not in the habit of carrying any arms about him, beyond those usually worn by the gentry of his day. But if he attempted to depart, he would in all probability be descried, and, being caught eaves-dropping, attacked. That they were robbers, he had determined in his own mind almost from the first, and what he had overhead confirmed him into certainty on that point; and in that lonely place, no outcry that he could raise was likely to be heard by any one. Under these circumstances, he thought it most prudent to be perfectly still, and he did not move a finger, lest he should alarm the gentlemen of the road.

"Immediately after I was out of sight of the fop," continued the person who had been recounting the above adventure, and who had spoken in so lively and amusing a manner, "I encountered his antipodes. A young man of handsome appearance, with a large, dark, splendid eye, and haughty brow, ' like Mars', to threaten and command,' met me. He was not tall; there was nothing, perhaps, particularly remarkable in his shape, and yet a grander or a more imposing form I never beheld; and when I heard him speak, the deep distinct tones of his manly voice, and the expression of his mournful, contemptuous, and intellectual face, convinced me that I should not be able to play a trick off on him. The young man was amused with my nonsense, as I rattled on to him, and he procured me, very politely, a passage through Captain Norton's park."

"I should not wonder, Bess," returned the other, suddenly, "if you were talking with the lad who stuck so hard to me, up yonder. There could hardly be two such, and you met him in the very direction he took, for I watched him as I hid myself in the thicket, after taking to my heels. I should have attacked him, I think, but that I saw he had a pistol, and I thought that the report of that would have brought others to his aid. I did not make much of that business, certainly—but the papers I have got may prove valuable. They reveal names in the conspiracy I told you is organizing, which are among the highest in the county. The lives of hundreds are at my mercy."

A thought here struck the mind of the Miser, which filled him with dismay. He felt in his bosom, and with difficulty suppressed a cry. Visions of ruin and destruction arose in ghastly array before his excited imagination. He heard the hooting of the multitude, he saw the fatal tree, he felt the hangman adjust the rope around his neck; and, unable any longer to restrain his desperation, he was on the point of rushing on the tall man, and endeavouring to wrest from him the papers, which he did not doubt were those he had lost, when abruptly springing on their horses, almost before the Miser anticipated their intention, they struck spurs into their horses, and were off like the wind, though he shouted to them, with all the might of his lungs, to stop.

Pursuing, and continuing to halloo, in the vain hope of staying the velocity of the robbers' movements, his attention, which had hitherto been so pre-occupied as to preclude his noticing all other sights and sounds, except those which immediately interested him, was on a sudden arrested by the sound of the hoofs of many horses, and presently he could distinguish a body of troops advancing upon him at a rapid rate; and his excited terrors taking a new turn, he instantly dashed into the midst of a thicket, losing his hat in the precipitation of his flight, and with his grey hair streaming about his head, franticly exerting all his speed, and fancying that he was closely followed by the cavalry. Nor were his fears altogether unfounded, although he did not stop to reason or reconnoitre; for observing that a man was flying with all his might and main to avoid coming in contact with the horse, and the suspicions of the local authorities having recently been excited by some vague information received through indirect channels, the officer in command, complying with the request of the magistracy, at once made an attempt to apprehend one who was so manifestly anxious to elude the cognizance of the military, and despatched some of the dragoons with orders to detain the fugitive.

But the Miser, winged with desperation, by long and prodigious efforts succeeded in baffling his pursuers, who had cut off his retreat in one direction; but had neglected to guard a pass at the extremity of the thicket, which led into a dangerous and rocky district, inaccessible to cavalry, and through which, at the imminent risk of his life, the Miser continued his headlong flight, until utterly spent and breathless. Fortunately for him, he had taken a measure which the coolest sagacity and presence of mind could not have surpassed for policy, though he had not calculated its results.

As soon as the dragoons perceived that they had made a mistake in allowing the fugitive to escape from the thicket where he must necessarily have been hemmed in and detected by so large a body of troops, they dismounted and pursued on foot; but not being remarkably agile, and having no particular motive to capture him, they did not gain ground; but dispersing in various directions, they contrived to cut off all visible retreat and progress from him by a short cut which he had not observed, and if he had continued his wild career it must have proved the means of his arrest.

But happily, as has been observed, Fortune favored the Miser better than foresight would have done, for he had, entirely through its instrumentality, come to a stop among the rocks, where they, arising to a great height, and in almost a pyramidal form, excluded him from sight, while he had time to recover from his exhaustion; and when the shouts of his enemies, who were evidently at fault, again urged him to flight, he perceived that there was an excavation in the rock, which promised a secure place of concealment, and instantly descending, he found that there was a subterraneous passage, the greater part of which was hewn out of the solid granite that principally composed the rock, and winding onwards conducted him, though nearly in utter darkness, into the open air, far from the range of the soldiers' vision, they imagining that the object of pursuit was yet lurking in the immediate vicinity of the place where he had disappeared. But as the distant echoes of the sounds he so much dreaded died away, and finally became quite inaudible in the distance, he saw two horsemen, about half a mile before him in the high-road, relaxing not in their speed, and thought he recognised in them the gigantic robbers who had first given rise to his fears.

END OF BOOK IV.

BOOK V.

Wisdom hath no celestial panoply,
But whilst she thinks she lies at closest ward
Opens herself to unsuspected danger.

G. Stephens.

Amid two seas, on one small point of land,
Wearied, uncertain, and amazed we stand ;
On either side our thoughts incessant turn,
Forward we dread, and looking back we mourn.

Prior.

—— Of most disastrous chances,
Of moving accidents by flood and field ;
Of hair-breadth 'scapes.   Shakspeare.

Nay, these are creatures of the air, and soon will disappear,
All phantoms of the passions which wither'd grow and sere.

From an unpublished Poem.

2 E

BOOK V.

CHAPTER I.

To fear—to love! What will not love and Fear, those tyrants
Of the spirit? To dark Death they urge, and yet Fear
Is ever flying Death, and Love is seeking everlasting LIFE.—*MS.*

THE MISER'S FLIGHT—THE ROBBERS IN THE DEN OF THE
ABSENT LION—WALSINGHAM AND ELLEN.

IT was within an hour of midnight, and the brightness of the empurpled heaven, with its stars and stillness, was softly and clearly glassed in the lake-like waters of the river, which extended through the middle of a clover field, into which the Miser had stealthily crept from the subterraneous passage, which had formerly been in frequent use, as it formed the road through a mine, which having been exhausted by long-continued operations, was now deserted, and its very existence nearly forgotten.

The smell of the newly-mown clover was fragrant and refreshing, and the song of the nightingale was borne on the breeze that scarcely stirred the leaves upon the willows which grew on the river's banks, and appeared to hang with melancholy fondness over their favourite stream. The Miser, however, was in no mood to contemplate the tranquil loveliness of the scene, nor to use his eyes for any purpose but the perception of peril to himself, and the figures of the horsemen, who being on high ground, figure for one moment; but at the distance which it was from him, it was impossible to discern which of the two rascals it was, as they were so similar in shape.

But it was no time for delay; and accordingly regaining his horse, he hastened to the lower part of the wall, which it was just possible for a good-leaping horse to clear. Could the little animal he bestrode accomplish such a feat? At all events, he would try his mettle; and bestowing a severe smack on the creature's hinder parts, he urged him over; and to his astonishment in one moment found himself where he wished to be,—as if he was on as fine a hunter as ever followed hounds—and very soon a little farther. For the spirited beast, indignant at treatment to which he was unaccustomed, and smarting from the effects of the smack he had received, fairly ran away with his rider. Useless were the efforts of the Miser, excellent horseman as he was, to obtain the mastery over the refractory animal, and he was carried along, infinitely disconcerted, and ignorant of whither, over a level country for the space of half an hour and of ten miles. The intellects of the Miser had by this time a little recovered themselves, and he could judge with a little more discrimination than he had hitherto displayed, the best mode of procedure.

The speed of the courser gradually abated, and when at last he arrived before a neat, pretty cottage embowered among trees, he came to a pause, and then halted altogether, sniffing the air with apparent satisfaction, and neighing with good-will.

Immediately another horse made a response from some little distance, and looking round, Everard Walsingham descried two steeds tied to an elm about a hundred yards from him, and which, he could not help thinking, were those of the robbers.

On nearer inspection suspicion became converted into conviction; and then he was about to hurry into the house in which— by a singular fortuity—he doubted not the scoundrels were, when he bethought himself whether it were not insanity to rush into the den of ruffians who might not scruple to cut his throat. But the papers;—they *must* be recovered. If Walter Danvers found he had lost them—at that idea the Miser trembled violently, and clammy and bead-like drops of perspiration stood on his brow. He was not by any means a coward, as far as his own personal safety was implicated, as his pursuit of the highwaymen evinced,

and at once summoning resolution, he strode rapidly to the house.
He must have been carried a considerable way, at the pace he
went, out of his direct road, as the robbers were before him; but
he did not consider this matter.

There was not a sound in the cottage that the Miser could perceive; and at first he almost imagined that, after all, the rascals
had not entered; but presently he found that they had effected
an entrance, in a manner by no means usual with those who go
into their own residences; and then it struck him, that a burglary
was taking place, in which those individuals he had so strangely
and ignorantly followed were principals. What was to be done?
Should he alarm the inmates? By so acting he must exasperate
the robbers against him, and it had been his object, all along, to
conciliate them, if possible, for they—or at all events, one of them
—possessed knowledge, which would destroy him, and many
others also, if revealed. He had permitted the animal which had
borne him so bravely to use its own discretion, when he quitted
its back, and to his no little amazement he found that the sagacious brute had trotted round to a stable in the vicinity of the
abode, and was endeavouring to open the door with its foot, as
if satisfied he was at home. A sudden and startling thought
darted on his brain. The horse he had been riding was remarkably like one he had seen Walter Danvers on a short time antecedently,—the place in which he was, tallied exactly with the
description he had been given of that dreaded person's dwelling,
at which he had an appointment the day following. The horse
of Danvers! Probably then *he* was there; and he would re-
possess himself of the papers held by the gigantic robber, if mortal could.

The Miser's heart beat quickly. More and more convinced of
the validity of his supposition, and anxious at once to assure himself of it, he entered the abode in the same way as the housebreakers had; and then stopped for a minute to consider the
best means of getting to Danvers. They *might* kill him, (Danvers,) and then—the flood of confused ideas that followed that
possibility was such as to blind and confuse the Miser's mind;
but dismissing them hastily, he continued the train of rapid reflection which they had interrupted. There might be many burglars in the cottage, and it was possible that if resistance were

offered, it would prove unavailing against numbers; but such reliance did the Miser repose in the great strength, courage, and capacity of his ancient friend, that he did not suppose but that he would find some means to possess himself of the important documents, to recover which was the only care of his soul. But if he himself were discovered, all might be lost, and he knew not in what direction to seek Danvers, nor how to turn in order to avoid coming into contact with the housebreakers.

With a cat-like step he stole fearfully along, and presently he thought he could distinguish voices. Yes, now he was certain—the voice of the taller robber whispered—

"No fear, Bess. I saw him, I tell you, in the clutches of my old regiment, and he was the only male in the house—the lad his son is out. You can stand guard over the women—I never trust myself to do *that*, you know, because with my ardent temperament, when I see a pretty girl in bed I should play the very—who the deuce coughed then, behind?"

The Miser had overheard this speech, and collecting from it that it was probable the redoubtable Walter Danvers was captured, he forgot his caution in the terror and anxiety which seized upon him, and did not try to stifle a cough which unseasonably attacked his lungs. He hastily retreated, and would very willingly have quitted the cottage on the instant, but perceived a figure approaching him from the other side.

The robbers were on the alert, and one of them swore with a terrific oath, that he would kill the person who was lurking about. Drawing his sword, the Miser was about to retreat into a room, the door of which was just ajar, when it was on a sudden thrown open, and a towering form with a flaming weapon and cocked pistol advanced from it.

Thus surrounded on every side, he could only stand on the defensive; and now he saw the housebreakers descending some stairs, and making towards him. Whether all that he had beheld were robbers or not he could not determine; but certainly he would be considered in the light of an enemy, in any case, by both parties, and his line of policy was not to offend either. In this most unpleasant " fix," with the probability of being mistaken for an inmate of the house by the burglars, and for a burglar by the inmates of the house, he could not make up his mind what course of conduct to pursue; for he was naturally wavering and undecided, and the events of the last few hours had not been of a description to endow him with the faculty he wanted.

But the crisis of the affair was at hand.

"What want you here?" exclaimed a tall, pale man in a night-gown, pointing a pistol at him; and ignorant who this person might be, the Miser was anxious not to provoke his hostility, either by silence or indiscretion. The gigantic robber who was in possession of the papers was now also within an arm's length, and pointing his sword at him, threatened to be his destruction if he uttered a word. A scream, evidently proceeding from a female, also assailed Everard Walsingham's ear, and a fair form rushed forwards like a ghost, and was presently clasped in the embrace of the pale personage in the nightgown. It was ludicrously terrible. None of the parties appeared to know in what way to act, for the presence of the Miser puzzled both, as he made no demonstrations of enmity either for or against either.

Let us retrograde a few minutes, and see what had been passing in the chamber of the individual in the nightgown, whose white cheek and lips, and indeed whose whole appearance, did not tend to make him formidable, from the idea they gave that he was suffering under severe illness. As may have been concluded, he was no other than Captain Walsingham, who having been disturbed out of a sweet vision of Ellen Danvers, by hearing an unusual noise, started up, and instantly heard an oath in a strange voice, accompanied with threats. Danger to the beloved of his heart was the first notion of Charles, and seizing his sword, and a brace of pistols, which lay beside his bed, weak as he was, arose and hurried to the door. Although, even in that short distance, he staggered, as the blood mounted to his head, and his feeble limbs almost refused to carry him, yet the image of Ellen used brutally by midnight ruffians so nerved and excited him, that each instant he acquired a factitious power, and when he perceived the Miser, and immediately afterwards the maiden, (for it was no other than her he loved who flung herself into his arms,) the proud spirit subdued the weakness of the clay, and the soldier stood with flashing face and hand grasping his faithful weapon as firmly and as formidably as ever in the battle field.

The first impulse of the gallant Captain was to kill Everard

2 F

Walsingham; and so true was his aim and so excellent the work-
manship of his pistol, that at so short a distance, the destruction
of that man would have been inevitable; but to his surprise, he
found that the stranger was an object of more than suspicion to
other persons, and that he did not seem in any way unfriendly
to him.

"Do not tremble, dearest," whispered Charles to Ellen, clasping her fondly to his breast, while she, terrified beyond the preservation of decorum, clung to the being in whom her young
afflictions were beginning to centre, as if for protection to herself,
and safety to him.

"I did not expect this, Bess," muttered the gigantic robber
to his colleague, who seemed at least equally indecisive. "What
shall I do, Bess?—Shoot that long one there, at any rate?"

"No, no," was the reply, "don't be rash," adding—"My
friends! you must know that this tall gentleman and myself are
in search of gold, silver, diamonds, or any other valuable substances, whether in rubies, emeralds, carbuncles, or even pearls.
So, whatever articles may be in your possession of such a description, we shall be infinitely indebted to you if you will deliver
up to us, without any fuss, and I promise on the word of a man
of honour that no harm shall come to you. If, on the contrary,
you oppose us, we have pistols and must use them, by sending a
bullet with our compliments to those empty heads which have not
wit enough to keep such brains as are in them safe and sound.
There is something in the business we don't exactly understand;
but as our only object is to possess ourselves——"

"Curse your insolence!" here interrupted Charles Walsingham, and levelling his pistol at the last speaker, that facetious
gentleman prudently retired a pace or two. The soldier continued—"If you do not instantly retire I shall discharge this
pistol."

While he was yet speaking, the gigantic housebreaker, imagining perhaps he should intimidate the invalid, fiercely advanced,
and threatened to blow out his brains,—a menace which was
practically returned by Charles, who fired at the head of the giant,
who was only saved from death, by stumbling and falling down.

He was on his legs again in an instant, and returned the fire;
but to his indignation and surprise his own companion, as he did

so, knocked up his arm, and the ball pierced the ceiling above the head of his assailant, whose faintness was now returning over him, in spite of all the desperate energies he had summoned to his assistance.

"No murder, Peter!" exclaimed the individual who had prevented the effectual transmission of the bullet; "we shall have it all our own way, directly. See! the pale man is reeling now; he is a brave fellow at any rate."

Sense had by this time deserted the sick soldier, and sinking against the wall, his sword fell from his hand. Simultaneously with the insensibility of Charles, the Miser, who thought that his time had arrived, sprang forwards, and seizing the arm of the giant, cried—

"Those papers! Give them to me, and I will reward you handsomely."

But the ruffian hurled him violently away, and said to his companion—

"You are right, Bess. Go and secure those valuables, and then we'll be off at once. I'll keep guard here. All that *we* care for is the *swag*. I don't understand that queer chap I've just sent sprawling there, and if he has any more of his impudence, I'll give him cold lead for his supper."

But the Miser was not so easily to be shaken off, and renewing his importunity, he said—

"What will you take for the papers you have got? They can be of no use to you, and—and I will give you anything in reason for them."

"Who the devil are you?" inquired the robber curiously. "I think I've seen you before somewhere. I suppose you are one of the chaps in the plot; but how do you know I have got the papers? Let me see—hum! What's your name, old boy?"

"That can be of no consequence to you," returned the Miser. "I only want the papers, for which I will give you £300; or if that is not sufficient, I will undertake—to double it to-morrow."

"O, you've got £300 about you in hard cash, eh? Give the blunt to me, and you shall have the papers—when I've done with them; I will not take £3000 now—nor even six."

"My excellent fellow! just calmly consider! Who will believe any statements that you may make? Who but will believe those

papers are forged documents, if they proceed directly, or even indirectly through channels which cannot be relied on. On the
other hand, honour, wealth, the station you have lost—for I see
that you are no vulgar robber—you may obtain if——"

" O, you be d—d, with your gammon and humbug;" responded
the housebreaker. "Come out with the £300, I've got plenty to
do, and little time before morning to do it in; if you don't instantly fork out, I'll run you through your lean carcase by——"

" No," answered the Miser, firmly; "not unless the documents
in your possession are delivered."

" We shall see about that," returned the fellow, suddenly rushing upon him, and before he could make any resistance, whirling
him round and throwing him to the ground, when kneeling on his
chest, despite his menaces, he ransacked his pockets.

By this time the other robber, who had vanished before the
Miser had made the vain attempt to regain the documents, had
returned, bearing various articles of value, and gazing at the still
insensible soldier and Ellen, who, with quivering hands and trembling frame was attempting, but fruitlessly, to restore him to life,
said compassionately—

" We've got enough here, Peter; don't touch the poor girl,
who, I dare say, has nothing about her."

" Very well," answered the gigantic rascal, bestowing a kick
on the prostrate Miser, and springing away; "have you secured
what I told you?"

" Yes, it's all right. Let us be off at once." And with these
words, the burglars took their departure.

The Miser, however, persevered in his endeavour to recover
the documents which implicated the safety of so many, and even
when the tall robber had foot in stirrup seized him by the arm;
but he was rewarded for his temerity by a blow dealt with the
butt-end of a heavy horse-pistol, which bereft him of life and
motion for some time; and when he recovered, no trace of the
burglars was left, and he found a pool of blood issuing from a
deep, if not dangerous wound, in his head. Dispirited and dejected by the result of his great and useless exertions, as well as by
the money he had lost, and the injury his cranium had sustained,
Everard Walsingham crawled away, and having with much difficulty reached a hay-stack at the distance of about half a mile

from the cottage, he ensconced himself in it, and was soon in a sleep which lasted till morning. Meanwhile Ellen Danvers was unremitting in her devoted attentions to the poor soldier, who was only insensible from excessive over-exertion in his debilitated state. If he could but have seen how the maiden wept over him—how she clasped his cold fingers in her little hand, pressing them to her lips and calling him kind names—friend, brother, protector. She thought him dead at one time, and then despair and agony were painted on her young forehead, and she called upon Heaven to restore him to life, and her own soul seemed ready to depart with anguish. Those few brief, yet long and lingering moments of suspense, dread, grief, terror and anxiety, did more for the love of the soldier than weeks spent in the common prosecution of a suit in ordinary circumstances. From that hour Ellen was all his own.

When he opened his eyes, she uttered a joyous cry, and murmured a prayer of gratitude. "Thank God !" she exclaimed, "you are saved !" And she burst into a violent and irrestrainable passion of tears.

"And you are safe !" whispered Charles, faintly. "Ellen, my own Ellen! First, last, best beloved !"

CHAPTER II.

Juan yet quickly understood their gesture,
    And being somewhat choleric and sudden,
Drew forth a pocket pistol from his vesture,
    And fired it into one assailant's pudding.
Don Juan, Canto XI.

Here is a woman now I warrant you,
Would sup with Satan, and her face by his—
Lit by the fires of Pandemonium—would
Look darker than the Arch-Fiend's! She is all
Blackness and wickedness, mind, heart and shape.
Old Play.

ELIZABETH HAINES AND HER ADVENTURE—MOTHER STOKES
AND THE ATTEMPTED ASSASSINATION—THE MONSTER.

THE dignified Mistress Elizabeth Haines, after quitting the
house of Danvers, half repented her of having left the gallant
warrior, and the tender, innocent, and confiding Ellen alone together; but as she hoped to be able to return in the course of a
few hours, she banished all misgivings from her mind, and when
she reached the nearest village, inquired for some one to officiate
as attendant on Captain Walsingham in her absence; but an
epidemic was raging in the place, and she could not induce any
person to leave the friends and relatives who were stretched on
the bed of sickness. As she dared not delay any longer, she
hired a vehicle to take her a few miles on her journey; but she
had not proceeded very far, when the miserable horse attached

to the cart in which she was sitting struck his foot against a large
stone that lay in the road, and was lamed so badly, that there
was not the slightest chance of his being able to render any service for many days.

Under these circumstances, Elizabeth, who though not a
young, was an extremely active woman, and accustomed to use
her legs, thought that she might make as good speed with them,
as if she waited until another horse could be procured, and quitting the crazy machine to which she had somewhat recklessly
entrusted her limbs, it being an excellent match to the disabled
brute, and as ancient as the date of such vehicles' introduction
into England, she stepped briskly forwards at the rate of four
miles an hour; and nothing occurred to impede her progress,
until she arrived at a sequestered spot, where the wild plants and
ugly and misshapen trees were thickly interwoven, and the bushes
and brambles were so dense as to prevent a passage through them.
As she was about to leave the rectangular road which she had
hitherto pursued, and strike into a circuitous path, which was so
very precipitous and rocky, that it would have been difficult for
a horse to ascend it, she happened to cast her eyes in the direction of some underwood which grew to her right, and was startled
by perceiving an object with which she was familiar. She hastened to the spot, and examining that which had attracted her
attention more closely, was certain that it had formed a portion
of the dress of Harry Danvers. There were marks of strife and
violence, and some blood on the ground and among the bushes,
as if a person had been dragged along in a wounded condition;
but these abruptly ceased, nor could Elizabeth discover any farther trace to aid her in her search. "Good God!" she exclaimed,
"some dire misfortune has befallen Harry—perhaps they have
killed him! O, he has been recognised by some of the minions
of the detested Elector of Hanover, and on his resisting, they have
murdered him! It must be so—Ah! what is this?" (picking up
something which lay on the ground)—"A heavy stick, with blood
and hair on it—that fair brown hair! it must be his! My poor
Harry! And yet he would not have received a blow from such a
weapon, if he was attacked by such as I was inclined to suspect.
Some darker agency is at work. I feel assured, that the malig-
nity of personal spite pursues Walter and those that belong to

him. He has many enemies;—but who knows him? Who
could have done this?" Cogitating thus, the ears of Elizabeth
were assailed by the neighing of a horse, and presently an animal,
in which she instantly recognised that which Harry usually rode,
cantered up to her and peered with friendliness into her face.

"This may possibly afford a clue," thought Mistress Haines,
as she patted the creature's neck. "This is a sagacious animal,
and attached to his master—Heaven grant he is yet alive!" But
the horse could not render any assistance to Elizabeth, further,
than on a gesture from her, he walked up to a spot where there
was a quantity of grass, and where he had been tied to a tree,
but having broken away, had been wandering disconsolately about,
until he perceived an old acquaintance.

"I am afraid I am only losing time," muttered Mrs. Haines to
herself. "I will mount this animal and hasten to ascertain the
fate of Walter, and then I shall soon learn whether Harry is in
the power of the lawful authorities, or not. If he have fallen—
vengeance alone remains. O, how I pant for the hour when my
deep and irremediable injuries shall be wiped away in the blood
of the false king and his slaves. My husband—my son—both
slaughtered! Widowed and childless, my whole life shall be con-
secrated to the one great object for which I suffer on—the restoration of that family to their legitimate rights, from which I am
myself sprung. Alas! I am a lone and withered thing! My
green hopes have perished; the verdant boughs which grew up
around me, and gave me back my blithe and radiant youth, in
hope, and promise, and beauty—all gone—all broken, and decayed!" And the stern woman's eyes filled with tears, as the
sense of the extreme desolation of her condition entered her heart;
but she dashed them hastily away, apparently almost with shame,
and with masculine agility mounting the horse of Harry Danvers,
hastened to repair to the village in which the Britannia Inn was
situated.

As she entered a narrow lane, however, extending from a desolate common to the place she was going to, a female of low
stature and swarthy face, the expression of which was not the
most attractive in the world, suddenly met her, and cried,

"What are you doing with that horse?" Then, seeming to

think she had said both too much and too little, added, " I saw
a gentleman tie that beast to a tree, a short time ago."

" Ha !" exclaimed Elizabeth, watching the changes depicted
on the countenance of the hag, " do you know aught of the
owner ?"

The female was evidently disconcerted at the directness of this
interrogatory, but replied, after a minute, with excessive effrontery, " Whether I know him or not is nothing to you. The law
won't allow you to seize on every horse you may find."

" I am perfectly aware of that fact," rejoined Mistress Haines
with composure; " but *I do* know the owner, and if he is not
speedily forthcoming, I shall take measures for your apprehension. It is evident you are acquainted with something relative to
the young gentleman I refer to———" Before she concluded
this sentence Elizabeth perceived that the woman was fumbling
for something in her dress, and anticipating her intention she
produced a pistol which she carried, and said, " I am accustomed to use fire-arms, and if you dare to raise a finger against
me, I will shoot you instantly."

The hag had indeed intended to act on the offensive against
Mrs. Haines; but finding that she had so resolute a person to
deal with, dissembled, and exclaimed, " I am a poor, decrepid
old creature, and can do no harm to you. I know nothing of the
owner of this horse, I have told you already; so I wish you a
good day ;" and thus saying, was hobbling away, but Elizabeth
prevented her by levelling her pistol, and exclaiming,

" Move one step, until I permit you so to do, and I will kill
you. I am persuaded you are fully aware of the fate of the gentleman I am seeking, and I see that your gown is stained with
blood ! You may well start !"

Here the suspected individual applied her fingers to her mouth,
and produced a shrill whistle, the design of which was not immediately perceptible; but Elizabeth was on her guard, and
fearing lest the female might have allies at hand, she thought it
most prudent to bring the affair to an end, and in a calm, commanding tone, said,

" I am not to be intimidated by anything you can do. Tell
me without delay what has become of the youth to whom this
horse belongs, or, by heaven !" and she menaced the woman with

the pistol she held. But a sound of swift feet approaching now
alarmed the Amazonian lady, and dreading lest she should. be
destroyed, and all knowledge of the fate of Harry thus oblite-
rated, she forced the beast she rode to gallop off.

"No, no," exclaimed the swarthy hag, ferociously, "it's my
turn now. I've got a pistol here; and you shall find I can use
it, if you don't stop, my stately dame!"

This threat was disregarded by Elizabeth, who with the nerves
of a man combined the long and practical experience to be acquired in camps and with those whose trade is war.

Not ignorant of the advantage of being mounted, she charged
her adversary, who had thrown herself in her way, and who fled
as she did so: but instantly turning round, fired, and succeeded
in wounding her terribly, though not dangerously, in the body.
But the pain of the wound did not retard the dauntless Elizabeth,
who, as the lane was only just wide enough to admit her horse to
thread it, without pains and caution, knocked down the other and
trampled on her as she went.

"Pursue her, boy!" vociferated the hag, hoarsely, and breathing with difficulty from the effect of the injuries she had sustained
from the horse: "she reels in the saddle, look! After her quick,
and knock her brains out if she should fall!"

But though sick from pain and the bleeding at her side, which
the ball had penetrated, Elizabeth maintained her seat: and it
was most fortunate that she could do so, and that her steed was
swift of foot; for a strange form was chasing her with the nim-
bleness of a forest beast in pursuit of prey. But she was sensible
that she could not long retain her faculties; for her head swam
and ice seemed gathering around her heart, while the muscles
almost refused to do their office ; and it was only by a fixed and
desperate exertion of mind, that she prevented herself from falling.
Another minute, and all would have been over with her, for her
pursuer was armed with a club, and appeared bent on destroying
her; when a figure which wanted a large portion of its proper
stature, from the absence of legs, entered the lane through a hedge
which shut out a corn-field, and as he did so, Mrs. Haines dropped
from the horse—which with true military training directly stood
still—and was caught in his arms. The wild creature, in whom
an old acquaintance will possibly be detected, did not hesitate

long how to act; but uttering a savage yell of exultation, sprang forwards, and aimed a blow with his club at the head of the life-less woman. The cripple perceived the savage's intention before it could be executed, and raising a thick cudgel which he carried, dextrously parried the blow, and with right good-will in his turn aimed another at the monster. He was immediately attacked with tiger-like rage and fierceness, and was compelled to deposit his inanimate burthen on the earth, and to defend himself against the miscreant. Though deprived of a considerable portion of his materiality, the cripple was not in the least weakened by his mis-fortune, and with a powerful arm, and excellent skill in the use of his cudgel, bestowed a severe drubbing on his wild foe. Still the monster, with the pertinacious courage of a bull-dog, refused to retreat, and the cripple was preparing to deal him a blow on the skull, which would probably have determined the contest by breaking that indispensable appurtenance, when a harsh voice screamed—

"What, Samuel Stokes, would you kill your own son?" and continued, while the cripple stood irresolute, "would you kill the poor child of Sally?"

"Whew!" whistled Sam, greatly disconcerted, as the hag, of whom the reader has peradventure formed his conjectures and identified with a most amiable being who has heretofore acted a highly conspicuous part in our drama on manifold occasions, spe-cification of which were supererogatory. "Why, aunt, where the devil did ye come from, and what the deuce d'ye mean by that there?"

"I mean what I say, you graceless, unfeeling, unnatural dog!" returned the reputed witch, breathless with the speed she had made, as well as the previous impression made on her by the horse. "This boy you have been so cruelly beating is yours! O, I could tear your eyes out—you wretch, you villain! The poor lad is almost dead from your treatment. How he is bleeding! Be assured for this I'll have revenge on you! You shall hang on a gallows and be drawn and quartered, hang you! My threats and curses are never in vain. Don't stand gaping there, but go about your business, and never let me see your ugly face again, or I'll scratch it till no one shall know it—I will!"

"But d'ye really mean to tell me, that there brute is mine and

Sally's? O, don't go for to gammon me! I know your old tricks,
Mother Stokes!—Ah, this poor creetur here, who seems badly
hurt, will soon *rekiver*. I wonder who fired that there pistol
which brought me here to see what it was!"

"*I* fired it!" exclaimed Mother Stokes, vehemently; "go,
and blab *that*; do, you villain! You want to have my daughter
for a wife, I hear! I would rather give her to Satan and his imps
for a strumpet!—Off with you, or I'll call them!"

"No, indeed, you black-hearted old wretch!" responded
Stokes, indignantly. "If I *don't* blab I shan't do my duty—you
fired at her, did ye?—Fired at her, did ye?—Shiver my timbers, if you wasn't Sally's mother, I'd kick you from here to h—!
There, I've said it! Be off with ye, at once, or—" (another oath,
which for the sake of our lady-readers shall be omitted, honest
Sam making use of expletives a dozen times in a sentence when
in a passion) "you'll see what I shall do to ye! I'm ashamed to
belong to your blood, I am! The poor creetur's a-opening her
eyes! Don't be alarmed, my good lady! If that old daughter
of a dog there dares to come nigher, she'll repent it, she will!—
How she bleeds, poor soul!—I'd better put her on the horse and
take her to the doctor's!"

"On your peril, do it!" exclaimed Mother Stokes, in a voice
almost suffocated with rage. "I have another loaded pistol here;
and I swear I will shoot you, if you were fifty times my nephew,
if you don't leave this woman to me, and promise never to divulge
the secret that I wounded her. You know me, Samuel! I'm a
desperate person, and now have gone too far to retreat."

"A fig for your ball and gunpowder," responded Sam, contemptuously. "I've been in twenty actions with cannon-balls
a-flying about my head by dozens and hundreds, and d'ye think
I care a d—n for a pistol in the hand of such a—" (a complimentary
epithet not in the 'Elegant Extracts,') "as you? Think you're
lucky I don't take you afore a justice. It ain't because you're
my aunt, as I doesn't do so, I promise ye!"

The hag found it was necessary to change her note, and with a
violent effort of mind swallowing the abuse which she longed to
retort, said in a wheedling, fawning tone—

"Nay, Sam, now, I was only in joke. You know I am your
own aunt, and the mother of your cousin Sally. It wasn't I that

wounded the female. Come, my dear boy, go along with you; and if you won't say a word of this business, I'll promise to make Sally your's again."

"O, you wicked old devil!" exclaimed Sam, whose incorruptible integrity was perfectly proof against the temptation with which he was assailed. "D'ye think I'd have Sal, much as I love her, if so be she wasn't willing herself? I don't think as I could take even Heaven itself as a gift from you. Go off. I shall take this poor, wounded person to have her hurts seen to, and you may think yourself precious well off, if I don't tell who did them."

"But Sam—but Sam!" said Mother Stokes, beseechingly, "hear me——"

"Don't Sam me," interrupted the sailor, as he raised Elizabeth, who was now in some measure recovered, in his sturdy arms, and was going to place her on the horse again.

"Nay then," exclaimed the hag, losing all command over herself, and firing at her nephew, but only grazing his head with the bullet. Scarcely had the report of the pistol subsided, when another person appeared on the scene of action, and the atrocious Mother Stokes no sooner saw him, than she fled, and was accompanied by the sorely-beaten savage.

"O, Master Francis, is it you, sir?" said Sam, who scarcely turned away as the pistol was discharged at him; "I'm a-going to the doctor's with this poor creetur, who's badly hurt. She's a-coming to her senses now. How d'ye feel, mum? You're safe and with friends."

As he spoke Mrs. Haines regained her faculties, and casting her eyes on the new comer, she cried—

"That must be a Walsingham! Young gentleman, I claim your assistance. Where is that woman?"

"O, she's off! don't be alarmed," said Samuel. "We'd better go, and get your hurts seen to at once, for them pistol balls sometimes play old gooseberry in the body. D'ye feel well enough to ride on, mum?"

The young man Mrs. Haines addressed now spoke—

"I am in ignorance of all that has previously passed, madam, but whatever help I can render, is yours."

"I fear that some foul deed has been recently perpetrated,"

returned Elizabeth, speaking with difficulty from the pain of the
wound, "and I would ask you to inquire into it. I fear that I
shall not be able to act now, with the requisite promptitude. If
you are the person I take you to be, young sir, I knew your father
well; and if you are as like one of the bravest men that ever lived,
in nature as in person, you will not refuse to grant a boon to a
helpless woman."

"I am Francis Walsingham," returned the youth, who was the
same mentioned in a former chapter as unexpectedly making his
appearance before Mr. Stokes, and with a heightened colour, as
he uttered his name, "and whatever service, consistent with the
honour of a gentleman, I can do you, I repeat, I will."

"Many thanks! Proceed to the nearest magistrate, and procure a warrant to seize on the person of that woman who wounded
me. I accuse her of some vile practice against the life or safety
of one Harry Danvers. Lose no time in doing this, while I get
my wound dressed, when I will make a deposition. Pray, come
to me, when you have been to the magistrate's; and Heaven reward you."

Exhausted with giving utterance to so many words, Mrs.
Haines suffered Samuel to place her on the horse, and he having
mounted behind, in order to support her, they repaired to the
nearest apothecary's, after Sam in an under-tone to young Francis Walsingham had pronounced, "The woman is Mother
Stokes." Meanwhile, that estimable lady, stricken with terror,
without waiting to form any plan of procedure, attended by the
savage, who was surly and sore with bruises, left the lane, and
crawled into the corn-field, which she hastily crossed, and followed
a path that took her away from her own home. Abating not her
speed, she sought the most unfrequented roads, and carefully
avoided every human being, until the shades of night began to
descend. Dire were the passions raging in her heart; but fear
was that which now urged her on, and made even revenge subordinate. But when on coming to a part of the country with which
she was acquainted, she found she was many miles from the locality
where the rencontre with Elizabeth had taken place, she ventured to seek the repose which her weary limbs needed, and to
deliberate on the best line of policy for the future.

"I must not return to my hut," she thought, "for they will

be sure to seek me there ; but they will not find the lad—ha, ha !"
And she laughed devilishly. "No one knows where to find him,
and he will starve to death. O, Master Walter! good news for
you." Having chuckled over this pleasant picture, she added to
herself—"And that woman and my nephew! I must wreak a full
revenge on them! O, that I had all my foes in my power! The
tortures I have heard of in foreign countries should be nothing to
the agonies I would devise for my victims. They should drag on
years of insufferable misery of mind and body, and eat the most
loathsome things that crawl the earth."

She finished with a mental oath, and was looking round to see
if there were any water near to assuage the thirst she felt, when
the savage uttered a cry, which she knew was of alarm. She
started up and listened. Yes, there were shouts of pursuit.
They had tracked her. She heard the galloping of horses; and
renewing her flight, still followed by the monster, hastened into
a thicket, in order to seek concealment.

Having gained the shelter where she hoped to remain undiscovered, Mother Stokes rapidly glanced round her, in order to
form a correct judgment of her exact position, and the amount
of difficulty there must be, in eluding the vigilance of pursuit.
It never for an instant struck her that she might have been mistaken in her supposition with regard to her peril from those who
were on the alert to detect and apprehend some person, and thus,
like many other guilty people, from precipitation and terror, took
the very means for exciting suspicion, by the timidity which she
displayed. The trees, though they did not grow to any extraordinary height, in her lurking-place, were of adequate density for
all purposes of concealment; but she did not calculate on any
other than the common and usual means of pursuing fugitives
from those she was in dread of, and so she couched down, together
with the savage, hoping the enemy would soon abandon the
search. On a sudden, after the lapse of a few minutes, her
wild companion arose, and running a few paces from the spot,
picked up something which he brought to his mistress, who, on
inspection, found that it was a hat of antique construction, and
not at all beautified by wear; and, indeed, it was so altogether
remarkable, that she was certain it was one she had before seen
on the head of a person with whom she was acquainted. An

idea flashed upon her, produced by an association connected with this object; and she thought "If I am taken I will betray the Miser, and so procure my own pardon. That woman whom I wounded must be a friend of Danvers. He is implicated in the treason which I intended should turn out profitably for me, and so the government will not care for her, should she die; and I have nothing to fear, unless they should discover the cave and search it; and, even then, there is no positive proof against me. But still I would much rather no inquiry should be made; I would not willingly be examined before a magistrate—"

Even as she was thus cogitating, she perceived the glittering of steel through the trees, as the moon shed more than common lustre on the earth, and suppressing a cry of alarm, was about to fly in the opposite direction, when the savage prevented her, and with his finger pointed out a similar cause for apprehension in the point whither she was about to repair. The noise of arms became more and more distinct, and at length the hag perceived she was gradually being hemmed in by soldiers, and that there was no possibility of escape.

All her terrors returned upon her with aggravated intensity, and creeping into a hollow tree she hid herself there, the wild boy still accompanying her. What dreadful moments of suspense are those which are passed in such a manner! The agonized doubts, the hopes and fears alternating, and minutes appearing to grow into hours. It is possible that anticipation may be more terrible than reality. And now the circle which the military had made was circumscribed to a few dozen yards, and she heard them beating the bushes with their swords.

"He is not here, that I can see," observed an officer. "I think he must have found some means of eluding us—though how I cannot guess, without there be some other subterraneous passage. I suppose we may as well conclude the search. After all, we know not whether we were correct in our conjectures concerning the man. He is a rascal, I make no doubt, but perhaps not the sort of one we want."

" Please your honour," exclaimed a non-commissioned officer, as the last speaker was just issuing the word of command to the dragoons to return to their horses, " here's a woman's shoe I've found.'

"A woman's shoe, you blockhead. And what the devil is that to me?"

"Why, sir, you see—hem—that though it's a man we are looking after—"

"Tut, tut, you stupid fellow, do you think he'd wear women's shoes?"

This dialogue had greatly relieved the mind of Mother Stokes, who had been listening intently to all that was passing. From the first moment when it was mentioned that a man was the object of pursuit, she knew that she could not be the person sought for; and she now recovered from the consternation into which she had been thrown, and began to devise the best method of acting. If she could have invented any plausible tale to account for her being where she was, she would have instantly left her hiding-place, lest she might still be discovered; but when she considered how suspicious were the circumstances of her position, and how probable it was she might be subjected to a further examination were she to make her appearance, after having palpably endeavoured to avoid observation, she resolved on remaining quiet and waiting the issue of events. But she was not allowed to exercise free will in the matter; for one of the soldiers thrust his sword, happily in the scabbard, into the hollow of the tree in which she was lurking, and struck the mouth of the savage with such force as to knock out two or three of his huge teeth, upon which, with a howl of rage and pain, he rushed out and retaliated on his unintentional assailant, by striking him with his club ferociously, and causing him to measure his length on the earth. But a dozen powerful hands were instantly laid upon him, and he was dragged into the midst of the soldiery amid jeers and cries of wonderment at his uncouth and strange appearance. Mother Stokes, convinced that she should be detected if she remained in the tree, now emerged from it, and made an attempt at an obeisance to the officer who had first spoken. In her hurry she had left behind her shoe, and as she had consequently but one, it seemed certain that she was the owner of that which had been just found.

"Well, we have a queer pair here, by Jove!" cried the chief of the party, no other than Norton's second in command, "Beauty and the beast—ha, ha?"

"An it please your honour," returned Mother Stokes, to whom this question was directed, " I am a poor, lone, widow woman, and this unhappy boy you have here—"

" Boy! I thought he was a brute. Do you mean to say he is really human, then ?"

" Yes, sir, he is a human being, and without the gift of speech. But he has been my faithful companion all his life, and I hope you won't do him any harm. We had just laid ourselves down to rest in that tree, and were fast asleep, when he had his teeth knocked out. We are homeless, and without money, and so we were going, as we often do, to pass the night where we were."

But the officer was by no means satisfied with this account.

" I must take you before a magistrate," he said, " your story, it is plain, is false. The noise which we have been recently making must have aroused you from any sleep, and the fact of your having left your shoe, as if in haste, looks bad. So you must both of you jump up behind two dragoons."

Mother Stokes finding that expostulation would be vain, sullenly yielded to necessity, and was taken up, not without grumbling, by a soldier, as soon as the troop was re-mounted. The savage likewise shared a similar fate, and having been deprived of his club, and his long arms pinioned, the troop proceeded at a brisk pace towards the county town for which it was destined. Mother Stokes deliberated whether it might not be her best plan without delay to reveal what she knew of the plot in which the Miser was involved to the commanding officer, especially as, from having found his hat, and the soldiers being in pursuit of some suspected person, it was probable her intelligence might be forestalled—and dreaded lest such should have been the case. But she was unacquainted with the officer's rank, and knew not if he had the power of giving any pledge for her safety, if she communicated her knowledge, which he could redeem ; and although she endeavoured to extract information from the soldier she rode with, the fellow was so surly at being obliged to have such an ugly old witch in his immediate proximity, that he only answered with oaths. The march was thus continued till midnight; and the troop had nearly reached its destination, when a horseman rode up to the commander, and spoke to him in a hurried tone. The officer uttered an exclamation of surprise, and then shouted,

"Right about face! We shall have some bloody work to-night, lads! The Jacobites are up in arms, and now within ten miles of us, in some force; but if they want to fight, we are the men to give them a bellyfull of hard blows!"

CHAPTER III.

This smooth discourse and mild behaviour oft
Conceal a traitor—something whispers me
All is not right. Beware of Lucius.—*Cato.*

Right loyal heart! This is a friend indeed—
A friend to feel for and remove the evil.
He who will sit contentedly to meat,
And reason calmly on a friend's distress,
Who dares not speak his thoughts with boldness out,
May give you wise advice, but nothing more.
Old Play.

THE MEETING OF THE JACOBITES — THE EMISSARY—JOHN
NORTON—THE FLIGHT.

IN a large and dreary apartment, the walls of which were covered with dust-begrimed portraits of grim old warriors and stately dames of the 16th and 17th centuries, and also with arms of various descriptions, such as the lance, the battle-axe, and the unwieldy two-handed sword, which had done service possibly in the wars of Palestine, together with the mace, the bow, the shield, and others, the use of which had long been exploded, with some rusty suits of armour and banners, which were victorious trophies, and were now dropping to pieces with age, were assembled a number of men, exceeding perhaps a score, in deep and earnest council. They were of all ages and of divers conditions, though very few were not entitled to rank among gentlemen. There was the proud and venerable nobleman, with his white hair and regular features, his tall stature, and his erect carriage, all demonstrative of his ancient lineage, and the innate and hereditary haughtiness of his nature. There was the stalwart 'Squire, with his sunburnt cheek and ruddy complexion, his broad and open chest and firm step, good nature, strength and manhood being impressed on his whole looks, countenance, and bearing. Of this latter description by far the greater number of the meeting was composed ; but here and there a sturdy yeoman, with the same general outward characteristics as the burly squire, but yet with more vulgarity of feature and figure, might be seen, while one common interest and one common danger levelled for a time the distinctions of rank ; and in their zeal for the cause they were met to support, the prejudices of class and station were forgotten. It need hardly be added, that this was an assemblage of Jacobites, convened for the purpose of carrying on some systematic operations for the restoration of the house of Stuart to the monarchy.

At the period in question, like almost every other period in the history of the world, there were numerous discontented spirits, ever ready to catch at change, for the mere sake of novelty, regardless of the consequences of revolution ; and in the efforts which were making in the cause of the royal exiles, the sincerity, and the heartfelt attachment and loyalty of their adherents was limited to a very small number. Nevertheless there was a sufficiency of general murmuring and sedition in the country to warrant the hope, that in any disorganization of the existing order of things, the conspiracy would become a popular movement ; and the subtle machinations of the Jesuits, and of the Roman Catholic denomination, almost universally, were unremittingly at work, for the destruction of the Hanoverian succession ; and while they fomented discontent among the masses, and secretly introduced dissension into the counsels of the deliberative assemblage of the nation—those representatives numbering among them members favourable to the ancient line of kings—the animosity of party spirit, and the rancour of religious bigotry, together with the envy and jealousy excited by the partiality of the reigning sovereign for foreign satellites, envenomed the minds of many of the higher orders, who by the persuasions of foreign emissaries became so disaffected, and so allured by the promises held out to them, that

they only awaited a favourable opportunity for throwing off
allegiance to George the First, and declaring for the Pretender.

Having thus cursorily remarked on the state of feeling that
subsisted in the country, and the elements in activity for rebellion, it may be as well to particularise the motive of the council
which had been assembling in the house of a fervent Jacobite on
the evening specified. The failure of the rising in 1715, in favour of the Stuarts, having damped the ardour, and depressed
the spirits and energies of those who were desirous that the direct line of the ancient monarchs should be rectified; it was a
matter of no very easy practicability to reanimate that high-pres-
sure enthusiasm, which the fate of the disastrous insurrection had
annihilated in the least sanguine, and diminished in others;
and although a numerous body of agents, foreign and otherwise,
had been employed for this purpose, the want of money and extensive influence of the great body of fervent Jacobites paralysed
the effect of the eloquence of the subtle and artful men selected
to accomplish the work in the hearts of those it was wished should
join the combination re-organizing against the house of Hanover.
A number of these foreign emissaries in England had suggested
the expediency of converting those not unfavourable to their
cause into available partisans, in order to collect as much money
as possible,—monetary resources, as affording the means of
bribery and corruption, being the chief means on which they relied,—for the carrying on and the better regulation of the movement; and several of these, sly, dark, keen-eyed individuals, for
the most part of foreign aspect, were collected in the chamber in
a little knot, which as soon as it dispersed, cunningly, and no
doubt by preconcertion, contrived that each member should
monopolise the attention of two or three of the most influential
persons present; and proceeded with caution to break to them
the necessity for an immediate outlay of their pecuniary assistance, to be repaid them, with a high rate of interest, as soon as
the restoration of the exiled family could be effected.

Perfectly aware, however, of the necessity for extreme circum-
spection in their exertions, where they tended to deprive their
partisans of the wealth which they so dearly prized, and anxious
in no way to damp the zeal of those adherents, and of others
less ardent in the cause, by a display of the narrowness of the

finances they possessed for the effectuation of so mighty an object as their ulterior purpose, they proceeded to break the ice with a sophistry and oiliness of tongue which deceived the well-natured country gentlemen to whom they were appealing, by representing that the resources of James Stuart were ample, and that it was a mere momentary pressure of urgent necessity, which rendered this application to them for money expedient. Nothing, however, so sharpens the wits and opens the eyes of the generality of mankind as a demand on their purse-strings; and the agents of the Pretender speedily perceived that the looks of many of their supporters were not at all indicative of satisfaction at the turn which affairs seemed taking against their own private pockets.

"What was the exigency," they murmured to each other, "which so imperatively called for this demand; and why was it not forseen and obviated before? They had no funds among them to be hazarded on some dark and mysterious scheme, which might, it was likely, be frustrated, before it could be ripened."

It was at this juncture that a man of rather diminutive appearance, and of about nine-and-twenty summers, entered the room, and was immediately greeted with a cordial welcome by the emissaries and others who were most zealous in their Toryism, who addressed him by the name of "Hugh Freestone."

"Where is Walter Danvers?" was the general interrogation, addressed to this personage as he proceeded to the centre of the apartment, and helped himself to a glass of wine from a huge bottle which stood upon the table. A physiognomist, by careful perusal of that somewhat sinister countenance, might have detected a lurking shade of displeasure darkening it, as such importance seemed attached to the appearance of the person inquired for: but disguising every outward emotion with a skill which has ever been carried to perfection in the subtle school to which he belonged, Freestone replied,

"He is unavoidably absent, and upon business which is of importance to us all. I should have been with you sooner, but that I have been delayed by two or three persons wavering in their allegiance to his Majesty, King James; and I was anxious to confirm them in their loyalty. Gentlemen, I have gratifying

intelligence to communicate to you collectively—to many, individually. I am commissioned to bear letters—which I will deliver presently—all promising the highest honors and emoluments
from our gracious Sovereign to such of his faithful subjects as
peril themselves for—"

"Ay, *promises!* Fine words butter no parsnips," observed
a coarse yeoman, who had been indulging in liquor, and grumbling, at the attempt on his purse.

Freestone appeared dubious whether to notice this interruption, and cast rapid and furtive glances to his coadjutors, to
gather their opinion ; but his glance wandering to others, and
observing that it did not fall without weight on the majority of
the meeting, and seemed to represent their sentiments on the subject, he said,

"A friend has been pleased to tell you that *promises* are all
which our Royal Master gives. I would ask the gentleman whether he is so unreasonable as to suppose that before he is re-
seated on his ancestral throne, our gracious monarch would
choose to make any large disbursement, save for the *general* good
of the cause ? But, indeed, a very considerable sum is actually
in the hands of Captain Danvers, and jewels to the value of
£3000, which have been sent by ladies of distinction to evince
their attachment, will be added to the treasury without delay.
Yet surely it behoves us to do something more than *talk* of our
willingness to serve his Majesty ! Let us unite heart and hand,
and endeavour to extend the influence of our party through all
the land. The measures proper to be adopted must be on so
large a scale as to require a supply of money commensurate with
the greatness——"

" No humbug !" here again interrupted the sturdy fellow who
had before, under the stirring power of drink, so freely expressed
his feelings. "Be more explicit, Master Freestone—we won't
grope in the dark."

" Our friend has evidently been quaffing of the best country
ale," remarked Freestone, annoyed at the bluff yeoman's bold
speaking, particularly as he found it more powerful than an
appeal of greater eloquence and less genuineness would have
been, while the pertinacity of the man's nature, he felt, was not
to be subdued by—what is expressively termed, now-a-days,

" flummery," or bullying. " I request him, for the sake of cour-
tesy, and if he be indeed sincere in his devotion to the interests
of our lawful King, to hear me with patience, and to be ' silent
that you may hear.' I will now proceed to peruse to you a
general letter from his Majesty, signed and sealed by himself, in
which he thanks you for all your noble and disinterested loyalty,
and when, by the grace of God, he again occupies the place
which Heaven and the laws of England entitle him to demand,
he will amply recompense you singly, and——"

While the speaker was yet in the middle of his sentence,
having produced a rather favourable impression on his audience,
more perhaps by the speciousness of his manner than the goodness of his matter, or any overpowering eloquence he possessed,
a person suddenly entered the apartment, and casting his eyes
around, exclaimed,

" Gentlemen, a pressing occasion must excuse ceremony on
my part. Your able and trust-worthy agent, Captain Walter
Danvers, in his untiring endeavours to serve the good cause, has
involved himself in peril; and it becomes us all as *men*, as
friends, and brethren joined in one common fraternity, to extricate him from the dangerous predicament in which he stands.
I need say no more, I am sure. You have swords and hands,
and *hearts* ever ready to throb for those that endanger life for
right against might !"

The new comer was a man of middle age, a trifle below the
ordinary height, and had been perceptibly riding fast and long,
his spurs being incarnadine with the blood of his horse. There
was an instant silence through all the meeting, and some who
were timorous turned pale with apprehension, and others who
were bold knit their brows and compressed their lips ; but many
who composed the assembly were personal friends of Danvers,
and the appeal which had been made to their courage and gallantry was soon visible in their actions. All appeals are effec-
tive where vanity enlists the sympathies.

" Walter Danvers !" ejaculated the emissary Freestone, "this
is indeed unexpected intelligence ! You are certain, Mr. John
Norton, that the news you bring is correct ?"

" There can be no doubt on the subject," answered Norton,
confidently. " I learned as I came hither to inform you that he

was in danger, that he has been made prisoner by a party of dragoons, who are now probably within a few miles of this place. I am sorry to add, that my own brother, who has lately resumed his military functions, after having abandoned them for so many years, is in all likelihood the chief instrument of Danvers' capture."

"We will rescue him or die," exclaimed several individuals warmly.

"Yes, Walter Danvers must be rescued," said Freestone. "But, gentlemen, we must not be either rash, or timorous. The chances of success and failure must be carefully balanced, before we engage in any measure which might inextricably involve the safety of all here present—some of whom have not pledged themselves as yet to support our cause, and whose names must be kept secret. Captain Danvers is one, whose own personal resources are so great, that it is highly probable he may devise some means of escape from the clutches of the enemy; and even if he should not be able to do so, do you think we are justified in endangering our own, our family's, and our king's well-being for his sake?"

This last reference to the selfish interests of the heart, threw a wet blanket on the ardour of the friends of Danvers: and many moved by their own fears and indecision, sneaked away towards the door, that they might quit the room with all speed on an emergency; yet still, with a lingering feeling of shame at the cowardice which prompted their desertion of a friend in the hour of need, remained at the entrance.

But John Norton, who was cordially attached to Walter, determined that a cold-blooded calculation should not sacrifice one whose great and extraordinary energies had been of such essential service to the Jacobite party, although he had no confidence in his own oratorical powers—his capacities of rhetoric and persuasion never having been called into action—urged by the exigency of the case, and endued by it with words and ideas, exclaimed—

"My friends! What you have just heard from Master Hugh Freestone, I own I was totally unprepared for. He said, when he first began to speak, that 'Walter Danvers *must* be rescued!' I reiterate those words again and again! I saw the generous enthusiasm expressed by your looks and gestures before it was

damped by cold and grovelling thoughts, and I am certain that
where it exists in the bosom, an occasion like this *must* call it
forth. You are all well aware of the unremitting efforts of that
gallant warrior—the best and bravest, I do not hesitate to assert,
among the good and brave, who adhere to his majesty King
James—to serve us at desperate risk; and I call upon you, as
men of honour, of feeling, and of courage, not to permit any mere
selfish considerations to interfere with your efforts in his behalf.
Who that is here present has made such exertions, and whose
exertions have been so eminently successful as those of our
absent friend? Remember, if you lose Walter Danvers, you lose
the right hand of our power in this country. He is acquainted
with all the movements of friends and enemies. He has possessed
himself of important information, of which he is the sole repository; and I am convinced, that were his majesty to know the
peril of this faithful servant, he would not for an instant allow
ulterior con——"

"I cannot allow you to proceed, Mr. Norton!" here broke in
Hugh Freestone. "The good of one, can never for an instant
be put in competition with the good of many. And even were
his majesty generous enough to wish us to emperil the success of
his cause, in order to rescue a single instrument of it, however
excellent, should we, his councillors and friends, be justified in
allowing such a procedure, without remonstrance? No. I pledge
my sacred word that whatever can be done to serve Captain
Danvers, with any regard to the interests of King James, shall
not be omitted: but in the prosecution of our great scheme, all
collateral points of regard and feeling must be sacrificed."

This truly Jesuitical speech, which like that of a certain great
living statesman promised "an infinite deal of nothing" not being
satisfactory to honest, straightforward John Norton, he said—

"I must ask you explicitly to state what you will do?"

"I must ask a few moments for thought," replied the emissary, confused at the blunt directness of the question, which did
not allow him a loophole for the exercise of his inventive, two-
meaning faculties. "We must remember the inconceivable importance of every trifling deed at this juncture."

"No," replied Norton, resolutely. "Caution at such a time
as this is but another name for dastardly treachery. Gentlemen,

I stand forth to demand your assistance for our friend Walter
Danvers. That hireling there, who is utterly regardless of the
lives of our best and bravest, I am persuaded, will not sway the
actions of the majority of those here present—of *one* honest heart
which has a throb for friendship, and a drop of English, unpolluted blood, to shed in the cause of manhood. Let those who
prefer their own safety to honour, justice, principle and bravery,
remain behind with Hugh Freestone—the paid agent of the
Jesuits—a coward of mongrel breed, with all the worst qualities
of the French and English character united—I am a plain, blunt
man that loves my friend, and for that friend speak boldly out—
he, who is afraid to venture anything for him who has ventured
all for us—he, who would behold a hero sacrificed for a few
scratches and bruises—he, who would dare to tell you that we
owe nothing to gallantry, that we owe nothing to our noblest bene-
factors :—but let the true men who can feel and dare, let all but
slaves, traitors and dastards follow me."

"Do you dare to call me dastard, John Norton?" cried Freestone, fiercely. "By heaven, sir! you shall live to repent such
words!" And his sallow cheek became flushed with crimson;
but he mastered his passion with wonderful self-control, and was
to all appearance perfectly cool; though there was a storm beneath, the existence of which might only be surmised by a slight
quivering of the thin and bloodless lip.

"I am quite ready to meet you hand to hand, Sir Agent!"
was the rejoinder of John Norton; "but now the cause of Walter
Danvers will not allow me to tarry. My friends, which of you
declares for me?"

Half-a-dozen individuals pressed round him and volunteered
their services, animated by that strong and fiery appeal to their
generosity which simple earnestness had furnished Norton with,
but the remainder, who could not probably have been moved by
the genius of Demosthenes, where their own interests militated
against what they knew became them to do, were moveless.

"'Tis well!" said Norton, "with these brave men, I shall be
able to effect more for Danvers, than if encumbered with those
who have neither a heart to feel, nor a hand to stir for honour's
sake. Freestone! We shall meet again!"

And with these words he was departing; but as his adherents
prepared to follow him, the emissary exclaimed—

"Ye are hastening to your own destruction, rash men! What are ye about to do? The disciplined soldiers of the Elector of Hanover must inevitably put you to flight or destroy you, even if you were equally matched in numbers. Hear me, and do not blindly yield yourselves to the guidance of that madman, whose only excuse for his extravagant conduct is hot-headed and undistinguishing regard for Captain Danvers. Were there the most remote probability that the efforts you meditate making for his rescue could be crowned with success, Hugh Freestone would be the first man to put foot in stirrup and accompany you. But if you will consider the matter dispassionately, you must perceive that the chances are immeasurably against you in every point of view; while ruin and destruction to the common cause must unavoidably ensue, if you persist in this wild and Quixotic enterprise, which I am convinced your cooler judgment must disapprove. Good friends! Noble supporters of a noble king! Return, I beseech you, and do not introduce division into the counsels, which with common care and discretion, will assuredly, sooner or later, triumph. There are many ways of serving Walter Danvers, without having vain recourse to arms; and those who are truly anxious to be of service to him will think discretion may now avail him better than zeal. Think, fathers and husbands, brothers and lovers, of your children, wives, sisters and mistresses—think, if you are taken, as in all human calculation you will be, the agonizing pangs you will inflict—"

"Hear him not," interrupted Norton, who saw tokens of returning indecision among two or three of those who had been about to follow him. "Or if you *do* hear him, recollect that your gallant friend Danvers is a father, and the tyrants of the land will not permit him to live, if they retain him in their grasp. We will not be rash, nor imprudent; but every feeling of honesty, of manhood and of chivalry must speak 'like angels trumpet-tongued,' peremptorily requiring us to render him all the assistance in our power."

Norton finished speaking, and was for a second time moving away, perceiving that his last outburst had been responded to in the hearts of his followers, when a man, pale and breathless, rushed into the council-chamber, and ejaculated—

"They come—the horse—we are discovered—betrayed, and the enemy in strong force are now at hand!"

Having managed to speak thus much, the affrighted messenger, who like a bird of ill-omen among superstitious men, had scattered dismay through the assemblage, paused to recover himself. All was instantaneously confusion and uproar. Swords and fire-arms were grasped; and some proposed resistance to the death; while others less daring were for yielding without a blow; and fruitless were all the attempts on the part of the leaders to restore order; for the panic seemed to have closed the ears of the greater number present; and in spite of vociferation and remonstrance, they ran hither and thither, now preparing for flight, and now for conceal-ment in dismayed and wavering fear and pusillanimity.

What a study for the close observer of human nature is a scene like that I have tried to sketch! How base, how lofty, how vary-ing, are its phases. In some you can observe the high resolve, and undaunted purpose, in some the clinging timidity, the shrink-ing terror; and in others the gross selfishness, which is the vilest cowardice of all. And thus is man in every age, great, mean, and unsteady of purpose; now he shall seem a worm, and now soar into a God. Hamlet's sublime panegyric is half hyperbole.

In the midst of all this hubbub, John Norton maintained the utmost coolness and composure. His was a nature, which with-out partaking of singular exaltation, was bold, firm, and energetic; and his nerves were as unshaken in storm as in calm.

"Brave men! on you again I call!" he cried, unconsciously adopting a measured vehicle for his thoughts, as many others will do, when the bosom swells with strong emotions of heroism and determination. "Follow me!" and added, as he hastened out of the apartment, "Delay at all events is the most dangerous path."

"Here they are!" was the exclamation, as a number of horse-men were seen approaching, as soon as those (who were consi-derably in the minority) who had listened to and approved the promptitude of Norton were in the court-yard where their horses stood.

"These are not regular soldiers," observed Norton, casting a rapid gaze at the advancing enemy—"ah! they are pursued, surely. See how they look behind them! Vault into your saddles, my men, and let us be prepared to act!"

A distant shout was now heard, and the approaching party accelerated their speed.

" Throw open the gates," cried John Norton, " *these* are friends, at all events. I know them now. They are a few who composed a meeting to be held in the open air this night, at the distance of a few miles. Let us be off at once. Our horses have had a rest, and these dragoons you may now see in pursuit, have, I doubt not, ridden far and hard. The moon is behind a cloud, and we shall not be seen in the darkness."

The flying party which had been mistaken for the foe, had now arrived ; but when Norton exclaimed, " I would not advise you to stay, my friends, you will assuredly be attacked by the military if you remain here," they joined him ; and in the course of a few minutes gained the shelter of a wood, just as the planet which had favoured their flight glanced brightly forth, and the dragoons, to the amount of thirty, became perfectly apparent.

" They are certain to attack the house ; but those who are in it are sufficiently numerous to defend it, if they do not yield ; and they have proved themselves so lukewarm and cowardly for their friends, that we are not bound to join issue with them."

As John Norton was yet speaking, the military drew up in a square before the house he and his followers had quitted ; and he, not being interested in the fate of those so cold in their attachment to one whom he admired beyond almost any other of his acquaintance, and whose services he rightly considered had been of inestimable benefit to the conspiracy, put spurs to his horse ; and with his more faithful train, now swelled to double the original number, lost no time in threading the intricacies of the wood.

CHAPTER IV.

A perfect transformation here displayed.—*Don Juan.*

By Jove, he was a noble fellow Johnson,
  And though his name than Ajax or Achilles
Sounds less harmonious, underneath the sun soon
  We shall not see his likeness; he could kill his
Man quite as quietly as blows the monsoon
  Her steady breath (which some months the same still is).
Seldom he varied feature, tone, or muscle,
And could be very busy without bustle.—*Ibid.*

WALTER DANVERS AND GEORGE—PERILOUS SITUATION—THE ESCAPE.

THE readers of this Chronicle may conceive it high time that they should no longer be kept in suspense with regard to the fate of Walter Danvers and George. As the former was on the verge of discovering himself, that he might rescue the child from the peril he was in from the soldier, who was about to hurl stones down the hollow tree, the trampling of horses was heard, and several dragoons, with a serjeant at their head, dashed among the drunken soldiers, and knocking down one or two in their headlong speed, cried vociferously,

" Arm, arm! The Jacobites have risen!"

Simultaneously with this, there arose a cry from the guardhouse (for such was the nature of the building in which Danvers had been incarcerated) of—

" The prisoner has escaped!"

The fugitive cast one look at the tree which the soldier had climbed, and found that he was descending with all expedition. So having only to provide for his own safety, he glanced quickly round, to determine the best means of flight or concealment. But he was at the height of thirty feet from the ground, and even could he have descended, it was hardly possible to escape obser-

vation; while, if he remained where he was, his recapture was
inevitable. He was startled by a whisper close to his ear, and
to his no little astonishment perceived George at his side.

"It is very dark now," said the boy, "and in all this confusion you will not be noticed, if you do as we proposed at first, or
—but trust to me. Hark! They have found out the way you
have escaped, and are breaking through the trap-door!"

George with all celerity jumped on the nearest branch of the
tree close to the building, and fixing the rope to a stronger
bough, threw it to Danvers, who instantly caught it.

"*This* will bear you," said George, in a low but distinct tone
of ventriloquism. Danvers perceived that the rope he held in his
hand was not the old, crazy one, which had previously broken;
and hearing the trap-door yield with a crash to a tremendous
blow from some heavy instrument, favoured by the darkness,
—although several soldiers were still standing immediately below,—reached the bough with a jump, and the boy instantly removing the cord, bade him make for the hollow, from which, he
added, escape was easy.

Scarcely had the fugitive reached the trunk of the tree—the
crash of the boughs having fortunately been unnoticed by the
soldiers below, who were absorbed in conversation—and discovered
the hole through which it was necessary for him to pass, when
he saw many persons gain the top of the house he had just
quitted, evidently expecting to find him there. "He is clean
off!" exclaimed one of the pursuers, while the drum beat to arms,
and the noise, the hubbub and the bustle distracted the keenness
of their wits.

They shouted to those below, whose senses were stupefied by
the libations they had been indulging in, aggravated by the unusual tumult, to close each avenue of escape; while George,
creeping among the branches, was soon again beside his friend,
and whispered, "Descend at once; and I will follow;" just as
one of those at the top of the house suggested that the fugitive
might be lurking in the hollow of the tree, where they actually
were. Danvers, therefore, hastily descended, while the soldiers
on the housetop, finding that they could not get to the tree,
shouted to those below to climb it.

"But I've just been up there, and no one's in it," remarked

the same fellow who had been going to throw stones down the
hollow trunk, " unless—" an idea striking him, and instantly
beginning to ascend, " unless I made a mistake about that there
thingum'y being a owl."

The fugitive by this time was at the bottom of the tree, and
discovered that there was a hole of about the size of a fox's in a
transverse direction there. George had now joined him, and
said, " Creep along, all's right;" and still trusting to the little
fellow's sagacity, he began to crawl quickly away, the boy at his
heels, exactly as the soldier had reached the hollow, and was
hurling stones down it, which fell innocuous behind the child.

" There's a hole, I think, at the bottom of the tree," cried one
on the house-top, " go down and see if the rascal's there." The
soldier being pot-valiant, descended, although he might have
hesitated to have so acted under ordinary circumstances, as he
was one who had witnessed the terrific power of Danvers. But
when he came to the hole, his heart failed him, and he did not
choose to enter it. As it was perfectly dark, too, he could see
nothing; but he threw some stones into it, which fell within a
trifling distance of George, who had not been able to make much
progress, Danvers finding some difficulty in getting on. But they
had not to proceed much farther, and Danvers having crept as
far as the limits of the hole would permit, and finding that he had
come in contact with the earthen walls, whispered,

" Now, what are we to do?"

" You are at the bottom of another tree now," returned
George, " and must climb up with your back and legs; you can
stand upright and will find you can see a ray of light. There—
that's well; now clamber up. You see I came along here the
moment the soldier got up the tree we've left behind, and then I
got down, and managed to climb up to you again, by the side of
the guard-house. Ah! they are crawling down the passage to
us; don't you hear their voices?"

" There is a quantity of hay lying below," exclaimed Danvers,
who was now outside the other tree, " we had better hide there."

" Just what I was thinking of," replied the boy, " make
haste; the darkness will soon be over, and then they would see
us directly."

Danvers accordingly dropped to the ground, and hastened to a

2 K

quantity of new hay, which was at the distance of two or three paces from him; but some person acquainted with the secret of the hole now rushed to the second tree, before little George, who had become entangled with the rope he carried with him, could imitate the example of his companion. The elder fugitive had concealed himself beneath the hay, but left a small hole for his eyes; so that he could perfectly discern all that followed; but where the boy was hiding he could not conjecture.

The darkness, as George had prognosticated would be the case, had now indeed vanished, and all was as bright as noonday, beneath the unusual splendour of the full moon. The pursuers, who had been crawling through the subterraneous passage, by this time were ascending the tree; and no sooner emerged from the hollow than they commenced a scrutiny among all the dense branches for the fugitive. They would very soon probably have discovered him; but a circumstance intervened which diverted their attention.

" He is not here! But what is that I see creeping by the side of that pile of stones?" cried one.

" It is a human being," exclaimed another, and in an instant every individual was chasing the object of suspicion. Now or never was the time for Danvers to escape, and quitting the shelter of the hay, he was making the best use of his legs, when he perceived an intoxicated soldier lying on the ground not three yards before him. A stratagem of war immediately suggested itself to the brain of the fugitive, ever fertile in such expedients, and stripping the drunken wretch with marvellous celerity—and he fortunately being a fat large-made man, so that his clothes were fully capacious enough to cover the broad chest and muscular frame which he owned himself—an exchange was in two or three minutes effected, and he instantly decamped in his metamorphosis. Meanwhile, the others had been giving chase to the person whom they saw creeping behind the pile of stones, who fled at their approach; and plunging into a broad river, which ran within a few furlongs of the guard-house, disappeared below the surface.

" That could not have been a man," observed a soldier, " he looked to my eyes quite a child."

A head was seen above the water for a second, and then

vanished, just as a musket-ball was flying in the air towards it, and those of the military who could swim prepared to jump into the river. Presently the head was seen again, but beyond gunshot; and in the course of another minute, a young boy was observed to quit the stream, gain the opposite banks; and mounting a pony which had been tied to a gate within a few paces of the place where he landed, dash away with a shout of exultation and defiance. That boy was George. Perceiving the man who was acquainted with the secret communication between the trees, as Danvers reached the shelter of the hay, fearing lest by following he might betray him to the pursuers, he dropped on the other side of the huge elm in which he was, and several smaller trees growing in one direction in a straight line, he managed, by darting from one to another, to escape unobserved, until he arrived at the pile of stones, where, perhaps, he purposely exposed himself, in order to favour the escape of Danvers, and where he was first seen. Having swam the river, and mounted the pony which he had left on that side, he felt that he was safe from capture; for the soldiers finding at once that it had not been the principal object of pursuit they had chased, and that the child at most had but assisted his escape, while such an accomplice could not be of great importance, and the drums still beating to arms, in addition to which a distant sound of musketry was distinguishable, abandoned the pursuit; and returning, fell into their ranks without further delay. A scout presently arrived with information, that it having been discovered a meeting for the purpose of sedition was to be held that night, a detachment of dragoons had attacked the rebels and put them to flight. The men who had before arrived, while Danvers was on the house-top, had intimated that they had been dispatched by their commanding officer from an adjacent town, to bring whatever force they could from the guard-house, where a company was stationed in addition to the dragoons who had been quartered there for a few hours, but who did not amount to above a dozen. It was said that the insurgents meditated an attack on that town, and the soldiery in it were inadequate to its protection. Rumour added that the whole country round about was ripe for revolt. The news of an insurrection had spread like wildfire among the country people, who all flocked to the guard-house; but none of them were permitted to enter the gates, at which sentinels were placed : and just as the drum ceased beating to arms, Captain Norton, who had been sent for with all speed, arrived and assumed the command of the troops as senior officer. He was immediately informed of the escape of the prisoner Walter Danvers, by his second in command, who had ordered every precaution to be taken in order to prevent the fugitive's quitting the precincts of the guard-house, if he were still lurking there.

" Escaped !" ejaculated Captain Norton, the intelligence seeming to fall on him so unexpectedly and fearfully as to stun his brain for the space of a minute. " A thousand guineas for his person, dead or alive !" he exclaimed vehemently. " How could he escape ? Where was the guard I ordered to be placed outside the door of his cell ?"

" The prisoner managed to pass through a trap-door which we knew not of."

" Death !" interrupted Norton, " I chose the sentinel I placed over him, because I considered him trustworthy; but he must have been treacherous or sleepy ! Accursed chance ! Let a corporal and four men be sent to patrole in every possible direction. I repeat, I will myself give a thousand guineas for his capture."

The position of Danvers meanwhile was anything rather than an enviable one. At first he thought of making for the river, and swimming across : but he found that there were many persons now on the other side, who must have detected him in the broad moonlight; and having no confidence in his speed of foot, he did not think it prudent to venture anything on that alone. Foes were around him, and dangers threatened each instant; but his coolness remained undisturbed ; and he watched every opportunity which might befriend him, as he stood behind a wall, concealed from observation. The muster-roll was now being called over, within pistol-shot of him ; and the intoxicated soldier remained totally insensible where he had left him under the shade of the tree ; and it occurred to the mind of the fugitive, that he would be missed, and inquiry instituted, which would probably lead to his discovery. It was difficult to decide how to act. To escape by the high wall which surrounded the guard-house was utterly impracticable, without detection ; or otherwise, mingling with the crowd outside, he might have made his escape easily :

and when he heard the large reward offered by Captain Norton
for his re-capture, (well aware of the efficacy of money in sharp-
ening the wits), and that a party was about to be sent to endeavour to take him, he almost gave himself up for lost. But he
had contrived to elude the vigilance of his foes, even in more
desperate cases, and his iron nerves were immoveably firm, so
that he did not betray himself, as many others might have done,
by hastiness or want of self-possession, for an instant. He had
observed that the drunken soldier in whose accoutrements he was
dressed, resembled him in age and face, though he was more
obese, and taller by two inches. Was it possible to pass for him
with his comrades? The difference of height and deficiency in a
few pounds of fat might be supplied without any very great difficulty, to appearance. Acting on the impulse of the moment, and
while he proceeded with his operations, thinking the matter over,
he seized some loose hay, and stuffed it into his inexpressibles for
a paunch. He placed some more in his shoes to give him stature,
and then stepping from behind the tree where he had performed
these things, he boldly advanced, and "fell in," assuming the air
of a man who is rendered merry by strong drink, although not
fuddled by it, and distorting his face into a broad grin, such as
he conceived it probable the fellow's he represented often wore.

"Ah! Jack Timmins," exclaimed a private to Danvers, as he
placed himself beside him, "what a rum dog you are, to be sure!
I was afraid you would be found in your old way when the drum
beat, and that you would get the cat horrible for't."

"O, Jack Timmins is my name," thought Walter, "I must
remember that. It is well I heard it." He got up another con-
tortion of the face, and when "John Timmins" was bawled out
from the muster-roll, he stoutly answered "Here."

"How precious jolly you got at the 'Cat and Fiddle,'" remarked the private who had before addressed Danvers, again
turning to him, as he shouldered his bayonet in first-rate military
style, and drew himself up to his extreme height, that his want
of it might escape observation among the strapping six feet
fellows who surrounded him.

"O, yes!" responded the pretended Timmins, "that I always
does, you know!" and as soon as the accents had escaped his lips
the word of command was given, "Quick march!" and the dra-

goons preceding the infantry among whose ranks the fugitive had introduced himself so audaciously, he speedily found himself without the gates of the guard-house. So good a soldier as Danvers was, of course felt at no loss to perform all the functions of a private of foot, though he had always been accustomed to serve with cavalry, and still holding himself as erect as possible he marched along with the rest gallantly. But he was aware that there is something in the bearing of every individual, which, even when known, is hardly to be exactly imitated; and he was upon thorns every minute lest he should commit himself by some inadvertent and inappropriate action. The soldier, who had twice accosted him, occasionally eyed him curiously, but whenever he observed him doing so, he gave a comical twist to his countenance, which completely answered the purpose for which it was intended; and if a momentary suspicion as to his identity, crossed the mind of his comrade, it was soon dissipated in the hurry and excitement of the hour.

It was generally expected that an engagement would ensue on their march; for report had magnified the numbers of the insurgents into thousands where there were but hundreds, and it appeared probable that they would make an attempt to intercept such a force as was now hastening to the small garrison town of G——, which including the dragoons and a handful of militia who had joined them on the way, did not amount to above a hundred men.

Danvers, in addition to other anxieties, experienced no little solicitude as to the fate of the fine little fellow who had rendered him such very important services; but he was certain that George would not suffer himself to be taken, if he could escape the clutches of his foes, and as he appeared tolerably well acquainted with the locality of the guard-house, and his sagacity, adroitness, and cleverness, had been so conspicuously manifest in perils which severely tested them, and his stability of purpose and courage also, he felt, that had he remained with him, he could have rendered him no aid: and was compelled to trust to fortune for his deliverance, hoping, in case of the worst, that the enemy would not deal hardly with so young a boy; but determined rather than that he should suffer anything on his account, to rescue him at the expence of life and liberty.

The troops had now entered a narrow pass betwixt two rows of trees, planted at right angles on either side, and were descending into a valley, the approach to which was between green banks, where creeping plants and lichens and brambles were growing profusely below the lordlier trees, while a cascade, whose waters glittered in the soft and yellow moonlight fell with a pleasant-sounding dash into the bosom of the quiet spot. The song of the tuneful bird of night and silence could be distinctly heard, as the heavy and measured tramp of the infantry, accompanied by the noisier, yet no less regular sound of the horse, disturbed and contrasted strangely with that sweet song and the rustling of the verdant boughs.

What a melancholy thing it does seem to contemplate a number of our fellow-beings proceeding through so fair a spot to spill the blood of their countrymen, without feeling animosity against them, many in all the glorious flush and pride of strength, of manhood, and animated spirits, in a few brief hours to be as the clods of earth on which they tread! How wretched and contemptible is the barbarous delight in honours thus acquired, at the expense of existence, at the desolation of pure, kind hearts, of affection, friendship, and the ties of consanguinity! Surely a time will arrive, when the extension of the lofty intelligence, and the development of the sublime ratiocinatory powers of mankind, will deem the soldier's trade but fit for butchers and for savages, and the universal world will glory more in a single disinterested, noble, and generous action, though performed by the lowliest of its sons, than in all the conquests of a Cæsar or a Napoleon acquired at the price of justice, humanity, science, virtue and religion, which must all be sacrificed as encumbrances by that ignorant demoralizer of himself, who imagines in his vanity that in reigning paramount for a few brief years over the earth, he is acting in conformity with the dictates of wisdom, and securing for himself happiness in life, and immortality of fame in death. Poor wretch!

> Behold the child, by Nature's kindly law,
> Pleased with a rattle, tickled with a straw,
> Some livelier plaything gives his youth delight,
> A little louder, but as empty quite,

Scarfs, garters, gold, amuse his riper age,
And beads and pray'r books are the toys of age ;
Pleased with this bauble still, as that before,
Till tired he sleeps and life's poor play is o'er.

But no, that is bad philosophy, though it is very fine poetry, (the most Shakspearian in diction and in power that Pope ever penned.) Ambition is a toy, and vanity is a play-thing, and wealth, and rank, and the *external* forms of religion are vain and hollow ; but there are joys too pure, there is happiness too divine, to be classified in one common category with these poor, worthless earthly things. All pursuits which have but personal aggrandizement for their goal, are indeed beneath the notice of a good and wise man ; unless they also conduce to objects which may promote the good of others, they only tend to deteriorate his condition ; but surely love, and truth and purity of feeling and fancy, can afford sacred transports and enjoyments here,—surely they must outlast the grave ; and from the depths of the charnel-house, and of certain though slow corruption, send forth bright and perennial flowers, which like the fabulous asphodels are of everlasting odour.

Every pursuit which tends to enlarge the scope of our charities, and expand the sphere of our humanization, refinement, and philanthropy—the love of nature, of art and of philosophy—and above all the love of the creature, which leads to the adoration of the Creator—though developed among the humblest and least aspiring of the plants of the garden of the great moral world— while they evince the existence of a principle in the human mind distinct from the utterly animal and sensual, dignify the work of heaven, and yield an unfailing proof of the indestructibility and eternity of the meek and gentle nature, which displays itself in cherishing and fostering even—what may be termed—the daisies and buttercups of the heart.

What folly to go out to subdue the world, and to neglect the vast and immortal universe within ! Surely the man who conceives he is greater by conquering others than himself, who finds more pleasure in external marks of homage than his own self-approbation, cannot think very highly of the mind he owns ! But it is great and glorious to subdue the strong enemies that fight with us in the spirit's ocean, and plucking out the rank weeds of evil, encourage with care and tenderness the household and smiling virtues, which will make an oasis, if not an Eden, in the dreariest deserts of this sad and stormy life. To return from this digression of ethics.

It was the intention of Danvers, as soon as he was able to escape from the ranks which he had been constrained to join, to quit them unceremoniously; but he found, much to his annoyance, and a little to his confusion, as they entered the defile to the valley, that attention was gradually being directed to him on all sides, the noise and confusion of the previous portion of the march having now subsided, and whispers of " Who is he?" " That can't be Jack Timmins," reached him. But he saw that it would have been vain to attempt leaving the enemy now, for he was placed in the very centre of the company, and, as general suspicion was aroused against him, the least movement on his part, which might increase it, must prove fatal to him.

But perceiving that the feeling of mistrust was increasing, and convinced that he should not long remain undetected, when the road enlarging admitted of a greater number marching abreast, he prepared himself for a struggle, while he swaggered impudently forward, his cool effrontery for the present serving to keep those who suspected him in uncertainty. What to do, however, he knew not; but he was determined not to be taken alive, with the certainty of an ignominious death before him, if he could elude it by the most desperate risk and exertion, deeming it infinitely preferable to die a soldier's death by the bullets of his foes, than to expiate his misdeeds like a felon on the gibbet.

At one moment he was half-inclined to spring up the precipitous bank by which he was passing into the valley, and could he have seen a horse anywhere to accelerate his flight, he would assuredly have attempted it; but he was no longer a boy, and his legs, though muscular, were far from being agile; and moreover he was ignorant of the country he was traversing. Every moment the danger of his predicament increased; but still he remained undecided what definite course to pursue, as he must necessarily act upon the spur of the moment, and the appearance of a favourable opportunity—when he fancied he heard a voice with which he was acquainted, if not familiar, singing above; and lifting up his eyes, was persuaded he beheld little George

2 L

seated like a bird on the topmost branch of a cedar, and making significant gestures to him. One minute more, and the infantry would march in the same manner as previously to their entering the defile, and he would be entirely open to observation. Suspicion would be converted into certainty, and he must be arrested. He took his resolution, and quitting the ranks in an instant, rushed up the banks, just as the officer in command cried " Halt !" and simultaneously those in the first rank exclaimed, " The enemy."

There was a clang of arms and a flash of light from a musket, and all was excitement and eagerness. Danvers was instantly missed of course, but he had fortunately chosen the most propitious moment for escape; and dashing into the thickest growth of trees, was uninjured by the balls sent after him, while the greater number of the military were too much occupied with the expectation of immediate action to notice the desertion of a solitary soldier.

Scarcely had he accomplished what he desired thus far, when Danvers was met by George, who bade him follow him down a precipitous road, among rocks and fallen trees; and it was well that he did not delay doing so, for an exclamation arose that " It was Walter Danvers who had just fled," and the tempting reward offered for his recovery was fresh in every mind. By command of an officer several privates instantly pursued him, while a discharge of fire-arms, in the van of the troops, announced that a brisk skirmish had commenced.

CHAPTER V.

Yes, Love indeed is light from Heaven,
  A spark of that immortal fire,
With angels shared, by Alla given,
  To lift from earth our low desire.—BYRON.

A something fixed on earth, yet not in Time!
  Nay as 'tis purified by grief it soars
Through the immensity of space, sublime,
  And in Eternity and Heaven adores.—MS.

" 'TIS LOVE THAT MAKES THE WORLD GO ROUND!"—ELLEN LEAVES CHARLES.

GENTLE maiden! whose smile and kindness I endeavoured to propitiate in the early part of this history by a promise which I have not by any means forgotten, do not think that I am unwilling to redeem the pledge which I gave you relative to the delineation of the softer passions which reign more especially paramount within the female bosom, to the exclusion of that restless fever which men call ambition, of avarice, of pride, and all 'that perilous stuff' which degrades the grosser nature of the Lords of the Creation, and makes them impassive to the poetry and romance of being.

How true is the aphorism of that very clever and beautiful novelist, Paul de Kock, whose occasional immorality is more than counterbalanced by the kindliness, nature and simplicity of his genuinely pathetic writing: " With man the principle of love is but an episode in his existence; with woman it is the history of her life." Those that despise this silly sentimentality, which only boys and girls—and but a few of *them*—for an instant cherish in this highly rational, utilitarian and enlightened nineteenth century, may skip two or three pages of this present chapter, and then they will peradventure find substance more pleasant to their Ainsworthian, excitement-loving appetites; for we must not forget that what is delectable to one is an antepast of purgatory to another; and that the milk or pure water which I, a Teetotaler, prefer to port and potent beer, will cause that red-faced gentleman who breakfasts on Barclay and Perkins's composition to make such wry faces, if set before him, as might well turn his beloved beverage into vinegar, if in the same proportion as physical sensations are operated upon by moral affections, they could change the state of decomposition in which so many are in the habit of swallowing their liquids. But you need not fear that I am about to bore you with a Lecture on Teetotalism. Cytherea's son, and not Father Mathew, now demands notice.

It must be remembered that Charles Walsingham and Ellen Danvers were not like the young men and girls of this day, and that they had been unaccustomed to the chilling convention of great cities and great people. They were Nature's children, and the position into which Fate had thrown them was peculiarly favourable to the growth of that passion which Childe Harold says, " overpowers the pencil and the pen," or some such thing; and though they might otherwise have lingered weeks and months without knowing the state of each other's minds, a few hours had extracted a declaration from the lips of the lover; and something very like a confession of a reciprocity of feeling ecstatified the soldier into the third heaven, as the pure, sweet girl hid her fair face, and wept—how deliciously! But all this was imminently dangerous to the material part of the sick man, however much it might conduce to the beatification and exaltation of his intellectual, *moral* [Come, purist! find me some word more appropriate !] and *spiritual* being.

I must say a few words in defence of the reason of Charles, whom some cold-hearted persons may think little better than a lunatic for making desperate love to a woman whose face he had not seen, save in his dreams, a day and night; and of whose connexions, history, rank, fortune, family, &c., which are of such inestimable importance to the " oi polloi," he was in utter ignorance. And I am the more anxious to offer an extenuation, as I wish to draw him with a great deal of common sense as well as lofty romance of character. Now suppose that something be conceded to the weakness of body—which must always affect the mind—superinduced by all he had undergone, suppose that the soldier was more likely to yield to the impulses of his heart in his feeble frame of body than when enjoying the robustness, strength and energy of his usual uninterrupted health, there can be no doubt that a man may know more of a female under some circumstances in ten minutes—though talking and being talked to without disturbance—than in some cases he could in ten hours. That postulate being granted, the whole argument is as clear and incontrovertible as any of the reasonings of the mathematicians. Suppose that a person were with the object of his admiration for three hours a day—a pretty good spell, surely—in one month that would amount to 84 hours; and no prudent, cautious, individual in the world would assert that a man might not see sufficient of a lady in that period to justify his offering to tie himself to her for a life-time. By another simple rule of arithmetic, supposing that Ellen and Charles had been in each other's society for ten hours only actually, and the minutes therein were equivalent to the others' hours, they might have been in fact, in the same ratio as the other parties, about two thirds of a year making love, or in other words getting into trouble. According to Cocker, then, the time they had been together was equivalent to eight times as much as that allowed by custom to be the orthodox period for a declaration: so that there can be no doubt that they were vastly better acquainted with each other's hearts than the conventional lady and her suitor: and when we take into consideration also the enormous balance in favour of the son and daughter of nature against those of art and disguise, when we look into the state of their feelings and sentiments, the result was not only probable, but certain. I believe that this is the first calculation in which multiplication has been applied to the business of god Cupid's house of exchange; but I have no hesitation in predicating that romance writers may better combat the prejudices of society by a little demonstration of the kind, than by all the logic of Aristotle and the dialecticians. And now to consider, though not in detail, the nature of that intercourse which led to such a consum-

mation. It has been observed that Charles and Ellen had exchanged but few opinions; but then what they *did* say had freer
scope in their hearts, and made a deeper impression than if they
had talked much.   Pity was the predominating feeling from the
first in the bosom of the maiden towards Walsingham.   She had
watched him when he was asleep; and his noble face, so eloquent
of the dreams in which he was enveloped, pleaded potently in his
cause. Now in a fashionable drawing-room "with all appliances
and means to boot" for the carrying on of what is termed a flir-
tation; with ottomans, easy and lounging chairs and sofas, where
the lady and her suitor "look marriage settlements, and wedding
dresses," of course compassion towards the suitor is not aroused
in the object of his love.   She thinks him, for the most part, a
very pleasant, polite, and well-looking man, if he be tolerably so,
and nothing more.   Neither is it usual for a man to doze in the
presence of his adored, so that she cannot contemplate him unobserved, while he is dreaming of her.   Again, she does not know
how patiently he can endure pain, while his soul is brightened by
her presence; she cannot see the smile quivering on his pale lip,
when noticing that she looks pitifully upon him.   Nor is there
an opportunity for the display of that victory of mind over matter,
which the soldier had just given an instance of in leaving his sick
bed at the imminent risk of his life in his anxiety for her he loved.
And now to discuss the opposite side.   A young lady of sixteen
is not in the habit of attending a fine fellow of six-and-twenty
and ministering medicine to him.   The sentiment of gratitude
therefore is not awakened in common life by benefits conferred.
A girl is not at liberty to *look* the least interest for him she likes,
until he has formally declared himself, and been accepted.   But
innocent, simple, gentle, loving Ellen disguised not that she was
anxious about the poor fellow, and she gave him his nasty physic
with such commiserating softness that—by Jove! it was irresistible!   Then although the accommodating, well-natured person,
who performs propriety by a third presence in a London drawing-
room, considerately retires to the most remote corner of it, every
person who has felt the annoyance of such a necessary "bore"
must acknowledge that it throws an awful damp on the impetuous
fire of passion, &c.   A man doesn't like to outpour the secret
things of his deepest spirit, if it can be possibly overheard by an

old fubsy, matter of fact, worsted-working aunt, who probably never had a tender thing addressed to her, (poor old soul, she was always so desperately dull and ugly!) in her monotonous existence. But why multiply examples and antitheses? The case is so very palpable and self-evident that illustration is supererogatory. Ellen and Charles were formed for each other, and it would have been the worst frigid stoicism on the part of the latter if he had not declared his conviction of the fact to her, and it would have argued an equal degree of frost in the area of the other's affections, if she had returned a chilling answer to the ardent breathing of it. With some difficulty, by the assistance of Ellen, who insisted on his leaning on her shoulder, when she found that the invalid tottered as he attempted to walk, he regained his bed.

"O that I should be in such a state as to be totally incapable of rendering the succour, I would almost peril my soul to afford you!" exclaimed Charles, his head once more resting on his pillow, and the unresisting hand of Ellen clasped feebly in his: presently conveying it to his faint lips, and pressing it as fervently as his weakness would allow.

"Do not talk, I entreat you," returned the trembling maiden, withdrawing her hand, but so gently, that Charles, presuming on his condition, again took it. "I dread lest this excitement should make you worse than ever.—May heaven avert such an evil! Now try and compose yourself to sleep again."

"My ministering angel!" cried Walsingham, passionately, "I could not sleep. My heart, brain, soul, and being are alive with the spirit of burning joy. Oh, Ellen, you will be mine? Do not turn away your eyes, dearest! They are to me like the light of heaven, and restore the fainting life within my bosom. That is kind of you, to look at me thus. Sweet one! For long, long years, a something most exquisite and lovely has visited me in my day-dreams—something full of passion, splendour, softness— a blending of every joy—a harmony of every sweet sound: but never anything like the realization of this Elysian hour. You smile upon me, you tremble, you blush! Dear smiles, and tremblings, and blushings, brighter and more beautiful than the Morning's, when she rises from the sleep of love, and her rosy tints appear instinct with immortal light. If I were a poet,

Ellen, how your face would inspire my genius! Its tenderness
and grace would sink into my soul, and open the well-springs of
its fancy, until they should pour out like silver water from a fountain with music and swiftness: but though I have no imagination,
though I am unable to immortalize you and myself also, like
Petrarch and Tasso their adored ones, I can feel all the purity
of your loveliness as acutely. It shines with such calm and
seraphic radiance, that it etherealises all my spirit, and leaves not
a taint of earth or dust behind, in the worship it offers to you.
I spring buoyant into the blue air, and breathe the atmosphere
of blessedness. There is nothing of the mortal in me now. I
could look into our Great Father's face, and adore its effulgence, without being blinded : for were there nothing but love
like mine for you, it must raise us to be only less than angels."

There was something approaching to delirium in this rhapsody
of the soldier's : but who can describe the emotions of Ellen, as
in a voice scarcely higher than a whisper, but distinct beyond the
thunders of a Cicero's eloquence, he poured forth the pent-up
feelings of his soul—earnest—intense, though wild in its enthusiasm, into her ear. He had passed his arm around her slender
waist, as she stood beside him—he looked imploringly in her
lovely face, and raising himself in his bed, he imprinted the kiss
of passion on that sweet mouth, and inhaled fragrance from it
more dear to him than the airs of Eden.

There are indeed moments so thrilling, so absorbing every
faculty of the mind, and every portion of the sentient being, so
divine in their unutterable bliss, so free from the corruption of
this dark charnel where we rot into nothingness, that it would
require a seraph's spirit in a human mind to communicate them
as they should be communicated. The humblest, the poorest, the
most wretched of earth's creatures have felt such a foretaste of
eternity, and forgotten for a few brief moments that we do not
exist in the everlasting spheres—that hope must wither, and
love must die, and passion, and truth and beauty consume away
like the summer flowers which *look* as if they did not bloom to
fade, but are so odorous and beautiful that when, as autumn
comes, we see their withered leaves and wasted glories, we could
almost weep, as if some portion of our own joy and happiness
were crumbling to dust. Alas! these glad things are frailer than

the lilies ; they are scattered, never to be regained on this side
Heaven, and like those snowy flowers, as they float down the
stream of Time uprooted by the storm—poor, faint, dying splendors, beneath the holy stars that mock them with their rays—
they quiver, they droop but too surely, and sink with weeds and
viler things into the gloomy and all-ingulfing ocean — the
nothing—to be remembered, wept—and forgotten.

The transports and delirious raptures of Charles Walsingham,
and the milder, but hardly less impassioned feelings of Ellen Danvers, had subsided ; and as the morning sun burst into majestic
radiance, their ecstacy glided into a hardly less delightful tranquillity of bliss, and the soldier painted their future prospects
with a glowing and yet subdued brightness ; colours of the heart,
soft, fine, and ethereal—expatiating upon the pure and unalloyed
pleasures of domestic life, contrasting them with the aims and
ends of avarice, ambition, and those wild and frenzied excite-
ments which the votaries of dissipation love—of that unrest
which men miscall delight : but the recollection of the critical
position of her father caused Ellen's fair young face to become
overshadowed and sad ; and the soldier contemplating it, and
finding that there was something in the mind of the maiden
which weighed heavily upon it, gradually became less energetic,
and with a sigh he relapsed into the silence which extreme exci-
tation alone had enabled him for so long a time to break. Yet
he had *not* spoken much, though he had said a great deal. His
tones, his looks were eloquent with a deep burthen of meaning,
till the evident uneasiness and despondency in Ellen's countenance put a stop to his tender speeches. Had Ellen dared, she
would have imparted her anxieties to her lover ; but fearful lest
by so doing she might unintentionally commit some fatal indiscretion, she with some difficulty restrained herself.

There is no portion of our existence here whose radiance is not
palled by some remote terror, some fearful apprehension, which
although it may possibly render the fleeting moments of actual
fruition more precious, serves like the needle ever to the pole, to
point to that better and more enduring state, where life and immortality are the being we trust to possess. Go where you will,
examine how you may, trace the course of events from the remo-
test period of time, and the most barbarous states of society, to

our present most artificial civilization, the same eternal cycle has
been evolving, and it is vain for the best, and greatest, and most
fortunate, to hope to escape the common lot.   If a God exist, is
it possible that He could suffer man alone of all created beings,
to perceive in the perspective years of sorrow and lamentation,
how often to be so darkly realized! to drag the dreary chain of
defeated projects, annihilated schemes, and all the sad category
of evils, "which patient merit of th' unworthy takes," and
give the lie to that aspiration after the immortal, the verification
of which must attest to us the goodness of that Power we adore.
If any one be insane enough to predicate such blasphemy as this,
which would reduce Omnipotence into a fiend more inhuman
than any that breathes in Hell, better far to adopt the Atheist's
dreary and most wretched negation, and live, and weep, and
perish, totally regardless of all things but the present, leading the
life of a brute, but never being so happy.   Those who laugh at
the idea of a divine revelation might reasonably ask themselves
the question, "Why has the Supreme Being left us in uncertainty
with respect to what shall become of us hereafter?   Surely, He
was bound to lend us some staff better than mere conjecture on
the most momentous of all subjects, and to help us with a support more sure than fallible reason can supply, when we are
afflicted with such dire calamities, and earth becomes nothing to
our souls."   For it is a fact altogether incontrovertible that there
is nothing to justify the idea of a God and a hereafter, analogical
or otherwise, *in* the universe, except such inductions of reason—
which are in the mind, but must be developed—as the philosopher alone is capable of deeply investigating.

Sweet Ellen Danvers! Pity that so kind and bright a nature
should have to buffet with adversity, and struggle with the cold
and boisterous winds against which such fragile plants are so ill
calculated to contend!   Yet frequently we may behold that stern
old rascal Boreas expending his violence against such gentle and
weakly things, and permitting the steadier and older trees to remain unscathed by his blasts.

Long and wearisome appeared the hours of that day to the
lovers; for Ellen, unskilled to disguise her feelings, absented herself as much as possible from the chamber of the invalid, and
wandered about the garden, anxiously awaiting some communi-

cation from Elizabeth, or the return of her little messenger. Suspense at length became almost insupportable, and she would herself have quitted the cottage in the hope of obtaining some intelligence of her father, if Walsingham had been in a fit state to be left alone. But, as might have been expected, the soldier was more feverish than he was the day before, after the extraordinary excitement and exertions he had undergone, and the accession of fever had been attended with a momentary aberration of mind, during which he said something about the mystery of Ellen's appearance and behaviour, inexpressibly distressing to her; for it implied a doubt on her candour and ingenuousness, which she felt must lower her in the opinion of the frank and open Charles.

"My father may be dying even now," thought the maiden, after allowing her imagination to lead her reason as it seemed proper to that important functionary from which half our woes and joys are derived, "and by delaying I may be prevented from receiving his dying benison. Ought any consideration to weigh for a single instant in the balance with me, when a fond parent, who has cherished me in his bosom for so many years, is perhaps longing to bestow his last caress upon his child? I love him—I *ought* to love him infinitely better than all the rest of the world united; for he has been both father and mother to me, although he has such a stern spirit, and such unbending pride and inflexibility. I am certain that I do not feel towards this acquaintance of an hour, anything in comparison with that I do for him!"

Oh, no; what is there like the love of a child for the being from whom she derives her existence? And yet Ellen, if truth must be spoken, was not absolutely convinced, in the sanctuary of her secret heart, of what she had just said. She felt herself colour, as her intellect turned inwards, and was angry that her feelings were for an instant rebellious against the dictates of duty and rectitude. She could not tolerate the idea of being so ungrateful to an affectionate parent.

It seems most strange that love has the power, in so short a time, of overpowering the strength of old ties and friendships, and if not uprooting entirely amity most dear, and connexions most close, at all events of making them as nothing when put in competition with its all-penetrating influence. But such is the law of nature; and those who love at all must acknowledge the supremacy of the sentiment over all other things that are sweetest, brightest, and most sacred on earth.

Ellen was in some measure relieved from her embarrassment (as the event gave her liberty over her own actions) by the appearance of a withered crone, whom she knew she could trust, and who had come from the adjacent village, having just lost the only friend and relative she had in the world, understanding she would be paid for attending on a sick person. Ellen had previously seen and conversed with the aged woman, and as her character was good, considering that she might be entrusted with the care of the invalid who had just fallen into a quiet sleep, which augured favourably for the renovation of his strength, she determined, though not without many a reluctant pang, to quit him: and acting on this resolution, she stole softly into her lover's chamber, and in the perfect innocence and guilelessness of her warm young heart, she kissed the wan hand which lay on the coverlet. "If I should never see him again!" thought Ellen. "Oh, Heaven, watch over him, guard him, love him, even as I would; and if it be thy decree that we meet no more in this life —and such a foreboding now dwells within my breast—do thou, O Father of Mercy—" The poor girl here felt sobs choaking her utterance at such a gloomy anticipation, and fearful lest she should disturb the invalid, she hastily quitted the apartment.

"Let me see," meditated Ellen, as soon as she was sufficiently composed to collect her thoughts; "if I go at this time of night in search of my father in female apparel, I may be exposed to great danger. What had I better do? It is past eight o'clock; but I will delay no longer. There is an old suit of Harry's which he has much outgrown, and will just fit me. I will dress myself in his clothes, and then I shall be safer." A feeling of modest repugnance at this plan for an instant occurred to the girl; but speedily conquering the natural delicacy and sensitiveness of her age and sex, the exigency of the case supplying her with an *animus* which she could never otherwise have gained, she proceeded to put on her brother's dress, and to sally forth.

"I must tell the old woman to inform Walsingham that I hope to return in a few hours," muttered Ellen to herself, "and— and—yes; he was asking me to bestow on him a ringlet of my hair. I will leave that for him, for fear we should never meet more;" and resolutely battling against the shrinking timidity which oppressed her as she thought of her beloved, she cut off a sunny curl and enclosed it for him in paper, simply writing— "C. W. FROM ELLEN."

She little recked of the misery, the separation, and protracted grief which were to pursue her for many years! She little recked as she delivered her parting gift to the crone to give to Walsingham when he awoke, that for long and desolate years of solitude, and pain and isolation, it would be cherished, kissed, and almost idolized as his chief solace by the being to whom she had rendered the inestimable gift, the treasure of faith and unchanging truth which emanated from the fountain of her first, pure love.

CHAPTER VI.

Snuff.—This disguise is for security sake, wench. I will try how I can kiss in this beard. O fie, fie! I will put it off, and then kiss.

The Atheist's Tragedy.

Dio.—By Jove! I'll play the hunter for thy life.
With all my force, pursuit and policy.
Æne.—And thou shalt hunt a lion that will fly
With his face backward.

Troilus and Cressida.

ELLEN'S ADVENTURES—THE DISGUISED PURITAN—THE FLIGHT AND THE PURSUIT—THE COMBAT.

IT may well be supposed by every one acquainted with the timid wavering heart of "the maiden of youthful sixteen" that Ellen Danvers did not contemplate the dangers to which she was about to expose her inexperience, without feelings of the liveliest alarm and apprehension; and nothing but her anxiety and doubt, which as every hour passed away, became more and more insupportable, could have enabled her to maintain her resolution of

going forth. Thus may strength be derived from weakness, para-
doxical as the fact may appear.   She had persuaded herself that
her trusty little messenger would have returned long before, and
she could not help dreading that some new and unexpected calamity having occurred to her father, George was unwilling to be
the bearer of bad news.   Ignorant of the peculiar situation of her
beloved parent, and aware that none but those he could implicitly
trust could be of any service to him, she was determined on seeking him perfectly alone ; and avoiding the village near which her
home was situate, she gained the road by which the child had
told her he was going to travel, without molestation, and indeed
without being noticed.   Her bosom had been palpitating with
fear for the first few minutes of her journey, especially when a
winding of the path she had taken quite hid from view her home.
Presently, however, she was again able to perceive the picturesque
little abode which contained one grown so dear to her, and mounted
a slight eminence to behold that beloved being's window.   She
lingered for a minute straining her eyes toward the vine-adorned
casement " to breathe a prayer for him," and then hastily descending, continued her walk.   The evening was far advanced,
but it was one by no means calculated to add to the terrors of
the young girl.   Peace and silence unbroken wrapt the scene, and
the declining twilight possessed a mysterious charm for Ellen, for
she was habituated to think that good spirits then visited the
earth, to protect the pure and virtuous, and naturally religious,
she was most inclined to be so at so holy and sublime an hour.
The last faint rays of the dying day, as they melt into darkness
and night, appear also to leave within the human breast deep and
secret feelings chastened by a melancholy and dreaminess, such as
are seldom felt in the brightness of morning, and Ellen indulged
them with more than ordinary abstraction from the world ; she
mingled devout aspirations and pious thoughts with the poetry
of feeling and passion, fancy and sentiment.   Although she possessed but little imagination, and even her fancy could not be said
to be either of a powerful or intense description, her nature was
such that it could not be devoid of the great first principle within
the soul of every fine and sensitive being, the feeling for beauty,
moral and material ; and she had now reached a locality which
she had never before visited, and whose wild and shadowy gran-

deur struck her with admiration, despite her own fears and suspense. At her feet there was a mimic cascade, which falling over
green banks in a sloping and gradual descent, mingled with a
dark and silent stream, overgrown with weeds and rushes. Above
there ascended to a height of nearly seventy feet, a mass of granite
with pointed heads, and nearly all the rock was covered with
shapes, some grotesque, some graceful, and some hideous—the
fossil remains of animals, reptiles and trees, which had become by
this time apparently a portion of the solid stone. But it was not
these which attracted the attention of Ellen. A mist ascending
from the valley below, clothed every object with its silvery exha-
lations, and reaching the gigantic trees which flanked the high
road seemed to embrace them with undulations of life and motion.
This vapour sweeping lightly through the dusky air, was now
tinged with the trembling moonlight, and now left to trace its way
through the pathless space in gloom—

> " More dark
> And dark the shades accumulate; the oak
> Expanding its immeasurable arms
> Embraces the light beech,—the pyramids
> Of the tall cedar, overarching, frame
> Most solemn domes within; and far below,
> Like clouds suspended in an emerald sky,
> The ash and the acacia floating hang,
> Tremulous and pale."

She recollected a short hymn which she had been taught in her
childhood,—and while she lingered in the quiet place—hoping
that she might meet George before she turned into another path—
the sensations excited by the time and scenery found vent in these
words, which she sang with extreme pathos and sweetness, if not
with science.

> "Thou who hast spread the hills above
> And robed them with such green,
> Father of mercy and of love!
> Unknown, yet not unseen.
>
> " Thou who dost make the very air
> So exquisite and pure,
> If Nature be so bright and fair,
> It makes the spirit sure.

" A world there is remov'd from sight—
A world of light and bliss—
Thy goodness Father for the light
Which gives us hope in this !"

" A godly song, well and piously sung !" exclaimed a voice
close by Ellen, as she concluded the third stanza of the hymn,
and a large hand was placed on her shoulder simultaneously with
the articulation of the first accents she heard. " It rejoices my
soul to hear a youth of thy years so religiously disposed. Verily
in these days there is a lack of wisdom, and when we behold the
young saplings bending the right way, we should be glad and give
praise to the Lord for disposing His babes to the faith."

These words, delivered in a nasal twang resonant of the con-
venticle, did not at all communicate the happiness they were intended to convey to Ellen, who on looking at the individual from
whom they proceeded perceived that he was an enormously tall
man, but stooped and was extremely awkward in his gait, and
his face did not indicate in any degree the benevolence and kindness which would have re-assured her at such a time and place.
He was of middle age to appearance, with long lank hair mingled
with gray, combed straight over his shoulders, and his complexion
was cadaverous, his figure thin, and his dress puritanical. " I
see that thou art about to travel the road that I am going, worthy
youth," said the stranger, finding that his new acquaintance,
muttering " a good evening" was about to quit him, " and with
thy leave I will bear thee company; for there are evil men abroad,
who go about like a roaring lion waylaying godly and peaceable
persons and robbing them ; but I place not my faith in the carnal
weapon ; but in the shield and buckler of the Lord, and my sword
and spear in the hand of His angel ! Verily the darkness accu-
mulateth, and the loneliness of the road even increaseth ; yet will
I not be afraid, for in Him I put my trust, and the robber and
assassin shall not prevail against me."

" I have heard there are many such villains as you describe
abroad," replied the disguised maiden, hastening onwards as fast
as possible.

" Yea, multitudes, fair youth ! I am journeying to a far town
to preach the word to the congregation of my brother Hezekiah
Showthefaith ; you may have heard of me—Gideon Killthedevil!"

Ellen opened her large eyes to their fullest extent. " Is that your name ?" she inquired, innocently.

" Not my name in the flesh you shall understand. I am called John Timkins out of my holy vocation. I have turned from the wrath to come and joined the Anabaptists. How happy should I be, if thou, who art so promising a youth, wouldst renounce the world, the flesh and the devil, and adopt the calling of a preacher of the truth."

The disguised girl was becoming a prey to unspeakable terrors as she hurried along, the fanatic close at her side, for the earnestness with which he gazed into her face, and the singular expression of his countenance went far to persuade her that she was detected—though she did not pause to ask herself how that was possible, when her companion was a perfect stranger—and the solitariness of the road at every step became more awful. Still he did not offer any violence to her, but continued to talk, although gradually he suffered his puritanical phraseology to drop, and he spoke with less of that nasal twang she so much disliked. There was something in the voice not quite unfamiliar to her, but she was certain she had never seen the man before. How odious was the cant with which he assailed her, when she was convinced that he was a hypocrite at heart !

" You are young to be walking so late, my pretty boy," observed the disagreeable object of Ellen's alarm ; " but I will protect you at any peril to myself—even wield the carnal weapon," he added with a half-laugh. " Ah, I see we shall have to cross a broad and deep river there ; for the bridge, which was thrown across it this morning, has been broken down. There is no occasion, however, for more than one to get wet."

" I thank you," hastily interrupted Ellen, " but I think I had better go round. I wish you a good evening," and with these words she was pacing away, when the puritan detained her, saying,

" Nay, there is no cause for fear. You cannot go into the road which lies across the water without walking for a mile and a half; and you will be obliged to pass through a thicket where there have been frequent robberies of late. Come along, and trust to me." Having thus spoken, the tall man took the disguised girl on his back, regardless of her entreaties to the con-

2 N

trary, and when in the very centre of the stream he suddenly threw his arms about her and exclaimed, "So, you thought I was a methodist preacher, and that you could gammon me you were a boy, my beauty! I know who you are. Give me a kiss, and upon my soul I won't do you any harm."

Vainly did Ellen scream and struggle. The water was up to the chest of the gigantic man in whose embrace she was, and he held her just as he would have dandled a baby, so that resistance was impossible.

"What's the use now of kicking up such a row, when there's no one to hear you?" remarked the fellow. "You see, I was as much in disguise as yourself. There," taking off the ugly wig he wore, and exposing a fine head of hair, "as you seem to have an invincible objection to kiss such a cursed, humbugging-looking rascal as I was——Whew! come along," he added, on a sudden, looking round, and instantly carrying the almost insensible Ellen to the other side, and then taking to his heels, as if a legion of fiends were behind him.

The girl, on sufficiently recovering to observe the cause of this precipitate flight on the part of the pretended preacher, discovered that a body of horse soldiers was within pistol-shot of the stream which she had just been carried over, and the vanguard, consisting of two or three men, were on the point of firing at the fugitive, while an officer spurring up to them ejaculated, "That is the long devil who robbed me so politely the other day, in conjunction with an accomplice. Ten guineas for the man that takes or shoots the scoundrel."

The tall fellow meanwhile had made the best use of his legs, and as a bullet from a carabine fell a few feet behind him, he plunged into another part of the winding river, and dived down to a considerable depth. All was bustle among the cavalry, and the word of command having been given, several dragoons plunged into the water, and when the deserter (for such he was) arose to the surface, they being mounted discharged their fire-arms at him, but it would seem without effect, for he instantly dived again, and did not show his head for a considerable time.

"There he is!" at length exclaimed one of the troopers, as the robber rose at a considerable distance from the place where he had vanished. The firing was incessantly continued, while the fugitive was in sight; and some of the shots flying within a little of his head, he thought it prudent again to disappear. "Where the deuce is he now?" cried several voices, not the slightest symptom of the deserter occurring after an interval of several minutes, "he must be drowned, surely." "No, no, see! that is he, hanging on the bough of the willow yonder. We shall have him in a minute." And, indeed, the fellow appeared to take the matter coolly enough; for there he sat, protected by the boughs only from the bullets directed against him, swallowing some liquor from a stone bottle which he carried in an enormous pocket.

"I've swallowed so much water, I must take a dram to qualify it," he muttered to himself; "ah, fire away! That ball was a d—d good shot; it came within an inch of my nose! Why, that's my brother who fired that—the precious scoundrel! Tom, you rascal, what the devil are you at?" he roared to a huge fellow within an inch of his own stature, and vastly bulkier in form, who having deliberately aimed at him, was now swimming his horse towards the tree. "I suppose it's time for me to be off now," added the deserter, suiting the deed to the word, as the Herculean soldier he had addressed approached to within a dozen yards; and dashing into the stream, with renewed vigour, he made for the distant bank.

"Cross over and intercept him!" cried an officer, who had just taken to the water, to those who were nearest to the other side—the willow being in the middle of the river—and his orders were instantly obeyed, two or three having gained the bank, and spurring forward to seize the deserter.

"It's always best to send one's nerves on a visit to the lower regions in these cases," thought the pursued to himself. "You won't catch me, my lads." Altering his course, and striking out for some green banks which were defended from the approach by land, by a little forest of underwood, which extended for two or three furlongs in a quadrangular form, and an opening in which on the river side afforded a retreat, he exerted all his powers. This manœuvre greatly delayed the dragoons sent round to take him, for they were obliged to dismount, and having done so, experienced no little difficulty in making their way through the

intricate trees, and when they had done so they discovered that
the deserter had effected a landing, and was scampering away
with might and main, but closely followed by the Hercules who
had nearly wounded him while he was in the willow. The path
which extended through the trees in that direction being broad
enough to admit of a horseman passing, the pursued manifested
no intention of dashing into the more labyrinthine portion of the
wood, a fact which surprised them all at first; but the mystery
was soon cleared up, for they perceived their comrades riding in
all directions, in order to surround the thicket.

"What legs the scamp has!" exclaimed a soldier, as he saw
the fugitive emerge from the shelter of the trees; and mounting
himself the tallest sapling at hand, perceived that he had just
eluded a party detached to intercept his egress from the place,
and escaped many shots which were aimed at him. The huge
dragoon, who from the circumstance of his great size the reader
may recognize as one with whom he has already some acquaintance, was close at the fugitive's heels; and a desperate chase it
was, the robber putting forth all his speed, and emulating a stag
or greyhound in celerity, while his pursuer buried his spurs in
his horse's flanks, and cheered the animal on, now with vehement
now with angry exclamations.

"Tom Jennings has been flogged to-day," remarked a private
to another, " and his blood is like hell-fire!—Whew! he is striking at his brother with his sabre! he'll kill him, if he can."

The deserter and his inveterate hunter soon left all behind
them, the road being favourable for the former, as it was extremely rugged; and gradually the sound of the voices of the
soldiery became indistinct, and finally undistinguishable. Still
neither party relaxed in his velocity, and the breath of the horse
and the human being endeavouring to outstrip him came thick
and fast. They had now entered a pleasant little valley, and all
traces of man and man's habitations had disappeared. It was
stillest night, and the faint plashing of a fountain placed in the
centre of the quiet spot was the loudest noise that disturbed it
until invaded by the robber and the trooper. On a sudden the
fugitive turned round, threw himself on the green earth, and
ejaculated composedly, though with some difficulty,

" I'll run no more, stap my vitals! Tom, you blackguard, how can you be such an unnatural villain as to attempt to take the life of your own brother!"

" Yield yourself, then, my boy, and quickly," responded the dragoon, in a hoarse voice, as he reined up his panting steed, " what cursed long sticks you have!"

" Pshaw, Tom, I'll make up the difference to you, as far as the reward offered for me goes—chance if you ever get it from that chap. Come and have a draught from this bottle; you must be thirsty with your hard ride."

" Don't gammon me," returned Tom, surlily. " You're a nice young gentleman you are, I must say for you, ——— you."

" Very, Tom. I'm going to have some spirits and water, I'm so dry. You really won't take a drop of this stuff, eh?"

" I shan't allow you any such liberty, you vagabond! Give me the bottle, and surrender yourself at once, or else if I don't put this cold steel into your belly, I'll be ——— "

" Keep a civil tongue in your head, though you are my elder brother, Mister Tom," rejoined the other. Remember that you haven't a dozen comrades here to back you."

" If I have not," answered the dragoon, fiercely, " I have often made you bite the dust, and will do it again."

" Well, if you will have a few hard blows to whet your appetite for supper, you know you are pretty equally matched with me at the broadsword. I prefer passes with a rapier—it's more gentlemanly—by way of amusement; but this is a trusty blade I've got here, and so come on, my worthy Thomas."

" Since you will have it," returned the dragoon, who displayed some surprise at finding that his foe was as well armed as himself, a long sword having been concealed beneath his large puritanically cut coat. And to it they went in earnest. They were excellent swordsmen, and perfectly matched. In mere brute strength, the bones and muscles of the dragoon were stronger than those of his adversary, but the temper and activity of the latter amply counterbalanced this advantage, as he very soon proved. The soldier had been necessitated to alight, in order to attack the deserter, or he must otherwise have ventured his horse among some huge fragments of rock and stumps of trees which were extremely dangerous. Thus being on equal terms, at all events in one respect, the fugitive took every advantage of his superior agility against "Tom," and the foot of that redoubtable personage stumbling among the stones and trees, he rushed upon him and threw him to the earth while he was striving to regain his centre of gravity, and pointed his sword to his chest.

"Strike, and be —— to you!" cried the fallen one, with a horrible oath, and with vain rage and hatred in his accents. "This has been a cursed day!"

"No, master Thomas, I've an idea you're not fit to die yet," responded the robber, feeling in his pocket with one hand; "but if you attempt to stir, my noble brother, I shall certainly make you crows' meat. Keep your overgrown carcase still—you won't, eh?" Suddenly, with the dexterous sleight of hand of a conjuror, the deserter passed some strong cords round the arms of his adversary, and in the course of two minutes succeeded in binding him hand and foot. "Good night, dear Tom," he added, in a jeering tone, "when I see you again, I hope you'll be in better humour."

In reply, the immense fellow vented awful imprecations on the other's head, who lightly springing on the back of the war-horse his relation had been obliged to desert, and blithely caroling an old Cavalier song, cantered briskly away, turning a deaf ear to the menaces and imprecatory expressions of his vanquished enemy.

CHAPTER VII.

Here's a brave fellow now ; his tongue, his hand,
His legs, and all his faculties combined,
He makes subservient to his roguish tricks!
He lies, fights, runs, and plays the hypocrite
With any man in England, I'll be sworn.—*Old Play.*

There is a holy fount in every breast,
Which, tho' defiled, the work of Heaven displays ;
Its waters gush, and make the worst the best,
And fill the soul with Love's supernal rays.—*MS.*

MOTHER STOKES AND FIGGINS—THE ROBBER—RENEWED
PURSUIT—THE CAVERN.

NOT unobserved had passed the combat between the two tall
men in the sequestered valley ; for, concealed by the thickness of
the intervening boughs, there sat three figures in a plantation of
young trees—a large, powerful man in a half-military dress, a
short, ill-featured woman, and a monstrous being, whom it would
have been a matter of some difficulty for a naturalist to classify,
though he had certainly two mis-shapen legs, and something
resembling a human head.

Previous to the contest, the man and woman had been speaking
together, and it may be as well to record the substance of their
conversation.

" Well, mother Stokes," said the military-looking man, who
had a quid of tobacco in his cheek, " you were telling me how
you escaped. By Jove, you had a narrow——Ha! I thought I
heard a distant firing then! there are parties of soldiers scouring
the country in every direction, searching for rebels."

" Yes, Figgins," answered the woman, in reply to the first part of his sentence, " you see, when I heard the word of command given to ' right about face,' and that there was a rising of the Jacobites, I thought I might yet have a chance of getting out of their hands. I was very much in the way, as you may suppose, and it was proposed to send two privates on with me and the boy to the town ;. but every man was of consequence, and so I was carried back. I had recovered my wits, and taking from my pocket a bottle of spirits which I had with me, I secretly dropped some powder into it, the effects of which I knew well. I was pretending to be about to take some of the liquor, when the soldier I was behind, as I had thought he would, caught hold of it, and drank off half the contents of the bottle at once. Calling me a polite name, he thanked me for the draught, and handed the rest to the man with whom the boy rode, who drank it ; and in the course of a few minutes they both grew sleepy. Small parties were now detached to scour the country, and I and the boy went with one of them, together with a corporal and two or three privates. Most luckily, we fell in with some suspicious-looking men, who on being questioned did not answer satisfactorily, and, such being the orders, the Corporal proceeded to arrest them ; but they resisted, and produced concealed arms. Finding that the dragoon I rode behind was quite overcome with drowsiness, I gave him a push, and looking at the boy as the sleepy soldier fell gently to the ground, I rode off. The horse I was on being as good as any in the troop, I had a fair chance of not being overtaken, the others being busy with the rebels ; and the boy having thrown himself from behind the other trooper, soon joined me. But chase was given, and so I abandoned the horse, and concealed myself here, where you found me."

" Yes," returned Figgins, " the dragoons encountered me, and asked me about you, but I put them on a wrong scent—What's this ? Keep close, old girl ! There'll be fighting yonder, directly, I see."

It was at this time that the soldier and the deserter made their appearance, and soon proceeded to the exchanging of blows, and Figgins, having nothing of the knight-errant in his composition, calmly looked on without interfering, although, when he recognised the combatants, he muttered, and seemed undecided how to act.

"I don't wish it to be known that I'm here," thought the Corporal. "In the first place, that old woman and the monster, if seen, would betray the fact that I deceived the soldiers; and —Ah, ha! I thought so—Tom is down; but I don't think his brother will do him harm! A good joke, upon my soul! He is tying the huge fellow's arms with cord. It's nothing to me. I'm not in the King's service now—that is, I'm not on active duty. I shall leave Tom where he is, and go my way. The long one is off now; the impudent rascal, he has taken the horse. I would not advise you, mother Stokes," he added, in a low voice, " to remain here. I must go and see after your niece Soph. By the bye, I hope you put some food and water into the cave with that stripling."

Mother Stokes grinned savagely, and shook her head.

"Good God! what a devil you are!" exclaimed Figgins, " the lad must be starved to death by this time;" and thus saying, not without something like horror, the Corporal hastily quitted his depraved companion, and walked away with rapid strides, while she gave some spirits to the savage and then drank a portion herself.

Meanwhile " the long one," having gained the victory, and seized on the horse, lost no time in getting over the ground; but he discovered that the animal was injured in the pastern, and having been tremendously worked for the last few hours, in carrying such a burthen as his late rider, over hills and precipices at so great a pace as he had been urged to, it was not possible for him to maintain the pace at which his new master wished him to proceed.

"I must try and rejoin Bess," said the robber to himself, " and then we will be off to London. I don't like to lose this horse. I could sell him for £50. in town, and I owe my troop a grudge, so I should like to take one of their best chargers from it. The devil! I had quite forgotten the accoutrements of the beast. I see some men standing there at that little public house, at the entrance to yonder village, which is still open, and where I wanted to have had some ale after my hard run, and they are inspecting me curiously. I'll speak to them; curse me, I must have my ale. Good evening, masters," he said courteously to the persons in question, " I am thirsty, and would thank any one to

2 O

tell the landlord to bring me a pint of his best home-brewed. I'm much obliged to you, Sir! You are open later than usual here."

"Yes, Sir Methodist," replied a jolly-looking fellow, "there are plenty of hard blows to-night going on, and they are apt to produce thirst."

"You conclude I am a methodist from my dress, eh?" returned the tall man. "I am a medical man, and attached to the dragoons, as you may perceive by the trappings of the horse. Oh, here is the ale! Your healths, gentlemen. Host, bring me some bread and cheese, and meat, with wherewithal to replenish my flask of brandy, and change for a guinea."

"There are some of your regiment, the —th, coming up now," observed the merry-seeming individual who had before spoken.

"I see," returned the deserter, with wonderful composure. "This is likely to prove an awkward affair," he thought. "I am quite tired of running, and the ground is entirely open here. Luckily my clothes are nearly dry with the violent exercise I've taken. D—n it, I will brazen it out, by ———!"

Although he did not trust to his disguise, which his remarkable stature indeed would have rendered unavailing, he yet hoped to escape, convinced that those now approaching did not belong to the party which had just pursued him, and that they could not know much about his appearance; but the unfortunate horse was certain to attract their notice. It was not a little, however, that could daunt his resolution, and as the dragoons approached to within a few feet of him, he exclaimed,

"Ah, my men, poor Tom Jennings! he's gone! all my efforts and skill were unavailing. The Doctor was present at his death, and said I had done all human ingenuity could effect to save him."

"Who the deuce are you?" inquired a Corporal in command of the little detachment, gazing with bewildered eyes at the tall person in black.

"Don't you recollect me. I have seen you before, I think. I am the Doctor's—Doctor Pillwell's assistant. I think I once pre-scribed for you, when you were ill."

"Never saw you in my life! What's become of Tom Jennings? Do you mean to say that big Tom's dead?"

"I have told you he is no more. There has been a terrible affray with the Jacobites, at which I suppose you were not present. Tom was the only man killed, but others are wounded."

"But you can't be Doctor Pillwell's assistant, unless you are newly appointed. I saw the assistant a week ago, and quite well."

"Little Jeffery, you mean? I am sorry to say he has been taken ill; and as I once officiated for him before, when he was sick, I've got his place; and I don't think that he can ever recover."

"This is a curious business! How d'ye come by Jennings's horse?"

The question thus put to 'the long one' was at first a poser; but straining his ingenuity to reply, he said, "Why, you see, the horse has been injured—you can examine the leg, if you like—and as I have considerable skill in horse surgery, and this is rather beyond the science of the superannuated old veterinarian of the regiment, I have taken it in hand. Well, landlord, you've brought change? Let these good fellows each have a draught of your ale—there's half a crown to pay for it. Good night to you all."

"But I really don't understand," said the non-commissioned officer, whose wit was not of the brightest.

"I hope we shall be better acquainted, Corporal," added the tall fellow, without heeding the interruption. "I am obliged now to go on to R——, where some of the wounded have been sent, and where Dr. Pillwell waits for me. You know the Doctor's a particular man, and would kick up a deuce of a rumpus if I were not punctual, or I should have been happy to drink a pot with you."

Thus saying, the modern Goliath slowly walked his horse away, and almost simultaneously he heard a trumpet which he knew signified troops were at hand. The danger was still imminent, and fearing lest he should be recognised by the party now so near, our fugitive put his steed into a trot, then into a canter, and finally into a full gallop.

"I think that fellow's a humbug," observed the jolly-looking man to the Corporal, "if you don't know him, depend on't he's trying to put a trick off on you."

"I think so, too," returned the person addressed, who all along had his misgivings; and when the tall man changed his brisk trot into a canter, at the second bray of the trumpet, was quite certain all was not right. "We must take that rogue," he said to his party, who were quaffing the strong ale which had been given them, "we shall soon see if he spoke truth." But though he belowed to the long gentleman to stop, his commands were disregarded, and the full gallop commenced; and ordering the soldiers under him to follow, the Corporal hastened after the fugitive.

To the chagrin of the robber, he found that the lameness of his steed increased so rapidly, that it was impossible he could bear him another mile at any pace; and as he stumbled and refused to obey the bit, his rider dismounted without loss of time, and once more trusted all to the length and speed of his legs. But an unexpected disaster now happened to him; and he discovered that in avoiding Scylla, he had been running on Charybis. Another small party of dragoons as he was turning an angle of the road at great speed, presented an appalling spectacle to his eyes; but he hoped that he had not been noticed, as an old oak in the centre of the road nearly hid him from view; and taking his determination at once, he crept into an enclosed common, and ran across it, when he perceived that he was in a rocky and almost impassable place, flanking the whole extent of the common, and in which there had been numerous excavations formerly, for mining purposes. But he had not been unnoticed while crossing the heath, and the Corporal who had pursued him having joined the rest, the sounds of his hunter's shouts soon reached him. The fugitive was aware that many of the excavations around him were exceedingly dangerous, but relying on himself, and perceiving that if he strove to renew his flight he must be seen and fired at, he determined on cautiously descending into one of the deserted hollows, which seemed to extend far into the earth. Slowly commencing his descent, he found that the excavation continued for the length of nearly a hundred feet, and then abruptly terminated in a semi-circle; but, when accustomed to the darkness of the cavern, he had sufficient light from above to show that there were several windings in the opposite direction, which probably communicated with other caves of smaller dimensions.

" He went this way," said a voice, which sounded so distinctly, as it awoke the loud echoes of the cavern, that it caused the robber to start.

" I have been seen then," he thought. " Ah! they are coming after me—neck or nothing! I will try this way," and he fled hastily, as several lights were kindled at the mouth of the excavation.

A stream passed through that part of the cavern which the fugitive had chosen to pursue, and following its sinuosities he for a short time left his pursuers far in the rear; but they speedily followed in the same direction as he had taken, and their shouts again became more and more distinct.

" They'll catch me at last, I shouldn't wonder," said the deserter to himself, in a gloomy tone. " But I won't be taken easily yet :—ah! what noise is that I hear ?—Blows as if from a pickaxe, and groans! What fearful cries !"

Proceeding a little farther, the robber discovered a low passage in which he could not nearly stand upright, and stooping several inches, he entered it and found that the sounds which had just met his ear became more audible for a minute, and then ceased altogether. The fugitive stood still; and now he heard his pursuers closer than ever. He could not advance above a dozen paces farther, and retreat by this time was cut off.

" There must be some place within," he thought, " whence those awful sounds came. I don't believe in ghosts, and if I could find that, I might yet baffle them :—but they are coming down the passage; what shall I do ?"

He looked around him, but saw nothing to facilitate his escape, and was preparing for the last desperate struggle for liberty, when a most fortunate and unexpected interposition in his favor occurred ; for while he was in despair of eluding capture, a huge mass of earth and rock, sufficient to have buried a hundred men under it, fell, with the noise of an avalanche, on a sudden, without any visible cause, having been detached from the heavy and rocky soil above, and closed up the passage which the military were on the point of entering, extending nearly to the spot where the fugitive stood. It would have required at least a week's labour from those without to have cleared the way again, as the passage was so narrow that it only admitted of the entrance of one at a time, and both sides were of hard stone and granite.

" If I were worth the notice of Heaven, I should call this a providential interference," thought the tall man, almost blinded and suffocated by the dust and rubbish near him. " Well, I'm the favourite of fortune, I suppose; but this is too much of a good thing. I am safe from capture, but by no means from death. I may, perhaps, die comfortably of starvation here."

While thus cogitating, again the robber heard a repetition of the groans from within. " Have we spectres here, or goblins, or devils, or what ?" asked the robber, of himself. " I wish the respectable individuals would not take it into their heads to make such dismal sounds. Upon my soul, they freeze my blood, though it is warmed with running and hot liquor." He listened, and again hearing the sound, and marking the direction it proceeded from, he sounded the walls with a stone, and was convinced that in one part they were hollow. " I'll pay a visit to this ghost—or whatsoever the gentleman in distress may be," said the robber, after some deliberation. " It seems that I cannot get out of this place by any outlet I can discover; and the locality —wedged up here as I am—is not so enchanting as to induce a fellow to make a long stay unnecessarily."

Taking up a vast stone, which it was not easy for him to lift, he dashed it against the part whence a hollow sound had come, and the wall fell with a tremendous crash like that of detonation—though nothing to what had preceded it. Drawing back to avoid the second blinding which the effects of this measure produced, as soon as the dust had subsided, he again stepped forwards, and perceived a sort of cell seemingly unoccupied : but on closer inspection he found a fair-haired youth lying in a senseless condition on the ground, evidently exhausted from long want of food.

" Poor boy, poor boy !" exclaimed the gigantic fellow, pouring some spirits down the throat of the solitary tenant of that gloomy abode, a tear gathering in his eye, and his strong hand shaking as he performed the friendly office.

What a mystery is the human heart ! The robber would not have hesitated to have taken a dozen lives in the prosecution of his nefarious profession, where his feelings were uninterested, for

the sake of a few wretched coins to spend in idleness and dissipation, and yet there was something in the forlorn condition of
the young and emaciated stranger, which, for the time, filled him
with as much of ' the milk of human kindness' as ever glowed
in the bosom of a Howard or a Fry. Compassion is usually
most powerfully excited by an unexpected appeal to the heart,
and in proportion as the feeling of pity becomes developed, a
thousand kinder and gentler thoughts and sentiments enter into
it. Yes, for the time, that man of blood and guilt (whom no
remorse nor compunctious visitings of nature deterred from his
iniquitous vocation), as he recalled the old familiar faces of his
childhood, and a thousand almost forgotten dreams and hopes
and aspirations returned upon him—who shall say by what
associations ?—forgot the past of crime—the broken faith—the
stained and dreaded hand—the degraded majesty of self-com-
mendation—the hatred, the shame and obloquy of the world—
and a future of useless regrets, accumulated ignominy, imprisonment, revilings, curses, and finally a felon's death—those awful
shadows of the spirit which ever drag down the wicked man's
soul to hell, vanished, and a new spring of tenderness and humanity, and all good and gentle feelings, gushed through his inmost
heart. For an appeal so tacit yet so omnipotent, as the forlorn
condition of the insensible youth must present to any one not
utterly devoid of that humanizing principle, which is an instinct
in every nature not totally brutalized by vice and sin, to act like
demons in the face of God—breaking down the structures the
fiend has raised, and dividing the links of that chain upheld by
stormy passions, so destroying the bridge over which the spectres
of the departed hurry to and fro (though these are all too soon
repaired by recurrence to the same evil practices), like the balmy
spell of a holy angel breathes a serene repose, redolent of the
lost Eden of Peace and Virtue.

Oh, if we could but operate upon the *heart* of the malefactor,
by setting in array before him the bright scenes of his innocent
childhood—of his happy boyhood, and joyous youth—his mother's sacred kiss, his sister's endearing smile—the kind words of
his youthful friends, the harmless pleasures he deserted for criminal delights, and forbidden joys—we should effect more than
by all the eloquence of the preacher launching forth into elegant

rhetorical periods on the shortness of life, the sin of the world, and the vanity of human pursuits—for we should open the avenues of the better nature—more than the philosophic sentences of the moralist, painting luminously the miseries of vice in its every phase, and the beauty of ethics and wisdom. Where is the great Poet—he *must* be somewhere—who shall apply the principles of Christianity to the feelings and affections with a Shakspeare's power, delineate the light and radiance of the former seraph changed into the haunting ghost of mourning and of desolation —the pure heart made foul and corrupt, and the abode of unsightly shapes, instead of God and Love, and only to be restored to its pristine tranquillity by the mercy of that heaven that loves the penitent, that pities the contrite, and pours forth ebullient joy in the empyrean, over one sinner that returneth to the bosom of his Father, who forgives and rewards!

CHAPTER VIII.

Chaos of Thought and Passion all confused;—
Sole judge of Truth, in endless error hurl'd,
The glory, jest, and riddle of the world.

ESSAY ON MAN.

Cal.—O ho, O ho! would *it* had been done!
Thou didst prevent me: I had peopled else
This isle with Calibans.

The Tempest.

ELLEN AGAIN—THE EPICUREAN'S PSYCHOMACHY—THE
SAVAGE IN LOVE—THE RESCUE.

AND what has become of poor Ellen Danvers all this time?
The tall robber having deposited her in safety on the other side
of the stream, she sank trembling and terrified, and almost unconscious of what was passing around, to the earth; and the
bullets which came whizzing within a few yards of her, after her
late companion, did not tend to allay her apprehensions, or
restore her to the possession of her senses. On seeing the
natural head of hair of the rascal who had offered such rudeness
to her, she was persuaded that she had seen him before: and at
last she entertained no doubt of the fact that he was one of the
burglars who had broken into her father's house a few hours
before.

"Well, and what are you, youngster?" inquired a rough voice
of Ellen, in an accent such as she had never heard addressed to
her before, "do you know anything of that long scoundrel there?"

Finding that it was an officer who addressed her, the disguised
girl mustered courage to answer—

2 P

"No, sir; I do not know aught of him, except that he is a ruffian. He accosted me a short time since, and insisted on walking by my side, and—and——"

The rising blushes on Ellen's fair face would have betrayed her sex to any one skilled in human nature; but the officer was obtuse. " And what made you set up that scream, my boy, when you were in the river, eh?"

The maiden knew not how to frame a reply; for she had an invincible repugnance to telling a falsehood, and if she betrayed the truth, she knew not what might be the consequence.

" Did he offer any violence? Did he try to rob you?" asked the officer.

" Yes, sir," replied Ellen, readily; for it was strictly true that the fellow wanted to steal—a kiss. " I am very thankful," she added, " that your troops arrived so seasonably; and I hope the villain will be taken?"

" A very likely tale the lad tells us," observed a pert young subaltern, who wanted to show his sagacity, having overheard the greater part of this dialogue. " In my humble opinion," the subaltern continued, " the tale he tells us bears its own contradiction on the face of it. For you will notice, sir, that the tall scoundrel met with no opposition from this boy till we were at hand."

" What would have been the use?" returned Ellen, with more spirit than she gave herself credit for, " when there was not a soul at hand to help me? Besides, in the disguise he wears, I did not recognise the wretch who—" she hesitated again, doubtful whether it would be then prudent to mention the circumstance of the previous night's robbery.

" In my judgment," remarked the subaltern, pragmatically, " this boy should be taken before a magistrate and examined. You perceive, now, he stammers and colours up. Depend upon it, sir, he is in league with that rascal we are now hunting."

" It is false!" exclaimed Ellen, indignantly, and with some of her father's haughty and commanding air; and her slight figure erect, and with flashing eye and dilated nostril, she would hardly have been known for the timid girl she really was, by any student of human nature; but circumstances evoke a strength of character and exaltation of mind which impart new features to the external appearance.

"Gentlemen," she continued, with calm firmness, "I am entirely at your mercy ; but I am now proceeding to inquire after a father whom I dearly love, and I hope as Christians and as soldiers bound by every humane and honourable sentiment—as parents—as children, if you be such—not to delay me."

As she appealed to the gentler feelings of those she addressed her voice lost its strength, and her eyes were suffused with tears. The elder man with a rugged exterior was not devoid of kindness, and replied—

"Go along, then, my lad. I am a father, and have a boy of your age ; God speed you."

With these words the veteran rode away, but the subaltern exclaimed—

"What an old fool that is, to be hoaxed by fine words. This lad is evidently an impostor—Ah! he has availed himself of the permission given him already ; but I'll ride up and put a few more cross-questions to him which will elicit the truth."

Fortunately for Ellen, the young man was here called upon to take the command of a party of dragoons, and she was suffered to pursue her way uninterrupted, though she was so overcome with the excitement and terror she had undergone, that she could hardly use her limbs. Arriving at a blacksmith's shop she made inquiries about Elizabeth, and learned the particulars of the first accident she had encountered, the smith being engaged in repairing the vehicle which had broken down with her. Ellen on receiving this intelligence, asked if there were any sort of conveyance at hand, desirous of accelerating her journey, but being answered in the negative, renewed her walk, and with "fainting steps and slow" contrived in the course of two more hours to progress a league. It was now growing very late, and the poor girl felt she must rest ere she could proceed farther. Sitting down beneath a sheltering ilex, she leant her head on her little hand, and gradually the effects of extreme weariness—for she had walked six miles—and the lateness of the hour, which was past that when she usually retired to rest, combined to frustrate her intention of not sleeping, and she soon slumbered the repose of health and innocence.

She had remained in this state of oblivion for about an hour, when the form of a man approached, and presently stood within a few feet of her. He was young—apparently not beyond earliest manhood—but there was something in his thoughtful face, and dark, large, luminous eye, which gave an expression, but seldom to be remarked in those of his age.

"Now," said the youth, after a silence of some minutes, during which it was clear his brain had not been idle, "now is 'the one half world' buried in sleep. Dreams! dreams! If we could see them all! Their fantastic meanness and folly—how vilely should we think of the intellectual beings around us! The desires which during the day had been distracted by the cares and business of life, occupy the heart and imagination. The proud man is dreaming—of what? of toys and baubles. Now some title is conferred upon him—which he affects to scorn—and how the poor wretch's heart does leap! The counterpane of his bed is set in motion by it! The wise man is dreaming. Is it of the delights of virtue? Pshaw! he hears the plaudits of fools and knaves, yet while he affects to curl his lip, he is happy. O, wonderful! *He* wise!—The lover sees his bright mistress—her he adores; but there is a brighter form just now before his mind's eye. A more tempting lip now courts his kiss—a more lustrous eye expresses desire. Go to—go to! If the vast curtain drawn over the secrets of the Life of Sleep were removed—in the sickly brain we should perceive a fever—typifying existence! restless, vain, perturbed. Disappointment, shadows, chimæras, death and annihilation. Ay, it is in the oblivion we sometimes gain in sleep, the happiest of all states of being is realized. Our nature is a corrupt, a vile one. But we made it not. There is no truth, no faith, no radiance, no purity in man. Best to be nothing. Look where you will, 'tis ever the same. In the savage, and the genius, advanced in civilization—the man of mind—the weak, vain woman—the boy—the child—all weeds—falsehood, misery!"

Again the disciple of Hegesias lapsed into silence; but in a few minutes broke it once more.

"Our nature being thus depraved by the almighty fiends we call circumstances, it is folly to talk of sin: for who or what organized those circumstances! who called them into existence? A good or evil principle? Neither; a blind one; for supposing the existence of an extra-mundane God, he must either *be* necessity, or else necessitated, and so only a secondary cause. For nothing can violate its own laws. A God could not be a brute, any more than a brute could be a God. Well, then, he is necessitated to be what he is, and so subject to a superior principle; and if so, the attribute of omnipotence is reduced to non-entity. It is impossible such should be the case. In the chain of being mind forms the nucleus into which the finest portions of matter enter;—without them it is empty. How far does this chain extend? Into Eternity? Has being limits? That is inconceivable. The vast Whole is Infinite. We are all a portion of that Whole."

Again he paused.

"What is the most perfect thing in nature?" he pursued. "Man! But he is also the most imperfect. Paradox of paradoxes! Irreconcilable anomaly! He can alone conceive the perfect; then why is he not so? What are the elements necessary for perfection? If we can conceive a thing, cannot we execute it? No, in proportion as the intellect of man is great, his passions appear powerful and overwhelming. He can never be aught but what he is."

Thus saying, the soliloquist was about to depart, when the recumbent form of Ellen caught his eye. The silvery moonbeams played upon her pure, calm face, and gave it an angel's beauty.

"Poor boy!" exclaimed the youth, compassionately, "is he then houseless? And so young, so innocent:—he *must* be innocent, to sleep like this. I cannot hear him breathe, and could almost believe him dead, but for that rosy glow on his cheek. He cannot be dreaming—and yet—hark! he speaks—what says he?"

Ellen murmured the name of Walsingham in her sleep.

"This is singular!" exclaimed the young man, "who can he be?" He continued to gaze on the sleeper, fixedly; but on a sudden the expression of his face altered. He examined the object of his notice more closely; he stooped down, and—yes, there could be no doubt of the fact. A bush which grew close to the spot where Ellen lay had disarranged her dress, and sufficient of her white bosom was exposed to proclaim her sex.

"A lovely creature!" cried the youth, breathless with surprise. He paced up and down with uncertain steps. Again he approached her. There was an inward struggle with him—being as he was of awful passions;—night, solitude, and his own nature contending against the young girl. What protection had she under such circumstances from an Atheist or a libertine? Yet when he gazed upon her modest charms—her serene young brow—her child-like look of purity, her sweet soft smile, and saw a tear trembling on her veined eyelid, the generous feelings of manhood prevailed : and fearful of trusting himself any longer in her presence he hastened away. Need it be added he was William Walsingham?

Those only of a similar temperament and opinions can exactly estimate the difficulty he found in leaving unpolluted and untouched the defenceless being who had so imprudently exposed herself to such peril. The passions of such a man are more inflamed by the unexpected appearance of loveliness in such a situation, than by the arts employed to raise the fancy and stimulate the blood of the sensualist. But at eighteen there may be a spark of humanity left even in the bosom of the fiercest libertine ; and though the Materialist was one who had left behind him entirely the youth of feeling, the poetry which supplies the absence of religion and morality in such a disposition had not quite evaporated. I fear that my feeble hand is incompetent to delineate the subtile lines and shadows in such a character—one most "antithetically mixed"— now violently struggling to be good, and again dragged down to evil. It is infinitely less difficult to pourtray an individual whose opinions and actions are decidedly enlisted on the side of Vice or Virtue, than one continually wavering between the two— one aiming at the loftiest objects this minute, and submitting himself to the grossest and meanest desires the next. I almost despair sometimes of developing anything original in the consummation of ideal individual mind, when I discover the difficulties attendant on doing so. Yet all have experienced similar passions—all wavered between and battled with the Powers of Light and Darkness, and by searching the depths of our own hearts something may be done. Shall the Epicurean live when his painter's feeble hand is mouldering below?

Poor Ellen had only escaped one danger to he assailed by another. A few minutes after the Materialist had disappeared, a hideous creature emerged from a clump of trees at the distance of a hundred yards from the spot where she lay, dreaming of *her* Walsingham ; and advancing to her, scrutinized her appearance with curious eyes. Presently he uttered a suppressed sound of delight, resembling nothing human in its wild, yell-like intonation, and kneeling down beside the maiden, he twisted the long tresses of her hair in his misshapen fingers. The scene would have forcibly recalled some of the pictures of nymphs and satyrs, which the old masters so frequently chose as subjects.

The glaring eyeballs of the monster wandered from the closed eyes of the sleeper to her little and exquisite mouth : then to her graceful throat, and lastly to her half-exposed breast. New feelings seemed contending in his mind, and his unsightly face became frightfully distorted with violent and brutal passions. Now he clasped the sleeping beauty round her gracile form, and was about to inflict a disgusting caress on her pure lips, when awaking with a start, and almost fancying she yet dreamed, Ellen screamed loudly and struggled to liberate herself. But though young and low of stature, the monster's strength was that of a man, and she vainly endeavoured to extricate herself from his long arms, which clasped her so tightly as to impede her breathing. Half lifeless with horror, and helpless in that sinewy grasp, the extremity of her danger alone gave her strength ; but the miscreant having raised her from the earth was carrying her away to the clump of trees whence he had issued. He had enough intellect to shape a course of action for himself, and he thought, " I will make her my mate, and keep her in a cave, and steal fruits and gather berries for her. I'll catch the birds that sing most sweetly, and confine them for her, but none must ever see her again except myself ; for I know I am loathsome to look at, and she will hate me if she see others."

Meditating thus, he conveyed his terrified burthen to the spot he had chosen, and compelling her to sit on the grass, and embracing her waist, he produced some fruit and offered it to her. It was his savage mode of making love. The monster's bodily powers were far in advance of his age, and his passions proportionately precocious : but these new sensations had abruptly come upon him, and overpowered the little reason and humanity he possessed. Something between a man and a brute, in mind as in shape, though not incapable of feeling as well as of reflection, his thoughts extended but little beyond what in beasts is instinct. There are three qualities of mind, sense, reason, and understanding. The first is passive and shared by all animals, the second is an attribute of man alone. The last, many brutes have a share of, and the savage was not deficient in it; but he could not carry out a train of ideas, probably from defects of education, as much as from weakness of judgment. Thus he had no notion of morality, and invariably, of course, followed the bent of his inclinations. After all, there may be intellectual beings far more fiendish in nature.

Ellen almost thought that she was abandoned of Heaven; but, as a last expedient, she strove to touch the heart of the hideous boy.

" I know not whether you can understand me," she at last faltered, " and I know not how to find strength to speak." [The monster made gestures signifying he comprehended.] " I am a forlorn girl," continued Ellen, " and have put on this disguise to seek my father. I beseech you, let me go. What would you have? I can be of no good to you."

The savage shook his head, and pointed to two pigeons, which were roosting together on the tree above. He gave her to understand that he wished they should live together like those birds, by his looks and gestures, and again pressed the fruit she had rejected on her.

" God help me!" exclaimed the poor girl, weeping, " what shall I do?"

The savage seemed sorry for her distress, but did not offer to release her. He attempted to kiss the tears from her cheek. She repulsed him with horror, and reiterated her cries for help. The monster at length appeared enraged at her screams, and putting his hand on her mouth dragged her down. It was at this juncture that the maiden beheld a woman approaching, and by a desperate effort managed to tear away the miscreant's hand from her lips, and to exclaim, " Help me for the love of God, help me from this demon!"

The new comer replied only by a sardonic and malicious grin, muttering, " Why should I interfere? I hate all youth and beauty. Let the boy treat her as he likes." Saying which, to the agony of Ellen, she retreated.

By a convulsed exertion of her remaining strength, the maiden regained her feet, but it was impossible to fly while her tormentor retained her by his claws of hands.

sand dogmas and fantasies incapable of demonstration, it extends no beacon, it affords no star to guide the weary soul to a haven of rest and happiness. Every system of philosophy which pretends to be founded on immutable truth, with the exception of this solitary monstrosity, also offers something to the amount of enjoyment or good, and affects to contain some principle which may elevate and sustain. But this from first to last is dreary negation of all that is sweet and consolatory to man.

" The weakness of superstition," says he, who denies the existence of a Creator, " is exploded for ever by Atheism ; and by the adoption of it, the universal earth might be emancipated from the shackles of error and falsehood."

But this is no principle at all, as any logician knows. Common sense informs us, that unless it can be proved that something can be substituted for something, which confers a degree of happiness, it is best to retain what has been tried. Did you ever know an Atheist happy ?—Wonderful hallucination! Is there no superstition in the negation so weakly advocated? The superstition (if it be so) of an extra-mundane God, is not one-millionth part so great as that of a blind power which is ever producing a combination of harmonic and certain results. And for the rest, all is obscurity, hopelessness and conjecture. Annihilation glares like a demon on us at every step, and despair stalks over the glorious universe ;—a phantom which must ever be dissipated by a firm credence in the immortal, which is implanted in us—even in the savage who worships vain idols.

To return to that miserable one, who, by a strange perversion of mind, believed we are all as brutes, indestructible only in the matter of which our bodies are composed, while the spark of thought, feeling, and reason is extinguished for ever by death.

He had entered the dwelling in which we now find him, and sought the lady who was holding earnest communion with her Maker. He stopped at the half-open door, on hearing her musical voice in prayerful accents, and listened in profound silence to the breathings of that seraphic spirit. There, far from every human being, as she supposed, unheard by any in the material world, she opened her secret heart, in the assurance of faith and love. Her splendid and unearthly beauty was irradiated with intense glory from the eloquent working of her perfect features,

2 Q

those large, and pure, and melancholy eyes, shaded by their silken lashes on which

> —— " Clear drops, which start like sacred dew
> From the twin lights her sweet soul darkens through—"

glowing with the majesty of her thoughts, the fervour of her aspirations, the rapture of her celestial hope.

A celebrated character of political eminence, who was a friend of a late eminent divine and scholar, had imbibed sceptical opinions. It happened he was staying with this worthy clergyman, and one night, having left that person in his own chamber, he remembered he had left something behind, which he had occasion for, and returned to the apartment. The pious man was on his knees, engaged in supplication, and the sceptic listened to him, and heard him seek the aid and sustentation of the Deity. He had entertained a notion that religion is but mere profession; but when he found how deep and heart-felt was his excellent friend's devotion, and when thus unknown to all he sought his Maker, he said, " that it did more to shake his doubts than all the arguments he had ever heard in favour of Christianity."[*]

And such for a short time was the case with that young Atheist, whom, it were superogatory to inform the reader, was William Walsingham. His unbelief, however, was too deeply rooted to be extirpated in a moment. Yet when he beheld the clasped hands, the upturned eyes, the parted lips, that quivered with emotion involuntarily, and were more exquisite in the enthusiasm they typified than the inspired hand of a Raffaelle ever pourtrayed in his pure saints and virgins, the prostrate form, the looks of divine feeling, the grandeur, the meekness, the pathos of her countenance, and heard the thrilling sweetness and love and enthusiastic hope of her accents and expressions, he was so touched, so subdued, so convinced that he saw all that was most true, sincere and undefiled, that tears of admiration trickled down his pale cheek, and rapid thoughts were evidently busy within him, from the shadows on his broad forehead; while he closed his eyes and stood motionless as a statue.

But his mood soon changed. The evil fiend of his nature re-

* This anecdote of Redhead Yorke and Dr. Valpy is from a private source.

sumed its sway, or, oh! how different a man he would probably
have become. Had such a mind devoted itself to religion and
virtue, it might have illuminated a world by its radiance, strength,
and fervour.

The suppliant arose, and encountered the cold, if not sarcastic
gaze of the Materialist. A slight blush was visible on her sculptured cheek, as she found she had been detected in her sanctuary
of thought, but it passed away like a cloud from before the sun, and
erect in all the placid dignity of worth, she confronted her visitor.

"You pray frequently, I suppose?" said William Walsingham
to Harriet.

"I find comfort in prayer," was the reply.

"And you think the invisible Power you worship requires to
be reminded of your wants and wishes?" he rejoined.

"If you heard what I lately said, you know to the contrary,"
answered Miss Walsingham. "God is certainly aware of all
that we require."

"Then why endeavour to change his purpose, why importune
him, when you know he is unchangeable,—for so you say he is—
if you conceive that he has any intention at all?"

Miss Walsingham did not speak, and William continued—

"Of course you must suppose this being has not created you
for nothing. Should you beg any gift from a generous and beneficent earthly person? Would not a benefactor anticipate your
wants and supply them, as he thought was most calculated to be
serviceable to you, without your reminding him of your depen-
dency? Well! Cannot you answer me a word?"

"Yes, William: but I must have a moment to reply to you in a
way commensurate with the importance of the subject. I always
reflect why I do everything; so you must not suppose that I am
doing so now for the first time; but I wish to collect my thoughts—
for they have not been engaged in mere reasoning. It appears to me,
in the first place, that whatsoever makes me happy, that must be
well and wise to do; for the search for happiness is the great law
of the human mind. God knows my heart, I admit, of course;
but He wishes I should know it. Is not that reasonable; if I
am accountable for my actions? He has also an immutable purpose with regard to me. But though nothing can change His
purpose, it does not therefore follow that I cannot change my

own; and what means so effectual can I use, as prayer? The human heart is prone to evil (at least I think so), and we want to direct it to good. I find that prayer purifies my heart: I am enjoined to pray, and if the results be such as I am told they will be, is it not rational to conclude the truth and divinity of its origin? It is reasonable to suppose, even if God had not ordained prayer as a means to an end, and not an end itself, that it is a wise method of elevating myself, and so rendering me acceptable in His eye. And for the gifts He bestows on me, I am grateful, and therefore I thank him. Could I do less to any one? And because I am weak, I ask Him to sustain and strengthen me? Is that absurd?"

" But if this Being exist, has he not pre-ordained all things? Is there not a necessity for everything? If there be not, then there is no necessity for a God. How could the moral government—as you term it—of the universe proceed, if the Power that rules all, did not ordain that specific causes should produce definite results? For if this were not so, all nature would be at war with herself. Then why attempt to divert the necessary purpose of this Creative Mind?"

" But I have the ability to will, and therefore am not a machine in the universe. Moral actions cannot be said to proceed from necessity; and it is no mistrust of the goodness of God to prefer our petitions to Him, that we may become better and more devoted to His will. Ah, William! you do not know the flood of joy and happiness which fervent prayer causes to gush through the heart. We are sublimated while we are abased by it. The smile of the Eternal rests upon us, and our belief becomes conviction and transport. There are great mysteries in all things, I admit, and I know not how the Eternal purpose of the Deity can be changed,—I do not think it can be: but this I know, while I believe He is immutable, and orders all the wonderful operations of nature, that the balm of His holy spirit falls on my bleeding heart and heals it sweetly."

" But you must think you can change the Eternal purpose by prayer, while, weak in your belief, you ask for a greater measure of it."

" I am not weak in *belief*, William—*that* comes by the grace of Heaven—but faith is more than mere belief. It sinks into the inmost life, and pours ecstatic thoughts into the breast. We bound through the deep azure space and gain our immortal wings before we become so. If God foresees, He does not compel our actions. I am necessitated to believe in the existence of my Creator; but faith is distinguished from that necessity by a broad line of demarcation. To give mere credence to a thing is not to make the object of credence a principle of action. But faith vivifies all holy thoughts, it inspires all devout adoration; it quickens the heart to virtue, and makes it a willing sacrifice—destroys the seeds of vice, annihilates all fear, bears the bright feelings to the realms of bliss, and lays them at the throne of Him that gave them. For what can we render back to the Supreme for all the benefits He heaps upon us? Gratitude is all that we can offer up, and He accepts it. But you, if you were a believer in the existence of a God, would take all he gives and never bend the head in acknowledgment of it! Is this your science? To tell me that you know God has predestined all, and therefore you can only work out the scheme of Providence?—Even as the atoms on which we tread are compelled to obey the laws of gravitation!—Is this your pride of intellect? To believe that you are nothing more than the engines framed by the hands of men, in the vast plan of creation? If so, give me ignorance. Let me be as the poor savage that is not enlightened by the beams of revelation, who understands not how the countless stars, which for ever glorify the skies, are measured, and the great globe revolves round the sun : but let me feel that I am something more than the gross matter of which my body is composed. *That* is *my* pride. If a Newton who explained those celestial laws with such all-piercing genius, if a Shakspeare who read all the complex mysteries of our fearful and marvellous nature, if a Milton whose mighty imagination soared through time and space, could humiliate themselves before the light of that religion I adore, the invectives of unbelief, and the sneers of pseudo-philosophy will not unfix my mind from bending in lowly worship, sustained by a consciousness which *you* cannot have, that the Being I address is truly present to me, and that the immortality I hope for will not be withheld."

With what energy and truthfulness did Harriet Walsingham thus defend the faith she held! A Cicero with his flowers of rhetoric could not have pleaded more convincingly than did that

woman with her lustrous eyes, her harmonious voice, her flashing
face, which awed into annihilation as she spoke the Atheism of
the youth. He was for the time staggered; but alas! not
shaken.

CHAPTER II.

The Atheist will tell you that all this harmonious, all this exquisite arrangement, is the result of a fortunate concurrence of fortuitous circumstances; for
the fool has said in his heart, "there is no Maker, there is no God." Can you,
will you believe him? Rather let us, compassionating his scepticism, admire
and wonder, let us reverence and adore.—Dr. BEDINGFIELD.

ATHEISM—WILLIAM'S VISIT TO LAWYER QUIRK—A NEW
CHARACTER.

ATHEISM has but one solitary stronghold, in the heart of the
great mystery of evil, whose origin we shall fruitlessly endeavour
to trace, since good alone is eternal.

Unbelief in general may be said to have two forts, viz., the
practical infidelity of the great body of nominal believers, and
the superstition which covers like a pall the fair face of Christianity among two-thirds of the civilized world. When, therefore, some bright and divine example of genuine piety is discovered
by the sceptic, among those whose tenets he ridicules, the eloquence of conviction which truth and sincerity carry to the mind
in spite of itself, effects more than all the syllogisms of theological
writers, and the elegant and forcible discourses of divines in the
pulpit. By one instance of goodness the Atheist's soul may be
borne into the source of good, and he will see evil in its true light,
instead of through the distorted medium of false philosophy.

He will see how vile immorality and crime of every species is, contrasted with the moral radiance he *must* admire, and that the sorrows with which humanity is afflicted, are far from being insupportable to those who believe in eternal rewards, and the beneficence of an overruling Providence, who never inflicts pain but for wise and merciful ends. But why afflict the virtuous?— Because they bear grief the best, and their example is like the voice of an angel, and breathes supernal love and holiness.

Dear one! whose enthusiastic love of God in all thy most severe and agonizing trials, affords an irrefragable argument for the power of religion in sustaining and in comforting, whose actions are indeed "like an angel's," whose aspirations are all of faith and hope, and adoration, pure and intense as the devotion of Harriet Walsingham, who like thee has suffered more than tongue can tell, but in the mind more than the body,—accept this poor, passing tribute of affection and admiration, though, respecting thy modesty, I refrain from giving to the world a name which should be immortal as the bright stars of Heaven, when the fame of Napoleon has expired with the memory of all the woes he caused. The imperishability of a nature like thine should be a beacon to the universe, guiding it to peace and joy, a memory immortal even here, where all is mortal, as it must be in Elysium, a flower that exhales eternal odours, gentle and sweet ; for man in forgetting such an example,

> " Like the base Judæan throws a pearl away
> Richer than all his tribe."

"It is well," said William Walsingham, after a pause, in reply to the fervent appeal of that pure mind in favour of the creed it held so firmly, "it is well. Behold! this life is a dark and stormy dream ; and thunders and lightnings boom and flash upon us, destroying our frail barks ; each hope is withered, each joy is crushed for ever! If you can believe that evil ever springs from good, I say, 'tis very well. I would *I* could delude myself with the idea of being happy for ever! Pray on ; weep on ! Poor dust! Thou art not strong enough for the most fiery spark within, that struggles, but to be extinguished. Better to be as the brutes that know nothing beyond the present, than have the insufficient knowledge we possess. How painful is the thought

that all we can do is vain, that death will clasp us in its icy arms,
and the heart cease to throb, and the soul of mighty thoughts be
hushed in everlasting silence! And yet, is it not better to be
nothing, than to feel the gigantic impulses to accomplish things
beyond our reach—to experience the bitter feelings of disappointed
ambition, of frustrated desires, of impotent grasping after the invisible,—mysterious longings and aspirations, unutterable thoughts
and visions, which vainly strive to burst from the womb of time,
and to cleave eternity,—things that mock us with their splendour
and power; for ever, for ever baffling our grasp?

> ' To die, to sleep,'

" Thus saith he who knew all *we* know—

> ' No more; and by a sleep to say we end
> The heart-ache, and the thousand natural shocks
> That flesh is heir to; 'tis a consummation
> Devoutly to be wish'd.'

" Ay, the dreamless slumber!"

It would be difficult to describe the profound mournfulness and
melancholy pathos with which the Materialist uttered those dark
words, which like the philosopher's of Cyrene, might have caused
those who thought as he did, to have rushed on annihilation;—
but Atheists seldom or never commit self-destruction;—words
which so accurately pourtrayed the sensations of a mind like his,
which must ever aspire to the eternal, whatever opinions it maintain. The lofty intellect warped by the cold negation of Atheism
is in antagonism with itself, and every sublime feeling must be
annihilated before the spirit can rest contented with a world so
corrupt and wretched as this.

Almost unconsciously he had given vent to his thoughts in
words—a habit which he had acquired by so frequently choosing
solitude, and holding monologues in his abstraction, which were
many of them singularly different in their matter, yet all tinged
with sadness and despondency of good.—Harriet Walsingham's
acute sensibility was deeply touched by the gentleness, the pathos,
and the absence of his usual bitter sarcasm, in what the young
Atheist had been saying, and taking his hand in her's, she exclaimed—

" My poor, deluded nephew! surely to be happy is the great

object of existence? Whatever tends to make one wretched must be founded in error. I love you very much—more even than I loved your father; and it grieves me deeply to see you unhappy. Dear William! you can struggle with yourself; you have great though dormant powers, and for my sake, in return for my affection, rouse yourself, will you not?"

Harriet clasped William's neck, and kissed him fondly.

The strong frame of the Atheist trembled violently, and he half repulsed his aunt, muttering indistinctly to himself, while he closed his eyes, and knit his brows, and seemed engaged in a desperate internal conflict.

"What is it that you say, dear boy?" she inquired, solicitously.

"There are two principles in the mind, it would seem," said William, regarding not the question which had been put to him, nor the presence of another; for he was in a state of mind wherein the visible and actual make a less powerful impression on the brain than the ideal. "Now we are led by the one, now by the other, as the omnipotencies of circumstance command. They are the antitypes of good and evil, yet in themselves are neither the one nor the other. They are but blind agents of necessity. Shall I yield at once, or still strive on? It will come at last!— Embrace me no longer. I am a base, unworthy wretch, bright one! I feel what I am when with thee, and hate myself. Yet there is a sacred radiance in thy presence which—" he hesitated, and added, "No matter."

So saying, with quivering hands, he was about to release himself from the circling arms of Harriet Walsingham and to depart in haste, when, as he was breaking from her, she cried—

"But, William! you have forgotten the object for which I sent you, and which has so long occupied your time."

The Epicurean pressed his shaking fingers on his hot brow and muttered—

"My blood boils as in a fever to-night."

"I have been sitting up expecting you for a long time," continued the lady; "and I almost feared you had met with some accident. You look ill, dear William—are you so? Your face flushes, and then becomes deadly pale, and you shake as if with ague," and again she put her arms round him.

"Do not touch me—I am well now," said the youth, shrinking

from his aunt's embrace, and with a fearful effort mastering himself. "I *had* forgotten the business you mention. I found out
the man to whom you sent me—a sly, subtle little rascal of advanced age, who, if he be not a villain, his face belies him foully.
What scoundrels those lawyers are! They are worse even than
the priests! That the world should have been so bamboozled
for so many centuries!"

"Well; and what did he say?—I am sure you are not well.
Your eyes still roll wildly. Let me send for the doctor?"

"No, I thank you. Neither priest, nor lawyer, nor physician
shall have aught to do with William Walsingham. The old fellow
said a great deal; but it was all humbug and nonsense. I discovered his residence, a shabby house in the centre of the town,
and having asked for 'Lawyer Quirk' I was ushered into a dark
room, where there were a few dirty pictures, a table with writing
utensils on it, and a couple of chairs, constituting the whole furniture. Presently the decrepid form of a man on the verge of
eighty, with a diabolical leer, half squint, half twinkle, with a
wrinkled forehead, and small, sharp eyes, but deeply sunken in
their sockets, entered the room. He was bent almost double,
and was dressed in a snuff-coloured suit which was well worn.

" 'You are lawyer Quirk, I suppose,' said I.

" 'Your servant, young gentleman,' he replied.

" 'My name is Walsingham,' I continued, 'and I come from
my aunt, Miss Walsingham, to communicate with you on a subject——'

" 'Ah, ha!' the old man interrupted. 'I see! I see! I shall
be happy to serve you. State the case.'

" 'I must first know what you can do, Master Quirk,' I said.
'It appears that some years ago you waited on Miss Walsingham,
and tendered your services to her on a matter of much delicacy.
You said you were acquainted with circumstances relative to a
person of the name of Danvers, which you would state for a specified sum, and moreover offered——'

"Here the old man broke in on what I was saying a second
time.

" 'I beg your pardon, young sir; in these matters we must
be precise; I spoke nothing positively. I only hinted—You see,
I should be loth to commit myself,—having a character to maintain in the eye of the law. Do you bring credentials with you?'

" ' Worthy Master Quirk,' was my rejoinder, ' if you think
you cannot trust me, I shall repose no confidence in you.'

" ' Don't be so hasty, young gentleman,' he cried. ' This is
a matter of much importance, and we must be cautious, *very*
cautious. I should like to see Miss Walsingham personally, and
will undertake to effect all that I promised to do many years ago,
if it should be necessary.—That escape was remarkably well
managed—not that I had any hand in it—God forbid! hem!'

" ' Well, I suppose you had better wait on Miss Walsingham
to-morrow; but you must not on any account reveal the place of
her abode——' "

" *That* does not matter now," muttered Harriet.

" ' Or that she is living, to any. Your services will be amply
compensated; but if you should dare to prove unfaithful, as I
live, I will slit your ears.'

" The old rogue made many protestations of fidelity, and talked
a great deal of absurdity wide from the purpose, which he intended
to deceive me; but I cut him short, and left him. Various accidents have delayed me, or I should have returned long ago. And
now adieu until to-morrow, when I shall be with you, in order to
be present at the interview with Quirk. I thank you for having
trusted me in this affair.—And yet," he said, in an under-tone,
" I would that it had not been! Though it must have come.
Yet!—well—think as well as you can of me, beloved aunt. I
value your good opinion far more than that of all the knaves and
fools who compose this busy world. I am what I am. With
towering passions and little self-controul, weak, but not wavering,
sensual, but not heartless; something between the God of our
Philosophers, and the evil one of superstitious fears. Again,
adieu."

Thus having spoken, the Materialist took the extended hand
of his aunt for an instant, then dropped it suddenly, and vanished.

" O, what a noble mind is here o'erthrown !" ejaculated Harriet Walsingham. " How great are all his sentiments when they
do not flow in the channels of his debasing materialism. May
Heaven change his heart and sentiments, and make him a wiser,
and happier man. With all his errors, I feel I love him beyond
all my other relatives !—I dread this interview with the lawyer;

but Walter's life is forfeited, and instant measures must be taken
—alas, alas! that fatal passion. Is he guilty, or innocent? I
cannot judge clearly of him. Why, why have I loved him thus?"

How often has that question been put to her soul by the splendid
aristocrat, who moves among the proudest of the earth, as well
as by the humble peasant to whom that love is sole wealth and
happiness. "Why have I loved him thus?" Painful, sorrowful
words, implying that the adored object of the being's best and
early affections is unworthy of them. What priceless treasures of
pure faith and passion are cast away by those whose breasts in-
sphere but the god of self! What a thing it is that the heart's
wealth should be lavished in vain! How exquisitely our Hemans
embodied that thought; how passionately she cries—"I depart
unknown!" And the most precious things are lost or squandered
—jewels, as it were, of unknown beauty, dropped from a brighter
sphere, and cast away by the dull and ignorant, never to be regained. "Why have I loved?" "Why have I not loved?" In
those two sentences are summed the greatest of miseries. But to
leave this apparent enigma unsolved, and return to our narrative.

Harriet was disturbed from the reverie into which she had
fallen, by hearing a sound in her apartment. Starting up, she
uttered a cry of alarm, as she beheld a strange-looking, little, old
man, who stood at the distance of a few feet from her, peering
around with his still sharp and cunning small eyes. He was just
such a figure as we associate in our fancy with the queer, diminutive personages of fairy tale, old, ugly, and of sly feature, with
intellects as much on the alert as they were in early youth.

"Do not be alarmed, madam," said this odd individual to
Harriet, making an obeisance. "I am lawyer Quirk. I hope
that you will pardon my thus intruding myself on your privacy;
but I have disclosures to make which I could only communicate
to you thus, unheard by any witness."

And with these words, the lawyer fumbled in his capacious
pocket, and produced some dirty, yellow papers.

CHAPTER III.

Truth ever lovely since the world began,
The foe of tyrants, and the friend of man,
How can thy words from balmy slumber start
Reposing Virtue, pillow'd on the heart!
Yet, if thy voice the note of thunder roll'd,
And that were true which Nature never told,
Let Wisdom smile not on her conquer'd field ;
No rapture dawns, no treasure is reveal'd !
Oh ! let her read nor loudly, nor elate,
The doom that bars us from a better fate ;
But, sad as angels for the good man's sin,
Weep to record, and blush to give it in.—CAMPBELL.

THE EPICUREAN ENCOUNTERS CAPTAIN NORTON—THE QUESTION—THE PURSUIT.

MEANWHILE William Walsingham, after leaving his aunt, pursued his way, lost in abstraction—as indeed, professed Materialist as he was, almost invariably was the case, when left to himself. He believed (singular anomaly as such a belief was in this instance) that he could only derive gratification through the medium of the senses, and yet no man was ever more occupied with analysis of the elements of thought and sensation. He despised metaphysics, which he considered a name for nothing, notwithstanding he found his own intellect a theme of engrossing interest. If you read the biography of men of similar opinions and like mental powers, you will find that his was by no means an isolated case ; and it demonstrates, in spite of all the materialistic tendencies of sensuality and epicureanism, that every fine mind is more or less absorbed with a study which is the most mysterious and profound of any we can take cognizance of. True, the man who devotes himself to the exact sciences, to politics, or to business, may be drawn away from very abstract reflections by necessity; but it will be perceived also, whenever the soul takes a higher flight than usual, the strange and incomprehensible essence of which it is composed is that to which it is attracted, as the needle to the pole. If you read the Elizabethan dramatists you will see such was their opinion. It were unnecessary to offer any farther defence of mental philosophy, as it thus would appear an undeniable fact, that in the highest and the most ethereal moods, the spirit exhausted with flights of fiery imagination and exalted aspirations, returns to the source whence all must emanate, the one great secret of what we are. What was the youth thinking about?

"I wish I could know the mode in which certain causes must operate to certain effects. If this *could* be defined, then, indeed, volition would not be a phantasma of the diseased fancy; for then we should know how to steer our course with certainty, whereas, at present, we have no star to light, no compass to direct us; we are in total ignorance of the 'to come!' Each circumstance produces a new train of ideas, and each new train of ideas evolves some stage of mind. There is no such thing as a state of sensation—that is an unaccountable thing when all *is* sensation!—could sensation for an instant be annihilated I should become another individual. It is evident, then, in order that identity may be preserved, that I should undergo continual progression; without progress nothing could exist,—and, therefore, progress is a law of development. These last few hours have produced many changes within me. I have been tempted to do that which I consider immoral—not because there is such an entity as vice, but because it would perhaps have made another miserable. What a heart this is! My head has no chance with it. Yet why so? Reason is in every action; otherwise I should be propelled in all things by desire. Am I so? My animal nature was evidently subdued by my intellectual one, for I was strongly tempted—twice tempted.—But still the strongest motive; ay, ay, the strongest motive!"

The Materialist folded his arms, and stood perfectly still, surveying the face of heaven, the grey of which was blending with a rosy hue, foretelling the dawn was at hand. In the anatomy of his mind above given, it has been endeavoured to give an insight into the recesses and springs of thought ; and, indeed, it is *here* that there is such an almost illimitable field for speculation and interest, greatly transcending that of *mere* action, which is but the body to the soul. Sir Edward Lytton Bulwer has been lately attempting something of this sort. He is a fine, beautiful novelist, and the effort was a noble one. But a public must be made before this is generally relished. Shakspeare made a public in an age far inferior to ours ; let us all *strive* at least to create in fiction a vehicle for the intellectual and moral exaltation of man. Blend the interest of thought and action, and the novel will rank as high as the essay. Its theatre is a larger one than the essay will ever command, its actors are passions which appeal to all hearts, and not ideas which require study and labour to abstract and generalise. Once more let us look into the sanctuary of the spirit !

" Even as the external universe is in eternal motion, whirling round and round according to its invariable laws, so is my being, which is a part of it," he thought. Walsingham paused for a moment, and added aloud—" I sleep, and yet each instant that I do so, my existence is varying. My ideas are in continual chaos, and have to be moulded into form, and they are moulded when I wake as when I sleep, without my exercising controul over them. I arise from the wild visions of sleep, and thoughts and passions crowd on my conscious brain. Again I enact the same scenes of unsatisfactory illusion, again the same feelings absorb me—I love, I hate, I lament, and all as vainly as when I dream. Harriet Walsingham ! If thou wert not, what should I be ? How different now ! But each unit that *is*, must be connected with some other in the vast whole. Why am I what I am ? Why may I not love where my wishes prompt ? If I were a brute now, and she also shared the same nature :—*she* a brute ! Nay, it is the mind, the lofty mind that dazzles while it attracts the greatest admiration, that subdues while it excites, and purifies while it makes impassioned, I worship. With nothing less could I be satisfied. What is this love ? An animal propensity ! It must be so ; but there is something in it I can scarcely comprehend. Absurd and contradictory are all the hypotheses of

genius and philosophy on the origin and nature of it. Has it
birth purely in the regions of intelligence? Certainly not. I
could not love, nor any one, but a mad poet—could love an abstract idea, a mere nympholepsy. *I* will not be afflicted with
such dreams. Well, then, is it as with other sentient beings?
They are content with sensual enjoyment—are *we* so? I'm weary
of conjecture! Certainty does not live in aught save the real
and actual. And yet I am fool enough to detest them. I!—
Poetry is the bane of science, and is a childish sport of misem-
ployed imagination. I'll have nothing more to do with it."

Such were the crude and confused mass of feelings and ideas
in the Epicurean's mind. The reader will perceive, from the frequent use of dramatic quotations in the Materialist's reveries, that
he had acquired a strong relish for that style of reading; and,
indeed, from childhood he had delighted in plays and poems,
and perhaps never felt better pleased than when some happy
image or striking metaphor engaged his attention. You may try
to dislike every vagary of fancy, as well as each undemonstrable
theory of intellect; but if you have either the one or the other,
depend upon it you may sometimes experience pleasure in giving
a rein to them—letting the fancy play with the understanding,
and *vice versâ;* and surely every pursuit calculated to refine or
strengthen a portion of that you *are* should not be contemned.

There was a soft hush diffused through all the earth. The
stars were still twinkling, still fading, one by one, from the sky,
and the moon was descending with slow and imperceptible movements beneath the horizon; and there was a slight rustling among
the trees, as the early larks unclosed their eyes, and began to
twitter and hop from branch to branch, a wonderfully truthful
description of which you may find in the singular poem of Peter
Bell. William continued his walk, half inclined to lie down and
sleep, for he had not taken any rest that night:—indeed, he
often wandered about like an unquiet spirit while all was calm
and still, uttering high and dark thoughts, and indulging in wild
dreams; and when the morning approached would sleep away
the hours until noon. This was one among several eccentric habits
of that uncommon youth.

He was met on a sudden, as he began to ascend a hill of some
altitude, along which poplars and other tall trees grew in parallel

order, just like a line of grenadiers, by a man who emerged from behind the shadow of those aspiring gentlemen, and whose appearance was haggard, if not ghastly, in the extreme. He could hardly recognise in him the person of Captain Norton. The recollection of the dead boy he had loved so well returned upon him, although it had been dismissed from his absent and ever dream-thronged soul, so that he had for a short time actually thought on in his usual way, as if the sad event had never been. But the Materialist was not *really* one to forget so soon. His feelings were profound; and measuring the bereaved parent's grief by his own—proportioning the loss to the closeness of the tie—he could hardly be surprised at the fearful and extraordinary change which intense anguish had produced in the Captain. He accosted him compassionately, saying—

"Why are you absent from your home at this hour, sir?"

"Home! home! Ay, those were words, dear and familiar to me once," cried the wretched man, in a hollow voice, and with his blood-shot eyes vacant and glassy. "What is time to me, now? Time was, and is; but I have left it—I am a blank now! And home!—that word was made for those that have children,—dear ties to bind them to it. He that hath them not, if not houseless, is homeless, in the true signification of that word; home is in the human heart. I suppose you know I have lost Percy? He loved you, next to me: now, tell me—you are an Atheist—do you think nothing more remains of him—the good, the gentle, and the noble—than that corruption which will soon be hidden from our abhorring eyes? *You* will abhor; but—I—could kiss what the worm will shrink from of him. O, God! If I thought *that*—I would not live. Do you not answer? Is it your belief Percy is annihilated?—No equivocation."

"This awful bereavement has unsettled the poor wretch's brain," muttered the youth.

"Indeed I am not mad, William Walsingham. Madness is happiness; and so denied so often to sinners. If aught in the world could convert me to your way of thinking, this death, this cruel death of one so good and young;—but then he is happy: and I alone am accursed!"

"You talk incoherently. Pray let me return to your home with you, sir?"

2 s

"Incoherently, do I? You may think so: but I am as calm as all this glorious Nature around.—I feel some pain though in the brain. Perhaps I *may* go mad; and that will save me much misery. Still, I want you to answer me. Do you think that it is possible a mind like Percy's can have become as nought?—a breath of music that is past!—a flame that is quenched!—answer me sincerely."

"Some other time we will speak," began the Materialist, unwilling to belie his real sentiments, and yet loth to torture the unhappy Norton by expressing them.

"No time so fit as the present," interrupted Norton. "I begin to doubt of every thing save my own desolation."

A celebrated author, recently alluded to, observes, "that is a peculiar incident that perhaps occurs to us at all times—viz.—to have a doubt of futurity at the very moment in which the present is most overcast, and to find this world at once stripped of its delusion, and the next of its consolation. It is, perhaps, for others, rather than ourselves that the fond heart requires an hereafter. The tranquil rest, the shadow and the silence, the mere pause of the wheel of life, have no terror for the wise, who know the due value of the world.

'—— After the billows of a stormy sea,
Sweet is at last the haven of repose.'

But not so when that stillness is to divide us eternally from others; when those we have loved with all the passion, the devotion, the watchful sanctity of the weak human heart, are to exist to us no more."

The author of "The Pilgrims of the Rhine" is certainly mistaken about the philosophy with which a wise man might meet annihilation; but with regard to the agony of believing the dearest one of this existence is lost to all eternity, that the mind whose thoughts were wont to make us joyous, and whose sentiments of affection were such treasures to our bosoms, his aphorism is entirely true.

The Atheist paused.

"Why will you compel me either to wound your feelings, or deviate from the line of conduct I consider right?" he said. "We must all die; but what is life, that we should value it?

'When the breath of man goes forth,' says the old Hebrew king, 'all his thoughts perish.' Be comforted! Percy—poor fellow! has been saved the sad and bitter things which ever await natures like his—envy of his fine qualities, hatred, malice, weariness and disgust of life. Then, at all events, *he* is the gainer by death.";

"O no, no, no!" cried Captain Norton, wildly. "I will not believe it. Tell me that yonder pale star, which is vanishing from the sky, will never shine again; that—Ha—there! look there! The murderer! seize him!"

With this abrupt exclamation Norton rushed away through the trees and the brambles which skirted them with extraordinary agility, considering his age, followed by William, who believed he was going mad, and feared he might do some injury to himself. But, despite his youth, he could scarcely keep his friend in view, particularly when he dashed into the midst of a thicket—which had many labyrinthine windings, shouting fiercely, "Villain! stop." That the poor distracted man pursued but the phantom of his brain he was convinced, for he had neither heard nor seen anything which could lead to such a frantic chase. He would now have lost all clue to the direction in which Captain Norton had gone, but for his vociferations; yet it was with much difficulty that he threaded the intricacies of the wood, with which he was imperfectly acquainted.

The morning broke, and still the pursuit was continued by the officer with unabated ardour, William still endeavouring to overtake him, that he might by his persuasions soothe his frenzy and induce him to return to his desolated home. How truly had the stricken wretch said that "from henceforth he had no home!" The spirit had deserted the temple, and all was dust and night. O world! O death! The world death's house; death, the dwelling of silence!

Norton's fierce cries subsided, and the Epicurean now knew not where to seek him. He raised his own voice and shouted; but no answer was returned. Long and weary was his search; but for hours it was unattended with the least success. There was no outlet that he knew of to the thicket in the direction he had taken, and he was certain that Captain Norton could not have returned from his wild pursuit, or he must have seen him. He was on the point of relinquishing his efforts, being thoroughly exhausted with the great exertions he had made, when he espied a portion of a broken sword, and marks of a desperate and recent struggle on the grass where it lay. But still he could perceive no traces of the officer. He had been pursuing then no phantom, but real, substantial flesh and blood. Renewing his quest, he followed the marks of the footsteps on the grass, until they led him to a spot where they abruptly terminated. It was nearly at the outskirts of the thicket, where bushes and brambles, mingled with underwood, grew thickly. Here there had been another struggle, for the impression of a body, which had fallen heavily to the earth, was visible; and examining the bushes, the youth perceived a ponderous stone, which, on his placing his foot upon it, rose, and revealed a cave of apparently some depth and extent. Hesitating but an instant here, the Epicurean descended into the bowels of the earth in total darkness; for the stone at the entrance was so constructed as to fall and close, when not upheld. His foot struck against a soft object, and stooping, he discovered it to be a human form.

Thus far, my friends, have we journeyed on together over hill and dale, now gazing up to the skies with the gladdened orbs of faith; now looking down into the black abysms of the earth, and beholding no light in the darkness. A little while and our brief drama will have run its little day, and may be consigned to oblivion, like many a nobler thing. Perchance, in years that lie deep in the womb of time, some greedy bookworm will seize upon this record of the past, and say, " Behold what things our ancestors read !" Yes, a brighter era will come; and though the human heart will be unchanged, a new spring of sweet affections and lovely thoughts will obliterate the remembrance of the old flowers of autumn. But, oh ! there is beauty, there is holiness, there is everlasting odour in what has once been loved.

> " A thing of beauty is a joy for ever;
> Its loveliness increaseth ; it will never
> Pass into nothingness ; but still will keep
> A bower quiet for us, and a sleep
> Full of sweet dreams, and health, and quiet breathing."

If there be aught loveable in this, my humble work, I am well content. It is a joyous feeling, although it be sad withal, to think that when the daisies are exhaling fragrance over our quiet dust, bright eyes will be weeping, and warm hearts throbbing over what has once been fostered in our own breasts. Give me one tear, O world! when I am beyond tears,—give me one sigh, when I am at peace, and breathe an atmosphere where the gale wafts no mournful sounds for ever.

CHAPTER IV.

I do not speak of fear, or flight, or death ;
But dare all imminence that gods and men
Address their dangers in.

Troilus and Cressida.

His back against a rock he bore,
And firmly placed one foot before ;
" Come one, come all, this rock shall fly
From its firm base as soon as I !"

SCOTT.

DANVERS AGAIN—THE CHASE—THE MISER—GEORGE—
NORTON—THE FLIGHT.

WALTER DANVERS, closely pursued, followed little George, whose speed of foot was almost miraculous, up rocks and banks, and over huge trees, which had been levelled with the earth by the axe, with difficulty maintaining his footing. Certain of being taken, and equally certain of being executed, if he did not strain every nerve to fly, he exerted himself to the uttermost ; but notwithstanding, some of his pursuers gained on him. There was no place at hand which afforded the means of concealment, and he could hardly hope, single-handed, to contend successfully against half-a-dozen well-armed men ; but he was determined rather to

die like a soldier by their swords, than to expire by the noose of
the hangman. Meanwhile the skirmish was kept up briskly at
a short distance, and he hoped that he should be able to reach
the party engaged against the cavalry and foot soldiers, which he
could not help trusting was composed of his friends the Jacobites.
This was his only chance of safety; for two or three of his pursuers were now within gunshot of him; and he had no hope of
outrunning them—indeed, he felt his breath was nearly spent.

" Come on," cried George to Danvers, " you see they are
fighting yonder; and if you run on, after you have got there,
these men behind will not dare to chase you."

The practised eye of Danvers followed the direction of George's
finger, and recognised some of the Jacobites in those who were
fighting with the military. He perceived that they were greatly
out-numbered by the soldiers, and that it was only possible for
them to maintain the contest while they were covered by the thick
trees behind which they fought, and which in some measure concealed their paucity from the enemy.

" With a good leader," he thought, " they might get safely
off; but, otherwise, they will all be taken.   Ah! there is honest
John Norton fighting like the devil—a fine soldier, but no general! Ha! they strike him down! God grant I may be in time
to save him!"

Gathering up all his powers, Danvers rushed on to render help
to his faithful friend, who had been felled by a heavy blow from
a clubbed musket, and was surrounded by four or five of the foe,
who were about to plunge their bayonets into his body, for he
refused to yield. Had his salvation depended on Danvers he
must have been lost: but a sturdy yeoman hastened to succour
him, and with some sweeping blows of his broadsword compelled
the soldiery to retreat a pace or two, enabling Norton, who had
only been stunned for half a moment, to regain his feet, and subsequently his saddle.

" Will you run, or fight?" asked George of Danvers, seeing
that he paused to recover breath, as soon as he saw John Norton
was rescued from impending death.

" Fight, my boy! Run away, and God bless you!" was the
reply.

But before Danvers could reach his friends, he was seen by

several of the enemy, who dashed forwards, with the intention of preventing him from joining them.

It must be understood that he had made a semi-circle, after quitting the ranks into which he had introduced himself, so that he had never been actually far distant from the foe. Armed with his bayonet, he made equal speed; but they who were striving to outrun him, had not to traverse so considerable a portion of ground as he had, and he saw himself surrounded, and with no option save that of fighting or surrendering. He had already taken his resolution which to do. The men who had previously pursued him were now at the distance of a few paces, numbering four or five, and others were coming up. His quick mind instantly conceived, that if these fellows attacked the Jacobites in flank, they must be routed immediately; for on that side they would have no defence, while the soldiers would be protected by the trees.

"By Jove!" he exclaimed, "I will not be the means of destroying my friends. O, for two stout hearts and four strong hands, like my own, to drive these rascal hirelings off."

"Here, Walter!" cried a voice, which made him start. "Here is a hand to aid you," and the form of Everard Walsingham, the Miser, emerged from behind a tree; but he looked so pale and weak that Danvers felt he could be of but little use. Still no aid was to be disregarded under such circumstances, and he knew that as far as personal courage was concerned, he could trust the Miser implicitly. He was not a little astonished, however, at his conduct, as well as by his sudden appearance in such a spot: and it was only a most transient feeling of honour which had communicated such an impulse to the bosom of Everard Walsingham. But he still retained in the midst of his meanness some of the high principles he had imbibed in youth relative to that bastard reputation which is commonly substituted for moral bravery, and he was unwilling to desert a friend in his extremity. Everard was still seeking the robber who had possessed himself by so singular an accident of the important papers, and had wandered accidentally to the place where he encountered his former associate. Being fatigued when he arrived there, no very long time previously, he sat himself down beneath the tree from which he had advanced, and was roused from his doze by the report of fire-arms. He saw the skirmishing betwixt the military and the Jacobites, and while deliberating what direction to take to be in safety himself, the form of Danvers became visible, pursued by several men. He repented him of his gallantry almost as soon as he had proffered his aid to Danvers. "Walter *might* be killed," thought the Miser, "killed without confession, and then I should be safe."

"Surrender!" shouted those who were behind Danvers, as the others who interposed between him and his friends approached. Without returning any answer, Danvers levelled his bayonet and fired. That unerring aim brought down the most formidable of his foes. "Charge!" vociferated the fugitive—fugitive no longer —as if to men behind the adjacent trees.

"Walsingham, take care of yourself, and do what you can to divert the enemy's attention."

"Are you mad?" cried the Miser, as he beheld Danvers quit the shelter of the tree, and dash against the foe. A dozen bullets whizzed through the air at Walter, but ere they could reach their destination he had thrown himself down, and they fell within a very trifling distance of him, while he, having re-loaded with marvellous celerity, again fired, and again shot a tall fellow who had reserved his fire, like a veteran, and was on the point of aiming at the prostrate Danvers as the ball entered his own brain.

All this was not done without forethought by the bold Danvers; for he hoped that the firing would lead the military to believe that another force of Jacobites was at hand, and cause them to fall back on their main body, who had not yet got fairly into action, but stood in a phalanx ready to charge as soon as the word of command was issued; nor was he disappointed. The main force seemed somewhat disconcerted, ignorant of the real state of the case; for report had magnified the numbers of the insurgents into thousands: and it was asserted that foreign auxiliaries all well armed and disciplined were among them. The amount of those who had quitted their ranks in order to capture Danvers had not been observed, and though it was of course known that several had been detached to retake him, they feared desertion had taken place, so that their disconcertion almost grew into a panic. The Jacobites continued firing, protected by the trees, and they could not be greatly harassed in return without an exposure of the troops, which their leaders considered would have been imprudent, as it was impossible to ascertain the numerical strength of the rebels.

"With a Serjeant's company now," thought Danvers, "I would put these rogues to flight. But they will soon discover how contemptible is the force opposed to them; for the soldiers dispatched to seize me, who are in the rear, can count every man on either side from that rising ground. I will lead them a chase, and if I can but get to my friends, a masterly retreat might be made, in the position they are in."

These thoughts passed like lightning through the brain of Walter, whose rapidity of judgment and swiftness of action were such as to baffle all pre-conception; and being safe for a few seconds, at all events, from the bullets of his pursuers, his stratagem having proved so successful, he arose, and fled again.

"If I had but Dickon now, I would dash through every obstacle," continued Danvers to himself. "Now, Walsingham," he said aloud to the Miser, as he returned to the spot where that person still stood inactive, "use your legs, man! I wonder," he thought, "where the boy has gone. *He* will not be taken, if I know him; but it is strange I can see him nowhere."

While Danvers sped onward, and Everard Walsingham, lost in indecision, remained rooted to the earth, the Jacobites were not idle. John Norton turned his eyes in the direction of the firing, and perceived a man fighting most desperately with the foe, but did not recognise Danvers, whose back was turned to him, at the instant. He felt it was necessary to act with prompt nerve, and to take advantage of the circumstance; but he wanted the ready intellect of Walter Danvers, though he lacked not any of his daring. Nevertheless, perceiving the dispirited looks of the troops opposed to him, and finding the courage of his own men rise in proportion to that depression, he proposed a charge; but this measure was strenuously discountenanced by the more prudent of the party.

"We cannot stay here," cried Norton. "A larger body of the regulars will soon arrive, and we shall be annihilated.—Ah! yonder is my brother among the enemy. He is holding a council with his officers. His tactics are, I believe, good, but he has no head for action, as I have none for tactics. O, for Walter Dan

2 T

vers, now! I'll be bound he would extricate us. We cannot return whence we came, for then we shall be encountered by great numbers of the enemy; the military prevent us from advancing. On one side we have a river which cannot be forded, and on the other, a country so hilly and rugged that our jaded horses will never be able to carry us over it. No, we must fight!"

"If you please, sir," here exclaimed the voice of a child close to Norton's ear, "if you want Mr. Danvers, that is him yonder, loading his gun and firing. O, he has killed *another* man! This is a dreadful scene!"

"Why, how came you here, my man?" said Norton, during this temporary cessation of battle, "and how do you know *that* is Walter Danvers?—By heaven, though, I think the boy is right! See! the brave fellow yonder is defending himself against half-a-dozen soldiers, he 'enacts more wonders than a man.' 'Tis Danvers; none but he, could fight thus.—Come, let us join him!"

Raising a loud shout, the little band of Jacobites hastened to the aid of the redoubted Walter, who maintained the unequal conflict with desperate valour, and thinking that his hour had come, with his back against a huge mass of granite, which had been detached from the rocks above, his lion mien undaunted, and his stern nerves as firm as in ordinary circumstances, he remained at bay, attacked by a dozen antagonists: for they poured on him from either side, like so many bull dogs on a bull.

"Bravely done, Walter!" shouted John Norton, spurring on with might and main to his assistance.

The soldiers turned to see who were advancing on them, hearing the clattering of the horses' hoofs; and as they did so, Danvers rushed through the midst of them, striking two or three down with the butt end of his weapon.

"Mount my horse!" exclaimed John Norton; "the troops are marching on us!"

Danvers, seeing that no time was to be lost, vaulted on the horse's back, which bore up nobly under this superincumbent weight of at least three-and-twenty stone. Danvers shook Norton cordially by the hand.

"We shall do with *you*, Walter!" he exclaimed.

"There is nothing for it but flight," replied Danvers. "As

soon as possible we must disband. There will be ten to one against us very soon. At all events the enemy labour under the same disadvantages as ourselves here from the roughness of the country, and regular troops are always tardy in their movements. —Spur on for your lives, my men !"

Passing over the trunks of trees, and leaping awful precipices, now dashing down nearly perpendicular hills, and now swimming rivers, the flying Jacobites pursued their headlong course. Nor were the troops of the government less daring, but dispersing in all directions, endeavoured to intercept the insurgents before they could gain the open country, which was at the distance of two or three miles.

"There is your brother, the Captain, John," observed Danvers to his companion, "among the very foremost. How madly he pursues. He will break his neck, if there be not a special Providence over him."

Captain Norton was, indeed, speeding after the Jacobites at a frantic rate. He had seized on one of the best horses of the regiment of dragoons, and his rowels were bloody, as he spurred the animal over precipices and enormous trunks, regardless of his own neck and of the knees of the charger, which bore him in advance of all others by the length of some roods. Never did huntsman dash along so furiously ; and he was now within a hundred yards of the fugitives.

" Every man for himself !" exclaimed Danvers, abruptly ; " the enemy are dispersed, but were we to attack any portion, the whole body of them would be on us instantly. Norton ; this horse will never carry us at such a pace another mile. One of us will probably be taken, but one *may* escape, if the beast can go on. I will leave you, and trust to fate."

"Why, Walter! what has come to you?" asked Norton, in amazement.

" Do you not see ?" whispered Danvers, " another large force is upon us? We are surrounded on every side, but they know not their advantage yet. There is a chance for those who can gain that opening yonder before the soldiers reach it."

" Wherefore conceal this ?"

"Nay, I know not. But I have noticed that unexpected difficulty damps the spirits of many men—especially when they fly.

You perceive many dragoons are coming up: the sun shines on many cuirasses through those trees. Fresh horses will be certain to overtake tired ones, if the men make no blunder. God bless you."

" But what do you propose to do, Walter? Wait an instant."

" I can delay some of the fellows who are pressing on you so hard," replied Danvers, quitting the steed of Norton. Before any remonstrance could be offered, Walter had with a swift bound gained the summit of a rocky knoll, where he was exposed to view, and shouted with all his might defiance to the foe. As might have been expected, attention was greatly directed to him, for he was of as much importance as all the rest collectively, while the large reward offered for his apprehension redoubled the ardour of the private soldiers in the chase. His object was thus gained in diverting attention from the Jacobites, who, with very few exceptions, got clear off: but his own peril became more imminent.

John Norton was resolved that he would not be less generous than Walter, and presently quitting his horse he ascended a low hill covered with trees, expecting from its summit to see him; but there was no trace of him, far or near. He hastened in the direction which he supposed the fugitive had taken, and plunged into a copse in which he concluded that he was hiding.

CHAPTER V.

If you will have revenge from hell, you shall:
Marry, for Justice, she is so employ'd,
He thinks with Jove in heaven, or somewhere else,
So that perforce you must needs stay a time.
                                        Titus Andronicus.

There are sorrows and dreams of death and woe,
But the Past is a Hell which the Guilty know.—*MS.*

THE MISER AND GEORGE—EVERARD WALSINGHAM'S EMOTION—THE CAVE.

THE stout-hearted little George having been bidden to betake himself to flight, reflected how he might again best serve Danvers; and foreseeing that it would be impossible for his friend, single-handed, to cope with the number of opponents that were pressing on him, and finding that Norton, whom he recognised instantly among the Jacobites, did not perceive who it was, fighting so fiercely and at such odds, he thought his best plan was, if possible, to get to the trees, under shelter of which the insurgents maintained the contest. With some difficulty and danger he accomplished this object, as the soldiers were busied with Danvers, and bullets came flying close to his head as he made for the Jacobites.

As soon as Norton had led away his confederates to the aid of Walter Danvers, George thought it right to look to his own safety, and running to the opposite trees, he ascended one of the largest elms among them, from which he had a complete view of all around. Captain Norton, as soon as the insurgents had quitted their ground, gave commands for instant pursuit, and was foremost in it himself, from the first; but when he recognised Danvers with his brother, he redoubled his speed, George escaping unnoticed in the elm. He had watched the succeeding events with breathless interest, and was on the point of descending to the ground, in order to witness more, when the intervening trees prevented his observing farther, when a tall, thin man, who looked almost like a ghost, advanced from behind an oak, which grew close to the place whither the child had repaired, and glanced around him. His eyes fell suddenly on George, and he uttered a cry of astonishment, which attracted the boy's notice. Advancing eagerly to him, Everard Walsingham—for it was he—exclaimed,

" Who—what are you? Tell me your name!"

" My name is George," was the reply, " what do you want?"

" God of heaven, how like!" said the Miser, wildly; " I cannot bear to look on him—and the voice, too—so musical, so plaintive! Do not leave me yet, child," he added, as George was about to depart. " It is such painful pleasure to look on you. I loved her—ah, I *did* love her—madly, doatingly. And yet I could strike at her sweet life like an assassin. But she was corrupt, and vile, and worthless. She died, she died! O misery, O despair!"

The Miser's eyes became fixed on vacancy, and George compassionating his condition, but anxious to learn the fate of Danvers, cried,

" I am sorry to leave you, but I can't stay any longer. Good bye!"

" Say that again!" ejaculated Everard, hearing only the last two words George had spoken. " ' Good bye!' Her very tones, looks, all! Oh, heaven, that a devil's heart should lurk beneath an angel's form. My wife, what wife!"

" What ails you?" asked the child gently, restraining his impatience to be gone.

" Again, again!" was the exclamation of the Miser. " So silvery is that sweetness it seems like that of a departed dream—remembered, and for ever! Would it could be forgotten! Life, life! what art thou? A delusion, a frenzy! There is madness in this brain, there is hell in this bosom, and yet that clear soft voice recals a heaven of peace and love—gone, gone, gone! The Paradise is ruined, the garden is made desolate—lost, lost, lost!"

"Poor man, he is distracted," murmured the child, "but I must leave him."

"Stay yet a little while," cried Everard, imploringly. "Young boy, thou art like an angel—thou resemblest strangely one that is dead, and my world, my universe, is buried with her! But thou—thou child—get thee gone! get thee gone! Things most divine in beauty, may be hollow and rotten within, like a tomb with fair marble outside, but dust and corruption all that it contains. If there were truth in aught, I could take thee to my bosom and be a father to thee: but I shall be deceived no more —never more. The brightness of earth is a mockery; its glories are like the mists of morning, and are dispersed by the Sun of Truth! Accursed sun! Oh, that I could live in darkness henceforth! I *will* live, believing there is no splendour, no holiness, no hope, joy, faith, sweetness, out of the immortal spheres."

The boy lingered a moment after the Miser had ended his incoherent speech, and then exclaiming, "God have mercy on him!" vanished.

"Just, just so, she spoke! The phantom has left me—all is a phantom!" cried the unhappy Everard. "Being may be nothing but a shadow—the mighty world may be a spectral illusion —life an imagination—death a chimera. Well—that is well!" and a bitter smile overshadowed his face. "If I could fancy now that all my past life has been a peopled vision—oh, what comfort it would be! Could an Idealist imagine such a thing? If so, his is a blessed creed!"

The Miser relapsed into intense abstraction. Though his was a mind, incapable, from its want of power, of grasping the philosophy which teaches wisdom and endurance, he was wont to speculate on the invisible, in order to divert his mind from the thronging and dismal shapes which haunted him day and night.

"And why may not all be a dream!" he muttered. "Is there reality in any thing? In happiness? Oh, no. In virtue? Never. In wisdom? The wisest have played the fool, and their knowledge is nothing. We wake to this existence, and none know how. Then, as it is so, why do we exist? Why believe

life is a fact? There is no real basis for doing so. Our senses
are ever cheating us, and our intellect can take cognizance of
nothing, save through the senses. If this be so, actions may be
nothing more than ideas! What are ideas? Sensible objects?
Impossible! If they are not of the same substance as the outward world, what are they? How connected with the universe?
They are dissimilar in essence from matter, and therefore cannot
be developed through its medium. Ha, ha! Now I am trying
with my reason to delude my reason; but I cannot. I do so,
day and night. I look at my gold, and as the glittering hoard
stares me in the face, I say to it, ' Thou art a lie !' and yet I
hug it to my heart, and forget everything but the dark irrevocable
past as I do so. We are the idiots of a fallen creation, walking
in the light of God's face, and seeing only ourselves and death
and time, instead of the eternal host, and life indestructible and
bliss undying. Eternity! I fear, and hate, and loathe the
thought. I cling to earth, while I detest myself, and all that is
beneath the canopy of heaven. If I could but quaff of the
Lethe stream which gives oblivion! where is it?" The Miser
groaned audibly.

" Your mind is sick, friend, if your body is not so," a mild
and gentle voice here interrupted the Miser. " I am neither physician of body nor soul, professionally, but I am a Christian, and
I cannot see you suffer without endeavouring to give you comfort. Why should any despair, and cling to pain, instead of
looking upward with hope?"

A little, hale old man, with a fishing-rod in his hand, was
addressing Everard Walsingham, who, on noticing him, replied,

" I need not thy help. Human wisdom, if I asked its succour, could avail me nothing."

" Nay, I know not that," replied the stranger. " I happened
to rise earlier even than usual, this morning, and I heard a firing
which brought me here. Seeing you motionless, I thought you
might be wounded, and hastened to you, when I heard you
dreaming aloud, as visionaries are wont to dream. But what
you said convinces me that you are suffering in the spirit grie-
vously, and I well know that mental far exceeds corporeal
agony. You strove to fancy that every thing is unreal, as if to
fly from the recollection of something that oppressed you—par

don me for listening to what you said. But why, instead of permitting this incubus to sit upon your heart, destroying the vitality of reason and judgment—why not rouse your soul, which can do all things it will? You are wretched; well, sorrow is the portion of humanity; but though the clouds of this life darken the bright effulgence of the ethereal day, this world is but as a night of vision, and the land of truth and immortality is the morning promised to us. From the shadow we rise to the substance, from the clouds, to the pure radiance of the heaven. You have done wrong, perhaps—where is the man that has not? In fact, we *must* err, whether we will or not. But the Eternal Goodness can pardon all things, if there is but sincere repentance, and is that so very difficult a thing to render?"

"All who sin, repent; but it is terror, and not love of God that makes them do so," replied the Miser, sullenly.

"Not always so," answered the old man. "From the frailty of our nature we must, as I said, be ever committing actions which grieve us to contemplate, and almost before they are beyond recal; but why is this? Conscience exclaims, 'you have done wrong;' and we are humbled in our own opinion. Now, the fear of retributive justice does not come upon us so soon as the mortification and abasement we must feel from falling in our own respect. Then, sin is hated from love—from love of virtue which is by nature implanted in the soul; and if we love virtue, we love God also, that is clear."

"If that be the case, why should men ever do wrong?" demanded Everard, from whose mind the appearance of George and the train of feelings consequent upon it, had effaced the events which had preceded them for the time entirely.

"His mind—his immaterial principle can alone take cognizance of abstract ideas," replied the stranger, (in whom the reader may recognise one previously known to him,) "and his body is organized in the same manner as that of all other animals. Man is a compound being; with feelings, thoughts and perceptions. His feelings being exclusively animal, and his perceptions utterly sensuous when the reason is not called into operation, he cannot possibly act according to moral laws, except by combating against inclination by the higher nature, by which he becomes elevated above the mere machine, and in proportion as he is virtuous, and

2 U

satisfied with his actions, he is happy. Now, if we regret that
we have done ill, it follows, that we must be unhappy until we
do what is good. *Mere* regret for the past is an unintellectual,
enervating and immoral thing; and if we persist in rendering
ourselves up to it, without arousing the purer and diviner energies which are the life of the spirit as the blood is to the body,
all must seem a blank, except the portion of being to which our
thoughts continually recur. Pardon me, then, if I say you are
acting most unwisely in lamenting over what you cannot recal,
and not seeking the comfort to be derived from striving to do as
much good as possible, in order to erase the bad from the great
book."

"Some things cannot be erased," returned the Miser, with a
trembling lip. "When you have murdered your own peace,
what can restore it? What can give life to the dead?"

"He that gave life," responded the old man, reverently. "But
what is this firing which I now hear again? I am afraid some
bloody business is going on."

"Ah! I had forgotten," exclaimed the Miser—"I must provide for my own safety at once," he thought to himself; and
hastily wishing the stranger farewell, he strode away in the opposite direction to that whence the report of musketry proceeded.

And what had become of Walter Danvers, whose disappearance was somewhat mysterious, in the interim? The copse into
which he had plunged after leaving John Norton (which he did
when he perceived his horse was weary with the exertions he had
made and could not be expected to bear up much longer under
the weight of two men) extended over some space, and the low
trees grew in great thickness in every direction. Stooping low,
he concealed himself under some furze, which grew beneath the
brushwood, for he heard Captain Norton, whom he had left but
a very short distance in the rear, bounding up the steep he had
just quitted, and he must have exposed himself to view, if he had
moved from his lurking place. Danvers had little hope of escaping; but he was one who never yielded to despair, and had frequently escaped from perils very nearly as great as those which
now beset him.

Captain Norton, fancying that the fugitive had reached a clump
of trees at a very short distance—which were insulated from the

rest—hastened in that direction. He had quitted his horse, of course, and with cocked pistol and bare sword, advanced, breathing vengeance against the destroyer of his son. It would have pleased him better to slay his hated enemy with his own hand at that moment than to have seen him die by the hand of the public executioner; for his heart was thirsting for the blood of the man who had made it desolate, as poor wretches thirst in the wilderness for water, and it seemed to him as if the ghost of his boy were crying out to him for instant retribution.

O, that miserable desire of revenge, which when it takes possession of the mind goads it to madness! How strange that we should care about the destruction of an insect like ourselves, whose ephemeral existence is not certain for an instant! Wretched nature of man, how mean, abject, despicable thou art! It *can* soar,—how high, let angels tell; it DOES fall—how low, you may read in the chronicles of perdition!

Meanwhile, Danvers was surprised to find a huge stone beneath the furze into which he had crept, and which seemed to cover what had once been a well. He found that by pressing the stone on one side, an opening was revealed; but it was so dark below that he was unable to determine to what depth the excavation descended. It occurred to him, however, that he might conceal himself in this place, as there was no water there, and remain undiscovered; and deliberating but a few seconds, he increased the pressure of his hand on the stone till the aperture was wide enough to admit of his body passing through. But how was he to accomplish the descent? He threw a small pebble down to ascertain the depth, and as it did not seem very great, and there was no water below, he resolved to work his way down with his back and knees at the risk of excoriation; but what was his surprise, when in commencing the descent, he discovered steps at regular intervals, by which he had no difficulty in effecting what he wished.

During this time Captain Norton had been beating the bushes in every direction, calling on the fugitive to come forth and meet him without success of course. Presently, however, he perceived the form of a man hastily making his way through the thicket, and not doubting it was Danvers, rushed furiously after him. The chase lasted some minutes, but at last he overtook the object of his pursuit, and seizing him with a ferocious grasp, was about to cut him down with his sabre, when the man turned and he ejaculated—

"How! my brother John!"

His uplifted arm fell, and the disappointment of unsatiated hate was expressed by his face.

The younger Norton confronted the captain boldly. "You were seeking Walter Danvers," he said.

"Ay, for the murderer of my gallant Percy!" replied the veteran officer. "Show me where he is! He shall fight me like a soldier, if he dare."

"He would fight the devil himself, if that were all," returned John; "but what did you say about his being a murderer! and Percy?"

"My son is dead, and fell by *his* bloody hand whom you hug to your heart," answered the captain.

"Impossible! Walter Danvers could not have raised an arm against a mere boy of fifteen! When—where was this, that you tell me of?"

"I have no time for explanations;—I shall go mad, if the monster escape. If you have one drop of blood in you which is warm in the cause of kindred, place him in my hands. I saw him riding behind you, and you must know where he is. If you do not this, although you *are* my brother——"

"I care not for your menaces," interrupted John Norton, as his brother glared upon him, and lifted his sword to a level with his head, "but this is, indeed, an awful calamity.—On my word, on my soul, I know not where Danvers is now! I was in search of him myself.—But there must be some mistake in this matter."

"I tell you he murdered him,—if not in cold blood, when the poor boy had no means of defence.—My child! my child! I hear your voice calling again on his accursed head the destruction I have sworn to fulfil! John! Conceal him not; you *must* know where he is. Walter Danvers and I cannot breathe the air of this earth together longer."

"I have pledged my sacred honour that I am ignorant of where he is," replied the younger Norton. "If he *have* murdered my poor Percy, by heaven! though he is my dearest friend on earth, I will have his heart's blood. I will deliver him to justice, I swear. If my nephew fell in honourable fight by his hand, I must forgive him; but will henceforth avoid his sight."

" Honourable fight! You said just now, he could not have raised his hand against a boy of fifteen! But I am losing precious time. You swear you have no idea where the murderer is lurking?"

" I have sworn," was the reply.

" Go, then, for this time; but if you have deceived me, I will kill you—as I will all that keep him from my sword. I have recorded an oath above that I will not close an eye, nor eat a morsel till he is discovered."

Thus having spoken, Captain Norton resumed his search, and plunged into the deepest parts of the thicket. John Norton also pursued his quest for Danvers, though not with the amicable feelings which he had been animated by previously. The main body of the troops had not perceived when Danvers and the Nortons had gone out of the direct road, and one and all were still chasing the flying Jacobites, it being supposed that Danvers had only ascended the bank for a minute to reconnoitre. Some more troops had now joined the others, and they dashed forward with the eagerness of fox-hunters, anxious, now that they perceived the handful of men before them, to retrieve the fame they had lost, in not having routed them instantly. But the insurgents (if they could strictly be called so) had a good start, and were better acquainted with the country than the military, so that they finally succeeded in baffling the foe—with the exception of one or two who were ill mounted,—and dispersed in all directions.

CHAPTER VI.

Yes, though thou hast destroyed my life of life,
And though existence now is dark and sear,
And this sad heart with memories is rife
Which are too deep to trickle in the tear,
I pardon thee, and wholly.—*From an unpublished Poem.*

To suffer woes which Hope thinks infinite;
To forgive wrongs, darker than Death or Night,
This, like thy glory, Titan, is to be
Great, good, and joyous, beautiful and free.
                    Prometheus Unbound.

GEORGE'S ADVENTURES—MOTHER STOKES AND ROGER
SIDNEY—THINGS PAST.

THE child George, after quitting Walsingham the Miser, hastened, if possible, to rejoin Danvers: but he could discover no clue to guide him to the place where he was.

"What shall I do?" he said to himself. "If I remain here, the soldiers will, it is likely, return and take me, and those papers will be found. I wanted to have returned with Mr. Danvers safe to his home—his daughter would have been so glad and grateful to me for getting him out of peril; but that is impossible at present, I am afraid. Miss Danvers will be very anxious about her father; so I will go to her at once."

Acting upon this resolution, George turned into a little valley reposing peacefully beneath green hills and rocks, down which a mimic cascade was pouring with sweet music—the only sound, except the chirruping of a bird, and now and then a faint and far-distant shout, to be distinguished. Here George had left his pony, tied to a young sapling, and mounting him without delay, with his habitual promptness of action, was cantering briskly away, when to his horror and dismay he perceived the monster, who had so nearly killed him when he was rescued by Danvers, his huge eyes fixed on him savagely, and his distorted face grinning with a demoniacal expression, as he was ascending the sloping ground which led out of the valley.

The savage was armed with a pole, and was covered with blood, so that altogether he looked most ferocious and terrible; but the brave child, who had conducted himself so dauntlessly through dangers which might have cowed the boldest man, and tried the strongest nerves, spurning the impulse which would have moved him to turn and fly when he beheld the monster, urged his pony on to a gallop, determining to force his way through every impediment: but his enemy seized the bridle with his powerful hand, and made menacing gestures, which expressed that he would destroy him, if he attempted to proceed. George, however, was not to be intimidated, and struggled to release himself from the grasp which the savage now placed on his shoulder, but his powers were utterly inadequate against one who possessed the bones and sinews of mature and even great strength, vigorous as he was for a young boy. The monster dragged him to the ground, and struck him with his unshapely hand; but the child fiercely returned the blows, and would probably have been killed for his temerity, had not Mother Stokes hobbled up, and exclaimed,

"What! Sophy's brat! How is this, eh?"

"This is the second time that devil has attacked me," replied George. "If I were a man, I would not let such a wretch live."

"Let him go," said Mother Stokes to the savage. "But I'll tell you what it is, young gentleman, if you don't take care you shall have such a beating as you will carry the marks of to your grave."

"I do not fear you," replied George firmly; "I know you are a very bad woman;" and so saying leaped on his pony, and was going instantly to continue his journey, but Mother Stokes prevented him.

"Not so fast, little sir," she cried. "As to your thinking me a bad woman, I don't care a pinch of snuff for your opinion; but I shall give you a lesson that will make you keep a civil tongue in your head. Go, and get some thistles," she added to the savage, while she detained the child with a strong hand. "I'll give him a flogging he shall remember."

George struggled violently, but to no purpose, and the thistles having been procured, the woman was about to administer the chastisement she had threatened, in the manner formerly practised at schools, when an old man stepped forward and exclaimed,

"Why are you going to punish the child in such a cruel way?"

Mother Stokes started at the sound of that voice, and when she turned her face to the speaker uttered an exclamation of surprise; and a shudder ran through the old man's frame as he beheld her.

"Wretch!" he cried, "I thought that you were gone to your great account."

"Indeed, Master Sidney! Well, I'm here alive, and at your service," returned the woman with a sneer, the most hideous imaginable. "When we meet in the lower regions, if my master Satan should appoint me servant to the fires, I shall take care to provide you with a very comfortable, everlasting roasting!" And she chuckled, as she concluded her benevolent speech, much as the kindly inhabitants of Pandemonium may.

"I pity you," replied Roger Sidney—for it was no other than the old Angler, who had just been conversing with the Miser— "you must be very wretched. But this young boy here you shall not touch. A miscreant, like you are, is unfit to chastise the worst of human beings, and such, I am sure, he is not."

"What right have you to interfere?" demanded Mother Stokes. "I would advise you to keep clear of this business, or I will set my monster on you. I think you have had enough of me to sicken you from interfering with such as I am. Roger Sidney, I yet owe you a return for many favours, and will pay them with interest ere I die."

"I am not so old and feeble, but that I can still strike a good blow, returned the Angler, surveying the savage with curiosity. "I bid you to release that boy directly."

"Never, at your command," cried Mother Stokes. "Sidney,

I hate you. Once, when my heart was full of vanity, and my face was not, as it is now, hideous and wrinkled, I would have given myself to you. Yes, I *did* love you as much as I detest you now. You scorned me, and I was revenged—deeply, bitterly revenged. The despised menial proved an enemy—"

" Oh, woman, woman!—If you indeed belong to that sex which is most like the angels when adorned with virtue—" here broke in the old man, " forbear to torture me! Why, why did you strike at that innocent life, pure and gentle as the sweet flowers that bloom for a few brief days, and send up their fragrant incense to the Creator! *She* never injured the meanest thing that crawled;—yet you, like an incarnate fiend, poisoned her bright existence, and devised the most accursed falsehood that was ever fabricated without the gates of hell! Her death, too, was most mysterious—grief does not kill at once. Tell me, know you how she died?"

" Probably by her own hand," replied Mother Stokes. " I dare say she swallowed poison; it may be taken in such a way that it cannot be detected afterwards."

" Liar!" cried Roger Sidney, indignantly. " She was a Christian, in all her thoughts, words and works, and could never have committed an action which might have endangered her eternal welfare. My Eliza! my first, and last, and only love! why didst thou leave me alone? We should have lived and died together!" The old Angler spoke with profound pathos and feeling; but his grief only increased the malice of the reputed witch.

" So, you think she wouldn't have killed herself, do you? And you believe, if she *did* so, she mightn't go to Heaven! I can't see, for myself, why she shouldn't do what she liked with her own.—Well, I won't make you miserable, by giving you proof of the fact. That she *did* die by poison there is not a doubt, though the surgeons could not say how it was taken, or what it was."

" Ay, and by whom was it administered?" exclaimed Sidney, quickly. As he spoke, he fixed his clear, penetrating eye, undimmed by age, on the woman, who quailed beneath it. " Indirectly you certainly *were*, and directly you *may* have been the cause of her untimely death! There is One who sees into the secrets of all hearts, and He alone knows thine. *I* do not judge thee, but from Him you will receive just and terrible punishment, if you do not repent of your accumulated crimes."

" I repent of nothing," returned Mother Stokes. " I glory in what I have done, and with my dying breath I will curse you. See, what you have made me. I was once admired and flattered; I am now ugly and loathed by all. I am grown old, but not so much with years, as from fierce passions consuming me—passions created by you; for I was not what I became until you crossed my path."

" Your character was infamous," replied Sidney, " before you entered into Miss Spenser's service. " Oh, if we had but known what you were, how great a load of agony might have been saved !"

" I live on the recollection of that glorious vengeance," exclaimed the woman, with savage exultation. " When I think upon it, the blood dances in my torpid heart, and rushes through my veins like a torrent, making me young again. I told a lie to destroy your bride. True! But why should she have believed me? If she really loved you, surely she—"

" I'll hear no more," interrupted Roger Sidney, with vehemence. " I shall forget myself, if I listen to you any longer. It is not for the blighting of existence that my soul hates you. I could have been content to have lost my Eliza, if she had believed me true. O God! O God! But she knows the truth now. She sees me from yon blue vault—soaring among the eternal host—and perceives that my whole spirit was devoted to her— perhaps more than it ought to have been, and so I was visited so heavily! For you, unhappy creature, dreadful, indeed, must be your misery! The pangs of a guilty conscience like yours must be a very antepast of damnation. Repent—repent, and I will forgive you all !"

Oh, the sublime heart of the believer! It leaves behind all this earth's littleness, and laughs at what man can do. Revenge, however dreadful, can do nothing against the peace of that mind whose hope is a world, whose faith a God, where shadows do not deceive, and falsehood disquiet. For the hope is in God, and the world is in the soul—that world a heaven, that God a Truth immutable !

So when the fiendish woman saw how that high faith baffled her petty malice, she ejaculated,

" Forgive me ! *You* forgive *me!* When Heaven forgives the peopled Hell ! I ask not forgiveness—I would be content to endure wretchedness myself for ever, so that you should share it. I pour on you again and again my maledictions. Forgiveness ! Ha, ha, ha ! Do you prate of that ? O rare ! When the snake is coiling around the heart, and inflicting tortures, pity and pardon him ! When the executioner is racking your limbs with agonies, extend to him the hand of friendship ! Reverse all the laws of nature—make the lamb fond of the wolf—the deer, of the savage hound—do all this, and then tell me of forgiveness !"

With these words, Mother Stokes, followed by the savage, hastily left the valley.

CHAPTER VII.

If I had a mind to be honest, I see Fortune would not let me; she drops booties in my mouth. Who knows how that may turn back to my advancement?—*Winter's Tale.*

> How the knave jostles by, and fools exclaim,
> " This man is wise!"   'Tis that they idiots are.
> *Old Play.*

MOTHER STOKES AND THE MISER—GEORGE AND ISAAC
QUIRK—SAM STOKES—THE PAPER.

THE passions which instigate all our actions, and from whose dominion none can escape, are the parents of all good, and of all evil likewise. Revenge is, perhaps, the darkest of all; and how often is it substituted for Justice, how often does it steal its name! Throw it away, like fine old Roger Sidney! If a man insult you, he is a blackguard, and you would degrade yourself by noticing him. What advantage do we reap, if we succeed in punishing a rascal? Will it put money in your pocket, give you a clear conscience, a *mens sana corpore sano*? Pooh!

We must now put ourselves in very villanous company for a short time, and return to Mother Stokes, taking up her adventures from the period when she effected her escape from the military. That escape had been effected with no great difficulty, and was in fact winked at by the officer who had taken her, and forgotten, in the hurry of action, to leave her at the town from which he had led his troops to encounter the Jacobites. It was

not long after this, that the circumstance of the monster falling
in love with Ellen Danvers occurred, and it was succeeded in the
course of a little period by that detailed in the preceding chapter.
Soldiers were scouring the country in every direction; and fearing lest she should be again taken, Mother Stokes concealed herself, as best she might, when the engagement betwixt the military
and the Jacobites took place.

What a tempest was in the bosom of that woman, when she
recognised the old Angler; and how vastly was it aggravated by
the conversation which supervened! She forgot the boy by
whom she had been incensed, she forgot the peril in which she
stood, and all her passions and thoughts were swallowed up in
the idea of Roger Sidney, whom she had not beheld for many
years. What a Pandemonium is the human heart, when the
fires of the dark volcanoes which smoulder there, are kindled by
that strong fire-creator which rules the being, as Lucifer his
kingdom, and they burst, and roar, and scatter destruction, tearing their own entrails, like him of the old fable, living on their
own vitals, in throes and convulsions!

Mother Stokes, very soon after she left Sidney, beheld the
form of Everard Walsingham—though the distance from his
house was considerable. The Miser, paler and more emaciated
than ever, was crawling along, with difficulty supporting himself
on his legs, from fatigue and loss of blood; and his mind was at
least as distracted as that of the reputed witch.

Mother Stokes accosted him, well disposed to torture one she
had in her power, and said—

" Good morrow to you, my lord !"

The Miser started and trembled, and the woman continued—

" I have some business with you, and we had better not defer
it. If you want to know the nature of it, I can inform you in one
word,—Treason."

" Ah !" cried the Miser, as if a serpent had stung him.

" Yes, you must give me money ; or I will reveal all."

" No, no, no," exclaimed Everard. " I am ruined already.
I defy you, woman—and yet—well, what would you say? I
know nothing of treason or you."

" Indeed !" replied Mother Stokes. " Don't you know Walter
Danvers, and a'nt you aware the Jacobites——"

The Miser suddenly seized Mother Stokes by the throat; but he released his grasp instantly, muttering—

"No, never again. I have no money to give—none!—Walter Danvers is nothing to me. You mistake me for another."

"Not I! It is well you left your gripe of my throat, or I have one here should have strangled *you*. Your name, I know, is Everard, Lord Walsingham."

"No, no, I tell you no no," answered the Miser. "I am a poor man—no lord; be assured, you are in error."

And he rushed away like a maniac. Mother Stokes gazed after him with one of her sardonic grins and said—

"I have you fast enough, old bird! You shall not escape from the net I have laid for you."

Meanwhile, Roger Sidney, as soon as Mother Stokes and the savage had disappeared, turned kindly to George, and said—

"Take care of yourself, my little fellow; and if you want a friend, here is my name and address. I cannot stay with you now."

Then putting some apples into his hand, of which he was very glad, the old man hurried away, to conceal from every eye the emotions which the words of Mother Stokes had excited in his bosom.

"Poor old man!" murmured the child, a tear starting to his eye, as the Angler left him—"poor, poor old man!"

But George was not to return to the house of Danvers; for as he was guiding his pony in that direction at a fast trot, he was descried by some dragoons, who had been ordered to scour the locality in which the engagement had been fought, as well as to see whether the enemy had left any wounded men among the trees. Unfortunately for George the soldiers were some of those who had attempted to capture him, when he swam the river, and instantly recognising him, raised a threatening shout, and gave chase; the boy urging his diminutive steed into a gallop, when he heard the foe's vociferations. A circumstance happened here, which impeded the progress of the soldiers: for as they were within a few yards of the young fugitive, who was striving with all his might to gain a labyrinth where he might, perhaps, baffle pursuit, a man started up from the ground, on which he had been lying, and fired at them.

This individual was no other than the sturdy yeoman, who had acted a conspicuous part at the Jacobite meeting, and had joined John Norton's party. His horse had been killed under him by a stray shot, and he had fallen, and been severely hurt. This was just as the Jacobites hastened to the aid of Danvers, and the yeoman, stunned and bruised, was overlooked by them. The bluff fellow's temper was exacerbated by the pain of his injuries, and he no sooner saw those by some of whom it was probable he had sustained such damage, than with an effort springing up, he discharged his pistol; but not with unerring accuracy of aim, for it revenged the death of his own steed by disabling the leg of that belonging to one of the dragoons, which fell, with his rider. The yeoman was surrounded and menaced with death, if he did not yield; but with a grim smile he hurled the pistol he had fired at one of the soldiers, and brandished his sword on high. The combat which ensued did not last long, for a sabre-cut in the head felled him to the earth, and he exclaimed with a groan—

"D—n you! You've done my business, properly. Here, you rascal (to the dragoon who had wounded him), you'd rob me after I'm dead, if I didn't give you my purse now. Go, and get drunk, if you like, and—and—"

His voice failed, and he gasped for breath; but he managed to exclaim—

"What a cursed fool I've been!" and expired.

> "Heroes must die, and by God's blessing 'tis
> Not long before the most of them go home."

All this, however, procured a famous start for George; but he was obliged to pursue a path opposite to that he had intended taking, and became involved in the intricate windings of the place. The soldiers continued their pursuit of him, but they also speedily became bewildered in the maze, and after some time abandoned the hope of capturing the child.

George, after hours spent in trying to extricate himself from the labyrinth, emerged in a direction far from that he wished to have found himself in; but he had eluded the soldiers, and was now in a solitary path, exposed to no observation. He had lost himself entirely, and overcome with the extraordinary exertions he had been making, he suffered the pony, no less fatigued, to

pursue the path he thought fit, and his weary eyes closed in sleep.
Dozing thus, but not quite unconscious, he was carried along by
his little steed for about an hour at a slow walk, along a road
between high embankments, whereon the wild thyme grew in
luxuriance, and made the air fragrant. The day was declining,
and the song of the birds grew less frequent, while the sheep
that might be seen grazing on the green hills with the kine, were
lying lazily, cropping the grass, their occasional bleating and bel-
lowing, mingled with the tinkling of the sheep bells, making a
pleasant sound in the distance. George was dreaming of happiness perhaps, never to be realized—wandering among Elysian
scenes,—among woodlands and rivers and valleys yet more lovely
than those which he now and then caught glimpses of through
his more than half-closed eyelids, when he was aroused by feeling
a rough hand placed on his shoulder, and a voice which he knew
exclaimed—

" So, my young chap, I've caught you at last, have I ?" and
he received a severe blow, which knocked him to the ground. On
looking up, he perceived that he was within a few yards of the
Britannia Inn, which was situated at the extremity of a straggling
village, picturesquely isolated, stood over by the stable boy, who
had pursued him vainly, and whom he had charged down when
he ran off with the pony, with clenched fists.

What boy but knows the village bully, with his ugly face, and
his sturdy form, from whom he has often received so unmerited
a drubbing, until he grew strong and tall and could fight his
battles manfully ?

George regained his feet, and feeling how vain it would be to
contend against the powerful lad, who was the little tyrant of the
little place, and from whose hand he had just sustained a blow
which might have prostrated one of double his age, he said—

" O, Isaac ! Why do you beat me ?"

But before he could proceed any farther, the bully again struck
him brutally, and the high and fiery blood within the child's
heart mounting to his pale cheek and brow, he returned the blow
with all his force. Isaac Quirk—for such was the appellation of
the stable boy—turned almost livid with rage, seized him by the
neck, and was going to dash him against a wall, when a hand
came in contact with his own face so forcibly as to cause him to
measure his length on the earth.

"'Pon my soul, Isaac, you're not a bit better nor that savage as they say is your cousin," cried Sam Stokes, who had been the means of rescuing George from the vengeance of the stable-boy. "Aint ye ashamed of yerself to hit a child like that there, you great lubberly blackguard?" continued the tar, as Isaac arose with sullen anger (if that be not an anomaly in terms) in his looks. "You're no nevy of mine, you rascal, you!"

"That young devil ran away with the powney," replied Isaac, in his defence, "and he deserves to have his precious head knocked off, he does!"

"I've a notion you desarves it most," returned the sailor, indignantly. "What chance had a little chap like that there against you? Thof I'm your uncle, I'm a Briton, and have sarved the king, and I'm—— if I lets you make use of the strength God has given ye to fight the foes of old England, as if ye was a savage Hingian, and not born and bred in the only country good for-tuppence under the sun."

A crowd was now collected round the sailor, the stable-boy and George, and some seemed inclined to side with Sam, some with Isaac.

"That boy ought to be well birched," cried the landlord, of "The Britannia," who was very wroth at having been so long robbed of his pony, at no slight inconvenience to himself.

"And if he ought—and I knows nothing of the rights of the business—is that any reason why a young, unhuman scoundrel should go for to dash him against a wall?" rejoined Samuel.

"I didn't dash him against the wall," answered Isaac, growing saucy when he saw his master was favourable to him.

"It's well I prevented ye," returned the cripple, while George, a little terrified at the threatening looks of the landlord, crept closer to his protector.

It was most strange that he who had undauntedly gone through such dangers lately should dread the ordinary correction of a refractory child: but it is said that a French soldier, who will fight bravely, has been known to sob when about to undergo the punishment of the lash; and it was on the same principle—the dread of ignominy, perhaps—that George shrank from chastisement.

2 Y

"Never fear, my man," said the tender-hearted Stokes, patting the child on his cheek, "you shan't be hurt."

While he was thus speaking, a burly form made way through the crowd, and George clung yet more nearly to Sam.

"You little rascal!" exclaimed the new comer, "your mother will give it you, when you go to her. Ah, Stokes! Is that you? How d'ye do?"

"Yes, Mr. Figgins! d'ye know this boy?"

"He's a young rogue, and I know nothing good of him," replied Corporal Figgins—for it was he. "Go home to your mother, sir, directly:" and seizing George by the collar, the Corporal dragged him away, though Sam Stokes seemed much inclined to interfere again in his behalf.

Isaac Quirk gazed after George with ill-disguised malice. He muttered something to himself in an inaudible tone, while Sam addressed him thus—

"If so be I ever see ye fighting with one less than yerself, d'ye see, I'll whack ye, shiver my timbers."

The stable-boy then proceeded to take the tired pony into the stable, but before he did so, he caught sight of a paper which George had dropped in the scuffle with him, and picked it up, though with what motive—as he could not read himself—is not quite clear. The crowd dispersed; Sam Stokes having accepted an invitation from the landlord of the "Britannia"—to whom he was a good customer—to take a pipe and tankard with him, and his sweetly-disposed nephew found himself alone outside the premises. He busied himself, with a sulky air, in his usual occupations, occasionally whistling, and mumbling—"I'll take care and pay you for it, Mr. Uncle Sam!" not noticing that he was narrowly watched by a little old man, to whom he bore a degree of resemblance, who was standing at the distance of a few paces from him, leaning on a staff.

This young Master Isaac Quirk before us, was the son of Samuel Stokes's sister, who married the son of a pettifogger, much against the said pettifogger's will. Both his parents died when he was a child, and he had been employed as an errand boy, and subsequently as a helper in the stable of the "Britannia," his grandfather, the lawyer, having declined to do anything for him. Indeed, he had never seen the attorney to whom he was so nearly related, and nature had endowed him with all the mental powers he possessed *in toto;* for he had never learned anything but what he taught himself—if that Hibernicism may pass. Nevertheless, Isaac was considered a sharp-witted fellow who had an eye to his own interest; and it was remarked he had usually more money in his pocket than the generality of lads in his station—a circumstance arising from the success he uniformly had in games of chance and skill, including marbles, chuck-farthing, &c. He was now advancing towards man's estate, and was debating with himself whether he might not procure some more profitable employment than that he now held.

"I shouldn't care," said Isaac, uttering his thoughts, "if I was a chimbley-sweeper, so I'd lots of cash. What's the use of this here life, if one han't the means to enjoy it? I'd stick at nuffin, not I, to have as much money as I wants. I'd beg, cheat, steal, rob—um!—I doesn't know as I'd do what'd risk my neck, 'cos one can't live without 'un. But I'd do it, if it wasn't for that. I must learn to read and write—one can't cheat on a large scale without being a bit of a scholard. That's the way rich folks keeps riches, or else if poor 'uns was as cunning—wouldn't they do 'em just! I wonder what this here paper is, now? It strikes me there's something unkimmon in it. It don't look like the writing of a uneddicated person."

While he was communing with himself, the little old man had carefully marked all he said, and seemingly with exultation.

"What's bred in the bone," he thought; and advancing close to Isaac, he cried—

"My lad, you should never think aloud—it's a bad practice. But I'm glad I overheard what you were saying: for it gives me an insight into your character. You are a very promising boy, and uncommonly like your father. What is your age, Isaac?"

"Who are you?" asked the stable-boy, much surprised at this address; and without deigning to notice the old man's interrogatory. "You're a queer-looking old fellow, you are!"

"Who should I be, but your grandfather, Lawyer Quirk? You may fancy I've been unkind, my lad, in not taking any notice of you, hitherto; but I'll explain the matter; and, with your native good sense and discernment, I am confident you will perceive my conduct was just. You see, my good Isaac, your father offended me by his imprudent marriage; and would have extracted sums of money from me, which I couldn't afford to lose. So I told him he must not come to my house: and as he was old enough to choose a wife for himself, I supposed he could also support her. Well, he took to drinking, and died in a fit, and your mother did not long survive him. Then I was importuned to provide for you. But, Isaac, my hands were full of business, and I could not be troubled with a squalling brat. Now, however, you are no longer a child, and I'll see what I can do for you, if you like to come with me."

"You're a rum old cock, and no mistake," answered Isaac; "but I'll see you don't try to flummux and gammon me! I understand you, dad, and I'll sarve you, so as you'll agree to pay me well."

"I like your sincerity," said the lawyer, "and will give you £10 a year for your services. But, Isaac, if you are sharp—as I think you are—you may double and treble that salary in such a situation. You shall be taught to read and write, and—cheat, my lad"—— he added, in an under-tone.

"Will'ee?" cried the stable-boy, with a grin. "I shan't want much teaching. So there's my hand on the bargain. I knows you wants some dirty work done; but I'm accustomed to *that* with my fingers, and why not with my brains? But as to your teaching me to cheat, dad, I've a notion I can do that without your help—only give me some humbugging words. If you'll engage to larn me to read and write, I'll thank'ee!"

"Sensibly spoken," replied Lawyer Quirk. "When I was your age, Isaac, I was only a travelling tinker, as my father was before me. I found that wasn't a thriving trade, so I took to begging: but having been sent to prison for that, turned my thoughts to something more reputable, and entered an attorney's office. This attorney was just such a man as I am now; he wanted a *good hard swearer*, who would stick at nothing—blush at nothing—just my case, Isaac!—I proved the best witness he ever had—stepped into his shoes when he died, and married his daughter, ha, ha! Follow in my footsteps, boy, and you'll get rich. You've a genius for roguery, I can see, by the twinkling of your little grey eyes. I like a grey eye!—I never knew a man possessed of one, devoid of cleverness or sense!"

"What a pity we didn't know each other afore," observed Isaac.

"Perhaps it is; perhaps it is: but no great time has been lost," returned Quirk.

"Can you read this thingumy?" inquired the stable-boy of his grandfather, handing to him the paper George had inadvertently dropped.

The old man putting on his large horn spectacles began to read at first with curiosity, then with interest and wonder.

"How did you get this?" he asked of the lad.

"O, just by chance! It was dropped by a cursed little brat as I means to drub a'most dead one day."

"I'll keep this, Isaac," said the old man, putting the paper in his immense pocket.

"That's of use to'ee, aint it?" asked Isaac.

"Y-e-es, it may be," was the reply.

"Then I won't take less nor a guinea for it, dad."

"Ha, ha, ha! you're a monstrous clever dog," chuckled old Quirk. "Why, what should the paper be, eh?"

"Something what you can make money of," said Isaac: "and nothing risk, nothing have."

"You shall have a guinea, Isaac," returned the aged man, approvingly. "I like to encourage rising talent."

"Yes, and the sooner the better," returned the young hopeful.

"Here, then, is a guinea," said the lawyer, after searching his pockets for some time.

Isaac threw the coin on a stone, instantly.

"Thought so!" he exclaimed—"counterfeit, by Jingo! That won't do, by no means, old cock,—nothing but copper gilt."

"Why, how old are you?" asked Quirk, with an air of intense admiration at this manifestation of his grandson's precocious genius.

"Sixteen," responded Isaac—"old enough to know what's what, I can tell 'ee. See, if you've a good guinea about ye."

"There's no deceiving him, I see," muttered the lawyer, "he's as sharp as steel. Then, you can come home with me, now?"

"Yes, but where's the guinea? I never takes promises— substance for shadder, anyhow.

"You'll make a first-rate man; if you've common industry," remarked Quirk, as he gave the required coin to Isaac.

"Ah! it's all right, *this* time. O yes, depend on't, dad, I shan't be long learning *your* sort of tricks. I des say they're not different from mine; all roguery's alike."

And thus ended the interview between two remarkable characters, who were about the most cunning and villanous of all that ever figured in the annals of rascality.

CHAPTER VIII.

> Love-quarrels oft in pleasing concord end,
> Not wedlock treachery endangering life.
>
> MILTON.

> There in a moment we may plunge our years
> In fatal penitence, and in the blight
> Of our own soul, turn all our blood to tears,
> And colour things to come with hues of Night.
>
> BYRON.

MORE ADVENTURES—DANVERS IN THE CAVE—THE SECRET DOOR—THE BLOW—CORPORAL FIGGINS.

WALTER DANVERS, after he had descended into the cave which he had discovered so fortunately, endeavoured to see what kind of place he was in; but the darkness was so intense, that it was impossible to discover anything. Even when his eyes, accustomed to the darkness became of some little use, all that he could perceive was, that he had entered into a subterranean passage, of apparently considerable extent, which was probably surrounded by water at one extremity, as several reptiles, which generally inhabit dark and stagnant pools, rushed past him in alarm.

There appeared to be no outlet large enough to admit of egress, except that by which he had entered; and, therefore, summoning patience to his aid, he seated himself on the ground, and gave himself up to thought. He was extremely sorry, now, that he had not taken the important papers he had entrusted to George from him, when he might have done so; for although he doubted not the integrity and discretion of that extraordinary child, he feared that some accident might befal him, and all be discovered. But the adventures of the last few hours had been so crowded together, there had been no time for reflection; and after all, he thought George was not exposed to so much peril as himself.

The hours glided slowly on, and at length Danvers, weary with his long confinement, away from the light and air, and anxious to be stirring, ventured to re-ascend, and look about him. All was apparently safe: the sounds of pursuit had ceased, and there was no trace of friend or foe, far as the eye could reach. He, therefore, sallied forth with caution, and walked along through the thick trees of the copse.

But as he was about to make for the high road, he turned his head sideways, and beheld two fierce and bloodshot eyes glaring like a wild beast's upon him; and conceiving that many other foes were at hand, he rushed back towards the cave.

Captain Norton—for his assailant was no other—attacked him with maniacal fury; but Danvers, warding off the blows aimed at him with his musket, by a well-directed stroke shivered the officer's sword into pieces, and clubbing his own weapon, knocked him down, and again made for the cave. Before he could disappear, Norton followed, exclaiming—" Villain ! Coward !" but in a voice almost inarticulate with intense passion. For a second time—the stone at the mouth of the cave delaying him—the fugitive was obliged to defend himself; and again felled his antagonist; but as he was once more descending into the earth, Norton seized him by the throat, and supplied with factitious strength by his frenzy, a fearful struggle ensued. The hard and enormous bones and iron muscles of Danvers at length prevailed, and he dashed his opponent senseless down the steps on which the contest had taken place, when, fancying that he heard others approaching, he closed the entrance, and crept through a passage only high enough to admit of his going through it on his hands and feet.

Captain Norton remained insensible for a long time, having sustained a severe injury in the head : and he was slowly returning to life, when William Walsingham entered the place, and trod on his body.

"His blood! his blood!" exclaimed Norton. "I will have the murderer's blood!"

He strove to regain his feet; but had it not been for the help of the youth he could not have done so, and when he had succeeded, he was so dizzy that he still needed William's support.

"O, this passion of revenge!" muttered the Materialist, "how unworthy it is of a rational being! What pleasure can there be in destroying a human being, because *he* has destroyed one previously?"

"I will tear his heart out!" ejaculated the officer, "and I will give his body to the dogs!"

"Be calm," said the young man, "this rage only exhausts you."

"I tell you I *must* find him," replied Norton, staggering along; and in spite of the remonstrances of his companion, crawling through the low passage by which Danvers had escaped. This being done with much difficulty, Norton found himself before a mass of solid rock. "He *must* have gone this way," said the officer to William, who had followed him.

"Nay, he might have escaped by the entrance while you were without sense—I beseech you, relinquish your unavailing search."

"Never! I will pursue him into hell!" replied the veteran soldier, vehemently. "Ah! see, what is here." And striking against what seemed the solid rock, a door, so constructed as to appear a portion of it, unclosed. "He must have gone this way!" almost screamed the officer, rushing away.

After taking several windings, he entered another narrow passage; but as he was proceeding to thread it, he received a blow on the face from a strong hand. With a shout of rage he sprang on the person who had struck him—concluding, of course, it was Danvers—but he soon found, though it was nearly pitch dark, such could not be the case; for the man who opposed him was a giant in stature, whereas the object of his resentment was of a very common height.

Danvers, meanwhile, having discovered the secret of the door in the rock, by accidentally falling against it in his hurry on leaving the low passage, lost no time in taking advantage of the circumstance, and continuing his flight, certain that such was his only means of safety. But instead of taking the turning by which Norton had come in collision with his tall adversary, he chose one which led him to the open air by many windings, through a circular hole of several feet in diameter, beneath which the river was gliding calmly; and hesitating not many seconds, he plunged in and swam to the opposite shore.

The cavern he had left behind was a deserted mine, which had been abandoned centuries before, and afforded shelter to the persecuted Protestants in the reign of Bloody Mary, who had increased its natural facilities of concealment by artificial means. Afterwards, it had been worked to a considerable extent, but its vein of metal was now quite exhausted, and for many years its proprietors had closed it.

Danvers was now terribly in need of refreshment; not having taken anything to eat for a great number of hours, many of which had been spent in excessive fatigue; but he did not think it prudent to expose himself to observation, by entering any inn or public house, if such there were in the vicinity. Yet he felt that if he did not procure food, he should not be able to undergo the exertions which would probably be requisite; and he thought his best plan would be to offer to pay for provisions at some cottage, and proceed on his way at once.

Night was now gradually approaching, and he was at a loss what direction to take. There appeared no vestige of a habitation on the side of the river he had swum to—and he could only have left the cave by taking to the water—but a little farther up on the opposite side, where there was a heath of some extent, he observed a hut, and resolved to proceed to it. He was very wet, of course, and being too tired to enjoy swimming—although the water had refreshed him—he walked across the stream, where, narrowing, it was shallow, and made for the squalid abode he had noticed.

He went up to the hovel, and knocked at the door, when a woman's voice, with which he was almost certain he was familiar, bade him "come in;" but in a tone so low that the sound of it alone was audible.

"O, Mother Stokes!" the voice exclaimed, as Danvers, with-

2 z

out standing on farther ceremony, entered—" so, you're come at
last !"

But as Danvers advanced, the woman who had spoken, and
who was extended on a bed, uttered a scream, while Walter stood
transfixed in horror and amazement.

" My wife !" he exclaimed.   " Merciful Heaven !   How came
you here ?"

And his brain reeled so that he could hardly stand ; but his
eye wandering to a cradle near the female, he saw a new-born infant asleep in it, and the truth flashed upon him.

" Thus, then, after long years, I find you !" cried Danvers,
addressing the woman, who was no other than the niece of Mother
Stokes, introduced to the reader in the early portion of this
Chronicle.   The woman made no reply.   " Abandoned wretch !
This is your child, then ?" said Walter Danvers.   " Who is its
father ?"

" That cannot matter to you," replied the female, recovering
her effrontery.   " I do not ask you to support it.   Pray, what
do you here at such a time ?   How did you know I was in this
place ?"

" Nay, chance has brought me to you !   I never wished to see
your face again," replied Danvers, bitterly.   " You have poisoned my existence, and made me guilty and despised.   O, how
I curse the hour that I first saw you !   What madness and infatuation it was in me to make you my wife !"

" It was !" returned Mrs. Danvers, (if it be thought she is
entitled to that appellation,) speaking with an icy sneer.   " You
certainly did not show the intellect you fancy you possess in marrying an actress, who had previously been kept by your friend
Mr. Walsingham, having had children——"

" Infamous creature !" interrupted Walter.   " You know that
you deceived me—wickedly deceived me.   My God ! that I
should have sacrificed the possession of one of the purest and
brightest angels that ever breathed, to be the cuckold of such a
vile harlot !"   And he struck his head with his clenched hand in
agony.

" Call me what names you please, _dear_ husband !" said Mrs.
Danvers, with mock humility and theatrical hyper-pathos, " I

deserve them all:" and then burst into a hoarse laugh, which irritated Danvers to madness.

"Hark you!" he cried, approaching close to her, and speaking in a voice little above a whisper, but preternaturally distinct and clear. She shrunk from him with a quivering lip, as he added, "There is a devil in my soul, now, which prompts me to that which I might fearfully repent. How easy now it were to place my hand upon your throat, out of which you have insulted me so vilely——"

"O, God of Heaven!" exclaimed the female, gazing at the bright, starting eyes of her husband, and shrinking from them appalled. "Do not murder me, Walter! Think how unfit I am to die! Spare me, spare me!"

Instead of the crimson flush which had for a minute covered his face, a deathly pallor had overspread the brow and cheek of Danvers. He moved not, he spoke not; but continued to glare with that awful look upon the now awed and trembling wretch, till her flesh crept and her blood congealed.

"There is no hope for me," thought Mrs. Danvers, "if the Corporal do not come directly. Why did I rouse the fiend in his desperate nature? That gaze of stony horror! Ah, Walter! have mercy!" she cried.

"What harm should I be doing?" muttered Danvers, still retaining the same immoveable rigidity of position. "Many a poor wretch has been executed for one half the crimes she has committed! I am tempted fiercely. It would be just, strictly just!"

"No, no, Walter!" exclaimed the woman, cold drops of mortal agony on her brow, throwing herself on her knees on the bed before him. "Remember I—was once your wife, and I bore children to you! On my soul, they are *yours!* Indeed, indeed, indeed!"

Well was it for the guilty creature that she had spoken those words; for the resentment of that man of mighty passions had been roused to such a pitch of frenzy by her taunts, and his violent, stern and sanguinary feelings, so preponderated over reason and humanity, that murder seemed nothing to him. But the appeal was perfectly successful.

"Ay, ay, they are my children, and hers, too—they are like me: you swear they are mine, Sophia?"

"O, yes, yes!" was the reply. "Pray, leave me—I am ill. You see I have just been delivered."

"God forgive you, for I cannot," returned Danvers, moving away. But just as he was on the point of leaving the hut, he was arrested by a Herculean grasp. Corporal Figgins opposed him. "What! she has fallen to be your strumpet, ha!" exclaimed Danvers, his eagle eye seeming to read the Corporal's soul.

"You are my prisoner!" said Figgins.

"Yours!" cried Walter, contemptuously. "Huge beast as you are, it would take a dozen like you to capture me."

"We shall see about that," returned the Corporal, stoutly. "What brought you here, to insult and terrify——"

"Scoundrel!" exclaimed Walter, the strength he had lost through hunger and fatigue, returning as if by magic, with the rage within his breast; and striking Figgins in the mouth, thereby dashing out several of his strong teeth. The blow was returned, and Danvers aimed his bayonet at the Corporal's heart. Figgins averted the weapon with a thick cudgel which he carried, and drawing his sword, attacked his foe.

"Kill him!" cried the woman, as the blows were given and parried. "Kill him, Figgins! he knows too much;" but the Corporal, with all his unwieldy strength and skill in the use of the broadsword, was unequal to cope with Danvers, armed as he was with the bayonet.

Therefore, though burning with passion, he was constrained to forego all hope of capturing his enemy, who compelled him to retire into the hut, and threatened to transfix him with his bayonet to the wall.

"I spare you this once, Mr. Figgins," he said, however, "but I warn you to beware, lest I should think no more of slitting that bull throat of yours, than of slaughtering a hog. Your paramour and you are well matched, and I leave you to yourselves." And so saying, he strode away.

CHAPTER IX.

And there was famine with his eager eye,
His staring bones, and ghastly look ; as though
A ghost had come from Hell with horrid tales.

Old Play.

" An honest rascal, eh, sir?   Know you him ?"

The Rogue's Comedy.

HARRY   DANVERS   AND   HIS   HORRIBLE   SITUATION—JEN-
NINGS—A STORY—A STRUGGLE.

A CONSIDERABLE time has now elapsed since young Harry
Danvers has appeared on the stage ; and lest the circumstances
in which he was left should be forgotten, let us return to him,
and see what turn the wheel of fortune has taken in his case.

Alas ! as we revolve on the everlasting axis of destiny, how
very, *very* seldom do the stern sisters give us a favourable turn ;
and how frequently are we left in a worse condition than that in
which we began !

Harry Danvers was left asleep, and if he could enjoy a rest so
dreamless, without the vain struggles, the guilt, and sorrow of
mortal existence, he was not to be pitied.   We should do well if
we could forget that we *are*, forget there are hearts hollow and
cold, forget there are hopes, joys, and despair ; supposing this
" might be the be-all, and the end-all here :" but we have sweet
and happy feelings, nestling themselves in the bosom of an immortality ; and they are blest, and bright, and beautiful in the
felicity they scatter, and the eternity they so eloquently predicate.
They purify and etherealise our being, and even in pain and disappointment will conduct our spirits to some angel sphere, where
the poetry of our young hearts may find realisation.

When the lad awoke, he felt the pangs of hunger, and he had
not the means of appeasing the demands of his appetite.   But,

nevertheless, he set himself to work with a strong and resolute
soul, and made some progress; but was at last obliged to stop,
from exhaustion. He threw himself on the ground once more,
and presently slept again; nature endeavouring thus to supply
the strength he could not obtain from external means. But at
length famine was preying on his vitals, and thirst was goading
him to madness. He raved and prayed by turns, till insensibility
kindly stole over him. O, the horror of such a situation, no
friendly word to comfort, no dear face to smile, to soothe—cut
off in the morning of existence, and none acquainted with that
dark and awful doom! But too frequently have there been such
cases unseen of all but the Omniscient eye. But Harry dreamed.
God's angel was in his bosom; and he thought he was in Elysian
fields, all lovely things around him, in the society of the beatified.
He might soon have been so, if no human succour had been at
hand: but he was aroused, after he had slept a very short time,
by a choking sensation in the throat, and opening his languid
eyes, beheld a most gigantic figure, the stature of which seemed
superhuman in the grey obscurity, supporting him. He gazed
around with bewildered looks.

"Water! O, water!" he cried, his tongue cleaving to his
palate, and his former pangs returning.

"Here is some soaked biscuit; try and eat it," said the man,
who was sustaining him.

Harry's heart leapt at the sound of that voice, for he had made
up his mind that he should never hear one again on earth, and
though he had been listening in imagination to the songs of
seraphs, I question whether he was not more delighted at hearing
what was not anything like heavenly music. Whatever Hobbes
and Mandeville may tell you to the contrary, depend upon it
man does *not* hate his species for the love of himself—an assertion
very well defended by Hazlitt, when he wrote against Helvetius.
O, how we cling to this old earth of ours! We are always abus-
ing it, and all that it contains, as if it were a pickpocket, or a
lady of ill fame; but we must in our hearts conceive it is a very
honest, amiable, and virtuous creature, just adapted to our wants
and wishes. Talk of evil, misery, &c. &c.! Bless your soul!
We must be very fond of them; or we should want to leave them

behind, since they are for ever pursuing us; but then we certainly
don't know if we all should do so. " There's the rub."

Harry gradually revived ; and in the course of a few minutes
was able to express his thanks to the friendly stranger, and inquire
how he happened to come to his assistance, how he got there,
and several other questions.

" An accident has brought me here," was the reply. " I suppose such has been your case ?"

" No," returned Harry, " foul treachery has brought me to
this pass; and but for you I should have perished."

They soon entered into familiar conversation; and Harry
found his companion a rather amusing person, with a large fund
of anecdote, which he was very willing to impart.

" We must set about, and try to release ourselves without
delay," said the tall man, Harry having regained his spirits under
the influence of his lively, rattling talk; " but you must rest
yourself first. Explain to me your position, and I may possibly
help you; for I have a good deal more power than you would
give me credit for, seeing me in this d——d methodistical dress."

Harry immediately communicated all that he prudently could
concerning himself to the stranger; who eyed him with curiosity,
and when he had finished, said—

" Well, I'll stand your friend, if I can, depend upon it. Now
suppose you try to get a little sleep, and I'll go to work and see
what I can do to release ourselves from this unpleasant predicament. I have got plenty of food in my pockets."

And so saying, the tall man produced some biscuits and meat
from his huge pockets, and partook of some himself.

" Thank you," cried Harry, " I can't sleep; but I don't know
that I could help you much in working."

" No, no," said the stranger, proceeding to examine the place
carefully; and added, " in an hour we may break through this
wall; but I feel rather tired myself, and there is no very great
hurry—" muttering, " they won't think of trying to get at me.—
As you have told me something of yourself," he continued, " I
will now relate some particulars of my life, which has been a
rather singular one; for I have seen ups and downs without
number; but laughed at the jade fortune—who is a cursed, fickle
wench, not worth caring about :—and drank, and made merry,

without giving a thought to the morrow. I am an easy, jovial sort of fellow, and scramble as I can through existence, never bestowing a second thought on what may come, after it is over."

THE HISTORY OF THE STRANGER.

" My maternal parent was a lady attached to a marching regiment, and married to a little wretch of a drummer, who, I must tell you, was my *reputed* parent. It is a devilish good plan to have a father who takes care of you, at all events. Mr. Jennings, the gentleman I have alluded to, was also a tailor, and indeed in person he was but the ninth part of a man; whereas my good mother was a strapping piece of feminine loveliness, standing six feet high.

" Now, there was a young fellow just entering life, who was a private in the regiment, named Figgins. He was, when Mr. and Mrs. Jennings were married, somewhere about your age, or maybe, a little older—but was a tall and sturdy lad, and his society was much liked : for he sang one of the best songs, and told some of the most facetious stories of any person I ever knew—and I have been so fortunate as to make the acquaintance of men of wit, humour and ability. You must pardon the rough way in which I tell my story—hopping from one thing to another without rounding a period, for I hate verbosity, and like variety. I don't know that the character of my sweet little mother was unimpeachable before she married ; but whispers were circulated, I have heard, to her disadvantage, after she had entered the state of holy matrimony ; and it was asserted that the boy Figgins ' twixt the sheets' of my father 'had done his office.' Certain it is, that in the course of time, my mother produced a bouncing boy, not in the least like good Mr. Jennings, but more resembling Figgins. This was my eldest brother, and myself and a sister followed as fast as nature permits—a deuced good job that human beings don't spawn like fish do, or we must all be cannibals—all three of us being remarkable for height and strength. Soon afterwards, Mr. Figgins quitted our regiment, and entered into the Horse Guards, who wanted some six feet fellows ; and that in which he had served, subsequently was ordered abroad. About the same time as the departure of this worthy, a singular circumstance occurred, which exercised a powerful influence on the destiny of my sister and myself. An eccentric medical man, who was always theorising and experimentalising, had a fierce dispute with the surgeon of the regiment I have alluded to, on the causes of the difference of stature among mankind. The military surgeon maintained that the cause of this diversity is the same as that from which springs superiority of mind—original organization—while the theorist stoutly asserted that it was the result of training, and offered to make a bet that he would create giants out of two children, if he had them under his care. This eccentric individual carried out his wager, and made choice of my sister and me for his experiment, though, as I have said, we were always remarkably tall; and so he might give a shrewd guess that we were likely to substantiate his hypothesis. Certainly, he succeeded in making me six feet four in my stockings, and my sister is but two inches less: but then my brother is full six feet three, and no training was bestowed on him. It seems to me, sir, that all these theories which distract the brains of our knowing ones—as they are esteemed—are so many humbugs, originated by quacks, and swallowed by fools, and that plain common sense is the only rational thing in the universe. But I am an exceedingly shallow and superficial fellow, and nothing but an empiric myself; so I don't pretend, by any means, to be infallible in the oracles I deliver. Opinions go flying about hither and thither, like leaves before the wind, and they don't stay any longer for the most part; so I have no opinions, no principles, but am ruled by my feelings—as, in *fact*, who isn't?

" Such were the circumstances, then, which attended my birth and early life. My parents, and particularly my father, was glad to be rid of such encumbrances as two hungry children : and, accordingly, my sister and I were taken under the roof of the excellent theorist, who, to do him justice, provided all things proper, both for our minds and bodies ; *only* he crammed us nuto bursting with soups, at one time, imagining that liquids are more conducive to the growth of the body than solids.* The old gen-

---

* Such was the supposition of a physician, a few years ago, who caused, it is said, a young Irish giant to reach seven feet by feeding him in this way.

tleman was a great Materialist (as I have heard those called who
say we have nothing but matter in us—though how we know
that, any more than other animals, if it is so, I don't pretend to
understand.) I am no philosopher, assuredly; but was always
a very idle rascal, and never bothered my head about what didn't
concern me.

" My mother, just before the regiment her husband belonged to
embarked for a foreign country, was drowned when in a state of
intoxication, and I never heard what became of my father; but
it was said that he never recovered the joy of losing his larger
half, and died of it by slow degrees. But I can't believe happiness has ever killed a man. Be this as it may, I grew up strong
and hearty; and was stuffed with a little Latin and Greek; but
I always hated them cordially, thinking them my natural enemies,
as good Englishmen do Frenchmen; so you may suppose I never
made much progress. The theoretical gentleman to whom I am
indebted for my education, and something maybe, of my inches,
would have bound me apprentice to him, and married me to a
little squint-eyed girl with whom he was trying a contrary experiment to that I was submitted to; but I relished not pestle and
mortar, nor four feet one of female ugliness, and thought my
brother—who had been taken care of by a relation, and was now
a private in a dragoon regiment, though only sixteen—a very
lucky chap: for he had never been obliged to learn so much as
to read. Thus do we estimate the blessings of fortune; and ever
by negatives: what I mean is, we do not feel grateful for benefits
enjoyed, but think how much happier we should be, if we had
what we cannot possess. However, I cut the fair dwarf, and
cutting limbs, and one fine morning I went off to London by myself, being then about fifteen, but taller than many men, by
several inches. Here I supported myself by my wits, now as an
auxiliary at one of the theatres, now as a street-musician; and
once as servant to a lady of fashion, who took a fancy to my
great height, and made a regular show of me. She wanted to
have all things remarkable about her, and all her servants were
dressed like ladies and gentlemen. I was a smart and dashing
fellow of pleasing appearance, and suited her exactly; but my
unfortunate predilection for the fair sex began to manifest itself
about this time, and I was discovered in the act of making love

to her eldest daughter, who would have run away with me, if we
had not been detected. I had reached the age of seventeen in
this manner, when my old protector died, leaving a thousand
pounds a piece to my sister, the squinting dwarf, and myself,
and writing me a gentle rebuke on my wildness, adding, if I were
wise I should marry the wife he had selected for me, and get a
fine family of children. 'For,' said he, 'perfection lies between
extremes, and I doubt not your offspring would be symmetrical
and beautiful.' This latter piece of advice, however, I declined
to profit by, and I fear his moral axioms were equally futile with
me. My sister came to live in London, and was very much
admired, though she had grown to an awful height for a woman.
I procured a situation as secretary to a gentleman of literary
reputation, who employed me to steal all the tit-bits from the
poets and others, and dress them up in a new fashion, in which
work I was aided by my sister, who has more brains than I have.
What a thing is fame, to be sure! Strange, that any one should
care leaving one behind him, when any pitiful pilferer can acquire
it, by paying a few pounds to another to do his dirty business!
But one day my employer had the audacity to take liberties with
my sister, she having come to visit me, and I being out, she
knocked him down. So I lost my situation. When I got the
legacy left me by my worthy old friend, you may suppose I soon
spent it. I kept horses, company, and mistresses, and very soon
found myself without a farthing. But I hoped to marry an
heiress, being a favourite with the ladies, and I doubt not, should
have succeeded, had I been able to carry on the war: but my
creditors were importunate, and I was obliged to quit London on
a sudden; and being very hard pushed, I enlisted as a trooper
in the regiment my brother was in. I became a favourite with
my comrades, having some of the qualities of Corporal Figgins,
thought more of than any others by soldiers—although not half so
clever a man: but the fair daughter of the quarter-master of the
regiment having engaged my affections, I wanted her to become
my wife.—O, these women! Ever since Eve was made, what mischief they have brought on mankind! The quarter-master hearing of this affair, came to me in a great passion, and swore he
would horsewhip me. Now I was known to be a man of some
education; and several of my officers had even associated with

me when I was a gay man in town, so that I was not looked upon in the light of a common soldier. I gave a challenge to the father of my beloved, who being a hot-blooded Irishman accepted it. Pistols were at hand, and we fired without the presence of witnesses, when I most unluckily shot my man through the heart. I was obliged to decamp without a minute's delay, and since that time have wandered about in various disguises, having had some hair-breadth escapes, which I will relate to you at some future time. Now I will go to work."

Thus Mr. Jennings concluded his history, which he told with great volubility, and Harry having thanked the tall man for the confidence he had reposed in him, that person, the pickaxe in his hand, shortly effected a breach in the wall.

"Now, then," he said, "I dare say that we shall find our way out; but I must assume another disguise. I learned this art when I was pursuing a theatrical occupation. I shall be lame and blind, now. With this wig" (producing one from his pocket, and putting it on) "and a few other alterations, no one will know me."

Harry was astonished at the metamorphosis which Jennings soon produced in his appearance, seeming a poor, feeble old man, very far advanced in life. His dress also he managed to transmogrify; but not to his own satisfaction. Looking around him, the long gentleman perceived an oak chest, old and rotten, and breaking it open with the pickaxe, he exclaimed—

"Here's luck! A lot of clothes of all sorts. You had better help yourself, for if you'll take my advice, *you'll* assume a disguise also."

From a heap of miscellaneous articles of apparel, Harry selected a cloak, which had once been handsome, and was not in a bad state of preservation considering the age it was apparently of. Jennings chose some other garments for himself, and then said—

"Now I will stain your face, if you like, with a preparation I have here; and you may then go where you will, and not be recognised."

So Harry, reflecting that he might prosecute his search after his father with greater safety, if he took the counsel of his new friend, submitted to have his fair face embrowned, and they then sallied forth, the youth declaring he felt quite strong again. But as they were proceeding through a dark passage, Jennings cried, "Hist!" Scarcely had the word escaped his lips when hasty footsteps were heard advancing.

"Stand here!" said Jennings, in a low voice. Even as he spoke the footsteps approached to within a few feet of them ; and the tall man bidding Harry follow him, noiselessly moved forward, and the passage being wide enough to admit but of one person threading it at a time, whispered, "We must fight for it :" and thrusting out his long arm, bestowed a terrible blow on a person within a yard of him. The stroke was returned ; but Jennings soon hurled his opponent to the earth, and with Harry at his heels, was proceeding again, when a second individual opposed them.

There was another brief, but strong struggle, when the tall man was for a second time victorious, and still accompanied by the youth hastened away, and met with no farther resistance. So we will leave them, and glance at some other of our acquaintances, whom we have not seen of late.

CHAPTER X.

Alas! our young affections run to waste,
Or water but the desart! Whence arise
But weeds of dark luxuriance—tares of haste,
Rank at the core, tho' tempting to the eyes.

BYRON.

CHARLES WALSINGHAM—MISTRESS HAINES---AND A PHILIPPIC AGAINST THE WORLD, WHICH CONCLUDES THIS EVENTFUL BOOK.

IT was a night of tempest and violence. The lurid lightning shot athwart the sky, succeeded by claps of thunder at rapid intervals, and the heavy sleet and rain descended without a moment's cessation. Some solitary star might occasionally be seen in the black vault above; but no moon gleamed through the heavy, gigantic clouds, and the wind whistling in dismal and fitful gusts, tended to aggravate the gloom and desolation of the scene.

But these things were little known by the occupants of a chamber in a lone country house—one of them being in a semi-dozing condition, and the other absorbed in stern and intense reverie.

The former of these persons was a handsome young man, who lay on a sofa—or rather a rustic bench, covered with cushions—with a pale face, and attenuated frame, seeming not yet recovered from severe and protracted illness. The other was a woman in the decline of life, with gray hair, and dark, fiery eyes, which were now, however, grave, and bent down, lines of thought and sorrow distinctly visible in her sunken cheek, and haughty and commanding brow.

At length the woman rose from the chair on which she had been sitting, and went to the window. She surveyed the scene without with a stern, unmoved countenance, muttering—

"What is the scathing hand of the tempest, to the desolation and destruction that rage in a human bosom? Nature will look fair, and put on her holiday smiles again: the sky will be blue and calm, and the glorious lights of Heaven will shine as if they were spiritual beings removed from change; but the soul which has lost its radiance once, pines and droops, until the silence of the grave closes over it."

Having thus said, she folded her arms across her chest, and stood in an attitude of contemplation for the space of some minutes, the lurid flames above throwing a ghastly and spectral hue upon her bold and striking lineaments. Presently she returned to the couch by which she had been resting, and scrutinized the features of the young man there.

"A splendid form,—in health, manly, vigorous and imposing," she said.

Her voice awoke the sleeper, who exclaimed—

"You are very good to take so much interest in me. In a few days I hope I shall not be obliged to trespass farther on your kindness."

"I am glad you feel you are getting better."

As the woman was thus speaking, a vivid flash of lightning revealed a miniature which she wore, and which had escaped from her bosom.

"How very strange!" said the sick man.

"What is very strange?" inquired the female.

"I was thinking you bear a wonderful resemblance to some picture that I have seen," was the reply, "and now I perceive you are the very image of the miniature you wear, which is evidently one of Charles the Second."

A flush of mingled pride and shame rose to the woman's brow.

"Yes, Captain Walsingham," she said, "that monarch was my father. He was a man with evil passions—with dark crimes it may be;—but yet he *had* virtues which shone forth from that darkness, like the flame of Heaven there from the gloom around. He was a man of intellect, and natural feeling ; but all his best qualities were perverted, and his abilities suffered to rust from neglect. He died almost before I saw the light, and I, who might have mingled with the most illustrious among the great, am now a poor, old, withered creature, mourning over great wrongs, and unable to right—to revenge myself. But there is a God above, who will redress the injuries of the widow; and the time is at hand, when I shall see the tyrant and the usurper dethroned, and the family to which I belong wielding the sceptre of their ancestors."

The daughter of a vicious king spoke with vehemence and rapidity, as if unable to stem the torrent of her feelings, and there was that about her which confirmed the truth of her assertion, not only in looks, but in words, and tones and gestures.

Walsingham (the invalid was he) regarding her compassionately, rejoined—

"To what injustice, may I ask, do you allude?"

"Listen," she answered, with that startling and abrupt manner which conceals and stifles passion. "I had once a son, the glory and pride and hope of my existence. I had once a husband, kind, brave, generous, and good. My son was even such a man as you are. The same height of stature and military bearing made him look like the descendant of a line of monarchs : the same fine, open features promised the firmness, sagacity, and courage which he had ; and if ever there lived one worthy of be-

ing called a hero—one worthy to stand among his fellow-men,
erect in the majesty of worth and mind,—he was pre-eminently
so. I think I see him now, poor boy! with his flashing eye and
powerful frame, ready to go forth to battle in the sacred cause of
Justice. I think I see him in all the flush of youth and valour,
each limb so strong, each beauty so magnificent! And then a
pale, stiff corse, livid with the marks of the hangman's hands.
They would not give him so much as a soldier's death. O God
of Heaven! thou alone knowest what I have endured! Thou
alone art conscious of the extent of the ruin and wretchedness
within me, and canst alone revenge my wrongs—my fearful, unutterable wrongs!"

Walsingham attempted to soothe the excited feelings of his
companion; but her frenzy rushed in a lava flood of violence
from her bursting heart, and she continued.

"In the fatal rebellion of 1715, my husband and son were
given commissions in the army under the Earl of Mar. They
had previously served in France as private soldiers; but their
bravery and prowess had attracted the attention of King James,
and I, through a friend who was in his household, having made
known to him that my boy was the grandson of the restored
Charles, he interested himself in his behalf. You know the termination of the war in Scotland; and you know also that many
brave men were taken and executed. My husband fell in battle,
as a soldier ought; and I wept for him, with tears of pride and
grief; but my child—my only child, was hanged like a felon;
and I shed no tears for *him*, but breathed a deep and bitter vow
of vengeance, which I will accomplish ere I die. My son had
attained the same rank in the army as you hold, and he was beloved and admired by all his comrades. Oh, he was so good, so
great! None can know the agony of a heart whose every throb,
hope, wish, is centered in a darling child—one always most affectionate, noble, and exalted,—when his death is attended with
infamy, and he is cut off when a proud career of honour is opening to him, in the vigour and blossom of his life;—a thousand
bright and radiant things, which are to the human soul what
angels are to heaven, destroyed for ever by his death. And I
have been like a tree struck by the ethereal fire—all joy and
splendour crushed and blasted within; and my only desire on

earth, a holy, an awful, and a consummate vengeance! Young
man, you serve the cause I hate; you are the minion of those
who cut off from me the tendrils which twined around my heart;
and when you hear my maledictions, you feel no goodwill for me.
But if you had experienced the dire and burning pangs which
have scorched up the very springs of this existence I bear, until
they have become like living fire, pouring torture and madness
through my veins, you would not think Elizabeth Haines a revengeful and bloodthirsty woman. You would not think my
words are those of gall; you would not wonder I am desperate
and frenzied."

The blood had mounted to the pallid cheek of the Hanoverian
soldier as Elizabeth poured forth her torrent of invective; but towards the climax of her speech, pity and tenderness were expressed
by his looks, and every vestige of anger, kindled by the dispa-
raging allusions to himself in connection with the existing government, vanished from his open forehead. "I sympathise with your
sorrows most sincerely," he said; "but surely it is our duty, as
Christians, hoping to receive mercy, and conscious for the necessity of the exercise of it toward ourselves, to forgive the injuries
with which we have been assailed, and to leave a righteous retribution to the infallible Judge of all."

Elizabeth vouchsafed no answer; and the young man added:
"Poor indeed is the good or evil, the mercy, or the justice man
can do; and for the virtuous dead, what care *they* for vengeance?
Are they not happy beyond conception? Can we add aught to
their felicity? The gallant husband and son you so deeply lament,
are perhaps enjoying even now the fruits of their good deeds on
earth, and you may possibly be giving them cause for sorrow—if
they *can* grieve—by fostering a sentiment inimical to religion on
their account. We all of us err, and must suffer; but there is
One who knows our weakness and commiserates——"

"Ay!" exclaimed Elizabeth; "but He makes man the instrument of His vengeance; or else, why should He have instituted
laws, which were to be vindicated with severity? And I have
sworn to seek justice, and I will have it, or die. Wherefore
should I forgive those who have so irremediably wronged me?
who cared not for my tears and prayers, and the youth and
gallantry of my heroic boy; who spurned me with insult and

3 B

treated me with indignity, though the last daughter of a king—
and tearing my son away from my widowed arms, consigned him
to the death of a common malefactor? Theirs are low and
slavish spirits who would not seek to be revenged for wrongs like
these! O, God of Eternity! that I should live and see him in
the convulsions of expiring mortality, without stirring, weeping,
speaking, and live—so long:—all the sap which supplied my inmost being with vitality, so cruelly drawn away from me; and
nothing left to support my agonized soul, my dreary and desolate
existence—except revenge—except that."

"Alas!" replied the soldier: "deep and terrible are the trials
with which we are afflicted; and it is only by enduring them with
that high and heavenly philosophy which Faith and Virtue can
supply, that we can hope to sustain them, and cause them to
operate to the purpose for which they were sent—our own purification and exaltation. Too often are we in the habit of calling
that just which harmonises with our passions. We must learn
to extract good from evil, and apply the poison as a wholesome
medicine, necessary to prepare us for a better state. I must acknowledge that the conduct of the government in the year when
that unhappy rebellion terminated was harsh, and perhaps sanguinary: but stringent measures were at that time indispensable,
and could not be carried out without the effusion of blood. Of
course the least guilty were sometimes immolated; but for the
sustentation of the monarchy——"

"What! do you justify the murder of my son?" burst out
Elizabeth, indignantly.

"I do not! I myself would have pardoned him and every other
valiant enemy freely," replied Charles. "It never would be with
satisfaction that I could take the life even of the basest; but a
painful sense of public duty must have compelled me to sacrifice
my individual feelings; and I think and hope that such a principle dictated the execution of your son."

"Talk not of execution!" exclaimed Elizabeth. "Call the
deed by its right name! It was inhuman, if legalised murder.—
Shall we say that a government has a right to commit any deeds,
when an accursed tribunal condemned the son of the Eternal to
die?—I speak it with all reverence!"

"O, no!" cried Walsingham. "But surely no parallel is to

be drawn between such cases. The Messiah shed no blood ; but these misguided men committed many atrocities."

His words were heeded not, and he desisted.

" My boy ! my boy ! how nobly he bore himself, even unto death !" cried the widow, passionately.—" Undaunted to the last, he raised his voice, and exclaimed against the injustice of the house of Hanover, and prayed Heaven to make the righteous cause triumph at last—And it shall—it shall !—He lived and died a hero, as lofty as was ever deified or immortalised in the ancient Roman days !"

Walsingham's eye fired at this description, and then became dim with tears.

" O, that I could have saved him !" he ejaculated with enthusiasm. " O, that the sacrifice of my life could have given to the world so brave and generous a spirit !—But, tell me : cannot I serve the gentleman under whose roof I now am ? Is he not in danger, from having acted with imprudence ?"

" If we should ever need your help," replied Elizabeth Haines, softened by the fervour she had elicited from Charles, by the picture she had drawn of her son ; " I will not fail to ask you to exert your influence in his behalf."

" I thank you cordially for that promise," said Walsingham. " Is there nothing I can do for *you*, also ?"

" Nothing," returned Elizabeth, rather haughtily ; " you do not owe me anything : and I would never willingly receive any benefit at the hands of an officer-of the Elector of Hanover."

The soldier coloured, but did not reply for some time. When he did so, he said—

" You will convey a short letter for me to the young lady, who was such a ministering angel to me :—you cannot refuse me this ·last request ?"

" I must not," said Mrs. Haines, though with more hesitation than was usual with her.

" Yes, yes," you will !" cried Charles. " I swear to you it shall contain nothing which the saints themselves might not read. I have centred all my fondest hopes and aspirations in that pure young being : and her absence has impeded the progress of my recovery. I need not add that my designs are honest. I would not wrong any woman that lives, and for *her*—I should as soon offer an insult to a seraph."

" Well, I will take your letter," replied Mrs. Haines; " but I warn you that she can never become your wife: there is an insurmountable barrier betwixt you."

Often, very often have those words sounded like a knell to the sweet bells, which chime like those of the Eastern Paradise, in youth, because the vile barriers of the world arise between pure loves, and fetter the limbs with iron,—which eats into the flesh more keenly than the chains of a tyrant! The end of all joy—the seal of all the aerial soarings, and pantings, the awakening from the sweet dream of passion, and the thrilling ecstasies which now are yours, O bright ones! such must be—such is the inexorable, universal destiny. And behold the poet and the visionary changed into the cold, heartless man of the world, sordid, and selfish, and sarcastic, without aught of the lofty and generous feeling which was kindled by the pure breath of affection! And lo, the gentle, tender girl, with her romance, her delicacy, her truthfulness, a dissipated, degraded, guilty creature, sacrificed by those who worshipped Mammon for dust—to which *they* have returned. Gold! gold! opinion, bigotry, and prejudice, what miseries have ye created! Dear Reader! What thing seems most desirable in your eyes? Power? O, bethink you how it has crumbled from the grasp of the mighty of old time! Love it not, seek it not, if to attain it you are required to give up a tittle of those humble household enjoyments, which you know not the value of until they are gone. Make of the smiles and *tears* which are in the spirit, friends,—for it is good to be happy, it is good to be sorrowful. But would you have wealth?—Find it in the *heart*. Are gold, diamonds, rubies, to be compared to the warm drops that flow in the human bosom? The *Penates*, of which the beautiful feelings of nature constitute the substance and the spirit, must not be hurled down, for the idols of the world—

" Whose root is earth, whose leaves and branches be
     The skies which rain their plagues on men, like dew."

END OF BOOK VI.

BOOK VII.

We are the fools of time and terror : Days
Steal on us and steal from us : yet we live
Loathing our life, and dreading still to die.

Manfred..

Down, reason then ; at least, vain reasonings down.

Milton.

Inspiring thought of rapture yet to be,
The tears of love were hopeless but for thee !

Campbell.

To-morrow and to-morrow, and—to-morrow,
Creeps in this petty space from day to day,
To the last syllable of recorded time !
And all our yesterdays have but lighted fools
The way to dusky death !—*Macbeth.*

CHAPTER I.

Here he was interrupted by a knife
With " D—n your eyes! your money or your life!"

BYRON.

THE PHILOSOPHER AND HIS MEDITATIONS—THE CHILDREN
—WALSINGHAM—THE ROBBERS—HARRY AND DANVERS.

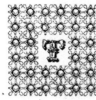HE sultry breath of the noonday was mingling
with soft and refreshing gales, and the long
shadows of the trees upon the grass indicated
that evening was at hand, though the royal
orb of day was still shining gloriously in the
western sky, and tinging the fantastically
shaped clouds with gorgeous hues of yellow,
pink, and crimson. The faint disk of the moon might be seen in
the soft, blue heaven, resembling some ideal image, rather than
aught substantial. A spirit of love and stillness seemed to hang
enamoured over the radiant scene, and the notes of the thrush
and the blackbird in the verdant hedges, which enclosed fields
and orchards abounding with corn and fruit, sounded sweetly
and harmoniously in the calm air; and Nature smiling solemnly

and tenderly, in the serenity of her dreamy soul, appeared to say, " We have had enough of darkness, of terror, and convulsion ; let us now remain for ever thus, and woo the divine beings who live in the everlasting effulgence to come and see how happy, how tranquil, all may be, even far away from the spheres of glory !"

Some such thoughts as these had probably been passing through the mind of a solitary mortal, who sat, enjoying the fragrant breeze, scented with the breath of dewy flowers, beneath an enormous elm, which overshadowed a pretty little cottage, nestled among woodlands, but commanding on one side a beautiful and extensive view of hill and valley, stream and pasture ; for as a shade of deep melancholy was visible on his face, he said, in a low voice—

" Yes, all is like Heaven, now ! Thus humanity, with peace within, and beauty, and love, and melody without, may for a few moments forget that there is such a thing as sorrow. But the history of all is DESOLATION ; the calm is only the forerunner of the tempest ; the storm gathers, and brings ruin with it ; and the dream disperses." The rest is silence.

What a man was there ! Though below the height, even of what is considered a diminutive person, though slight, and pale, and fragile, the intense and eager spirit within illuminating his white cheek, and breathing on his parted lip—the deep and majestic character of intellect so vividly impressed on each feature and each line of his eloquent countenance, denoted one of those master spirits, which soar on immortal pinions to the stars, and commune with feelings, desires, and aspirations, which are not bounded by time and space.

But if the splendour of his other features was remarkable, much more so was the God-like effulgence of his forehead, which was covered with a skin so delicate, that every vein in it was perceptible ; and the subtile workings of the brain seemed equally visible, as the thronging, clear, and aspiring thoughts were busy in that organ where all sensation is : and which looked forth a world of infinite things from his large, luminous, and piercing eyes, that, but for the long lashes which shaded them, would have been almost insufferably brilliant. Intellect and imagination were the predominating characteristics of that wonderful face ;

but sensibility and gentleness, with a mixture of that quiet sadness which is now more like thought than melancholy, and now the reverse, pervaded its general expression. The head was exquisitely formed, and covered with fair hair, such as that which Milton is represented to have possessed, and although his age was not above six-and-thirty, he was a little grey, and lines of sorrow blended with those of reflection on his brow. His frame, as has been remarked, was very small and delicate; but would have been decidedly symmetrical, but for a slight and nearly imperceptible crookedness in the left shoulder. He might have looked contemptible by the side of a giant, if the size of his person alone were taken into consideration; but the blaze of his face was such, that few indeed among the children of men could have borne comparison with its continuous light. Yet there was repose in each look, and tranquil dignity in each gesture, which mellowed the brightness of his countenance, and imparted lofty grandeur even to his puny form.* Inward and frequent communing with his soul, was evidently a delight to him; and he was now engaged in profound meditations, which were partly embodied in the following words:—

" ' The rest is *silence!*' So said *Hamlet*, when he expired. So, after the turmoil of this being, there is not a breath to disturb or to excite! The end of Life is Death. Is Death nothing? When we gaze on the rigid lineaments, the stiffened body, the glazed eyes, the dull, heavy forehead, we ask, Is this, then, all? Where is the mind which informed those now motionless features? Is the mind nothing? For it must be so, or else an essence of itself. Whatsoever *exists* is indestructible. The forms of things may perish, but the substance cannot be destroyed. It is possible, then, that form is the creation of our mind, as matter is the affection of the senses. Both exist; otherwise it is impossible to conceive the intellect or the senses as existing. Then Death is an entity. It has form, if it have no substance; but it is in the mind—an idea which is universal. Life also exists; and in these things are the arch-mysteries of

---

* This description is long and minute: but, to my mind, there is something deeply interesting in the study of the outward form, which almost without exception conveys the image of the mental shape.

Being. Beautiful Life! With all thy music and visions of stupendous magnificence, thine ethereal grace and motion, what art thou? Thy looks are as an angel's, and thou must come from none less than God. Then what is Death? Who made the horrible corruption, the foul smell, the loathsomeness, the *silence* wherein thou dwellest? Does the Creator of life blast his own sublime work? Does He change the loveliness into deformity, the symmetry and perfect excellence into a heap of shapeless ashes? The Sculptor does not break the statue on which he has expended his thought and labour: but Time is the iconoclast. Say, whence is Death? Is there some evil, as well as some good Omnipotence? Two Omnipotences? Impossible! One, or none at all.

"Then Death is from God? He created not Death, but the elements of Death; and we must ask wherefore? Reason, haughty Reason! answer thou this. Solve the problem, explain the necessity! Look at the agonies which follow in the steps of Death—did a merciful Creator inflict them? Did he make the poor widow desolate, and the innocent children orphans, for nothing? Death itself a good man will not fear; but to leave those he loves to a cold world is hard indeed. Is Death the end of Life? After a "fitful fever" of many painful diseases of mind and body,—hopes annihilated, and joys crushed unsparingly, is "Silence," I ask, the consummation of all? Is the goodness of the Eternal evinced in Evil? If this were a sweet and a pleasant existence, to be succeeded by a sleep from which there is no waking, it were well; we should have nothing to complain of but the cessation of joy. Though, even then, it is not possible to conceive that in the infinite design, where nothing is lost or wasted, the human mind, which is the most exalted work of all, should sink into nothingness; while dull matter exists for ever. Great Being! Incomprehensible are thy ways; but to me that incomprehensibility is a manifestation of thy divinity and my weakness. Wisdom in vain would fathom thy mysterious operations, and Genius penetrate into thy secret councils. But I thank Thee for the conviction of a surpassing eternity, stamped in thy divinest characters on my soul! I bless thee that I exist; I thank thee that I suffer; for I know that if Thou art, I am to live, when Universes have passed away."

Such were the feelings and contemplations of a philosopher. He had read and thought with all the power of a strong, a vigorous, and original understanding ; and his conviction of the immortality of the soul, was mighty to sustain and comfort him. We invariably find that the finest and noblest spirits are ever most clingingly attached to the idea of their Eternal Destiny; and while others may pursue the phantoms of a vain ambition, and a worldly lust, how striking is the contrast between their gross and miserable Idols, and the bright Deities which are the objects of the true philosopher's adoration ! There is something, to me, divine and affecting in the worship of that truth, of which we possess both so much and so little, and the affectionate endearments which are so profusely lavished on the ideal and invisible. Those who had no Revelation to guide them were always reasoning on the probability of a future state of existence, and there was a passionate desire to demonstrate this high argument, which invests the philosophy of the ancients with its greatest charm. At the present time, we rather confute the theses of sceptics, than advance new reasons. The genius of the metaphysics of the Greeks and Romans was, abstractedly, affirmation ; but the re-action produced by the study of those sciences from which we derive much of our civilization, from their materialistic tendencies has been negation. We seldom recur to first principles now : and when such is the case we shall be likely to think little of aught beyond the actual. But then it is on the other hand advanced, that these philosophers idolize their own theories. True, great thinkers, from Plato down to Schelling, *have* idolized—Virtue, Wisdom, Love, and Immortality, the essence of the One Eternal. Only sciolists adore what is not IN the Creator.

On the bench on which the reasoner was seated, there were some volumes, the nature of whose contents indicated the bent of his mind and studies. There was the inspired disciple of Socrates, there was the lofty Cicero, the subtile Aristotle, and the moralising Seneca, together with the acute Locke, the spiritual Berkeley, the erudite Cudworth, and the ingenious Clarke.

" And yet," continued the thinker, " the assumptions and reasonings of all philosophers were inconclusive and insufficient for our assurance, without the promises of God. They confirm

what is true, they do not certify what is probable. For why
should we be left uncertain of our future destiny, if it could be
revealed to us? True, we might hereafter receive a heaven;
but is it compatible with the benevolence we must ascribe to
Deity, to withhold the only knowledge that can comfort us under
every calamity? No; the belief is stamped on the soul, the
certainty is conveyed from above. Far happier is the religionist
than the speculator: the hopes of the one are fixed and immutable; the other's, varying and uncertain. These are great minds
I have been communing with; and their arguments for immortality are good and rational: but Revelation affords irrefragable proof to the believer."

The psychologist now proceeded to examine some notes he
had been making on the authors whose works were his favourite
study—notes which contained novel, fine, and original criticism,
analytical, and comprising a philosophy of Eclecticism. Victor
Cousin was not then born: but the embryo of his excellent system was in being, and his views and those of that noble thinker
were in many points similar.

A few words here must be introduced in favour of the doctrines of the Eclectics, to which I am inclined to assent, and
then we will eschew abstract discussion. There can be no
doubt that there is but one true philosophy : and it is also manifest that there is no system so comprehensive as to embrace all
Truth. Every writer has a theory of his own; but each such
theory must necessarily contain portions of what has gone before,
and for this reason : the human mind is so constituted, that it is
essentially re-productive; there is a chain of universal ideas, all
of which are shared in by each individual. The same thoughts
will cross every intellect, though in a variety of phases, as the
same objects will create similar associations. Now this universal
chain of ideas is broken in the individual mind into separate
links; and error consists rather in separation from the whole,
than the creation of a false totality.

This distinction is of importance in defending Eclecticism.
For it is true that Eclecticism is itself a system: but it is not
confined to one hypothesis, as many doctrines are. But is the
truth of this philosophy contingent, or necessary? Is truth in
itself absolute and universal? An absolute universal truth implies

an absolute, universal being, who is not a recipient but a Creator : and it is certain that man is not such. Then show me this universal truth, apart from Deity. I maintain, we can only find it in parts, and on the putting of them together well or ill depends the amount of its greatness or the converse. If we cannot create illimitable truth, amid the multiplicity of errors which the confusion of parts with the whole has caused, our only method of arriving at it is to join the divided links, observing where they have been broken : and I apprehend that as far as finite reason will permit, Eclecticism searches for those segments, and by placing them in the circle, connects the divided links, and erects a philosophy, not by searching for new worlds, but by reproducing the materials of the old ones, and combining and harmonizing, instead of wandering in the mazes which ourselves create, adding difficulties to the elucidation of the true more frequently than finding a means of separating the false and certain.

Such were the opinions of the character we are now in contact with : and they will be diffused in proportion to the progress of science, and impartial investigation. There may be errors in judgment among Eclectics : but they will not be tied down to particular and exclusive dogmas ; and will not substitute the jargon of the schools for honest sense, for lucid logic, and for long experience.

I must not trespass too far on the patience of my readers ; but it is requisite to point out the peculiar sentiments of the philosopher, and not to permit those who differ from him in opinion to suppose that he had adopted them without adequate grounds. And now to return to the real and substantial, which somehow is relished by the generality far better than the abstract and ideal. It would seem that for the most part our feelings are susceptible of greater satisfaction than our reasoning faculties. The heart against the head " all the world to nothing."

The thinker's cogitations were interrupted by the sound of gay laughter, and lifting his eyes from his book, he directed them to the spot from which it proceeded. Two childish forms were bounding towards him, and he gazed with deep fondness on their young and radiant faces. Those who had seen that look could not have mistaken it for any but a father's. O, how different it is, in its mingled pride and love from all others! There is a poetry of half human weakness, half divine affection in it.

The children were respectively of the ages of six and seven, and the youngest was very like her parent. The other was darker, with large, dark, oriental eyes, full of liquid sensibility, and even of romance, her figure light and airy as a little sylph's: yet even as she sped along, scarce touching the ground, and her beautiful face wreathed with smiles, there was an expression of mournfulness in it singular to behold in one of her age, when the heart is so light, and the spirits so high and wildly blithe, and not a dream of sorrow overshadows the pure soul. There was a world of melancholy in those dreamy, soft, bright orbs, which foretold that her destiny was not among the happy and joyous, and even in her very smile there was something that made one sad. Her beauty was strange and unearthly, but yet it was winning, it was irresistible, every look of her features being full of eloquence and passion. There was no promise, perhaps, of very great intellect in her countenance, but imagination, fancy and feeling were imprinted on the whole of it. Her long, dark tresses floated over her exquisite throat and shoulders; and if they had not been confined would almost have swept the ground—for she was of low stature for her years—and her polished limbs were extraordinary elastic and gracile.

The other, though equally lovely, had no remarkable character in her appearance; but she seemed gentle, docile, and affectionate: and, as has been observed, was extremely like her father, but without the mighty intellect which flashed such radiance over his face. She was very little also—even in a greater degree than her sister, and her hair, which was of equal length with the other tiny creature's, was of an almost flaxen hue. A poet who had seen them on a sudden might have thought fairies were not the creation of his brain.

"O, my dear father!" said the elder of the children, running up breathless to the philosopher, and throwing her arms round his neck: "there is such a fine horse—such a fine man coming up the hill. Lolah and I have been running to tell you: but she has no chance with me!—Dear Lolah! how pretty she looks with her flushed cheeks, and sparkling eyes, doesn't she?" And the varying countenance of the child changed from gladness to deep melancholy, though without the least apparent cause.

"My own Adah!" exclaimed the philosopher, clasping the bright creature to his heart with unutterable love, and then embracing Lolah also—as fondly, perhaps, but not so passionately. The eyes of Adah swam with tears at the tenderness of her father's caresses: Lolah's looks were but of love.

"Strange!" muttered the thinker to himself; "what can bring those tears to her eyes?"

"Ah!" cried Adah, whose ears—as indeed every other sense —were marvellously quick, overhearing her father. "I shed tears because I am so happy to have your love. I would not lose it to be the queen of the stars of heaven. But happiness is such delicious sadness!"

"And you would like to be queen of those orbs, sweet?"

"O, yes! they are so bright to look upon. I could weep for a long, long time, when I gaze at them, and yet I know not why —for the sun is brighter, and I do not weep to look at *that :* but then, you know, it is *another* brightness. What joy it would be to have an angel's wings and fly up to those dear worlds, which you tell me are like the earth,—but they must be *more* beautiful! To take you with me, my father, and Lolah, and the flowers and birds I love, and leave all the sorrow which you say exists on earth—sin, and pain and death behind for ever!"

"I hope you will one day live in worlds more bright than those, my child!—more full of bliss and beauty," said the philosopher, playing with the dark ringlets of Adah's hair.

"Nothing *can* have more brightness," returned Adah, shaking her head—"*that* is like the light of the soul—do you understand me? But sometimes I fancy that they look sorrowful. Have the stars souls, think you? They could not be so beautiful without them, surely?"

"My little poetess!" said the fond father, smiling, adding to himself—"Children are all Idealists: and their thoughts seem fresh from heaven." Then a shade of melancholy like that on his child's April face passed over his own, as he murmured—"I remember Harriet once asked me the same question, when she was no older than Adah. I could almost believe in the Platonic theory of the pre-existence of the spirit."

" Why do you look *so* ?" asked the child who had just spoken, the tears now trickling down her cheeks, as she anxiously watched the shadows on that loved and splendid countenance bending over her. " Your eyes are as mournful as my own."

Lolah also regarded her father wistfully : but spoke not a syllable.

" Some thoughts of the past !" replied the philosopher gently; and turning the conversation to the channel which it had proceeded from, added, " Lolah, when I kissed her did not shed tears, nor must you, my Adah !" and he dried the drops on that soft cheek with his lips ; but they only sprang into her eyes the more abundantly.

Adah's answer was remarkable.

" Lolah is very good and kind, and very fond of you ; but she conceals her feelings, as a rosebud hides the dews, and I cannot hide mine. I would sooner be Lolah than myself: she has more command over her heart, though it is full of love and sweetness."

Children have an intuition into children's minds, which we never reach by reason. Often did the philosopher ponder those distinctions which his eldest child had drawn ; and in after years he found them singularly verified.

As this scene was passing, a solitary horseman, of dignified mien and erect carriage, who appeared scarcely to have recovered from a severe illness, was climbing a steep hill, whose summit was within a few yards of the philosopher's cottage ; and by the time Adah had finished speaking, he was within view.

" That *must* be Charles Walsingham !" exclaimed the owner of the dwelling. " What a height he is ! Well ! the giant and the dwarf lie ' i' th' same fashion in the earth !' What a difference a foot of stature, or so, will make! But the mind may have as lofty thoughts in a poor, weak, diminutive form like mine, as in a grand and vigorous frame which will require six feet two of earth to bury it."

Thus speaking, he quitted the bench on which he had been sitting, and advanced to meet the traveller, who perceived, and recognised him, and greeted him frankly, saying—

" Mr. Spenser ! I have not seen you for many years ! You are well, I hope ?" And he extended his hand.

"I thank you, yes! Welcome to Uskedale. You will make the hearts of your good relations blithe, though you have delayed long."

"Are these your children?" asked Walsingham.

"They are!" replied Spenser: "this one, Adah, is the image of her poor mother, after whom she is named."

"She must have been very lovely," said Charles, as he patted the child's velvet cheek. "But has she always so pensive a look?'

"She never looks so gay as her sister Lolah," was the response.

"They are well—all of them—at Walsingham Hall?" asked our old friend Charles, having noticed Spenser's children with much interest.

"All well: but they have been very anxious about you. I will not stop you longer, but I hope I shall see you to morrow. Good bye."

Walsingham once more shook hands with Spenser, and promising to visit him as soon as possible, continued his way.

"I like his looks," thought Spenser: "if they do not belie him, he has a royal soul."

The soldier was now within a few miles of his journey's end: but the scenery through which he was passing evoked so many sweet associations of boyhood, that he lingered at many a familiar spot, until the sun was lost below the horizon, and a lovely twilight succeeded. The delicious calm of the evening was hardly disturbed by any living sound, and the distant jingle of the sheep-bells was the only music that blended with that of the faint gale. Spenser's cottage was far removed from any other human habitation, and the loneliness of the road increased as Walsingham proceeded. Many thoughts were stirring within his bosom, and the solitude was a luxury to his spirit: so that he suffered his horse to advance at whatever pace he chose, and resigned himself to reverie. But he had not journeyed above half a league from the dwelling of the philosopher, when as the moon arose from behind a cluster of poplars, behind which there was a romantic lake, that glided serenely on among rocks and hills and banks—and on whose bosom there rested many a fairy island tenanted by aquatic birds—he was arrested by a voice, crying—"Stand and deliver."

With true military promptness, Walsingham drew his sword and a pistol with either hand; and sternly gazed on the man who had addressed him. Two fellows, mounted on large, bony horses were in his direct path, a third was coming up from behind the poplars with cocked pistols, and three others emerged from another clump of trees at a short distance, also armed.

"Give way!" said the soldier, as he sat rigid and immoveable as a statue in his saddle, not a muscle of his face working, as he spurred on his fiery charger.

"Down with him!" exclaimed one of the robbers.

And swords were crossed in an instant, while Charles levelled his pistol and fired, but the ball missed one of his assailant's head by a hair's breadth. Opposed to these fearful odds, the high and haughty courage, and cool presence of mind of Captain Walsingham did not for an instant desert him. Wheeling round rapidly, he caused his horse to rear, and dealt blows in all direc--tions with incredible quickness: but just as he was about to charge his two first antagonists, one of the highwaymen raised his hand, unseen by the soldier, and taking steady aim, would in all probability have shot him through the heart, when a horse-man galloped swiftly up, unheard by the villain, and struck the weapon from his hand.

"Cowards!" exclaimed the new comer, "desist."

"Ah!" cried the robber, whose object had been thus frus-trated, turning round, and perceiving a slight young man of some seventeen years of age beside him. "You're not my mas-ter; and you had better keep out of the way. We have had no wages for a long time, and must now help ourselves."

So saying, the fellow turned to assail Walsingham again.

"I dare you to disobey my orders!" exclaimed the youth, in a calm, commanding voice. "Who lifts a hand against this gentleman, I will shoot him."

"Big words, Master Harry," returned the ruffian to whom he had before addressed himself, while the other men desisted from their attack; "but I am not going to be led by a boy like you. On him, comrades!"

With these words, the robber once more raised his arm against the Captain, when the young man, whose peremptory commands he had slighted, drew a pistol from his pocket, and without utter-

ing a word, discharged it. The bullet entered the brain of the
rascal who was so determined on obtaining Walsingham's purse:
and with a deep groan he fell and expired, at the same instant as
another horseman arrived on the scene of action.

"Thus," said the young man, who had acted with such stern
decision, "thus will I punish every man who dares to turn
assassin, instead of acting up to the orders he has received from
his employer. My father!—have I not done well?"

"Yes, Harry," said a deep, manly voice, in which Walsingham recognised that of Ellen's father; "you have acted as I
would myself. You," he added to the robbers, "take that cur-
rion away; and be prepared to act better for the future.—Captain Walsingham, I am very sorry this has occurred. These men
are in my employ; and have most infamously behaved in quitting
the honourable service I gave them, to turn marauders. But I
cannot tarry any longer. I will communicate with you at some
future time:—farewell!"

And without permitting the soldier to answer a word, Danvers,
accompanied by Harry, cantered briskly away.

CHAPTER II.

Ill deeds will rise,
Though all the earth o'erwhelm them to men's eyes.

SHAKSPEARE.

THE ADVENTURES OF DANVERS—MOTHER STOKES AND SAM
STOKES—MRS. HAINES AND ELLEN—ROGER SIDNEY.

IT is necessary now to retrograde some time, and to detail the
adventures of Walter Danvers since we lost sight of him. When
he quitted the dwelling of infamy and guilt, where the woman
who was once his wife remained with her paramour, he strode
hastily away, and plunged into the deepest solitude he could
find: and so violent was the conflict in his bosom, that for
many minutes he was as one struggling between life and death,

his iron frame shaking, and the muscles of his face quivering involuntarily; while the convulsed movement of his lip, and the writhing of his cheek, demonstrated how terrible was the inward struggle. Such natures as his, if not so exquisitely sensitive as those of highly nervous temperament, have intense feelings: and their passions are not only quick and furious, but deep and enduring. He had loved one as far above him in virtue, as the woman he now loathed, was more deeply steeped in crime; and his grief and despair were aggravated by the consciousness of his own misconduct—to call it by no harsher name—and the conviction that he had irrevocably wronged a woman richer in all the gifts of mind and heart and soul than those most eminently endowed with them among all he knew.

"O, my Harriet!" he exclaimed, in accents of despair, "that I should have lost thee by having tied myself indissolubly to one I detest—a fiend—a devil! Curses on her!—And, yet, have *I* not need of forgiveness? I, who have made *her* miserable, than whom there is not a purer and diviner saint in the courts of Heaven!"

At last, worn out by excessive fatigue of frame and mind, Danvers cast himself on the earth, and groaned aloud in all the bitterness of despair. Shall human eloquence accurately paint the fearful hell raging within that stern spirit? It was the Titan in his agony: but the hero of the immortal Greek was supported by his own mind. Danvers, on the contrary, had no great principle to sustain him. He suffered for crime, and not for virtue. The good man can bear all things, the bad one nothing.

While thus grovelling on the earth, a female approached, and glared on him with eyes of devilish malice. She broke out into a hoarse, chuckling laugh, after a minute, spent apparently in ineffable gratification, as she beheld the hopeless misery of Walter, and said—

"This is rare luck! Hu, ha! Worthy Danvers! How happy you seem! O, I delight in seeing you look so pleased and joyful! Pray, don't rise! I dare say, when you've heard some more good news that I've got to tell you, your face will be bright as heaven's!"

"What mean you, woman?" demanded Danvers, fiercely, returning the glare of hate fixed on him, with another so full of fire, that it seemed to blast its object, like lightning scathing a withered oak.

Mother Stokes (for it was no other) soon recovered the dark power which was in her horrid nature to torment, and resuming the effrontery which had shrunk under the awful glance of Danvers, replied—

"I'm in no haste, and so I will stay and talk with you a bit. I love your society—Ha, ha, ha!"

"Trifle not with me," cried Walter, from between his clenched teeth. "If you have aught to say, speak at once."

"O, if you are so anxious to hear the good intelligence, far be it from me to withhold it! You had a son a few years ago—a likely lad enough!—I suppose you were fond of him?"

"I *had* a son. Do you know aught of him, foul hag?"

"I do, sweet Master Walter! Blessed are those that die young! Ha, ha! He may be in the highest heaven by this time! Isn't that glorious news for a good father?"

"Mistress Stokes! speak out at once; or I may do you mischief. I am almost mad already. What of my son?"

Mother Stokes loved, like the cat, to torment her victims before she destroyed them: and would have delayed still longer to impart what she knew about Harry, but Walter looked dangerous, and his bayonet glittered brightly in the moonbeams, so that—knowing his desperate character, she at length said—

"Well, to relieve your anxiety, I have to inform you that your son is certainly no more. In looking after you he fell down a steep—"

"What! what! Where, where? O, agony! Take me to him! O God! This is more than I can bear!"

"But, after all, he might not have been your son, Walter Danvers! There is some comfort in that!"

Danvers seized the vile woman by the throat, and she shrieked with terror; she felt that her love of vengeance, and the pleasure she felt in beholding her mortal foe's pangs had carried her too far. He relaxed his grasp in a moment, however, and said in a husky voice—

"Take me to the body, then, and I will spare you!"

"Indeed, I know not where it is! Perhaps they have taken it to the Britannia to await a coroner's inquest."

No sooner had she spoken, than Danvers released her entirely, and rushed franticly from the place. As he did so, the monster, having heard the squeak of his grandmother, joined her.

"We will be revenged, boy! we *are* revenged!" she exclaimed; "but our vengeance is yet incomplete. He must be taken if he goes to the inn; and then he will be hanged—ha, ha! Good, good! I have not felt so merry for many a year—never since Roger Sidney lost his bride! Now, then, you go to the hut, and see what is taking place there. If you should see those who are likely to detain you, run instantly away. I'll wait for you where I am. Bring Figgins to me, if you can."

The savage obeyed, first having shaken his huge fist at the now distant form of Danvers.

That unhappy person, heedless of the consequences, was now hastening to the Britannia, scarcely being left the use of reason, to ascertain the fate of his son; but before he had taken a step which would have been irrevocable, a suspicion that he had been cajoled darted on his brain.

"I will not be rash," he muttered. "God grant that the woman has spoken falsely. O, I was ungrateful when I wished for death just now! Harry may live—Ellen *does* live!—I may regain my honour—obtain a divorce from that wretch, and—and —Harriet may still be mine! I love her more than ever."

This wild transition from abject despair to the most exalted hope kindled new energies in the heart of Danvers. It is a most strange thing that the mind always flies to extremes; and the fact evinces that it moves in a cycle, so that its changes are necessarily not gradual, but sudden. If it were not so, it is inconceivable that the mighty revulsions of feeling which are so often evolved instantaneously, should not undergo modification. They would be slow and gradual, and would not convulse the central being, if they were constrained to traverse a considerable space ere they could reach the opposite extreme.

But this is a subject too recondite for profound investigation at this time. To give an impetus to thought is all the novelist can expect.

Danvers, as soon as he could regain his cooler judgment, began to ask himself how he should now proceed. He must obtain news of Harry; but how to do so, he knew not, without exposing himself to imminent danger. Irresolute as to the measures to pursue, he made for a neat little abode, at the porch of which there sat a crippled man with but stumps of legs, to whom he addressed himself.

" I would thank you, friend," he said, " to sell me something to eat. I am hungry, and have to journey far."

" You shall have it, messmate, with all my heart," replied the maimed tar with alacrity. " Here is some bread and cheese, and I'll go and mix you some grog."

" No, I thank you ! I will take nothing but a draught of water," returned Walter, whose stomach was now making dire remonstrances, in spite of all his anxiety ; for the fatigue he had undergone without tasting a morsel, was immense. " Can you tell me if the body of a youth, who was lately thrown down a precipice, has been carried to the Britannia ?" inquired Danvers, hardly knowing how to open the subject his heart was set upon, and eager to do so, without betraying himself.

" No, I'm sure it wasn't an hour ago," was the reply.

" Thank Heaven !" cried Danvers. " But has any one been severely hurt in this part of the country, very lately ?"

" Why a woman has been wounded," returned the cripple. " She *would* give me this here thingumy, when I went to see——"

" How !" interrupted Danvers, attracted by a little trinket which the tar held between his finger and thumb.

" Ay, and a sweet young lady as is with her now—she's as pretty a creetur as ever was, she says, says she, ' You've been very kind to my poor nurse, and must accept this locket for my sake.'"

And the honest fellow, in the pardonable vanity of his heart, exhibited a locket with hair in it, which removed all doubt from Walter's mind.

" It is very strange !" he thought. " I was not certain about the other trinket; but this—! You say that the woman was wounded. How did it happen ?"

" Why, I hardly likes to tell 'ee ; 'cos as how a person I'm related to, fired the pistol at her. Mayhap you're acquainted with the poor body who's hurt ?"

" Yes, I must go directly to her. Can you guide me to the place where she is ?"

"That I can," replied the sailor; "and I'll go with 'ee, as it aint fur off."

"I suppose Elizabeth and Ellen have come in quest of me," thought Danvers; adding, aloud, "The wound is not dangerous, then. But why did this woman fire at her, good friend?"

"It's a long story, and I don't quite know the rights on't," returned the cripple. "But what I can make out is this.—The good lady as is wounded found out as a young gen'l'man she knows has been murdered—and—why, what ails ye, sir? You quite staggers!"

"Go on—quick!" cried Danvers, gasping for breath, and all his worst apprehensions returning.

"Well, then, this here aunt o' mine, Mother Stokes, 't would seem, knows more than she ought about the death of this poor lad; and the lady what's wounded, accused her, and so she tried for to send a bullet through her, the—wretch!"

"Ah! I see! I see!" exclaimed Walter, in a choking voice. "That infernal woman lied to me! It was she who killed him! By Heaven! I'll be revenged! My son, my son!"

"Lord bless us!" cried Sam Stokes, "be you then, the father of the youth? Poor boy! He's gone aloft, I fear. But, bear up, brother. It aint *certain* he's dead. If, as how, you're the father of the young gen'l'man, though, you're the very chap they're all a looking arter; and a terrible price is on your head. They do say," (and Sam recoiled a step as he spoke the last words) "you're a murderer!"

"It is false!" exclaimed Danvers. "But I care not for myself if Harry is gone! O, my boy! my own brave boy! Now I feel all the agony I inflicted on the heart of Norton!"

"Hark ye!" cried Stokes. "I doesn't believe as you're a murderer; or ye wouldn't feel so for your own son being killed. But take my advice. *I've* got enough rhino myself:—and if I was as poor as the devil, I wouldn't betray ye; but others might: and so—"

"I cannot remain in suspense, my friend! Pray make haste: I care not if I am taken! O God!"

"Well; it's so late now, ye mayn't be observed, and see, yonder's where yer friend is!"

Elizabeth had been taken, after she had seen the apothecary, to a small public-house, at no great distance from the Britannia; and Stokes managed to smuggle Danvers into it, without his being noticed by any. Cautiously he opened the door of Mrs. Haines's apartment, and then left his companion, who advancing into the middle of the room, perceived Elizabeth stretched on a bed, dozing; and Ellen, buried in thought, sitting close beside her. He clasped his daughter in his arms, placing his hand on her mouth, to prevent her crying aloud with sudden fright.

" Harry !" he gasped—" have you heard anything of him ?"

" Oh, my father," cried Ellen, " how glad I am that you are here safe! We know not yet poor Harry's fate, but have hopes ; —oh, Elizabeth, you are awake! My father is here!"

" You are in great peril in this place, Walter!" said Mrs. Haines. " But I rejoice you have escaped so far. We know not yet, whether Harry be alive or dead. The proper authorities have been applied to, and a young man of the name of Francis Walsingham has promised to give us the earliest intelligence possible. He is, even now, investigating the circumstances of the case, though doing so is fraught with risk to himself. Nothing is yet more than surmise."

As Mrs. Haines concluded, a footstep was heard on the stairs, succeeded by a tap at the door.

" Here he is," cried Ellen. " My father had better, perhaps, step into the closet." Danvers accordingly having concealed himself, the visitor was admitted by Ellen.

" Pardon my intrusion at this late hour," said Francis Walsingham, as he entered. " I have not very good news to give you. But the hut of this woman Stokes has been searched, and this pistol, marked with a crest, which I have remarked on a ring you wear, discovered. The wretch herself cannot be found. There is a female in the dwelling, who is her niece ; but she cannot, or will not, give any account of her. I hope that our invalid here finds herself better now."

" Yes, I thank you," replied Elizabeth. " Nothing has yet been ascertained then, positively ?"

" Nothing ; but, I beseech you, hope for the best."

While the young man spoke, he gazed with deep and earnest sympathy on the anxious face of Ellen ; and a close observer

3 E

might have detected in that glance the incipient passion which
manifests itself in ardent but respectful admiration.

" Well, then, I will wish you good night," said Mrs. Haines,
desirous of talking with Danvers, uninterruptedly. " It is very
late, and I must take some sleep. I am much, very much indebted to you for the kind interest you have evinced for me."

Francis Walsingham pressed the extended hand of the invalid,
and taking that of Ellen, ventured to press it to his lips, and departed. As soon as he was gone, Danvers emerged from the
closet. An earnest conversation ensued, Mrs. Haines briefly relating her adventures on the road, and expressing her belief that
Mother Stokes had attempted the life of Harry, though for what
reason she could not understand. Still there was some room, however slight, for hope, and they clung to it like drowning wretches
to a reed, though Danvers, remembering the malignant looks of
the reputed witch, felt sick at heart.

" I must go and look for him myself," he said.

" But you must rest first. You seem terribly fatigued, my
dear father !" said Ellen. " O, if my beloved Harry be indeed
lost, you are all I have of kindred on earth ! For my sake be
cautious then."

" I believe I must rest for a short time," replied Danvers ;
" but in two or three hours I must depart. That time I will
spend in sleep ; for it is absolutely necessary I should gain all the
strength possible for to-morrow. God in Heaven bless you, sweet
child ! If He think proper to deprive you of your father, remember He is the parent of the orphan."

How is the sentiment of religion expanded by adversity ! It
may *bloom* and look bright amid prosperous fortunes ; but it is
the winter of grief which prepares the eternal spring of joy !

Kissing his daughter affectionately, Danvers lay down on the
floor, and was almost instantly buried in profound repose. Mrs.
Haines too was in a few minutes fast asleep, and Ellen was left
the sole watcher in the apartment. Long and wistfully she gazed
on the calm features of her father, now so calm, so motionless,
that they were like those of the dead ; and her imagination conjured all the evils to which she might be exposed, if deprived of
him. Yet not for those evils did she care. Her pious and gentle
spirit relied on the protection of that Heaven where such pure

beings find friends innumerable : but the desolation of existence without the fond ties of kindred was a thought she could hardly endure.

"Nevertheless," she murmured, in the humble, trusting words of that One, before whose virtues all human excellence is dim, "not as I will ; but as Thou wilt !" raising her swimming eyes to the starry vault, and addressing Him who is above the firmament. And she recalled the last words that the earthly author of her being had spoken. "God is the parent of the orphan."

It was seldom indeed that Danvers spoke a word appertaining to religion ; for though not a sceptic, it was a rare thing for his thoughts to soar above this world ; and they had the more weight on Ellen's heart from that circumstance.

It is most strange that the majority of mankind should think so lightly of their immortal, in comparison with their mortal destiny ; when all around speaks in sad and solemn accents of the shortness of all earthly pleasures, and the nihility of man's pursuits. But that high spirit which probed all the secrets of the human bosom,—the Shakspeare, whose genius appeared to have the gift of Omniscience, in nearly every character he has delineated, has markedly depicted the aversion of men in general to contemplate the Eternity which is All or Nothing. If it do not exist, the longest life would be utter vanity and hollowness, though crowned with magnificence and glory : but if it be indeed the goal of virtue, then how easily may every sorrow be compensated, and every grief annihilated in the presence of the glorified of the incomprehensible Uncreate. Yet even in this melancholy fact, that man should neglect the future, a design is evident : for if we were only alive to the Hereafter, the affairs of this life would be neglected utterly :—and there can be but little doubt, that we should pursue the path to eternity, without despising the mercies we possess, or affixing too high a value to the transitory enjoyment of all things here.

The hours passed away, and before the morning broke, Danvers arose.

"My child !" he said to Ellen ; "I cannot tarry to relate what has befallen me since we parted, but I hope to see you again in the course of a few hours. I will now take some bread and meat, if you have them, in my hand, and depart at once."

"I know not why," returned Ellen; "but all along I have had a hope that Harry is safe. But you, my dear father, must be very cautious. Could you not disguise yourself in some way? I wore Harry's clothes till a few hours ago, when I procured these from the village."

"It might be well if I could do so; but I can stay no longer. I shall not be recognised in this obscure light. I am glad Elizabeth is asleep; bid her adieu for me:" and so saying, having received some provision from Ellen, Danvers stole down the stairs, followed by his daughter, who locked the outer door after him.

He then directed his steps towards the spot Mrs. Haines had described to him, as being that where she had remarked the blood, and found a portion of Harry's dress, and in the course of about an hour he reached it—though it was with some difficulty he recognised the place from Elizabeth's description.

The sun was rising gloriously, and the morning lark carolled its joyous hymns as it mounted the liquid heaven; but distracting feelings in the breast of Danvers, caused all the grand and majestic spectacle of nature, and the melody of her multitudinous voices to jar on his brain. At one moment, it might be elated with hope, his eye would sparkle, and his heavy step become elastic; but the next, gloom and despondency overgrew his spirit, and he felt almost weary of struggling with fortune. How gladly in that quiet spot, when all was so blithe and radiant, could he have resigned existence, with its pageantry and mockeries. Well, it is all the same now! All our actors have left not a trace behind, and *we* also hasten to oblivion.

The news of a murder having recently been perpetrated had on the previous day attracted numbers to the place where Elizabeth had discovered the tracks of blood, and they were now almost entirely effaced; but Danvers followed them as far as possible, and then set his head to work to find something farther.

"If he *have* been murdered, what could the assassin have done with the body?" he asked himself. A sudden thought flashed on him. "It was at no great distance from this place that Walsingham was murdered!" he exclaimed; "and I have always suspected that Mother Stokes was in some way accessory to that deed, which has been so falsely ascribed to me, Walsingham's body—if his body it really were—was found in the river—the very river which I see yonder between the trees, about half a mile hence, and which I now perceive was that I crossed yesterday. That very cave I was in may contain something to throw a light upon the deed. I will take some dry wood with me, and kindle a blaze in the place."

Danvers had his bayonet—though not the musket to which it was attached—with him, and a pistol which belonged to Elizabeth also, so that he had not the least difficulty in procuring a light; and forthwith gathering up some decayed wood, he proceeded towards the cave. When he arrived at the water, he perceived an old man arranging his fishing materials, and eating a biscuit as he did so: and it struck him forcibly, before he saw the Angler's face, that he knew him, but as he did not wish to be seen by an acquaintance, he was stealing away, when the old man turned his head, and caught a view of his side-face.

"What! Walter Danvers!" he cried in amazement.

Danvers at this salutation stood still, and looking at the Angler, said—

"Mr. Sidney! I am glad to see you!"

"Ah, Walter; I have heard that you have suffered much, since I saw you last," exclaimed the old man, who was no other than our friend of the rod, who has before figured on several occasions.

"I have, indeed," was the reply.

"You were found guilty of a crime, Walter, which I am certain it was not in your nature to commit," rejoined Sidney. "I read—and carefully read, all the evidence on the trial, though I was then at a great distance from this part of the world. I know public opinion was against you; but after all, it appeared that the body could hardly be identified.—Pardon me, if I pain you by alluding to such a subject; but I want to say something about it, which may be of importance. That devil, Mother Stokes—"

"Ha!" cried Danvers, "what of her?"

"She could be guilty of any crime, I am convinced: and of course you know that she lived, at the time of Mr. Walsingham's murder, at a very short distance from the place where you said you found him, wounded and insensible. I have just been thinking over the matter—for it was not far from hence that the body was found—and some notions have entered my old head, which

I will tell you. Poor Mr. Walsingham was known to have had money and valuables about him to a large amount when he was murdered. You are not a person to care for money—supposing it possible you *could* have perpetrated such a deed—but what more likely than that this woman, when you left Walsingham in order to procure assistance, should have been tempted to rob him; for if you remember, your little boy, who happened to be passing soon after you were gone, said, that he saw a demon stabbing the wounded man, and was so horror-stricken, that he fled on the instant, was seen by a woman who was also near the body; and that this woman and the little demon pursued him; but he was too nimble for them. I never believed for an instant, as was suggested by the counsel opposed to you, that the boy either spoke falsely, or was terrified by some phantom of the mind : for though he was only seven years old, he appeared an intelligent child ; and his statement could not be shaken by all the rigid cross-examination he was subjected to. Mother Stokes, it was said, was very ill at the time, and in fact confined to her bed ; but that might have been an artful trick of her's. As for the demon, I beheld a creature with Mother Stokes, yesterday, which may easily account for the child imagining him such—so strange and hideous is it. I have made inquiries, and find that he is a semi-human being, and the grandson of Mother Stokes ; and that he runs about the woods with an old ape in a savage state."

"I have seen him!" exclaimed Walter Danvers. "O, if I could but prove my innocence of that accursed deed! I thank you cordially for your belief in my perfect guiltlessness, and for your good suggestions also. Harry's story was so vague and wild, that I was inclined myself to doubt the accuracy of it; and it never struck me until you started the supposition, that this monster could be the demon Harry alluded to, and which he stoutly maintained, had stabbed Walsingham. The story was improbable, and there was strong circumstantial evidence against me. But now I fear this fiendish woman has destroyed my only son. Will you accompany me a short distance? I am proceeding to search a cave, which I accidentally discovered yesterday, in which there may be something, perhaps, to throw a light on these transactions. You will be an excellent witness for me, if we should find aught to justify our suspicions."

Roger Sidney at once assented to Danvers's request, and they walked on together, the latter relating the extraordinary circumstances of the last few days, as far as they concerned the business on which they had been talking.

In former years, when Walter was a lad, Roger Sidney had been very kind to him; and so many generous and noble traits had he observed in the youth's character, that nothing had been able to shake his conviction that he was innocent of the foul charge of murder of which he had been found guilty, after a protracted deliberation, by a jury of his countrymen. He was a fine old fellow—that Roger Sidney, though eccentric, and strangely devoted to so frivolous a pastime as that of angling, and retained all the freshness and verdure of feeling which usually departs from the bosom with youth and joy.

Danvers had originally possessed a fine though very faulty nature; and except that he was somewhat sanguinary, and that his ambition was not of that exalted kind which excludes self from its dreams and aspirations, he was still capable of great and lofty deeds. One crime, one deadly crime, which he bitterly and with agony repented, was an indelible blot on his honour and reputation. Almost all persons of his character have committed some foul act, which all their other virtues cannot wipe away. Brutus—the patriotic Brutus murdered Cæsar in cold blood, and with the basest ingratitude, whatsoever the crimes of that mighty conqueror:—the amiable, but misguided Charles the First, who had many of the qualities of Danvers, can never be forgiven for his conduct relative to Strafford, and deadly and innumerable errors have been committed by persons capable of high and valorous deeds. Yet this is not any palliation of such offences; but only evinces the weakness of human nature when it is severely tried. And Danvers had been tempted far more dreadfully than the Roman patriot, or the British monarch.

Sidney and Danvers found no difficulty in entering the cave, where the father had so lately and narrowly missed his son; and having lighted some wood, commenced their examination. Each held a withered branch alight in his hand, which burned with tolerable brightness; and at length they entered the cave where

Harry first found himself on recovering his senses. Here Danvers lingered, while Sidney crawled through the aperture which Harry had recently made; but the former was soon called to the old man's side by a cry of horror from him.

"Look! that skeleton!" exclaimed Roger Sidney,—as Walter, every drop of blood seeming to congeal within him, appeared,—pointing to an object at a short distance.

"Ha!" cried Danvers, after looking at the unsightly thing for a few moments, murmuring a prayer of thankfulness that he stood not by the lifeless corse of his child. A glance at the skeleton sufficed to show that the first stage of decomposition had long ceased. "By heaven!" cried Danvers, "these are the remains of poor Walsingham. The very height of the stature, the very form of the skull—the hair, some of which you may see, of a peculiar auburn hue, and the shape of one leg, which is slightly warped from his having broken it when he was a boy. I think there can be no reasonable doubt of the fact. But we shall find more directly. Ha! see! this sword, though very rusty, I can swear to; for I exchanged it with Walsingham for one of his, and on the trial it was thought a strong evidence of my guilt that a part of the blade—see, it is broken off at the point!—was found in the body. Well, I don't think there is any trace of Harry, unless—ha! there is something at your foot. It is part of a letter directed to him in Norton's hand-writing. Oh, God! my boy!" Danvers clasped his hands together on his brow, and stood, an image of despair, for a minute or two.

"Be of good cheer," at length exclaimed Sidney, "we have found nothing else of your son's; and this may have been dropped by Mother Stokes. He may not have been here."

Danvers shook his head, but answered nothing. "Now," he thought, "let fate do its worst. What is life to me?"

"Come, let us search every corner," said the old man, "and then, at all events, you may be relieved from this awful state of suspense."

In compliance with this suggestion Walter resumed the search, but he could find nothing else of Harry's. There appeared, however, at no great distance from the skeleton the marks of recent gore; and with a hopeless spirit, the agonised father quitted the cave with Sidney.

CHAPTER III.

There live, alas! of heaven-directed mien,
Of cultured soul, and sapient eye serene,
Who hail thee, man! the pilgrim of a day,
Spouse of the worm, and brother of the clay,
Frail as the leaf in Autumn's yellow bower,
Dust in the wind, or dew upon the flower;
A friendly slave, a child without a sire,
Whose mortal life, and momentary fire,
Lights to the grave his chance created form.

CAMPBELL.

DANVERS AND OLD QUIRK—THE EPICUREAN'S BOOK—THE
MISER AND THE LOST PAPERS.

"WE must now consider what further steps are expedient,"
said Roger Sidney. "I have been informed that the authorities
have been in pursuit of this wretch, Stokes; but all in vain. It
is clear, however, that she cannot be far hence. I will go and
make a deposition before the nearest magistrate, and you can
continue your quest for your son. Keep a good heart, I beseech
you, and trust in the goodness of Providence."

"At all events," replied Danvers, "Heaven is good to my boy.
If he is no more, he is happy. But O! It is a dreadful thing to
be bereaved of one we love so dearly! God bless you, sir! I
think the course you have marked out will be the best to pursue.
And—and—if I should perish, worthy Mr. Sidney,—I have a
daughter—a good and lovely child, who will be left without protection in the world. May I ask you to extend your friendly hand
to her? There is no one whom I could trust—unless it be my
honest John Norton, who must provide for his own safety—like
you."

"I will be a father to her!" returned Sidney, grasping the
hand of Danvers. "But I hope you may be preserved yet. And
consider, Walter, whether in the dangerous schemes, in which it

3 F

seems you are involved, you are not depriving her of one she so much needs. I know not the nature of the service in which you are engaged; but I have heard rumours of treason—"

" No more of that, I pray you," exclaimed Danvers. "Whatever betide, I am bound heart and soul to the cause I now serve. Once more adieu, and accept my cordial thanks for your goodness."

Thus parted those two old friends, the most opposite in character imaginable, and yet, though with widely diverse views and interests, linked together by bonds which could not be broken by time or circumstance. The friends of youth—sincerely so,—are ever most deeply interested in our welfare: and they must sympathise with our sorrows the more profoundly, that we are blended with their own early associations. True, old friends are ever ready to assist us, " when all around grows dark and dim," and others forsake, neglect, and forget us.

Walter Danvers continued his solitary way, without any fixed plan of action. He entertained but small hopes that he should ever behold Harry again alive: but reluctant to abandon the search, he walked forwards at a rapid pace, buried in gloomy reverie. Thus he had advanced for the space of about a mile, when he was met by a little old man, who gazed at him curiously; and then, doffing his hat, accosted him, saying,

" Master Danvers! A good day t'ye, sir."

"Ha! old Quirk!" exclaimed Walter, with some surprise, "I did not think you were in the land of the living!"

"Oh, yes," answered the lawyer, with whom the Reader is already acquainted, "such rogues as I am don't die so early as the good. Ha, ha! Well, sir, I think I know something you would be pleased to hear. And I could give you information, if remunerated handsomely, which might be of great importance to you."

Danvers smiled bitterly. "I see you are the same old grasping fellow as ever, now that you have one foot in the grave," he said; " but it is your nature. What have you to say to me?"

The lawyer grinned. " I find," he replied, " that the beautiful Miss Harriet Walsingham is still much interested for you."

" Ah!" cried Danvers, " what of her?" And he spoke so

eagerly, that the cunning attorney felt he had that to impart which would unloose the purse-strings of Danvers.

"Why," returned Quirk, "you are in a very perilous predicament, having been found guilty of the murder of Mr. Walsingham, the lady's own brother; and Miss Harriet supposing you were in prison, sent for me to communicate on the subject. Now, what will you give me, if I relate what passed in that interview?"

"Nothing," replied Danvers, with an effort. "What she confided to you, she did not intend should reach my ear; and therefore I should consider myself most base in bestowing a bribe on an untrustworthy agent, to learn a secret which honour forbids me seeking out."

"Well, as you like on that point," returned the old fellow; "but I was not a little astonished that she should betray so much feeling for one who was supposed—pardon me for saying it—to have injured her deeply, in more than one respect. I am at this time retained by her for you, and I have no doubt I shall be able to make out a case, proving your innocence of the death of Mr. Walsingham. But I shall be at a great expense, a very great expense, Master Danvers!"

"Strange," muttered Walter, "most strange!"

"What is strange?" asked Quirk, peering into the other's face.

"That she should have applied to you, who are known to be one of the greatest rascals in the kingdom.

Quirk chuckled. "That is the very reason I am so often applied to," he said. "You see, sir, I have constituted myself Attorney-General to all the scoundrels in England; and as it is known I possess their secrets, I am frequently sought by persons of reputation and even rank, when they want to circumvent the machinations of villains. I am a low, pettifogging lawyer. What of that? I make £3,000 a year, and am not more mercenary than statesmen and others. I work best for those who pay me best. Surely that's right?"

"Most undoubtedly," replied Danvers, sarcastically. "But do not the rascals you work for often cheat you?"

"Cheat their lawyer! Ha, ha, ha! Do the minor devils cheat Satan? Preposterous! Well, sir, to return to the matter we have digressed from. What will you give me, if I prove you

guiltless of that murder? I suppose you want to stand clear in
the eyes of the world, and especially in the eyes of Miss Walsingham?"

"Yes, I do," was the answer. "I will give you £100, when
you can establish the innocence which avails me not. And,
Quirk, you have sagacity and shrewdness. I will now give you a
fee to deal with an old wretch of the name of Stokes." The
lawyer started. "She knows something of Walsingham's murder, I am convinced, as we shall prove hereafter: but now I
would have you discover the fate of my son, who, I suspect, has
met his death at her hands."

"Indeed!" cried Quirk, as Danvers placed in his hand ten
guineas, which instantly disappeared.

"But she is not to be found," added Danvers.

"Ah, not by *you*, perhaps," answered the lawyer, with a
smile; "but *I* shall soon find her. "I will see her immediately,
and try to elicit the truth from her. You know I monopolise all
the rogues. And *this* has been my plan through life. I have
uniformly endeavoured to establish a reputation for consummate
villany. I would not stop half way, and keep something like the
semblance of a character with the world. No, no. I have remarked that your half-and-half rascals always are believed to be
as great ones as others, but yet they are not bold and decided
enough to please the scoundrels. Well, state your case to me,
and I will then see what I can do for you."

Danvers proceeded to relate the facts of Harry's disappearance,
and of his having searched the cave himself; and when he had
finished, the decrepid but cunning lawyer cried,

"I see! I see! No time is to be lost. Meanwhile, Master
Danvers, I would advise you, as you have been so lucky as to
escape, to keep close. You do not care to hear further of Miss
Walsingham, I suppose?"

Danvers, desirous of hearing Harriet's opinion of him, and
wherefore she had sent to the attorney, but determined not to
arrive at the knowledge by underhand means, replied, "Tell me,
what does she think of me?" but added, "I will hear no breach
of confidence."

"She firmly believes you are not lost to virtue," returned
Quirk, with a sneer, laying an emphasis on the word Virtue,

which he no more believed in than Robert Owen, though from a different principle. "Between you and myself, I can't conceive that one man is better than another. Some may appear worse; but that is all. Farewell for the present."

"I will meet you here at this time to-morrow," cried Danvers.

"If you will take my advice," answered Quirk, "you'll do no such thing. I'll find you out, depend upon't, when I have anything to communicate to you." And so ended the interview.

"Harriet still loves me," thought Danvers, "in spite of all my villany. But her love partakes of pity more than of any other sentiment. Alas! I can never hope to regain what I have lost."

While thus cogitating, he continued his walk, with many corroding feelings in his bosom, to add to the grief and agony which his more recent probable affliction occasioned; and, heeding not whither he went, he reached the very spot where he encountered the Epicurean a few days previously. He stopped, when he found where he was. Casting his eyes on the ground, he saw a book lying beneath a tree, and remembered to have seen the young philosopher with such an one in his hand. The whole of that singular meeting rose up to his mind. What vast changes had those few hours which had elapsed made in his fortunes and being! He recalled the dark and melancholy words of the strange boy who appeared to have adopted such Hegesian views of human life and destiny, and murmured to himself, " I wonder who he was!" Picking up the volume, he opened it, and found it to be a Greek Plato, with the name of " William Walsingham" written on a blank page.

"What!" exclaimed Danvers, " the son of the man whose murder is ascribed to me! Most marvellous! Such must be the case. I remember I was struck with a resemblance which I could not define."

Beneath the name which William Walsingham had written in a large bold hand, very peculiar and significant of his character, there was a Latin sentence, which Danvers had just sufficient scholarship to understand, in the same writing as the autograph. It was to this effect: " Here you may read the aspirations of a mind too soaring for earth, and yet too low for that which it aspired after. Vainly does the heart pant to leave its cage, as an

imprisoned bird that would soar into the liquid air. Genius is
the light of the world, and darkness encompasses it like a pall.
He that would enjoy life, must tread the path of others. Enjoyment—vain, idle word! To enjoy is but to avoid pain! He that
would do this must gratify his senses, and repress the longings
of his heart for perfection, and of his intellect for the unattainable. He must grasp power, and wealth and glory, if he is
ambitious; he must bask in the smiles of women, if a sensualist,
he must eat, drink, and sleep, like the other animals: and when
he has done all this—when he has drunk of the cup of pleasure
to satiety—when he has gained the acclamations, the envy, the
admiration of the Universe—when he has raised himself to the
station of a God by his genius, and made for himself the paradise he longed for—behold, it passes away like a vision. And
though an immortality of fame may irradiate his memory after
death, all will be naught to him! Oh, what is greatness, love,
passion, glory, ambition, hope, and life? In the words of the
philosopher, all but as *A lucernarum extinctu!*"

"With the putting out of candles! What a simile!" thought
Danvers. "I hardly comprehend what the youth is. We are
as meteor lights, that is certain, and fall into the black abyss of
Death, the secrets of which no traveller can tell."

Turning over the leaves of the book, he found a paper in the
same character, on the works of Epicurus and Lucretius, in comparison with those of Plato. It was masterly and brilliant,
indicating a perfect knowledge of the subject, and abounding
with deep and sombre thoughts, grand, shadowy and sublime.
It was the writing of one deeply versed in the secrets of the
human heart by intuition, more than experience. "We may
observe," wrote the critic, "a singular feature in the writings of
the disciple of Socrates—an ardent belief in immortality, though
vague and indistinct in its intimations; in those of Epicurus and
Lucretius a firm conviction of the non-existence of anything of
the conscious being after death. The visible and invisible worlds
constitute in the mind of Plato a species of phantasma, in which
his thoughts are continually involved. Yet of what consequence
is it to contend for the indestructibility of the mind? for, of
course, it is the merest axiom to say that it is not eternal in its
present state. To be eternal, then, it must undergo a change in

essence, and therefore could not remain the same mind. No; the present is All: and that All, if calmly and dispassionately considered, amounts to—Nothing."

" Wonderful!" thought Danvers, " to contend thus for annihilation, and to deny the entity of the present in the same breath. If I thought annihilation possible—if I were certain now that my Harry ceased to be—that I might never, never see him more—oh, death!"

Danvers had been comforting himself with the belief, that if his son were dead, he was happier far than if he had continued on earth ; and somehow the essay of the Atheist had made a more powerful impression on him than he liked to own to himself. There are certain states of mental progress, when we are apt to doubt of everything. conducive to felicity ; and Danvers, it has been said, was not a religious man. Irreligion is more frequently manifested in dull indifference than disbelief, and though it may not sap the foundations of morality so speedily in the former phase, it takes away the prop which sustains, and slowly plunges its votaries into the depths of wretchedness. Walter, from his occupations, and the original bias of his nature, had been immersed in thoughts which ever distracted his mind from the contemplation of eternity. The fevered dreams of ambition, and the hot unrest of mighty passions, continually absorbed his spirit. All men of the world more or less resemble him. The doctrine of annihilation is necessarily such, that it excludes from the soul every sweet hope and thought directed into the future— even on earth. If there were no other argument against it than its restriction to the present—when no rational person will assert that the present is sufficient for the happiness of man—and that he must ever desire what cannot be attained, as a law of his being—it were a cogent reason for rejecting it *in toto:* but when we are torn from those we love, when we behold our bright ones scattered, " like sear and yellow leaves," by the blast of desolation, oh, how agonizing would be the reflection, that the most virtuous, and pure, and cherished have become but as the matter which is wasting to ashes; " for none can say to the grave ' restore to me my beloved,' nor to corruption, ' give me back my darling.' " In the words of the eloquent Bulwer, " when after long years of desertion and widowhood on earth, there is

to be no hope of re-union in that Invisible beyond the stars,
where the torch not of life only, but of love, must be quenched in
the Dark Fountain ; and the grave that we would fain hope is
the great restorer of broken ties, is but the dumb seal of hopeless, utter, inexorable separation.   Blessed be the faith which
removes these terrors.   Listen not to those who would destroy
the poetry of the affections, with the pure religion of the heart."

Plunging into yet deeper meditation, Danvers now pursued his
way across a more sterile and uncultivated portion of the country
than that which he had hitherto traversed.   And presently he
found himself in a narrow path, winding betwixt hills and rocks
which rose to a considerable altitude in a semicircular form.   A
wild torrent rushed down a channel which it had made for itself
in the hard, stony earth, and spent its fury in hollow and mournful,
yet angry tumult in a valley which lay below.   Descending into
this valley, he descried a thin form, crawling along with uncertain
steps, and recognised in it that of the Miser, Everard Walsingham,
from whose residence he was now at no very great distance.
Hastening his pace, he would soon have overtaken Everard ; but
the Miser turning his head, no sooner beheld him, than he rushed
away at a furious rate, regardless of the shouts of Danvers to
stop.   But, unluckily for the fugitive, in dashing down a hill
which he was at the ascent to, when Walter first observed him,
he fell, and sprained his leg so severely that he could scarcely
limp along.

"In the fiend's name," cried Danvers impatiently, as soon as
he reached his former friend, who was groaning, as much from
fear as pain, " what ails thee ?"

"Oh, Walter," replied the Miser imploringly, " indeed I did
not betray your trust.   I am unable to tell you how I lost ;—
you know—that is—" and he stopped abruptly, hardly daring
to look Danvers in the face.   But his was a countenance which
betrayed the secrets of the soul even to a superficial observer,
and the keen eye of Danvers read it almost as a book, from
custom.

"You have not dared to breathe a word of what I confided to
you, to living man, Everard Walsingham ?" said Danvers, sternly
regarding the Miser.

"No, no! indeed not I!" replied Everard, frantic with fear,

and losing all thought, but of the danger he was in from the terrible resentment of that dreaded man; for the events of the last few days had almost reduced his feeble mind to idiotcy. " I dropped the papers, and a robber has got possession of them. He broke into your house at midnight, and, and—"

" Wretched fool!" interrupted Danvers, " I told you of the infinite importance of those papers." And as he spoke he recollected those documents which he had entrusted to little George. The feelings of the father gave way before those of the partisan, and he exclaimed, " We are undone." He thought to himself, " Those papers put together with mine, if discovered, will destroy every hope that we have. I must think no more of private sorrows; but bestir myself at once . . . . Walsingham," he said aloud, " you have been, at all events, shamefully careless: but if I find that you have done worse, expect my heaviest vengeance on your head; you shall die, by heaven!" And with these menaces, turning a deaf ear to the prayers and entreaties of the Miser, who was now driven to the very verge of desperation, and half drew a pistol from his bosom, when he found Walter heeded him not—but returned it to its place again instantly— Danvers left him.

" Oh, it has come at last," ejaculated Everard, " my fearfullest dreams are on the point of verification. What shall I do? My reason seems to totter. Ha, he is gone, and I—and I!" He left the sentence unfinished, and fell back with a piercing cry of anguish.

CHAPTER IV.

My noble boy, and have I found thee thus?
When that I thought the grave had o'er thee closed!
Oh, joy—Off, villains, off—a father's love
Will make this arm omnipotent!—*New Drama.*

HARRY DANVERS—FREESTONE—THE STRUGGLE—WALTER
DANVERS—HARRY'S DEPARTURE.

MEANWHILE Harry Danvers and his tall friend, Jennings,
having escaped from the cave in safety, took the first turning of
the road which led to it; and then held a consultation together.
"Perhaps we had better separate for the present," said Jennings;
"but meet me again here to-morrow, or the next day, if possible. But if that cannot be, here is my address in London. I
will give you a helping hand in any difficulty you may get into,
depend on't. And now I must commence my transformation.
Good bye."

Thus having spoken, Jennings began to limp away, turning up
his eyes in a peculiar manner, as a chance traveller made his
appearance—to whom he made application for alms in a whining
voice. Harry instantly strode away in the direction of the Britannia: but he found he was weaker than he thought possible.
When he had gained the shelter of a wood at the distance of
about half a mile, he stopped to rest for a few minutes, as well as
to drink from a brook which coursed gently, and without a ripple, through the place. Having refreshed himself, he arose, and
pursued his way; but he had not proceeded many furlongs, when
a man rushed up to him, breathless with the speed he had been
using, and exclaimed,

"I do beseech you, exchange your cloak and hat with me. I
am desperate, and if you refuse, I must take them by force. My
own are in better condition by far than—"

" Ha ! your name is Freestone ?" ejaculated Harry, before the man had finished his sentence ; and he himself being disguised, was not recognised by the other.

" Yes, yes, your voice is familiar to me, but I know you not. There is no time to waste. If you would befriend me, make the exchange."

" I suppose you are pursued," said Harry, as he proceeded to divest himself of his cloak and hat—the latter article of dress he had lost, when he was knocked down while contending with Mother Stokes and the savage, and it had been replaced with one as old as his years—and he gave them to Freestone.

" I think I know you now," exclaimed the emissary, a dark cloud gathering on his brow for an instant. " I have been pursued until almost exhausted. The great meeting you have heard of, as about to be convened, a 'short time since, was discovered, and a number of military attacked us. We were basely deserted by Norton and many others in our extremity ; but, with the most daring, I made a sally, and together with two or three others cut my way through the enemy. But I have been pursued, with scarcely any intermission, ever since. My horse has fallen under me from fatigue, and the hunters are now almost within sight."

Generously resolving to incur peril himself, in order to save one of the principal instruments of the cause he was attached to, the youth said, " I will try to mislead the persons who pursue you. At a distance we might easily be mistaken for each other. You can conceal yourself among yonder bushes, and I'll appear to fly. But, before we part, I must express my conviction that you are in error with regard to Norton ; he is the best, bravest, noblest fellow in existence."

" I cannot stay to dispute the point," returned Freestone. " I thank you for your help ;" saying which he immediately disappeared.

Harry, however, did not wish to be taken, though he would probably have been suffered to go at large, after some delay ; for he was anxious to gain tidings of his father, and to be at liberty to assist him, if necessary : and therefore, as soon as he heard the sounds of pursuit, he knew that he was perceived, and started off. After running for about ten minutes, when his strength

and wind failed him, he plunged into the thickest of the wood,
closely followed by two or three men, who were on horseback;
but who quitted their steeds, and tied them to a tree, in order to
follow the fugitive, who they imagined was at hand. The exertion
that he had made, quite knocked up Harry, after all he had
undergone; and he crept under some tall grass, overhung by
bushes, and lay concealed there. The pursuers were very close,
and would probably have discovered Harry, had not their attention been diverted by the appearance of two men, the one wild
and haggard in his looks, with blood streaming down his face,
the other a well-looking youth of about eighteen.

"Have you seen the villain?" demanded the first of these
persons of one of the soldiers, who seemed much fatigued with a
protracted chase.

"Does your honour mean the Jacobite, Hugh Freestone?"
inquired the soldier, doffing his cap.

"No, no," answered the officer, who was no other than Captain Norton, and who had been pursuing Danvers with desperate
eagerness, while William Walsingham, unwilling to desert him
while he laboured under such a frenzy of excitement, remained
with him. "I am in search of the miscreant, Walter Danvers,"
continued the Captain, "for whose head—and you are at liberty
to kill him for a felon and a traitor—I will give a thousand
pounds."

"I wish I could clap my hand on him," replied the man, who
was heartily sick of pursuing Freestone, and did not suppose that
he should take him without great difficulty yet,—the emissary
having slightly wounded him with a pistol-ball already. "Shall
I assist your honour to look for this rascal? Tom and Jack there
will see after t'other."

Captain Norton accepted the man's services, and William
Walsingham, bidding the soldier not to quit the officer's side,
departed. The two soldiers left behind were in no humour to
continue the pursuit in which they had been engaged; and as
soon as the other man, who was their Corporal, had followed
Captain Norton away, they proposed to "wet their whistles"
before they did anything further. Accordingly they seated themselves on the ground, and began to drink from a flask of spirits
which one of them carried, and to refresh themselves with some

hard biscuit, while they gathered the nuts and berries which grew near them. They were very weary, and the turf being soft, and the spot a pleasant one, realizing those pictures which Poussin delighted in—quiet and shady and romantic—they did not seem likely to quit it speedily.

Harry remained in a state of suspense and anxiety far from being enviable, while the soldiers regaled themselves, lazily recumbent; but he did not dare to stir, lest he should be discovered. He was a bold fellow, and, in ordinary circumstances, would not have hesitated to encounter them in fight, but now he was so faint and weak, that he felt he should be mad to do so.

"Well, I think I shall take a snooze," said one fellow, the refreshments being demolished. "It's of no use to try and catch that d——d runaway."

"You may do as you like," replied his comrade; "but I haven't done eating these berries and nuts. I shall pick all I can, and carry them to my sweetheart."

"Sweethearts be hanged!" returned the first speaker, who was soon snoring.

A whole hour was consumed in this manner, much to the annoyance of Harry; and at last his impatience getting the better of his prudence, leaving behind the hat and cloak of Freestone, as soon as the back of the soldier who was gathering wild fruits was turned, he crept out: but he had hardly done so, when he was descried by the man who was giving a proof of the sincerity of his passion, after having plentifully supplied his own wants; and with a shout, he pursued him, although he saw at a glance he was not the person he had been in search of.

It was evident, however, that Harry wished to elude observation, and that he had been lurking near for no good purpose, that he was not suffered to escape as he might have been, had he put a bold face on the matter, and (being without Freestone's habiliments) stepped boldly away. The sleeping soldier was aroused by the shout of his comrade, and joined in the chase, saying—

"Perhaps this is the fellow Captain Norton offered the reward for!"

The notion of the possibility of such a thing, gave wings to the feet of the pursuers; and Harry, though a fleet runner, would

have had but little chance of escaping, if the intricacies of the
wood had not befriended him : for he was now nearly exhausted,
and needed rest and food. Still he held on with might and
main ; and at one time imagined that the soldiers had abandoned
the hope of capturing him, a darkness having arisen, and envelop-
ing every object in obscurity.

It was with this idea that he quitted the shelter of the wood,
and paused to recover breath ; but it appeared the soldiers had
only been involved in a maze, from which it was some time ere
they could extricate themselves : and seeing Harry, renewed the
chase. Knowing that he should soon be overtaken in the open
road, in his tired condition, the youth darted away in a transverse
direction ; and gathering together all his energies, turned an angle, which hid him from view, and regained the thicket, before
his pursuers could perceive the path he had taken. There was
only a choice of two paths in that direction, and the soldiers
separating, rushed onwards.

I have uniformly observed, that whatever is most difficult of
attainment is most eagerly pursued by mankind ; and the efforts
which Harry made to escape, redoubled those of his enemies, so
that he was not much better off than before, unless he chose to
fight for it ; and being unarmed, in the state he was, what chance
could he have had with the stalwart fellow who was behind him?
But it was fortunate for Harry that he had acted as has been
described ; for he was now within a few hundred yards of the
place where the dragoons had left their horses. The youth
immediately scanned the appearance of the three animals, who
were tied up and grazing, and his practised eye soon discovered
which was the best and least fatigued horse. Having made his
selection, he bounded along, almost staggering from extreme exhaustion, vaulted into the saddle ; and in another instant was
galloping away at a tremendous pace.

Still labouring under the impression that he might be the man,
for whose capture so tempting a reward had been offered, the
troopers relaxed not their exertions, the more Harry endeavoured
to outspeed them, convinced that he was of importance. It was
almost dark when Harry once more quitted the thicket, no twilight having ushered in evening. Though hotly pressed, it was
evident he had the advantage, his steed being in better condition

than the soldiers', and himself a much lighter weight than those ponderous dragoons. But he felt he should not be able to support himself much longer, and even the animal he rode could not maintain the speed to which he was urging him, after the previous exertions he had been compelled to make. He was some minutes' gallop in advance of the soldiers; and he hoped that in the darkness of night he should be able to elude them by pursuing several cross-roads nigh at hand. Nor was he disappointed; but his head swam in such a manner, and he was so faint, that he could scarcely keep his seat. The horse of the foremost dragoon, a man of immense weight, had failed him, so that Harry thus gained another advantage: but now his face became perfectly white, and his eyes grew dim; and finally he fell insensible from his saddle, happily for him upon some straw which was laid for a dunghill.

The pursuers found themselves at fault, when they came to three roads which intersected the highway they had previously been traversing: and the atmosphere was now so thick, and the approaching night so dark, that it was impossible to distinguish objects at any distance, or to trace the hoof-prints of Harry's horse. One of the troopers had dismounted, his steed panting for breath, and led the beast along, while the other, though still retaining his saddle, was obliged to proceed at a walk. The spot where Harry lay being about a mile, or nearly so, in advance, he was thus for the present safe from his pursuers, if they but happened to err in the choice of their road; for it was a lonely part of the country, and they were not likely to meet those who could give them the least information. And fortune favoured the youth; for the dragoons determined on following the two paths, neither of which he had taken: and for hours prosecuted an unavailing search.

It was early morning when Harry recovered his senses. Looking about with much bewilderment, he perceived a farm-house at the distance of a furlong or so, and the horse which had proved so useful to him a few hours before, standing a little way from him, making a repast of some hay from a stack. Harry still felt weak and feeble: but he thought that a good meal would restore his strength; and he determined on walking to the farm-house, and procuring a breakfast there, if possible. So taking the dra-

goon's horse by the bridle, and leaning on him for support, Harry
with fainting steps and slow, proceeded towards the dwelling so
opportunely near him, trusting that he had baffled the vigilance
of pursuit, and might now continue his way as he thought fit. He
gained the rustic abode, the inhabitants of which were already
stirring, as it was harvest-time; and found no difficulty in procuring wherewithal to appease the cravings of his appetite.   He
inquired where he was; for, in the precipitation of the chase, he
had not marked the direction he had taken: and found that he
was farther from the thicket where the latter part of his yesterday's adventures had taken place than he supposed possible; for
in the course of half an hour, which the gallop might have occupied, at least seven good miles had been left behind; and the
chargers of that day were not remarkable, for the most part, for
speed.   Harry, having partaken of the rustic cheer hospitably
pressed upon him, was on the point of taking his departure; but
the heavy meal on his empty stomach caused a return of illness,
and for several hours he was constrained to remain where he was.

At length, having recovered, he sallied forth: but a scene had
just occurred, which involved him in fresh difficulty.   The soldier
Captain Norton had taken with him, having been sent back a
short time previously by the officer, as nothing could be seen or
heard of Danvers,—he took the road in which the farm-house
was situated wherein Harry had taken up his quarters, and on
arriving at the locality, he perceived the horse which Harry had
brought thither, standing outside.   He immediately asked of a
rosy urchin to whom it belonged, for the purpose of eliciting the
truth, and was told " To a young gentleman within."

" O, indeed!" he said, drawing his sabre, " I must see this
gentleman."

But as he spoke, the worthy mistress of the house, who had
heard the preceding question and answer, having taken a great
liking to the youth, came out, and finding the soldier with his
drawn sword, seized a pitchfork, and in a threatening voice cried,

" If you dare to lay a hand on him, I'll run you through, you
great, ugly lobster:" and seeing Harry, who was sallying forth,
added, " Run, young gentleman! I'll keep this rascal off."

Harry, however, had too much of his father's spirit to run from
mortal man, when there was the least probability of fighting with

success: and a second pitchfork being at hand, as he saw he had but one foe to deal with, he firmly stood his ground. Those people in the farm-house who were not gone to work in the fields, now gathered about them: but intimidated by the presence of the burly soldier, in spite of the commands of their mistress to drive him off, remained neutral.

"That young rogue is a thief, if he is nothing more," cried the soldier: "and I order you, in the king's name, to assist me to arrest him. The horse that stands there, belongs to my regiment."

The worthy dame who had so stoutly arrayed herself in Harry's cause, was somewhat staggered at this intimation, especially as she beheld two other dragoons advancing towards the house. These were no others than those who had so hardly pressed Harry the day before, having returned from a fruitless expedition: but on making inquiries of some labourers attached to the farm, receiving intelligence of the fugitive's whereabouts, they had hastened thither. Still the old woman did not absolutely desert her favourite, who remained undaunted, and beholding the soldiers, who were by this time within a hundred yards, sprang towards the horse, with the hopes of being able to reach him before he could be prevented from mounting; but the corporal of dragoons was too quick for him, and seized his arm with a powerful hand. Vainly did Harry struggle, vainly endeavour to release himself from that Herculean grasp; and he had given all up for lost, as he heard the shouts of exultation the dragoons raised within gunshot of him, when a form bounded over a hedge which stood opposite, uttered a cry of joy in a well-known voice, and struck down the strong man, against whom the immature powers of Harry availed nothing, as if he had been a stripling.

"Ha! my father!" exclaimed the youth.

"My own boy!" ejaculated Walter Danvers, as he stood with flashing eyes over the man he had struck. "Mount, Harry; and I will vault up behind you! My dear, dear Harry!" said he.

"Stop!" vociferated the soldiers, fiercely, as they came up.

"Dare not attempt to impede our way," cried Danvers, in his stern, deep voice, calm and awful as the thunder, as he levelled a pistol, "or I shall fire."

"That is the man for whom the reward is offered!" exclaimed the prostrate Corporal.

3 H

Harry Danvers was now in the saddle; and his father leapt up behind him. Having recovered the son he had nearly given up for dead, Walter Danvers felt invincible; and so terrible was the flashing of his lion-like countenance, so lit up with fierce radiance and daring, high chivalry, and transport, that it awed even the stout hearts of gallant British soldiers. Yet the reward to be gained was great, and they made a stand: but urging his horse on to a gallop, Danvers charged them down, Harry knocking one to the ground with the pitchfork, and off they dashed triumphantly. The chargers of the soldiers were quite spent and blown, while that on which the father and son were riding, was now quite fresh, and displayed a brave spirit; so that, in the course of a few minutes, they left the shouts of the enemy behind them; and before half an hour had elapsed were many miles distant.

That the joy of Danvers at recovering his son was intense, may easily be supposed, and that of Harry at seeing his father was little inferior. Beautiful is the love of parent and child, when there is confidence and fervour; it is "like moonlight" in its purity, and is potent to give consolation, to develope the best feelings of the heart, to strengthen, to subdue!

Harry having related his adventures since he parted with his father, Danvers gave him a hasty outline of the prominent features of his own in return, and then added—

"We must waste no time in idleness. It was lucky that I recognised you, my Harry, in that disguise; and I think it would baffle any but a father's eye. I must procure something of the same sort for myself, and communicate with our adherents in this part of the country, among whom I fear the result of the late disastrous meeting has struck a panic. You I must send forward to London with despatches, if you feel well enough to undertake a journey. I sent the men to intercept a mail which will depart from the metropolis with state papers of importance. If you can do so, try and see them before they proceed in that business; but do not mix yourself up with it, or you may be branded with the name of robber. I will now return to Ellen and Elizabeth, who must be extremely anxious: and then I must try and recover the documents which have been lost. I cannot return to our house; for probably that has been discovered by the authorities, despite the precautions I have taken. Do what you can also in London. Thus far you are in the road to the metropolis ; but here we must part. God bless you, my beloved boy ! How grateful I should be, that you are spared to me. There *is* a Providence over all."

And embracing his son, Walter Danvers dismounted ; and Harry, manning himself to undergo the fatigue of the journey, to which he was hardly competent, cantered off. A load was now removed from the heart of Danvers, and brighter hopes and feelings than had stirred within him of late took possession of his soul. He ate some coarse bread, and drank of some clear water, and felt he was equal to any exertion. It would not have been prudent in him, however, to have entered the village where Mrs. Haines and Ellen were, in the broad daylight : and so he resolved to visit a partisan of the cause he served, who lived in the vicinity. Thither, accordingly, he repaired ; and procured minute intelligence of the recent discomfiture of the Jacobites, and spent a long time in laying schemes with the zealous adherent of their common party for the reparation of the mischief which the late events must occasion to it. As soon as twilight began, he proceeded toward the " Britannia :" but his quick eye detected a lad dodging him, among some trees, before he entered the village. Danvers feigned not to perceive him ; but on coming to a sequestered spot, suddenly turned, darted on " the Artful Dodger," and in spite of his cries and kicks, soon bound him hand and foot ; having done which, he proceeded unmolested to the inn, where he had left Mrs. Haines and Ellen : and was fortunate enough to enter it, and reach the room they occupied, without being seen.

CHAPTER V.

Are these the pompous tidings ye proclaim,
Lights of the world, and demi-gods of Fame?
Is this your triumph, this your proud applause,
Children of Truth, and champions of her cause?
Oh, star-eyed Science, hast thou wander'd there
To waft us home the message of despair?

                                        CAMPBELL.

WALTER DANVERS — CHARLES WALSINGHAM AND HIS COU-
        SIN WILLIAM—OPPOSITE SENTIMENTS.

IT may easily be supposed how rejoiced Elizabeth and Ellen
were to behold Danvers, and to hear the good news he brought
of Harry's safety; but he did not stay above a couple of hours:
when, singularly metamorphosed in external appearance, he departed. Ellen had procured a woman's dress, during his
absence, exactly similar to that worn by Mrs. Haines, which she
pretended was for that person; and insisted on her father's
wearing it over his own clothes. A lady's wig concealed his
hair; and she painted and patched his face in such a manner
that his identity would indeed have been difficult to establish. A
boy, belonging to the public-house where the females still
remained, perceived Danvers, as he left it; and amazed at his
strange appearance, and the manner in which he stalked along,
which, as may be supposed, was most unfeminine, the time being
midnight, was convinced that he saw a ghost: for he was
certain that no such person was in the place; and fled on the
instant, with a terrified exclamation.

Danvers heeded him not, however, but made for a place of
rendezvous, which he had appointed with the individual in whose
house he had spent the greater part of the day, who had
promised to collect some of the principal conspirators by one

o'clock in the morning. When he arrived there, it was not easy
for him to make them understand whom he really was; and,
satisfied with his disguise, he determined on retaining it for the
present. But a circumstance occurred very soon afterwards,
which disgusted him with his female attire : for he was met by a
semi-intoxicated, rustic libertine, after quitting the meeting,
without effecting much, who having a somewhat strange taste
for coarse and masculine beauties, made overtures of an amatory
nature to the supposed lady, who almost killed him in his rage
and vexation, with a blow on the face, which was the sole reply
he vouchsafed. Some boon companions of the tipsy man came
up at this juncture, and being flushed with liquor, heedless of the
signal discomfiture of their friend, set upon Danvers, and tried
to tear his gown off his back. Never was there such a scene,
when Danvers, wrenching a cudgel from one fellow's hand, commenced breaking the heads of every man of the party, who
thinking that the devil himself had put on petticoats, at last
decamped at full speed. Having procured a horse of a friend
whom he visited after this curious incident, he tied his female
attire into a bundle, and carried it in his hand. But his subsequent adventures were not of sufficient interest to be recorded
here. Once more only had he been able to visit Ellen in the
period which intervened between this time and when he encountered Captain Walsingham, Harry, and his men ; and was
informed by his daughter that Mrs. Haines, having wonderfully
recovered, had gone to see after the invalid officer, as well as to
transact some other business at home ; and she thought it would
be better for herself to remain where she was. This she said
with a sigh. Danvers, after thinking a minute, seemed to agree
with Mrs. Haines, by whose advice Ellen acted, on this point,
but the girl seemed melancholy—of *course*, at being left alone.
It was a few days after this that the prevented highway robbery
occurred ; and having thus glanced at the circumstances which
had taken place during the interval in question, let us follow
Charles Walsingham's history at once.

As soon as Danvers and Harry had disappeared, the soldier
continued his journey, though at a slow pace ; for the recent
adventure had given him much food for thought. He had already
imbibed strong suspicions that Danvers was engaged in some

hazardous and unlawful business; but his conjectures as to the
nature of it had not been similar to those which now forced
themselves on his mind. It was not to be disputed that Ellen's
father exercised control over robbers, who would have murdered
him; and the deductions to be drawn from this, made Charles
feel sick at heart. Three days had elapsed since the scene which
had occurred with Mrs. Haines, who left him very soon afterwards; and he had lingered on in the hope of seeing Ellen, but
in vain. He could not prevail on the stern and haughty woman,
who was so nearly allied to one of England's kings, though
occupying a subordinate station in society, even to inform him
where her he loved might be found; and all his affections were
now so bound up with Ellen, that he felt existence would be a
dreary blank to him, if not filled by her beloved presence.
Though returning health made him feel an elasticity of frame
which he had not for long experienced, the idea of being eternally divided from Ellen was so intolerable, that he felt an infinitely greater depression and despondency than in the worst part
of his illness. What though the sanguine tides of life course
through the veins, and the proud spirit of youth and manhood
impart aspirations too lofty for the earth, though strength, and
sense, and all personal and intellectual advantages be combined;
when the cherished object of the heart's best hopes is departing
from us, sickness, age, and debility are more endurable. Who
hath not felt the vanity of pride of mind, and power of body,
when joys are crumbling to dust, and dreams are melting into
bubbles, bubbles into air? *Sic transit gloria mundi.*

But as Charles was revolving these bitter things, which were
gall and aconite to his spirit, about a mile from the spot where
the scene of the attempted robbery had passed, he encountered a
young man with a book in his hand, which, though open, it was
evident he did not read; for he was so lost in reverie that he did
not even perceive the horseman, until he had nearly run up
against him.

"Ah," said the soldier, perceiving the youth, "surely I have
seen you before, young sir? May I ask your name?"

The moon was streaming over the pale face of the young man
with a brightness which gave it a peculiar hue of melancholy,
softening the lines of thought already visible in that young brow,

and imparting to the whole countenance a gentleness such as it seldom wore. The youth gazed a moment into Charles's face, and apparently recognizing him, exclaimed, " You must be no other than Captain Walsingham. My name is William."

He did not, however, hold forth his hand, but Charles took it, saying, " Who could have thought to see you so manly, my dear cousin! when I left you a little urchin, scarcely to be called a boy. I am very glad to see you again." Frankly did Charles Walsingham shake William's hand, but the Epicurean did not return the pressure with equal warmth. " Well, how are the good folks at Walsingham Hall?" asked the soldier, endeavouring to throw off his melancholy ; " all well, I hope ?"

" Quite so," replied the youth. " But, of course, you will find great alterations in them, after having been absent so many years."

" I have almost forgotten their very characters, being but a thoughtless lad of sixteen when I left England. My good old grandmother, who must now be of immense age, how is she ?"

" Hale and hearty still," replied William Walsingham. " She will yet entertain you with her reminiscences of the Conquest, if you like to listen to her."

Charles smiled. " I recollect," he said, " the dear old lady used to take the family history very far back. And your aunt— my uncle's wife, the pretty, amiable Fanny, does she look young ?"

" Still more so than she is," returned the Epicurean. " She will have to present her little daughter to you, who promises to possess even more beauty than her mother—at least, a more intellectual style of loveliness."

" I am anxious to see my little cousin. And what has become of poor Harriet? I fear she has never recovered the effects of that unfortunate attachment?'

" Ah, she will see you : but she lives at some distance from this locality, entirely secluded from the world, even having taken her mother's maiden name, that her dwelling might not be discovered by friends or others. It is generally supposed among her former acquaintance that she is dead. She is a glorious being."

" She must be very wretched," remarked the soldier.

" You do not know her," replied William, shaking his head. " She seems to spurn from her the cares and sorrows which oppress the hearts of common mortals, and to live in a world of her own creation, pure and bright as herself. Her mind is like a bird at morning, springing upwards, and heeding not the earth it leaves."

"I know she is a poetess. She was a noble creature when a girl. That any man could act so villanously towards such a woman as did that Walter Danvers! It is a bad world, William!"

The Atheist smiled darkly. There was something painful and disagreeable in the sneer, which generally accompanied that smile; from which Charles, willing to be favourably impressed with his young kinsman, averted his eyes. It reminded one that looked upon a picture of a fallen angel, that the heaven had sunk into the hell. The image which arises to our minds, when we study Goethe's strange and wonderful creation of Mephisto-philes, cold, keen, and sarcastic, realized that look.

"This world," said the Materialist, in reply, "contains many things which men call evil, knowing not what evil really is."

"And can you explain the enigma?" inquired the soldier, desirous to sound the depth of his cousin's mind, but unprepared for its powerful grasp and precocity.

"I think I can," answered William. "I do not agree with the sentiment expressed in Pope's last work, the Essay on Man, which I have here, to the effect, 'that whatever wrong we call, may, must be right as relative to all.'"—He continued, "partial evil, according to him, being 'universal good,' it is reduced to nothing more than a relative term. We know nothing of evil, it is asserted, except by antagonistic properties in some other essence. I deny the fact. Evil is an entity, *per se*, or it is nothing at all; and for this reason: we do not feel by contraries only; since contraries imply that other qualities inhere in their opposites. If it were not so, there would be no dissimilarities at all; and good and evil would never have started into existence. But it is said that what is a curse to one, is a blessing to another; and what is virtue here, is vice there. What is the inference? Why, that they individually co-exist in the idea, from their painful or plea-surable effects. Which is equivalent to saying that virtue and vice, pleasure and pain, have no being in themselves, but are true and real in their material operation. There is no other standard of morality."

"I should say," cried Charles, "that they do exist most positively as intuitions—I believe that is the term—from the very circumstance of their receiving different appellations at various times and places. It seems an universal idea among all men that these states of morality are ever in being."

"Very well," returned the Materialist. "But what is the cause of that idea. Sweet is sweet, and bitter, bitter, everywhere. Evil must of course consist in painful sensations of mind or body, which may be produced from their action on separate organizations in different degrees. Here is this new work of Pope's now, which I have just received. Some will believe its philosophy good, others will think it vile. Here is the same cause producing diverse effects. But then we must consider the preceding sensations which modified the subsequent sensations of the recipient. What is good? That which produces benefit to mankind. But the question is not as to the results of good,—for that is begging the question; but what creates the benefits themselves. I say truth is, and falsehood is an idea; but not a necessary and universal principle implanted by Nature. Then each individual pursues the path of inclination, whether he will or not. Opinion is nothing more. I contend that this is the only morality: for if there be restrictions on the enjoyments of mankind, beyond such as Nature makes imperative, an evil is caused, from which other evils must arise. If the despotism be removed, a good is created, and from good, or in other terms from liberty, more must spring."

"I do not understand you," said Charles: "nor do I perceive how what you have been saying bears on the subject."

The worthy soldier was not versed in controversy, and was unable to pierce the mystery of a chain of argument, made up of sophistry, such as the mode in which his cousin marked out his theory. But he was soon enlightened. The Materialist rejoined thus—

"Virtue, so called, must have had a beginning in the mind. And what was its primary cause? Is it conceivable that it could have arisen from any other belief than that it tended to create pleasurable sensations? For, in the first stages of society, when men are barbarous and uncivilized, they must judge of all things by their immediate sequences. And it appears to me that these barbarians arrived at a truth from nature: as we do from induc-

3 I

tion. I believe a thing is thus; and I do so because it pleases my mind most to do so: and I have no option; for all actions of thought—so to speak—must proceed from the operation of external laws on my organization. The first law of nature must be the best: and that is, to gratify the feelings which she has implanted in us. Those feelings are perverted by circumstance, and produce injury to others. The good is the fruition, the evil is the perversion. If we had but all things in common, these passions would not be."

The Materialist paused for a reply: for he was for the most part ever ready to hear an objection; but his cousin remaining silent, he finished thus—

"The light of nature is the only true light. All others must be factitious. The ideas of vice and virtue are not intuitions, but pain and pleasure are. What you think is pleasant in your morality, I think the converse. It is evident then that the cause of those ideas must have been from the different impression of external objects on dissimilar natures. The same cause thus operating on two opinions—as is the case in optics—where nothing can be seen in a similar phasis by different persons—a diverse effect is produced. I infer that there cannot possibly be a standard of morals, because no two individuals will agree on the same point. Absolute and contingent truths are supposed to admit of a division: but to my mind they seem the manifestations of the same principle. I conceive that they move in one cycle, and are parts of a whole. In that Henry Spenser is right. If this be a just inference, what we denominate good and evil, must bear the same analogy; viz. that they are the emanations of one thing, and true to the individual: but specific, and not universal. They do not admit of separation—out of their immediate physical laws—the one necessarily following the other. They are distinct in relations, they are identical in derivations. My *ultimatum* is this—That good and evil are the same in kind, but not in degree; and it is from allowing too much to the one, and too little to the other, that all the confusion about them has arisen. In other words, 'GOOD IS EVIL, AND EVIL GOOD, ACCORDING TO THE MEASURE WE TAKE OF THEM.'"

"According to the measures we take of them!" exclaimed Charles, when the Materialist had thus concluded his argument

for the non-entity of a moral standard—which has been given
rather to show the contradictions of Necessitarians, than to display the full scope of William's almost mature philosophy—crude,
but metaphysically so, in its deep paradoxes and anomalies.
For materialism is always unripe; it is only the fruit shaken
down, and rotting into decay, not ripening into sweetness. " Yet
you allow," added the soldier, " that good and evil are diverse ;
one cause having two specific properties in effect."

The Materialist replied thus—

" How much which might be productive of good, is lost by
pseudo-philosophy ! I told you I believe good and evil inhere in
the same substance: but it is in the application of them, we
wander at present without card or compass. By following the
dictates of nature, we cannot do wrong. Man should move in
harmony with the universe. He should study the analogies which
exist in the world ; and he will perceive a beautiful system of
morality ; which can alone be really conducive to happiness.
Abjuring then the idea, that by permitting man to be wretched in
some respects, we are promoting his weal in others ; partial evil
being allowed to exist only as it does in the matter of which we
are a portion ; governing ourselves by the rooted conviction that
each one is acting according to necessity, how much pain, crime,
and misery may be avoided ! Let us *not* believe that the evil of
one is the benefit of another ; but rather, in permitting it, we
cause a larger amount, as by cultivating good we create more. Is
it not so with matter ? Let us endeavour universally to promote
the greatest amount of happiness, as we cultivate land so that it
may produce the most fruit ; and it must follow. Alas ! for
man. For ages and ages he has been lost in the dark windings
of an inextricable labyrinth, disputing about words which never
had nor can have any ideas attached to them ; and fancying that
in those eternal logomachies, he is elucidating the mysteries of
being,—and indicating which path leads to felicity, and which to
perdition. Let us but return to that sublime philosophy which
is ever evolving around us : and casting away the stern dogmas
which would restrain all the gentle influences and exquisite impulses of universal charity and uncorrupted feeling to a Stoic's
dungeon bosom, live as the stars of heaven, radiant, and divine,
and mild, resembling them in all save their immortality."

William spoke with enthusiasm, though his usual manner was calm, cold, and even cynical : and although much which he had spoken was very far removed from the principles of the soldier, he could not but admire his elevated views of the universe, apart from their materialism, unaware that he was conversing with one who saw all things through a distorted medium, who believed that the shrine was without its divinity, who was persuaded that the dear light of the everlasting was nihility, pure faith mere foolishness, and her sister virtue in *personal* action a chimera : that all the majestic feelings and aspirations of the spirit are to end with this life ; and that there exists neither good nor evil save in the brute sensations.

Had he been a controversialist, or a deep thinker, Charles would easily have perceived the tendency of his cousin's opinions ; but he now only esteemed them the sentiments of a visionary, who had adopted some false views, which were blended with others, ennobling, poetical, and in some degree, original. He was pleased on the whole with the youth, who, when he chose to permit his sarcasm to sleep, and to speak with the natural fervour, zeal and energy of his mighty heart, was one whom no person with any power of appreciating him could listen to without being fascinated and delighted. It was seldom, in truth, that the Materialist allowed himself to utter the real sentiments of his bosom, which apart from his Atheistic and Epicurean principles, were noble and philanthropic : but then some shadow would cross his mind in the midst of his Utopian dreams, and he would sneer even at himself.

Charles Walsingham replied—

"It were well, I acknowledge, if we could establish universal love and peace : but at the same time, I cannot think, that to yield like the Sybarite to gross indolence and luxury is wise. Like the ancient Spartans, I would have the soul disciplined to scorn all things for the sake of virtue and patriotism ; and having lived well and nobly, continually sacrificing self, and mortifying our evil passions, how much more glorious were our existence than the stars !—how much more bright and like to the angels ! Our bodies may perish ; but we may live with the wise, and great, and good,—among the incorruptible spirits of the blessed !"

The Materialist gazed sadly earthwards: and after a short pause, exclaimed—

" All visions : we have both been dreaming. I know not how it is. I laugh at metaphysics, believing they consist but of verbiage : yet, living as we do among old systems, we are obliged to meet our opponents with their own weapons. Ay," he continued, with increased mournfulness, " this life, though it have smiles of entrancing sweetness; though it have radiance and ethereal glory ; though it have music which binds the heart with a spell of love, and passionate and thrilling rapture, has nothing which can endure for an hour. The busy world goes round in all its panoply of pride, its restless energies, its ambition, struggles, and despair. Beauty buds around us, and its blossoms are cut off. Where shall we look for them ? Go to the tomb, and behold all—all that remains of sweetness and freshness which were joy to the senses. The towering mind of genius, the tender breast which once it were transport to recline upon, love, hope, wisdom, power, hushed in the stillness of eternal sleep !"

O, that voice—those words ! Never were there any such but those which have proceeded from one steeped in crime, or one even like to the Materialist.

" And yet not so !" returned Charles, the latent poetry and enthusiasm of his nature aroused by the melancholy and despairing ideas of his cousin, so chilling in themselves, but kindling the loftiest hopes and aspirations in the soul of faith. The Epicurean had spoken, as if soliloquising : but the soldier replied with unconscious elocution and fire. " There are things which endure for more than an hour. There are things which breathe of their immortal origin, and flash celestial morning over the night of earth. When the icy hand of death is laid upon the moral hero's bosom, when the soul of greatness is struggling with the last pangs of mortality, when the patriot dies in sacred freedom's cause, though the axe may sever the head, and corruption destroy, and the earth conceal all that is earthly in him, a spirit of truth and power, a spirit of admiration and love goes forth, and attests the indestructibility of the beautiful. And though the light of truth may be obscured, though virtue may be forgotten, and humble merit be buried in oblivion, they exert an eternal influence, transmitted to posterity : and their example creates a religion of

charity, an atmosphere of purity, an odour of peace, a redolence
of happiness—which cause the spirit to look upward for the consummation of hope, to trust intensely, firmly, and meekly in the
beneficence of the All-wise and holy : and to endure, to soar, to
forgive, to believe—to repose in the terrors of the tempest, and
remain serene, though all things around may perish :—to die as
to be assured of softest sleep, and a waking of unimaginable
bliss ; and in that tranquil death, to point out fortitude and resignation, and that of all-sustaining love which smiles doubt and
fear to annihilation."

Probably the Atheist conceived that the eloquence which his
zeal and sincerity lent to his kinsman was the merest rhapsody
and extravagance : but it was a remarkable feature in the character of that youth, that if an appeal were made to the heart
more than to the head, he heard it in silence and respect : but
when a logical sequency of reasoning was directed against him,
he answered with coldness and contempt of fine feeling. Those
who argue with unbelievers may be assured, that if there is any
of the right staple of humanity left in them, they may get at the
head more frequently through the feelings than either by asperity,
ridicule, or hard arguments derived from facts or induction.

"Well," he said, as the soldier concluded his harangue, "here
is your destination.   Yonder old, dusky pile between the trees is
Walsingham Hall."

CHAPTER VI.

What from this barren being do we reap?
  Our senses narrow, and our reason frail,
  Life short, and truth a gem which loves the deep,
And all things weigh'd in custom's falsest scale,
  Opinion on omnipotence, whose veil
Mantles the earth with darkness, until right
  And wrong are accidents, and men grow pale
Lest their own judgments should become too bright,
And their free thoughts be crimes, and earth have too much light.
                                                BYRON.

WALSINGHAM HALL—FAMILY MATTERS—THE CHILD—THE
HOUSEKEEPER—CHARLES AND WILLIAM—DESPAIR.

WALSINGHAM HALL was a large, quadrangular building, of considerable strength and solidity, having formerly been castellated, and defended by a drawbridge and moat. It had originally been built by the founder of the family, a valiant Norman knight, who came to England with the Conqueror: but great additions had been made in the reign of the Virgin Queen, when its possessor was ennobled, and extensive lands attached to it by a royal grant, so that its architectural appearance was of the Elizabethan era more than of any other.   During the civil wars the Walsingham who was the head of the family at that time, being a staunch Royalist, his mansion was attacked by the Roundheads, and, although it was stoutly defended, taken, and its fortifications destroyed.   After it was thus dismantled, it had been deserted for many years; and though, after the Restoration, occasionally visited, it remained in a ruinous condition, until a Walsingham in the reign of William and Mary entirely repaired it.   Altogether, it was comfortable and handsome, though not magnificent; and its green lawns, its verdant pastures, its noble parks, in which herds of deer were reposing, its enclosures, gardens, woods and fertilizing streams, formed a whole, which would have pleased any eye, and, of course, was peculiarly gratifying to a person who could boast his lineage as belonging to one of the most ancient and honourable families in England.

Charles Walsingham, although not a high aristocrat, was proud of his ancestry, and few indeed could claim lineal descent from persons of such exalted character as many of the early Walsingham's had made. Its present possessor—or rather, tenant—was a sister of Harriet Walsingham, who had married very early in life the head of the family : but having only a daughter, on her husband's decease (which occurred many years antecedent to the date of our tale) she was only permitted to reside in it during her life, the estates being entailed. Her husband, however, left a competency behind him, which amply provided for his daughter, while the provision made by law for his widow, if not a splendid, was a handsome income.

In a vast, gothic apartment—which was almost the only one in the house which remained of the original building—were seated three persons of very different ages and appearance. The first, an extremely aged woman, of remarkable exterior, was seated in a huge arm-chair, beneath trophies of war, and surrounded by portraits of haughty warriors and ancient dames, some of which she bore a strong resemblance to herself. She was dressed in an old-fashioned manner, plainly, but handsomely, and though there was much good nature in her still fine features, and though her once tall form was greatly bent, so as not to reach the stature of a short female, there was courtliness and dignity in her appearance. She had been a celebrated beauty in the reign of Charles the Second, and, indeed, anterior to the accession of that monarch to the throne, though that was seventy years previous ; and had moved in the court as an attendant on royalty during the sovereignties of the merry monarch, of James the Second, William and Mary, and Anne : and her dress was a heterogeneous mixture of the fashions of the last half century, each fashion in good taste, but contrasting oddly with the others, so as to present, as it were, an epitome of the best modes of dress for a long time.

The second personage was a lady of about seven-and-twenty, lovely, elegant, and exquisitely formed, who was Lady Walsingham, Harriet's sister, and the other, a child of some eight years of age, who was her daughter. The dowager Lady Walsingham, grandmother to the younger, both by blood and marriage, was explaining some matter of genealogy, while she knitted away with untiring zeal; her granddaughter was embroidering, and apparently not very much interested in what her aged relative was saying: and the young child was endeavouring to paint, not without promise of taste and skill, at a solid mahogany table which was placed in the centre of the spacious chamber.

"You see, my dear," the old lady was saying, "my grandmother's sister was married to the first Lord Walsingham in the year 1605. Sir Everard was the only son of the first lord; and was knighted by Elizabeth for his services in battle; and you know I was the youngest child of that union. My father expired in the same year that King Charles the Martyr was executed—I was then only eighteen—and I shall never forget his death. His last words to me were, 'My Eliza, never, I charge you, marry a canting Roundhead, as you value my dying blessing.' He was a brave Cavalier."

"So I have often heard you say," replied the younger lady.

"Well, two of my cousins, John and William, contended for my hand. You know I married my poor, dear John: and William, a gallant youth, as ever drew sword, was sadly disappointed, but he married in the same year as I did, Anne, the daughter of Sir Roger Stevens. My eldest son, poor Charles Rupert, was united to his cousin, the second child of William, and they had three children. The eldest of these, a daughter, you remember, died in giving birth to a child, the second married your father's sister—the mother of dear Charles—(who ought to be here ere now), and the third——"

"My dear grandmother," interrupted the younger Lady Walsingham, "do not fatigue yourself by talking. I know doing so increases your cough."

"Not at all, child," replied the old lady; "let me see; where was I? O, I recollect! The third was united to my niece, your mother's aunt. Your father was my third child, you know, and your mother—I remember her a lovely girl of fifteen, when I was at the Court of William and Mary—your mother was the second

3 K

cousin of your mother's aunt's son's wife, the daughter of the
Duke of Leinster——"

"What a memory you have at your age!" exclaimed the
young widow.

"Oh, but it fails me frequently," returned the 'fine old English lady.' "I made a sad mistake the other day when the dowager Marchioness of Clanricarde called on me. The Marchioness
recollects better than I do. The intermarriages in our family have
been numerous, and I sometimes forget—though I was perfectly
acquainted with them all. It is singular that dear Charles, who
is but a year younger than yourself, should be my great grandson;
but my eldest child married into another branch of the family
when young, whereas your father was middle-aged when you
were born. My eldest daughter, then, Charles's grandmother,
whose son—the father of Charles, when he was quite a boy,
married—ah! I am confusing myself! Well, his wife died soon
after giving birth to Charles. She was a pretty, amiable woman,
and had a fortune of £3000 per annum; but the greater part of
the money was lost in an unfortunate speculation—I don't like
anything but landed or funded property—and it has dwindled
down through mismanagement, I fear, to much less—so that poor
Charles in fact is anything but rich."

The younger Lady Walsingham resigned herself to her fate
with a sigh, knowing from experience, that her grandmother
never wearied on the subject of their genealogy, &c. But fortunately for her, there was now a tap at the door, and on Lady
Walsingham saying, "Come in," a female of pleasing appearance,
somewhat past middle age, entered. She was a little, slight
woman, with grey hair, a gentle and pensive face, and neatly and
tastefully attired.

"Well, Mrs. Oakleigh, have you had Master Charles's bed
aired?" inquired the ancient lady of the housekeeper,—for such
was the office of the new comer.

"I have, my lady," replied Mrs. Oakleigh, in a low, sweet,
and distinct voice, which, although the centenarian was rather
deaf, she heard perfectly. "I have come," she added, "to inform your ladyships of something which it is painful to me to
impart; but it is my duty to do so. The young woman, Sarah
Stokes—"

" Yes," interrupted the old lady, " your cousin's cousin."

" Sarah Stokes," continued the housekeeper, her lip slightly quivering, " has not conducted herself with the propriety I could wish." She paused, as if considering how to proceed.

" O, I hope it is nothing serious?" said Lady Walsingham.

" The subject is one which must be as painful to your ladyship as myself; and perhaps Miss Helen will go and play on the lawn while I speak to you."

" Go, my dear," said the younger lady to her daughter, who obeyed immediately.

" I shall relate the facts at once," proceeded Mrs. Oakleigh. " I hope she has not acted *criminally*, in its worst sense; but she certainly has most imprudently. A few hours ago, I was going up the back stairs to the upper rooms, when I saw Sarah, permitting herself to be kissed by---by Master William."

" Indeed!" exclaimed both ladies at once.

" Some words were spoken, the meaning of which I did not exactly comprehend : but Sarah denied some imputation strongly, saying, ' My mother knows nothing, I am sure.' As the words were yet on her lips, they both saw me, and went away in confusion. I told Sarah to come to me in my room; and she was very impertinent when I addressed her seriously on the levity of her conduct; but I *might* have passed it over, hoping she would never misbehave again, if I had not received information from one of the other servants, which leads me to suspect that such familiarities have before occurred. I would not put the worst construction on the affair; but I must leave that to your ladyship's judgment. I can only express my deep regret, my lady, that I should have been the means of introducing into your household, one who seems to have conducted herself so ill. It was from a wish to take her away from her bad old mother, and at the solicitation of my nephew Smith, that I gave her, with your ladyship's permission, the situation she has now filled so long. I think, if I may venture to give my opinion to your ladyships, that Sarah must no longer remain in the house with Master William, lest evil come of it. And I can only hope that you will forgive me for having brought one into the family who has proved so indiscreet."

" I am sure, Oakleigh, you have not been to blame," said the aged lady. "I will speak both to Master William and Sarah; but I will not---and I think that my granddaughter will not---dismiss the girl, without giving her a chance of retrieving her character. Without reputation, young women are driven to despair. She is related to you, and I feel interested in her. What has become of her old sweetheart, Samuel Stokes, your cousin, lately?"

"I think I saw him a minute ago, talking with Corporal Figgins outside," answered Mrs. Oakleigh. "As I have now done my duty, I will go and speak to him; but I hope your ladyship, through kindness to my feelings, will not extend too great a degree of lenity to Sarah."

"You have been a faithful servant, Oakleigh, and we should be most ungrateful if we were not kind to you," returned Lady Walsingham. "For thirty years you have been attached to our house, and I look upon you as a friend. But we must ponder well before we decide. Ah! what was that shout?"

"Oh, mamma," exclaimed little Helen Walsingham, as she rushed into the room, breathless with haste. "Here is cousin Charles, at last." And while she yet spoke, a tall and martial form was seen at the door, and the aged lady cried,

"What, can that be Charles?"

"My dear grandmother," said Captain Walsingham, advancing quickly, and embracing the venerable woman, "your hundred years have visited you lightly indeed. My cousin Fanny, and my aunt, right glad am I to see your sweet face again! And is this little Helen? Kiss me, my pretty one! Ah, worthy Oakleigh, I must kiss you, too—the best-hearted creature alive!"

While these greetings were going on, there was one who stood at the threshold—behind which numerous eager faces might be seen—who appeared not to participate in the general hilarity. It was William Walsingham; who presently quitted the scene and the house in moody reverie.

"What a fine fellow William is grown!" exclaimed Charles. "I forgot to ask about Francis."

"Frank is at sea, you know," said Lady Fanny, her cheek colouring slightly as she spoke to her husband's nephew.

"I have been long coming, but you were informed of the cause of my delay?" said Charles.

"Oh yes, but why did you not let us know where you were, that we might send to you, or come and nurse you?"

Charles was taken aback at this question, which he was not prepared to answer; for, indeed, he was not aware that his relations were unacquainted with his recent abode, and had thought it at the time unkind that they had not sent to inquire after him: he was, however, so occupied with Ellen that he did not bestow much thought on aught beside. But supposing that Ellen's father might have some secret motive for desiring his residence might not be known to any, he returned an evasive answer; and had no difficulty in turning the conversation, with the multiplicity of things he had to talk about.

Meanwhile, William Walsingham had wandered forth without any definite purpose, unless to indulge his gloomy feelings unobserved. It was a lovely moonlight, and though it was late, the radiance of the planet compensated for the beams of the sun, and silvered every object with its mellow floods of lustre. He observed, as he quitted the precincts of the grounds immediately attached to the mansion, Corporal Figgins engaged in conversation with a cripple; but without stopping for an instant even to return the salutation of the former, he strode onwards, many bitter and passionate things within him. At length, having reached an old hollow tree, which grew at the extremity of a fine park, he stopped and leant against it; when without any apparent cause, he suddenly broke forth into a fit of his strange, unnatural laughter, which was like nothing earthly; but it was more strange and hollow even than usual.

"All the world is mad at times," he exclaimed, "I am convinced! What is it to me that this same cousin of mine was born after a certain legal ceremony had been performed between his father and mother? And yet, forsooth, I am troubling my dull brain about it. Poor blockhead that I am! Let the fools and knaves whom custom and cunning have made rich and courted, and *noble*—save the mark!—pay honour to the cant and humbug whereby they live. But oh, it were most vile for one who has drank of the streams of high philosophy, to trouble his heart that such things are. Let Time perform its everlasting cycle, and let the bubbles which float upon its tide burst as they list. Flow on, dark river, flow on! Thou art sprung from tears, dreams, and *empty* smiles! Thou art peopled with delusions, falsehood, wretchedness, and error." Tears were starting into the Atheist's eyes, but he suffered them to roll unheeded down his sallow cheeks, and continued his melancholy monologue. " Millions of years have passed, and worlds have been destroyed, and new ones reproduced. Thus will it ever be! What is it that a solitary worm must hug the chain of woe to his desolate bosom? What matters it that all should seem to him a chaos, a wilderness, and a void? There are smiles of love around, there is merry laughter, and wild excitement. Perhaps the wisest, because the wildest thing for such as I am to do, is to plunge headlong into the engulphing ocean, where all is lost, sooner or later. Let me bask in the light of splendid beauty, with kisses in which there may be deadly poison, but in which there is frenzied joy also ; let me quaff to the dregs of pleasure, let me love, let me drink of the wine cup, until the veins run with a perpetual lava stream, careless of death, careless of annihilation ; let me see the roses, but not the thorns, inflame my heart, debase my intellect ; crush all that is lofty, all that is sublime within me ; and when at last the hand of destruction is on my being, render up my breath, certain never to draw it more!"

Oh, Walsingham, thou erring, noble, sinful being! That one so like an angel in thy original brightness should have fallen as thou didst fall! Not yet, indeed, had the Eternal Night closed upon thy spirit :—thou hadst still thy mighty thoughts, thy dreams, and aspirations ; and despite the wretched creed which thou didst hold—like the divine creation of Milton, of which thou art in some degree a resemblance (the mortal, instead of the immortal fallen!)—thou appearedst less only than Archangel ruined! If all the gushing tenderness of thy soul had been centred in the pure and beautiful, though sorrow might have settled on thee, and affliction crushed thy youth's dear hopes, thou wouldst have soared to the throne of Love, and reclined thy throbbing brain upon a pillow smoothed by the hands of guardian spirits, and sweetened by thine eternal Father's smile. O blessed balm, which can alone heal the bruised heart, and restore the wounded peace! Seraphs would have comforted thee, Virtue would have been present—Heaven would have crowned, most assuredly, thy existence.

But it might not be. There *may* be pardon for all ; but thou wert guilty, debased, and lost. . . . . It is the will of God that there should be crime and error in the world. *He* did not create them : for He is indeed free from all taint, or possibility of it. But it is evident, for some inscrutable purpose, He does not exert His Omnipotence to crush what is bad : and therefore even out of evil, such as that of a great mind overthrown, good must come. We must solace ourselves, when we look abroad, and see the awful calamities which the wretched passions of our fallen nature occasion, that every thing must work to an end which Providence has foreseen. If not a sparrow fall, nor a lily of the field be clothed with beauty, without the hand of Divinity has directed it should be so ; surely the Uncreated One has a purpose inconceivably great in suffering these sad things to be. The good and loving man who reflects on these mysteries, may deplore the effects of guilt, but he is certain that virtue will shine the brighter in the darkness ; and worship what seemeth wise to him, the more he perceives the misery of vice. It may be, " 'twere to inquire too curiously," to plunge into the speculative theories of those who have written on the origin of evil. Nothing satisfactory can be advanced either on the one side, or the other ; but it is obvious that perfect beneficence would not have permitted evil, merely to try a helpless creature whose actions he foresees ; or to let him fall lower than the brutes, without some ulterior end, unsearchable and divine. Here let us pause. And before we venture to question the existence of that Being whose attributes are all holy and perfect, let us look at the state of the Atheist's mind when he is led to doubt, then to deny, and compare it with that of the believer.

The solemn stars were advancing from " the vasty depths" wherein they abide immortal, while all other things fade and die. The Materialist contemplated them with a stern and mournful and meditative eye, and said, " It is well—I will weep no more, I will despair no more. I will exclude from my mind every painful sensation, and live and die regardless of all, except myself. Myriads of miles divide us, oh ye stars ! But my career shall be radiant as yours, while it lasts ! A few, brief years, and I shall be sleeping quietly below, while the silent worm is nestling in this outworn heart—this prematurely destroyed and subtile brain

—for I feel I am sinking, and shall not rise again. I dismiss from my dreams all hopes for man; let others cherish a vain Utopia; but give me the Actual, and I will make an Ideal out of it as beautiful, and—as worthless as a poet's visions. I will be no more Walsingham the Dreamer; but Walsingham the Sensualist. And when the cold world sneers, I will sneer again; I will laugh with it, jest with it, spurn, smile, loathe with it—return curse for curse, jeer for jeer, vengeance for vengeance: and having exhausted all passions and sensations of this stale being, sleep, to wake no more."

CHAPTER VII.

A startling paradox is passion, sir ;—
Wormwood and honey :—brief as mortal thought,—
Eternal as the everlasting word.—GEORGE STEPHENS.

FIGGINS AND STOKES—THE DISCOVERY—THE EPICUREAN—
SALLY—SAM STOKES'S LOVE—THE REVENGE.

WHEN Corporal Figgins and Sam Stokes were conferring as the Epicurean passed by them, they were engaged in a conversation, which it is requisite to record.

"You don't think as I've any reas'nable hope, then, Corporal?" exclaimed Samuel.

"Why, Stokes! women are odd creatures, and take funny fancies into their heads sometimes; but I can't say I think at present you've any chance with Sally. And I'll tell you, if you'll be secret, why. I don't believe she cares much about your legs, as you suppose is the case; but she's in love with somebody else."

Poor Sam here heaved a sigh from the bottom of his heart; and then his eye kindled for a moment, as he said—

"I'll fight the rogue as has stole her love away from me. My eyes! Who is he, Corporal?"

"Nay of that I am ignorant," replied Figgins. "I would

have been civil to her myself, when it was thought you had slipped the cable; but she saucily told me, 'she was food for my betters.' "

"Did she!" ejaculated Sam, thoughtfully. And while he was so speaking, William Walsingham passed, and the sailor's brow darkened ominously when they encountered him. "Food for your betters!" he muttered, "then I see how the land lays. O, my poor Sally! P'rhaps she's been sedooced already by that young blackguard. If so be she has, thof he has high and good blood in his veins, I'll—I'll—well—!"

"Nay, Sam!" cried Figgins, who had his reasons for not wishing the truth to be then known, "you are mistaken there. That Walsingham lad is as proud as the devil; and he wouldn't stoop to what you imagine."

"Wouldn't he!" exclaimed Samuel. "You knows better nor that, Mr. Figgins, sharp as *you* are, and for this reason. Gentlefolks has the same bad passions as others has, and they don't care how they gratifies them; but a poor man is thought the worse of if he does anythink of the kind with a innercent girl. But a gentleman may go and break a hundred hearts, and folks say, 'O, he's got lots of pluck!' and likes him all the better."

Figgins mused.

"If," he thought, "I could get rid of this lad by exposing him, I should lose a troublesome fellow, who reads me through. But at present I must keep terms with him; for he is able to undo me. Stokes," he said, aloud, "don't be rash in your conclusions. The young gentleman is yet quite a boy, and Sally, though still a pretty woman, almost old enough to be his mother."

"She is but nine-and-twenty," returned the sailor, "and don't look even *that*. No, no; there's no such vast difference in their age, Corporal, and poor Sally always had high notions. But if I hadn't led her astray, she mightn't have gone wrong. I shall never forgive myself, you knows how she stands succumstanced, and you knows when a gal has once been imprudent, she's likely to be so twice."

There was a native shrewdness and sagacity in the simple logic of Samuel, which, if Figgins had been a far greater dialectician than he was, would have puzzled him; and truth even in the mouth of the ignorant will confound the sophistry of the wise. But he replied—

"Well, possibly she may have been indiscreet with some person—nothing more—but there are many others beside the youth you have fixed on as the party. She has never said anything about him to you?"

"No," responded Sam, "but look ye here. They lives in the same house together. The boy is a handsome boy, and, thof he was born on the wrong side the blanket, a gentleman bred, anyhow. Sally likes gentlemen, and she's a pretty, saucy woman. They often meets in coorse, and he says something to her, and she will laugh and joke with him. He kisses her—all gentlemen kisses pretty servants, if they'll let 'em,—and what's the consekence?"

"You jump to your conclusions too quickly," said Figgins, laughing. "In the first place, your premises are false. _All_ gentlemen don't kiss pretty servants, even if they would allow it; and this boy, I repeat, though a bastard, is deucedly proud—proud of his intellect, his science, and all that. In addition to which, he is but eighteen, and lads of that age are not up to what we old hands are. Sally, I own, is still a young woman; but not likely to attract the admiration of one such as he is; for he would think her coarse and vulgar."

"Ah!" responded Sam, "what if so be he _is_ as proud as Lucifer? Pride won't make a man more nor less nor sich. I've remarked too, that women, when they gets towards the sharp corner, is fond of boys. And, besides, look at that youth. He's made like a man—broad, deep chest, and firm-set figure! He's got a face of genus—I thinks they call it genus—sich lots of thought there is in it—and for the matter of his not being up to snuff, he's as much so as a chap of thirty. You and I, Corporal, has lived now to middle age, as you says, and know what women is. We're not angels, Mr. Figgins, if so be we aint devils, and flesh and blood is flesh and blood, —— me."

"That's an axiom, as scholars would say," Figgins answered when Sam had clenched his argument with his favourite benediction on himself. "But all I advise you is, by no means to betray what you fancy. I think you're mistaken: so, good night. I've got business to transact before I go to sleep."

Thus saying, the Corporal rolled away, like an elephant, and

Stokes was going into the house, when he suddenly turned, and said—

"What has become of that there little boy, as you took away with 'ee t'other day?"

"O, he's safe with his mother," replied Figgins, turning on his heel for a minute, and then continuing his way.

He took the same path which had previously been pursued by the young philosopher; and having walked for about a quarter of an hour, he abruptly came upon him, just as he finished the soliloquy which ends the last chapter, a dark, yet sublime expression on the face, which Sam had characterised as one of *genus,* which the Corporal perused aright.

A painter could not have wished a better countenance to study, if he had wished to delineate the Satan of Milton (a subject which it seems all artists have hitherto shrunk from) as he pronounced the awful imprecation in the Address to the Sun, which rivals, if it does not surpass, the mightiest poetry of the ancients. There was power, and pride, and pain, and passion in every line of that singular and intellectual face; but not a ray of hope or peace was there: all darkness, like a grand and shadowy night, when strange phantoms appear to float over the ebon sky, starless, moonless: yet the very clouds were magnificent in their gloom.

"Good evening to you, Master William," said the Corporal, putting on his best manners.

"Well," returned the youth, gazing fixedly into the broad, red face of Figgins, who could sometimes affect sentiment, though the very antipodes of a sentimental person, and was preparing a remark, to open a conversation. And the Materialist's eye was yet brighter than the one which glittered beneath the wide, massive forehead of the Corporal.

"It is a beautiful night," said Figgins, "and I suppose that it's splendour has tempted you away from the Hall? I don't wonder, sir, that you, who have such great dreams and ideas, should love solitude in such a spot, and to pour out the heart in deep abstraction from the world. Even I, when I look up to those glorious orbs that shine on us so solemnly, feel thoughts which I cannot define."

It must be observed, that Figgins had caught the phraseology used by scholars, as well as by men of the world, and with ready cleverness could repeat sentiments he had heard, or adapt those he had read.

"Can you describe aught of the nature of those thoughts?" sneered William, who was convinced of the hypocrisy of the Corporal's character.

"Perhaps I can, better than you think," returned Figgins, nettled at the contempt of the youth. "When I gaze into the dark space, which is illuminated with more magnificence than the halls of an earthly palace—quenchless fires, which have glowed with glory when the heroes and conquerors of the past were in the zenith of their greatness, I ask what are they, and whence are they? Who supports them in that vast dome? what mighty hand guides them through the firmament for ever? They may contain men like ourselves, with great intellect, and petty aims, with a soul which can grasp a world; and with a heart which cares for nothing but the present, with its transient light, its fading beauty, its waning pleasures. Or they may be the worlds of creatures whose powers are proportioned to their aspirings, who can enjoy existence, not as *we* enjoy it; but live among unfading raptures, with bright women, and delicious wine, like the Gods of old; all beauty and passion theirs; revelling in scenes of luscious joy, without a dream of pain."

"Ha, ha, ha!" laughed the Epicurean; "pity you have not tried to write poetry, Figgins. Pshaw, man! I know you. You are a shrewd, sordid rascal, whose thoughts never wander from their centre—your amiable self—who cheat the fools, and laugh with the knaves,—who eat, drink, wench, and are content. A great rogue, but a clever one! How like you your portrait?"

"I thought," said Figgins, in some degree returning the sarcasm of the Materialist, "that you consider there is no such thing as vice or virtue?"

"Well, Corporal! Are you going to philosophize, as well as launch forth into the poetics? Take my advice, man, and stick to the earth—the good, old, dirty, foul, rotten earth, which is well enough for such as you are. Why were any others ever born? You are a most wonderful man, truly. But O, sagacious Figgius! you understand not the distinctions of science. A bad act *is* a bad act: you could not help performing it; but whatever is inimical to morality is, of course, a vile thing. All is either foul or fair in its nature."

"If I were to cut your throat, of course I couldn't help it," returned the Corporal. "Circumstances, over which I have no control, you know!"

"Sly dog! you are a wit!" replied the Epicurean. "But if I have no control over circumstances, I can create them. And whenever I discover roguery, I think it incumbent on me to unmask it."

"Of a verity," responded Figgins, assuming a sanctimonious air. "But look you, Master William Walsingham,"—here again changing his manner—" we know each other. You are an intellectual, and I a sensible man. We know the world; you from reflection, I from experience. You wish for pleasure;—that is natural at your age. I wish for money, being almost sick of what you're seeking. We are acquainted with some of each other's doings—"

"Do you dare," cried William, fiercely striding up to Figgins, and hissing his words through his clenched teeth, with a voice low, but distinct, in spite of its suppressed passion, "do you dare, low scoundrel that you are! to insult me?"

For an instant the stout spirit of the veteran soldier failed him, as he beheld the flashing eyes, the dilated nostril and haughty brow of the Materialist, and heard the fierce accents of his wrath; but he was not a man to tremble beneath the frown of breathing mortal: and he replied—

"Come, come; don't let us get into a passion! That's never of any use. Hear me out calmly. Not only do *I know;* but others suspect your intrigue with Sally—"

"What!" exclaimed William, seizing Figgins by the throat with ungovernable rage, and shaking him, huge man as he was, as if he had been a stripling, in a convulsion of passion.

The Corporal, with no slight exertion of his strength, shook off his boyish assailant; and said—

"Now, be calm, and let us reason the matter like men together. If you don't want it to be known, well and good. I won't blab. Only be more prudent than you have been. I myself have engaged in a hundred such affairs; but have managed them all with perfect secrecy. Take counsel from an old stager; and when you kiss, let it be where none can peep at you. The cook saw you kissing Sally the other day."

"Excellent!" cried the Epicurean, in his usual cold, sarcastic way. "What a joke for all the servants!" Then he added, bitterly, "To be grinned at by a parcel of ignorant boors, and coarse country wenches! Well, you want me to keep your secrets, Mr. Figgins! But it seems *my* secret is out!"

"O," said the Corporal, slyly, "I see you are no greenhorn! But look you here. Every servant in Walsingham Hall has done something which none of them would like known. It has always been my plan to possess myself of those little mysteries; they give one more power than you'd believe. I have all these domestics under my thumb, and I'll take care they shall not annoy you."

The Epicurean paced up and down with an uncertain air, and with gall and aconite in his heart.

"No; I will leave the place," he muttered. And without saying another word to Figgins, he stalked away.

"He's a clever fellow, hang him!" said the Corporal to himself. I hate him from my soul; but I daren't do what I wish. It isn't often that we can: but a time will come."

While this scene was acting, and determining the destiny of the Materialist, Sam Stokes had entered Walsingham Hall, intent on seeing his cousin, whom he found in the kitchen, saying to the cook, "What a fine man the Captain is, to be sure."

"Ah, I suppose he'll take master William's place in your heart," sneered the cook.

"Hold your tongue, you saucy slut," replied Sally, angrily.

While the words trembled on her lips she beheld Sam, gazing mournfully upon her. She was a pretty, rosy-cheeked woman, with a laughing eye, dark brown hair, a low but well-formed figure, and much impudence in her face. Though her features were not regular—the nose being inclined to the snub formation, and the mouth being large, and not finely moulded—yet the teeth were so white, and the eyes so mirthful, and the whole countenance so bright and animated, that she was exactly the style of beauty calculated to attract the vulgar, who can admire coarseness and rude vivacity.

"Can I speak with 'ee alone, Sally?" asked Samuel, without lifting his eyes from the ground on which he had fixed them.

"Oh, if you wish it; but I wish you wouldn't come bothering me," she replied, leading the way into the pantry, he murmuring, "I shan't bother her long," as he followed; and, the door being closed, he exclaimed, with much emotion,

"Sally, I have been faithful to you, these many, many years; and, before I lost my legs, women as pretty to look on—though not so pretty to me—would have been happy to let me court 'em: but I wouldn't, Sally; for I always considered you my wife, in all but the name. I saw that unhappy creetur of ourn t'other day. And, wretch thof he be, I'll love him, Sally, for your sake, if I can. He shall come and live with me: your mother has made him what he is with her deviltries. But, oh! I can't bear to find as you've given yourself to that young Walsingham————"

"Impudence!" here interrupted the woman, "who told you that lie?"

"It's no use for to deny it, Sally,—I *knows* it," returned the sailor. "In coorse, you've a right to do as you likes; and since I've met with my misfortin, I can't well expect you should marry me. But I'd have had *you*, Sally, without legs, or arms, or precious eyes. But oh, Sally, live decent and honest. I've got a little cash, which I'll give you as a marriage portion, if so be you'll take some worthy man for your husband, and return to vartue once more. I hopes some one will love and cherish you as I would! I knows I did very wrong to betray you, by taking advantage of your affection for me—you *did* love me once, cousin dear! And I wish to make some amends to you, for I thinks it may be from having once fallen, you've done so again. Oh, Sally, dear Sally!"

"Don't dear Sally me!" exclaimed the woman indignantly, turning away from Stokes.

"Yes, *dear* Sally," continued Sam, "think how wrong it is! This here lad will desert ye, and you'll lose for ever your k'racter. What can ye do then? Leave this house, Sally: and don't go to your mother's—she's a bad un. But try to get some other place; and here's a purse for ye."

A little affected by the genuine tenderness and kindness of the poor sailor, Sally answered, "Your fancies are wide of the mark, Sam. Put up your purse; I won't take it. It aint be-

cause you're so maimed I refuse to marry you. I think you're a
good-hearted chap, and I always thought so. Ah, there's the
bell. I must leave you. Ask the butler to give you something
to drink, and then go home. There, we part friends; your hand;
good night.",

"Stay a moment, Sally," cried Sam, despairingly. "We once
was all the world to each other. I love you still, Sally, far more
than this old shatfered hull, in which the heart beats as warmly
as ever. When I'm dead and gone, and the worms crawl in my
cold bussum, you'll sometimes think, 'Poor feller, *he* was true
to me.' Yes, thof the world called ye bad names, and druv ye to
despair, ye should find a home in my breast, a port in my arms.
If I could die for ye, I would gladly. Oh, Sally, if ye feel anythink still for me, take my advice; and you'll be happy yet."

"No, no," was the reply, "I cannot. Besides, if I left my
place now, it would seem as if I was sent away; and I don't
know but what I shall be, as it is. Sam, I'm very wretched!"
And she burst into a flood of tears. "I feign what I don't feel
when I speak so audaciously. My heart sometimes seems as if
it was breaking."

"My own Sally! now you are my own loved girl," said Sam,
taking her hand, while his own shook terribly, strong as were his
nerves. "Listen," he continued, with deep feeling, "you, as
well as me, believes there's a great God aloft, and that He par-
dons those as repents. None as does wrong *can* be happy, however rich and great they be. But if we tries to do well, Sally, as
much as our poor natur lets, what a sweet thing it is to know
we've a friend in Heaven who loves us like his children,—when
all's sorrow and storm around. My dear cousin, you've done
wrong like me; I can't never forgive myself, 'cos I feels that
I've been the cause of all this here. But you'll be forgiven, as I
hopes I shall, and in the arms of some honest man you'll be
happy—very happy!" And sobs heaved the broad chest of the
sailor.

Fine, rough son of Nature, thou wert a nobler being far than
the elegant, accomplished, polished slave of empty fashions and
hollow forms, without the heart to despise the little follies of the
crowd, without a soul to soar above the atmosphere breathed by
the Helots of thy tribe! Talk not of munificent charities, of

splendid gifts, of disinterested patronage. Lord of a million, come here, and look upon this picture! The truth, fervour, devotion, of a brave single-minded tar should make thee sink into nothingness in thine own esteem, unless thou canst act and feel like him. The poet may eulogize a hero's courage, a patriot's firm and unwavering love of his country; but to love like Samuel Stokes—without hope, without a thought of self—by heaven, it was sublime!

The misguided Sally was also weeping; but she checked her tears, which gushed forth the more abundantly as she felt what a treasure of fidelity she had thrown away, and said, "I thank you, Sam, for all your kindness; but it is too late. God bless you! I am a lost, guilty woman; but I will pray for you, if ever I pray again."

The appeal of Sam had not been vain. He had touched the right chord, and Sally stood humbled and heart-broken before him. The eloquence of the pulpit would not have availed, the terrors of religion would not have awed her; but there is almost always ' something of the angel left,' when the soul has fallen from the purity of its heaven.

" I need your prayers," quoth Sam ; " but why don't you say them now ?"

"Of what use is it to pray, when you know you are doing evil? I have been as much to blame as him—more so. He was a mere boy, and I, no girl; but I musn't go on." And with these words, Sally, fearful lest she should reveal all, having unburthened her heart so far, ran out of the pantry, and Sam, with an aching heart, stumped off.

There is something calculated to move every soul in the withering of the hopes of the young visionary, when he perceives the fallacy of his early aspirations, and droops and dies of disappointment. The spectacle of a great man struggling with the storms of fate, and pursuing the course of rectitude in the face of peril and calamity, until ingratitude stabs home to his central life, is lofty and divine. But, if than these less beautiful and august, the desolation of a generous heart and simple nature, unsupported by any philosophy save that derived from its integrity and virtue, is not less affecting, and to be commiserated. Indeed, what has the humble, the lowly being, who can never obtain

3 M

posthumous fame, to sustain him in misfortune like that which now visited the sailor? In many a dire disaster, his love had lent him strength; and he had struggled on, when pain nearly made life insupportable, in the hope of pressing a faithful mistress to his bosom; but Sam, like more ambitious men, was doomed to experience all the misery of blighted love, and to see an existence before him, uncheered by affection, and unblessed by sympathy, maimed as he was, and no longer young, the buoyancy of his spirit crushed, and not one pleasant ray to lend sunshine to his breast, and impart the elasticity and hopefulness he had lost. The philosopher may call stoicism to his aid; the poet, like gentle, glorious Keats, our well-beloved, may see " the daisies growing o'er his grave," may behold maidens weeping over his sorrows and untimely death, and fine and ethereal spirits like his own, not born to rot in the corruption of a dunghill worldliness, mourning for him with sincerity; but one like the poor tar, without knowledge, without the panting desire for future admiration, could only sigh over his departed dreams, and lament the falsehood which brought him to such a pass.

"Poor soul!" thought Sam, his thoughts dwelling with pitying fondness on his unworthy cousin, " after all, who should blame her? She was but fifteen, when I left her, and it warn't likely she'd be true to me, thinking as I was dead."

A few words are necessary to explain the exact position of Stokes and Sally, at this place. The sailor had formerly been a carpenter; but not liking his trade, went to sea, when quite a youth. On returning, after a very long absence, he found Sally, whom he had left a child, grown womanly in appearance, though a mere girl, and she being pretty, and her cousin's heart of inflammable materials, " not being that ill-favoured" then, they formed an attachment for each other. They were to have been married shortly; and, indeed, Sam had actually bought the wedding ring: but fate ordained that they should not then be united. They were imprudent before their union had taken place, and the week before the proposed celebration of their nuptials, Sam having gone to a small sea-port to see an old messmate, a pressgang bore him away; and he was soon hundreds of miles distant from the shores of England. A few months after his departure, Sally was delivered of the unhappy being whom we have seen in the monster; and intelligence reached her that the ship in which Sam was, had foundered. Sally was much grieved at this news; but she was then a light-hearted girl; and she soon got over her loss, and entered into the service of Lady Walsingham. But few were acquainted with the indiscretion of which she had been guilty, her mother living at some distance from any habitation, and the miserable offspring, who was at this time more hideously misshapen, if possible, than afterwards, was seldom seen abroad, when able to go alone. Sally had conceived such a horror to her unhappy child, that no persuasions could induce her to nurse it; and the ape of which mention has been made several times (a present of Sam's—who brought the creature from abroad—to his aunt) being with young, she suckled the boy, who grew very strong, and before he had attained the age of three years, was at least equal in vigour to children of double his age, running about in the woods with his wet-nurse, and climbing enormous trees with no less agility than the monkey.

But, to return to Sally. She conducted herself with perfect propriety for many years, in the service of Lady Walsingham, and though she was what is termed a flirt, nothing was observed in her which could excite even the animadversion of the worthy housekeeper. At the age of fourteen, William Walsingham quitted school, his master asserting that he had discovered him delivering lectures in favour of atheism to the other boys, and that he was quite unmanageable. A man in mind, and almost one in appearance, even at that early age, with violent passions, and such principles as he had adopted, he was thrown in the way of Sally Stokes, and it was not likely he should resist temptation. Sally and he were equally culpable: and the result of their intimacy was now fast approaching to a crisis.

Sam stumped along briskly, considering the loss of his legs, and soon left the Hall at a great distance behind him; when, just as he was about to get over a gate, midway between the mansion of the Walsinghams and his own little cabin, he beheld the being through whose instrumentality all his joys had been wrested from him, and all his hopes in life defeated, engaged in moody thought at the distance of a few yards. The dark demon which lurk in the breast even of the most virtuous, was busy

within the heart of Stokes at this encounter, inflamed as his passions were, after his recent interview with his old sweetheart, and
seizing the Epicurean by the arm, as he came up to him, he exclaimed in a hoarse voice, half-choked with wrath and vehemence—

"We have met, have we, Master William Walsingham! I
want to speak to ye."

William raised his hand, with the intention of striking the
rude person who had thus grasped him, to the earth; but when
he beheld his maimed condition, merely said, "What would
you have with me?" And he remained motionless, in expectation
of the rejoinder of the sailor.

CHAPTER VIII.

Come, then, my masters, let's be merry all!
If Life is short, 'tis best we make the best
Of what we can; and drink, and jest, and sing.
Old Play.

THE STRUGGLE—DANVERS IN DISGUISE—THE CAPTURE—
MOTHER STOKES AND THE SAVAGE.

"Look ye," returned Samuel. "After an absence of fourteen
years, I came back to England, with Mr. Spenser. Mayhap
you've heard of Sam Stokes—mayhap not; but that's no matter. I knew your father, the Admiral—as brave and true a
heart as ever lived, and I've dandled you in my arms, when you
was a babby. But listen. My cousin, Sally Stokes, was my
sweetheart; and I loved her more than all this airth—loved as
you never *could* have done, by ———!"

"Ha! Well?" exclaimed William, with stifled emotion.

"Yes, I thought she should be my wife; and we should have
pretty children to comfort us in old age; and when I'd got
enough to make us comfortable,—when there wasn't any reason
why she shouldn't be my wife, for she *would* have taken me, I

know, even as I am now—I find you've crossed my path like a dark sarpent, and here I am, riding at the marcy of the gale, without mast, sail, or compass. You've made this wreck of me! Oh, Master Walsingham, it may seem a small matter to you, to crush a honest heart—to bring a woman to shame...." Here Sam's voice became inarticulate from suffocating passion; but at length he was able to add, " You have your larning, your wisdom, and all that which rules this world in cleverness and understanding, and power and mind. But I have no parts, I have no knowledge; and I only thinks as my conscience pilots me, and acts as I thinks right, without argufying; but if I could act as you've acted, I should think myself one of the blackest-hearted villains as ever lived. You may frown and colour—well you may blush for your misdeeds; but I don't care."

"Release me!" cried William Walsingham, in his deep, calm, thrilling voice, " or I may commit murder. Man, I caution you that what you say is rousing terrible things within me. I will not be held thus by you!"

"You *shall* hear me out," said the sailor, with suppressed fierceness in his tone; "great thof you think yourself, you shall hear my mind. We are here, man and man, with the great God above us, and stand equal in his sight. I don't care for your threats. I have stood against a hundred bristling pikes, and have got as many scars on my breast."

Ay, there they were, with awful human passions, in the holy stillness of that lovely evening, and the stars shone as sweetly and tenderly on them as on the spirit soaring to beatitude.

The face of the Epicurean grew livid, then white, then red, and then again pale as death, as he struggled in the grasp of Stokes, who seemed now to possess the strength of a Hercules, as he tightened his iron grasp.

"Death!" shouted Walsingham, the proud and impetuous blood of the haughty Normans from whom he was descended conquering all his philosophy, and boasted love of equality. " Death! I will not be restrained by a low dog, like you!'

And he dealt Stokes a blow which would have struck him down on the instant, had not the tar averted it with his fist. The passions of both men were furiously excited, and they hardly knew what they did. A struggle ensued: but Stokes laboured under the disadvantage of want of height from the loss of his legs, as well as being less firm on his stumps than he would have been, of course, on his feet; and by a great effort William dashed him to the earth, when he struck his head against the gate so desperately as to stun himself. In an instant the expression of the young man's face altered.

"Poor wretch!" he cried; "what have I done? Base villain that I am! O," he continued, as Sam recovered, "forgive me, Stokes! I am indeed a scoundrel! I hope you are not much hurt.—Begone all pride of intellect, of birth and education—begone my principles of necessity—everything—gallant fellow, forgive me!"

"Nay, nay," exclaimed the tar. "I didn't intend to do what I've done. You haven't wronged me; but you've wronged Sally, and yourself, and society, and God."

"Well, well!" returned William, "I wish you good night. Can I make you any reparation for the injury I have done you? I will go to Sally—she told me you wished to marry her—and plead your cause, if you will let me."

"No, no," answered the sailor, his weather-beaten face flushing, "not *that*. Pray to the Lord to pardon you;—for such a worm as me has nothing to pardon."

"I would do so," replied William, "even at your suggestion, if I believed such a Being existed. Once more, good night."

"What! You don't think there's a God!" ejaculated Sam. "Ah, sir! Then I can easy account for all you've done. From my soul I pity ye."

"Pity me, good fellow! But you are right. I *am* to be pitied— I accept even your pity. You know not how I have sunk in my own esteem to-day. Farewell! May you be happy!"

Thus the Atheist left Stokes, who gazed after him, and thought, "There's a fine heart in him yet! Not believe in a God! Then he thinks as how there's no heaven, and when we die we perish, like brutes. What a strange belief in what is to make one miserable. I'm glad I'm not larned."

Leaving Sam Stokes, and his humble feelings, our chronicle must now resume the thread which had been broken off, and return to more important personages.

So necessary had the papers which he had entrusted to little

George become to Danvers, that he resolved to risk everything to ascertain their fate; and convinced of the fidelity and trust-worthiness of his clever little friend, he was fearful that his share in effecting his own liberation had been discovered, and he was in consequence imprisoned. Old Quirk, the lawyer, had been taken suddenly ill, but he had sent him a letter, (though how he discovered his whereabouts was a mystery), in which he made great promises of assistance to him, in clearing his character from the stigma of the murder he had been condemned for. Mother Stokes, added the attorney, was lying concealed, but he should be able to find means to communicate with her ere long.

Some days after the occurrences narrated in the foregoing chapter, after having visited all the influential Jacobites in the country, Danvers repaired at a late hour to the inn where his daughter was; having given up the house he had previously occupied, on receiving intimation that it was known as his to the authorities. Mrs. Haines had returned, after removing various articles of furniture; and they only waited for Harry ere they departed to another residence at the distance of a few miles from the quarters they occupied at this time. It was dusk when Danvers, once more having donned his female attire, entered the inn, and proceeded to his daughter's apartment. Not unseen did he enter the place; for a smartly, but vulgarly dressed lad of about sixteen, was standing at a few paces from the door by which he made his ingress, and gazed at him scrutinizingly. Danvers did not see him, or he would have noticed the same boy he had bound hand and foot some days before, though much better attired. But the disguise Walter wore was good, and might have baffled even the keen eyes of young Isaac Quirk—for he it was—if other circumstances had not militated against him.

"Betty, my dear!" said Isaac, to a red-cheeked chamber-maid of about his own age,—to whom he used to make love when a stable-boy at the Britannia—entering the house, "I want to speak with ye a minute. Haven't ye got two ladies staying here?"

"Ay, to be sure. They've been here ever so long."

"Very good. Does any one come to them, my love?"

"No, not as I knows of. But I'll tell you a cur'ous sucam-stance. T'other morning I see the prints of a man's shoe—which

Boots says as how he don't believe was mortal—from their room
door down the back stairs. Now our young Boots says he see a
ghost the night afore pass out o' that there door to which the
steps lead. But I've an idea ther's no sich thing as ghosts; and
they're no better nor they should be."

"O, indeed! How did he describe the ghost, my love?"

"Why, it were something like a man, and something like a
woman, but in a woman's dress, he says."

"Ah! *I* never see a ghost," returned Isaac, "and I never
heard of a ghost leaving the mark of a dirty step behind. You
didn't see that there female as went up the back stairs just now?"

"No, I didn't," answered the chamber-maid.

"So: there's a shilling, and there's a kiss for you," said Isaac.

"Impudence!" giggled Betty, who was very civil to her old
lover, now that he was rising in the world.

Young Quirk left Betty, and put the thumb of his right hand
to his nose. The nose and the thumb were moulded much alike,
only that the former had a comical twist upwards, yet there was
something in that fat snub indicating a keen scent.

"There's no reason as I knows of why I shouldn't do a job on
my own account," he muttered. He produced a paper from his
pocket, and read, 'Walter Danvers—description of. He is of
middle height, but strongly made, with a scar on the forehead.'
"Jist so!" said Isaac to himself. "'Prominent features; age,
about eight-and-thirty.' It must be him," thought Mr. Quirk,
junior. "'In addition to the original reward of £100 offered
for his apprehension, Captain Norton promises the sum of £1000
for his person.'" Isaac chuckled. "I'll have him!" he exclaimed,
"before he be one hour older."

Accordingly, young Isaac strutted away: and leaving him for
the present, our narrative must return to Danvers.

After answering the anxious inquiries of Ellen and Elizabeth,
he announced his intention of going in disguise to the Britannia,
and endeavouring to discover the whereabouts of little George;
and though his resolution was strongly opposed, Mrs. Haines
offering to repair to the inn herself, and gather what intelligence
she could, Danvers replied that he should run no risk, and at that
hour the Britannia was not a place fit for a decent woman to
enter. Its character, indeed, had become notoriously bad, and it

was nearly deserted by all respectable persons. In addition to this, Danvers thought he should more easily trace George than Mrs. Haines could; so he substituted for his female attire a new disguise, which he had sent to Elizabeth from a neighbouring town the day before in a parcel. This dress consisted of an old-fashioned suit, such as was worn twenty years before, a large wig, a slouching hat, which concealed the upper part of his face; with sundry other articles of minor importance; and when he had placed some patches on his cheek, and assumed the gait of an elderly man, it would have been difficult to recognise the stout, bold, Walter Danvers in any light less broad than that of day; and even then none but those intimate with him could have detected the cheat. As it was now nearly dark, Walter sallied forth, promising to return in the course of an hour, and assuming the airs of a faded beau, who had flourished in the preceding century, hastened to the Britannia.

As he approached the inn, he could hear shouts of boisterous laughter, accompanied by oaths and screams, and on entering the tap-room, where he thought he should be able to procure the desired information of the landlord, he beheld a scene of confusion and uproar which baffles all description.

It was the annual meeting of an association called the "Jolly Boys," and consisting of all the rustic Roués, and sporting characters for some miles around. Of these, some were already drunk, and lying under the table, chairs having been overset, and candles and mugs dashed down, with crockery and wine bottles. Others were roaring snatches of hunting songs; and some, with loose women seated on their knees, were playing off practical jokes, exceedingly relished by the spectators, which were retaliated with interest; while a few, whose brains were not so excited by liquor, were talking and laughing and looking around, much diverted, and smoking, and drinking, and eating with little interruption, by turns.

At the head of a huge table, distinguished by his size, and jolly visage, sat an individual, in whom Danvers had no difficulty in recognising Figgins. His stentorian lungs could be heard distinctly above all the din; and he was amusing the company with some indecency, which set them all in a roar.

"Come! I'll give you a song, my lads, if you'll make a little

3 N

less noise!" vociferated the Corporal, who was chairman on the
occasion—not because he was the wealthiest or most important
person there (for the "Jolly Club" admitted of no such distinctions)—but from his well-known convivial qualities. "I'll make
a song on you all," cried Figgins, commencing—

> " Here are gathered the young, and the old, and the bright;
> How delighted they all are this glorious night!
> How they talk and they laugh, drink, kiss, smoke, smile, and swear,
> And with shouts of good fellowship rend all the air!
> 'Tis the Night of good fellows, the Night of all joys!
> Come, then, join in the chorus, my own Jolly Boys!
> There is time both for singing, for swearing, and love!
> Ev'ry thought, every feeling is brilliant, by Jove!
>
> " Look at yonder old fellow who reels in his chair!
> We'll give him sweet thunder to rouse him up there!
> How he turns up his eyes, like a duck in a storm—
> Hoist him up, Boys! Ha! ha! what a big-bellied form!
> There's a gallon of old ale, I bet, 'neath his vest!
> Give him more! give him more! Make him drunkenly blest!
> There ne'er was a sinner so fond of the stuff!
> By St. Thomas! for once we will give him enough!
>
> " Look at yonder young fellow, his girl on his knee!
> I'll warrant he'd go to old Nick, sirs, for she——"

" None of your jokes on me!" here interrupted the last person
alluded to in the extemporaneous effusion of the Corporal's genius,
—who was a strapping farmer, noted for his pugilistic powers,
and his prowess in drinking and every other vice,—with an oath.
" I'll beat the breath out of your big body, Tom Figgins——"

" Ah! give it him!" exclaimed several of the assembly who
were pot-valiant: but as soon as the redoubtable farmer fixed his
eyes firmly on those who wished Figgins to fight, they became
suddenly mute.

" Nay, an ye threaten, fighting Tim, I'm your man!" quoth
the Corporal, coolly tossing off a bumper, while the young farmer, inflamed with copious libations, and knowing that Figgins
intended another practical joke, similar to that which had been
played off on the old fellow who had been drenched with his
favourite beverage, on himself, strode up to him, and shook his
fist in his face. The Corporal rose up in a moment, seized the

sturdy farmer by the neck and breech, and tossed him to the
other end of the room.

"Bravo, Corporal!" shouted the admirers of Figgins, after
he had made this prodigious display of strength, as they clustered
round him, and patted him on the back, although they had not
previously dared to brave the wrath of ' fighting Tim.'

Meantime, Danvers looked vainly for the landlord, who was,
in fact, overcome with his own powerful liquor, and snoring
beneath the table, and Walter meditated a retreat, in order to see
if he could not find some one who could satisfy his anxiety about
George, when the keen eye of Figgins perceived him, and he exclaimed—

"That's a specimen of the fashion of Queen Anne's day!
Bring him here, my masters, and we'll have some sport with him!
I see ' fighting Tim' has broken his thick head in his fall."

"Nay," said Danvers, as several persons were about to put
the wishes of Figgins into execution; and drawing a pistol from
his coat pocket, "I always return practical jokes, and if any one
touches me, I shall shoot him."

One man, who was a sporting character, and was considered
the best wrestler in the county, desirous of imitating the example
Corporal Figgins had set, here shouted—

"Leave the old chap to me, lads! What say you to a tussle,
my ancient cock? You've got a broad pair of shoulders, anyhow.
Put that cursed bull-dog up, and let's see if you've got the manli-
ness to stand up for yourself without making it bark."

"O, if you wish it!" responded Danvers, still speaking in the
voice of an elderly personage, and suiting the word to the deed.
"Now, Sir Bully, though I'm no longer a young man, I'll wrestle
with you."

A space was cleared, and the sporting character advanced,
thinking to serve his opponent in the same way Figgins had
treated his man; but to the astonishment of all present, the apparently antiquated beau raised the sturdy wrestler in his arms, and
bumped him against the wall, as if he had been a child. A shout
of laughter succeeded the discomfiture of the boasting fellow, who
having overthrown a great numbers of stalwart antagonists, was
wont to play the bully over all; and Danvers, having punished

his insolence sufficiently, threw him down, and was about to leave
the tap-room, when several individuals cried—

"You must drink one bumper with us! We will give you a
draught fit for a king."

"I thank you, no," returned Danvers, once more about to quit
the place, much disgusted with the vice, excess and extravagance
he had witnessed, when he was met by two constables, accompanied by Isaac Quirk; and the latter exclaimed—

"That must be him! Seize him!"

"Ha!" ejaculated Figgins, who had been watching Danvers
closely, but could not penetrate his disguise, springing instantly
to the door. He was just in time to frustrate the escape of
Walter, who had knocked down the constables with his fists, and
was rushing away, though Isaac Quirk attempted to catch him by
the leg, when the Corporal grasped his arm. "Now, then, brave
Master Walter Danvers!" he said, straining every muscle to hold
him, "now we've got you!"

It was in vain that Danvers struggled to release himself, for
Isaac had got between his legs, to which he clung with dogged
tenacity, despite the terrible kicks he received, and Figgins had
pinioned his arms behind: but though numbers swarmed like bees
around him, and he was clutched on every side, it was not without
a desperate struggle that he was secured.

"Remember," cried Isaac Quirk, when the prisoner was at
length overcome, "I gave the information, and I claim the reward."
Danvers was led away handcuffed; and Figgins quitting the fes-
tive scene, mounted a horse which he had brought with him, and
galloped from the inn.

As the crowd which followed Danvers and the constables from
the Britannia passed through the village it was located in, an old
woman, who had ensconced herself behind a hedge, and who was
accompanied by a misshapen being, hardly human in form,—was
gazing through a hedge which concealed her from view in the
gloom of night; and by the light of a torch, carried by a constable, she descried Danvers a prisoner. As soon as she beheld him,
she rubbed her hands with unutterable glee, and pointed out the
captive to the strange creature she was accompanied by, who
answered her look of exultation with a grin of savage malice. As
soon as the crowd had disappeared, the female and her companion

crept under the hedge, and walked away; but they had not proceeded above a mile, and were crossing a field which led away
from the Britannia in a westerly direction, when they were met
by a youth, whose face denoted abstraction and gloomy reverie,
and whom the savage no sooner beheld, than he ran up to him,
knelt down, and pointed towards a heath which could be dimly
seen in the distance; at the same time making violent gesticulations, and attempting to speak. His whole hideous face was imploring and earnest; and the young man he attempted to make
understand, looked at him with commiseration and interest, and
addressing the female he was with, said—

"Well, Mother Stokes! what is it that this poor wretch would
say to me?"

"Why," answered the woman, "the fact is, my poor ape has
been very ill ever since she was brutally treated by a villain—who
I hope will soon be at the devil!—and is at the point of death.
I can hardly get this boy to leave her; and you having once doc-
tored her before, he thinks, I suppose, you can do so again."

William Walsingham—for it was no other now in conversation
with Mother Stokes—seemed to muse deeply on what had been
said. "He is human still," he muttered.

"Ay," cried the woman, overhearing what William said, "and
a great deal better than many other human devils. Human!
I don't know why we should think better of men than of beasts.
Except that we've more mind, we're just the same."

The Epicurean looked down, and thought, "Exactly! but I
hate to hear this woman say so. . . . I will walk with you," cried
William, plunging into inward metaphysics.

"If you like," replied the amiable lady, "you can come," and
on they went.

"Have you seen your daughter lately?" asked the Epicurean,
after a pause.

"Yes, you know she has left the Hall; but I don't know
where she is now."

"Indeed! I have been absent for some days, and did not know
it. So, this wretched creature is Sally's child?" said William.

"Yes; but she won't own the fact," returned Mother Stokes.

"I must see Sally, if I can, once more. Do you think she
would like me to take the boy under my protection? She might

never see him again ; but he should go wherever I went, and I would clothe and feed him, and do what I could to cultivate the little intellect he has."

The monster started at this proposition, and made gestures to his grandmother.

" Well," exclaimed mother Stokes, " Sally would have no objection ; and I find he's in my way sometimes. But what can you possibly want with such a one as he is? I shouldn't like him to be made a show of."

" What does he wish you to understand by his signs?" asked William, paying no attention to what the reputed witch said.

" He means to say, he would go with you ; but he would not leave his mother—so he calls the ape, who was his wet-nurse, and has been his companion from childhood."

" Then he is capable of strong affection? I should like to try the experiment !" he muttered to himself.

" I would not part with the boy, if I thought you would not treat him well."

" I will pledge myself to that ;" was the reply. " I am going to quit England—perhaps never to return—and I should like to take this strange being with me. In the cultivation of his intellect, I should be able to trace the nature of man from its lowest state."

While thus speaking, they arrived at a hovel, the door of which opening with a latch, Mother Stokes entered, and motioned to the Epicurean to do likewise. He did so, and beheld a female of considerable personal attractions, though past the prime of beauty, her dress in a state of dishabille, with an infant in her arms.

CHAPTER IX.

Heav'n help us all from mothers, still say I!
Why can't we come into the world without
Thus being visited for others' sins?
A plague on honesty! If all were vile,
My birth would not thus foully reek.—*The Bastard.*

WILLIAM WALSINGHAM DISCOVERS HIS MOTHER—THE MON-
STER'S DESPAIR—HARRIET—THE ATHEIST'S AVOWAL.

MOTHER STOKES whispered something to this person, who
gazed on the young man with manifest curiosity, and said, " He
is like his father!" The pale cheek of William flushed at this
allusion to him; but the crimson disappeared from his face
immediately, and he spoke not a word.

" Your worthy husband is safe in prison by this time," said
Mother Stokes in a low voice to the other woman. "They'll
keep him safe this time, I warrant."

The attention of the young philosopher meanwhile was directed
to a wretched ape, who was lying on some straw at the farther
end of the room, evidently in a dying state, while the savage was
standing beside the animal, and making a sad moaning in answer
to the feeble groans of the poor brute. The spectacle was one
intensely interesting to William; and occupied in watching the
mournful countenance of the monster, he forgot that there were
any in the lowly dwelling, except himself and the object of immediate perception. But the two females were making their remarks upon him, the younger one, it was evident, with some
peculiar interest, whispering to and questioning mother Stokes
repeatedly. Their conversation was interrupted by the sound of
the Materialist's voice; for in his absence of mind, as usual, he
embodied his thoughts in words.

" Yes," he said, " thus the chain of being extends through

the sentient world. The highest mind only differs from the lowest in the scale of intelligence in degree—it is, in fact, only the most sublimated portion of matter. This poor creature now here, differs from the expiring brute in little but the feelings of the heart, and even these are exhibited but in different phases; and a sagacious dog will manifest the same affection towards its master as *he* does to the beast. See! now the mortal agony is upon the ape. It pants, it struggles: and the wild being who once derived sustenance from her breast, is weeping over her! No doubt his feelings are as strong as those of a child mourning the death of his parent. Ah! the ape's limbs stiffen; its eyes are glazed: now all is over!"

A wild scream from the savage now rang through the place; and throwing himself on the dead ape, he lavished embraces on her, mingled with tears and groans: then he arose, and motioned to Walsingham to approach still nearer to the body, and looked up beseechingly into his face.

"I can do nothing," replied the Epicurean, "the poor ape's life is annihilated."

The savage uttered a dismal howl, which died away in a low moan, and Mother Stokes going to him, attempted to soothe his despair and agony. By degrees, the violence of his grief subsided; and at length he made signs to his grandmother, which she interpreted to William, as purporting that now the ape was dead, he was ready to go with him.

"I will befriend the wretched being to the best of my ability," said the Materialist, preparing to depart.

"You don't know who that is," said Mother Stokes to the youth, pointing to the other female.

"I have not the pleasure of her acquaintance," answered William indifferently.

The woman alluded to burst into a fit of laughter. "I have often heard," she said, "'that it is a wise child that knows its own father;' but no one ever said, 'it is a wise child that knows its own mother! You are one of my numerous sons, I believe."

The Materialist started as if stung by a serpent, and his face became very pale. "*You!* my mother!" he cried. "Impossible! Quite impossible! I thought she was dead; and you— you?"

"No; all that I know about it is, that if you are the son of Admiral Walsingham, you are mine, too?"

"I am proud of my maternity," said William, with a bitter smile. " *You*, my mother! Well! what does it matter? How many children have you, may I ask?"

"A few days ago," replied the abandoned woman, in whom will be recognised the wife of Danvers, "I had six, with this babe here. But, Percy Norton having been killed by my husband, I have but five now."

"What! Percy Norton? Great Heaven! *He* also your child? Then, he was my brother! I always loved him as such."

"Why not, my dear son? My handsome second-born! Do you see anything so unprepossessing in my appearance, that I should not be the mother of a goodly progeny?"

"No, no," replied William, hastily. "And so you are still leading a life of infamy? Here, take this purse—quit your paramour, whoever he be, and amend if possible—farewell. You have, in me, given birth to one of the most miserable wretches that ever breathed." The Epicurean covered his brow with his hands, compressing it tightly, as if with great pain, and hastily stepped toward the threshold; but stopped abruptly, and said, "Can that poor savage go with me now?"

"Yes," answered Mother Stokes. Then turning to her grandson, she added, "Good bye, boy!—There, you've been long enough crying over the ape. Your howling won't bring it back to life. Go along with the gentleman—he is your third cousin; and I hope he'll be kind to you." But the monster still lingered, and made signs to his grandmother. "It shall be as you wish," she answered impatiently.

"What does he say?" asked the Materialist, who, notwithstanding the unwelcome and unexpected disclosure which had just been made, was deeply interested in the exhibition of the savage's feelings.

"He asks me to bury the ape in some pretty spot," replied Mother Stokes, "and where he may find the grave, if he should ever return."

"Poor thing! poor, poor thing!" ejaculated Walsingham.

"I am much obliged to you for this purse, William," began Mrs. Danvers. "I never received money before except from—"

But the Epicurean cut her short. " Come along," he said to the monster in a gentle tone, and the unhappy being moved away from the corpse, as if to obey his new master ; but returned to it again instantly, gazed fondly on the mutilated features of the only creature that had ever loved him and regarded not his deformity, and kissed them repeatedly : then bursting into a passion of agonized sorrow, he embraced the motionless form, and tearing himself away, rushed out of the hut.

William walked from the hovel with rapid strides, a chaos of whirling thoughts in his brain ; but in the course of a few minutes, he reached a vehicle, in which a man was seated, waiting for him.

" Take this poor creature with you," said the young man to the driver, " and convey him to the Inn where I slept last night, and where the coach to London, if I mistake not, starts from, at noon to-morrow." So saying, the Epicurean departed.

* * * * * * * *

Seated in an antique arm chair, with open window, her eyes raised to the calm, dark, starless, firmament, with a lamp diffusing a soft and subdued light through the apartment, was Harriet Walsingham. She looked more beautiful than ever ; and so passionless was the lofty expression of her surpassing countenance, and so unearthly the elevation of its character, that it was hardly possible to think of her as one of the race of weak, sinful mortals, who are continually tempest-tossed by their errors and misdoings. On a table before her were a lute, some papers and drawings, together with books, writing materials, and a few flowers which were dying fast. The papers consisted of some beautiful poetry, which none but a woman could have written, imbued with all that fervour, feeling, and imagination which constituted the chief charm of our lamented Hemans' verses, to which they were equal in power, and not inferior in composition. The drawings were executed with masculine grandeur of conception, and delicacy of style ; some on sacred subjects, some on historical ones, and others purely fanciful. They also were from the hand of the poetess. The books consisted of the works of those great minds which attest the immortality they are the exponents of, by thoughts and feelings which are not of this world ; but there were some also of human interest, pathetic, lovely, and tender. Why are not more of them composed? Why, when we attempt to imitate a Milton, who is so immeasurably above us that we can never hope to rival him, do we not strive to follow in the steps of those sweet bards, who are the pride of England, and the pleasure of the world? Who touch the human part, " and with the lofty dignify the low."

A few faint stars were now visible in the purple heaven, and gradually became more and more bright and glorious. Having contemplated those ethereal orbs for a minute or two, with that pure delight which such high spirits know in meditating on the eternal and the infinite, Harriet turned her eyes towards the drooping flowers on the table, and said—anticipating a fine idea of a fine modern poet—" Stars are the flowers of Heaven, and they fade not like those of Earth." It is a pleasant thing (it may here be remarked, digressively) to *all* but an author, to find we share the same sensations and aspirations as the mighty dead, or the illustrious living ; and even though a person who has adopted literature as a profession may be mortified, when he discovers, like the Hibernian, that " the rascals have stolen all one's best ideas before they came into his head ;" to know that the dignity of our nature necessarily leads to the same trains of thought and association in all reflecting minds, is a fine and exalting feeling.

Harriet was a musician, as well as a poetess ; and, taking up her lute, she ran her white fingers over the strings with careless skill ; and presently her voice was heard mingling with the symphony. Never was a voice more clear and sweet and thrilling, as it ascended joyous and passionate, like the morning lark's, then sunk into a sweet and solemn lament, resembling the last notes of the nightingale, and embodied her fine aspirations in words and music prompted by the emotions which were then swelling in her bosom. The melody was simple, and the words by no means equal to those she had often composed ; but it is impossible to describe their blended effect, as they poured in a gushing flood of harmony through the lonely chamber, in that still and solemn hour, almost seraphic in their intense pathos and sublime earnestness. They appeared the emanations of a loving spirit soaring through the interstellar space, at first elate, then plaintive, faint, or triumphant.

" Breath of my being, Hope! What wouldst thou whisper me?
Thou tellest of the raptures which can never, never be!
Thou tellest of the words of Love, whose presence is a dream,
And the wild, the glowing, and divine, which are a meteor gleam!

" Life of my heart! whose symphony is sweeter than the gale
On which is borne the dying swan's all passion-breathing wail,
While zephyrs hang enamoured on the strain they hear above,
Floating,—dispersing in the sky, why whisper ye of Love?

" I tell thee, oh, deluding Hope! Love was not form'd to die;
And therefore cannot leave its own bright immortality!
Some rays may fall upon us here, like Heaven's approving smile,
But we are drooping, dying, lost, in too great bliss the while!

" Tell me no more of Love, false Hope, beneath the stars: but oh,
Let me not droop in blank despair, and in envenomed woe.
Still speak to me: thine eloquence should raise the fainting heart—
A friend, a balm, a melody, a comforter thou art.

" But whisper not those words again, and linger not, sweet, *here;*
The empyrean is alone thy true, befitting sphere;
Lend me but wings to soar above the sad, dark path I've trod,
And I will call thee ' ANGEL' sent to help me up to God!"

" If there *be* an angel," exclaimed a deep and scarcely less
thrilling voice than the minstrel's, when she had finished her
song, and with parted lips, and eyes which seemed to swim in
their sea of liquid light, permitted imagination to paint the glories
and wonders of that spiritual universe which she had been alluding to, " if there *be* an angel, then thou art one."

" What, William!" cried Harriet Walsingham. " Why have
you absented yourself so long from home? I saw my sister a
little while ago, and—and—she said that all should be buried in
oblivion——"

" You know then what has happened?" interrupted the Epicurean quickly, " you know it all! Well, I deserve to be despised,
hated, pointed at! The Universe is now my home—or rather, I
shall have none." And he paced up and down the room, struggling violently to master the fearful passions within, but nearly
convulsed with them. " Yes," he continued, with rising vehemence, " spurn me, if you will, hate me, deem me all that is
accursed, vile, and despicable. Look you, Harriet Walsingham!
If you think I am the meanest thing that ever trod, and contami-

nated the earth, you do not think worse of me than I do myself. Yet, if *you* cast me from you with loathing, I shall go mad—I am almost mad already! Feel my brow, how it burns! There is living fire within my brain, and the blood is boiling like the fabled streams of Hell! Yet there is ice crawling over me, and freezing life. O agony!"

" Be calm, William! I do not hate you. I feel you have done very wrong ; but if you repent of evil——"

" What can repentance do ?" exclaimed the young man wildly. " Can it tear from my memory the ignominious stamp written in characters of flame upon it, like a felon's brand ? Can it restore me to my own good opinion—which is the only God I acknowledge ? But I could not have done otherwise! How is it conceivable that I could ? There is no virtue, and no vice.   Why do you prate to me of things you understand not? Rend the spheres of Heaven and show me infinity! Demonstrate the possibility of the mind not acting in conformity to certain eternal laws which govern the universe ; each atom convulsed or quiescent according to unalterable Necessity?" and he seemed to forget he was speaking to another, and addressed some imaginary being in his mind.   " I laugh you to scorn, hollow bugbear! which fools and madmen have erected to awe the great spirit of liberty and strong thought. Poor Phantom Conscience!—the idlest breath of superstition and ignorance! Ha, ha! avaunt!—Hear me, Harriet! I have much to tell you—much that may in your opinion palliate —and yet I know not—but hear me.   You know not what I have been—none know what I have been from my early childhood."

He approached close to his aunt, and continued, with suppressed excitement in his looks and accents, thus—" I was born a bastard—the child of a low woman, without one feeling of modesty, or decency.   I speak to you in the common parlance of mankind.   I adore universal love ; but prostitution of the person I abhor from my very heart.   Why is it that we must check the natural impulses we feel, and restrain all that can conduce to the small amount of pleasure man may experience ?   I had fearful passions, which consumed me when I was little beyond an infant. I could love, and I could hate as mortal never loved, nor hated before, at such an age.   If I were punished for a bad action, I cherished deep, bitter vengeance against the person who punished me. If treated with affection, I used to think I could endure damnation for the sake of those who were kind to me. My father died when I was a child; and I was placed under the protection of his mother. I was sent, when young, to school, and was tyrannized over, and beaten, until my whole nature was perverted. I began to hate the world, and to ask myself the cause of the wretchedness I saw and felt. But I had strength and intellect beyond my years; and, by degrees, I emancipated myself from the cruel despotism of my schoolfellows. Thought was ripening too fast, and character developing too early. And now I come to the point, on which all my fate has turned. By some means it became known that I was a bastard—though the fact had been concealed from me—and I was taunted on my illegitimacy by one I hated. Oh, the agony of despair and shame I felt! I almost meditated self-destruction; for my schoolmates, finding how sensitive I was on the subject of my birth, on every occasion sought to torment me—for such is the bias of the mind in the present state of things—until I thought all the world my foes. I used to seek some solitary spot and sit for hours together buried in deep and gloomy reverie, regardless of the fair face of nature, and of every thing but my own unhappiness. I struggled on, however, though the iron had entered into my inmost being; I resolved on conquering all: but neglected first to subdue myself, until it was too late. My companions began to shun and fear me; for I beat them all into utter, abject subjection, and the power of my arm was felt by the strongest. They used to whisper whenever then saw me; and I laughed inwardly as I beheld their cowardice, and knew their slavish spirits. From that school I went to another: and now I felt that I was no longer a boy, though in fact but thirteen. I was vigorous in body as well as in mind, and I began to reflect more and more intensely. After six months' hard, unintermitting study, to which I dedicated all my leisure hours, after pondering over the works of various authors, and frequent inward meditation, during the hours others devoted to sleep, I embraced the opinions which I now hold: and was in the habit of collecting my elder schoolfellows together, and inviting discussions on religion, for I conceived that to be the bane of society, and exerted all my powers to show its fallacy. Well, I was sent away from school on account of my Atheism, my master admitting at the same time that he could teach me nothing more —that I was as good a scholar as himself. I came to Walsingham Hall, and continued my studies with greater avidity than ever. I exercised mind and body with violent action, and always until exhausted. At length I became weary of this incessant thought, and new feelings and passions took possession of me. The woman I seduced—for I *did*, I suppose, seduce her—was thrown in my way. Though I felt I was doing wrong, I had no motive for exertion, and yielded to temptation; excusing my conduct to myself by the usual sophistries of men; but the more I reflected, the more I was ashamed of that low connexion."

"Feeling so, why did you continue it?" inquired Harriet, in accents of mild reproof, perceiving her nephew paused.

"Because I yielded myself up to fatalism, a doctrine I am now induced to think as unphilosophical as demoralizing; and persuaded myself that it was all in the course of that blind necessity against which it is useless to strive. My mind was then in a chaotic confusion; and the elements had not mingled, so that I adopted many absurd notions, and many crude hypotheses of my own without sufficient investigation. I admit that I knew the pretexts which I invented to excuse my actions to myself were so flimsy that a child would laugh at them. But I became disgusted with all things. For me there was no longer freshness in the air of spring, in the perfumed flowers no sweetness, in the cooling breezes no invigoration. Even my books were neglected by me. Occasionally I took lessons in Mathematics, and other branches of science; but I cared not for them. I was a man almost before I was a boy, and seemed to have exhausted every enjoyment of existence. Your society alone afforded me pleasure. I have met with men of learning and ability, and discussed abstruse questions with them, in some cases coming off victorious; but in you alone are united all the qualities of feeling and intellect, which I can admire with all my heart. In you alone I found something beyond that poor humanity which I pity while I despise, knowing how vile a thing I am myself. But gradually," continued William, in a hollow voice, "strange thoughts and sensations, and a flood of perpetual excitement entered my bosom. I loved, Harriet Walsingham, and I knew loved vainly, wildly. I struggled with all

my strength against this fatal passion—I in some measure subdued, but could not extinguish it.   I even sought the society of
the low woman I never cared for, in order to divert my mind
from brooding on that image which was despair.   You told me of
Walter Danvers——It *will* come," he muttered to himself, " and
yet she will think the worse of me !   No matter.,   I shall see her
no more."

"What has Walter Danvers to do with the subject' of. your
love ?" asked Harriet, with emotion, no suspicion of the truth
entering her pure heart, " you never told me that you felt an
attachment for any one.   Tell me who it was ; and if it be in my
power to make you happy, I will' beggar myself to do so.   I
should not consider any sacrifice too great for your sake.   If you
but loved and were happy, I know it would reclaim you.   Say,
who was the object of your hopeless passion ?"

" *You !*" exclaimed the Epicurean with startling quickness.
" I knew it would come to this—I felt it must be so.   I am going
away from you for ever, and it boots not whether you curse or
commiserate me.   When I found your whole heart was given to
another irrevocably ; when I found that your soul's beloved had
appeared to you, the last refuge of my hope disappeared.   I
said to myself, she will abhor me for this feeling which she will
deem so guilty and unnatural, and I determined never to whisper
a word of it.   Turn not from me with such lofty disdain ; but hear
me out.   ' Why,' said I to myself, ' may I not purify and etherealise this love I bear for her, until it become the realization of the
old Platonic Idea ?   If my love be not sensual, it cannot be offensive
even to her.   I will adore her as some pure being of the mind—a
nympholepsy—a dream of no earthly passion.'   I liked the notion ;
but while I cherished an adoring admiration of your mind, I saw
not that I was deluding myself into desperate error. * * * You
have heard my confession—you despise me.   You think I have
uttered words so gross that they are the foulest insult and injury
ever offered to woman.   I tell you that I love you ; but I say it in
despair.   If it had been possible to have possessed you, I might
indeed have been reclaimed.   I know your worship of the Idols
which ignorance and superstition have set up : and so farewell,
Harriet.   We shall never meet again.   Never, never, never !"
And he clasped his hands and groaned deeply.

CHAPTER X.

Pause yet awhile—oh pause, misguided heart!
Angels deplore the fallen thing thou art!
Turn from the gulf—oh, see, it yawns beneath!
And fly from sin, from agony, and death!
Come to the home where all are safe and blest,
And let the seraph's pen record the rest.
Oh, quit the threshold ere 'tis not too late,—
The key is dropp'd——and Mercy shuts her gate.—*MS.*

HARRIET'S REPLY — THE EPICUREAN DEPARTS — CAPTAIN
NORTON ORDERS HARRIET TO BE TAKEN TO PRISON.

OH, the wretchedness that man may feel! To think of parting
for ever from the object of all the spirit's worshipped visions,
and to believe in annihilation! That thought continually recurs
to my mind, and I see in it the dull torpor which may possess the
soul of one wandering through eternity, hopeless of Heaven. To
be parted *for ever* from the Alpha and Omega of desire! The
Atheist ended thus,

"Forget that such a wretch as I am exists:—but yet remember the bitterness of my misguided life, remember my sufferings,
my passions, my principles, and try, O try! to pardon me."

The changes on Miss Walsingham's splendid face, during the
confession of her nephew, were manifold. Now haughty pride
and anger flushed her white cheek and brow, dilated her nostril,
and imparted a loftier grandeur to her perfect form, whose swelling outlines, whose majestic and statuesque proportions, were
those of a Grecian Goddess, erect in immortal beauty, and then
pity mingled with her resentment, and she looked more like a
seraph reproving a fallen mortal. She spoke, after a long pause,
which he interpreted as emanating from hate and scorn, and was
moving slowly away with drooping head, when she prevented him
by laying her hand on his arm, and thus speaking—

3 P

" I *do* pardon you, weak and sinful young man! I have heard you with patience, and will reply without indignation, wrath, or contempt: though such feelings have been strongly excited in my breast by your frenzied words, I will speak to you as a friend, and forget that I am the object of your avowal. William, I have loved you as my son—as my brother; and have endeavoured to be mother, sister, and counsellor to you. I have seen your noble mind bound in darkness by the errors of a vile and false philosophy; and while I have deplored the perversion of your judgment, I have sought, in some measure, to counteract the influence of it on your intellect, by appealing to the originally excellent heart you possessed. You stand now upon the verge of an awful abyss; and I must subdue my natural feelings as a woman, which must be those of repugnance toward you, after that horrid confession, to reason, to expostulate with you, and strive, ere it be too late, to induce you to renounce the immorality and iniquity to which your detestable creed conducts of necessity. Oh, if mine were the inspired breath which reaches the depths of the secret spirit, if mine were the profound wisdom which exposes the hollowness and sophistry of the theories of scepticism and unbelief, you would not leave me without being convinced; for I would strain every nerve to save you; but I have no eloquence, no wisdom. My words are those of a feeble woman; my understanding cannot pierce the subtleties of logic, and wrestle with the difficulties of sophists, which perplex themselves, and cannot enlighten others. I can only hope to attain my object by touching those latent feelings which are the holiest and highest, while they meekly confess themselves the humblest portion of our complicated being. To your best feelings then suffer me now to appeal. Consider, William, how many you may make wretched by indulging in your sensuality; how many fond hopes you may blight by giving way to your vices and your libertinism. It is impossible not to create misery by yielding to unbridled passion, as it is certain by treading the path of virtue, and rooting out from the heart all that is corrupt, infinite benefit must accrue to the mass of mankind. I will not speak to you of religion; but I will of morality. You acknowledge the first great principle of ethics is, that every man is bound to do nothing which can create wretchedness in another. Pause then, I beseech you, that you may not

have a death-bed of unavailing remorse ; that you may not, when
the parting hour come, behold a ghastly array of victims reproaching you as the cause of their crimes—spectres that will
haunt you in life, and if there be another, cause perdition to all
felicity. What is this existence, William ? Is it not all vanity
and sorrow ? To what does it tend, if there is nothing beyond the
grave ? Behold a scene of tears and lamentation, bright dreams
dispersed, and goodness trampled upon, and vice triumphant!
Behold famine, pestilence, war, and every appalling shape of
pain. Is it wise to reject the belief of a hereafter, which shall recompense mortality for suffering? Is it wise to scoff at the
idea of an eternity of happiness, when we know that temporary
enjoyment is so fleeting and uncertain ? Is it well to take this
consolatory anticipation from others, and trample all the opinions
which the best and noblest hold, under foot?"

" I know not," answered the Materialist, without raising his
eyes. " I *have* thought that if the dogmas of antiquity were exploded, there would be a dawning of beauty and felicity for all
the earth. I *have* thought that a state might arrive, when the
universal mind would be free from prejudice and superstition ;
and all be united in love, truth, and charity. But I distrust myself, my principles—all things. I am wretched, but have no haven
to seek shelter in, and snakes are gnawing my vitals ; but there is
nothing for me save endurance. If I turn to your religion for an
instant, I am sickened at its ghastly terrors : if I embrace the
religion of philosophy, I am involved in endless anomalies and
difficulties. Yet I confess I am not satisfied with my present
negation ; I confess that annihilation is painful to my contemplations—scarcely less so than eternal condemnation."

" True," said Harriet, " the natural religion which is vaunted
by metaphysicians is empty and unsatisfactory. Take that of
Plato, the best of all human systems ; and behold its continual
problems, its inextricable mazes, its speculations, and absurdities.
It is to draw the mind to virtue, most undoubtedly, that religion
was instituted ; and if it have the power of meliorating the heart,
its value as a means to an end cannot be disputed."

" And what has it been able to effect for humanity ?"

" I thank you for that question, William. I myself have—oh,
how much—to thank Heaven for its sweet solace. It has raised

the sinking spirits of those who pine beneath accumulated misfortunes, and beaconed with certain radiance to the rock of safety, which has withstood the desolations and destruction of ages. Upon that rock it has placed the foot of the penitent, and guided him upwards when he would have sunk with diffidence and despondency. In the night of unutterable anguish, it has poured supernal light into his soul; it has raised him above doubt, it has dispelled the gloom, it has opened a world of light more pure than all of human origin, and stores of wisdom, of poetry, and beauty which could not have been constructed by the thought of man. In the power of Faith lies the secret of patience; and while the efforts of the greatest minds are unable materially to alleviate the calamities to which humanity is exposed, has it not poured balm into all wounds, and afforded a certainty of an incorruptible inheritance—mansions of glory and skies of unclouded loveliness, transcending all the dreams of enthusiasm, and the wild imaginations of love and passion? There is no uncertainty for the believer: the speculator, even though not an Atheist, can be assured of nothing. Judge of all things by their fruits. If religion conduce to the happiness, or virtue of mankind, then it must be an essence necessarily opposed to falsehood. For is it not an absurdity to assert that it promotes the morality, and sustains the framework of society, if it is composed of fallacy, if its foundations are infirm, and fabric unsubstantial? Yet statesmen, irreligious as yourself, have considered this system requisite to maintain order, and to conserve the laws. And it were as reasonable to say that the material world could be sustained by laws unfixed and inadequate, as that the moral universe can be governed by false and evil principles. It is not yet too late for you to avert your steps from the precipice, beneath which there is a stupendous eternity, it is not yet too late for you to worship what you now despise, and seek all truth, fortitude and hope."

The Epicurean shook his head. "No," he said slowly, "I can renounce nothing, and receive nothing—I shall die as I have lived. Belief or unbelief is no effort of what you call volition. I confess I have done very wrong; and I repent me of the past. But it is of no avail to stay longer with you. Bless you, glorious woman! A few little years, and you will be dust, and I shall be rotting among the worms. There, the breath of this foul world will not trouble me, and the veil of external darkness will be drawn over my misdeeds and woes! To tell you how I loved, would be disgusting to your pure ears. But I have suffered greatly, if you think I have sinned deeply. Once more then farewell. I shall leave England in a very few days."

"Whither would you go, my poor, deluded boy?" asked Harriet, moved to tears by the inexpressible dejection in her nephew's looks and words.

"I shall visit the mighty monuments of the past, and my thoughts shall be with the great dead—and you. I will write to you, when I reach London; but I must never return to your presence."

The youth pressed his aunt's cold hand to his parched lips, and dropped one tear—one bitter tear—upon it. He relinquished it, and moved away; and when Harriet lifted her eyes from the floor, he was gone.

"Lost! lost!" she exclaimed, with a sob. "Oh, what a mind, what a mind, is ruined for ever here! God pity him! Poor, poor mortality!" She watched the retreating form of the Atheist from her window, until it was lost in darkness and distance : and then she knelt and prayed.

Though all her holy and angelic feelings had been outraged by hearing she was the object of a guilty and degrading passion, though she abhored from her soul the principles of the Materialist, and was indignant at his actions and sentiments, it were difficult to describe her anguish at thus parting from one she had loved, when she herself had scarcely entered her girlhood; and for whom her tenderest solicitude had been excited during the years in which he was advancing towards man's estate. As for opposing the course which William Walsingham had marked out for himself, though he was only eighteen, no person acquainted with him would have attempted such a thing by coercion; and she felt persuasion would have been vain. Indeed, she acknowledged to herself that she could never admit him to her presence again, on the same terms of intimacy as heretofore; and therefore his absence, while it pained, would relieve her from constraint. But still there was so much to love and admire in William, despite his errors, despite his hatred of all the religion and morality which Harriet deemed so sacred, so firmly had those fine qualities of mind and heart entwined themselves around her warm enthusiastic spirit, that she could not have grieved more profoundly over any affliction that could now befal her—save *one*—than she did over his fall, his irretrievable error and misery. She could only pray that the intervention of a power greater than any earth could supply would yet accomplish all her hopes for him : and earnestly did she implore Omnipotence to make him wiser, better, and happier. Whether, when we pray for others, our intercessions are heard, we know not : but in imploring forgiveness for our enemies, and beseeching drops of consolation to visit the afflicted, and requesting rectitude to the erring and guilty, so much beautiful philanthropy, love and piety are evolved, that it cannot be displeasing to the Creator that we should do so.

About an hour had been consumed in this painful, and distressing interview with her nephew ; and Harriet was preparing to retire to rest—though after the excitement she had undergone, she could hardly hope to sleep—when her intention was diverted by the galloping of a horse at a short distance from her house ; and surprised, in the retired spot where she lived, that any person should be passing so late—for it had struck ten o'clock— she again looked out of window, with a presentiment that something extraordinary was about to happen. She was far from being a superstitious woman—one so fervently, yet rationally religious as she was, could not be so—but still sometimes a foreboding will enter the bosom, and she trembled with a vague fear that some dire misfortune was about to happen. It was so dark, that she could not recognise the horseman ; but presently her ear distinguished the trampling of the hoofs of another horse ; and as the first person she descried hastily alighted at her door, a second became dimly visible in the distance.

Before another minute had elapsed, a quick step was heard on the stairs, the door of her apartment was thrown open ; and Captain Norton (but so wild and haggard that she could scarcely believe his identity) entered, and stood before her. The image of Walter Danvers instantly rose to her mind. She had heard of his escape, and thanked Heaven most devoutedly for it : but a thousand terrors now assailed her fancy ; and she gasped—

" What—what of him ? Pray, speak !"

Norton had been glaring round the chamber like a tiger, and

exclaimed sternly and savagely, " You will not deceive me now
by your dissimulation, woman !" And a wild fire was gleaming
in his eye, which indicated the species of suspicion ordinarily
exhibited by incipient insanity, as he added in a sepulchral voice,
which struggled with intense passion. " You had better deliver
him up to justice at once. I am convinced you have concealed
him here."

" What ! Walter Danvers !" cried Miss Walsingham.

" Ay, even that miscreant of hell !" cried the officer fiercely.
" I have been seeking for him day and night, and a spirit whispered to me in a dream, which I had a few hours ago, ' Seek
him at the house where he hid himself before.' Again I command
you to render him up to justice. Resistance will be vain. See,
here is a soldier ; and there are two constables at hand."

" On my word of honor, he is not here !" exclaimed Harriet
earnestly.

" You told a deliberate lie once, and I doubt not would do so
again," returned Norton, directing the soldier, who now made
his appearance, to search every corner of the house. By this
time, the constables also, to whom he had alluded, were heard
below, and it was manifest that nothing Miss Walsingham could
say would deter the officer from acting as he had determined, for
his whole appearance and actions were so wild and incoherent,
that reasoning with him would have been useless.

" As you will," said Harriet. " I can only repeat that Walter
Danvers is not in this house."

" We shall see that, speedily," replied Norton. " If he be not
forthcoming, I warn you, a warrant for your committal to prison
will be put in execution. I am a magistrate, and—Ha !—Isn't
he in that room, Williams? Well, we shall find the villain presently, I'll bet a hundred pounds. Ha, ha ! The spirit told me it
should be so. He was a spirit sent from on high, and would not
dare to deceive me ! Here, Constables, enter and do your duty.
Never mind a woman's presence—no, nor an angel's !"

" Poor man ! he is mad !" exclaimed Harriet, " his affliction
has driven reason utterly from his brain."

Norton overheard these words, and glaring terribly on her, said,
" You shall find if I am mad. I am quite sane enough to expose
your infamous conduct in harbouring a murderer—the murderer
of my boy, my Percy ! He is to be buried to-morrow—and he

must be avenged before then, or he would not lie in the earth. He smells foully now. I thought for a long time corruption would not seize upon him—he is so very beautiful; but it has come at last! Well, cannot you find him?" he cried impatiently, addressing the men he had brought with him. " He *must* be here, I tell you. I will look for him, myself."

Accordingly Captain Norton resumed the search in person; but he was no more successful than his followers: and his resentment kindling against Harriet by the conviction that she was acquainted with the place where Danvers was lurking, he said, " If you will not confess where he is concealed, we shall find means to force you to speak. Constables, do your duty. Here is your warrant. Take her hence."

" Surely," exclaimed Harriet, as the officials advanced to execute their orders, " you perceive he is distracted, that he knows not what he does."

But the constables attended not to her expostulations.

" To prison with her," cried Captain Norton. " We shall be able to extort the truth from her. Oh, that the rack were not abolished in England!"

The constables led Miss Walsingham down stairs, and shutting their ears to all her arguments on this most unjustifiable seizure, they placed her on one of their horses; and accompanied by the officer and the soldier, the latter riding behind their beautiful prisoner, they rode from the cottage. Harriet resigned herself to her fate without further effort, and was soon far away from that peaceful home, where for long and dreary years she had buried her sorrows. Forgotten by a world for which she was too lofty and too good, devoting herself to Heaven and to study, pouring comfort into the hearts of the sorrowful, and denying herself all the luxuries to which she had been accustomed, in order to minister to the necessities of the poor, had lived the gifted, the brilliant, the glorious Harriet Walsingham. Oh, Woman, woman! without thee our divine aspirations would find no ark on earth; but would

" Convulse us and consume us, day by day,
And cold hopes swarm like worms within our living clay."

END OF BOOK VII.

BOOK VIII.

" This is the history of man !
He wanders forth amid enormous wilds,—
No star his guide,—save *one* he will not see ;
He gazes hopeless on the darksome scene,
And wonders if 'twas Heaven that placed him there ;
Until at length black shadows close upon him,
And on the Desert's verge th' eternal night
Disperses, and the STAR gives light—he dies!—*MS.*

CHAPTER I.

Thus may you see successive Vice and Virtue;
The one is acted by material things
That breathe in Time, and die like brutish swine;
The other breathes the atmosphere divine
Of its own high eternity.—*Old Play.*

THE CHILD RESCUED — THE LETTER — ISAAC QUIRK AND
CORPORAL FIGGINS—DIAMOND CUT DIAMOND.

"H E L P, help!" screamed a female, in accents of agonized distress. "My child! my child, God of mercy, save my child!"

These words proceeded from a lovely woman, who stood wringing her hands on the bank of a deep and rapid stream. But nothing was to be discerned in the water, and all was as bright in the ethereal sky, and all as tranquil on the beautiful earth, the birds sang as blithely, as if that scene of horror and dismay had not been. Verily, the heart of Nature is of stone!

A few minutes previously a young child had been walking by the side of the lady whose distress was so heart-rending; and attracted—as children ever will be—by the radiant glories of a butterfly, she chased the splendid insect to the verge of the river, when her foot slipped, and she was precipitated into the water.

And now she rose to the surface in the middle of the river. There stood her mother, helpless and frantic, and apparently no human aid at hand. What tongue shall utter, what pen describe the feelings of a parent at such a moment? She looks up to Heaven, and there is the firmament calm and holy, looking as full of happiness as an angel's face; but no answer to the appeal.

She accuses Providence of indifference to her agony, because there is no special interposition in her behalf. The current bore the child away, and in another minute she must have been irrecoverably lost, when a little boy ran up, beheld the drowning child, as her fairy form rose for a second time, and plunged in without a moment's hesitation. Bravely done, young swimmer! He grasps the child by her long hair, and in spite of the swiftness of the tide, buffets the waters, and reaches land with his burthen. " She's saved! she's saved!" exclaimed the mother of the little girl, and rushing up clasped her in her passionate embrace. Oh, that joy; the despair changed into ecstasy, the anguish into transport! Is it not almost worth while to suffer *such* pain, to enjoy transcendant bliss?

The boy who had so gallantly rescued the little girl, stood panting, and shaking himself, but perfectly collected, as if he had done the commonest thing possible, though he was a mere child in years; but she whom he had preserved as yet exhibited no symptoms of returning consciousness, the powers of life being suspended. The boy then exclaimed, " Let us lose no time. Something must be done directly."

" Ah!" exclaimed the lady, who in her joy noticed not that her kisses were unreturned, " run for help, for God's sake. Oh, she will die! Is there no aid near?"

" None," returned the boy. " Do you think you could open a vein in her arm?"

" Oh, no, no," was the reply.

The boy produced a pen-knife from his pocket, and tearing his handkerchief into strips, cried, " I think I can do it!"

" *You!*" ejaculated the lady, "you are little older than my child."

" It's a case of life and death," returned the resolute little fellow, " not even a barber lives within three miles. Will you let me try to bleed her, or do so yourself?"

" I cannot, you cannot?" answered the distracted mother, all her agony returning with aggravated intensity.

" I am certain I can do it. I have often seen persons bled. You see she shows no sign of life! Another minute may be too late."

Well," said the lady, who after witnessing the extraordinary courage and presence of mind displayed by the young boy could not but feel some confidence in him. Without waiting for further permission than was implied by the monosyllable the little fellow took the round and dimpled arm of the child.

"I saw a man recovered from drowning, by being bled the other day," he said. "Now, ma'am, we'll bandage the arm very tight, and then I'll cut this vein a little just here—so, that's well. Luckily this pen-knife is sharp." And he made a slight incision, from which blood lazily trickled and presently the patient gasped, and opened her large, lustrous eyes with a wondering look. She sighed painfully and murmured, "I thought I was in Heaven with my dear mamma. Oh! what is it that pains me?"

"Thank God!" ejaculated the little doctor. And he tied up the wound quite scientifically, and stood gazing with deep interest on the beautiful being he had saved from a watery grave. "It is the very same," muttered he, "the young lady who gave me the cake a few weeks ago, when the savage attacked me."

The child spoke once more. "Oh, my dear, dear mamma!" she exclaimed, "I have been so happy! I was up there (pointing to the skies) with you."

Beautiful—altogether beautiful and pure is the love of a child for its mother, and it is a human instinct, after infancy; the affection of a believer for his God, without the awe of adoration, trusting, hoping, looking for all joy from that sacred source. The mother covered her beloved child with kisses. She murmured a prayer of gratitude, and silence spake the rest.

"Now, ma'am, hadn't we better carry the young lady home?" asked the prompt and stout-hearted boy, who had throughout acted with the decision of a man, and of a brave man too. "She is so light we can easily manage to do it." While these words were being spoken, a young man approached, and the lady recognising him uttered an exclamation of surprise.

"What! my nephew Frank?" she cried. The individual thus apostrophized advanced, and took the lady's hand.

"What has been the matter here?" he inquired, looking at the little girl so marvellously saved from death.

"This is my daughter. She fell into the water, and was only rescued by Heaven's interposition. Will you carry her for me?" The young man immediately took up the slight burthen in his strong arms.

"Which way shall I carry her?" he asked.

"Towards Walsingham Hall—Noble boy," (to the preserver of the young child) "you will come with me! Henceforth you shall be to me as a son."

But the little fellow shook his head. "I cannot go with you now, ma'am," he said.

"What is your name, then? Where do you live?" said the lady.

"My name is George. If you live at Walsingham Hall I'll call on you very soon, as you are kind enough to wish to see me." And with these words the boy disappeared. Of course the reader has established in his own mind his identity with the "George" who has acted so conspicuously before in our chronicle.

"And how came you here, Francis?" questioned the lady, as she walked on, holding one of the child's tiny hands with the pressure of a mother, loving and rejoicing. "I thought you were far away at sea?"

"The facts are these?" was the reply. "About two months ago, when cruising in the Mediterranean, I had a quarrel with the first lieutenant of my ship. You are acquainted with my position as far as this; that I ran away from school about six years ago, and became a common sailor. You also know that I was raised to the rank of midshipman not very long afterwards for some unworthy services of mine, in action. Subsequently my name and rank were discovered by my Captain, who was an old friend of my father, and he was very kind to me. But this man with whom I quarrelled was jealous of the notice taken of me, and seized every opportunity to annoy and insult me. My Utopian dreams of what a sailor's life may be—so full of liberty, so bright and joyous—have certainly not been realised hitherto; for in no position of life is tyranny so odious and perfect—one can never escape from it. I bore the enmity and petty malice of my foe uncomplainingly for years; but on one occasion the vile scoundrel taunted me on the circumstance of my unfortunate birth. My hanger was in my hand, and I called on him to draw. We fought, and he was wounded. I was instantly put in irons: but I had a friend in the surgeon's mate. He told me he feared the injury my foe had sustained would prove mortal, and advised me to attempt an escape. I believe the Captain winked at my departure, and I leapt overboard (my fetters having been removed by the surgeon's mate) and swam to a merchant vessel bound for England. By means of a bribe I induced the commander to aid me, and I arrived in safety at Portsmouth ; but was unwilling to make my appearance at Walsingham Hall, for several reasons."

By this time the young sailor and his companions had arrived at a small cottage, which was no other than that of Stokes, and here they resolved on staying while they sent Sam to Walsingham Hall for a vehicle. The little girl was placed in the hammock which our friend Stokes had slung in his snug cabin, and he being at home was very willing to perform the service required, and stumped off without delay to bring the carriage for Lady Walsingham and her daughter.

Meanwhile the boy who had rendered so important a service to them pursued his way along the sinuous banks of the river until he reached a rudely constructed bridge, over which he was about to pass, when his eyes fell on a horseman. He uttered an exclamation of pleasure, and ran up to him.

" Ah! my brave lad," said the youth to whom he so eagerly went up extending his hand.

" I am very glad to see you," said George ; " but I must tell you bad news. Your father is taken again, and is now in prison, and I was going to him when I saw you. I have been put into confinement by my mother, and could only make my escape this morning."

" Where is my father now then ?" asked Harry anxiously. " By what ill fate was he taken ?"

" I can tell you but little," replied George. " I will get up behind you, if you have no objection, and then we can ride towards the place where Mr. Danvers now is." Accordingly the youth took him up, and they proceeded at a trot while George added. "A fellow named Figgins who—lives with my mother" (he stammered and blushed deeply when he said this, and tears started into his eyes) " found out the part I had taken in helping your father, which you may have heard of ; and I was confined so strictly, that I thought it would have been impossible to get away. Last night I overheard a conversation between my mother and Figgins, and among other things which I didn't clearly understand they talked about some murder, and mentioned the name of Walsingham. Then my mother went away, and an old woman named Stokes came and talked with Figgins, and I thought that they mentioned you and a cave where you had been taken; and they thought you were starved to death; but I could not overhear all. Figgins and this mother Stokes are going to the cave to-night, at all events, for some purpose."

"Ha!" cried Harry, "then I will be there too."

"And here are some papers, which I have managed to conceal. They were given to me by your father to keep safe. Several times I feared they would have been discovered."

"Thank you, my young hero! a thousand times thank you! We owe you more than we can ever repay. I shall now go to Mrs. Haines and my sister. If you like to accompany me we will protect you, and you shall never want a home while we have one."

"Oh! will you take me to live with you!" exclaimed George, with sparkling eyes and joyous voice. "I will serve and love you with all my heart and soul!" But a gloom overshadowed his face when he had finished speaking, and he muttered. "She is still my mother." Poor fellow! He is not an isolated instance of that beautiful spring of life which never, never can return being blighted by the withering frowns of coldness and unkindness. "Ah!" he ejaculated, "there is Mrs. Haines coming this way. Perhaps she has heard of what has befallen your father."

Harry put his horse into a gallop, and hastened to meet Elizabeth. She had just heard the same news as he had, and was proceeding to visit Danvers in prison. So they sent George on to Ellen, and Mrs. Haines mounting behind Harry, they hastened in the direction of the gaol where Walter was confined.

"I fear it will be impossible for my father to escape again," said Harry to Elizabeth."

"He must attempt to do so at all events," answered Mrs. Haines, "otherwise he will assuredly die. A government founded on usurpation is always merciless."

They proceeded at a gallop, and had left a couple of miles behind them, when in turning out of a lane they met a cripple and Elizabeth exclaimed—

"Ah! my worthy Stokes! This is a person to whom we are much indebted," she said to Harry. "There is not an honester heart alive."

Stokes returned the salutation of Elizabeth and inquired after Ellen. A thought struck Harry relative to the communication of George he had resolved to act on, and he cried, " Perhaps this good fellow will accompany me a few hours hence to a place not far distant from this spot. I want to gain some insight into a dark affair, and cannot trust the execution of my scheme to the laws. There is a cave in the vicinity, and two persons are going there for what purpose I can only guess. But we must be very cautious and take arms with us. I only want a witness."

" I'll go with 'ee with all my heart," returned Sam.

" Then meet me here as soon as it is dark," said Harry. " I will bring a lantern with me, and provide myself with arms."

" What are you going to do ?" inquired Elizabeth solicitously. " You had better take more assistance with you. I must go to some of our friends immediately and can engage some."

" No," answered the youth, " we must not let the business get wind. Come, now let us proceed to ——. A deed of blood shall be brought to light ere many hours have passed."

As they continued their progress Harry intimated to Elizabeth the intelligence he had received from George, and concluded by saying that he trusted a new light would be thrown on that deed of darkness of which his father had been unjustly found guilty.

" Even if we could accomplish such a thing," returned Mrs. Haines moodily, " your father would suffer death as a rebel. But I know how it would rejoice his heart to be proved innocent of a crime so diabolical."

" We must now consider what steps it is expedient to take in order to secure my father's escape," said Harry. " Do you know the place in which he is imprisoned ?"

" No ; but I have heard it is a gaol of great strength. We are now fast approaching it. I fear, however, we shall not be allowed to see him."

" Perhaps we may be able to get a letter to him. I have some ink which cannot be discerned, that I brought from France, but which may be seen when it is exposed to fire, and my father knows the secret. But here we are at the entrance to ——"

Here Mrs. Haines and Harry dismounted and put up the horse at an obscure ale-house. A letter was written forthwith with the ink Harry had alluded to, containing some sort of plan for his

3 R

deliverance, and the rest in the usual way and of such a nature as was probable to come from a son to his father. Having taken this precaution they hastened to the prison, but as they expected were refused admittance to Danvers. The prisoner, it seemed, from the intimation of the turnkey was to see no one until after his examination on the morrow. By administering a bribe, and showing the man that the letter which had been written contained merely inquiries after his health &c., the great object of their going there was accomplished, and they departed perfectly satisfied with the success of their stratagem. As they left the gaol, they were remarked by a vulgar, flashy, cunning-looking young fellow, who appeared particularly struck with the appearance of Harry, and when he was out of sight he rang the prison bell and asked to speak with the turnkey.

"Ah, Master Quirk!" said that functionary making his appearance, after having delivered the letter to Danvers. "How's the old buck to-day?"

"The old boy's nigh well," responded the youth. "It has been touch and go with him. But I want to speak with you about those people there who just left the gaol (Mr. Isaac Quirk's phraseology was rapidly improving). Did you remark how uncommon like the young man is to Danvers?"

The man colored and stammered something in the affirmative.

"Take care he don't play you none of his d—d tricks," said Quirk junior. "Ah, what! Corporal Figgins! Good morning."

It was no less a personage than the redoubtable Corporal who now entered the place where young Quirk and the turnkey were conferring.

"I bring you an order, Mr. Gaoler," said Figgins, "for the person of Walter Danvers, signed by Captain Norton. He is to be removed to A—— and kept in the guard-house till to-morrow; when he will in all probability be consigned to the hangman's hands, after it has been proved he is the person who was condemned for murder. There is a guard outside and in half-an-hour we'll set off. Well, Isaac," addressing the ex-stable boy. "I congratulate you on your good fortune, lad."

"Thank'ee, Corporal! I would advise you to take precious good care of Danvers or he'll slip through your hands."

"Don't teach your grandmother to suck eggs," responded Figgins with supreme disdain.

"I should like to talk with you a bit, Corporal," returned Isaac. "I know a few things which might astonish you, clever chap though you be. Do you think that this here Danvers committed that murder, eh?"

"Of course," replied Figgins, coolly.

"Indeed!" said Isaac Quirk, laying an emphasis on the word. "But I'll see you before evening, and then we'll have some jaw." And the very precocious young gentleman turned on his heel and departed.

CHAPTER II.

How wonderful is Death!
Death, and his brother, Sleep!—SHELLEY.

MEETING OF HARRIET WALSINGHAM AND DANVERS—THE
CORPSE—CHARLES AND ELLEN.

HARRIET WALSINGHAM was in prison. Captain Norton having given directions to a constable to lodge her in safety, had galloped away before reaching the gaol, and thus missed the news of Danvers's capture. No questions were asked by the governor of the prison—a drunken, stupid beast—about Miss Walsingham, though such a vision surprised for a moment even that low sot; but having glanced at the signature of a magistrate in the warrant for her detention, caused her to be conducted to a cell, which happened to be the only one unoccupied, and there she was left alone.

How majestically, how sublimely beautiful did she look in that dreary place, her calm and serene countenance, like nothing in earth or heaven, upturned to the firmament, of which she could catch but a slight glimpse, her lips moving, but otherwise motionless as death. The faint light of the moon streamed through the grated window of the prison, and revealed the stone walls and pavement, the straw, and the massive chains, which made it look so gloomy; but that lofty presence with its living light, its faultless loveliness, seemed like "the splendour of the sun," to cast a glory upon all.

" How many," thought Harriet, " have entered this cell with a load of guilt on their hearts, which has pressed more heavily on the conscience than manacles on the body. I *might* have been here a criminal, weighed down to death with remorse! I believe I could sleep even now!"

The bell of a church tolled the hour of midnight, and its deep, heavy sound boomed dismally in the silence. What an isolation must it appear to be confined in prison, not a voice, not a breath to be heard! The feelings of a wicked man so circumstanced must be an antepast of perdition! Show me a guilty wretch, who can be calm when he is left alone, when he thinks none can behold him, and I will acknowledge he may be courageous, not till then. Any villain may die boldly if he have iron nerves; but to live alone bravely—I cannot conceive it possible.

Harriet sank upon the straw, and although she did not sleep she fell into a species of doze, from which she was startled by hearing the rattling of chains. A moment before, those brief and radiant shapes, which sometimes come upon us ere we drop asleep: scenes of joy, and music, and melancholly lulling fancies, had peopled her spirit; but that grating sound disturbed her rest. " Poor wretch!" she murmured, a tear gathering in her eye; for she had sympathy for all men.

She arose, and looking around her, perceived there was a door at the extremity of the cell. Singularly enough this door had a small sliding panel, which on that side it was possible to push aside; for the place in which Miss Walsingham was confined was not commonly used as a prison, although very secure, and the gaolers were in the habit of passing the scanty food allowed to prisoners in the next cell through this panel. Again the chains rattled. The sound touched a chord in Harriet's heart which vibrated deeply. " Shall I try and speak comfort to the poor creature?" she murmured. " If he is guilty, he needs consolation!" A third time the fetters were heard, and this time the noise was accompanied by the sound of a voice which electrified the heart of Harriet. Was it possible that Walter Danvers was imprisoned there? She listened in breathless silence. You might have heard the pulsations in her breast. Hush! what says he?

" A few short hours, and I shall know more than the wisest of mortals ever knew. Science cannot acquire the wisdom beyond

the grave ; philosophy can teach us nothing, even religion reveals
not the great mystery. But the veil will be torn asunder, and
the vast secrets of existence, the wheels of the universe, the
enigma of eternity be made clear as day. Oh, Harriet, my lost
Harriet ! In that better world may I be forgiven, and be loved
by thee once more !"——

There broke a sob on the stillness of that hour—a low stifled
sob, such as we hear not in mourning and desolation, but yet the
relief of a bursting heart—a *woman's* sob. The prisoner fancied
he heard a sound of woe, but he was not certain, and muttered,
" How many are still more miserable than myself in this accursed
place. There is the feeble, worn-out wretch, clenching his bony
hands and groaning in bitterness of spirit that he may not drag
on a few months of vile being. There is the brawny ruffian
thinking of the joys of a carousal, and starting from sleep with
blasphemies, because he has been dreaming of death. I do not
fear to die ; yet I would I were on the battle-field, that I might
meet the enemy of life like a soldier ! But I have little to make
me cling to earth ! I have robbed myself of a heaven—have been
the suicide of my being's hope."

He became silent. Burying his face in his hands he gave himself up to despondent thought, and heard and saw nothing in the
visible Universe. What worlds of feeling and conception rush like
a torrent through the brain of the unhappy captive, who is in expectation of being launched into eternity ! How memory recurs
to scenes of deep felicity, to haunting visions of boyhood, to
smiles and pleasures, and the busy brain conjures up, like a magician, all that has been, all that may be. And then the anguish
of thinking what might have been accomplished so easily ; but
which can never now be done ! Forwards, backwards flies the
spirit ! There are the friends of infancy, there are the placid hours
that flew on wings of serene delight, the spots which were so
dear and sanctified by the steps of those beyond expression loved,
the familiar voices, the lovely forms—gone for ever ! And then
arise from their tombs the passionate and brief excitement—a
very dream then, but now how strangely real—the wild enthusiasm,
the intense, and burning, and aspiring ardours of youth. All is
a phantasm ; but how vivid, how more than actual ! The Ideal
invests the past with a glory not its own ; at such a time the

pinions of imagination have the swiftness of light, and rush through Time and Space as if they were not. Innumerable forms people the void, schemes of ambition, aspirations after happiness projects for exaltation, and thoughts of things cherished beyond life, flashing upon the swift and whirling soul, and going as rapidly as they came. What joy and anguish alternately rise to view— now all as vain, as empty as if they had never been. Memory is the house of death, and all it brings are spectres that come and go we know not how nor whither.

"Walter!" cried a voice close to the ear of Danvers.

"Ah! whence that sound?" he exclaimed, starting from the floor, and gazing wildly about him. "Answer, whatever thou art! It must have been a phantasy! Oh, that I could see and hear her truly once more ere I depart."

"It is I, Harriet Walsingham, Walter, who thus———"

"God of Heaven!" interrupted Danvers. "Where are you?"

"Give me your hand," replied Miss Walsingham. "You cannot see me—there is no light."

"I cannot move my hand: but touch me that I may know my sense cheats me not."

"Ah! you are manacled!" Harriet stretched forth her arm through the panel, and placed her fingers on the hot brow of Walter. They lingered there for a moment, like the touch of an angel, and were then withdrawn.

"Oh, Harriet! My last and only love," exclaimed Danvers, in tones tremulous with tenderness, and grief, and passion. "How came you here? God has heard my prayer that I might see you once more before I die."

"Talk not of death," returned Harriet, with deep emotion. "Walter, I did not think to find you here. I have been brought to this place for abetting your escape."

"How! have they dared?" said the prisoner, fiercely. "Heaven and earth! that you should suffer this indignity on my account!"

"I am glad that it has so chanced; for now we can converse freely together. Probably this is the last time we shall ever meet on earth, Walter. But you must not die—oh, no, no, no! that would drive me mad, were you to perish on the scaffold."

"Bless you, adored! pardon me that I speak so. My love

has grown unearthly. Oh, that I might press your hand to these parched lips—*not* with passion! Extend it to me once again, in token of forgiveness. God reward you! They will release you immediately, of course?"

"Yes, now that you are taken; but I wish——"

"What do you wish, sweet saint? Why do you not reply?"

"I wish, then, that I might take your place. Is it not possible that I could get to you, and that you might pass from prison, wrapped in my cloak?"

"Not for ten thousand worlds!" ejaculated Danvers, absolutely shaking with emotion. "Noble woman, I feel like a reptile when I think on what has been; when the purity and radiance of your presence abases my soul, and I curse the villany——"

"Hush, hush, Walter! Not to a poor, wretched mortal, sinful as yourself, must such words be addressed. Let us forget the past and think only of the present."

"Forget the past! Bid me to forget Heaven and Eternity! I loved you, Harriet—I must speak—I swear I loved you better than my life—my spirit. My very iniquity proved the extent of my love. I sacrificed the honor I prized so highly for the sake of that guilty passion. Oh, pardon me!" Sobs, convulsing sobs heaved the mighty chest of Walter Danvers; and he hid his face —though it was pitchy dark in his dungeon—in his manacled hands, almost suffocated with emotions, better conceived than described. That a woman should be able to crush that stern spirit to dust with words of kindness.

"I pardon you from my heart of hearts, Walter!" answered Harriet, much moved. She mastered her feelings, however, wonderfully and added, "Let us not talk on this subject. It must be painful to both of us."

"But you believe me guiltier even than I am. You think I am a murderer?"

"No, Walter, of that dreadful deed I am now convinced you are guiltless."

"Joy!" shouted Danvers vehemently, till the echoes of the prison reverberated with that unusual cry of exulting rapture. "Joy, joy! If *you* think me innocent, let the harsh world load me with infamy and shame, and let my memory be execrated: let the finger of scorn and hate be pointed at me as I writhe in

death, yet I will smile as proudly as if God himself proclaimed
my guiltlessness aloud."

"I beseech you, speak not thus, Walter! You distress me
more than I can tell you. I hope to prove to all men you are no
murderer. But you have done wrong, very wrong in much. Why
did you kill that poor boy who so rashly attacked you?"

"It was a foul and bloody deed; but I meant it not. I would
give my life to undo it."

"Oh, that we could recal the past!" said Harriet. "But that
is beyond Omnipotence." She was silent for a little time, but
added, "You must try and escape, Walter, if all other means fail.
I would not have you die, to be assured myself of eternal joy."

Danvers groaned audibly. "I have cast this treasure from me
with wanton madness!" he exclaimed. "Heaven was within my
grasp, and, maniac-like, I chose damnation."

"These are wild words, Walter, wild and sinful. I beseech
you be calm; let us discuss your present position calmly."

But Danvers heard her not. There are states of mind when the
past is more vividly felt than the present, and he was absorbed in
the gone, murmuring, "She came upon me like a passionate
dream on the poet's thought, and while in her presence I recked
not of ought beside. She was my world, my idol, and I locked
up every feeling in her. I lived as in a vision, and it was only
when alone that I awoke to my crime. Ah, Harriet! my soul is
not here. It is buried with those blest scenes of thrilling, mad-
dening transport, when it hung enamoured on thy pure breath,
and heard the sweet accents which made me imperil eternity for
the sake of dwelling on them. Dost thou remember when thou
didst first make the confession of mutual love, while we went
along the banks of that stream whose music never was so harmonious as thy tongue's? Oh, God! oh, God! Thou didst give
unto me a jewel more priceless than the universe; thou didst
entrust the brightest gem in thy crown into a villain's keeping,
and he——"

"Stop, I conjure you, Walter!" interrupted Harriet, in a voice
of stifled agony, large drops of perspiration bitterer than blood
standing on her marble brow. "Why will you needlessly harrow
up the wounds of our weak hearts with these awful memories—
for they *are* awful, because unholy. How vain to regret! How

vain to weep! I thought I was beyond earthly passion : but I feel, now, how feeble, frail a thing I am. You pour poison into my spirit, speaking thus."—O, Love! O, Death! Time cannot conquer ye! Yet Love is stronger than Death, and weaker than weakness ;

> " Wormwood and honey; brief as mortal thought,
> Eternal as the everlasting word."

"Forgive me, blessed woman," answered Danvers. "I know not what I say. I am almost distracted. God grant I may die —that all recollection of me may be blotted from earth. I *had* thought of making a fame which might outlast this perishable frame, and glow with light when ages had elapsed. When this mortality was mouldering to ashes, I thought my deeds might be a beacon to light a world. But I dismiss such fancies now as vainest vanity. All is worthless that man can do. Come, let us talk calmly, if possible. If I die, Harriet, shed no tear for me. Visit my grave, if you will, sometimes, and murmur a prayer or blessing ; say, 'The misguided heart is silent, and corruption clings about him, and may the immortal in him find peace—and oblivion.'"

"Father of mercy!" ejaculated Harriet Walsingham, clasping her hands, and restraining the tears which swelled her bosom almost to bursting, "to this poor, stricken penitent send thine angel now to speak comfort which *I* cannot speak. Pity our infirmity, kind Heaven, and give us strength and hope. Let us pray, Walter! You know not the unspeakable blessedness and felicity which prayer has ever infused into my being." And she knelt and offered up a petition to the Throne of Grace, simple short, and earnest, to this effect. "We ask Thee, our Creator! to help us. We implore Thee to be present to our secret souls! Pardon the poor sinners who would return into thy bosom, and open the fold once more to the strayed sheep. Bless us, Thou eternal one! Make us purer, wiser, happier! And grant these supplications for the sake of Him whose sacred name we join with Thine, our hope, our assurance, and salvation."

She ceased to speak ; but her lips still moved, the inspired breath (the inspiration of sincerity) seemed to hover on them, her eyes were still raised, her hands clasped ; and the deep and solemn "Amen," of Danvers was heard. He then remained mute and hushed ; but his mind was active, and thronging thoughts replaced those which had occupied him a few minutes before. He was not a religious man, he was not of that enthusiastic and poetic temperament which makes a species of natural religion ; he was of the world : but the sound of that musical voice which had ceased, and the fervour of that pure and profound devotion, the simplicity of that exalted piety, in the loneliness and silence of that dreary prison, had an indescribable effect. Those who think what has been written here hyperbolical, must place themselves in the same circumstances, must listen to that sublime earnestness, in idea—which Milton thinks the secret of eloquence—and in the solitary night communing with themselves, they will perceive no extravagance in it. The watches of the night sublimate even the earthly : for there is a deep melancholy in the beauty of the stars, in the darkness of the moveless vault, and the stillness of nature, which raises us to the immortal and the infinite. Yes, Danvers prayed, and tears rolled down his brown cheek ; but they were not tears of gall. The bitterness of remorse had passed away, and he felt calm, collected, and resigned to all things. At length Harriet arose.

"What did you add that I could not hear?" inquired Walter in an altered voice.

"I will tell you," she replied. "I prayed that the love I feel for you may never more be such but as the Angels might not deem impure. My prayer has been heard ; and now I can converse as freely with you as if that which has been had not. What can I do for you, Walter? Is there any one whom you wish to know of your fate?"

"I have two children, Harriet. They are the son and daughter of that wretched woman who was once my wife : but they are mine also. They are good, they are all I could wish. Should I leave them, will you extend a friendly hand to them for my sake? I hardly liked to ask this of you ; but I know your angelic nature."

"I will love them as my children," interrupted Harriet, "if you die. But hark! I hear a step. I must close the panel for some one is coming. Farewell, Walter, farewell."

"God in Heaven bless you!" cried Walter, as the panel was

shut, seeming to close the gate of Paradise on him. "I am happy, now."

The gaoler had come to bring Danvers some water, and having given it to him, proceeded to the place where Miss Walsingham was confined.

"An order has just come from Captain Norton for your liberation, madam," said the man. "But he wishes to see you before you go. His messenger informed me that the Captain had received the information of Mr. Danvers's capture half an hour ago, and sent off immediately to bid us release you. He requests, however, as a favor, that you will wait a short time in some other place than this. Some military business detains him."

Harriet bowed her head, and followed the gaoler into another part of the building, when he left her in an apartment belonging to the governor of the prison. He had hardly departed, when a quick, irregular step was heard, the door was thrown open, and the haggard form of Norton appeared. He removed his hat, and made a reverential bow in his old fashion to the lady, his face expressing much contrition. He seemed to expect that Harriet would return a stately and female salutation; but without hesitating an instant she advanced and took his withered hand in hers, and said—

"I am sorry, Captain Norton, that by one action I have made you doubt my sacred word; but I do not wonder that it is so."

"Nay, Miss Walsingham!" exclaimed the old man, "I must supplicate your forgiveness for a rash and cruel deed. But my misery has almost driven me mad. You know I had a son—such a son! Ah, me! I will not talk of it; for I am old, and weak, and lonely. He is going to be buried. I would not part with him until corruption had commenced its work; and for long, death seemed afraid to touch aught so beautiful! Yes, I am going to part with him for ever. I shall never look upon his face again. Forgive me, madam! I am grown a poor old driveller— and—and my brain is outworn. Percy was my life, my heart, my hope. A few hours more, and all will be over for me on this side the grave. I shall walk the earth like a ghost!"

Captain Norton passed his hands across his forehead, as if to clear his mind, and Harriet, deeply affected, offered a few words of consolation, but he heard her not.

"I am going to see him once more!" cried the veteran, abruptly. "Should you like to gaze on him? You will not see such a work of art, if all the treasures of ancient genius were restored.—God's own statuary without His living breath!—There is a vehicle at the gate, which I ordered for your convenience. O, forgive me that I treated you with such rude indignity; but over my brain is a dark cloud, and on my heart, despair!"

And the officer led Miss Walsingham out of the prison, and handed her into one of those huge coaches our ancestors rumbled about in. He followed her into the vehicle, and they rolled away in the direction of Harriet's house. But in the course of half an hour they stopped at the residence of Norton, which was but a little out of the parallel road to her home.

"Will you come?" said he to his beautiful companion.

She silently assented, and they were soon in a darkened room of large size, in which there was a solitary lamp placed beside a bier.

"There!" exclaimed the old man, raising the lid of a coffin, and exposing all that remained of the young, the bright, the glorious Percy. "You see that the Destroyer has not been able to efface the stamp of the Everlasting on that high brow, so full of candour, and mind, and courage! Ah! a worm is crawling in the hair! Foul thing!" and he stamped it under foot, and kissed the luxuriant curls of his boy. "Why is it," he continued, "that decay can overtake beauty which is all of the soul? He smells now—O, horrible!"

The remains of the ill-fated youth were now, indeed, offensive, having been kept several weeks. As he had died in perfect health, however, decomposition had proceeded very slowly, and even now, though "worms were alive in his golden hair," he retained much of his singular and exquisite beauty.

"O, thou!" murmured Captain Norton, "once so loved! Am I about to consign thee to the loathsome chamber of death?—I, who gave thee life, and deemed thee a more precious part of mine own! But it must be—it must be!"

So saying, the old man proceeded to cut a single lock of those luxuriant ringlets, and to place it in his bosom. He had scarcely done this, when a messenger arrived in haste, requiring his immediate presence on some affair of great importance; and, as it was yet feared there might be a powerful rising of the Jacobites, though the government affected to make light of the recent disturbances, Captain Norton, apologizing hastily to Miss Walsingham for not accompanying her home, gathered up his energies and departed with the messenger. She did not follow him from the chamber of death, but taking up a pencil and paper approached closer to the corpse. All were asleep in the house, and not a sound, a breath could be distinguished. Calmly did she contemplate those perfect and beautiful features for some minutes, scanning the fair wreck with the eye of poet, painter, Christian.

"And art thou all then left," she said, "of buoyant youth, and elastic life, and intellect? I gaze upon thee, and methinks I hear that voice, for ever silent, singing blithely as the lark that carols in the sky. But the troubled stream of life thou hadst scarcely entered, thou hast left behind, and art gliding down the river of infinitude!" She paused a moment ere she added—"The mysteries of life and death what human heart can feel, what tongue can utter? The argument of the inspired thinker of Greece for the indestructibility of the soul, is this—' A contrary cannot receive a contrary. Life is the contrary of death; and therefore cannot receive death.' It may be death is nothing but a name: the soul lives not in Time; and, therefore, when dissolution takes place, it is only the separation of Time from Eternity."

Thronging, deep and religious feelings filled the mind of the Christian poetess, as she proceeded to her self-imposed task. Whatever scepticism may say to the contrary, there are thoughts and sensations which philosophy cannot embody, because they do not belong to the external; they are the shadows of things unseen, mystic, lofty and ethereal. Though the smell of the dead body was powerful, and disgusting, Harriet proceeded with her strange labour unshrinkingly, her face irradiated with a divine tenderness from the workings of her spirit. And the night wore away, and the faint beams of early morning streamed through the half-closed shutters, ere she had finished. There is something in the look of the dead which tranquillizes while it saddens, and as Harriet put down her pencil and murmured—

"What a wreck is here!" she inwardly exclaimed, "and when this dust, this animated dust around my soul is like this senseless form, God's smile will be on *me!*" She closed the coffin gently, saying—"Poor boy! sweet is his sleep!"

And she glanced from the motionless clay, while the lid of the coffin was not quite shut, to the portrait she had drawn. A low sob startled her, and turning round she beheld Norton contemplating her. He advanced eagerly, and seizing her hand, devoured it with kisses. Tears relieved him, while he cried—

"O, Miss Walsingham! This is more than kind of you! And not only to forgive the wrong I did you, but thus to undertake such a work. I understand it all. Angel! bless you!"

Harriet gave the drawing, which was replete with matchless beauty and fidelity, into the old man's hands; and then proceeded homewards. To return good for evil is the Christian doctrine, but among a million professed followers of Christ, who practises *his* precept? The business on which Captain Norton had been called away proved a false alarm, caused by the report of another insurrection; and on his return, he found the driver of the coach he had procured for Harriet asleep on the box, and repaired to the room where he had left her.

On reaching her house, Harriet sat down and wrote several letters, one of which she dispatched to a neighbouring town by a trusty messenger, and then, unaccompanied, sallied forth. She was met by Sam Stokes, who was returning from Walsingham Hall, and who knew her but by sight—though well acquainted with her family—having witnessed some of the numerous acts of charity she constantly performed. He made a profound inclination of his head to her, and she gave him a kind "good morning," and a smile which did the honest sailor's heart good. The poor and the sorrowful used to say that that smile rested like a sunbeam in their hearts, when she visited them.

"She's a mortial angel, that there lady!" muttered Stokes, as he trudged on. "I wonders who she be!"

Harriet continued her walk; and after some time reached a secluded cottage, which is already known to the reader as that of Henry Spenser, the philosopher. Entering without ceremony she found the contemplatist in a small room which he made his study, with open books, and scattered papers before him. He rose to give her greeting with some surprise, and taking her hand in his own—which was quite as small and delicate—he pressed it, saying—

"This is kind of you, Harriet. I was thinking of walking to your house this morning."

There was something in the eye of the philosopher when he regarded Harriet, at variance, perhaps, with the serenity and calmness of his ordinary demeanour, and his hand shook a little when it touched hers; but he resumed his usual quiet air, and she addressed him thus—

"I am come to ask a great favour of you, Henry. You were going to London in the course of a few days: will you hasten your departure and proceed thither, now?"

"I will go wherever you wish me," returned Spenser. "What can I do to serve you?

"You know my history, Henry; and you know Walter Danvers." She coloured slightly as she mentioned him dearest to her on earth, and the philosopher half turned away from her: but he looked her full in the face again, with steadfast eyes, when she proceeded—"Walter Danvers is now in prison; and his life is forfeited. But he must not die—O, no—he must not die! I had once powerful friends, and I have written to some of them to ask them to interest themselves in his behalf. Will you plead my cause with these people, whom I have not seen, nor communicated with for many years?"

"That will I," replied Spenser, with alacrity. "I would I had eloquence which could avail you; but I have little confidence in my persuasive powers. I fear these persons will not be very ready to serve you, although they once professed so much; but I can endeavour to strike a spark out of them."

"Yes, even flint gives fire; here are the letters," said Harriet. "If you can procure an interview with the King, do so. Represent to him that there are circumstances connected with the crime of which Walter Danvers has been found guilty, which in justice should be investigated; and endeavour to obtain an immediate reprieve. On my sacred word he is innocent. If you spoke with him you could not doubt the fact."

"We cannot look into the soul," returned Spenser, musingly; "but the soul *will* manifest itself. If I should fail in effecting what you desire, you must go in person, Harriet; for a woman's eloquence is most irresistible with men, and *you* might do almost anything. How long will it be ere the authorities think of putting the sentence of the law on Danvers in execution?"

"He will probably be examined to-morrow: but as yet I am in ignorance of all. There is an old lawyer of the name of Quirk who has promised to do much: but what he has revealed to me is vague and unsatisfactory. I am quite convinced, however, that he knows more than he will tell."

"I will go to him before I proceed to London. I am so little a man of the world that I hardly know how to set about doing you any service; but I will try to make up in zeal for what I want in discretion."

"You are all kindness, and are the most valued and valuable friend I have. No time is to be lost; but neither must we be hasty. Write to me immediately after you reach London, if you think my presence can be of use. You cannot conceive the state of suspense and dread I am now in."

"Yes I can," said Spenser. "I know full well that those who love vainly, often love the most intensely. Danvers was a noble fellow once, with all his faults: and I wonder not that he gained even such a heart as yours."

"O, there is still much good left in him," replied Harriet. "I have seen him within these last few hours, and conversed with him for a long time."

"Indeed!—I hope that I may return with his pardon; but do not buoy yourself up too much with that notion, Harriet. I dread lest——"

"Nay," interrupted Miss Walsingham, "I have made up my mind to all things. Only, he must not die, if all I have on earth —reputation, health, life, can save him. All *but* that God would help me to bear. How I have loved that man He alone can tell. I can confess this to you, Henry, without a blush, for you understand me. But let us not waste precious time. Seek out Quirk, and elicit what you can from him. Take this purse; for the sordid wretch cares for nothing but gold; and then make ready for your journey to London. My very existence hangs on the issue of this event."

Spenser sighed deeply, took up his hat, and having received Quirk's direction, instantly set off. Harriet resolved to await his

return where she was, and utterly exhausted with all she had undergone during the last few hours, lay down, and attempted to
snatch a few minutes sleep to enable her to endure the fatigues
that might yet await her. And she did fall into an uneasy slumber, which continued for a short time: but was startled from it
by an occurrence which shall be presently narrated.

It is now necessary to leave her fortunes, and to return to
Charles Walsingham. A little while, and the curtain will descend,
and these our actors fall into oblivion. We are *all* hastening
from this troubled stage of life, having performed our part in its
brief pageant, and shall be no more soon, even than these beings
of the mind who strut and fret their little hour so vainly! There
is to my heart something solemn in the conclusion of all things.
We hope, we fear, aspire, despair; and after all (as in life) the
whole " signifies nothing."

" To Captain Charles Walsingham.

" O, Charles ! My poor father ! All disguise is now useless.
Help him, if you love me. His name will put you in possession
of all I have to say. He is Walter Danvers. That you love me
I am certain: fly, then, to his succour. He is innocent; but the
facts are strong against him; and man judges by what *seems,*
and not what *is.* God knows my dear father's innocence; appearances are as nothing to *him;* and if you knew my father you
would say he must be guiltless of such a deed. You know he
was condemned to death many years ago. He made his escape
to France, and entered the service of that country. He was induced some months since to undertake a secret mission to England; and at my entreaty I came with him. Death stares him
in the face on every side: and if he perish, how shall I survive?
He has been so kind, so fond a father to me :—never denied me
a wish. He has supplied the place of both parents—for my mother died, I believe, when I was an infant. I have missed you
very much, dear Charles, (I write as my heart dictates, though I
know not if it is right), and would have addressed a letter to you
had I dared. But I promised my good nurse, when she gave me
the letter you sent by her, not to answer it. You ask me to become your wife; but *that* can never be, until the unjust stigma

3 T

on my father's name is removed. I would not bring the shadow
of disgrace on you for the universe—you are *my* universe, noblest,
loftiest, best! This is a cold, heartless world, and everything
evil, I have heard, is believed, while nothing that is good is
allowed. I can hardly believe this, though; for *I* can scarcely
credit what is *bad* ;—you know what I mean, but want words to
express. You, I am certain, are not one of those more ready to
condemn than pity, to suspect than confide. *You* will believe my
father's innocence without proof; but Heaven in its own good
time will clear the dreadful mystery which hangs over the fate of
your murdered relative up. I know not where I shall be when
you receive this letter; but will let you know how to find me in
a few hours. Strain every nerve, for my sake, to save my father.
He will be examined, I hear, to-morrow. It is of the utmost
importance we should get time to collect proof. But even if it
should be made apparent that he is guiltless of the crime of murder imputed to him, I fear his life will be forfeited on account of
the part he has taken in the recent insurrection. Let me hear
from you without delay. O, Charles! I would that I were queen
of all this earth, that I might give you the fairest lands and the
brightest spots upon it! But I am poor and helpless, and can
give nothing to you but my weak, foolish heart. It is not worth
your having, Charles; but I will cultivate it, as you would possess
it. How very incoherent and ill-written this letter is! How it
is blotted with my tears! Our loves have not begun under happy
auspices; but a fairer day may dawn. To all good angels I now
commend you. I have thought of you, I have prayed for you,
day and night. While the breath of life warms my heart, you
will be dear to Ellen.—None know I have written to you; but I
could not refrain from doing so; my heart is nearly breaking!"

CHAPTER III.

In this old rascal world, my friend, we see
At every turn some treachery or guile;
At every winding Sorrow meets the ear,
And Truth and Virtue weep, and Vice elate
Looks to the skies and swears Jove is not there!

Old Play.

CHARLES FINDS A MYSTERY—THE SECRET CONFERENCE—
FRANK AND HIS MESSAGE—A SURPRISE—ELLEN.

"My own, own Ellen!" exclaimed Charles Walsingham, kissing the simple and affectionate letter he had just received from the maiden of his heart repeatedly. "I will go to thee, instantly, and will never be divided from thee more! What an age it seems since we parted!"

Our old friend, Charles, had just returned from a long walk, which he had taken for the purpose of discovering the present dwelling of Ellen; but—as was the case every day since he had left the house of Danvers—fruitlessly. He was almost in despair of ever hearing more of her; when a servant put this letter into his hand, and informed him that a little, ragged urchin left it a few minutes before, but ran away as soon as he had put it into his hand. But the joy of Charles was soon damped, when he reflected on the contents of the epistle. His Ellen was the daughter of a malefactor condemned for the murder of a near relative of his own! His opinion had always been strongly against Danvers, though his judgment was formed by report; and the pride which was almost the strongest passion in his nature—a just, and honourable pride—revolted at the idea of uniting himself with a felon's child: but the image of the helpless and unprotected girl, so young, so innocent, so lovely and forlorn, rose to his mind and he exclaimed—

"I care not! I will seek some desert with her as my bride, and forget there are any others than ourselves in existence."

How different is the love of man from that of woman! Ellen,

if Charles had been placed in a position similar to herself, would have dared the scorn and ignominy of the world, gentle, timid thing as she was.   Men have more physical bravery than women ; but the very delicacy of a woman's soul—her tenderness and devotion—appear to gift her with moral courage.   Yet the soldier was an excellent fellow in his way !

It was now evening, and the young officer sallied forth again ; for there was a weight on his heart, which, it seemed, could not be relieved in the atmosphere of a house.   In sorrow and felicity do we not seek solitude?   But in sorrow we feel all things irksome, in felicity the dumb woods have voices deep and thrilling ;—*all* is beauty.   Heeding not the path he took, Charles walked rapidly on, and in the course of an hour found himself in a secluded spot, where the brushwood grew thickly : and leaning his back against a low tree, satisfied that none could see him, he resigned himself to dreamy thought.

" Ah !" ran his reverie, " I could be happy with *her* in an uninhabited island, even if it were dreary and sterile, and the bare necessaries of life must be earned with toil and wearisomeness. What real pleasures are there in the wreathed smiles of the crowd, in the false and artificial usages of the world.—No ; I am resolved on this, if Ellen consent to embrace such a step !—And yet, why should I be ashamed of presenting her to society as my wife? The gold is not the less valuable because it has come from the dark bowels of the earth encrusted with dirt, and she is not to suffer for the sins of her father.   Out on this proud spirit I bear ! Am I such a moral coward as to fear the reproaches, the sneers and the sarcasms of the cold, the vile, and heartless ?   But then, to shield her from the misery of being pointed at.   Ah, there it is !   I could not endure *that !*   No, we will leave the haunts of men, and be the world to each other !   Fair children shall spring up unto us, and we will train them in the paths of virtue.   Their endearments will be ample amends for all the sweet flattering things man can say !"

The soldier's meditations were interrupted by a confused sound of voices, but looking around he could see no one.   The spot in which he found himself was remote from every human dwelling, and the pleached boughs of the trees formed an impenetrable barrier to further progress in the direction he had unconsciously taken. But diverging somewhat to the left, at the distance of a few paces, was a path, by pursuing which it was possible to thread the intricacies of the labyrinth—which was the same already alluded to in a former portion of the narrative.

There was a little, ruinous building, of about ten feet in height, long since deserted, and which was close to the spot where Charles heard the sound of voices; but so dense was the underwood, that it was hardly possible to catch a glimpse of this ruin through the intertwined branches. The curiosity of the soldier was in some measure excited: but it is most likely he would have overmastered it, had he not distinguished the name of Danvers. It was impossible, however, to catch more than a word here and there by the intensest listening, where Charles stood: and instigated by some presentiment that he should discover something of importance connected with Ellen, he smothered the high-minded scruples which deterred him from acting any part that had a shadow of meanness, and cautiously treading, he went round to the ruin, and stationed himself outside (for the voices now came from the interior of the building) so that it was not probable he should be seen, if those who were now conferring came out, and passed near him. There was a small hole in the wall of the ruin, by looking through which, Charles could see two men engaged in earnest conversation. One of them was very old and rather decrepid; but he could not see his face, which was turned from him. The other was a person a trifle, perhaps, his own senior, of slight, but not ungraceful figure, and low stature, with a face in which there was some shrewdness and power, mingled with dark and gloomy passion; and he was speaking in a harsh, suppressed voice to the other person, when the soldier first saw him.

" You shall have the money," old man, he said ; " but not before you have fulfilled your portion of the contract. I cannot trust you, if I pay you the reward at once; but I will give you a promise in writing, if you wish."

" Nay, Master Freestone," was the reply, " that were of no use to me. Rogues must be content to pay for what they want at once—excuse me. Ha, ha! I will do nothing for you, I repeat, if you do not pay me down £300 on the instant. If you like the terms on which I am willing to serve you, well and good :

if not, say so, and I will go my way; for it is getting late and I have business to transact."

"Three hundred pounds is a large sum," returned the younger individual. "What assurance have I, if I give you the money, that I can depend on you?"

"None, whatsoever; except the word of a rascal; but my motto is—'Honesty among thieves!' Ha, ha! But it matters not to me. I shall be paid well, if I get him off."

"That must not be. Three hundred pounds is more than I can well afford to lose for nothing; but if you can show me that there is a rational prospect of my finding the agreement fulfilled, here's the sum."

"Three hundred pounds, as you remark, *is* a good bit of money; but nothing less would satisfy my conscience. Well, then, look you here, sir. I engage to perform what you want for a stipulated amount; and am retained on the other side at the same time. You pay me beforehand: well. It is evident to you that if I can get more by being honest than a scoundrel, I shall cheat you. Very good. I will let you know, if I am likely to do so; but if not, it is plain I have no interest to defraud you. I have a conscience, Master Freestone, though it is a rogue's conscience. It has got a d—d ugly twist, I admit, but still there it is. Are you satisfied, or not?"

"I suppose I *must* be satisfied. There, take the money. I must now quit this part of the country—but shall be present at the examination to-morrow, and narrowly watch you—and, if you fail to fulfil your promise, as the Lord liveth, I will return and slit your ears directly. If I am satisfied with you, I will not stint the remuneration even to what I have given you. You know something of my character, perhaps, and if not, may form some estimate of it by what has already passed."

"Ah! I can't feel or understand that desire of vengeance to no purpose. For my own part, I always make my feelings and passions secondary to my interest. But every man according to his humour!"

"I have an interest beyond the gratification of hate, here," was the rejoinder. "This man has stolen from me the rewards and praises which of right belong to me. Besides, if I did not hate him from my soul, and had no other motive to urge me on, his life is justly forfeited."

"How do you make that out, sir?"

"He has been guilty of innumerable crimes. I am convinced he is a traitor to the cause he pretends to serve, and—and—d—n him! He has crossed me in my path, like a serpent; he is a clever devil; and so no more. Good night. Remember, if you fail me, I'll take your miserable life!"

"Ha, ha! Take matters coolly, master Freestone, and don't threaten; it's a bad practice, depend on't! Good night.—Ah, Isaac! What do you want with me?"

While the old man had been speaking, the personage he called Freestone, wrapping a cloak around him, apparently for the purpose of disguise, walked moodily away; and a lad of about sixteen entered the place, and exclaimed,

"Mother Stokes wants to see ye as soon as possible; she's in a great quandary. I met her by accident arter you left me, and she says she's afraid there'll be old Nick to pay, and wants your advice. She'll pay you a guinea."

"I'll go to her," said the old man, and immediately moved away, followed by the boy.

"What can this mean?" thought the soldier to himself. "I certainly heard the name of Danvers; and if coupled with what I have overheard, there is something mysterious lurking beneath the affair of that murder. Yet I fear the murderer was Ellen's father. *She* a murderer's child! It seems as probable an angel should proceed from a devil."

And resolved to sift the business to the bottom he followed the retreating forms of the aged man and the lad. But night was fast falling, and he was unacquainted with the locality to which he had wandered, so that not being able to follow close on the heels of those he pursued, lest he should be seen, he mistook a turning they had taken, and was speedily involved in the mazes of the wood. Provoked with himself at having missed an opportunity of discovering an affair teeming to him with the intensest interest, he made violent efforts to extricate himself from the labyrinth; but the more he did so, was he bewildered. There was no clue to the Dædalian mystery of the place; and he had resigned himself to despair, and made up his mind to passing the

night in the open air, when he distinguished voices at no great
distance, and presently a struggle ensued. Hastily pushing his
way through the trees which impeded his sight, he found a young
man defending himself against half-a-dozen fellows in sailors'
dresses; but he was knocked down and pinioned as he arrived on
the scene of action.

"Ha!" cried Charles Walsingham, striding up to the men who
were busy securing the captive, with that generous impulse which
prompts us to take part with the weaker side, without inquiring
into the merits of the case. "What is this?"

The youth who had so vainly struggled against overpowering
numbers turned to Charles at this query, and it would seem instantly knew him, for he said,

"Do not interfere in my behalf, Captain Walsingham. These
men have authority for what they do, and you would only get
yourself into trouble by helping me."

"What! my cousin Frank? It can be no other. By Heaven!
If you say the word I will rescue you, or die."

"Strike him down," cried the leader of the sailors, raising a
cutlass against the soldier; but the prisoner exclaimed,

"No, for God's sake let the laws take their course, Charles;
your whole future prospects would be blighted for ever by your
unthinking generosity. I submit to my fate. But will you take
a message for me to a lady who lives at yonder house you may
see at the distance of a mile on the acclivity?"

"Certainly; but if you are taken, Frank, I fear death awaits
you. My cousin Fanny told me your story a few hours ago."

"Fear not for me; but proceed to that cottage and state the
predicament I am in to the young lady you will see, and say that
I have been to her father——"

"We can't allow you to jaw no more," interrupted the warrant
officer who had previously spoken. "If you won't heave anchor
at once, we must take you in tow."

"Only another word. Say for me I have been to her father
and he may see her to-morrow."

The young man thus having spoken was led away, and Charles
murmured,

"Poor fellow! I fear it will go hardly with him. But I will
hasten to London, and see what I can do both for him, and

Ellen's guilty parent. What a thought of horror it is that she whom I adore should have sprung from such a wretch. I cannot, will not believe it. But he is guilty ; yes, I must not allow myself to be led away by passion. I will marry her if she will consent to become mine ; but perfectly aware that by doing so I must forfeit my place in society. It is a cruel thing that erring man should make the innocent pay the penalty of the guilty! Oh, Ellen, Ellen! Have I then found thee at last! Poor, gentle flower ! this heavy blow will crush thy frail existence, unless a careful hand guard thee from the chilling blasts with which thou wilt shortly be assailed, unless there be one devoted to thee who will pillow thy head upon his bosom ! I were a wretch to hesitate in what way to act. I will sacrifice my station, and despise all the icy maxims of the vulgar crowd, and attach myself undividedly to thee. This proud heart will have to struggle greatly yet ; but when I see her, when I hear her sweet voice, and look on her fair and innocent face, I shall rejoice in the evils I encounter for her sake. Yes, Ellen! I will dry thy tears, and soothe thy sorrows, continually whisper fondest words into thine ear ; and while others shrink from the murderer's daughter, will clasp thee to my heart as a treasure vaster than all God's radiant universe. Hear my vow, O ye stars ! that now come glistening into your soft evening life, looking so holy that ye purify what is corrupt within our souls ! hear me, O ye woods, that speak a language of divine accents in still, trembling whispers ! I will make my existence, my passions, my dreams and aspirations hers only. Oh, thou eternal cause of all ! help me to pour balm into my pure angel's stricken breast, and direct me how to keep her free even from a breath of pain."

In the constitution of the mind of man innumerable elements are eternally at work : and there is not a single moment of existence that a change is not effected—however imperceptible it may be—in the individual. Yet the " Ego" remains the same, while the building is piled up ; it is as unchangeable in essence as God. Charles Walsingham was not a man of extraordinary intellect ; and though his resolution was not vacillating, his feelings were so ardent, that while his mind remained firm, his heart was always galloping as fast as it could go, carried away along rocks and precipices by its enthusiasm and poetry. But the strife within

3 U

him at this moment was great—love and pride were contending
against each other most ferociously : but the heart against the
head in such a nature " all the world to nothing." Oh, Love !
sacred Love ! How sublime thou canst make our low humanity !
Thou art no poet's unattainable vision, no idealist's beautiful abstraction : but continually liftest up the soul ; and from the well-
spring of thy pure life pourest most precious waters into the
channels of our secret being. If the character of Charles was not
of that exalted kind which unassisted soars above the weaknesses
of mortality, and he clung with the ardour of honorable ambition
to fame and reputation ; yet what were they in the balance with
that supreme affection which truth and innocence had inspired ?
The wise man said well, surely : " Love is strong as death," it
must be stronger than life, stronger than *all* save death, the arch-
victor over us !   " Ah," says the man who has loved in vain, " it
is an illusion ; it is selfish, HUMAN."   The happy lover replies,
" It is true, *un*selfish, DIVINE !"   It is ALL these ! Paradox of
paradoxes ! The false and the true, selfish and unselfish, human
and divine, commingled.   What a splendid fellow the soldier then
looked, as the lofty aspirations of his spirit painted with the glory
of enthusiasm his flashing face, and his noble form, so full of life
and strength and fiery manhood, dilated to its fullest stature with
the fervor of his heart ! Never did a conqueror flushed with
triumph after some bloody field, never did warrior crowned with
laurel after leaving the scene of ' the red pestilence' exhibit such
proud majesty of bearing, as the passionate lover then did, his
face turned up to Heaven, and his soul discoursing with invisible
spirits that seemed to throng the air, and approve his high
resolve; and when the mind is in such a condition it seems to
delight in recurring to what is beyond " the reaching of our
souls."

" Beautiful beings !" he exclaimed, his excited fancy (fancy
and feeling are nearly identical) evoking the unseen and spiritual
into actuality, " *ye* are blessed with immortality, with nothing to
cloud your happiness ; but ye are not more joyous than I shall
be with my Ellen, more felicitous than we will be with God !"

By this time Charles had arrived at the house to which he had
promised to bear a message from Frank ; and for the first time
descending from those imaginative heights, he bethought himself

that he had omitted to inquire the name of the lady to whom the
message was to be delivered. " I suppose she is some flame of
my young cousin," he muttered ; " but how am I to inquire for
her ? Ah, there is a light in that room, and the door is ajar. I
will enter, and trust to chance."

Taking his resolution, Charles approached, and after some
hesitation on the threshold, lest he should be mistaken for a thief,
proceeded into the house. He almost repented he had adopted
such a course when he reached the door of the chamber from
which he had seen the light ; but he had gone too far to recede.
This door also was not closed, and looking into the apartment he
saw a female form in the attitude of prayer. A murmur reached
his ear, at first indistinct, but which grew into an articulate
sound. He had been unwilling to disturb the fair suppliant at
such a time ; but when he heard that voice, he with difficulty
suppressed a loud exclamation of astonishment.

" Preserve my father, gracious Lord," were the accents which
reached the soldier's ear, " and shield him from the dreadful fate
impending over him ! Strengthen me to bear all things, and help
me, for I am very weak. But, oh, in all the trials I am doomed
to sustain, let me never, never know that he I love is unhappy ;
but give him all the felicity Thou canst give, and shower blessings, blessings—" ;

The prayer abruptly terminated in a shriek of terror, but it
speedily changed to a cry of transport, for she found herself encircled in those arms where she fancied no grief could reach her.
And burning, passionate kisses were pressed upon her lips, pure
and devoid of all sensuality as ever such kisses were ; but " with
other eloquence than words," conveying the depth and intensity
of the love that glowed in the soldier's bosom.

" My life, world, angel !" said Charles, while Ellen suffered
his warm caresses with trembling frame, and then throwing herself on his breast indulged in copious floods of tears. Poor
child ! trustful and simple as an infant clinging to a mother !

" Look up, my own Ellen," said Walsingham, in the most
thrilling voice that love inspires, " look up, my own, my beautiful ! Why were you silent so long, sweet ? Oh, it has seemed a
dreary time since I last beheld you ! Yet, though you have not
been present, bodily, love, you have haunted my spirit day and

night, like some strain of blessed music not of earth." —
Still she wept on; but was ever ringing laughter, were ever
joyous smiles fraught with so deep a burthen of transporting
bliss? Give me such tears in heaven! There are fountains in our
nature which manifest themselves in the most opposite ways—
there are streams which course through the centre of our being,
and are seen not in the light of their beauty, not visible " from
extreme loveliness" but in the deep, deep holiness of their eternity; mystic, spiritual, incomprehensible, assuring us of a heaven
removed from grief and mortality. For in this our life the earthly
and divine are separated by so slight a barrier, that when we
spring elate into blessedness the mortal weeps for the immortal's
power. Thus a tear and a smile may emanate from the same
cause. The ebullition of joy and woe is a manifestation of the
spiritual and material, and when the feelings are overwrought
how can they be relieved by smiles? Oh, no; tears proceed
from the deepest springs of joy; smiles are the April beams,
happy, not overflowing. If it were possible such ecstasies could
endure, however, the feeble powers of vitality would be soon
exhausted; and the lovers lapsed into a medium state of felicity,
in some degree overshadowed by the uncertainty in which they
were involved.

" You will be my wife now, Ellen?" said Charles, as the
maiden, in the guilelessness of her young heart, clung to the
being who supported her.

" Ah, no," returned Ellen, " that cannot be. My father's life
is in peril, and I would not desert him to be the happiest mortal
that ever lived. But he is innocent, I am certain; you, too,
believe him innocent?"

Walsingham evaded the direct question of his beloved. " I
will proceed to London immediately, and use all my influence to
procure his pardon," he said.

There was something in the tone he spoke in which caused a
pang of disappointment to shoot through the maiden's breast;
but she would not suspect that *her* Walsingham could believe her
father guilty of the darkest crime in the decalogue. Alas, she
was soon to be undeceived.

" You will go and see my father, Charles—you will go with
me?" said Ellen. " Mrs. Haines—she who nursed you in your

illness—has told me that he would never consent to our union, because your political principles are so widely different from his. But she knows not his noble nature; and when—and when I tell him that my happiness depends on his blessing our marriage, I am sure he will do so; for he loves me so fondly! He will be acquitted, and then there will be no bar to my becoming yours, provided your relations will receive a lowly maid into their house." The soldier averted his eyes uneasily. "What are you thinking of, Charles?" asked Ellen. "Do you not think that my father—"

"Yes, yes, I hope all will be well, love. I have been thinking we may spend our lives in some fair spot, where the din and turmoil of the world cannot disturb the serene happiness of our lives."

"But my father, Charles—my poor father. Your manner fills me with apprehension. You think there is not a chance of saving his life?"

"I will save him, or perish!" cried the soldier. "Oh, Ellen, to preserve you from sorrow I would throw rank, fame, and connexions from me as worthless gauds in comparison with thy wellbeing. But the facts were strong against him, you are aware—"

"Ah," ejaculated Ellen, a new light breaking in upon her, and striking her brain with anguish, "you are among those who have doubted his innocence. But I tell you, if you had watched him for years as I have, you would feel assured he could not have been the criminal—"

"Speak no more of this, my beloved," interrupted Charles. "Let us think of the best measures to save him."

"But assure me you believe now he is innocent," said the young girl, anxiously.

"I will try to do so, dearest. I have doubted, I own; but think not, if he were the greatest wretch that ever walked this earth, his crimes could create any diminution in my love for you. But I had forgotten something. Do you know a youth named Francis Walsingham, who has just sent a message by me to the effect that he had been to your father, and that you might see him to-morrow?" A slight, a very slight degree of jealousy sprang up in the soldier's bosom as he said this.

"Ah, yes, we will go together, Charles. You will tell my father you believe he is not guilty?"

One of the strongest traits in Walsingham's high character was his love of truth, without the most distant prevarication. He had already outstepped the boundary which he thought he might with a strict regard to conscience; and he was silent. Ellen gazed intently into her lover's face, and then turned away to conceal the silent tears that were trickling down her cheek. The cup of bliss was thus in a few moments dashed away from their lips, and during the long hours they spent in each other's society they were grave, sad, and dejected. O earth, O earth! Must all thy matchless fruition end in this? First, the elysium, all bright, all heavenly. Then the dark shadow stealing over the ethereal sky, until at last the whole vanishes into thin air, and of passion and rapture, and thrilling bliss is left not " a wreck behind!"

CHAPTER IV.

There's wisdom to be gather'd from the dead.—*MS.*

THE CAVE AND THE STRUGGLE—MYSTERY—FIGGINS.

At length, Charles Walsingham quitted Ellen, promising to return in a short time and accompany her to the examination to which her father was about to be subjected. It was midnight when he quitted the cottage where dwelt the treasure of his heart, and the weather had greatly changed since he entered the dwelling. A thick black cloud concealed the moon, and huge masses of vapour floated across the sable heaven; while ever and anon the summer lightning darted athwart the sky in transient blazes, and the distant thunder rumbled mournfully. At such a time, Creation appears to weep, and the very beauty of the scene is like a dream of lovely desolation. But Walsingham heeded not the elements, absorbed as he was in his own meditations, and walked onwards with rapid strides, his temples throbbing, and his blood feverish. Charles could not but perceive how sharp a pang he had inflicted on the sensitive heart of Ellen by refusing to declare what he did not feel—a conviction of her father's innocence: but for years he had made up his mind to the guilt of Danvers, and it was not possible that so rooted an opinion could change in a moment. As for the conference he had accidentally overheard, it made but little impression on him now; and he was inclined to think his ear had cheated him when he fancied he heard the name of Danvers pronounced. "O truth! truth!" exclaimed the soldier, "brightest of essences—what an inexorable tyrant thou art! When by one little word I might have made the being I adore happy, why could I not do so? I will study casuistry, and persuade myself that thou art stern and unlovely, when thou wouldst check the warm impulses of the heart, and create pain to the good and pure!"

While engaged in this train of thought, the soldier had reached the skirts of the wood where he overheard the conference just alluded to. The rain was descending rapidly, and instead of taking the direct road Charles preferred pursuing the way through the wood, as he might there be sheltered, while he continued walking. It was so dark, however, that but for the lightning he would have again become entangled in the labyrinth, and he half repented him of having chosen the path he now pursued. He wished to return to Walsingham Hall, to relieve any uneasiness that might be felt at his absence, and then ride back to Ellen, and proceed with her to the town in the prison of which Danvers was confined. But having scarcely recovered from the effects of his recent severe illness, the excitement he had undergone created a feeling of sickness and exhaustion such as he was unaccustomed to experience in the hardest campaigns. He paused to recover himself, and leaning against the withered trunk of a gnarled oak he looked up to the immeasurable vault, which was illuminated with splendour every minute by the lambent lightning, that seemed to fly like a winged horse over the pathless ether, and measured the dark space with a sensation of insignificance in the immensity of the stupendous universe. But not long did the soldier fix his gaze on the magnificent dome above, not long did his soul cleave the immensity of space, for the sound of footsteps and voices, and the light of a lantern at no very great distance excited his surprise. "Perhaps," he thought, "here may be some solution of the enigma which baffled me a few hours ago," and retiring behind the tree, he watched the per-

sons who were advancing. But the lightning ceased, and the
dark lantern was turned away from him, so that he only saw the
outlines of the figures that approached. The first form was that
of a large, powerful man, wrapped in a cloak, who carried something of considerable size underneath his mantle, and the other was
a decrepid woman's; but more than this Charles was unable to
discover. They conversed in a smothered tone, so that he could
only catch a word here and there; but he fancied the name of
Walsingham once reached his ear. Determined that he would
sift this business to the bottom, in the vague hope that his own
happiness would be secured thereby, he cautiously followed the
man and woman: but fearful lest he should lose them in the
darkness, as he had previously lost the others, he did not allow
them to get beyond pistol-shot from him; and it was difficult to
make his way through the crackling boughs which interposed,
without betraying his proximity. Thus he proceeded for about a
furlong and a half, when the individuals he followed suddenly
turned into a path which diverged from that they had hitherto
pursued, and then took another turning, ere Walsingham was prepared. Fearful lest he should be again too late, he quickened his
pace, and in another second he was convinced he saw some one
descending, as it were, into the bowels of the earth, when the
light disappeared. But he had seen enough to guide him to the
spot, and he found a huge stone beneath some brambles, which,
after some difficulty, he was successful in removing entirely,
and discovered a flight of steps, which he descended instantly.
He had pistols with him, and cocking one of them, and drawing
his sword, he advanced quickly in the direction of the retreating
footsteps. But the cave he had entered presented as many difficulties as the labyrinth; and he found he was going away from
the persons he pursued, having advanced into a passage from
which there was no outlet. But as he was retreading the way a
sound greeted his ear. He stopped and listened.

"This way," said a voice in a whisper, which rang through
the subterranean passage, "I heard a step go this way."

The crisis was at hand, and Charles conceiving it probable
that a mortal struggle might ensue if his suspicions were correct,
stood prepared for action behind a projection that was found in
the excavation.

" I thinks as how you be mistaken, sir," said a second voice, " but your hearing maybe's quicker than mine."

" Hark !" returned the other. " Hush ! what noise was that ?"

There was a distant sound, as of the falling of some heavy substance, and then all was still, strangely still. The individual in the vicinity of the soldier was now within arm's length of him ; but what was his astonishment as the light of the lantern which the foremost carried fell upon his face, to perceive the youth who had pistolled the robber when he was attacked after leaving Danvers's house, and who, from his resemblance to that person, he had concluded was nearly related to him. But he had mentioned nothing of that affair to Ellen, for reasons which may be guessed. The other man was a cripple, who had a naked cutlass in one hand, and he had no difficulty in recognising Sam Stokes in him. A dark suspicion entered the mind of Walsingham, which induced him to remain motionless, and the young man and the tar passed by without noticing his presence. He followed close at their heels, and presently they stopped before a door which resisted their efforts to open it for some time; but by their united strength they succeeded in forcing a passage.

But they were now at fault evidently, for they held a whispered consultation together. It was at this juncture a heavy footstep was heard in a passage adjoining that they were in, and hurrying in the direction of it, they stumbled against some person, who uttered a scream, and fled.

" That was my cursed aunt's voice !" exclaimed Stokes. " You go arter her, as you're the most nimble, and I'll foller t'other— Whew ! there's another behind us !"

But the youth sprang away without heeding his companion, and poor Sam, in his haste, stumbled and fell. Charles rushed past him with great rapidity, and bounded away. He heard the sound of water, and then a heavy plash, close beside him ; then there was a brief struggle, and a curse, and a groan—and a fall. Another second, and Charles Walsingham seized a brawny fellow by the throat, and cried,

" Move but a step, and I will kill you."

But before he was prepared, the fellow struck him with some sharp weapon, which wounded him in the shoulder, and by a mighty effort succeeded in freeing himself from his powerful

3 x

grasp. Ere he had fled a dozen paces, however, Charles discharged a pistol after him, which evidently took some effect, as it was succeeded by a slight cry of pain. Walsingham again pursued, but totally unacquainted with the place, which was pitchy dark, although a more active man than the fugitive, he could not overtake him. He reached the open air with some puzzling, and perceived some recent marks of gore in the direction of the maze; but they soon terminated, and he gave up the pursuit.

He returned to the cave, and entered it for a second time, determined that he would not allow the opportunity which presented itself of clearing up the mystery to pass by ; but he found it abandoned, and finally relinquished the hope he had entertained, and quitted the cavern. The wound which he had received, though not material, was now bleeding profusely, and he was unable to staunch it. He looked about him for some house to enter ; but it was now so dark, that he could distinguish no object at any distance. He walked on, somewhat faint and exhausted, and at last was obliged to stop, from weakness. Scarcely had he done so, when he heard the sound of a muffled drum, and presently the trampling of horses. He next distinguished a dead march, and in the course of a few minutes a funereal military procession swept past him, and proceeded towards a churchyard, at the distance of a few hundred yards.

In the person of the chief mourner he recognised Captain Norton, whom he had known years before. He was acquainted with the melancholy facts connected with Percy's death : and instigated by a feeling higher than mere curiosity, he followed the procession into the burial-place. The family vault of the Nortons was in the church, but the ashes of the ill-fated boy were to be deposited in the burying ground, and when they arrived there the troop dismounted, and walked slowly to the church. Many a rough heart was subdued, and many a weather-beaten cheek wet among the troop that followed the remains of the young officer to their last long home, and hands which had not trembled when grasping the sabre in the deadly charge, shook as they loosened the matchlocks preparatory to firing over the grave.

Captain Norton had induced the clergyman of the place to officiate at night : for he had an invincible repugnance to see a vulgar, gaping crowd attracted by the military display which accompanied the solemnity. And where was he during the ceremony in the sacred edifice, previous to depositing the corpse in the earth? The bereaved father then stood calm and motionless, his white hair, his wrinkled brow, his shrivelled form all seeming to belong not to a living man, every function of animal existence seeming suspended while the words of faith and consolation were being uttered by the officiating minister in a solemn tone. A superficial observer would have thought he was an unmoved spectator of the scene, if he had not been so very close to the coffin: but those fixed, glassy eyes, those contracted brows, and that compressed mouth told a world of agonized and voiceless suffering to the student of man.

Not for one instant did the veteran remove his eyes from the coffin which contained all that was left on earth of the beloved and lost. It was a piteous spectacle to behold the withered figure of the hopeless old man, those snowy hairs which a few weeks had changed from grey to silver, and the deep furrows that short interval had made in his blanched cheek, together with the unspeakable gaze of mingled love and despair which appeared to pierce through the obstacles that interposed between him and the being who was beyond sorrow.

Close by Captain Norton's side stood a figure muffled in a cloak, which was that of his brother John, who had requested to be present on the occasion: and it was with difficulty the honest John stifled the sobs which rose to his throat. But to the last, while they remained in the church, the chief mourner maintained his preternatural composure—but now they moved to the grave, and the awful obsequies drew to a close. The coffin was lowered slowly; and then a change came over the appearance of Captain Norton. He advanced to the brink of the grave.

"O God!" he cried, "oh God, why must I bear this?"

His brother attempted to whisper some words of comfort into his ear, but they reached not the stony sense. Every fibre of his being was drawn up, every sensation and thought fixed with excruciating tension in the engrossing idea of being separated for ever from his boy; and he gasped, staggered, and would have fallen, had he not been supported. "Dust to dust; ashes to ashes!" Hark, the musketry! But the wretched Norton heard it not. The rattling of the gravel on the coffin-lid seemed to strike like an ice-bolt to his heart. He stamped, he raved, and tore his white hair like a maniac—that *cold*, formal man—and then, with one long, protracted cry, one fearful scream—once heard, never to be forgotten—a scream that rose above the din of the musketry, and thrilled the blood of the most apathetic present, he threw himself out of the arms of his brother, and fell without sense or motion to the earth. A man's scream, a *courageous* man's scream is the most fearful thing in nature, and for years many of those present heard it in their dreams, and shuddered. But he was insensible : happy oblivion ! and he was carried away by some troopers. The heart-rending scene was over.

Charles Walsingham departed, full of grave and saddening feelings. The grey dawn was on the point of breaking when he reached his house. All was hushed around him, and but for the unquiet beatings of his heart he could almost have imagined that those stormy human passions and convulsions of nature he had left behind were chimerical. As Walsingham was crossing the lawn before the house, he noticed a figure at a short distance, and knew it to be that of Corporal Figgins.

"Ah, Corporal," he cried, " I want to say a few words to you."

Figgins somewhat unwillingly obeyed, and Charles spoke a few words to him, requesting him to inform Lady Walsingham in the morning that he was absent on unavoidable business. " What is the matter with your hand, Figgins?" he said, as the Corporal was about to leave him.

" I had a casualty, your honour," replied Figgins, " while cleaning a pistol, which went off and shattered one of my fingers."

" Strange !" muttered Charles to himself, when having entered the house he sat down to write a few lines to an influential friend in London in behalf both of Danvers and Frank. " It is very strange ! But I do the Corporal injustice to harbour such a doubt against him. Why must we suspect all things in this world ?"

Charles soon completed his letter, and having snatched a hasty repast, proceeded to the residence of Ellen. She had not been to bed, but was sitting, pale and anxious, on a couch, the traces of recent tears on her wan cheek. Charles advanced and kissed her. He then gave her a hasty sketch of his adventures in the cavern, and sat down to write a note to the nearest magistrate; when he had finished it, Ellen took his arm, and they quitted the cottage.

CHAPTER V.

Madness and Passion! Frenzy lives and dies
In this wild whirl when Reason trembling flies.—*MS.*

THE IDIOT—THE MONSTER—THE ATHEIST'S LETTER.

WE left Harriet Walsingham, a few hours before the period when the last chapter concludes, at the habitation of Spenser the philosopher, a circumstance having happened which shall now be chronicled. But in order to present the scene clearly to the reader, we must quit Harriet's side for a few minutes, and relate the events in due sequency. At the distance of a stone's throw from the abode of the metaphysician was an immense tree of great age, which from time immemorial had afforded a grateful shade from the summer heats to the foot-sore wayfarer, or the passing rustic. Beneath this venerable giant of the forest was lying a singular-looking personage. He was young, it was evident; but in some respects he looked much older, in others younger than he really was. There were white hairs in his long, light brown tresses, though he had not long left very childhood behind him; but his form was that of a little boy. Yet it seemed probable that he had attained the greatest stature he would ever reach; and, indeed, "Mad Willy," as he was called, had on a sudden ceased to grow when a child of eleven or twelve; and, except that his face was more pensive, and his hair streaked with grey, he was in no respect altered since that age. There was something sweet and gentle in his countenance, although the light of reason but seldom beamed in it: but occasionally a ray of intelligence lit up his soft blue eye, and then he looked the ideal of a poet. He wandered about, sometimes singing, sometimes dancing, or playing wild antics: but he was more frequently to be found dull and torpid, and all had pity on the poor lunatic. . . . . . But as he was enjoying the fragrant breeze which fanned his thin face, gazing with lack-lustre eye up at the sun-lit heaven, he was on a sudden ferociously seized upon by a monstrous creature, who seemed delighted to have thus caught him, and proceeded to pull his long hair, and to plague him in various ways, while the poor idiot boy uttered cries of terror or of pain, without attempting to struggle with his powerful tormentor. But as the savage was about to inflict severer punishment on the unhappy being, who lay unresisting but with imploring eyes, a noble dog of enormous size, uttering a deep-mouthed bark, sprang over the fence that guarded Spenser's cottage, and fastened on the monster, who was obliged to relinquish his hold of the lunatic, to defend himself from the fangs of the dog. He succeeded in extricating himself from the jaws of the formidable animal, and taking up a huge stone was hurling it at him, when Harriet, accompanied by Spenser's daughters, appeared, drawn to the scene of action by the cries: and the savage, throwing down the stone, produced a letter, and put it in her hand. With a growl as angry and full of defiance as that which the dog barked forth when he turned his back upon him, that ugly and monstrous phemonenon disappeared. Not a little astonished was Harriet at this affair, and at the behaviour of the savage; and on looking at the superscription of the letter he had given her, was surprised beyond measure to perceive the hand-writing of William. She opened it, and read as follows :—

"It is past! I have taken an eternal farewell of her to whom this weak and wretched heart clung, as others cling to the faith in immortality. I have looked upon her for the last time; and the dull, heavy torpor of despair weighs like lead upon my conscious brain. Alive, and hopeless!—well, let it be so. The struggle is over, and the passionate dream vanished in black night for ever! . . . . Harriet! I wanted to have written much that I could not speak : but *now* I can scarcely conceive anything; the power of thought seems numbed within, and the fierce tides within my breast are frozen; so that I am like a dead man, over whose body the worms creep; for even my griefs touch me not so as to affect the sense. I can feel nothing now. This may seem to you the language of exaggeration; but it is not so. I never lied, nor dissembled. The vile *Atheist*, at all events, worshipped truth as his God. I wish I were a brute beast, to exist in the light of your presence, and to be caressed by your hand. Of what advantage to us is this boasted Reason, which instinct, in fact, surpasses in its degree, since beasts of lowest intellect are so much happier than we? It is night—but I shall not sleep; for the calm and apathy have left me, and I am feverish and restless. What a strange thing it is that our feelings thus alternate! I see you before me—distinctly, powerfully: were I not a Materialist, by Heaven! I could believe it *is* you. Your image haunts me like a ghost, wherever I turn my eyes. If I look up to the burning stars, that glow with ethereal poetry, that face is there: those orbs, so pure, and bright, and melancholy, are more beautiful than the Host of Lights that have shone in the dark immensity before our thought can shape that which we call Time—a name for nothing. But all is a dream, all is a phantom. I wanted to have told you many things, and they have vanished from my memory, or present themselves in such chaotic, whirling masses that to abstract and generalise out of their crude elements is impossible. You once said to me, ' Your genius, William, is not your own. It is a shadowy demon that leads you over the great universe, and you follow like the blind. You want a strong WILL.' But I have a strong *will*, as you term what you cannot define; and so I will struggle like a hero against these oppressive feelings, and address you as rationally as if I were arguing against Spenser's abstruse metaphysics. Not death could separate us more widely than the great gulf I myself have placed betwixt us. This I know: but I must write to you sometimes, and you must receive my letters as if they came from the dead to the living. If I could embody all the passions, the pangs, the dreams, thoughts, and mighty feelings which urged me to become what I did, I think I could plead an extenuation for myself, which, anti-necessitarian as you are, you must admit to be valid. But I cannot do it now. And, besides, to what purpose if I could? No, Harriet, though I wish not to stand so low in your esteem, as you would place me, were I to allow you to think that I have acted, without attempting to stem the tide of my passions, I will not

debase myself, like your fabled Adam in the garden when asked
why he had taken the forbidden fruit, by laying the *onus* of the
matter on a weak woman. You think we are stronger than circumstances: but if you could anatomize my nature your opinion
might alter. I used to impose on myself the task of thinking of
you in the light of a mother—sister—oh, vainly! Where am I
wandering? My curse on this maddened brain, dull block!
which *will* reel like a drunkard's! I do not often take wine, but now
I will quaff the sweet poison, and see whether it will not appease
the fever; for as when we are cold we take ice in our hands, fire
to fire, perhaps, may extinguish the lava flames! .... Ay, the
wine, the wine! the honest, friendly wine! Light of the tombs!
Burn in this outworn heart, and give it vitality. Ha, ha! Now
I *am* mad. I mean to be happy. I will drink and eat, and shout,
and live like a good old Epicurean. I will become a drunkard,
and roar and laugh like the merriest devil that ever rejoiced in
Hell over the queer antices of his victims in the fires. The heart
of a Nero is in my bosom now; I could hug the red pestilence, and
fight like a savage! Well, I have drunk myself mad! How do
you like me now? I see you with that mild and majestic face, so
like one of your Saints, looking sorrowfully on me, reproaching
me with looks, not words. Oh, I could weep, yes, *weep*, to
think that I have lost that love I prized beyond life!—No more!"

"Unhappy being!" murmured Harriet. "I will go to him;
for I fear his brain is turning. What an awful letter! But there
is more here."

" . . . . . I have seen you enter the house of Spenser. After
I concluded what I wrote last night, I lay down and slept. Oh,
such a sleep! I thought I was in the infernal regions, and ages
had passed, and ages still went on. It was pain, pain, pain!
No cessation for an instant! And all this was crowded into a
few hours! Then you came and wept over me, and the briny
drops from your eyes moistened my blistered tongue; and,
though it was still agony, it was comparative Heaven. . . . I arose
at last, as if from a bed of sickness, and the pain I felt, the
racking pain, equalled that of my dreams. I would not have you
see me. You would hardly know me after that cursed debauch.
I wrote something *then* in addition to what is now before you,

which I could kill myself for having penned. The wildest licence of the Bacchanals never equalled it. But *that* shall not offend your eye. I hurry away, I know not to what! I shall plunge into the ocean of pleasure, perchance, and drink of it to satiety. I shall pursue the phantom of science,—write a work which may make me immortal, it may be; and then—welcome annihilation! It has no dread for me now. Were I happy, were I only *less* wretched than I am, I should shrink from death; but I will now believe it is the greatest good. Once more, farewell! In a few minutes I shall be gone. But write to me, I beseech you, write to me. I shall stay some days in London."

When Harriet finished reading this frenzied letter she concealed it, resolved that none but herself should ever see it, and as she did so, beheld Spenser returning. He had sought Quirk in vain.

"Then I must myself seek him," said Harriet. "He told me of a place where I might always hear of him in case of emergency, but he forbade me to take or direct others thither."

Harriet, quitting her friend, bent her steps in the direction Spenser had previously taken, regardless of his remonstrances on her imprudence in exposing herself, totally defenceless, to the power of such a known rascal as the lawyer. He was hesitating whether to follow Miss Walsingham, or not, when the form of an old man approaching caught his eye.

"I should know that person," he thought. "Who can it be? What! Is it possible? Old Roger Sidney! It *can* be no other." While the philosopher was speaking, our old friend of the rod ascended a hill to the right of Spenser's cottage, and was now within musket-shot of him. Spenser hastened to meet him with out-stretched arms. "Where have you been all these years, my dear cousin," he said. "I am very, very glad to see you once more."

"Ah, Henry, you are as much changed in aspect as I am. It was by the merest accident I heard you were living here, a few minutes since. I was certain it could be no other than yourself, from the description of your ' wonderful bright eye.' The light of that is not dimmed at all events."

While this conversation was going on, Spenser's little daughters were intent on watching the poor lunatic the noble dog had rescued from the savage. He was uttering wild, but hardly articu-

3 Y

late sounds, and muttering much in the intervals between his cries, having picked up something from the ground, which had been dropped by the monster inadvertently. It was the head of a riding whip, curiously formed, in which there was a whistle, used probably for recalling dogs in the chase; and presently Mad Willy began blowing at it with might and main.

"Yes, yes, it is the very same!" he exclaimed, speaking coherently. "I heard him whistling before the light had left my brain quite—and I am certain of everything before that time. I must tell it before I forget. Who shall I tell?" The poor creature's eye fell on Henry Spenser, and hastening up to him, he cried breathlessly, "I pray you, attend to me, sir. I am not crazed now. Look at this handle with a crest upon it—isn't it called a crest? This belonged to a person I saw murdered. I recollect it all; but it is fast melting from me. I was a child when it happened—a young child. Ah, the veil is coming over my brain." He pressed his little girlish hands across his fair low forehead, and then the expression of hopeless idiotcy, which for a minute or more had given place to a look almost of intelligence, vanished, and he gazed vacantly around, seeming not to be aware he had spoken.

The philosopher examined the handle of the whip curiously. "This is the crest of the Walsinghams," he said. "I wonder how this poor creature obtained the handle."

His eldest child was by his side, and was able to afford an explanation of the matter, having seen the whistle fall from the breast of the savage, where it had been concealed in a skin he wore. Sidney turned to the maniac, and attempted to extract a rational answer from him, but he only looked him vacantly in the face, and broke into a monotonous chaunt.

"I was almost in hopes that this circumstance might afford some clue to the murder of poor Walsingham. This unhappy being, little more than an infant at the time, surely appears to recollect dimly, as in a vision, something connected with that dark deed. But come, let us enter the house. I must present my children to you. Come hither, Lolah!"

"They are pretty creatures; but I was not aware you had married," said Sidney.

The colour rose to the pale cheek of Spenser, but immediately subsided. "I will relate my history to you presently," he replied. "I have undergone many vicissitudes since we parted. Captivity, slavery, and suffering have weighed heavily on me."

Sidney occupied himself with the beautiful children of Spenser, and their engaging prattle rejuvenated the old man's heart. Blessed are the feelings excited by the innocent questions and remarks of those bright young beings, with their freshness, their purity, and freedom from all the chilling convention and austerity practised in this heartless world; where all that is sweetest and holiest in us is enslaved by "the law of fools," who feel not the gushing poetry, who practise not the tenderness and cordiality, the human, natural feelings which lend a charm even to this earth.

"Ah," said Roger Sidney to Spenser, as he entered the dwelling of the latter, "happy indeed is childhood. To me there is an atmosphere sacred as religion itself in their gentle presence! I have often longed to be a father! How exquisite and delicious a feeling it must be, when you see the fair bud expand, the sweet blossom open, and reveal the bright consummate flower! But I was not ordained to experience such joys as these."

In familiar conversation the old friends passed the day, and when the shades of night were falling, and the children had gone to bed, Spenser was reminded by the worthy Sidney of the promise he had given him of relating his history. The philosopher gazed mournfully earthwards.

"I will fulfil that promise," he said, "since you wish it; but to do so I must draw aside the curtain which hangs over the past, and reveal things that will cost me a pang to tell."

As Spenser was on the point of commencing his narrative, he was interrupted by the abrupt entrance of the idiot, who approached him with eager eyes and parted lips, ejaculating,

"I have found it! I have found it!"

"Ah, well, proceed!" said Spenser.

"Yes," returned the lunatic, "an angel came down and whispered it into my ear. He bade me come unto you and say——" The unhappy boy paused: and added at length, "Yes, he bade me say, 'There are tears on earth which bedew the softest cheeks; but there is a sun in Elysium to dry them.'"

"Poor thing!" murmured Spenser. "Many cry 'Eureka,' and light not on anything so true as this. I must have him with me, and see if I cannot elicit something, in his momentary lucid intervals, about that murder. This matter his mind always recurs to when his feeble brain is in healthy action, it would seem. It should have been a fine instrument—that mind,—but a string has been broken; and it produces faint and broken sounds, instead of continuous harmony."

The lunatic retired as suddenly as he came, and might be observed making mouths at the moon when he was in the open air again. Mysterious principle of mind! what art thou? Materialist! show me what it is; analyse its component parts, if it have such. It was a hopeless case. He had always been a strange child: and some occurrence, the nature of which none could precisely understand, quite destroyed the equipoise of his intellect, when he was too young to have acquired any stock of ideas. But sometimes he would utter things a poet might not have blushed to enunciate; and he was not devoid of the liveliest feelings of gratitude and affection, when a gleam of reason flashed on him. He was the child of poor parents, who died when he was a child, and he had been nurtured on charity; but, previous to his insanity becoming confirmed, he had manifested a quickness of capacity really astonishing.

" I should like to see if I could not open the doors of this lad's mind," said Spenser to Sidney. " I think I could do much to remove the mists that hang over his poor brain. In my opinion, the mental physician (so to speak) might effect more than any other, if he would direct his attention to the phenomena of insanity."

" Very probably," returned Sidney. " But, for the most part, you metaphysicians are too apt to contemn the actual for the ideal. It is a great thing to discover a faculty of the mind; but a yet greater privilege to remove an evil, and make an intelligent and rational being out of one organically diseased."

The philosopher resumed the seat he had left when the lunatic entered, and then began the narration which will be found in the next chapter.

END OF BOOK VIII.

BOOK IX.

The Tragedy here ends. The *truly* tragic
Is not the seal of death, when grief is o'er.
Life is the solemn, melancholy theme,
Which should excite our tears ; beyond, there is
Sweet Silence---awful, but yet passing sweet.
                                        Old Play.

Mutinous passions, and conflicting fears,
And hopes that sate themselves on dust, and die!
                                        HELLAS.

CHAPTER I.

—— Men convinced
That Life is love and immortality.——
This is the genuine course, the end and aim
Of prescient Reason; all conclusions else
Are abject, vain, presumptuous, and perverse.

WORDSWORTH.

THE HISTORY OF A MIND.

H E history of the Individual Mind affords as vast a scope for thought and analysis, as that of an epoch, a nation, an universe. It has its eras and its cycles; and each atom of the sentient being is in itself a world in miniature. I hold, therefore, that every history is imperfect and worthless, which does not embrace the minute philosophy of the one being it pretends to elucidate. I compare myself to a fabric erected by no earthly hands, each part of which is in the abstract sense a whole; and therefore I shall endeavour, as I proceed, to give you some insight into the manner in which God has built me up to be what I am. O, that stupendous Architect! What intellect shall conceive the infinity of his resources, what study enable us to arrive at a just estimate of what we are, when considered in relation to that which has made us? But the dignity of our nature transcends our finite comprehension. We are told in that Book which contains the secrets of the divine economy, that we were created by the Eternal in his own image; by which I am persuaded we are to understand we are each of us possessed in our finity of the qualities

possessed by God in his infinity: the infinite in the Creator necessarily perfect, the finite in the creature necessarily imperfect.
Thus He is wisdom and love in the immensity of their significance; we are will and understanding in the finity of their
essence; wisdom comprehending perfect will, but not subject to
the sovereignty of law (for law is in time, not in eternity), only to
love, or its own liberty, without which infinite mind would be in
thraldom.   For will is nothing without love, and love is a mere
abstraction without wisdom.   Take one away and you destroy
all.   But by will, which raises man so high that he is God to
himself, as much as God is to God, love is caused to flow into
its just activities, understanding is directed into truth; and so, by
the union of the human and divine, by the everlasting flow of
thought, by the creativeness of mind, and the illimitability of
faculties, there is a likeness of the imperfect to the perfect, of
humanity to divinity.   We shall return to the source whence we
came, and be transformed ALTOGETHER into a spiritual, instead
of a material and spiritual existence.   Image of Deity!   What a
thought is that?   And yet it must be so; for God in creating
must stamp his own likeness on his creation, even as we do on
ours!   This philosophy, the germs of which are floating on the
ocean of thought everywhere, has enabled me to overcome many
difficulties in metaphysical theology, and has had a powerful influence in forming the elements of my mature character.   I am
both less mystic and more so than I was, when young.

    "You know that, at one time, when I was a mere boy, I em-
braced the theory of Berkeley : but though I still believe there is
much beautiful truth in idealism, I see my error in confusing
thought and sensation; I cannot consider it as a perfect system ;
and am now writing a work which is to reconcile the apparent
irreconcilability of the two great philosophers of the soul and the
senses, and trying to erect a theory on the bases of Locke and
Berkeley.   They have embodied nearly all the arguments for
matter and for mind, but have totally neglected to analyse the
reasons which may be adduced for their co-existence.   I am also
attempting to show the connexion between the science of mind
and morality, a branch of philosophy which by some strange
oversight has hitherto been disregarded, and to vindicate abstract
thought from the charge of inutility.   What is useless that God

has made? How idle is it to say that we are not to investigate the nature of the subtle principle of intelligence and the range of its powers, because such knowledge is not revealed to us from above; when neither is there a single science we have not to discover, and we know just as much of intellect as of matter! I wish you to understand that I am not now anatomizing the formation of my character, and the progress of my mind from one opinion to another, but laying bare some of the secrets of the soul as well as the heart—giving you my whole history in analysis. Materialism had made immense progress when Locke carried out the system of Descartes, and as a mischievous tendency downwards—for the effects of materialism are demoralizing to the masses—was manifesting itself in our metaphysics, Berkeley was raised up to give a check to the dogmatism of the Cartesians; and I among many others was carried away by the re-action that ensued, into a sea of error. Creation I doubted to be possible, because mind perceives (so says Berkeley), and does not create: but I did not consider that what in the finite is *perception*, in the infinite is *creation*. I looked upon this colossal universe as the phantasm of the brain, and all design and intelligence which are visible in it as but in ideas—that neither space nor time are in themselves entities, and that matter can only be a shadow impinged on sense—in fact an optical illusion. I now consider space in this view, namely that it is in the mind, and out of it; that although the ordinary idea of it is incorrect, it is, it must be. Time is rather the mutation ourselves undergo than that of outward change, or in other words it is duration with succession, while eternity is duration itself.

"You perceive that my opinions have undergone a great transformation since I was a young man; and I shall show you presently how this change affected my other feelings and sentiments. My father, your old companion and schoolfellow, you will recollect was a Socratic Theist. He was a good man, a noble man, a man with great deep passions, but a soul to subdue himself to reason; but his errors of judgment at one time exerted a great influence over me, and led me into deadly peril. I was educated for Theism; but I ended in Scepticism the most universal, a state of mind infinitely more unhappy than that of total unbelief. My father was a correspondent of the great thinkers of his time,

and their society was, when I was a boy, my chief delight. How
eagerly I used to listen to the long arguments which were carried
on in my father's house, on the most abstruse questions of
philosophy, before I had well mastered the meaning of the terms
employed in such controversies! I cannot describe to you the
pleasure—the more than mere pleasure—which I felt in associating with those great men, who command the stream of Time to
flow in the channels which the Immutable has appointed; and
before I was eighteen, I had argued nearly all the problems of the
most abstract science in agitation at the period among the most
enlightened artificers of civilisation and opinion. I burned to become another Plato: and my father fed the ardor within my
heart, until it overleapt the boundaries of moderation. He was as
enthusiastic a worshipper of metaphysical truth, though past
middle age, as in his early manhood: and we often used to sit
up whole nights when we entered into a discussion on some important point, until fairly exhausted with intense elaboration of
ideas.

"Probably never did boy become man in thought so early as I
did; but in many respects my character was unformed and feeble.
While my intellect was occupied with the great problem of
human destiny, I forgot the moral in the mental, instead of pursuing them together---which is the solution, to my mature judgment, of the mystery. Scepticism certainly indicates a tendency
towards irresolution, if it do not manifest some weakness of understanding.

"There are truths which do not admit of demonstration, which
we must receive, or remain for ever ignorant;—a child-like faith
generally marks the true, powerful thinker: he never doubts
except on good grounds, while the shallow sciolist denies everything at once which cannot be proved to his satisfaction. I was
continually renouncing some untenable position, and attacking
some prominent dogma of theorists. But in the course of time—
the rectifier of all things—I saw my error, and determined on
adopting a system for myself. Thought has a necessary tendency
to correct itself, provided a man be sincere. I searched antiquity,
I pored over the inspired sages until my eyes were dim and my
brain seething, and I was weary with the inward communing they
excited. Alas! for the man who has no pilot to guide the vessel

of his thoughts into a harbour of safety. Better not to think at all, than never to trust, to believe. I was dissatisfied with all things, and most of all with myself. My father strove to reason with me. He saw I was not happy, and warmly endeavoured to draw me to the religion of Socrates : but I pointed out so much that is incongruous and absurd in that wonderful but most preposterous chain of reasoning for which we are indebted to Plato, that I made him almost as sceptical as myself. He might have been a great, as he was a fine and lofty character, if his thoughts had taken the turn which the Creator has turned mine into, giving me peace and hope. At this time, you know, you were absent from England, having left it to be a wanderer when I was little more than a child ; and when you returned I was at college. I then went abroad, and we were separated for years.

"You are aware that my father was the guardian of Harriet Walsingham and her sister, having been a dear friend of their father. After having studied man and nature in the most glorious countries of the world, imbuing my soul with more poetry than I would once have confessed to, I came back, and found Harriet had grown into womanhood. I had known her from her infancy, and often carried her in these arms, heaping endearments on her in those unruffled days when I was a quiet, dreamy boy, loving solitude and silence. I once loved her as I should a sister ; and now that I was thrown into her society, new and thrilling feelings entered into my soul. I asked myself if love were not the object of life. For the first time, I deplored my poor, miserable appearance, when I found she had become much taller than myself : for the first time since boyhood, I gave up my books and devoted myself to a woman. My intercourse with her taught me what a fine creature God has given man for his helpmate, and what bliss and elevation passion can impart to the spirit. I must not dwell on this portion of my life ; suffice it, that I found too late Harriet loved Walter Danvers : and then resigned myself to all the bitterness of black despair.

"How vain is our boasted philosophy to support the heart in those trials which Heaven has ordained for our purification and exaltation ! I despised it—nay laughed at it, and rushed into pleasure to steep my soul in oblivion. From a Platonist I became an Epicurean. But deserting the foul haunts of vice with disgust

—though I sought not a brighter element, I listlessly went from place to place, seeking peace, and finding none; until at last I proposed to myself to write a work exposing popular errors in religion and philosophy, exploding Christianity, which I considered the bane of free inquiry, and setting up a better morality in its stead. Strange inconsistency! When I found that no human wisdom was efficient in relieving my own sorrows, what could I substitute for religion?

"I have opened to you, my dear old friend, the *arcana* of my spirit: but you must strictly preserve my confidence as regards Harriet Walsingham. That is all over now, and I love her as a dear friend, a sister. The struggle has been deep, but salutary—as what struggle is not? To return to my narrative.

"My new pursuit, of course, obliged me to apply myself diligently to the study of the Christian system; and to my astonishment, after a period, I found myself unable to answer some of the difficulties that presented themselves to my mind on the negative side. Why was this? I never experienced the same labor in overthrowing any of the hypotheses of philosophers. I became suddenly interested in this new occupation: it assumed an importance in my eyes that I thought nothing human again could; and finally, instead of attacking the *grounds* of religion, I wrote an essay unequivocally in favor of them, contra-distinguished from ethics. But I was only half a believer, for all this. The pride of intellect had to be subdued within me, fostered as it was for years by speculation. I looked on the Bible as partly true and partly false; some doctrines I received, and some I repudiated; I was strongly inclined to Socinianism. The humanly moral I did not sufficiently separate (if at all) from the divinely moral, much as I was inclined to believe Theology is not Ontology. But I found after some time that this humanized religion was cold and formal and unsatisfactory; and I set myself to inquire why it was so. Was the imperfection, I asked my soul, in myself, or the religion? I could not reply to this self-interrogatory, and began a diligent examination of my own mind. After long, deep, laborious research I found the secret out. I was very proud, and preferred the devices of my own fallible reason, to the infallible revealings of God. My philosophy became *subservient* to my religion, instead of the converse, I adored the supernal brightness, and wondered at my previous infatuation. I was at last the only rational believer —the entire one. Blessed be that great Being who has sustained me by the faith I have chosen for so long a time; blessed, thrice blessed the creed that opens immortality to all.

"Thus far I have devoted my confession to the history of mind rather than human action;—oh, the biography of the *soul* renders all other stale, and earthly!—but I shall now have to take up my narrative from the period when I quitted England, which was the month preceding that reported as fixed for the nuptials of Harriet Walsingham. I could not endure to see her the wife of another, even though I had *that* to support me which I had not formerly possessed, and accordingly I embarked for the East, in order to pursue some inquiries connected with religion in Palestine. I was wrecked off the coast of Algiers; and found myself a wretched slave, tasked beyond my powers of body, with no hope of deliverance. But I yielded not to despair, convinced that this misfortune was to terminate in my good, if I availed myself of the opportunities it afforded.

"If I had remained a sceptic, or even a speculator, I should have sunk under the burthens imposed on me by a severe task-master; but I was resigned, contented, cheerful; and my submissiveness procured me in the course of time some degree of favor in the eyes of the barbarian I was compelled to serve. He availed himself of my knowledge and understanding to effect some projects he wished consummated; and I at length became his favorite slave, so that I hoped he would restore me to liberty. But by doing so he would have deprived himself of a valuable servant, and therefore I was subjected to the closest imprisonment, while I shared all the delicacies of my master's table. An unexpected circumstance, however, occurred, which I will at once relate.

"The only daughter of my tyrant, a lovely creature betrothed to a powerful prince of the country, fell ill; and the physicians who attended her despaired of her recovery. Her father, confiding deeply in my universal science, bade me prescribe for her. I possessed some slight medical knowledge, for I always thought it a moral duty to study the preservation of health, as well as to be able, in case of emergency, to afford help to others: so I went to the young girl, and perceiving the nature of her malady, gave her some medicine. The effect of this was happy, and after some weeks I had the satisfaction of seeing my beautiful patient convalescent. The interest that she excited in me by her fortitude and resignation in illness, was strong; and I found her so intelligent and warm-hearted, in spite of her ignorance and superstition in some respects, that I wished to enlighten her with the beams of truth. Her mother, who was a Greek captive, was dead; and, when a child, she had imbibed from her some crude notions of Christianity, which she had mixed up with the religion of her country. At no time, and amongst no people, has there existed a state of utter darkness with regard to the destiny of man: the idea of an eternity is evidently stamped on the mind, to afford consolation to the savage as to the philosopher. I was able to impart to my master's child some of the religious opinions I had but recently adopted; and she was so eager for information, particularly on this all-important subject, that I had some difficulty in answering all the questions she put to me. I believe, if I had never seen Harriet Walsingham, I should have loved with my whole soul this beautiful and tender-hearted creature; for she clung to me in such an endearing way, that I could not but feel affection towards her, although the passion I had cherished for Harriet was not extinguished. If there *be* such a thing as second love, it can never resemble the first in its intensity and power; first love is like waking to the loveliness of being, things we never dreamed of flash upon us.

" Isolated as I was from all I knew, and severed from all the ties which bound me to the civilized portion of mankind, my interest and feelings were centred in my patient, whose health daily improved, insomuch that it was intimated to me I must no longer visit her—in a short time she was to become a bride. The young girl was in despair, when she found she was to see me no more, and besought her stern father to admit me to her presence; but taking alarm when he found that her gratitude was ripening into a warmer sentiment towards his slave, he was inexorable to her tears and entreaties. A week passed; and one night, as I was sitting alone in the place appropriated to me, engrossed with melancholy thoughts, I was surprised to hear my name breathed in a soft tone close beside me; and, looking up, beheld her in whom I was so much interested.

" 'Christian,' she said, 'I am come to bid you an eternal farewell. To-morrow I am to leave my father's roof to wed a hated lord; but I would not depart without speaking once more to him to whom I owe life itself.'

" Sobs choaked her utterance, and hiding her face in her hands she indulged her grief. I could say little to comfort her; but her despair wrought on me to suggest a plan to her which I thought feasible. 'Hear me, my sweet sister,' I said; 'if we could pass the guard stationed at the gate of the garden, we might seize on a galley and put out to sea. If you prefer incurring such a risk to becoming the wife of this barbarian, I am ready to accompany you.'

" The young girl eagerly embraced this proposition, and I was successful in introducing an opiate into the supper of the guard. The drug soon took effect, and shortly after midnight we went forth, I and my beautiful friend. We reached the sea-shore unseen, and entered a galley; but the wind, which had been rising for a long time, now blew so violently that I hesitated to put out to sea. I pointed out the peril to her, but added I was ready to brave death for her and freedom.

" ' Light of my soul!' she exclaimed, passionately, ' death has no terrors while thou art near me!'

" With reluctance I consented to the wishes of my companion, while the gale lashed the billows into fury indescribable. Never shall I forget that night. The Spirit of the Storm was abroad, and the winds became so awful that the ocean seemed lashed into one universal mountain of foam; and it was miraculous that our frail bark could live for a single minute in such a sea. On, on, we swept, the vivid lightning illuminating the whole extent of the ocean, and the thunders uttering their giant voices almost without intermission. And the maiden clung to me, her large meek eyes turned up to heaven, and questioned me, when her voice could be heard, on the mysteries of the Great Hereafter. We prayed together, in momentary expectation of death. Perhaps at these times, more than any other, we catch glimpses of most majestic truth; we know our material insignificance, we feel our spiritual glory. The veil is rent from before our eyes, and we know death and time are but as the portal and the vestibule of life and immortality.

"Gradually, the violence of the storm abated, and we were saved. But we were snatched from one form of destruction, only to be exposed to it in another yet more fearful. Our little stock of provisions was soon exhausted, and I saw no hope of the expectation I had formed of meeting some friendly vessel being realised. I repented greatly of my precipitation in taking away the poor girl; but she looked up into my face, and smiled like morning.

"'Am I not with *you*, beloved?' she cried. 'Behold, the skies are blue, and the air serene, and the great God is looking down upon us. You have taught me faith, and love supports me, as it sustains the world. Let death come, if I can expire in the radiance of your presence, and the peace of your arms. Talk to me of heaven, as you alone can speak.'

"Then I knew how I was loved—not with a childish, feeble passion, but with all the pure depth of a devoted woman's heart, and I made an inward vow, that if we were spared, since I had been the means of depriving her of kindred, I would be all the world to her. Ay, home and wealth, friends and country may all be supplied by the richness of true passion, which is a light of inextinguishable purity, when affection supplies the fuel. We were almost starving, while, around and above us, all was exceeding tranquillity and beauty, as if to mock our pangs; and my courage forsook me when I thought of the horrors of our doom. But the maiden threw her arms round my neck, and said,

"'It is sweet to die in hope—as sweet as to live in joy: if we pass through this ordeal without distrusting the Providence of God, we shall be in Elysium in another night."

"So strong was that simple child's belief! Woman's faith is more perfect, loving, pious, than man's. But on a sudden we descried land at no great distance, and our parched tongues moved in thanksgiving. We hoped that all our difficulties would now be over, and I said,

"'Dearest, you will now become my wife, and I will take you to that England you have so often heard me mention. Can you consent to be the partner of such a poor, wretched being as myself?'

"'*You*, poor and wretched!' was her reply. 'I would take you for my husband, joyfully take you, though I should see no other during my whole life, and you were the most hideously deformed of men. I love your *soul*, breath of my spirit!—it is the soul alone which is God's high likeness, and His inspiration burns and glows within thee!' And she clasped me in her arms, with her wild, eastern passion, and nestled to my bosom—poor thing!

"Could I be insensible to such intense devotion as this? No, though I loved her not with that passion which filled *her* being, she was inexpressibly dear to me; and for years she was my all of happiness. We reached the shore in safety; but we discovered it was an uninhabited island, and many were the privations and sufferings we endured. Can you wonder that under such circumstances, without a hope of being rescued from our predicament, I became a husband to her? I myself was the priest who implored a blessing on our union; and it was not withheld. Two children were born unto us; but, from the time the youngest came into the world, the health of my sweet wife declined. She lingered on, month after month: but I felt the fiat had gone forth, and that she was to be taken from me. I was surprised one day, when addressing me she said,

" 'I wish I could behold your native land before I die. What say you, my beloved? The boat in which we came hither can easily be repaired; and we can store it with provisions. Let us trust in God, who has been so good to us, and depart. If you were to die also, what would be the condition of our helpless babes?'

"After some deliberation I agreed to put to sea, though I could have been contented to live on in that lonely isle, far from the sight of crime and woe. For many days the weather was favourable; but I perceived indications of a coming tempest, and knew we were at a great distance from any land. Fortunately, however, this storm was less violent than that we had once encountered; but my gentle partner's death was accelerated by the soaking of the waves and rains, possibly. I knew that she must be soon taken from me, and I wept. Oh, she was so kind, so fervent, so simple, I must have been a brute if I had not loved her!

" 'Why do you weep?' she asked, while she fondled our children, who had slumbered through the tempest. 'Have you not told me, and do I not *feel* I shall soon reach that bright and

4 A

happy shore, the spirit of whose holy radiance is our great Father's smile !'

" ' Beautiful, thrice beautiful was thy piety, my truest, my lamented; and perfect as ever angel's was thy love—how undeserved! She expired without a sigh, like an infant dropping asleep. The breath had scarcely left the body of my wife, when I descried a vessel bearing down upon us. I hailed it with pleasure for my children's sake; but as for myself, I then felt weary of my life, and longed to enter the eternity beyond. My gentle wife had been so much my companion in the utter isolation in which we had been placed, and had entwined herself around my heart by such innumerable endearing ties, that I felt, when she was gone, as if the better part of my being were departed from me. But small time was left me to indulge my sorrow; for the ship I had seen soon arrived within a few cables' length of my boat, and I found too late it was a pirate vessel.

" I was sold to slavery again; but now my feeble powers were not overtasked, and as we had all been purchased of the pirates by the same person, my children were not taken from me. Years rolled on, and the fierce passions which had threatened to wreck my peace while I was in the world, were thoroughly subdued. The last thing that we learn is submission to the Divine will, and we cannot acquire perfect, uncomplaining obedience to Omnipotence except by passing through the fire which is ordained for such a purifying purpose. But I had a fellow-slave in an honest British sailor named Samuel Stokes, who wished me to attempt to escape; and as my children were now old enough to miss the blessings of liberty, I was induced to comply with his solicitations. We laid our plans successfully; but we had not long put out to sea in an open boat, when a vessel gave us chase; and we must inevitably have been taken, if an English merchantman had not noticed the signal of distress we raised, and made sail to our succour. The galley which pursued us was directed towards the vessel which afforded us protection, and our preservers were menaced with death if we were not delivered up. At the same time we saw a large vessel bearing down upon us from shore; and our only hope was in flight. We crowded on every stitch of canvas we could carry; and for hours the chase was continued, when the enemy visibly gained on us. A fearful contest ensued, our brave countrymen being determined to defend us with their lives : but it was to the skill, the courage, and energy of Stokes, the seaman I have mentioned, that we were indebted for freedom. Seeing that the British were falling fast, and there was but slight chance of their successfully opposing the numbers of the foe, he managed to set fire to the privateer, and by a clever manœuvre to get clear off from it : but the gallant fellow had hardly accomplished this—even as we heard an awful explosion in the enemy's ship—when a ball took off his legs, and he fell close to my side. But every man on board the privateer was destroyed, and although our own vessel was greatly crippled, and the crew terribly reduced, we were able to continue our homeward course, and finally reached England in safety. The noble-hearted Stokes recovered in spite of his dreadful injuries, and I had the satisfaction of placing him in a cottage at no great distance from my own, a few months since. I have thus, my dear friend, hastily sketched my autobiography ; and now, as it is midnight, let me show you to your chamber. I shall rise with the dawn, and we will proceed together to the examination of Danvers." Thus the old friends separated.

CHAPTER II.

—— These our actors
Are melted into air, into thin air.
—— We are such stuff
As dreams are made of ; and our little life
Is rounded with a sleep.—SHAKESPEARE.

A LONG HISTORY OF THE PAST, EXPLAINING MANY THINGS
THAT HAVE HITHERTO REMAINED IN THE SHADE.

THE Reader must now permit his imagination to wander back to the peopled past, when " these our actors " were in the heyday of youth and beauty, when all was bright, all was joyous, and none dreamed of the dreary shadows which now stretched across the sky.

About eighteen years ere the date of this history's commencement, Walter Danvers was a dashing, light-hearted young fellow, with great animal spirits, much cleverness, and kindness of heart, but without that decision and depth of mind which it has been my aim to delineate when he was on the verge of middle age. His passions were strong, and unregulated by those high principles of morality which can alone afford a check to the ebullitions of such a nature; worshipping pleasure above rectitude, and immersed in dissipation, he seemed to consider such enjoyment as it could afford the sole object of existence. The iron of his character had not yet manifested itself; but there were times when he panted to break the bondage of the senses, and to distinguish himself in some honourable path of life: but the force of habit was too strong for the counter-force of ambition, and he became deeply and more deeply the slave of vicious and demoralizing enjoyments.

The parents of Danvers had died when he was young, and there was no one to control his inclinations, or to remonstrate with him on his depraved habits. His father was the son of a farmer of moderate fortune, and had from a private soldier risen to be a distinguished officer. He married a lady somewhat above himself in rank, and Walter was the sole fruit of their union. Mrs. Haines supplied the place of a mother to him, she, previous to her becoming a wife, having lived as housekeeper with his maternal parent. So much for the birth, disposition, and mode of life of Danvers. Among his gay companions were the brother of Harriet Walsingham, and Everard, who was of a very opposite character to that he had become when first known to the reader. The former of these persons, a young man at the period in question, was possessed of considerable wealth, a fine person, a good understanding, and many other advantages; but he was at least as dissipated, with less nobility to redeem his vices, as Walter Danvers. Everard, the younger brother of the head of the family at the time, though but a youth, was initiated in all the vices of manhood. Nine-tenths of the gentry of the day, if Fielding and Smollett are right, were men of pleasure. To be ignorant was no stigma; to be virtuous was to be ridiculed, as a natural consequence of prevailing ignorance.

Everard was a gamester and a libertine; but his cousin, John

Walsingham, as he shall be called, was the most depraved of the two. Indeed, at that time, before the sordid love of money had taken possession of Everard's soul, he was generally liked in society; for he was courteous, gentlemanly, of a pleasing exterior, and if not intellectual and high-minded, he was gallant and accomplished. John Walsingham had a taste for theatricals, and infused a love of them into the minds of his kinsman and Danvers. They were all three of them good actors in their relative ways; and from the love of novelty played in various theatres under assumed names. There was a fair, gentle creature among the company of a provincial establishment, who acted the heroines of tragedy, and was considered to possess merit. Everard Walsingham became enamoured of her, and made dishonorable proposals, which were indignantly rejected. His love conquered his pride, and ultimately he privately made her his wife, but with strict injunctions not to reveal their marriage.

Meanwhile the fortunes of Walter Danvers were at a low ebb, from his having lost considerable sums of money to John Walsingham at the gaming-table; and his *friend* (Heaven save the mark!) advised him to repair his losses by marrying a woman with property. He added that he was acquainted with a lady, who was a widow, with great personal attractions, and of good fortune, to whom he would introduce him, if he wished. Danvers accepted the proposal, and proceeded with his friend to a handsome house, at which the latter asked for " Mrs. Williamson," and they were ushered into a room elegantly furnished, where, reclining on a sofa, was a lady of some nine-and-twenty. She was very beautiful, but it was evident she had recently been suffering from severe illness. Danvers was enchanted with the handsome widow, who, if not very refined, was one of all others to captivate the senses of such a youth; and he appeared to make a favourable impression on her. Not to dwell on particulars, at the end of a fortnight he was an accepted lover; and they were united in wedlock at the expiration of a month.

John Walsingham then went to sea, having first procured a commission in the army for Danvers. But Walter soon discovered he had been miserably duped, and that his wife did not possess a farthing; so that—embarrassed with debt as he was—he saw no prospect but that of a prison before him. Yet he never said an unkind word to his partner, who pretended great affection for him, and only lamented to her he could not support her in the way to which she had been accustomed. When at length Danvers was compelled to hide himself from his creditors, his wife suggested to him that, since their finances were so low, she might, perhaps, better their condition by going on the stage, adding that at one time she had studied for such a profession, when Mr. Williamson became enamoured of her, and made her his wife. Danvers at first objected to this proposition, well knowing what the profession of an actress then was; but his scruples were overruled, and his wife became a leading actress of comedy in the country; while he, having sold his commission in the army, entered into theatrical speculations. Fortune favoured him, and for some years he sailed prosperously on the sea of life, having become the father of two children.

After a long absence from England, John Walsingham came back, with an addition of rank and fortune. He sought out Danvers, regretted he had misled him with regard to the fortune of his wife, but said with a laugh, " she was a fortune in herself." During this time Everard Walsingham had travelled on the continent with his wife—whom all persons believed to be his mistress—and returned to England about the same time as his cousin. They all resumed their former intimacy, and played high, with various success. Mrs. Danvers had been absent from her husband for several months, fulfilling some engagements in distant parts of the country; and Walter having satiated of her society experienced no regret that she was not inclined to remain with him, and he never urged her to do so. She was once seen casually by him some months after she had left him; but eventually they scarcely ever met, and when they did so, their intercourse was cold and formal.

" Some years rolled on; and at length Danvers like all other gamesters found himself a ruined man, with no hope of retrieving his fortunes. About this time an accident introduced him to the family of the Walsinghams, and he beheld Harriet, then a lovely girl in her teens. Sudden and violent was the change this circumstance created in the heart of Walter Danvers. He deserted his old haunts, his old companions; his mind rose above the low pursuits which had hitherto engrossed him: but a darker crime

than he had ever committed in the heat of passion and excess—
the deepest stain on his character—was prompted by the feelings
Harriet excited. John Walsingham had never introduced Danvers
to his family; and his services being required in a distant part of
the world (for he was in the Navy), he quitted England without
knowing that his associate had become the friend of his family.
Many were the struggles in the heart of Danvers against the
iniquity of winning the affections of such a being as Harriet Walsingham, when he was irrevocably tied to another: but he was
disgusted with his wife, with all things in which he had hitherto
found pleasure; and hurried away by passion, he committed one
of the greatest crimes not contained in the decalogue. He did
not for an instant contemplate attempting the virtue of Harriet:
the sanctity of her pure presence was such that a demon could
hardly have been so malignant as to harbour a thought of wrong-
ing in such a way so exalted a creature; but he sophistically
disguised to himself his real feelings, and friendship was the
pretext he invented to cover his designs from his conscience and
God. But he could only be satisfied with the love, the utter, un-
divided love of Harriet. He was not interrupted by Everard
Walsingham, for he never visited his relations, nor had any communication with them; and months rolled on, and the heart of
that divine woman was his for ever.

Wonderful indeed was the alteration effected in the nature of
Danvers by his intercourse with this matchless being; and his
remorse at the villany of his conduct was sometimes so great,
that he was on the point of confessing all to her: but then he
could not bear the idea of becoming an object of hatred and contempt to her. But he made a determination, when all the mischief
was done, to tear himself away from his beloved; and instigated
by his foster-mother joined the inauspicious insurrection which
broke out about this time in favor of the Pretender. His fortunes
were desperate, his love unhallowed, and he hoped to win a
soldier's grave as the happiest consummation of his fate. But he
survived, and rose high in the estimation of his generals; and
after the total destruction of the hopes of the Jacobites, he was
offered a commission in the service of the king of France; which
he accepted.

He wrote a letter to Harriet, telling her he was a ruined man,

beseeching her to pity and forget him; and then repaired to
France, leaving his wife and children in Britain. But the devotion
and love of Harriet assumed a deeper and more manifest character,
when she learned the calamities of Walter; and in a letter
breathing with all that bright poetry which raises woman almost
to the angel (only it is better to be a perfect woman than an indifferent seraph), she besought him to return, and informed him
she had procured his pardon for the part he had taken in the
rebellion. But he remained stedfast in his resolution of remaining
away from her, though he could not make up his mind to break
off all communication with her, and sometimes wrote and received
answers in return. At length he came back to England on a secret
mission in some degree corresponding to that in which he was
engaged in after years. Once more he beheld Harriet; and all
his good resolutions vanished like mists before the sun, when the
magic of her presence was upon him. His passion had been fed
by absence and despair, and she loved him more than ever: for
woman's love is made more strong by pity, it grows more passionate by sympathy. How Walter cursed with bitterness of heart
his imprudent marriage, which debarred him from uniting himself
with the only woman his spirit ever worshipped. But it was
vain.

News now arrived that John Walsingham was about to return
to England, and Danvers feared discovery would be inevitable.
Racked with uncertainty what course of action to pursue, he
quitted Harriet, and repaired to London, where he encountered
Everard Walsingham. They renewed once more their broken intimacy, and Danvers was taken by Everard to a house he had
hired a few miles from town, where his wife had been recently
delivered of a boy. To distract his mind from brooding on the
agonizing thought that Harriet would soon know all his hypocrisy
and guile, he again became a gamester. For some time his star
was in the ascendant, and he won considerable sums, while
Everard, who generally accompanied him to the gaming-table,
was fortunate in his play. But this luck began to fluctuate; and
it was at this precise time that John Walsingham arrived in
England: and on the first night of his return went to the place
where Everard and Walter were staking large sums of money.
The love of play was a ruling passion still with John Walsingham;

and his cousin, Danvers and himself were soon engaged with the dice, when Everard and Walter lost to him the greater part of all they possessed. As John Walsingham had business in London, he accepted the offer of Danvers to share his lodging; and it may be supposed that Walter, like a drowning wretch catching at every straw, was anxious to detain him from Harriet, who was at this time with her sister, then recently married. They played on with various success, and John Walsingham, on the plea of business, put off his visit to his relations in the country. But he had another motive besides that of gaming for remaining in the metropolis: he had become enamoured of the wife of Everard— who would never allow the legality of his marriage—and made her the most splendid offers if she would live with him. He was repulsed; but under the impression she was only the mistress of Everard, he redoubled his efforts to win her. Everard had contracted a debt to the amount of several hundred pounds to his cousin, and was unable to pay it; so that he invited him to his house, and paid him all attention, while his gentle wife, fearful of producing the effusion of blood, if she communicated to her husband the conduct of his kinsman towards her, was necessitated to endure his society. But the climax was at hand.

The wife of Danvers, now past the first bloom of youth, endeavored to gain the attention of John Walsingham, now a very rich man, who met her advances with contempt. Stung to the quick by this disdain, she inwardly vowed revenge against him. The reader must now be informed that this woman was in fact the sister of Everard's wife: but her disposition was the very antithesis of hers. There never existed a creature more utterly infamous; for she had lived as mistress to John Walsingham previous to her marriage with Danvers, and bore him two children, Francis and William, and he being weary of her imposed the trick on his friend, which he had not in the generosity of his nature suspected him of. But it was not merely before her union with Danvers that this truly infamous woman had prostituted herself. For during her absence from him in the provinces, Captain Norton having conceived a passion for her, and ignorant of whom or what she was, she intrigued with him, and the consequence of their illicit amour was the birth of poor Percy. But this fact did not

reach the ear of Danvers, or he might have sued for a divorce.
To proceed,

Mrs. Danvers discovered that John Walsingham had transferred
the passion he entertained at one time for herself to her own sister,
whom she had not seen for many years : and one of the most
diabolical plots ever concocted out of hell entered her foul mind.
She frequently saw Everard, and artfully worked upon him, to
believe that his wife encouraged the advances of John Walsingham : but persuaded him to adopt some scheme of revenge which
should be more sure and deadly than any he could accomplish in
a duel. Hating her sister cordially, as she had ever done, envious
of her loveliness, and feeling her virtuous superiority (for *she* knew
she was married) she advised Everard to take his child away from
its mother, and promised to take charge of it herself. This was
what she called " killing two birds with one stone." So the child
was torn from its mother's arms, without any cause being assigned
for such a cruel measure (the infant not having been weaned);
for Mrs. Danvers advised him not to breathe a word of his suspicions to any—not even to the principal delinquent herself—in
order that he might have proof of the guilt of the parties. Everard
was easily worked upon to believe anything, and the artifice of the
abandoned Mrs. Danvers was consummate. Her object was to
cause Everard to murder his cousin, and to break her sister's
heart,&for having been the innocent cause of winning the affections
of the man to whom she had first surrendered her virtue.

Well, John Walsingham, Everard, and Danvers were assembled
together at the gaming-table, the second of those persons being
anxious to clear himself of his debt to his cousin : the fortunes of
the two latter were at the lowest ebb, while those of the former
were flourishing. They drank, they staked—though Everard and
Danvers played on credit—and they quarrelled. Everard quitted
the hell in a state of desperation and semi-intoxication, and went
to the house of Mrs. Danvers. But John Walsingham, flushed
with wine, resented an expression of Danvers dropped in the heat
of the moment, and called him, " Cuckold !" Danvers stalked up
to his insulter, and grasping his arm, with his brow crimsoned
and the veins swoln like whipcord, commanded him to unsay the
word. Those who saw the flushed forehead, and heard the voice
of Danvers, were fully persuaded he would only be satisfied with

Walsingham's blood. "Prove the truth of what you say, if you
will not retract," said Walter, who would have been content to
have borne any ignominy to obtain a legal separation from the
woman he now loathed with bitterness.

John Walsingham was mad with drink and passion, and he
answered Danvers that previous to his marriage his wife had been
the mother of two children, and had not recovered from her last
confinement when he saw her as Mrs. Williamson, adding in-
sultingly, he thought he had proved he was cajoled, and might
guess it was he who had fooled him. This was in a public room,
before a dozen persons, and swords were drawn between John
Walsingham and Walter; but Danvers slipped, and was wounded
in the right arm ere he could make a lunge.

"By —! John Walsingham," said Danvers, as he was separated from his antagonist, "you shall repent this." And he
quitted the gaming-house with his blood on fire.

But he was secretly rejoiced to find that his wife was such an
atrocious character, and flattered himself he should be able to
procure a divorce from her, and marry Harriet. Elated with this
hope he resolved on visiting the idol of his heart, and within an
hour after parting from John Walsingham he was on his road to
Harriet, resolved to see her again before her brother could do so.
John Walsingham, still inflamed with liquor, now determined to
put in execution a scheme he had for some time entertained, and
proceeding to Everard's house he procured admittance, and stole
up to the chamber of his cousin's wife. He entered, and found
her asleep; but his passions were somewhat cooler, and that
look of innocence mingled with sadness occasioned by Everard's
harsh conduct, which the poor creature's face wore, so subdued
and touched him, vile libertine as he was, that his purpose
changed, and he crept away; but Everard, who had returned
home, saw him leave the chamber, and gnashed his teeth with
rage. Mrs. Danvers, however, had so wrought upon his mind
that he suppressed the ebullition of his wrath towards John, and
rushing to his wife he violently reproached and brutally struck
her, when, without waiting to hear aught she could say in excul-
pation of the supposed crime, he swore never to see her again,
and quitted the house. He virtually murdered her; for she died
of a broken heart within three weeks of that time.

John Walsingham meanwhile had taken horse, determined to abandon his pursuit of his cousin's wife, and Everard doing likewise, in an admirable disguise tracked the man whom he believed to have so grossly wronged him. It so happened, from accidental occurrences, that at every inn where John Walsingham stopped, Danvers had stopped also; and on the subsequent trial, this was one of the arguments adduced to prove that he had waylaid Walsingham, and murdered him. But of this more anon. Everard on the contrary took his measures in such a way that none suspected him, and it was generally supposed he had departed for the Continent before his cousin's death. Thus the whole weight of circumstantial evidence, in the subsequent investigation, was thrown on the shoulders of Danvers: first, it was proved that he had a violent quarrel with John Walsingham, that they had fought and he had been worsted, that he had lost a large sum of money to him, that he had vowed revenge, and preceded him by a very short time, and, in addition to all this, other circumstances followed which proved his guilt, in the opinion of many, beyond doubt.

Harry Danvers (so it happened) had been placed at a school a short distance from the spot which was the theatre of the posterior events, and having played the truant one fine summer's day, he was wandering about in a wood, when he heard a cry at no great distance from him. The child—he was then about eight years old—though somewhat alarmed at such a sound, conquered his timidity, and proceeded in the direction it came from. But it is necessary to retrograde some minutes, to explain the whole occurrence clearly.

In a lonely spot near the wood where the little fellow was wandering might have been seen the figure of a horseman, of powerful and athletic make, who was humming the air of a popular song not remarkable for morality as he slowly wended his way; when he was attacked on a sudden by a man whose face was masked, also mounted, who wounded him in the body with a sword ere he could defend himself; and when with a groan he fell senseless to the ground, the assassin fled, as if pursued by fiends. That man was Everard.

It is requisite here to mention simply the fact that Danvers once discovered Everard used loaded dice: but as he had sacredly promised never to do so again, Danvers refrained from exposing him : but from that cause he had exerted a powerful influence over him. This circumstance will explain the secret which Walter held *in terrorem* over the Miser in after days ; but Everard imagined, when Danvers threatened him, that he alluded to a very different matter. For he had not proceeded above a quarter of a mile from the place where he had attacked his cousin, when he descried Danvers approaching by a cross-road, and redoubled his speed, supposing that he was recognised by him. But Danvers, though he saw a flying figure, knew not that it was Everard. He had been delayed on his road by his horse going lame, and was pursuing his way on foot. Just as the Miser vanished, Danvers beheld a horse without a rider galloping away, and concluded something was amiss. He speedily arrived at the place where John Walsingham was lying insensible, but not dead ; and (concluding a robber had attempted his life) he endeavoured to resuscitate him, but in vain, and hastened away to procure assistance.

Scarcely had he disappeared, when a woman and a strange, semi-human child advanced, and the former perceiving that the wounded man wore a rich gold chain, despoiled him of it. The hideous child took up a silver-mounted riding-whip the wounded man had dropped, and blew several notes on it—for it had a whistle. John Walsingham recovered from his stupor at this juncture, and finding the hand of the female in his pocket, struggled with her. Then that woman stabbed him with a knife, and he uttered the cry of agony Harry had overheard ; and the monstrous child struck him with a stone on the head. In a few moments the unhappy man expired, and, as he breathed his last, Harry came upon the fearful scene ; and overcome with horror, uttered a scream, and ran away.

The murderess dragged away the corpse, and descended with it into the cave—of which such repeated mention has been made —so that when Danvers returned to the place with a person on horseback he had casually met, there was no trace of the body. Information was given to the local authorities immediately, and Danvers arrested on suspicion. He was tried and condemned—a body having been found previous to the trial in a river in the vicinity, and some one identified it as that of John Walsingham—

whose else, it was argued, could it be?—though it was in such a
state of decomposition that the features could hardly be sworn to,
and a surgeon even thought it was probably that of a person who
pre-deceased Walsingham by some weeks.

Walter Danvers escaped—his wife led an abandoned life, keeping the child of Everard Walsingham (little George) for infants'
parts in the theatre; and Danvers's two children were conveyed
by Mrs. Haines to France. For Harriet Walsingham, she resolved to shut herself out from the world, and in the most private
manner removed from the roof of her sister to the house she had
ever since occupied, and where she devoted herself to Heaven with
all the tempered grief and pious resignation of her pure soul.

A few days after the perpetration of that dread crime which
he had but half accomplished, the wife of Everard died, and was
privately buried in a little country church-yard; he then left
England, and did not return to it for years. Walter Danvers
again served in the armies of France; and, nine years after he
made his escape from prison, returned on the mission he was
engaged in when he first made his appearance on the stage. Harriet Walsingham he, in common with many others, had heard
was dead; but he loved her memory with a sacred passion, and
often reproached himself as the cause of her decease. It is only
necessary to add that John Walsingham's children were taken
care of by his sister.

CHAPTER III.

> " Justice! Oh, 'tis a word God *only* understands!
> Man's justice is most impotent indeed
> To punish,—how much more so to reward!"

THE EXAMINATION OF DANVERS.

AT an early hour of the day, every part of the place where
the examination of Danvers was to be held was thronged; and it
was with no little difficulty that the officers of the court made
their way through the crowd, and assisted those personally interested in the proceedings to the places reserved for them.

The Hall of Justice was of considerable size, and at the farther end was a platform on which the magistrates took their
seats. Immediately below, railed off from the crowd, was the
bar, and beside it the witness-box, and at either side were
benches appropriated to lawyers and persons engaged in the
business of the court. Some of the prisoner's friends were conducted to their places, and might be seen—anxiously looking for
his appearance. The bench nearest to the spot where Danvers
would stand was occupied by several persons who claim acquaintance with the reader.

The tall figure of Elizabeth Haines was conspicuous among
them, and at her right hand was Harry Danvers. Sidney and
Spenser sat together in the middle of the bench ; and nearest to
the latter, beautiful as sculptor's or painter's dreams, a pale,
glorious face, on which the bright sun shone down, and seemed to
crown it as with a halo, might be seen. But not a trace of emotion was upon it : there was something even sublime in its repose,—and but for the eager straining of the eye towards the
door where the prisoner would appear, it might have been
thought she was an uninterested spectator in the scene. It was,
of course, Harriet Walsingham. Presently, a martial form, and a
fair, girlish figure advanced, with eyes bent on the earth, and
trembling visibly. Harry Danvers rose and took her hand.
" Ellen," he said, " why are you here ?" and his glance wandered to Charles Walsingham who accompanied her. But ere
she could reply, there arose an universal exclamation, for it was
thought the prisoner was coming.

It appeared, however, that it was the magistrates, who passed
to the platform, and sat down. Among them was Captain Norton, looking like a walking skeleton, but with a wild, restless fire
in his eye which gave a strange and ghastly expression to his
marble face. He sat like a statue, with compressed lips and
clasped hands, scarcely seeming to breathe ; the stillness he
maintained was most awful. There were present also the younger
Lady Walsingham, who occupied a seat a short distance from
Harriet, and a young lawyer, the friend of Charles once alluded
to, while a few less important personages were seated behind.
At the other side, a little below the platform, might be perceived
a little old man and a lad, the expression of whose features was

remarkably similar, full of vulgar cunning and shrewdness. These were the two Quirks: and at the distance of a yard from them stood two individuals, whom it is not probable the reader should recognise in the disguise they wore. The former was John Norton, dressed in an old-fashioned style with " spectacles on nose." The other was a foreign-looking man with a beard, of dark, saturnine aspect, who leant on a staff, and never raised his eyes. He was Hugh Freestone.

In a corner of the hall crouched a figure of really tall stature, but his height appeared below the ordinary, as he stood in the shadow of a pillar, and glanced fearfully towards the door at which Danvers was to enter. This was no other than Everard Walsingham—or Lord Walsingham (for such he was) who in spite of his terrors was led by intense anxiety to the place, in order to know the worst that could befal him. That Walter Danvers had not previously confessed the truth, Everard could not account for, except that the knowledge he possessed gave him such almost unlimited power over him. But now there was no chance of Walter's escaping, and he did not believe his generosity would sacrifice life for him. Sam Stokes, Corporal Figgins and little Mr. Smith intervened betwixt the Miser and the Quirks.

" Why is not the prisoner here?" asked one of the magistrates of an officer, who was leaving the court to hasten the appearance of Danvers, when there arose a shout, a hissing shout, a yell, from the street through which Danvers was passing from prison, and then there was a rush into the already crowded court, and shrieks and oaths resounded through the place, while the prisoner, strongly guarded, was conducted to the bar.

He looked somewhat pale and haggard ; but his undaunted spirit quailed not, and he stood with dignified composure, power, pride, command on his tranquil brow for a minute, until his eyes fell on Harriet Walsingham and his children. Then the strong man was subdued—while Harriet was hardly able to maintain her seat—and a tremor ran through his frame ; but it subsided, and the investigation proceeded. The chief magistrate having examined the depositions spoke—

" Prisoner, you are charged with being the same person who was condemned for the murder of John Walsingham, on the — day of —— 17 —, and made his escape from prison on the day previous to that fixed for his execution. Do you wish to say anything before I examine the witnesses who swear to your identity ?"

"Nothing," replied Danvers, in a steady, strong voice, which thrilled the hearts of many present.

"Who swears to the fact of this man being that same Walter Danvers ?" inquired the magistrate.

"I acknowledge the fact," said the prisoner calmly, as several persons were on the point of establishing the identity.

"Then," rejoined the magistrate, "the sentence of the law will be executed on you without further delay."

Here the young lawyer, who had undertaken to do what was possible for Danvers, rose and said, "I have to request that the execution of the prisoner be delayed till after an inquiry has been instituted into circumstances which have recently transpired relative to the murder of which the prisoner has been found guilty, and also that the witnesses of these facts may be now examined."

The young barrister had but just finished speaking, when old Quirk advanced, and addressing the chief-magistrate, said, "I have also to lay before your worship some matters connected with the same affair ; and I think, when you have heard the depositions, you will admit there is sufficient reason for delaying the sentence——"

"What!" interrupted a hoarse voice proceeding from the side of the chief magistrate. "After the lapse of nine years, is there to be more delay ?"

"Pray, Captain Norton," cried the magistrate who had conducted the examination, "allow me to hear the witnesses, and if we do not think what they urge against the present execution of the prisoner valid——"

"I am silent," cried Captain Norton, sullenly. "But you are aware this man murdered my son in cold blood, and that he is a notorious Jacobite."

"We must not prejudice the minds of our brother magistrates against this man, that of which he stands condemned being a capital offence," said the chief magistrate. "We must remember the importance of the matter, and listen to the facts to be adduced with patience. What witnesses," (addressing the barrister) "have you to bring forward ?"

4 c

"I am hardly prepared," began the young lawyer; but Roger Sidney and Harry Danvers, as well as Charles Walsingham and Sam Stokes, simultaneously arose. Roger Sidney was known to the presiding magistrate, and was first called upon for his testimony.

"I had made a deposition before one of the magistrates of the county," said the old Angler, "concerning the discovery of a skeleton which there are strong reasons for believing to be that of the same person for whose murder the prisoner has been found guilty; but the authorities, it seems, took no notice of the matter." A magistrate replied to this that the rising of the Jacobites had been so sudden and formidable that it had diverted the attention of himself and others from business of less emergency, every constable having been employed since the information given by Mr. Sidney: but that he would immediately send officers to investigate the mysterious affair.

"Nay," cried Harry Danvers, "that were useless now. You must cause the river to be dragged, if you would find the corpse alluded to." Harry then recounted the particulars of his midnight visit to the cave, and added that Sam Stokes had found him after he was wounded (fortunately but slightly—though he was stunned by his fall) and called on the tar to corroborate his statement—which Sam instantly did. Charles then begged for a hearing, and related the singular coincidence by which he had become a witness of the dark scene in the cave, and when he had ended, officers were dispatched to the locality where the plashing in the water was heard, and which was described by Harry Danvers. They had orders to have the river instantly dragged, and to return with all speed to the Court.

Captain Norton then spoke. "Can either of the witnesses," he asked, "point out the probable persons concerned in the occurrences of last night?"

"We have our suspicions," answered Harry Danvers, glancing at Corporal Figgins; who bore the look with bold effrontery, "but we can state nothing positively."

"And to whom do your suspicions point?"

"To a woman named Stokes, who lives in the vicinity of the cave, and whom I should wish apprehended, and to another person who is here present."

" Who is that person ?"

Harry pointed to Figgins, and related what George had told him. The Corporal advanced and confronted his accuser.

" A likely story," exclaimed Figgins, " when the murdered gentleman was my benefactor, and I now am the servant of his sister, Lady Walsingham. It is plainly trumped up out of spite because I captured the prisoner."

" Of this, more anon," said a magistrate.

Old Quirk then spoke. " As I am to consider master Danvers my client," he began, " I wish to elicit something farther than has yet been stated. I have no doubt we shall be able to make it appear that the skeleton which has been referred to is that of the person of whose murder Walter Danvers has been condemned, in which case he must be released : it was, doubtless, thrown into the water by the real murderer, who had discovered people had visited the cave where it was deposited. I am aware that the skeleton of the unfortunate gentleman was supposed to have been found soon after his death : but we are so often deceived in the identity of a skeleton—of those who have been dead some——"

" I must interrupt you, Mr. Attorney !" exclaimed the young barrister who had previously spoken in behalf of Danvers, " unless you are authorised to plead in the case, your reasoning is so jesuitical, that while you speak in favor of the prisoner, you endeavour to throw doubts on the validity of the testimony received. Am I right," looking at the Walsinghams, " in thus interfering ?"

" Certainly," said Charles, " with Mr. Danvers' approbation."

Old Quirk turned, a little disconcerted at the exposure of his double-dealing ; but his effrontery returned, and he said, " I will of course resign the matter into the hands of those who are chosen by my employers to defend the prisoner ; but I deny I have acted indiscreetly, as, if I had not been interrupted, I should have proved. I have some evidence to adduce, which is important ; but it is hardly yet digested."

" We will hear that evidence whenever you like to lay it before us," said the chief magistrate. " Is there any other witness present ?"

" Let us pass," here cried the voice of a young boy, " pray let us pass."

" Who is this ?" demanded a magistrate.

" I have got something of consequence to say," cried the little
fellow who had spoken. The officers made way for the new
comers; and a child of nine or ten years old, leading a mute
being some years older, advanced and exclaimed, " This boy has
been talking to me : for I met him coming here, and he said if I
would go with him he would show me how the gentleman was
murdered."

" What does all this mean ?" asked the presiding magistrate.

" I will tell you, sir," returned the young boy, breathless with
hurry and excitement. " I thought that what I heard from this
poor fellow was strange ; and he led me to a wood, some miles
from this place, when he told me that long, long ago, when he
was a little child, a person was murdered there. He said it had
cost him dear, for it had broken the music of his brain—that
scene—with fear : he described to me how the murder was done.
He said, he was lying under a tree, when he saw a man hiding—"

" Ha !" said a voice in the court, here ; but no one saw the
speaker.

The boy continued—" And then a gentleman came that way on
horseback, and the man who had hid himself killed him, and then
ran away. And presently another person came, and tried to help
the gentleman who was dead, or dying ; but it was no good, and
he departed. Afterwards others came, and as this boy says, killed
the gentleman again ; but I could not understand him when he
got so far."

" This is a strong corroboration of what the son of the prisoner
said on the trial," observed Sidney aloud.

" But the statement is so incoherent," returned one of the
bench, " that nothing can be made of it. Is this boy accompanying the child an idiot ?"

" I think not, sir," said little George—for it was he who came
up with " Mad Willy."

But the mysterious life of reason again was dormant, and the
lunatic could tell nothing. After a short time, the officers who
had been sent to ascertain if a body had been thrown into the
river where Harry described, returned with the news that it had
been dragged ineffectually, only a large stone having been found.
Corporal Figgins had seemed uneasy when the officers re-entered,
but having heard the result of their search, his brow cleared.

"I think," said the chief magistrate, " there is enough mystery here to justify the delay of the prisoner's execution. Let him be taken back to prison, and placed in strict confinement. I will represent the affair to the Home Secretary."

Thus closed the examination, and Danvers was removed strongly guarded. The crowded court was soon empty, and the sounds of human life were silenced.

CHAPTER IV.*

What! is it in the power of threescore years
To push eternity from human thought,
And quench the mind immortal in the dust?

YOUNG.

A CHAPTER FOR THINKERS—POPE AND BOLINGBROKE.

IT was evening, and the crowded thoroughfares of the metropolis were thinning, and the crowds gradually passing to their homes or pleasures. The day had been sultry, but a cool breeze was rising, and the stars became visible in the soft, misty blue of the

* The introduction in this chapter of a species of writing usually confined to a work avowedly metaphysical, requires some apology. The reasons why I have introduced such abstract speculation are manifold. First, the development of mind, which is all along the chief object of my Tale, is assisted by it. I maintain that the pivot on which character moves is not practical but theoretical —that theory precedes action, even in the thoughtless, generally. The next reason to be mentioned is—because the individual is the growth of his times, just in the same way as a plant is the production of a specific soil and atmosphere. The philosophy of this age is not that of a century ago, but is indivisibly connected with it. England at the era in question was rich in the abstract, but not in the ideal. The genius of our literature necessarily partook of the spirit of the age, and that was not to the poetical. Now, whatever may be said to the contrary, we are highly idealised. A state had preceded us full of the artificial, and redolent of the hot-house. Even the poetry of Pope has for the most part no vital imagination in it. But Pope will not satisfy our poetical wants ; we crave more ethereal food. We are advancing to the last stage of civilization fast. The limits of a note do not permit me to state all that I wish in connexion with this subject; but I have something to add, lest those who are desirous of checking thought—when it is thought run mad—condemn me for

autumnal sky. A diminutive man, who had scarcely reached middle age, was walking slowly along in that quarter of the town frequented by the gay and the brilliant of that time, but now nearly deserted by the fashionable world; was recognised with smiles and greetings by many of the most distinguished personages he encountered. But though he returned them, a sneer would gather round his mouth ever and anon, in spite of all the studious honor paid to him, though why it was difficult to define; for he did not seem at all in the condition of one made cynical by envy of the good things others enjoyed, and he himself did not possess; but a slight deformity—an almost imperceptible crookedness in the back—might, perhaps, in some measure account for the acerbity of temper he exhibited.

"Ah! my dear Pope," cried a handsome, gentlemanly personage more advanced in life than the little person with the crooked shoulder, who came out of a house inhabited by a great man of the time, now nearly forgotten, "I am sorry to see you do not look so well as you ought."

"Your lordship is going to sup with the pretty foreign singer, I suppose?"

"Not to-night. I shall be present at the discussion, and probably take part in it. You will be there?"

"Certainly, if your lordship speak. That young Atheist would have hit any but yourself rather hard the other night. He is a monstrous clever lad."

"Hang him! But I mean to pull to pieces his philosophy presently. Good bye for the present."

"Lord Bolingbroke is coming into office again, Pope, I hear," said a young man of fashion, addressing the crook-backed individual, as soon as the person alluded to was out of sight.

"Is he?" replied the other. "I heard that you were going to reside more out of the open air than is your custom. People *will* talk."

giving publicity to sentiments (in the mouths of William Walsingham and Lord Bolingbroke) inimical to Natural and Revealed Religion. My conviction is, that the more reason is excited, rational Christianity—pure, bright, effulgent, and tolerant—is promulged. That cause must indeed be bad, which can dread the attacks of its foes so much, as to wish its friends to shut their eyes and close their ears—to believe in their IGNORANCE.

"Going to gaol, eh ?" returned the young man. "That's a cursed lie." And he sauntered away.

Pope sneered in his bitter fashion, and was probably thinking of writing a satire, when a man of about his own size, and nearly of his age, with a countenance full of intellect and splendor met him. "What! Do I see Henry Spenser?" exclaimed the poet. "It can be no other; though it is years since I saw you."

"I am glad to meet you, my dear Pope," replied Spenser, cordially shaking the hand that was extended to him. And the two diminutive men, respectively perhaps the best living poet and philosopher of that day, walked on together.

"Here we are at a house," said Pope, "where thinking men of the day meet once a week to discuss important questions. Will you accompany me in ? The question to-night is the Origin of Evil. Bolingbroke will speak, and you will probably also hear a rather extraordinary youth, who advocates the atheistical side." Spenser still loved controversy, still loved to exercise his mighty spirit in the mysteries of things, and to throw in truth wherever it was possible to do so ; and assenting to the proposition of Pope, who was one of his earliest acquaintances, and whose fame he had predicted (when he was a boy himself) would increase more and more, he observed as he entered the house, which was open to the public, and much frequented by the wits of the day—"I cannot understand what Atheism means. It is a name for nothing ; a term which is a mere negative to an affirmative cannot be said to comprise a logical entity." They ascended some stairs in the tavern ; and were admitted into an apartment—when a singular scene was presented to their sight.

The room itself was spacious, and at the extremity was a sort of stage, from which some person was addressing the meeting. Altogether there might have been as many as thirty persons present, many of whom were evidently above the middle classes. Among these were the old and the young, the grave and the gay, the philosopher and the wit, the man of science and the man of pleasure ; and a better subject for a picture can hardly be imagined. The number of intelligent faces, the variety of expression in them, as the lamps cast down their effulgence from above, —being suspended to the ceiling,—plentifully scattered over the apartment, the look of mirth on this man's countenance as a brilliant wit whispered some biting jest on the company into his ear, or the solemn attention of this individual's saturnine physiognomy, presented so powerful and striking a contrast that words can but inadequately describe it. " SI DEUS EST, UNDE MALUM ?" was inscribed in large letters on a board in the front of the stage, such being the precise theme for discussion on that evening.

" Gentlemen," said the person who was speaking when Pope and Spencer entered, " I have the honour to announce that Lord Bolingbroke will open the debate this evening, and is prepared to show that all Evil tends to Good. Any person will be at liberty to take part in the discussion, provided he will conform to the regulation of not speaking above a quarter of an hour at a time."

Here Lord Bolingbroke came forward and was received with strong tokens of approbation by those who were inclined to his opinions, he being considered the head of the Deistical philosophers of the period. 'Silence' was proclaimed by the chairman, and at that talismanic word, the hum of voices subsided. All was deep attention, as the celebrated St. John prepared to speak.

What a vast power there is in discussion for directing the minds of men ! How opinions are gradually formed or uprooted, and truth or error received for all eternity ! And when intelligent and rational beings meet to inquire into the great subjects of deity, and the mysteries which are connected with our complex being, how infinite the importance of every look, and word and action ! But the battle of mind *must* be fought, and whether it be in the crowded arena where intellectual gladiators strive, or in the solitary soul with silence around, the result will be the same, the eternal purpose of God be developed. But what a thing to contemplate the mirrors of the heart in the lineaments of the listeners, as some prejudice is attacked, some feeling outraged, some faith shaken to the centre ! Here and there a man who has exhausted all the worlds of opinion may be seen cold and listless, but to behold the masses is to see all the mutations of intellect. Oh, it is more tremendous to the thinker than the strife of armies battling for continents !

Bolingbroke commenced thus—" The origin of evil is a subject which the sophistries of divines, and the false reasoning of atheists have so confused and obscured, that it is with difficulty the minds of the mass of mankind can receive the principles of the first philosophy. In this respect the civilized world is in the same condition as the man who lived in a dark cave, and was so accustomed to the obscurity, that he loved it better than the light. Gentlemen, I maintain, in pursuance of the argument we held the other night when we met here, that all evil is the creation of man—that it is in idea, not in reality. Either man's ignorance or his madness have diverted the order of nature—which moves in perfect harmony, if undisturbed by the action of secondary agents. In other words, there is no such thing as evil in nature; there is but one substance in the universe, which is *good;* and from the existence of it, we are led to conclude it was formed by a Being infinitely perfect and wise, in Himself unchangeable and eternal; but out of whom all is necessarily imperfection; that is, relative good, and not absolute good. Before I proceed any farther, will any one question my premises? If so, let him rise!"

There was a little knot of Atheists—then much rarer than in the present day—but none of them had the hardihood to attack the noble Deist, but a young, a *very* young man, seated opposite to Bolingbroke rose, and a murmur of applause broke from the atheistical party. Fixing his large, dark eye on Bolingbroke, the youth opened his lips.

"The noble lord," he said, in his cold, passionless manner, "appears to have strange notions of good in its relation with evil. What, if he required a tooth drawn! would it not be as much positive evil to endure the pain, as positive good to be in a healthful state, free from suffering? He tells you there is but one substance in the universe, which is perfectly good, and yet in the same breath informed you that *evil* is the creation of man. Surely it is an evil to have such an idea! I want to know—if there be but one substance in nature—why it should undergo decomposition and mutation? For if that substance be good, it cannot admit evil into it, on the principle that a contrary cannot receive a contrary. A unity of substance must be indecomposable and immutable. Unless, then, he can shew me that good and evil are mere arbitrary terms, and in fact manifestations of the same principle, his argument is utterly worthless. 'The order of nature,' he tells you, 'moves in perfect harmony, if not disturbed by secondary causes.' Well, I grant it. But then, I ask, what those secondary causes are? Did the *perfect harmony* of nature pro-

4 D

duce them, or not? If nature produced them, she must have
been at war with herself, and therefore could not move in harmony :
and if otherwise, it must be admitted there is another agent than
good in existence—the opposite of good, *not* relative at all."

"Our young friend," returned Bolingbroke, "in his hasty
empiricism, rushes at once to conclusions, unjustified by his premises. I repeat, there is but one substance in nature : but out of
this substance may proceed diverse qualities, as from the mind of
man emanate a variety of actions. I know he will reply, that if
this substance be perfectly good in itself, it cannot produce evil :
but it is the perfection of the organization of good which neces-
sitates mutation. Otherwise, we know, that flowing on in one
never-changing stream, the beautiful equipoise of the universe
would seem stale and dull. Suppose that we had one perpetual
summer, should we not grow weary of it, and long for the most
frigid winter? We can enjoy nothing except by the force of contrast, which immutability cannot afford. We must be immutable
beings to enjoy eternity, and only Deity can be so. I say, then,
that if we could reconcile such an anomaly as duration without
succession in time, and realize a perfect state, such a condition
would be the greatest curse to us possible. So that the question
resolves itself into this, namely, whether, as a state of change is
inevitable, we do not reap benefit from it?"

"Lord Bolingbroke has shifted his ground already," was the
rejoinder of the boyish philosopher. "He wants now to prove
that we are benefited by evil, when he told you in direct terms
there is no such entity at all. For the secession from absolute
good in the individual, is the point on which we are at issue.
Why is the mind so constituted that it is not susceptible of continuous happiness? The question of secondary causes he has deserted. He knows he is unable to satisfy the objection that evil
and good cannot co-exist in one substance, and so he wishes to
prove that evil is a manifestation of good. Earthquakes and tempests are beneficial in their effects, but yet they are a positive
evil. You cannot say it is good that a thousand innocent persons
are destroyed for the benefit of a million! Co-existence of good
and evil together demonstrates nothing but that they preserve a
poise, at the most. As wise were it to say that because there is
water there *must* be air, because there is fire there *must* be earth,

if the elements were divided, as that because there is happiness there must be misery. For a contrary never produced its contrary; life never made death, nor action inaction. Whence are these states of being then? Were they produced by an intelligent and beneficent first cause for a specific purpose—for the good of all? A perfect organization of good implies a perfect author of it, and therefore an imperfect organization an imperfect one. Unless then it can be demonstrated that the design of the universe is perfect, there can have been no infinite mind concerned in it, and the idea of a God is preposterous."

Bolingbroke looked puzzled; for he had not prepared himself for such an opponent, and the youth sat down, a low buz of applause running through the knot of Atheists, who had collected round their champion; but as the last speaker, confident of victory, looked for a reply, he encountered the blaze of an eye whose resplendency had never been darkened by all the powers of reasoning possessed by a William Walsingham. Ere Bolingbroke could frame a satisfactory answer, a clear, distinct voice said,

"Gentlemen, if I may be permitted to speak, a short time will suffice to invalidate the atheistical arguments you have heard." Bolingbroke seeing Spenser, who had thus spoken, was with Pope, nodded to the new speaker, who proceeded thus:—
"Every rational man acknowledges there is pain and pleasure, joy and grief, knowledge and ignorance, and so on. It was not the one state that created the other, but it is manifest there must be antagonism, or nothing but the thing experienced could be known. If then we allow good, we allow evil also, unless we say they are both without entity;—and we have to investigate their origin. What is the idea of happiness? No one can answer me. Our knowledge is simply negative, and built on antitheses. Show me a pure idea, independent of its antetype, and I will allow I labour under error."

William Walsingham rose to reply. "We are to conclude, then," said the Epicurean, "that the same power which created good, created evil also. What a comfort for the murderer to know that his crime—if he conceive crime exists—was the action of a Being who uses him as a machine! For if there be a God, it is obvious nothing can exist without his will. So that, if he knows a crime is about to be committed, and does not prevent it,

surely, at all events, he is an accessary before the fact. Now this
with a finite being would imply equal guilt, but with an infinite
one it assumes a different aspect. I put it to all here present
whether it would not be a moral dereliction, not to prevent evil,
if it is possible to do so ?"

"But if," said Spenser, "by preventing one evil a greater is
caused, is it not better to suffer the least."

The Epicurean smiled darkly. "What a God must that be
who is shut up in difficulties," he said. "In order to create happiness he must permit evil, according to you. You say God is
omnipotent, and yet not so. Is not this an anomaly?"

"It is evident," observed Lord Bolingbroke, "that God could
not create a God. A being less than infinite must be liable to
unhappiness."

"Very well, then," returned the Atheist, "the creation of an
imperfect being is nothing less than that of evil; and I deny that
it were justifiable to cause the *possibility* of evil. If we were to
act upon the same principle, would it be right? Knowing that
crime would ensue from a certain action of our own, would it not
be better to remain inactive? Where is the difference between
creating the elements of, and causing, a thing?" He ended.

"But," interposed Bolingbroke, "we are not to measure God
by our understandings. It is possible for him to exist in a mode,
and act in a way incomprehensible to us. When we employ the
finite to take the circumference of the infinite, we act as wisely as
a man about to pass a cord round the globe. We may fancy we
can do it, in the pride of intellect, but it is a mathematical
absurdity."

"Why reason, then, on what is incomprehensible? Why tell
me that God cannot do this, cannot do that, if you are unable to
shew me what his resources are?"

"Because," answered Bolingbroke, "I can demonstrate what
he is *not*, though not what he *is*. He must possess infinite power,
but we cannot tell what the infinite may be. We are to reason
therefore on what we know, not on what we cannot comprehend.
The finite is the scope of our faculties, and we cannot err within
its circle."

"Lord Bolingbroke, then," said William, "confesses his
ignorance of Deity. He is driven to allow mystery, even when he

is here avowedly to disprove its existence. I ask him whence is evil: and he can give me no solution. Well then, we are told, this infinite God cannot create a perfect being, which implies that he is under a necessity and therefore *inferior* to necessity. *My* God is then the strongest power."

"Exactly so," said Spenser. "Necessity, though inferior to yourself—being but a blind agent—is the Omnipotence *you* adore! But define what you mean by necessity; for I hold that God is unnecessitated—that all principles in existence find in him their centre, and therefore this necessity can be but a portion of his immense being. But God containing, and not contained by necessity, is subject only to himself. You cannot inform me of the nature of this abstract principle you adore (which must have had a cause, if it be not a Creator), and therefore it is rational to conclude it to be an arbitrary term, a name, vague, and undefined ; so that the dispute resolves itself at last into logomachy."

"And you attack me," returned the Epicurean, "with the same weapons as I used against you. There is no word we can use, in fact, that is not an arbitrary term."

"The admission is conclusive. The idea, then, must be antecedent to the word, as the touch of a player upon an instrument precedes the sound produced. You have an idea of necessity, but you did not gain it through words—not from without, but from within. Your materialism is untenable, if you cannot shew the converse ; and necessity can only be deduced from such a system of philosophy."

"I pretend not to define the nature of ideas ; but how is it possible to acquire knowledge save through the senses? We are now in a different line of argument from that we set out with, my opponents apparently having given up the position that they know more than I do !"

"You must shew me what the senses are," replied Spenser, without heeding the taunt. "For I hold a coal is heat as much as sense is knowledge, or the medium of it. Admitting that we derive all we know from the impression of external objects on our organization, you cannot demonstrate the identity of thought and sensation."

"No ; but I can evince they are phases of the same principle. Who ever knew colour but by the eye, body but through the touch ?"

" These are material objects. If you go to subjects, I defy you to show the senses made us acquainted with them. Can any combination of the elements form thought ?"

" But what is the immense difference between subjects and objects ?"

" That of Facts and Truths !"

" You admit that there must be facts on which to build truths ?"

" Certainly not. We know the universe exists as a universe of matter through sense: but we did not attain the idea of God in the same way. Rational beings alone have a conception of him. We understand by such a Being, one with all power, wisdom, goodness, unseen, eternal, in whose love is life and immortality."

" Has he ever denied himself, to do good to man, as his injunction, by the moral law, you would assert, is, to us ?"

" Yes. The Deist's God may be stern and inexorable; but not so the Christian's. Never was there a greater mistake than to predicate the contrary. The Deist tells us he knows nothing of Deity beyond the finite; the Christian believes God has revealed himself in infinity, which is the basis of the scheme of revelation. Controlled not, but controlling, we believe he exists, his laws absolute goodness, his power infinite wisdom."

" And that power is not a necessitating permeation ?"

" It pervades all the framework of creation, which is sustained thereby; but where there is a being capable of reasoning, reason alone constrains."

" Necessity, it appears to me, is a law of all the universe. If there were no necessity, how could there be a law? If there were no law, how could there be a world at all? So, if you admit the fact of a sensible universe, you must perforce acknowledge that it is controlled by the principle inherent in all nature, and superior to all nature. If you suppose there is no such thing as necessity, you allow that the elements are the creatures of chance, although there is an undeviating harmony preserved, except in those convulsions of matter, the cause of which is attributable to certain properties in the constitution of the original law."

" But what is law? Does law create necessity, or not? Is necessity a God superior to all law, or is it itself unnecessitated and omnipotent? If it be not an intellectual, guiding principle, it must be subject to law. Then it cannot be a first cause, but must be an agent. I would ask you, Gentlemen, if you ever saw necessity, or conceived it in any shape material or otherwise? Did you ever behold it organizing the operations of all nature, and shaping human action? I think that the Materialist is bound to shew to my senses all that he asserts, until he can demonstrate that there is that in the existence of matter uncognisable by sense."

" Not at all. The Materialist concedes the fact that there are qualities in matter which he does not understand. But what is the use of reason? Surely not to argue without *data*; and where are we to procure *data* but in the objects of our sensuous experience?"

" I will admit no mystery in matter;" said Spenser, " at least not in what we see, feel, touch, smell, or taste. The Materialist tells us we have no inlets of knowledge but through these senses, and then asserts there is mystery in matter. Then why is Materialism more rational than any other system, if on the threshold of inquiry it sets out with an enigma? Will any one define what matter is?"

" There is reason to suppose there are properties in the elements, which cannot be analysed at present from the defects of chemical science."

" The argument is tantamount to nothing at all: for chemistry is founded upon certain principles which, if based on observations of sense, cannot be shewn to be material. The facts of science are purely physical, but the truths thereof always metaphysical. Facts are for the being in time, truths for the being breathing eternity."

" What is the difference between the two?"

" The fact is the immediate evidence of sense, such as we share with other animals: the truth results alone from reasoning—a faculty with which none but man is endued."

" But what if the truth is the carrying out of the fact which is antecedent to it?"

" I deny," was the reply, " that fact always precedes truth. On the contrary there are many sciences which could not exist without *à priori* knowledge."

" Mention one," said William.

" Mathematics."

"Why all our ideas of numbers must be derived from sense."

"Ideas are not the product of the senses at all."

"Then what are they?"

"The combinations of mind. I compare the senses to the notes of an instrument, each of which has a separate office, a peculiar property: but who ever heard of an instrument playing of itself?"

"So then the sound came from without, and not from within, and the analogy favors me!"

"But what precedes the sound?ii asked Spenser. "Why, the touch of the player's fingers! The material action produces the phenomena of sensation, but the ideas were in mind only. Not to pursue this subject too far on this occasion—though I think if we destroy the common theory of ideas, we annihilate materialistic necessity,—(which would make an intelligent God a devil), let us return to the point from which we started. If there is a God, from whence is evil? Did it emanate from man, nature, or deity? It is manifest Omnipotence was under no necessity of doing anything: otherwise he would be no better than a blind agent, such as the Atheist deifies. Now if we suppose a great, good man were given power to create, what would he do? He would lay out a plan first. He would form intelligent beings: but if he laid them under inexorable necessity, they would be unable to assimilate themselves to a standard of good. Morally they would be no better than the atoms compelled to act according to the laws given to them. To what purpose such a creation?"

"Would it not be sufficient if the creature were happy?"

"Yes, but if intelligent, he must desire to be like the highest intelligence. If he had not will, he could not be happy, unless indeed he were ignorant, as our first parents once were.ii

"Blessed ignorance!" cried William, bitterly. "Why not remain so?"

"And lose all these majestic mental powers, these sublime feelings, these capacities of virtue?"

"Ay, if there can be no universal good *with* them."

"But if the only consummate, God-like happiness be in the use of mind?"

"The discussion is exceeding its limits—another night we will resume the debate," said the chairman. "It is now past midnight."

"The Epicurean murmured to himself. "A few hours more, and I shall be far away."

Spenser was engaged in conversation by Lord Bolingbroke for a minute, immediately after the discussion—the two philosophers having been introduced to each other by Pope—and during that minute the Materialist passed from the room : and years elapsed ere Spenser saw him again. And when he did so—" O, what a falling off was there."

CHAPTER V.

The love-dream vanishes, and o'er her soul
There comes the bitterness and the despair.—*MS.*

ELLEN DANVERS—HARRY—MOTHER STOKES—THE MISER.

ALONE in the solitude of her little chamber, with deep melancholy imprinted on her fair young face, sat Ellen Danvers. It was very late, and the lamp on the table before her burned faintly, throwing a sickly and uncertain light on her gentle and innocent countenance, lovely as one of Raffaelle's virgins. There was an open letter spread before her, and ever and anon she fixed her eyes upon it, and then pressed her hands upon her bosom, to stifle the sobs which almost suffocated her. But she resolutely suppressed every outbreak of feeling, and raising her glance to the starlight heaven, she murmured,

"Help me, O my Father! I am so weak! Thou hast made this heart, with all its feebleness and errors, and though I am alone the erring one, my nature is from thee!"

She relapsed into silence, and not a sound was heard, save her gentle respiration ; for the very winds were still, and the starry peace appeared to sink into the bosom of the universe, and to tranquillise all things. Yet there was that pure young creature, so sad, so miserable, finding not hope or consolation in the brightness of the lamps of Heaven—that seem as if they could not shine on aught save joy :—but only in that faith in the lofty and Invisible, which faith, virtue, and piety can alone supply. Deep are the sorrows with which mortality is afflicted : and oh, how profound they are when they flash for the first time on the soul of youth, hitherto alive but to gladness, for as the young

4 E

experience more intense and exquisite delight in pleasures which pall upon the taste of those who have exhausted feeling, so, pain from its freshness is most acute and insupportable, where the poetry of life, bright and elastic, has not been tempered with the grave philosophy misfortune teaches. Among all our griefs what more dreadful than those arising from the unsparing frost which nips the blossoms of life's spring—ever of love—the earliest, most beautiful, and most elysian of the passionate illusions we embrace as if they were indeed the substance, and not the shadow of eternity ?

"Yes," said Ellen, resolutely, "it shall be so! Never, never, to possess Heaven itself, would I let him degrade himself; and it is clear he thinks to wed me is degradation." She re-perused the letter, for the hundredth time. Its contents ran thus:

"Useless have been all my exertions, dearest Ellen, to procure a pardon for your father; and a few hours after you receive this letter, I shall be on my way back.. I had an interview with the Prime Minister yesterday; and although he was kind and friendly, he would not hold out to me the most distant hope of procuring the remission of that dreadful sentence which blasts all our happiness, and makes this glorious world a desert to us. But, sweetest one, we can quit the crowded haunts of men, and seek some distant solitude across the sea. We shall be all in all to each other, like two branches intertwined, apart from all others; and Heaven will smile on us. Pardon this hasty scrawl, and its ill-connected wording. I am to see one of the Royal Family presently, but I will not delude you with hope. Keep up your spirits, Ellen, for the sake of your—CHARLES WALSINGHAM."

Thus ended the epistle. "He mentions not a syllable of his own belief in my father's innocence," said Ellen to herself. "No, he is persuaded I am the child of a murderer, and yet he would marry me!" There was something inexpressibly consolatory in that last thought of the maiden. How perfect must be that affection which could urge Charles Walsingham to resign all earthly considerations, despite his conviction of the parent's guilt, for the love of the child! "But never, never," cried Ellen with energy, "will I marry, while a stigma so dark remains on my father's name!"

"That is my own Ellen," said the voice of Harry—who had

entered his sister's apartment, booted and spurred, without her hearing him, so engrossed was she with her own thoughts. "Ellen," exclaimed the youth, "since fate contends against us, and an accursed train of circumstances condemns our noble father to death, I am resolved to put in execution the scheme I hinted to you, without delay. To-morrow he is sentenced to die; but I will rescue him, or perish. Cheer up, my dear sister. As for this Hanoverian soldier, you must try to forget him, and give your true little heart to a good, honest Jacobite, who will love you better than this man. Farewell!" He then kissed his sister, and left the room.

Ellen paced to and fro for a minute, and then sat down and wrote as follows :—"Adieu, Charles! you may never see me more in this world ; but oh, remember me, though you think that I am a murderer's child. There is an eternity beyond the grave, and we shall meet again in that purer state of being reserved for us ; and then you will know all the earthly love that gushed out from my spirit as from a well to meet yours. You will know that if ever passion were perfect, in its weakness,— if ever affection were pure in its mortality, you possessed, you still possess the deepest, sincerest, and most enduring love that ever woman rendered unto man. I know not how to write the last word—the last word I shall ever address to you! But we must think no more of each other. My brain reels, and my hand shakes. I am ill, very ill. But if I should die, all will be well. Once more bless you, my own love!"

O, that aught in this world could be weighed against such a matchless treasure as that girl's affection! Poor—poor Ellen! Thou art not a character that may live with the sublime heroines of fiction—there is little to attract, nothing to dazzle the imagination in thee : but thou art truly such a being as we may search for vainly during years. But we must now follow Harry Danvers after he quitted Ellen, determined to save his father from an ignominious death. Harry having mounted his horse, rode briskly forwards in the London road from his home ; and having cantered for about half an hour, arrived at a public house, when he stopped, and addressed a person loitering about in a low voice.

"The men be all gone," replied the person he addressed, "and they said as how they should never come back at all, but take to the road."

While the words yet lingered on the man's lips, the form of John Norton on horseback became visible (but still disguised), and in the course of a minute he was by the side of Harry, who briefly explained the course he intended to pursue in order to rescue his father, and it was agreed that they should meet again at nightfall.

Harry in a short time was at the gaol where his father was confined. It is requisite to mention that nothing could be found of the skeleton supposed to be that of the murdered Walsingham, and the popular mind was so excited against Danvers—who was represented by his foes to be a monster of guilt—that there was no hope of his being pardoned, though his friends were all busy in his behalf. The government thought that by the prompt execution of the prime agent of the malcontents they should strike at the root of all the enterprises of the Jacobites; and they were not willing to look into the evidence in favour of him they had so much just reason to dread.

The interview between Harry and his father was short: but he contrived to slip the file he took with him into his hand unobserved, and to whisper a word significant of his intention to attempt his deliverance, although the gaoler was in the cell all the time.

Harry quitted the prison, and was soon in the open country, when, as he was crossing a narrow lane, a man emerged from it, saying, " Ah ! my young friend, well met." Turning at this salutation, Harry recognised the tall man who had rescued him from a lingering death in the cave; and took the hand extended to him, with frank cordiality.

" I saw you go into the gaol a short time since," said the gigantic fellow; " and I was told you are the son of the prisoner, Walter Danvers. Is it so? I wonder you should venture to show your face, if it be."

" Your information is correct: I incur no risk now from being known, as my father is taken," was the reply.

The tall man mused a moment.

" You are going to attempt to get him out of prison?" he observed.

" Ha!" exclaimed Harry, " who has betrayed——"

" Come, do not fear to trust me. I am a terrible rascal, I own; but I like you, and am willing to lend a helping hand—"

"Many thanks!" interrupted Harry. "But are you sincere? —Well, I believe you are. If you like to assist me in this enterprise, this purse is yours: and my gratitude shall always follow you."

"Put up your purse. I can afford to be generous, for I have been in luck's way lately, and expect to enrich myself still more by some knowledge I possess. Tell me your plan of operations; and then I will consider if I can suggest a better."

Harry briefly informed his new confederate of the scheme he had concocted for his father's deliverance.

"It will never do," said Jennings. "But I'll tell you what I'll try. The soldiers would never be taken from the prison on the report of an insurrection, and even if they were, you would still have the battle to fight. I will forge a document, purporting to be from the colonel of the regiment to which the soldiers belong (my old regiment) and go with it to the prison. This document shall recommend me as a trustworthy person to supersede a drunken rascal, whom, I know, is one of the turnkeys. The colonel is a patron of the governor, and I can imitate his handwriting easily. I shall thus obtain instant admittance to the gaol. This effected, I can possess myself of the keys, and release your father; and you will be in readiness with your rope-ladder. Trust all to me."——

The narrative returns to Everard Walsingham, who, after the examination of Danvers, was in a state of mind it is impossible to describe. He neither ate nor slept, and the powers of his intellect seemed prostrated to imbecility the most abject. He never left his dwelling; but remained mute and motionless, his wild eyes strained fearfully in the direction of the place where Danvers was confined, until they appeared starting from their sockets.—— But on the morning antecedent to that when Walter's sentence was to be executed, a change came over him; and he walked up and down his small apartment, muttering to himself—

"He will die: and if he do not confess, I am safe. But will his lips remain sealed? Ay, there it is!"

Such was his state of mind, when he was startled by hearing his own name uttered, and on raising his eyes, he beheld a woman past middle age and of stunted stature, who had entered by the door unobserved by him.

"What do you want?" gasped Everard, turning livid with fear.

"Be not discourteous to your loving aunt," was the response; and the female grinned broadly and hideously: "for, indeed, my lord, I have the greatest love and affection for your lordship. Ha, ha! Come, I won't keep you in suspense. I am the aunt of your wife; and a secret of yours has come——"

"How!" exclaimed the Miser, trembling in every limb.

"Has come to my knowledge," continued the woman. "But, fortunately, your lordship possesses some of that golden plaister so effectual in sealing the lips up; and I will be silent as the grave, if you are generous."

Everard groaned audibly.

"Do you alone know this—this secret you talk of, woman?"

"I and Walter Danvers."

"Walter Danvers! He has confessed then?" interrupted Everard, vehemently. "O, earth, open and swallow me up! Ye mountains fall, and crush me into dust!"

He became silent, and stood statue-like, with his wasted hands clenched together, and his features ghastly as a corpse's. Can human eloquence depict the agony and horror of that man, now that he thought his long-cherished secret was revealed, and his name branded with infamy for ever? Pride had been the ruling passion of the Miser, when he was a young man, and in some measure redeemed his character from utter, grovelling meanness; and this passion had been centred in the distinction of belonging to a family, and representing a name which had never been tarnished. On the death of the husband of the younger Lady Walsingham, he succeeded to the title, and although he chose to remain unknown, he was not insensible to the dignity he possessed; and under any other circumstances would have wished his rank blazoned abroad. Even when the vice of avarice, after a long career of dissipation, absorbed his soul, the pride of birth was not eradicated, though other feelings and habits vanished; and now he beheld the idol crumbling, and shame and ignominy heaped upon him. He writhed beneath the thought, more than under that of death, while the hag, gazing on him with malicious gratification, cried—

"You do not like it should be known, then, my lord?"

"Ah! And you say it is known but to yourself and Danvers? What proof of that can you supply?"

"Plenty of proof, my good lord. It is my interest not to blab, if your lordship will pay for my silence; and Danvers would hardly be indiscreet."

"I know not that. It is true he has been silent hitherto—and perhaps—ay, perhaps, he might not be believed!—But how came you by this knowledge, then?"

"Simply by using my ears. I can convince you that I know all, if you wish; and that it was not Danvers who let out the secret."

"Well, well! your price. You must take an oath of secresy, if I give you money,—a most solemn oath."

"If you desire it, my lord; but I shan't keep a promise any the better for swearing to it. An oath is but a word to me. You ask what I require. A hundred pounds will suffice."

Mother Stokes (the reader has concluded it was that amiable woman) had expected that the Miser would think her demand enormous, and not give her half the sum, but he seemed surprised that she should be so moderate in her requirement; and taking some coins out of a box, placed them in her hand.

"There, begone!" he exclaimed. "If you will let me know where to send it, I will forward a similar sum to you every year; but you will wring nothing more from me. If possible, never let me behold your face again. It is so odious to me, that I could almost find it in my heart—But, no. No more blood! No more blood!"

The last few words were pronounced in a whisper.

"I comply with your request, my lord," said Mother Stokes, and immediately departed.

"I will leave England," said the Miser, "leave it immediately. If the worst come to the worst, I shall then be safe from the fangs of justice, though I forfeit my property. I have accumulated £30,000; but then, Walter Danvers, if he should escape, would rob me of it all, if he could find me. And he *will* escape—yes, yes, I am persuaded of that. He would elude the vigilance of the Devil, and get out of Hell! Wretched man that I am!"

He closed and barred the door; and opening his strong box

took out some piles of gold. He gazed upon them for some time with a quivering lip, and breaking silence exclaimed, "Thou that hast been my bane—thou that I have hugged to my heart, when all other joys had left it—thou fair, damned, hollow, and glorious brightness, for the present we must part! Oh, to be divided from thee is anguish; but I could not keep thee safe. I should be robbed."

The reason of the Miser was affected by the accumulated horrors he had undergone, and his judgment, never strong, was for a season utterly lost. But with the cunning of incipient insanity, he determined on hiding his hoard, and it was soon buried in the bowels of the earth. Twilight had commenced when he quitted his cottage, and went on his way. He walked swiftly along, the Life and Death of Intellect struggling in his soul; and before it was quite dark he was in the very thicket where the murder of John Walsingham was perpetrated. His eyes wandered over the ground until they rested on the spot where his cousin had fallen, and a gleam of awful memory—the last he had for many months, that was not distorted and unreal—struggled through the mists which overspread his consciousness, and he fled like a hell-doomed wretch pursued by an unrelenting demon. "Murder! murder!" he shouted, and the distant echoes returned the sound. "His ghost tracks me! Ha, ha, ha!" and he fell senseless and stupefied to the earth, where he remained for hours. Miserable being! Great had been his crime, and tremendous was his punishment. His insanity, which endured for years, was peopled with dreadful spectres; his sleep was haunted with hated shapes, and his morbid fancy presented nothing but things of nameless horror. Over the globe he wandered, and his lucid intervals were more pregnant with utter wretchedness even than his insanity.

After Harry had quitted his father, Danvers remained sad and dispirited, with his face buried in his hands. Bitterly, at that hour, did he repent his past life, and fervently did he promise himself to strike out another path, if he succeeded in escaping the death which threatened him.

"Yes," he exclaimed, "I will endeavour to become such a man as Harriet would wish to see me. I will not seek to distinguish myself henceforth for courage or capacity; but earnestly set about reforming this heart which clings so stubbornly to the earthly and the temporal."

As if to support him in the determination he had made to renounce the evil of his ways, and to seek the pure and eternal, it was announced to him that a clergyman was without, and wished to speak with him. It so happened that the chaplain of the gaol had been taken ill the day preceding that to which our tale relates; and no other minister of religion was near; and the prisoner being willing to see him, he was admitted immediately to the dungeon. He was elderly in appearance, and stooped considerably, but, nevertheless, was above the medium height; and his voice was gentle, and hardly manly, while there was something in the brightness and expression of his fine hazel eye, certainly not in accordance with his age and calling.

"Will you leave the prisoner and myself together?" said Walter's visitor to the gaoler. After a little hesitation the man withdrew, and the clergyman cried, in a very sonorous voice, "Though grievous have been thy sins, my dear brother, if you but sincerely repent, you will be pardoned and saved."

Danvers bowed his head, and replied—

"I thank you, sir, for coming to visit me, and shall be greatly indebted for your counsels and instruction; for, though I am innocent, as God is my witness, of the crime imputed to me, I have sinned much and deeply".

To the astonishment and indignation of Danvers, the supposed clergyman was now struggling with suppressed and almost uncontrollable laughter.

"Hush!" he said, as Danvers was about to break forth into an exclamation of astonishment at this unseemly conduct. "I am not what I seem. I am here for the purpose of releasing you; but let us now seem to pray." Accordingly, the pretended priest again raised his voice in prayer, and made a long, rambling, extemporaneous discourse, while he said in an under tone, "I suspect there are listeners." Fumbling in his pocket at the same time, he produced a small phial. "This," he whispered, "is a liquid which, by pouring on your chains, will enable you to work easily, and without noise; and here is a file." The sentinel was pacing up and down outside, and whenever he came to the door, the false minister began to pray the more devoutly; but his back

turned, he added—"My ghostly counsels you will not derive
much benefit from—for I am an arrant rascal—but I will set you
free, I wager you a hundred guineas—which sum I have, in fact,
received already for the job. I shall procure admittance again
at night; and as soon as it is dark, you had better commence
filing at your fetters. In the course of three hours, you will have
accomplished the business, and then I shall be with you. Only
be prepared, and we will outwit your foes."

The gaoler again approached, and the pretended priest pro-
nouncing a blessing, took his departure.

CHAPTER VI.

If the assassination
Could trammel up the consequences,
And catch with his surcease success.—SHAKSPEARE.

DANVERS—THE GUARD—FIGGINS—THE PARDON—MRS. DAN-
VERS—THE PROPOSED MURDER.

ONCE more Danvers was alone. The sun was now sinking
beneath the horizon; but so few were the rays of light admitted
to the noisome dungeon through the closely-grated windows, that
day and night were nearly the same there.

About an hour after the pretended priest left Danvers was the
customary time with the gaoler to bring him his supper, and he
impatiently waited till then, as he could not commence his operations before. At length the gaoler made his appearance, placed
the provisions he had brought before Danvers, and with a muttered "Good night" withdrew. The sentinel outside was changed
immediately afterwards; and Walter applying the liquid he had
been given to his fetters, filed away; and in the course of a few
minutes divided a chain which bound his arm. With what fierce
eagerness did he continue that work for life or death, and with
what joy did he behold the massive chains fall one after another
from his limbs! The human mind is eternally assuming new

changes, it "never continueth in one stay." Though Danvers cared not for existence, negatively speaking, he feared to meet death like a felon amid the execrations of the populace—for he was not a *moral* hero—he had no martyr's zeal to sustain him, and was oppressed with the consciousness of many misdeeds.

Danvers was startled from the occupation on which he was so intent, by hearing an indistinct sound of voices outside his dungeon door. He listened; but could only catch a murmur, and presently he distinguished retreating footsteps;—then all was still. He resumed his operations: and in about half an hour, had the satisfaction of finding both his arms free: but the manacles on his legs were yet more ponderous than the others; and after he had filed through them there was an immense chain that would take an hour to cut away, it being passed round his body, and secured with a huge padlock.

He had but recently commenced filing at the fetters on his legs, when the heavy step of his guard approached. The man paused at the door; and Danvers fearing lest by possibility he had heard something which awakened his suspicions, concealed the file he had been using, together with the liquid, in his bosom.

"I may have to struggle for it," thought the prisoner, "if this fellow have overheard me filing. I wonder the disguised priest is not here."

But the door opened with a dull noise, and a vast form appeared. It was the dragoon whom Danvers had encountered on more than one occasion, the gigantic Jennings, and there was something in his aspect so hellish that a sudden suspicion of his fell design darted through the brain of Danvers. He advanced in silence until he was within arm's length of the captive, having previously closed the dungeon-door after him. It was manifest that he had been drinking, though not so large a quantity of liquor as to incapacitate him for his duty, but he smelt powerfully of brandy, as one who had recently taken a vast dram.

Drawing himself up to his full height, Danvers returned the glare of the soldier's eye with a stern, unquailing, and haughty gaze. The fellow indulged in a hoarse, savage laugh, while the captive confronted him.

"What want you here?" cried Walter Danvers, with a brow of menace.

"I wish to enjoy your society for a little, as it is your last night on earth," answered the ruffianly dragoon.

The suspicions of the prisoner were confirmed, and he glanced hastily round the narrow dungeon for some weapon of defence. The soldier supposed his hands were fettered; but Walter, though he held them in such a position as to make them appear so, the reader knows was now perfectly clear in that particular. The sentinel perceived that quick look, and interpreted it aright. He chuckled ferociously.

"Well, I am going to save you from the gallows," he exclaimed; and raised his arm.

We must look back a short time, in order to explain the motive of the murderous intention of the soldier, and return to Corporal Figgins.

The character of this man was thoroughly unprincipled and heartless; but he was not of that revengeful or malicious nature which delights in making others wretched from the gratification found in witnessing misery. He was simply a bad man, such as may be found, probably, in every hundred human beings, on the average, without redeeming good qualities, but certainly not a demon.

The connexion between Figgins and the detestable wife of Danvers, is, of course, explicit; and the influence which she exercised over him, though less intellectual than himself, was extremely powerful. Perhaps it is not *always* the strongest mind which directs; for the passions so often interfere with the judgment, that whatsoever power operates on them is the prime engine of good or evil. Never, perhaps, was there a greater blot on humanity than this Mrs. Danvers. She was the very epitome of all that is odious in woman; yet there was a fascination in her arts few men could resist. Her hatred against her husband after the interview which has been recorded between them, grew deadly and fiendish; and nothing would have pleased her more than to see him writhing in the agonies of death.

It had happened some hours before the time when our narrative breaks off, that Corporal Figgins was walking, at no great distance from the house of Miss Walsingham, when he noticed a horseman, in whom he recognised Captain Walsingham, advancing from the London road: and from some motive which may possibly be conceived, he turned into a field, where he was hid from view by the height of the hedge. Presently, Miss Walsingham also was descried by the Corporal, and she met Charles within a short distance of the place where Figgins stood.

"What news?" asked Harriet, eagerly, when her cousin was within earshot.

"I have not brought a reprieve," was the reply; "but I have hope it will arrive to-morrow morning."

That was all Figgins heard; for the relatives walked on together, and were soon out of sight: but Charles afterwards added, "Alas! he may be saved from death; but he may prefer to die; his sentence will be eternal banishment with felons. Even so much mercy can hardly be extended to him."

"Poor, poor Walter!" exclaimed Harriet. "But," she inwardly murmured, "he may yet be saved. O, God! in mercy spare him."

"Pardon Danvers! The devil!" growled Corporal Figgins. "What a thing it is to have influential friends! If it had been a poor devil of a sheep-stealer, they would have hung him up without any more ceremony than if he had been a dog."

He quitted the field, evidently in ill-humour; and had walked about half a mile, when he met his paramour with the hapless child of their guilty intrigue in her arms. He at once informed her of what he had overheard.

"And shall he escape after all?" she ejaculated.

"I suppose he will," muttered Figgins.

"I shouldn't wonder at all——" began Mrs. Danvers, and stopped short.

"What?" asked the Corporal.

"Doesn't he know something about you? At present you have triumphed over the accusations brought against you at the examination, but Danvers is vindictive as the devil."

"Why, yes," returned Figgins, in reply to the first part of Mrs. Danvers's speech. "I'll tell you what it is, as we have no secrets from each other. He caught me out in a little bit of swindling a few years ago; but I promised I'd never do the like again, and he didn't blab."

"Ah!" muttered Mrs. Danvers, "it was the same with Everard." She added aloud, "But he will blab, Figgins, when he is out of his present pickle, depend on't. He will owe all to these Walsinghams, and if he hears you are the steward on the estate, will think it imperative in him to warn them against you. Then all your fine projects will be blown into air. He is a murderer, we know, even if innocent of all participation in the murder of John Walsingham—and who but he could have stabbed him in the first instance? If we procured the carrying out of his sentence by giving him poison, or taking his life somehow? You have access to the prison, and might even induce him to commit suicide; for if I know aught of his nature, he would do anything to avoid a public execution."

"No," said Figgins, his red face turning very pale, "I'll have no hand in it."

"You fear to do it," sneered Mrs. Danvers.

"That sneer," observed the Corporal, "would have done for Lady Macbeth. I might get into a damnable mess, and I don't profess to be a Quixote."

"Pshaw! If you are cautious you need not implicate yourself."

"Ill give him no poison," returned Figgins, decisively.

"Is not that great brute of a son of yours one of the guard appointed by old Norton?" inquired the lady, as if struck with a sudden notion.

"Yes," answered the Corporal.

"Don't you think he could be induced to strangle him; and then it would appear as if Walter had committed self-destruction."

"Hum! Why do you thirst for his death with such tiger-like ferocity?"

"Look you, Figgins, I hate him; and he is in my way. I want to chalk out a new course of life. I want to catch some old drivelling fool for a husband—perhaps Norton would do—or, if not he, some one who would further your interests."

"What! You want to marry?"

"Yes, it would be a good speculation. I could then procure you a commission, and you might be a gentleman, as such clever fellows as you are, deserve to be."

"Well, I'll speak to Tom; but I won't promise anything."

"Didn't Tom get a horrible whipping for having suffered Walter to escape?"

"He did: and he is a spiteful, revengeful fellow, who doesn't forget."

" Give him some strong drink, then—he is fond of drinking—
tell him what you have told me, work up his passions, and inflame
his anger against Danvers. You can easily get a key to fit the
dungeon door, and give it to Tom. None will suspect you ; and
indeed the general opinion is against Dauvers so much, that his
death by his own hands (as it must appear) will be rejoiced at
when it is known a pardon has been granted. No person, it will
be supposed, could have a motive for destroying the prisoner ;
none will hear his groans, and as he is so heavily fettered, Tom
can easily throttle him."

"I do not like the job," muttered Figgins, as he separated
from the iniquitous creature, by associating with whom he had
fallen a step never to be recovered, and who had proposed such
horrible measures. " She is the very devil, that woman ; but I
wish he were out of the way—she talks rationally."

Thus cogitating, he walked in the direction of the town where
Danvers's prison was located, and stopped at a public-house,
where he procured some spirits in a bottle. He then went to a
locksmith's, and bought a peculiarly formed instrument, well
known to thieves and burglars. He invented some likely story
for requiring this article—used also by locksmiths themselves for
picking difficult locks—and then took his path to another public-
house, where he fortified himself with liquor. As soon as it was
drawing toward night, he walked to the gaol, one of the turnkeys
of which was a boon companion of his, and easily procured admission. His friend, the turnkey, had already taken as much
potent ale as he ought, but the Corporal easily induced him to
renew his devotions to the jolly god, and in less than an hour he
was drunk, and Figgins himself more elevated than usual. Cautiously looking about him to certify himself that he was not
observed, the Corporal then stole to that part of the prison where
Danvers was confined ; and on seeing the burly sentinel, he held
up the partially empty bottle of spirits he had bought, and said,

" I have laid a wager, Tom, that you could drink this off at a
swig."

"I should think I could," replied Jennings, taking the proffered
bottle, and gulping down the contents.

The quantity of alcohol thus taken would have maddened an
ordinary man, and it made the stolid brain of the huge Jennings
reel, so that he was obliged to lean on his carbine for support.

"Has your back healed, yet, of the cursed flogging, Tom?"
inquired Figgins of the dragoon. Jennings muttered an oath,
and resumed his walk up and down with an unsteady step, and
brow as black as midnight. "It was all through the murderer
you are now guarding that you got so punished," observed Figgins.

"He will be hanged to-morrow," growled the savage Jennings
from between his teeth.

"No, he won't," returned the Corporal.

"Won't be hanged!" cried Jennings, looking ferociously at the
other.

"I'll be bound Captain Norton would give half his fortune to
have him dead," returned the Corporal.

"By G—! I shouldn't mind strangling him," said the enormous fellow, his wolfish temper exasperated by the recollection of
his disgraceful punishment, and the quantity of raw spirit he had
swallowed.

"It might be done without any danger," observed Figgins.
"If he were throttled, and hung up as if he had done it himself,
who but would suppose he had destroyed himself to avoid death
on the gallows? But you are scrupulous, I know."

"Am I?" answered Jennings, with a hyena laugh.

"He is almost more than your match, that fellow," remarked
Figgins.

He touched a chord here which he well knew would vibrate on
the instant. The ruffian, devoid of mind, was only proud of his
colossal strength, and he rightly believed there was hardly a living
man of greater corporeal powers.

"I would bet a thousand guineas, if I had them, I could knock
his life out of him," exclaimed Jennings. "Blood and thunder!
I should like to do it."

The Corporal felt his advantage, and followed it up, although
it was not without compunction.

"A gentleman I met just now says he would give ten guineas
to the man bold enough to kill Danvers," he said. "All the people hate him: but he will get off scot and lot free."

"We shall see about that," returned Jennings.

The Corporal put some money into the guard's hand, and added
to what he had said—

" I shouldn't wonder if a subscription were raised for the man hardy enough to execute justice on this Danvers—if he chose to say he had done it—he was so hooted at the other day."

Figgins was certain he had worked up the mind of the brutal Jennings to the pitch he wanted, and concluded by giving him the instrument he had purchased. "This will open any lock, if you should want to do it," he said, and then departed.

CHAPTER VII.

Spouse! Sister! Angel! Pilot of the Fate
Whose course has been so starless! O, too late,
Beloved! O too soon adored by me!
For in the fields of immortality
My spirit should at first have worshipped thine,
A divine presence in a place divine ;
But not as now :—I love thee.—SHELLEY.

CONTAINING A GREAT DEAL—THE ESCAPE—THE CONTEST—
CHARLES WALSINGHAM—THE PARTING.

THE position of Walter Danvers was extremely critical. No cry that he could raise was likely to be heard in the remote quarter of the prison where his dungeon was placed, and there was that armed savage, equal to himself in strength, while no weapon of defence was near him. But, taking his resolution promptly, he rushed on the soldier, and griping him in his vast arms strove to hurl him down.

"Ha! you have got the use of your hands, have you?" exclaimed Jennings, attempting by a prodigious effort to release himself from that mighty hold. But Danvers felt that if the soldier once got from him, his fate was sealed, and tightened his gripe.

What an awful struggle it was! Both men knew that it was for life or death, and every iron muscle, every vast sinew was strained to the uttermost. The height of the dragoon gave him an advantage, and Danvers' legs were still fettered, and as they fell, the chains entangled the prisoner, and he was undermost.

"Devil!" cried Walter, as the giant planted his knee upon his chest, so as to impede his breathing ; and he thought his hour

4 G

was come. Useless were his convulsed exertions to throw off his vast foe, and the ruffian was trying to compress his throat with one enormous hand, so as to strangle him. Another second, and he might have been in eternity; when the ruffian received such an awful blow on the forehead, that he was laid prostrate, instantaneously; and a voice exclaimed—

"What a precious scoundrel you are, Mister Tom!" Then a rope was passed round the muscular arms of the insensible ruffian, and a gag was thrust into his mouth, while Danvers, recovering, beheld a man of singular stature before him, who was with the utmost coolness and self-possession employed in securing the baffled assassin.

"He's a thorough blackguard, that Tom, if ever there lived one," muttered the tall stranger. "He hasn't one gentlemanly idea in his thick skull. Mr. Danvers, I congratulate you on your escape. I am come to set you free. Your son is outside the prison, and we will be off at once.—Ah! that padlock! I have a key here which will unlock it.—There, now you are free. Take the sword of that low rascal, and let us be off."

Walter, accustomed to act in emergency, followed the tall person who had saved his life through several passages, which he threaded with the most perfect ease and rapidity, and up a flight of stone steps, having ascended which they found themselves at a grated window.

"There, if you look out, you'll see your son," said the tall highwayman. "He is just behind that lofty wall."

"But how are we to get out?" demanded Danvers.

"Why, let us try these bars.—It's all right. One of them is loose! I'll have that out in a jiffy.—Whew! what's that noise?"

"He has escaped! The prisoner has escaped!" vociferated a turnkey.

"Here's a go!" exclaimed the tall man. "But this way!"

And he dashed up a second flight of stairs at a break-neck pace, Danvers exerting all his speed to follow. The bold Jennings was soon at the top of the stairs; and made for a gallery, at the extremity of which was a trap-door, at the height of seven feet from the ground. Withdrawing the bolts which secured it in an instant, he darted through the aperture, and extended his hand to Danvers. The steps of many men could be heard ascending ; but the fugitives were through the trap-door before they were descried.

"Follow me!" said the tall man, running across the roof of the prison, as if he were a monkey ; and then producing a rope, he attached it to a chimney-stack. The shouts of the soldiers below reached their ears, as the rope was securely fastened, and "Long Peter Jennings" bidding Danvers steady it with his hand, slid down, and reached the high wall which surrounded the gaol. Danvers followed his example ; but he heard the enemy above, and had hardly descended, when their forms were apparent on the roof.

"Neck or nothing!" cried Peter Jennings. "I wish that d—d rope could be got off the chimney ; but we must leave it. Here, my lad," addressing some one beneath, in whom Danvers recognised Harry, "up with the ladder. Confound those fellows ! They are firing. All the town will be raised ; but we shall do them."

Bullets were, indeed, whizzing over the heads of the fugitives ; but they regarded them not ; and the tall Peter, holding the ladder which Harry had thrown up, bade Danvers descend, who, at once complied, and reached the ground in safety.

"Thank heaven!" said Harry, catching his father's hand. "Here are the horses. Let us mount and away!"

"But I will not desert my preserver," returned Walter.

"Fly!" shouted the tall man, with an oath. "I see hundreds hastening to stop you. I'll take care of myself, I tell you."

Danvers and his son leapt on their horses' backs, and dashed from the prison : for it was true that numbers were prepared to stop them. Bells were ringing, drums were beating to arms, guns firing, men shouting and swearing, women shrieking, and a cry of "The Jacobites! the Jacobites!" became universal. The tall Jennings was in an ecstacy of mirth, as he made the dangerous descent from the wall—no person being below to steady the rope ladder, which he tied to the cord that yet depended from the chimney : but an expression of anxiety overspread his face, when he saw a soldier was dividing it with his sword, just as he quitted the wall. "Here goes for a jump !" he cried, as the rope gave way, when he was yet twenty feet from the earth. He escaped with a sprained ancle, and tried to limp to a horse which was in readiness for him. But ere he could mount, half-a-dozen men arriving, laid their hands upon him.

"Down with them!" shouted a voice, as the gallant fellow defended himself against his assailants; and a horseman, dressed in a cassock, and mounted on a fiery steed charged the tall man's adversaries, sword in hand. They gave way, supposing that a whole host of Jacobites were at hand: and the deliverer of Danvers taking prompt advantage of the panic, vaulted on his horse's back, and exclaiming, " Bravo, Bess! *You* are the parson, then!" galloped fiercely off, followed by his ally.

The way in which the escape of the prisoner was discovered so soon was this. Some presentiment entered the heart of Captain Norton that all was not well, despite the great precautions he had taken to secure the captive; and rising on the spur of the moment from the seat he occupied in the barracks appropriated to his troop, he ordered some privates to accompany him, and hastened to the prison. Of course, on entering the prisoner's cell, they found Tom Jennings bound and gagged, and the bird flown; and instantly raised an alarm. Captain Norton vaulted on his charger's back, and pursued: and Jennings and one or two others also mounted. But the fugitive was on his own Dickon once more, and Harry was nearly as well mounted, so that they did not lose the start they had gained. The father and son then were first by a hundred yards; then came Captain Norton, Tony Jennings, and two dragoons; then a quarter of a mile behind, the tall fellow and "Bess;" and again, behind them, some horsemen, a little beyond gunshot, and among these last Corporal Figgins, who, attracted to the prison, reached it as Norton took horse.

Miles and miles were left behind, and the foremost fugitives found themselves at length in a solitary path, greatly in advance of the pursuers.

"Let us wait a minute to breathe our steeds," said Danvers to Harry: but as he spoke he noticed two persons, about a furlong to their right, engaged in deadly conflict. "By Heaven! That is John Norton, with his face to us!" exclaimed Danvers; "and his opponent must be Hugh Freestone." He again put Dickon to a gallop, and was soon on the ground occupied by the combatants. "My friends! how is this?" cried Walter, beating down the weapons of the two Jacobites.

Freestone turned deadly pale at Danvers' apparition, but John Norton uttered an exclamation of surprise and pleasure.

"I am glad to see you here!" he said. "I met Master Freestone by accident, and we agreed to settle a dispute of some standing on the spot."

"You may have plenty of fighting, if you wish, with the enemies of King James, without quarrelling with his friends," cried Walter. "Lo! even as I speak, they come."

And sweeping onwards, like a hurricane, came Captain Norton and his followers. There was brief time for counsel; and Danvers and Harry stationed themselves on a rising ground, while the younger Norton and Freestone remained inactive. Before another minute had elapsed Danvers was contending against Jennings and another dragoon, and Harry encountered a third; but Captain Norton was so exhausted by all the exertions he had made, that he was compelled to rest a moment.

"I will not see an old friend at these odds, without lifting an arm in his cause," cried John Norton. "There will be more here, anon. Hugh Freestone! If you have a spark of manhood left in your icy heart, to the rescue!"

The Jesuit did advance; but it was to array himself against his former friends. And so they fought man to man, until Captain Norton hurled himself against Danvers. That redoubtable warrior, gladdened and inspirated with air and liberty after so long a confinement, performed feats of soldiership equal to any achieved in the days of chivalry; and the dragoons were beaten back, even as the two individuals who had hitherto been behind —Peter Jennings and "Bess"—came up and swelled the numbers of the little band who fought on Walter's side. Captain Norton and Freestone were but indifferent soldiers; but actuated by violent passions, they had pressed fiercely on Danvers, while he was still engaged with Tom Jennings. Wheeling and striking, feinting, and parrying blows with marvellous celerity, however, Walter outdid himself. The blood of Danvers was up, and he felt a demi-god now that he had a prospect of freedom, and had escaped from such manifold perils. In spite of the superiority of numbers, and the *animus* which inspired them, those three mortal enemies of Danvers were obliged to retreat: and John Norton and Harry were no less successful in their strife with the dragoons, so that when fresh allies were added to their force, they were irresistible. "On them, lads!" exclaimed Danvers, following up the advantage; and with a shout they charged, and dispersed the foe. But ere the rout was complete, the burly form of Corporal Figgins, and with him four or five dragoons, changed the odds again, and the Jacobites and their friends renewed their flight. By a strange chance they were now within a little distance of the house where Danvers supposed Ellen and Elizabeth still to be: and, in fact, they had quitted it but a short time before.

"Shall we make a stand here?" asked Harry of his father. "The great body of our foes are far in the rear."

It was as he said. Captain Norton and Freestone—the latter mounted on a hunter—both being exceedingly light men, were almost within gunshot; Figgins and Jennings were considerably behind, their vast bulk retarding their speed: and for the other dragoons, they were nowhere to be seen. Once more Captain Norton rushed on with the fury of a maniac, as soon as he saw Danvers prepared to receive his attack; but Freestone was not so blinded by rage but that he felt the insanity of assaulting the Jacobites then, and he drew in his rein. Danvers, by a well-directed blow, shivered the blade of Captain Norton, as it was descending on his head, and as the old officer was drawing a pistol to discharge it at his hated enemy, Danvers wrenched it from his hand, and whirled him round as if but a reed. But he did not dash him to the earth, as he might have done, never to rise again: but dropped him gently, and then spurred on against the treacherous Jesuit. But Freestone turned and fled. Jennings and Figgins, however, continued to advance, and the Jesuit joining them, they charged the party of Danvers. Walter fired at Freestone, but narrowly missed him: then hurling the empty pistol at the traitor, he knocked him from his horse and engaged with Figgins. Fortunately for the Corporal and the dragoon the remainder of their friends were at hand, and the strife for the last time became deadly and doubtful.

It was at this juncture that a solitary horseman might be seen advancing; and so equal was the contest that a child might have almost turned the scales. It was Charles Walsingham. He had but a short time previously been at the house of Danvers, and found it deserted, and he was, after a fruitless search for Ellen, returning to see if she might not have come back : when he observed the contending parties ; and recognised Walter in the hottest of the fray. He paused, fearfully irresolute. His duty was to join the foes of Ellen's father, his heart bade him strike for him.

"Cruel fate!" exclaimed Charles, "Why hast thou brought me here? Love or honour must be sacrificed."—He saw the lynx eye of Corporal Figgins had perceived him, and knew his reputation was for ever lost, if he did not unite himself with the military. But there was Danvers, fighting like a lion against Tom Jennings and a second dragoon, and Harry was unhorsed, and contending with a powerful man also on foot, while honest John Norton was sustaining an unequal conflict with Figgins. The two tall individuals had their hands full ; and Hugh Freestone, recovering, was about to attack Danvers from behind.

The life of that being so dear to Ellen was at stake, and the Spartan spirit, which for a moment animated Charles to sacrifice love to fame, vanished instantly. He was not one to coolly calculate chances, or he might have thought if Danvers thus died, much obloquy might be saved, and all further impediment to his union with Ellen removed. But if such a thought flashed on the officer's mind, it was dismissed indignantly ; and he spurred on to strike the cowardly assailant of Walter down. Had he done so, all his prospects in life would have been blasted : but, suddenly, a shout was heard at a short distance, and a dozen horsemen, followed by others, were seen galloping up.

"Huzza!" exclaimed the Jacobites. "Friends, friends!"

Charles Walsingham turned, and saw that a strong party of armed men were arriving, and his purpose changed. Now, he would fight against the Jacobites to the death. The soldiers of the government perceiving that fearful odds were likely to be opposed to them, fled in dismay. But Hugh Freestone, as he sprang into his saddle, after being dismounted, discharged a pistol at Danvers, which whizzed past him and struck the horse Charles Walsingham rode. The animal, maddened with fear and pain, dashed away, and vain were all the efforts of his rider to restrain him. He was carried several miles before he regained the mastery over the brute ; and when he returned to the place where the late conflict had occurred, there was no trace of the

Jacobites, far or near. He again went to the house which the family of Danvers had occupied, but was no more successful in finding them. Thus he lost all clue to Ellen; and although he sought her for days and weeks could discover nothing concerning her.—At length in despair he went abroad, and did not return to England for many years. Honour and rank he gained; but what were they without his heart's beloved?

Many were the thanks which Danvers and Harry heaped on Peter Jennings and Bess: but they would receive no money from them, and they parted with mutual good wishes. John Norton had absented himself, but as Walter and Harry were left alone he returned to them.

"My brother," he said, "has burst a blood-vessel, and is now lying in a cottage about a mile away. O, Danvers!" he added, "We must never meet again. I fear you are the murderer of my brother as well as my nephew. Farewell! I loved you once."

"Noble heart!" exclaimed Danvers, sorrowfully. "And must I lose thee too? O, what a treasure is a faithful friend!—But I did not injure your brother in the fight!"

"No: but he became insensible after you dropped him, and he was borne away by the soldiers. God knows, Walter, I bear no enmity against you. But I ought not to grasp that hand red with my nearest kindred's blood."

"Nay," said Walter, "I would cut off this right hand readily to give back that poor boy to you. He died young, and not ingloriously. Perhaps I shall soon follow."

John Norton brushed away a tear, and then extended his hand to Danvers.

"May Heaven bless you, gallant warrior!" he cried. "No crime is upon your head."

Then embracing Harry, sadly he went his way.

"O, what a friend have I lost!" exclaimed Danvers, bitterly.

Harry could not console him. They rode on in silence for some minutes.—What a Night of Gloom and Desolation was in Walter's soul!

*   *   *   *   *   *   *

Danvers was able to baffle the exertions of his foes to recapture him: and about a week after his escape from prison, hired a small vessel to convey him and Harry across the channel.

All was soon ready for the embarkation of Walter; but he would not quit England until he had taken a final adieu of her who was all the world to him. His love of Harriet Walsingham was now almost worthy of that bright being: for when the passion is not purely sensual, it has so much essential and necessary holiness in it, that it must ultimately correct itself, and ennoble and sublimate the heart of man.

Danvers, then, one glorious autumn day, as the hues of the gorgeous noon were mingling with the softer and milder tints of twilight, when the world seemed breathing of peace and love, and the very air was melody, pursued his path to the residence of Harriet. What a revolution had the last two months effected in all his thoughts and associations! The affliction he had endured was salutary, although severe; and he felt, if not a wiser, a better man.

He reached the house, and tying his horse to a tree, entered the garden. There, in a natural arbour, the birds all singing harmoniously from grove and shade, through which the gushing breeze swept deliciously, her white hand supporting her beautiful head, sat Harriet Walsingham.

"Harriet!" whispered Danvers.

At that thrilling sound, she started to her feet, and the blood deserted her cheek, always pale, and then spread vermillion over it for an instant: but she quickly recovered herself, and extended her hand to her first and only love.

"Thank God!" she murmured, tears trickling down her face. "Thank God you were saved from that death of horror. I see you are disguised, and well, too, Walter; but I knew your voice directly."

Danvers pressed her hand reverentially to his lips; and a warm drop of love and gratitude fell upon it.

"I am come to bless you for all your goodness, Harriet; to hear you forgive me once again; and then to pronounce an eternal adieu."

His voice trembled, and he was afraid to trust himself to speak more.

"I hope you will be happy, Walter," said Harriet Walsingham; and a choking sensation in her throat also prevented her from speaking farther. They were silent; but yet that silence

4 H

was eloquent of what words can never describe. Harriet was the
first to breathe a word again. " Walter, my friend, my brother!"
she cried, with scarcely any embarrassment. " I want to disbur-
then my heait of the feelings which crowd upon it; but their
multiplicity bewilders me. Be a good man, I beseech you; and
then you will know what *felicity* really is. O, believe me, all
happiness on earth is but anticipation of heaven, and the love of
our Father in Heaven! He is with us, now, dear Walter. His
spirit is busy in my spirit, and bids me tell you to cherish faith
and virtue, and your reward shall be great, your bliss most certain. *I* have had to bear some sorrows; but God has given me
strength to endure them, as if they were the lightest breath of
grief; and no desolation clings to my spirit now."

Sobs convulsed the mighty chest of Danvers, and he turned
away, vainly struggling with emotion. Harriet pressed his hand
with sisterly affection. Holy and beautiful as ever angel's was
that serene and unearthly countenance. Her body was in Time:
but her soul was in Eternity.

" Lo!" said the Christian poetess, with deep enthusiasm; "all
our worshipped visions *here* vanish, never to return. The ambitious man weeps at the futility of all his gigantic schemes, even
when they are consummated; for consummation is the end, *not*
the perfection of happiness;—the scientific man deplores the
narrowness of his accumulated knowledge, seeing that it plunges
him but into error: the wise man sighs, because he is certain that
philosophy can give no comfort to the sorrowing, nor satiate that
panting for joy which is the law of existence. Joy;—it is but
the summer gale, flying—ah, whither? But the believer is not
bound to the low being whose scope is not in the eternal: he
sees a world above the stars, he beholds an universe in his own
mind more sublime than all this stupendous creation. This is
felicity; to breathe the ether of heaven, and to inhale the atmosphere of the Seraphim. Trust in God, O trust in God! And
the veil will fall from before your eyes, and the naked loveliness
of immortality and love will be revealed. You will learn to despise this earth, to feel all is vanity that does not aspire to a purer
life, full of all rapture, promise, assurance!"

"I will try," murmured Danvers; " but I can never be blessed
like you, after all the sins I have committed."

" Never believe it !" exclaimed Harriet, with energy. "The Christianity of the Gospel assures you to the contrary. Nay, it is possible that in proportion to your grief for the past may be the joy of your hope for the future. As a parting gift take this Book from me. It is *the* Book, and the one from which I have derived such inexpressible comfort. You will find some notes I have made placed between the leaves. They reveal some of the thoughts, the joys, and fears I have undergone, and on that account you may prize them."

" Yes, as I prize my life," returned Walter, pressing the sacred volume fervently to his heart. " It shall never leave my bosom until I die."

" May it sink deeply into it !" returned Harriet. " May its truths be like the stars, to light you through the night of life. I have known one, who was most dear to me," she added, sadly, " who laughed to scorn all that is contained in this inspired work : but he was the most wretched of mortals. Strange! that man should throw away the truest gems in all the universe, and cherish mere useless gewgaws made by human hands."

" If I am not mistaken," replied Danvers, his mind recurring to the young Epicurean by a sudden association of ideas—who shall say precisely how ?—" I know the person you allude to. I met him accidentally, but a very few hours before I discovered that you were not gathered to the dead."

" Poor, erring boy ! If you should ever meet him again, be kind to him for my sake."

" And he is the son of your ill-fated brother! I wish I had the power of serving him. What has become of young Francis, whom, I heard, was thrown into prison ?"

" The officer he wounded (I suppose you know his story ?) was not killed, and Frank has been pardoned, and was released the very morning that brought no reprieve for you.—Ah ! I see him coming up the hill even now. You had better not be seen."

" I must indeed depart, inestimable woman ! for my time is short. May all the choicest blessings the Almighty can bestow be showered on your head ! O, farewell, Harriet ! Sweet sister ! Grant me still one last request."

" I will, Walter ; for I am certain you will ask nothing I ought not to bestow."

"Grant me one kiss of that glorious brow—that shall one day be enriched with a seraph's crown—which I shall never see again, bright with earthly lustre."

Harriet met the lips of Danvers with her spotless forehead without a blush, without the quivering of a lip, and clasping her hands together, murmured a benediction. It was a solemn and affecting spectacle, though all was so calm, so quiet, so subdued. It was death in life.

"O, I must touch your lips!" exclaimed Danvers, in agony— he *was* agonized, beyond outward show—" farewell, farewell!"

And imprinting a lingering, despairing kiss on her lips, which she resisted not, he tore himself away, and rushed to his horse. Then, and not *till* then, the high and sublime fortitude of Harriet deserted her, and she burst into a passion of tears and sobs.

"O, my heart!" she cried, "O, my heart! Protect him, great God of Heaven!"

Can human eloquence give an idea of the workings of that exalted spirit at that hour? No; there is that within us which finds no voice, which the vulgar understand not, the lofty can but dream of. She sunk upon the rude bench of the arbour, and a coldness like that of death came over her. The struggle was awful; but the radiant soul roused itself from its torpor, and she knelt, and poured out her grief into the bosom of the Eternal. Long, deep, and earnest were her supplications; and into the solemn mysteries thereof the genius of ethereal beings alone can penetrate: but when she arose, as the pale evening star came trembling into life in the purple sky, she was as bright, as calm, and tearless as aught out of heaven!

CHAPTER VIII.

The actors have all vanished from the scene,—
Leaving behind them tears:—the tragic tale
Of human passions is a lofty theme—
The loftiest, and the lowest we can find.—*MS.*

DANVERS—FRANCIS WALSINGHAM—GEORGE—THE CHARACTERS OF THE TALE DISPOSED OF.

ERE Walter left England, however, he had still a few affairs to arrange, and foremost of all to see George, and proffer his protection to him. A theatrical performance was about to take place in the village of Uskedale, and George was to be engaged in it. He was found without much difficulty by Danvers, who ventured in disguise to a sequestered spot near the village, and employed a trustworthy person to bring the child to him. George came, and expressed himself delighted at beholding Walter once more.

"And where is your daughter?" he asked. "I loved her very much. She went away on a sudden from the house where I left her."

"Yes, my brave little fellow; but if you like, you shall go to her with me, and we'll take care of you."

George sighed heavily. "I must not leave my mother," he said. "No, Mr. Danvers, I am grateful to you for your kind offer; and I wish I might go and see your dear daughter and live with you and her: but my mother,—she is still my mother."

"What a noble heart is here!" murmured Danvers. "My dear boy," he added aloud, "I have no pleasant home to offer you, and if you were to live with me, it might injure you in after life: but still to escape from harsh treatment——"

"God bless you," returned George with a choking voice. "Leave me now, or I *might* be tempted. Oh, sir! There has been a sunny spot on my life since I knew you—I have been loved and pitied! As for disgrace—do not think I believe you guilty: and I should not fear to share your fate. But it cannot be. Good bye—good bye!"

The heart of poor George was full, but he restrained his tears, while Danvers gazing sadly into his fair young face, said, "My preserver! My young hero! What do I not owe you? Alas! I cannot return all the benefits you have rendered me. Noble boy! I will not induce you to follow my desperate fortunes; but I must hear of you sometimes. There is a direction to a house in London, and you must write to me—you can write? You must let me know where you are to be found. And now take this purse."

"No, no, I cannot," cried the child, "do not ask me. Leave me now; for you are in danger here. Take my love, my dear love to Miss Ellen, and tell her I will write to her soon. Ask her to do the same to me. Oh, she will be your comfort, your joy! May you be happy, my good friend, very happy—as, feeling innocent, you must. Farewell!"

Danvers kissed the boy fondly, and tears rolled down his cheek. " But keep this watch in remembrance of me, as you will not accept my purse," he said. And after much pressing, the child was induced to receive one of those huge warming-pans, called watches, in existence about a century ago, and then they parted.

Francis Walsingham and Danvers left England together. It was not a little comfort to Walter to find that so many believed him guiltless of the foul crime for which he had been condemned, for although the voice of conscience, the voice of Heaven, may acquit, yet we cling to the opinion of this poor world as if it could know all. Frank Walsingham was deeply enamoured of Ellen, and was convinced of her father's innocence ; but Danvers —when he urged his suit for Ellen with him—represented how he would suffer in the eyes of men if he sought to unite himself with her; and dissuaded him from seeing her. But the young man insisted on receiving his rejection from the maiden's lips, and speedily had the desired opportunity. He learned too late that Ellen had given her heart to his cousin Charles, and left her in despair. He procured an appointment to a vessel bound for a distant station, and it was years before he returned to England. Alas for love!

One more scene, and then our Drama must close. The performances at the barn which had been hired for the representation of a tragedy by some strolling actors, was far better attended than is usual on similar occasions. The great attraction of the evening was the appearance of a ' lady ' and a child. Mrs. Danvers was the ' lady :' for she was no longer able to procure the same engagements as formerly—younger and prettier women having stepped into the profession. A space was railed off in front of the stage for the Walsingham family, under whose patronage the performance took place. The younger Lady Walsingham and her daughter, attended by some friends, entered before the curtain rose, and took their seats. The little girl was all smiles and joy, but her mother looked pale and sad. It must be mentioned that inquiries had been made after George by Lady Walsingham, when he did not come, as she had desired him, to her house, but in vain, and she reproached herself, after the signal service the boy had rendered her, for not having at once taken him under her protection. She was not a little surprised, when, on the curtain rising, George came forward, and delivered an address with much grace and sense. The performance proceeded. Not one of the actors there displayed one half the cleverness, the fidelity, and even the power, of that precocious boy. There was the stamp of mind and originality on his acting; it was evident that he had not been tutored, but that he spoke as much from the head as the heart. It was the performance of a young boy, but of one who possessed the true deep spirit of dramatic passion, who thought and felt for himself, and would not be restricted to rules. He was loudly cheered, and at the conclusion of the play an agent of a London manager, who was recruiting in the country offered Mrs. Danvers and her gifted child an engagement. But ere she accepted the terms Lady Walsingham dispatched Corporal Figgins to her with a message. The Corporal had managed to triumphantly clear himself from the suspicions which had been raised against him on the examination of Danvers, and he was so able a man of business that Lady Walsingham would have been loth to part with him, unless his guilt could have been proved.

Mrs. Danvers waited on Lady Walsingham, who was pleased with her specious manners and good address. She put some questions about George to her, and then asked if she were willing to part with him, adding, that if she would consent to do so, she would adopt him as her son. Mrs. Danvers replied that she could not consent to part with her only child. In short, Lady Walsingham was induced to offer to take Mrs. Danvers (who, of course, went by an assumed name) into her house, the artful wretch pretending that she was tired of a theatrical life, and moreover wished to escape from what "she was compelled to acknowledge was an indelicate profession for a woman." Accordingly, she was received into the mansion of Lady Walsingham, Corporal Figgins having "made inquiries" as to the character of the actress, and found it was unimpeachable.

It was not long, however, that the lady remained at Walsingham Hall: for a rich old gentleman paid a visit to the mistress of the place, and after staying a week, took off with him the *ci-devant* favourite of Thalia—not a little to the chagrin of Mr. Figgins, who thought he had done a very clever thing in gulling Lady Walsingham.

But George remained, and became endeared to the family, while Figgins soon afterwards accepted the post of quarter-master in the regiment of which the elder Norton was now a major.

Major Norton was never seen to smile after the death of his son. He had recovered from a severe illness which the frenzied excitement he for a long time laboured under produced; but he moved among men like a spectre. The quarter-master was his only companion, his brother having gone abroad and entered into a foreign service.

And Harriet Walsingham—the pure, the bright, the perfect *woman*, who had endured so much, loved so much, felt so much—where was she? A short time after Danvers had effected his escape from England, she changed her residence, and hired a cottage about a mile distant from that of Spenser, the philosopher. They were much together, and Harriet delighted in imparting the rich stores of her cultivated mind to the children of her early friend, as well as to her sister's daughter. Those two lofty beings—the thinker and the poetess—found deep consolation in being together, and exchanging thoughts, which are not of this world, sympathising with each other's sorrows, and mourning for each other's afflictions. Old Roger Sidney frequently stayed for months with Spenser, but he still roved about in pursuit of his favourite pastime, age appearing to make no inroads on his constitution.

For the minor characters of our eventful history—Sam Stokes became a husband. At the end of a year after she left Walsingham Hall, his cousin Sally became his bride. Sam used to say, she might have done wrong, but he was "sartain" she would stick to the old ship for the future; and very happy they were together. They had several children, and Sam was as much pleased with fathership as he was with husbandhood. Peter Jennings and his sister were not heard of as being engaged in any predatory exploits for a long time. The former wrung sums of money from some Jacobites over whom he possessed a power which he did not scruple to use, and once more—to use a forcible slang-ism—" cut it flash" in town. Mother Stokes could not be found, and it was generally supposed that she was dead; her relations not being desirous of finding her, gave themselves no concern about her. One character must be mentioned, ere

the pen is laid down, and that is the poor lunatic who was introduced a few chapters since. Spenser took him under his roof,
and endeavoured to develope his intellect ; but although the unhappy creature evinced gleams of reason, and even a superior
quality of mind to the generality, he never by any means became
a rational being.

Ah! who is thankful enough for that blessing of a reasonable
soul—the greatest, loftiest boon Eternity can impart? By this
divine faculty we live beyond time, by this sublime power we
know that we are immortal, and that our heritage is beyond the
stars. But for reason, creation were a blank!—There might be
beauty, but where would it exist? Of what use would be the
glory of the heavens, the magnificence of the firmament? Would
it elevate the senses, would it exalt the pleasures of the animal to
behold the splendor of the universe? No: reason is the highest
in man, the highest in angels, the divinest in divinity. By reason
we have faith, by reason we have hope, by reason we have virtue,
by reason we have happiness—*these* are the majesty, the wonder,
and sublimity of being. We have sorrows too deep for tears, we
have woes too profound for expression; but the mighty reason
sustains, the august essence of Deity sinks not; but soars for
ever !

This has been the object of "THE MISER'S SON,"—to evince
that mind can rise superior to all things, that sense cannot
strengthen the moral faculties, that by aspiring with the spirit
there is peace and rest, and by suffering the physical to subdue
the mental, all is darkness and desolation. And this is the question which must divide philosophers "to the last syllable of recorded time." Are we to seek felicity in the mind, or in the
body? If in the mind, *there* is eternity enthroned. Around it
is infinite space, above it are the harmonies of immortality. The
light of worlds is dim before its radiance, the true, the abstract,
and the divine, are the atmosphere it breathes. Genius can sing
its melodies, and despair cannot groan its agonies to the ethereal
soul. It cannot rest, it cannot cease to rise, but there is a peace
and a calm in every sound, in every syllable, and tongue of life—
for they utter love!—"The very pain is sweet," for whence is
pain? From Heaven? No! There is no pain *there*: but it
comes to purify the sight, which otherwise is alive only to the

5 I

sensual. It must be by pain we can attain to blessedness.—And shall we desert the privilege of reason, and eat, drink, sleep, and die?—O, I will not paint the corruption, the wretchedness, the nothingness of the things of sense!—There is a corpse—loathsome and foul—*there* is a soul—bright—*how* bright!

FINIS.

NOTE.

My Readers have scarcely, perhaps, been satisfied with the answers given to the Atheism of the Epicurean. It has been my object to develope the character of that person *below*, rather than *above*: I have attempted to analyse the springs of passion, and to trace effects to their causes; it was therefore necessary to show the principles of the Materialist, and the question of the expediency of introducing such discussions into fiction—as those between Sidney and William, Spenser, Bolingbroke &c.—resolves itself into whether the character should be *at all* introduced. To this I answer, that *all* truths are good. But Atheism is false? Well: it contrasts religion; it is the shadow to the light; and is in fact a sublime illustration, rather than a subtle enemy to Christianity! This paradox is easily explained; look at the atheist's life,—look at the true believer's! I assert, that the existence of such a being as Harriet Walsingham is the best answer possible to all the arguments of the unbeliever. At the same time, I did not wish to mis-state anything. I have given the reasonings of William fairly; and supposing them all true, ask to what does the system lead? Behold the man! If ever there were a miserable person, with fine intellect, and naturally noble heart, the Atheist is one. It was impossible to advance all that might be said morally and metaphysically against Atheism in the limits of a few chapters, but the *facts* recorded become great *truths*; for they are matters of every-day history—the want of a *moral basis* is destructive of all happiness. Still, I believe, I have not left the philosophical arguments of William Walsingham unanswered: but every one who has thought on the subject is aware that to overthrow Atheism, we must allow it full scope.

Now then, as we are not Deists, and do not profess to see no mystery in the order of things, we discover, with some surprise, at first, that these very objections of the *extreme* unbeliever are the *bulwarks* of the Religionist of Revelation, and the *batteries* against the Religionist of Nature. Bolingbroke perceived that Christianity was the only answer to Atheism; he felt he could not stand against the God-negation, without Revelation; and therefore had recourse to the miserable sophistry of asserting there was a league between Divines and Atheists to destroy the One religion! Of course, if there were no evil in the world, there would be no mystery to explain, and the first principle of Revealed Truth is to reconcile the apparent contradiction of an antagonistic power to God; it declares immortality to be the solution of the problem. So, I have left the objection against the equal distribution of happiness as it is;—metaphysically it is not difficult to prove " whatever is is right," but the Materialist wants to take a ground of course with which metaphysics have nothing to do; he says, " use the *senses*, and good is unequally divided." To reply, " use the *mind*, and you find the balance of good and evil just," is not philosophical, it is begging the question: and as Materialism exists, however contradictory it may be, the *Moral* must be the answer to it. Morality is the best, and most conclusive argument against Materialism; and the ' Miser's Son' is an ethical work. The Epicurean objects to morality, he worships sense—he calls pleasure the only good, and consequently it was requisite to answer this practically: and finding virtue could not be denied, William plunges into the abstract, and here he is met by the profound ontology of Spenser.

CPSIA information can be obtained at www.ICGtesting.com
Printed in the USA
BVOW03s1304270415

397857BV00024B/472/P